# INSIDE AUTOCAD 2005

**BY**
David J. Harrington

1249 Eighth Street, Berkeley, California 94710

An Imprint of Peachpit Press

Boston ● Indianapolis ● London ● Munich ● New York ● San Francisco

# Inside AutoCAD 2005

International Standard Book Number: 0-7357-1439-8

Library of Congress Catalog Card Number: 2004105957

Printed in the United States of America

First printing: June 2004

09  08  07  06  05  04                    7  6  5  4  3  2  1

Interpretation of the printing code: The rightmost double-digit number is the year of the book's printing; the rightmost single-digit number is the number of the book's printing. For example, the printing code 04-1 shows that the first printing of the book occurred in 2004.

## Trademarks

All terms mentioned in this book that are known to be trademarks or service marks have been appropriately capitalized. New Riders Publishing cannot attest to the accuracy of this information. Use of a term in this book should not be regarded as affecting the validity of any trademark or service mark.

## Warning and Disclaimer

Every effort has been made to make this book as complete and as accurate as possible, but no warranty of fitness is implied. The information is provided on an as-is basis. The authors and New Riders Publishing shall have neither liability nor responsibility to any person or entity with respect to any loss or damages arising from the information contained in this book or from the use of the CD or programs that may accompany it.

**Associate Publisher**
*Stephanie Wall*

**Production Manager**
*Gina Kanouse*

**Acquisitions Editor**
*Elise Walter*

**Senior Development Editor**
*Jennifer Eberhardt*

**Senior Project Editor**
*Sarah Kearns*

**Copy Editor**
*Ben Lawson*

**Indexer**
*Angie Bess*

**Proofreader**
*Sheri Cain*

**Composition**
*Gloria Schurick*

**Manufacturing Coordinator**
*Dan Uhrig*

**Cover Designer**
*Aren Howell*

**Media Developer**
*Jay Payne*

**Marketing**
*Scott Cowlin*
*Tammy Detrich*

# Contents at a Glance

## .ng New Projects

## Planning and Organizing Projects                                    28

## Part IV    Annotating, Dimensioning, and Plotting

### 14    Text and Mtext Annotation                                    396

xviii    Inside AutoCAD 2005

# About the Author

**David J. Harrington** is the office computer manager at Walter P. Moore and Associates, Inc., a structural engineering company in Tampa, where he specializes in commercial structural computer-aided drafting and design work. Although now doing structural work using AutoCAD, his drafting experiences range from landscape irrigation design to retrofitting Launch Pad 39B for NASA at the Kennedy Space Center.

He has been active in the AutoCAD local user group community for more than 14 years, holding offices for the Tampa Bay AutoCAD User Group as newsletter editor, treasurer, content director, and president. Beginning in 1994, Harrington was elected to the board of directors for Autodesk User Group International (formally NAAUG). There he served as the Local User Group representative, AEC Industry Group chair, Vice President, Senior Vice President, and also President.

Harrington first used AutoCAD in 1987 when he began working with AutoCAD Release 2.6. He is well-versed in AutoLISP, having created hundreds of programs, and is the original creator of REVCLOUD—now a feature within core AutoCAD. An avid writer, Harrington has authored numerous articles for national trade magazines, as well as AUGI user group publications *PaperSpace*, *WorldView*, and *AUGIWORLD* magazine. He is also currently on staff with *AUGIWORLD* as technical editor. Harrington has been granted AutoCAD Level II certification from Autodesk. Additionally, Harrington has won the *CADENCE* magazine Top Gun AutoCAD contest and the *CADalyst* Challenge AutoCAD contest. These awards attest to his grasp of the software and his ability to make the program work for him. He is also a member of the faculty for Autodesk University, regularly speaking and instructing at the event.

In addition to this book, Harrington also technical edited *Inside AutoCAD Release 14* and co-authored/technical edited *Inside AutoCAD 2000* and *Inside AutoCAD 2000, Limited Edition*. He also was author-et-al for the previous book in this series, *Inside AutoCAD 2002*.

# Acknowledgments

I wish to thank my parents; my Mom for always encouraging me to accomplish whatever I wanted to do and for teaching me, by example, about sharing knowledge to help others; my Dad for never getting too angry when I took some electrical "thing" apart and lost half the screws in the process, and for guiding me to take a path into drafting, in which I have managed to support myself and family for 20 years.

I also want to thank those at Walter P. Moore and Associates for their continued support though the years for my extracurricular writing activities. Because of them, I was able to follow the leading edge of technology and learn along the way.

I would like to thank Autodesk User Group International (AUGI), the Board of Directors, and all the volunteers who make this great organization beneficial to all who partake of it. I extend a thank you to all the AutoCAD user groups throughout the world for helping spread the word about this great program and for providing opportunities to share your knowledge.

Of course, I thank Autodesk for continuing to make a program worth loving and worth writing about. Thanks to the Autodesk Beta Programs group who make it possible to produce a book during the software development cycle. A special thanks also to Shaan Hurley for helping to clear up all my late-night AutoCAD confusions.

I want to thank the technical editors, Christina Baldwin, Bob Bell, and Aaron White, for sharing their knowledge and giving their time to help make the book even better! I thank Jennifer Eberhardt and Sarah Kearns, for their valuable editorial advice and skills as well as the encouragement to follow my heart when editorial issues arose. I wish to thank Elise Walter for providing authoring guidance under very unique publication pressures and allowing me to make this book mine. And I thank Steve Weiss at New Riders for having the confidence in me again with another authoring opportunity. I would also like to recognize Dave Pitzer and Bill Burchard for their contributions to this book series through the many years.

Special thanks to Robert Unanue for sharing his knowledge so many years ago. He helped improve my drafting and design skills and kick-started my professional career.

—David J. Harrington

## About the Technical Reviewers

Developing technically accurate books is a priority at New Riders/Peachpit Press. We rely on the skills and advice of technical experts to guide the authors in the creation and development of their manuscripts. The following reviewers have provided their input— and we offer our thanks for their hard work and dedication.

**Christina Baldwin** has been working with AutoCAD for 15 years. She started as a "pup" piping designer and now owns a consulting business specializing in AutoCAD training programs and technical services. Christina's experience includes thousands of hours training drafters, designers, architects, and engineers in AutoCAD and other CAD applications. She is lucky enough to have attended and presented at the last several Autodesk Universities…if you attend this year, she welcomes you to seek her out to say hi and introduce yourself! Christina currently lives in the Pacific Northwest.

**R. Robert Bell** works for MW Consulting Engineers in Spokane WA US as its network administrator/programmer. The in-house customization covers the Electrical/Lighting, Plumbing/Piping, and HVAC disciplines and general drawing utilities. He has used AutoCAD since 1987. He develops applications for AutoCAD as a consultant and is active on Autodesk's programming-related newsgroups. He is also on the Board of Directors for AUGI.

**Aaron White**, P.E. is a structural engineer with the Tampa, Florida office of Walter P. Moore and Associates. He specializes in the design of long-span steel structures and has worked on the design of large projects such as the Boston Convention and Exhibition Center, the Orange County Convention Center (Phase V), the Puerto Rico Convention Center, the new McCormick Convention Center Expansion (Mc4W) in Chicago, IL, and the retractable roof for the new Arizona Cardinals stadium. He has more than 10 years of experience with AutoCAD, including teaching courses at Cornell University. Aaron lives in Clearwater, Florida with his wife Elizabeth.

# Reviewer Acknowledgments

First, I'd like to acknowledge Miles Merwin, mentor and friend, without whom I don't think I could have gotten through the last few months. I'd also like to acknowledge Brian Singer, my first and most important mentor, but mostly my staunchest supporter. And lastly, I'd like to acknowledge Bob Morse and the Bellingham Users Group for being my biggest fans and being my presentation guinea pigs!

—Christina Baldwin

I would like to thank my wife, Tonya, and my son, Nicholas, for the support they gave me during this project. Your understanding while I put in those extra hours did not go unnoticed. I also want to thank my grandfather, Woody, for inspiring me to always seek the answers; and my grandmother, Emma, for teaching me how to care. You have influenced me more than you know.

—R. Robert Bell

I wish to thank Elizabeth (and Estebhan) for their patience for my long nights and multiple deadlines over several weeks, while still putting up with travel for my day job. I also wish to thank my parents, Paul and Maryann. Without their support and sacrifices over the past 30 years, I certainly wouldn't be where I am in life, doing what I'm doing, while enjoying nearly every minute.

—Aaron White

# *Introduction*

AutoCAD is a Computer Aided Drafting and Design software phenomenon; its users far out-number those of any other CAD system, and its reach extends around the globe. AutoCAD has grown from a micro-curiosity to a complete CAD system by any set of measure.

AutoCAD also has grown from a relatively simple program to a large and complex one, but its size and complexity should not intimidate you. Millions of designers and drafters have learned to use AutoCAD with the help of Inside AutoCAD, a best-selling AutoCAD book for more than 16 years.

## Who Should Read This Book

*Inside AutoCAD 2005* is an updated and streamlined version of the most popular AutoCAD book series. The tutorials provide step-by-step instructions to help average AutoCAD users learn more quickly. Users with experience will find many unique and helpful concepts to better leverage the tools they already know. Of course, this book covers the fantastic new features of AutoCAD 2005 in a real-world scenario that all users will find familiar and applicable. This book is for anyone who wants to take a base level of AutoCAD knowledge and build upon it.

## Who This Book Is Not For

This book purposely does not cover the very basics of AutoCAD, such as how to use the LINE command and the various object snap mode descriptions, for example. It does cover what you can do after you have a collection of objects, from editing to annotating to modeling to plotting, and many other things.

## How This Book Is Organized

This book is organized into parts to help you digest the many features of AutoCAD 2005.

### Part I: Introducing AutoCAD 2005

Welcome to AutoCAD 2005, the newest release of the world's most popular Computer Aided Drawing and Design software package. Part I is devoted to a broad overview of the many new features of this version of AutoCAD—features that include new commands, new interface functionality, and a host of added capabilities that increase your productivity by making your work more efficient. The remaining parts of this book consist of groups of chapters devoted to specific aspects of AutoCAD. They are designed both for easy reference and to present AutoCAD 2005 in a logical, easy-to-use, and understandable manner.

## Part II: Starting New Projects

In Part II, you learn how to set up and control the AutoCAD environment to work efficiently. Also covered is the new AutoCAD 2005 Sheet Set manager. You learn how to use AutoCAD's layers to organize your drawings and your projects. You learn how to control an object's appearance using AutoCAD's linetypes, and you also learn how to effectively use lineweights. In addition, you learn how to use AutoCAD's coordinate system to draw accurately.

## Part III: Creating and Editing Drawings

In Part III, you learn the tools for obtaining information from objects as well as how to select and modify them. You learn how to properly create and use blocks, block attributes, and external references (xrefs) to harness the incredible power they offer. You also learn about AutoCAD's DesignCenter, a powerful tool that allows you to search for objects in drawing files and automatically insert their data into the current drawing, all without opening the original source drawings. You also discover unique aspects of hatch patterns and tools for your hatching needs.

## Part IV: Annotating, Dimensioning, and Plotting

In Part IV, you learn about AutoCAD's annotation type objects—text and mtext. We also cover using other Windows application data within AutoCAD via Object Linking and Embedding (OLE). You learn how to use AutoCAD's dimensioning objects and tools, powerful features that help describe your design to others. You learn how to use model space and paper space and how to take advantage of an AutoCAD feature called Layout, which makes working in paper space easier. You also learn how to create plots of your drawings using AutoCAD 2005's revolutionary plotting paradigm, which uses plotter configuration files, plot style tables, and page setups.

## Part V: Customizing and Advanced Concepts

Part V covers several advanced topics, such as specialized plotting features and the new Publish tool. Also discussed are the new AutoCAD 2005 Field text concept and the new Table objects. You learn how to customize your AutoCAD 2005 interface to make it work more efficiently for your needs and environment. In addition, you learn about the AutoCAD CAD Standards mechanism.

## Part VI: Three-Dimensional Techniques

In Part VI, you are introduced to the world of 3D modeling in AutoCAD 2005. Many features make building your AutoCAD models in three dimensions easy and time-efficient. The final chapter in this section introduces you to rendering and making photorealistic presentations of your models.

# *Part I*

# Introducing AutoCAD 2005

# Chapter 1

# What's New in AutoCAD 2005

Congratulations! If you are spending the time to read this book, you are probably a proud new user of the next version of Autodesk's flagship product, AutoCAD 2005. Each and every new release of AutoCAD comes with a multitude of features and enhancements. With very few exceptions, the software program just gets bigger and bigger with each big release; nothing gets removed. So key to leveraging the significant investment made in the software is making an honest effort to learn about the new features. It is rare to be able to apply all the new features on day one; productivity often cannot afford to be hampered trying to figure out how to implement a new concept. And with AutoCAD 2005, there are a number of areas with new features and enhancements to discover:

- User interface improvements
- Increased productivity
- Drawing management
- Display system enhancements
- Drawing sets
- Plotting and output

This chapter presents an overview of features introduced in AutoCAD 2005. Such a chapter should prove useful to veteran AutoCAD users as each feature or usability improvement is briefly described and, where appropriate, illustrated. The major features are of course covered in more detail in later chapters, and chapter references are included.

**I**NSIDER **N**OTE _____

> Many users skip a release or two between upgrades. If this describes your situation, you can also learn about what was added in AutoCAD 2004 by using the New Features Workshop found under the Help pull-down menu and by choosing Previous Release.

A primary question from users who upgrade is, "How is the file compatibility?". AutoCAD 2005 has the same file format options as AutoCAD 2004. "What about the upgrade process, how hard will it be?" Once again, check off this concern. AutoCAD 2005 comes with a great new utility for helping you transition to the new release. As shown in Figure 1.1, the Migrate Custom Settings dialog box can copy over various custom settings from your older installation. And because AutoCAD 2005 can sit side-by-side with other releases, even after you upgrade, you can still fall back if needed in a pinch.

**Figure 1.1**    The Migrate Custom Settings dialog enables you to determine which specific user customizations are ported over to AutoCAD 2005 when you first begin to use it.

The following sections delve into specific areas of enhancements and common applications.

# User Interface Improvements

A *user interface* (UI) is the human communication mechanism that you utilize to instruct the computer system to act in a certain way. AutoCAD 2005 has a number of improvements to the new Tool Palette interface, which was originally introduced as an extension to AutoCAD 2004.

## Tool Palettes

Toolbars have been the UI of choice ever since AutoCAD moved to the Windows operating system platform. Many would never have guessed that anything could come close to the productivity gain toolbars have provided, but Tool Palettes do—and provide the chance to facilitate even greater gains. As shown in Figure 1.2, at first they seem way too big for the number of tools they provide. But their advantage isn't how many buttons can be crammed into a given space (that is addressed next), but how easy they are to use. Because they accept so many types of customization, you can change your work process to be much more intuitive and action-based.

In spite of how large this interface is, it is surprisingly easy to tune to your specific needs. The palette interface is non-modal, which means it can exist outside of the AutoCAD application interface. If you are lucky enough to have a large monitor, or better yet, two displays, you can move any non-modal dialog into an area where it isn't in the way. But even if your screen space is limited, you can adjust how the palette displays. It can be docked on the side of the graphics area, after any toolbars. It can also be set to hide itself (see Figure 1.3 left), collapsing to just the vertical title bar. It also has the capability to be somewhat translucent (see Figure 1.3 right), enabling you to see things underneath.

**Figure 1.2**
The new Tool Palette interface is very user-friendly.

Also, you are not severely limited in the amount of written information you can provide. Because the palette can have its size and width adjusted, you can thin it up, as shown in Figure 1.3 (right).

After you start developing a number of palettes, you can then take advantage of palette groups. Basically, palette grouping enables you to create section tags that contain individual palettes in them. If you need to draw details, you can switch to a series of detail-orientated palettes, turning off plan-related palettes automatically.

## Tool Types

The Tool Palettes come with a number of predefined palettes with blocks and hatches, which is what the feature was introduced with. When included with AutoCAD 2005, however, it was enhanced further by the inclusion of various command type tool options. As shown in Figure 1.4, you have the ability to executing basic draw commands such as LINE. You can access dimension objects, text, and even gradient hatches to go along with normal hatch objects. New to AutoCAD 2005 are tables objects, and they too can be created with a tool palette. But the real interesting tool format is the Visual Lisp Expression. Don't let this fool you; Visual LISP can be used, but so can normal menu type operations. You can do the same kind of customization you do in a menu file here as well.

You can discover more about the Tool Palettes user interface in Chapter 22, "Customizing Without Programming."

# Increased Productivity

Changes are usually made to the software in each new release that aid your productivity in small ways. Of course, AutoCAD 2005 comes with a number of tweaks worth mentioning that, when utilized, would be sorely missed otherwise.

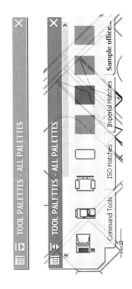

**Figure 1.3**
The hidden and transparent Tool Palette stays out of the way.

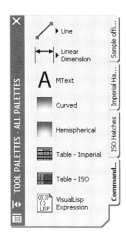

**Figure 1.4**
The new Tool Palettes in AutoCAD 2005 support object types and menu and Visual LISP Expressions.

# Hatch Enhancements

The hatching mechanism in AutoCAD 2005 got the lion's share of pick-me-ups, with three entirely different improvements, and all of them are key to using hatch effectively.

## Bridging the Hatch Gap

When you begin to hatch areas in AutoCAD, depending on who did the boundary creation, you may experience difficulty in utilizing the "pick point" method of hatching. This is where you can just pick inside an area, and AutoCAD determines the closest closed boundary in which to fill with hatch. However, if your boundary objects don't fully close, AutoCAD couldn't do it—until this latest version.

As shown in Figure 1.5, there is a control on the Advanced tab of the Boundary Hatch and Fill dialog. AutoCAD uses the value you provide as a "fuzz factor" when trying to close the area you picked within.

**Figure 1.5**
The Gap Tolerance enables you to work with not-so-perfect geometry.

## Trim Your Hatch

Perhaps sometimes you need to just reduce the hatch to a smaller area. AutoCAD 2005 introduced the capability to trim an Associative hatch. However, it cannot increase, filling new areas, but by using the TRIM command and a cutting edge, you can pick on the hatch object, and it cuts back to match. This can be a real time-saver because your original boundary does not have to be manipulated to achieve the desired results.

## Don't Osnap the Hatch

Many users create their hatching last to avoid having the hatch interfere with their active object snap modes. If this sounds familiar, then take advantage of the Ignore hatch objects control, as shown in Figure 1.6, found under the Drafting tab on the Options dialog. When this is on, AutoCAD simply ignores any and all hatch objects when determining osnap coordinates.

Learn more about the features of hatching in Chapter 13, "Drawing Hatch Patterns."

**Figure 1.6**
You can ignore hatch objects from the osnap mechanism. No more stray geometry from accidentally picking an internal hatch component.

## Middle Between Two Points Osnap

A quick feature for aiding the drafting process is a new object snap mechanism named M2P, or middle between two points. It is only available during a command either by using the right-click shortcut menu and selecting Mid Between Two Points or by typing **M2P** at a `Pick Point` prompt.

## Object Zooming

While you are working AutoCAD, you may find yourself using the ZOOM command to make whatever you are working on visibly larger. Normally, a ZOOM Window suffices, but using the new ZOOM Object option may fit the bill on occasion. Just select the objects you want to focus on and choose the Zoom, Object option from the View pull-down menu. Instantly, AutoCAD brings the display to the limits of the objects you have selected. You can also use the ZOOM Object command-line method.

## Editing Annotation Objects

A small enhancement is the recognition that it is difficult for a user to know if a piece of text is actually text or if it is an attribute or an attribute definition. Now in AutoCAD 2005, the DDEDIT command initiates the proper editing command depending on the text object selected. You can also just double-click on any text type object, and AutoCAD opens the appropriate editor.

Find out more about text objects and attributes in Chapter 14, "Text and Mtext Annotation," and Chapter 10, "Creating and Using Blocks."

# Drawing Management

Managing your drawing content, structure, properties, setup, and standards is probably the most tedious AutoCAD-related activity there is. Everyone wants to be drawing new lines and circles and not fixing problems caused by poor AutoCAD practice. Well, AutoCAD 2005 does not solve this problem by itself, but it does extend a few features to help in certain aspects of drawing management. By utilizing these features, you undoubtedly help improve your consistency and reduce the level of rework or correction.

## Markups

Often, the person who needs to relay changes to be made on a drawing is not AutoCAD-literate. They don't have the time to learn it, have no frequent need to use it, or perhaps have no license in which to use it. So they may be interested in using Autodesk DWF Composer, where they can embed *redlines* into a DWF file that it manipulates. Then you, using the MARKUP command, can import their markup DWF file. As shown in Figure 1.7, it overlays your drawing, enabling you to see both the redline and the actual drawing you need to edit.

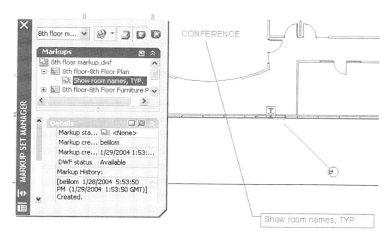

**Figure 1.7**    Viewing a markup created by Autodesk DWF Composer in AutoCAD 2005.

## New Layer Functionality

Can you imagine using AutoCAD without layering? I doubt anyone would want that, and even today, the layering system in AutoCAD continues to be improved.

### New Layer Properties Manager

Within AutoCAD 2005 now exists a more concise layer dialog, although it is fundamentally not all that different from before. As shown in Figure 1.8, the biggest changes are the new icon buttons across the top and the TreeView for layer filters. The buttons control creating new layers, deleting an empty layer, or setting a layer to be current. Also interesting is the new Status column, the lighter color symbol represents an unused layer that is available for deleting. In addition, at the far right is a new layer property for providing a description. This can help others grasp your layer standard if the actual naming convention isn't all that clear.

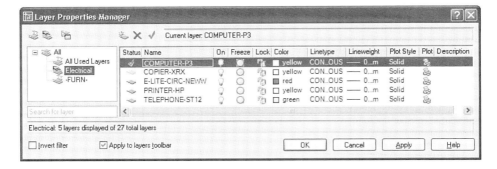

**Figure 1.8**    AutoCAD 2005 has a redesigned Layer Properties Manager dialog box.

### Layers Groups

If you look back at Figure 1.8, over to the left is a new Filter tree area and it also contains the new Group feature. Whereas a Filter enables layers that have at least one similar trait to be filtered and listed in the main dialog, a Group enables you to place specific layers that you choose into a collection for recall later when needed.

You can read more about using layers in Chapter 5, "Organizing a Drawing with Layers."

## External References

As the projects you create with AutoCAD get more complicated, so do your methods of organizing the data. By using external references (xrefs), you can break up large amounts of data into small, more manageable individual files. This presents its own challenge, though—organizing the xrefs. Fortunately, AutoCAD 2005 comes with a few new tools to help users of xrefs.

### Attachment Preference

A small but helpful new benefit to using AutoCAD 2005 is that it now remembers the previous xref attachments method used. So as you repeatedly xref in a drawing, even into different drawings, AutoCAD always presets the attachment type to what you did last.

### *Xref Uniform Scaling and Pathing*

A new feature to the XREF command, as shown in Figure 1.9, is the Uniform Scale option on the External Reference dialog box. This basically helps match the size from one value box to the other, eliminating the need to copy and paste the scale factors. You should note that you can also use a fraction as the scale, although that isn't new to AutoCAD 2005.

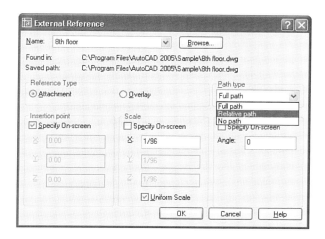

**Figure 1.9**    The External Reference dialog box eliminates inputting repetitive scale values as well as determining how best to record the xref path.

Something else to note on the External Reference dialog is the capability to determine how best to attach your xrefs to the current drawing. You still have the Full path and No path options, but now you can also attach using a relative path. This gives you the benefit of the subdirectory structure and enables you to relocate the entire project tree as needed. This feature was added in AutoCAD 2004 but is worth noting here.

More in-depth coverage of xrefs can be found in Chapter 11, "Working with External References."

## Image Relative Paths

Similar to xrefs, when you attach an image in AutoCAD 2005, you can stipulate to record a Full path, No path, or a Relative path. Because any file that gets attached to a drawing must be able to be found when loaded, utilizing this feature for your images enables you to relocate your project files, including raster images.

Understanding how to attach and adjust images in AutoCAD is covered in Chapter 9, "Object Selection and Manipulation."

## OLE Text Scaling

Users of Object Linking and Embedding (OLE) already know the benefits of doing so. You can utilize the best application for the type of data you are preparing. Spreadsheets are often best done in Microsoft Excel rather than AutoCAD—especially those that use macros. But after this data was brought into AutoCAD, getting it to follow some sense of size or standard was problematic. However, now with AutoCAD 2005, you can use the OLE Text Size dialog, as shown in Figure 1.10, to help AutoCAD adjust your OLE object within AutoCAD.

**Figure 1.10**    Scaling an OLE object based on its text size.

Learn more about using OLE objects with AutoCAD in Chapter 15, "Applications for OLE Objects."

# Display System Enhancements

With AutoCAD, you use the keyboard to type in data or issue commands. You use the mouse to pick points or buttons instructing AutoCAD to act. But without the AutoCAD display, you wouldn't be able to create anything of value. So it is to be expected that AutoCAD 2005 would come with improvements to its visual interface.

## Display Order

When you have AutoCAD create an object, it is stacked onto the drawing database, one after another. It is the order in which things exist in the database that somewhat controls how they appear in the drawing. Therefore, objects with internal volume such as a polyline with a width applied or a hatch object using the Solid pattern definition can often hide things you need to work with. Nothing is more annoying than not being able to select something because something else is *above* it. However, the DRAWORDER command enables you to raise or lower objects in the display system. And now in AutoCAD 2005, these adjustments stay after the current drawing session is closed or when the drawing is used as an xref.

# 3D Orbit Enhancements

As you create 3D models, you will undoubtedly become familiar with the 3DORBIT command. If nothing else, it is fun to spin and zoom around your model in a 3D user interface. But some serious work can be accomplished in the command. It has a clipping mechanism that can be used to generate views of your model. The new addition is the capability to zoom and pan from within this clipping interface, as shown in Figure 1.11.

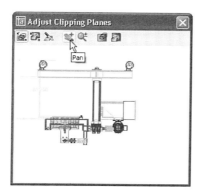

**Figure 1.11**    The new Zoom and Pan features found on the Adjust Clipping Planes dialog of the 3DORBIT command.

The 3DORBIT command is discussed in Chapter 25, "Introduction to 3D."

# Maximize a Viewport

As the use of layouts increases, tools that make working in layouts easier are welcome. To that end, AutoCAD 2005 comes with a handy Status bar tool that enables you to use your entire display screen when editing model space objects from within a viewport. It is a little tough to get used to, but finding the icon is easy enough, as shown in Figure 1.12. The primary button turns on the feature, creating an enlarged, dotted red bordered viewport that is maximized in your display area. Then the navigation buttons to either side become available. These let you alternate which viewport is maximized— if you have more than one.

**Figure 1.12**    There are new buttons on the Status bar while in a layout, used to maximize the viewport in which you're working.

You can learn more about using layouts in Chapter 18, "Paper Space Layouts."

# New Object Concepts

What would an AutoCAD update be without a few new objects to play with? Lucky for us, AutoCAD 2005 comes with a number of new ways to make an object, as well as a number of qualified new objects. It is becoming apparent through these features that there are new ways of using the object forms that already exist, so the key is understanding when and where to apply them.

## Symbols in Mtext

Every discipline that works with AutoCAD has a series of symbols used to describe its particular field of expertise. AutoCAD 2005 has finally begun to address these needs by providing symbols that can be inserted within an mtext object. As shown in Figure 1.13, there are quite a few, and several of those have meanings that can bridge different disciplines. They are simple to use; just click on the desired symbol description, and it is placed into the current mtext editing session.

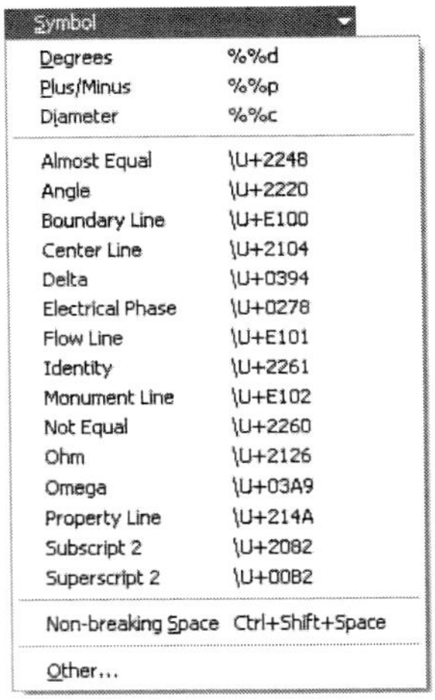

## Backgrounds for Mtext

At times, you may need to place text in a crowded drawing that would otherwise be obscured by other objects. Mtext now has a background property. It enables you to assign a color to the area or boundary box of an mtext object. In fact, you can assign the AutoCAD background color as well. This provides you with the ability to block or hide objects that are behind the mtext object. Now, if you have a very dense hatch and need to place information within it, you don't have to erase the hatch and then rehatch along with the mtext (creating the hatch void for the text). Just place the mtext object as needed, assign the background color to match that of the display, and use the DRAWORDER command if necessary to bring the text above the hatch.

**Figure 1.13**
Mtext can now use specialized symbols that address your documentation needs.

## Create a Table

Getting tabular type data into AutoCAD has always been as simple as drawing lines and text—lots of lines and text. Simple, yes, but extremely time-consuming. Now, with AutoCAD 2005 and its new object type, table, you can create a single object and manipulate the contents as needed. As shown in Figure 1.14, the Insert Table dialog box enables you to choose from your custom list of table styles, adjust the rows and columns as needed, and place the table into the drawing exactly where you want.

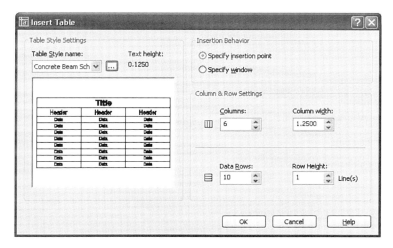

**Figure 1.14**    The new table object in AutoCAD can display spreadsheet-like information.

After you create your table, additional tools enable you to manipulate the structure and cells as required. You can use Copy in Excel and Paste Special in AutoCAD 2005 to place data as a table object. After the data is in AutoCAD as a table, you can further tweak it as needed to get the best-looking schedule you have ever created.

Experience the new table feature in Chapter 21, "Using Fields and Tables."

## Field Codes

Fields are not an object, but rather a new addition to text-based objects, such as mtext and attributes. Fields retrieve data from sources such as the drawing and the operating system and display the data as text dynamically. Thus, if the value of the data the field is linked to changes, the text updates to the new value. Figure 1.15 shows the multitude of field data types as well as a typical use of the Date field and how it looks in a drawing.

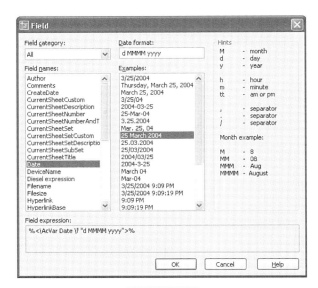

25 March 2004

**Figure 1.15**    The new Field dialog box has many, many different field data applications.

Notice the shaded background. The shade indicates a field in the text-based object. That functionality is controlled through the User Preferences tab on the Options dialog, along with settings on when to update field data.

Learn more about fields and their applications in Chapter 21.

## Revision Cloud

OK, I'm slipping in another non-object here. When you use the REVCLOUD command, you end up with a polyline object with a really neat bumpy effect that is perfect for pointing out revisions on a drawing. It also is good for making shrubberies (for the Knights who say "Ni!") for those in landscaping. But seriously, the REVCLOUD command is now a core part of AutoCAD, no longer an Express Tool, and has the added capability to reverse direction as well provide the calligraphy look it had when it was an Express Tool.

# Drawing Sets

Within AutoCAD 2005 is a new feature called the Sheet Set Manager. This one addition has the potential to rewrite how you create, organize, manage, plot, edit, label, reuse, store, and transmit your drawings. It is so fundamentally different that it will take time for users to understand the benefits it can provide.

## Sheet Set Overview

The primary component of the Sheet Set Manager is the palette dialog interface. As shown in Figure 1.16, this looks simple, but it contains a wealth of features and controls to help you manage your drawing data.

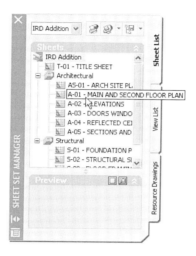

**Figure 1.16**    The main Sheet Set Manager dialog with a project loaded.

## Creating a Sheet

Before you can place content onto a sheet to plot it, you need to create a sheet. This is done through the New Sheet dialog, as shown in Figure 1.17, and enables you to determine how your sheet is numbered and named independently of the drawing filename.

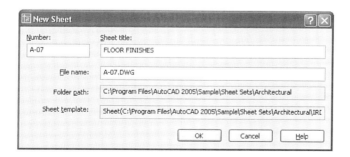

**Figure 1.17**    You use the New Sheet dialog to create blank, ready-to-use sheets from a drawing template.

For sheet drawings you already have, you can utilize the Import Layout as Sheet option from the right-click shortcut menu within the Sheet Set Manager. It enables you to locate a drawing and choose which layouts to use as sheets.

## Placing a View

Creating a sheet is only part of the process; you next must add information to the blank sheet. The Sheet Set Manager enables you to place a view from a resource drawing into the sheet, automatically xrefing the resource drawing, creating the viewport, matching layer settings, scaling and placing the viewport, and finally labeling the view! As shown in the sample in Figure 1.18, setting the scale for a viewport is extremely easy.

## Cross-Referenced Views

A new concept in drawing organization available in the Sheet Set Manager is the capability to easily renumber or rename viewports (which are used to display details and plans, for instance). By using the View List tab on the Sheet Set Manager, you can rename and renumber a placed view, as shown in Figure 1.19, and the Sheet Set Manager and the drawing reflect the change automatically. By using fields in your label blocks, you can create connections to your sheet set properties and views.

```
3/32"=1'
1/8"=1'
3/16"=1'
1/4"=1'
3/8"=1'
1/2"=1'
✓ 3/4"=1'
1"=1'
1-1/2"=1'
3"=1'
6"=1'
1'=1'
```

**Figure 1.18**
A partial list of the right-click Insert at Scale option.

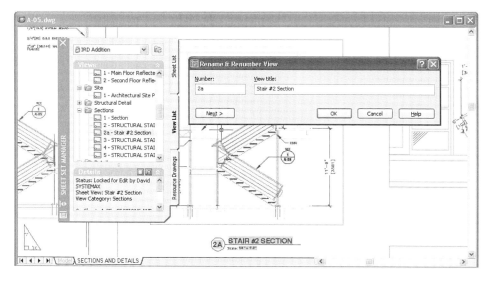

**Figure 1.19**    Managing a detail's number and title from the Sheet Set Manager, which are automatically updated by using field codes.

You can also use the View List tab on the Sheet Set Manager to open your sheets directly, bypassing the standard AutoCAD OPEN command. Views are easy to locate and open from the list, and then they can be edited as needed and closed.

## Sheet List Tables

The Sheet Set Manager takes advantage of another new AutoCAD 2005 addition in its Sheet List Table feature. Based on the new table object in AutoCAD, with one click from the right-click shortcut menu (see Figure 1.20), you can create a table listing all the sheets in your project, which you can update with one click as you add, renumber, or remove sheets.

| Sheet List Table | |
|---|---|
| **Sheet Number** | **Sheet Title** |
| T-01 | TITLE SHEET |
| AS-01 | ARCH SITE PLAN |
| A-01 | MAIN AND SECOND FLOOR PLAN |
| A-02 | ELEVATIONS |
| A-03 | DOORS WINDOWS AND ROOMS |
| A-04 | REFLECTED CEILING PLANS |
| A-05 | SECTIONS AND DETAILS |
| A-07 | FLOOR FINISHES |
| S-01 | FOUNDATION PLAN |
| S-02 | STRUCTURAL SECTIONS AND DETAILS |
| S-03 | FLOOR FRAMING PLAN AND SECTIONS |
| S-04 | STRUCTURAL SECTIONS |

**Figure 1.20**   Making an accurate sheet list has never been so easy.

## Archive and Transmitting

At some stage, you either will have to archive your project or send your drawings to someone else. Prior to AutoCAD 2005 and the Sheet Set Manager, making sure you had all the files you needed for your project set was very difficult and time-consuming. The concept was there, in the ETRANSMIT command, but it still required you to get your drawings together properly. With the new Archive feature of the Sheet Set Manager, as shown in Figure 1.21, you can easily archive your projects at important milestones.

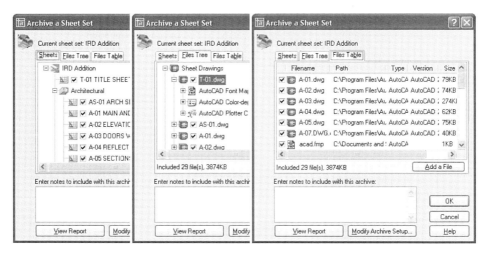

**Figure 1.21**    The Archive a Sheet Set dialog interface provides precise control of your archive set.

The Etransmit feature within the Sheet Set Manager provides much the same interface as Archive, except it's geared for the transmission of the files or ZIP file afterward.

Included in the new Sheet Set Manager is the capability to produce output documents of your individual sheets or the entire set. The Publish utility is actually very similar to the normal PUBLISH command within AutoCAD, which has been updated for AutoCAD 2005 and is described in the following section.

# Plotting and Output

Nearly every drawing that is created must be plotted at some point. The key to success is to spend less time trying to complete the plot than you spent drawing the content. AutoCAD 2005 introduces the first major change to the plotting system since AutoCAD 2000.

## New and Improved Plot Dialog

Plotting since the AutoCAD 2000 addition of page setups and CTB/STB files has been very good for most users. But after using that system for a week or two, you soon realize the negative effect that comes with a tabbed dialog. So, in AutoCAD 2005, the Plot dialog has been redesigned, and the tab panels have been eliminated. Now you can see 100% of the options needed to plot successfully, all in one dialog. In fact, as shown in Figure 1.22, using the little arrow button on the lower right collapses the right side, dramatically reducing the overall width of the dialog box. After you begin using page setups, the detailed section becomes somewhat redundant anyway.

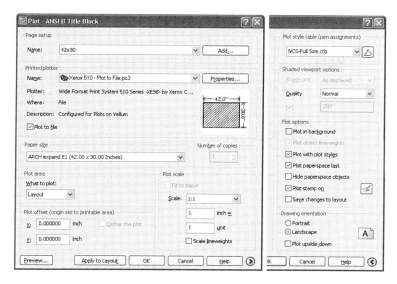

**Figure 1.22**    The new Plot dialog box interface provides a single display for configuring for a successful plot.

Page setups go hand-and-hand with the new PLOT command dialog box. The interface for page setups has been redesigned and is very similar to the Plot dialog. As shown in Figure 1.23, the new Page Setup dialog is big but contains all the elements needed to configure your page setups properly.

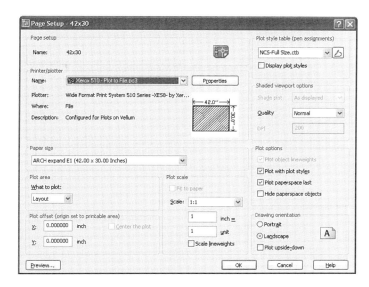

**Figure 1.23**    The new Page Setup dialog box is similar to that of the PLOT command to facilitate quicker editing.

Learn about plotting in AutoCAD 2005 in both Chapter 19, "Productive Plotting," and Chapter 20, "Advanced Plotting."

## Background Plotting

Many Windows applications have the capability to generate prints in the background, enabling you to return to work sooner, and now AutoCAD touts the same productivity gain. The software isn't necessarily plotting faster than before; it is just doing it without forcing you to witness the process. This feature is controlled through the Options dialog under the Plot and Publish tab, as shown in Figure 1.24, and can be adjusted to your preference.

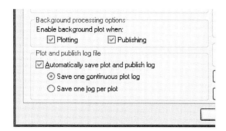

**Figure 1.24**    You can determine when AutoCAD should background plot through the Options dialog box.

## Publish Plot Sets

The way to batch plot many drawings at once is the new Publish dialog box. As shown in Figure 1.25, you can add sheets by way of the Add Sheets button, list layouts or model space only or both, and check the status of each drawing's readiness for plotting.

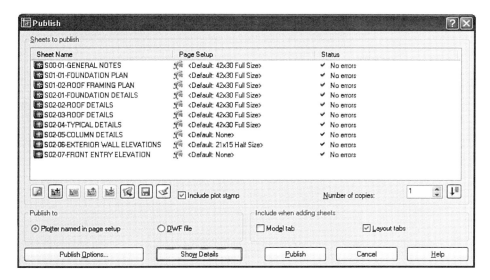

**Figure 1.25**   The new PUBLISH command replaces the old Batch Plot mechanism.

## Publish *DWF* Sets

Many users today are beginning to take advantage of the DWF technology. The capability to place DWF files on a web page, their small size format, and the ease of transmission make them perfect for remote users of your design data. Located on the Publish dialog box is the option to produce DWF files (see Figure 1.25). This uses all configured plot settings but sends the data to the DWF6 ePlot.pc3 plotter configuration, thereby creating DWF files very easily. The big benefit from this is that you don't have to define separate page setups for DWF plotting.

# Summary

In so many ways, the new features in AutoCAD 2005 reflect the changing needs of AutoCAD users worldwide in a quickly evolving Information Age. On the other hand, many new features and capabilities are the result of user requests for an even easier-to-use computer-aided drafting and design platform. No matter what your specific CAD needs are, AutoCAD 2005 stands as a worthy successor to the preceding releases of the world's most popular CAD software package.

# Part II

# Starting New Projects

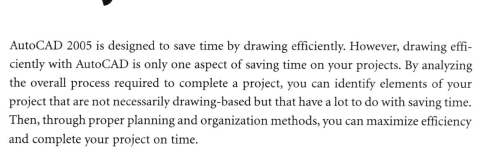

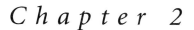*Chapter 2*

# Planning and Organizing Projects

AutoCAD 2005 is designed to save time by drawing efficiently. However, drawing efficiently with AutoCAD is only one aspect of saving time on your projects. By analyzing the overall process required to complete a project, you can identify elements of your project that are not necessarily drawing-based but that have a lot to do with saving time. Then, through proper planning and organization methods, you can maximize efficiency and complete your project on time.

In this chapter, you learn about techniques for both AutoCAD and the Microsoft Windows environment to help you work more efficiently. Among the topics discussed are the following:

- Key organization factors
- Initial drawing setup
- AutoCAD project organization features
- Creating title blocks and template files

# Getting Started: Key Factors to Organize First

The ultimate goal of project organization is to save time by working efficiently. In general, there is one simple rule to keep in mind that will help you work efficiently and save time:

Reduce repetition: Don't repeat what you have already done.

Before you can reduce repetition, you must first identify the organizational elements of your project. The following sections discuss various organizational issues that you should consider prior to beginning your project. Determine your specific organizational needs by asking the following questions:

- How many drawings are needed to complete the project?
- How much detail is required on each drawing?
- What is an efficient method of workflow management?
- How many different ways will you display the drawing?
- Which project elements can be used more than once?

## Determining How Many Drawings Are Necessary

When you start drawing a project, one of your earliest tasks is to determine how many and what type of drawings you will need. You also should compare the available computing power with the drawing size factor. Computing power consists of storage space, both long-term (such as with a hard disk, backup method, and network server) and short-term (such as how much RAM you have), coupled with the speed of your graphics card and CPU. Autodesk and other experts toss about many factors relating to how much memory and hard disk you need to handle each megabyte of drawing. Unfortunately, no hard-and-fast rule exists. If you use xrefs, extended entity data, attributes, and 3D solids, and if you will need to open multiple drawings in AutoCAD at once, then your needs vary substantially from someone who stores 2D vector information in a single drawing without any bells and whistles. Therefore, you must ascertain your ideal drawing size through experience and simple trial and error.

When you have a good feel for how large your drawings can be before the performance of your system hinders your work, you can determine how you want to organize your drawing data into individual drawings. The following examples discuss various options for organizing a project into drawings with AutoCAD:

- Your model exists in one drawing, and you can view the model through various layouts (with Paper Space viewports). Keep in mind that a model can be 3D or 2D. The model can then be viewed and annotated differently in each Layout page. See Chapter 18, "Paper Space Layouts," for more on the use of paper space.

- Each of your drawings may comprise a very detailed portion of a much larger product. You then assemble the various portions into a single model using external references (xrefs). The xrefs help you organize your drawings by listing the location of and relationship between each drawing. See Chapter 11, "Working with External References," to learn about xrefs and their application.

- Your drawings are only a small portion of your project documentation, and the drawings are linked to text documents, images, and other files using Object Linking and Embedding (OLE). See Chapter 15, "Applications for OLE Objects," for more on Object Linking and Embedding in AutoCAD 2005.

It is important to consider a variety of approaches when creating your drawings and to develop a tried-and-true method that delivers exactly what you need a majority of the time. After you develop your approach to building your drawings, you can begin to predict how many drawings you will need, what their contents will be, and how they will relate to each other. This process is critical to estimating how long a given project will take to complete.

### *Developing Drawing and Task Lists*

After you have developed your approach to building your drawings, you should develop a list of your project's drawings and then a task list that goes with each drawing. This list of drawings and their associated task lists should be flexible and expandable. Spreadsheet applications such as Microsoft Excel are excellent tools for creating task lists.

A convenient way to associate a task list with a drawing is to link a spreadsheet into the drawing's Paper Space layout. By linking the task list in the drawing, you create a drawing-specific storehouse for your task list that is visible in each drawing. You also can plot this task list with your drawing so that you can easily measure your progress when you create progress prints of your project. Finally, you can update this task list as you work in each drawing. By using a linked spreadsheet, you can quickly add and edit tasks in your list while working in the drawing.

**INSIDER NOTE**

A new feature of AutoCAD 2005 is *Tables*. These are annotation-filled "spreadsheets" that can be developed and saved for later use. In addition, with the added use of Fields, they can be dynamic for generating sheet lists of your drawings. Learn more about Tables and Fields in Chapter 21, "Using Fields and Tables."

You will learn some simple steps for creating a linked spreadsheet task list in Exercise 2.1 in the section "Using Object Linking and Embedding (OLE)." Figure 2.1 shows a sample task list, and Figure 2.2 shows the placement of the spreadsheet task list within a drawing.

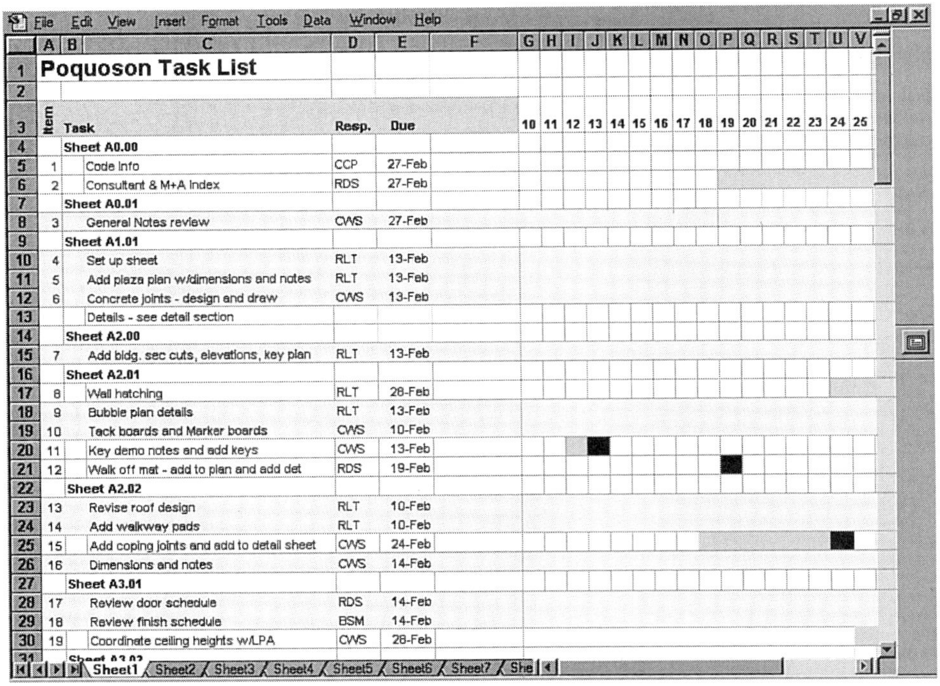

Poquoson Task List

| Item | Task | Resp. | Due |
|---|---|---|---|
| | **Sheet A0.00** | | |
| 1 | Code info | CCP | 27-Feb |
| 2 | Consultant & M+A index | RDS | 27-Feb |
| | **Sheet A0.01** | | |
| 3 | General Notes review | CWS | 27-Feb |
| | **Sheet A1.01** | | |
| 4 | Set up sheet | RLT | 13-Feb |
| 5 | Add plaza plan w/dimensions and notes | RLT | 13-Feb |
| 6 | Concrete joints - design and draw | CWS | 13-Feb |
| | Details - see detail section | | |
| | **Sheet A2.00** | | |
| 7 | Add bldg. sec cuts, elevations, key plan | RLT | 13-Feb |
| | **Sheet A2.01** | | |
| 8 | Wall hatching | RLT | 28-Feb |
| 9 | Bubble plan details | RLT | 13-Feb |
| 10 | Tack boards and Marker boards | CWS | 10-Feb |
| 11 | Key demo notes and add keys | CWS | 13-Feb |
| 12 | Walk off mat - add to plan and add det | RDS | 19-Feb |
| | **Sheet A2.02** | | |
| 13 | Revise roof design | RLT | 10-Feb |
| 14 | Add walkway pads | RLT | 10-Feb |
| 15 | Add coping joints and add to detail sheet | CWS | 24-Feb |
| 16 | Dimensions and notes | CWS | 14-Feb |
| | **Sheet A3.01** | | |
| 17 | Review door schedule | RDS | 14-Feb |
| 18 | Review finish schedule | BSM | 14-Feb |
| 19 | Coordinate ceiling heights w/LPA | CWS | 28-Feb |



**Figure 2.1** A sample task list for a series of drawings.

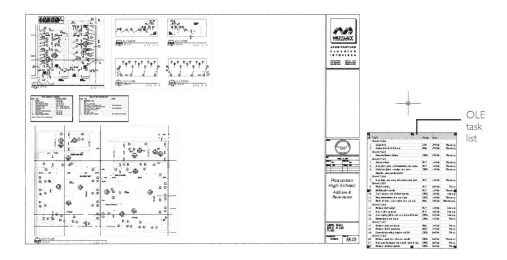

OLE task list

**Figure 2.2**   You can insert the task list as an OLE object on a unique layer and then use the layer plot option or OLEHIDE system variable to control its plotting visibility. Alternatively, you could use the thaw/freeze or on/off layer controls as well to control visibility.

## Determining How Much Detail Is Required

Another important factor in the organization of your project is determining how much detail is required for the drawing. Because AutoCAD is so accurate, you can easily fall into the trap of creating minuscule details that might not have anything to do with the actual production of your project from your drawings. It is important to implement only what the final user of your drawing(s) will need to accomplish the specific job. In addition, you should keep in mind that the person actually creating your project might have better, more effective methods of building the product in the field than you do on the drawing. You should ask yourself these questions:

- What should be documented?
- When should it be implemented?
- How should it be approached?
- Who should explain it?
- Where should it be presented?

The answers to these questions might seem obvious to you at first glance, but after you look at how they affect your project's organization, you may realize the questions aren't as simple as they may seem.

### *Answering the Questions*

In answering the first question, "What should be documented?," you should be concerned with more than just the parts of your project that you will draw. You also should consider how to organize your drawings in a way that describes your project in the most efficient and effective manner. For example, you might need to define a continuous chamfer that surrounds a faceplate, as well as the location of the holes in the faceplate and the specific location of tooling on the faceplate. To adequately describe these conditions, you would need two sections—one horizontal and one vertical through the faceplate—as well as a front view of the faceplate. Two isometric views can accomplish the same thing with one fewer drawing required.

The second question, "When should it be implemented?," might mean that you won't need to draw some details of your project at all because you will get back a set of shop drawings from a vendor that determines how the detailing will be done. Answering this second question also might determine the order of the drawings within a set of project drawings.

It might seem obvious to you that the third question, "How should it be approached?," concerns the type of drawing (such as isometric or plan and section drawings) that you need. However, you also should think about using photographs, annotation, and shaded 3D models as part of the explanation.

The fourth question, "Who should explain it?", might mean that you have a vendor finishing your work for you in the form of shop drawings, but it also involves finding a person within the project team to work on the design. A conceptual designer, for example, might not have the CAD skills that are needed to complete a detailed 3D model. Therefore, you might have to alter your preferred choice of drawing technique based upon who is doing the design and who is doing the drawing.

After you have completed the first four questions, you are prepared to ask the fifth and final question, "Where should it be presented?", which ultimately determines the organization of your drawings. For example, you must determine whether you have so many details that they must be displayed on their own detail sheets, or whether these details will fit as blow-ups on the same sheets that display your working model. You also must establish a systematic approach to the order of your drawings that works for every project. Furthermore, you should address whether you can readily insert new drawings into the drawing sequence if you discover that one is needed well into your project. Two key concepts that can help you manage this portion of your effort are as follows:

- Developing an efficient numbering system used within the drawings
- Developing a file/folder-naming system that corresponds with the drawing numbering system

### *Developing an Efficient Numbering System*

You need a way to name or number your drawings that works the same way every time and creates flexibility in the order of your drawings and the number of each type of drawing. A perfect example of a system that works this way is a library catalogue system, better known as the Dewey Decimal System. If you organize your drawings into categories and then sequence the drawings within a category, this type of system can work for you. Generally, each specific industry has its own organizational standard. For example, in the AEC industry, drawings have categories, such as Cover Sheet and General Information Sheets, Floor Plans, Elevations, and Sections. Each category might contain a sequence of drawings, such as the First Floor Plan and the Second Floor Plan. Following this format, you could define a drawing numbering system that meets the goals of predictability, flexibility, and expandability. The following list details a numbering system you could implement:

| | |
|---|---|
| 0.00, 0.01, 0.02, and so on | Cover Sheets and General Information |
| 1.00, 1.01, 1.02, and so on | Floor Plans |
| 2.00, 2.01, 2.02, and so on | Elevations |
| 3.00, 3.01, 3.02, and so on | Sections |
| …and so forth. | |

**I NSIDER NOTE**

Note that a new floor plan drawing can be added to the end of the Floor Plans category at any time without adversely affecting the drawing numbers in the categories that follow, such as the Elevations category. The limitation with the numbering system as shown is that a maximum of nine drawing categories and a maximum of 99 drawings in each category can be created. If you need more, simply add more numbers to your filenames, such as 01.000.

**I**NSIDER CAUTION

When developing a naming convention for files, unless it's really needed, it would be wise to avoid using "." in your filenames. Use it only as a separator between the filename and the extension. There have problems in the past with use of the periods causing software and file system incompatibilities. Better safe than sorry.

## Developing a File- and Folder-Naming System

You can carry the numbering system shown in the previous section a bit further and use it to name the drawing files while also adding project numbers and a drawing description. The only limitations in Windows operating systems are that the filename can't contain more than 255 characters, and it can't contain any of the following characters: \ / : * ? " < > |. Therefore, a responsible file-naming system might include a project or work-order number, a drawing number, and a predictable maximum number of characters for a description. The following example illustrates the format of a filename using this system:

```
<project number>-<drawing number>-<revision number><drawing owner>-<sheet
➥title>.dwg
0301-1.00-01cws-OVERALL BUILDING PLAN.dwg
```

Note that Windows operating systems also "remember" the uppercase letters separately from lowercase letters. Also note that the final extension for the filename is always .dwg for drawings. Even if you can see only the first 15 characters of this filename, you would know that the file belongs to project number 0301, that it's a plan of some type, that it's revision number 1, and that someone with the initials "cws" originated the drawing. This file-naming convention also sorts the drawing files first by project number, then by drawing number, then by revision, and then by author. Figure 2.3 shows an example of what the results might be.

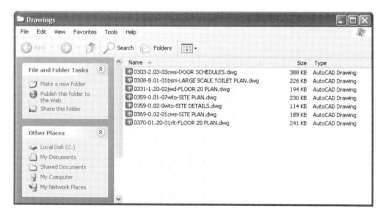

**Figure 2.3** Using filenames with logical naming saves you time and helps organize your project.

**I** NSIDER  NOTE

> If you create new drawings on a regular basis, an involved filename can become coun-
> terproductive. In other words, the amount of information that you include in your
> filename is partly based upon the shelf life of your drawings.

If you organize your drawings into folders that have some logical hierarchy to them, the
filenames also can become simpler. For instance, the previous example could have a
folder structure similar to the one shown in Figure 2.4. Using the folders in Figure 2.4,
the filename used previously could become 02EX01.dwg.

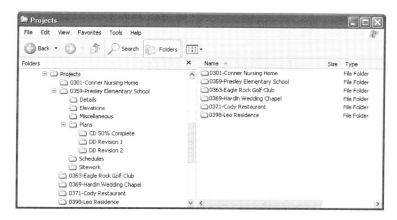

**Figure 2.4**   The judicious use of folders can simplify file-naming needs.

It's always a good idea to keep the project number or work order number as part of the
drawing filename so that drawings that might be accidentally misplaced can be tied to
their project with relative ease. You also must consider how many versions of any one portion of the filename you might have. For example, the project number 0301 enables you to
have 99 projects in 2003. If you think you will have more than 99 projects, you should use
a number with five digits, such as 03001. Likewise, 1.00 means that only 99 floors can exist
in the building (1.01 through 1.99), and using 01 for a revision marker means that up to
99 revisions can exist. Additionally, with the passing of the year 2000, it may be useful
to include the full year numeric value for project numbers, such as 2003001.

Make sure that you don't limit yourself to having to change your file-naming scheme in
a year or two. Take the time to study the types and number of events that you need to
record in your filename by looking over past projects that you or other members of your
company have completed. Don't hesitate to run your ideas by others to see if they can
spot any shortcomings.

**I**NSIDER **N**OTE

> Depending on the other people that need to work with your files, especially outside of your network system, developing an agreed-upon directory structure can ease the transition of data files between all team members.

## Determining How Your Drawings Relate

This topic can become very complex, because not only can AutoCAD drawings be linked to other documents and other documents be linked to your drawings, but complex relationships can also exist between the drawings themselves. You can organize your thoughts about the interrelationships between your drawings and other drawings or documents by asking a few simple questions:

- What information must be shared between drawings?
- What other documents will be included in the drawings?
- What other documents will the drawings be included within?

At this point, it's usually a good idea to create a mock-up set of drawings using a standard form. If you have a number of drawings and documents that make up your project, and your sheets are standard and uniformly sized, then a mock-up is easy to do and can be beneficial. If, however, your projects are small in terms of document count or widely varied in document format and size, you may not find a mock-up on a form to be very helpful.

You can create this mock-up as a basis for your drawing set in AutoCAD, or you can draw a free-hand mock-up using preprinted sheets and a pencil. Creating digital mock-ups of your project will be helpful in the long run because the effort contributes to the creation of the final documents.

However you choose to create a mock-up, it should organize key information. In the section, "Determining Which Elements Can Be Used More Than Once," Figure 2.8 shows an example of a mock-up form that contains places that provide the information to answer the three questions just reviewed. This shared information is placed in the drawing window on the form by using callouts (or bubbles) that reference another drawing. Additionally, such useful information as drawing number, drawing name, date, project name, and author is included on the form.

If you want to create your mock-ups digitally, you can place the mock-up right on the drawing to aid in its creation. This can be set up ahead of time by using a form in place of a title block in a template drawing. After the mock-up has served its purpose, you can substitute a real title block for the mock-up form. If you keep your mock-ups separate from your drawings, then it's a good idea to create your mock-up as an 8 1/2×11-inch sheet so that you can plot "mini" sets of your entire project until you complete the production drawing set.

**I**NSIDER **T**IP

> Digital or graphic mock-ups are a great way to manage drawing sets that are being created by a large group of people. For example, mock-ups of how detail sheets are to be organized can be created in Excel and stored in a public area (server) where multiple people can access them. This avoids duplication and reworking and aids in producing higher-quality documents.

## Using Object Linking and Embedding (OLE)

When you insert a document within your AutoCAD drawing, you can use Object Linking and Embedding (OLE). By using OLE, you can either link the inserted object to the original document or embed it as a duplicate of the original document. If you link the inserted object to the original document, every time the drawing is opened, AutoCAD automatically locates the original document and then updates the inserted object based on the latest version of the original document. By linking the inserted object to the original document, you ensure that the latest version of the original document is always displayed in your drawing, which is a very useful feature if the original document is being edited on a regular basis. Figure 2.5 shows an example of a document being inserted as a linked object in an AutoCAD drawing.

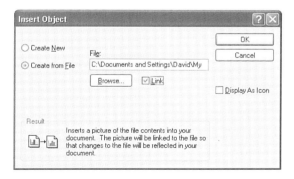

**Figure 2.5**    Linking an object to the original document when inserting it into an AutoCAD drawing using OLE.

Embedding an object, on the other hand, inserts a duplicate of the original document but does not link the inserted object to the original document. Consequently, any edits made to the original document are not reflected when the drawing is reopened. This feature is useful if you want to insert a copy of the original document without fear of the copy being overwritten by an updated version. Exercise 2.1 illustrates how to create a task list and insert it into a drawing using OLE.

**I**NSIDER **N**OTE

This exercise uses a spreadsheet to create a task list because a spreadsheet makes the insertion and numbering of tasks relatively simple. If you don't have a spreadsheet product, you can use WordPad (which comes with Windows operating systems) to accomplish the same goal.

### Exercise 2.1    Using OLE to Embed Task Lists in Your Drawings

1. First, use a spreadsheet application to create a task list with a few items listed. If you have a current project for which you need a task list, that would be a good place to start—otherwise, just make one up. The task list can be any width and length, but using something approximately 8 1/2×11-inch will produce typical results.

2. After you create and save the task list, highlight the tasks by clicking and dragging your cursor over them, and then open the application's Edit pull-down menu and choose Copy. The highlighted items are copied to the clipboard.

3. Launch AutoCAD 2005. AutoCAD by default provides a blank drawing using a template as a starting point. Because we need something specific, choose New from the File pull-down menu.

4. From the Template list, scroll down to the Ansi D - Named Plot Styles.dwt and click it, and AutoCAD loads the template file, already in a layout view.

5. From the Edit pull-down menu, choose Paste Special. From the Paste Special dialog box, click Paste Link. Now only your spreadsheet application is listed in the dialog box. Click OK. AutoCAD inserts your task list OLE object into the drawing.

6. Move your cursor into the center of the OLE object and select the object.

7. Right-click, and using the context menu that appears, choose the Move option. Now drag the task list object to the right of the drawing area.

8. Select the object again, move the cursor over one of the corner grips, and click. Now, moving the cursor resizes the object.

9. Click as desired to set a new size. The result should appear similar to Figure 2.2, shown earlier in this chapter. Using this technique, you can insert any variety of objects into your drawing from the Windows clipboard.

   Close AutoCAD without saving.

## Developing Efficient Workflow Management

If more than one person is going to work on a drawing, you must determine how each person will know which drawing is the current one. This aspect of project delivery is known as workflow management. Consider a scenario, for example, in which outside consultants or contractors work on your drawings, and you want to make changes to those drawings. How do you know if the drawing you have contains the most recent information? If you do not address this concern, you might edit an outdated drawing.

Another problem you may encounter is one in which two people need to work on the same drawing at the same time. By applying workflow management to your project, you can avoid conflicts and limit mistakes.

**I**NSIDER **T**IP

> The WHOHAS command in AutoCAD 2005 enables you to determine who has a drawing open for editing. When you're armed with this information, you can contact that individual and tell him or her to exit the drawing so you can open it. This functionality is also provided when you simply try to open a drawing. If someone has opened the drawing you want, AutoCAD reports the user's basic computer and user name.

### Proper Network File Control

Your organization of the project and its documents and your management of file access are crucial to avoiding a disaster with multiple document users or authors. If you work on a network that provides multiple user access to a drawing, then your network software must support file locking. Most contemporary network products enable you to open files in Read Only mode and won't let you overwrite the file on which someone else is working. Proper network file control means that the first person to open a drawing is the only editor that can actually save changes to the drawing. All subsequent users can open the drawing only in Read Only mode. If someone absolutely must record changes to a drawing that is currently open by someone else, he must save his changes as a new drawing. Recording these changes on a unique layer name and saving the changes as a new drawing enables the changes to be merged with the original drawing later.

---

**I**NSIDER **N**OTE

AutoCAD 2005 has a feature called *in-place reference editing*, which enables users to edit blocks and xrefs without having to leave the current drawing, and save changes back to the original object or drawing file. The REFEDIT command is discussed in detail in Chapter 11, "Working with External References."

---

## Using Redlines

Users also can record redlines on a unique layer that can be merged with a drawing. Redlines list comments, questions, and editing instructions for a drawing that are acted upon by someone else later. Figure 2.6 shows an example of redlines.

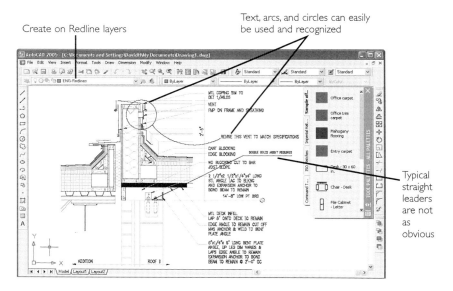

**Figure 2.6** Inserting redline revision instructions does not require sophisticated AutoCAD commands.

---

**I**NSIDER **T**IP

Because redlines can be created using basic AutoCAD commands, you could create your own toolbar that contains basic redlining commands such as text, lines, arcs, circles, and leaders. In this way, individuals who are not sophisticated AutoCAD users can still contribute to your drawings electronically, saving time and paper.

---

An alternative to creating a new redline layer in the current drawing is to xref the drawing into a new drawing and create redlines in the new drawing. In either event, you should name the drawing file and the layers used for redlines based on a standard. For example, the filename or layer name could include the editor's initials, a date, and the term REDLINES in its name. This simplifies the identification of your redline objects.

## Determining Which Elements Can Be Used More Than Once

As mentioned earlier, you can use xrefs to create more than one drawing from the same drawing. Although the use of xrefs can help ensure that numerous drawings contain exactly the same information and reduce total project drawing storage needs, xrefs also can help you avoid creating drawing elements more than once.

If you use a drawing template, as demonstrated in the previous exercise, you might not want to include a drawing border in the template drawing. Instead, you could devise a project border sheet that contains the project name, issue date, project number, project address, your firm's logo, address, and other information and insert it into drawings as an xref. Therefore, each new project drawing would include the border as an xref, and changes to the border would need to be made only once in the original xref.

**I**NSIDER NOTE

> Using this method, you should design the xref so that it contains only the information common to all project drawings. For example, elements like issue date and sheet revision data would stay unique to the drawing file and not appear in the xref file.

Using an element more than once can mean more than creating an exact duplicate of objects. You might want to use different guides in all your project drawings, such as the format of text, a key plan with different portions hatched in each drawing, or a sheet grid that doesn't plot. For example, you can create a block that contains only attributes that fill in your title block. The drawing author, checker, sheet number, sheet name, and date can be filled in separately for each drawing, but such elements as the text style, height, and layer will always be the same. (You will learn more about blocks in Chapter 10, "Creating and Using Blocks.") Suppose your projects usually involve a large number of drawings. By combining the use of block attributes inside blocks and xref drawings, you can increase efficiency by creating a template drawing that contains the border as an xref, the sheet-specific text as attributes, and a sheet grid on a non-plot layer. Figure 2.7 shows an example of a template drawing that incorporates a number of unifying features.

Firm information

Repetitive title
block information

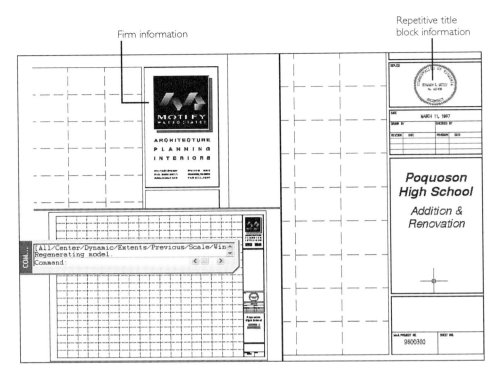

**Figure 2.7** A template drawing can contain project-specific information if you create a new template for each of your projects.

At the start of a project, you must map out as many multiple-use opportunities as you can. This includes organizing portions of drawings that you can reuse from earlier projects or from standard drawings that you have developed over numerous projects. Using the mock-up set discussed earlier, you should also map out the use of viewports to display the necessary views of your model. Figure 2.8 shows an example of a mock-up of a portion of an architectural project.

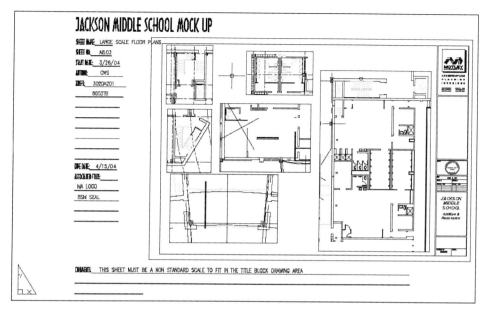

**Figure 2.8**   A mock-up of a project.

# Determining How a Drawing Will Be Displayed

The final, and possibly most complex, issue to consider when laying out a project is the number of ways that a drawing will be displayed. AutoCAD enables you to publish your drawings on the Internet with the Publish to Web feature. In addition, you might need to plot the drawing on a number of different sheet sizes, or you might need to create both drawings and renderings of the drawings for the project. Finally, as is the case for many drawings in this book, you might need to publish your drawings in a shop manual or a technical publication. As you can imagine, large drawings with a significant amount of detail aren't easily viewable on computer screens; if they were, the ZOOM command wouldn't exist!

If you create documents that will be displayed on the Internet, published in a technical publication, and plotted on a sheet of paper, something will have to give. You might need to create completely different drawings for each type of media due to one single factor: Your text and symbols won't work for each and every possible publishing method. Although a perfect solution doesn't exist for these broad publishing requirements, planning for the project's needs from the start can save a lot of time and headaches.

If your publication must vary from project to project, it might be a good idea to obtain a drawing from a previous project that is similar to the one you will use for the current project. Using this drawing, you could try to publish it under all the conditions that you must meet. This process will help you uncover any problems that you might encounter.

# Setting Up Your Drawing

After you have pondered each of the issues discussed so far, it is time to set up your drawings. You must follow a sequential set of steps to determine how you can accomplish this task. If you use the following steps, you will avoid revising text sizes, drawing configurations, and a number of other complications later in a project, such as:

- Determining paper size
- Determining drawing scale
- Developing title blocks
- Determining units and angles

## Determining Paper Size

The determination you must make first and foremost is the final plot size of your drawings. If you plot your drawings to paper, the paper sizes that your plotter handles define your options for the drawing size. Using a mock-up process—whether a formal one, such as the process discussed earlier, or simply figuring out how much paper area is required for an appropriate scale of your drawings—is the first step. Paper comes in an extensive set of sizes, and each industry generally settles on a set of standard sizes. One important factor to consider about paper is whether you can create a modular approach to your paper sizes. Figure 2.9 shows a progression of paper sizes that can expand or contract between sheet sizes while maintaining the same aspect ratio between sheets. Maintaining the same aspect ratio means that you can enlarge or minimize your drawings without concern for whether the drawing will fit the same way on a larger or smaller sheet.

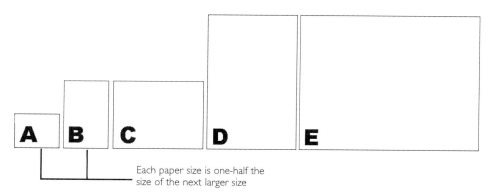

Each paper size is one-half the size of the next larger size

**Figure 2.9** Using paper sizes that are modular can aid in your documentation process.

Obtaining modular sheet sizes might not be an easy task. If you are in the Architecture/Engineering/Construction industry, for example, nothing about standard AEC sheet sizes is modular. The AEC industry is hopelessly antiquated in this area and is making no rapid movement toward changing the system. Although they have a modular set, no copier or standard envelope will use a 9×12-inch paper size. Table 2.1 lists standard paper sizes that are available.

**Table 2.1   Standard Paper**

| Paper Size | Standard | MM | In |
|---|---|---|---|
| Eight Crown | IMP | 1461 × 1060 | 57 1/2 × 41 3/4 |
| Antiquarian | IMP | 1346 × 533 | 53 × 21 |
| Quad Demy | IMP | 1118 × 826 | 44 × 32 1/2 |
| Double Princess | IMP | 1118 × 711 | 44 × 28 |
| Quad Crown | IMP | 1016 × 762 | 40 × 30 |
| Double Elephant | IMP | 1016 × 686 | 40 × 27 |
| B0 | ISO | 1000 × 1414 | 39.37 × 55.67 |
| Arch-E | USA | 914 × 1,219 | 36 × 48 |
| Double Demy | IMP | 889 × 572 | 35 × 22 1/2 |
| E | ANSI | 864 × 1118 | 34 × 44 |
| A0 | ISO | 841 × 1189 | 33.11 × 46.81 |
| Imperial | IMP | 762 × 559 | 30 × 22 |
| Princess | IMP | 711 × 546 | 28 × 21 12 |
| B1 | ISO | 707 × 1000 | 27.83 × 39.37 |
| Arch-D | USA | 610 × 914 | 24 × 36 |
| A1 | ISO | 594 × 841 | 23.39 × 33.11 |
| Demy | IMP | 584 × 470 | 23 × 18 1/2 |
| D | ANSI | 559 × 864 | 22 × 34 |

*continues* ▶

### Table 2.1  Continued

| Paper Size | Standard | MM | In |
|---|---|---|---|
| B2 | ISO | $500 \times 707$ | $19.68 \times 27.83$ |
| Arch-C | USA | $457 \times 610$ | $18 \times 24$ |
| C | ANSI | $432 \times 559$ | $17 \times 22$ |
| A2 | ISO | $420 \times 594$ | $16.54 \times 23.39$ |
| B3 | ISO | $353 \times 500$ | $13.90 \times 19.68$ |
| Brief | IMP | $333 \times 470$ | 13 1/8 × 18 1/2 |
| Foolscap Folio | IMP | $333 \times 210$ | 13 1/8 × 8 1/4 |
| Arch-B | USA | $305 \times 457$ | $12 \times 18$ |
| A3 | ISO | $297 \times 420$ | $11.69 \times 16.54$ |
| B | ANSI | $279 \times 432$ | $11 \times 17$ |
| Demy quarto | IMP | $273 \times 216$ | 10 3/4 × 8 1/2 |
| B4 | ISO | $250 \times 353$ | $9.84 \times 13.90$ |
| Crown quarto | IMP | $241 \times 184$ | 9 1/2 × 7 1/4 |
| Royal octavo | IMP | $241 \times 152$ | 9 1/2 × 6 |
| Arch-A | USA | $229 \times 305$ | $9 \times 12$ |
| Demy octavo | IMP | $222 \times 137$ | 8 3/4 × 5 3/8 |
| A | ANSI | $216 \times 279$ | $8.5 \times 11$ |
| Legal | USA | $216 \times 356$ | $8.5 \times 14$ |
| A4 | ISO | $210 \times 297$ | $8.27 \times 11.69$ |
| Foolscap quarto | IMP | $206 \times 165$ | 8 1/8 × 6 1/2 |
| Crown Octavo | IMP | $181 \times 121$ | 7 1/8 × 4 1/4 |
| B5 | ISO | $176 \times 250$ | $6.93 \times 9.84$ |
| A5 | ISO | $148 \times 210$ | $5.83 \times 8.27$ |
| | USA | $140 \times 216$ | $5.5 \times 8.5$ |
| | USA | $127 \times 178$ | $5 \times 7$ |
| A6 | ISO | $105 \times 148$ | $4.13 \times 5.83$ |
| | USA | $102 \times 127$ | $4 \times 5$ |
| | USA | $76 \times 102$ | $3 \times 5$ |
| A7 | ISO | $74 \times 105$ | $2.91 \times 4.13$ |
| A8 | ISO | $52 \times 74$ | $2.05 \times 2.91$ |
| A9 | ISO | $37 \times 52$ | $1.46 \times 2.05$ |
| A10 | ISO | $26 \times 37$ | $1.02 \times 1.46$ |

# Determining Drawing Scale

After the paper sizes have been established, the next step is to determine the appropriate scale for your drawings. The scale of a drawing is a deceptively simple concept, and it involves more than simply figuring out what size your drawing must be to fit on the paper. The real issue about drawing scale is that the information contained on the drawing must be legible, yet the drawing scale must be standard in your industry, and the sheet size must be as convenient to handle as possible. Your drawing must place the model, notes, dimensions, hatching, and symbols in their most favorable and legible light. If you have to cram a drawing full of symbols and text, the line work that represents the object of your drawing may become difficult to discern. Creating the drawing at the appropriate scale allows for space between text, dimensions, and symbols both within and around your drawing.

Of course, if you always create drawings at full scale, then the only option you are faced with is the selection of the sheet size for your paper. Using full scale might require you to cut up your drawing into sections rather than display the entire model on one sheet of paper. You might think that a drawing spanning more than one sheet seems inconvenient, but legibility is more important in this case.

## Using Paper Space Viewports to Scale a Model

When plotting, you can set the scale of your model in two ways. You can either provide a scale factor at plot time or "rescale" your model through Paper Space viewports. However, because both result in a drawing that is plotted at the appropriate scale, which one is the best choice?

A major advantage to using Paper Space viewports is that you get instant feedback from your drawing as to what drawing scale fits on your sheet because you immediately see what your plotted sheet will look like in your layout. Another advantage is that you somewhat guarantee how others will plot the drawing. If your drawing is plotted from model space with a scale factor, it's up to the user to determine the scale factor, which could easily vary. By setting up a scaled viewport, there's less chance of the plot view being misscaled. Therefore, scaling views of your model in Paper Space viewports is the better choice.

To use a Paper Space viewport for plotting to scale, you must zoom in on your model at a predetermined scale factor. The following steps summarize the entire process of determining and setting the proper zoom-scale factor:

1. Calculate the required scale factor. If your drawings use a decimal scale, this is a relatively simple feat. For example, a drawing created at 1:10 uses a scale factor of 0.10. The AEC industry uses Imperial scale factors, however, and the calculation requires a few more steps. A 1/8-inch = 1 foot scale drawing requires a scale factor of 1/96. To convert Imperial scales, simply multiply your drawing scale (in this case, 1/8) by 1/12 (12.0/0.125). Therefore, the scale factor for a 1/4-inch = 1 foot drawing is 1/48, and a 3-inch = 1 foot drawing is 1/4.

2. Click inside the Paper Space viewport to make it the focus.

3. Perform a Zoom Extents to see your entire model.

4. Perform a Zoom Center and select a point on the model that you want to be in the middle of the viewport.

5. When you are prompted for magnification or height, type your scale factor, followed by XP, as shown in Figure 2.10.

   The area of the drawing you selected is centered in the viewport at the desired scale, as shown in Figure 2.11.

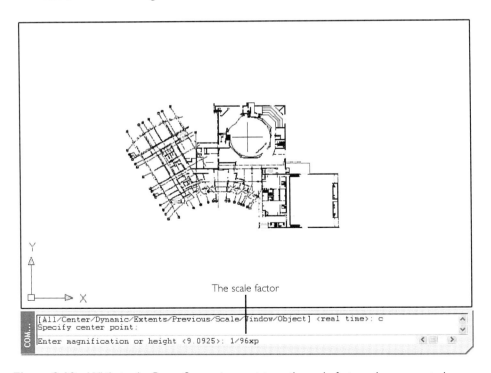

**Figure 2.10**   While in the Paper Space viewport, type the scale factor when prompted, followed by XP.

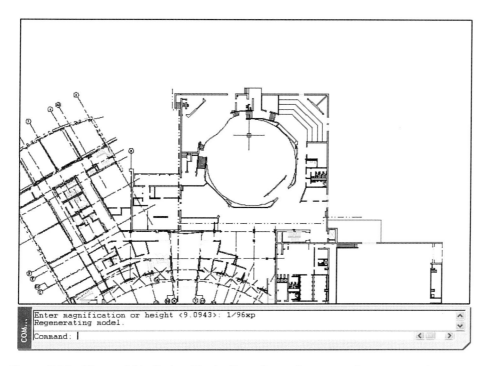

**Figure 2.11**   The model is displayed in the Paper Space viewport at the correct scale.

Using this technique, you can set up numerous plot scales of your drawing for any specific needs that you might have. Note also that any text, symbols, or other elements placed in model space will be scaled as well. If you want to display the same model at different scales, you must create symbols, dimensions, and text on different layers and at appropriate sizes for each scale, or draw them all in paper space. The great thing about drawing symbols, text, or other elements in paper space is that you can create them at their actual size without having to convert for scale. This means, for example, that text that is 1/8-inch high is the same height in all drawings, no matter what scale is used to plot the model. Be mindful, however, that if the objects in model space move at all, the relative position of the annotation objects in paper space and the model will be changed and may no longer align properly.

## Developing Title Blocks

Almost any drawing, whether a work order, a maintenance drawing, or a sophisticated manufacturing document, should have a title block. A title block provides informational—and often legally required—verification of what the drawing represents in terms of the object of the drawing, the time of day the drawing was created, and the origin of the drawing. If you only publish your drawings electronically, then the title block might differ considerably from one that eventually will be used for plotting or printing. For now, it is assumed that a paper plot is the ultimate goal of an AutoCAD drawing. The following list serves as a guide for the elements your title block should include:

- The name, address, and phone numbers of the firm originating the drawing
- The names, addresses, and phone numbers of any consultants working on the drawing
- The date on which the drawing was originally created and approved for use
- A revision history, including who performed the revision, what the revision was, and when the revision occurred
- A drawing title
- A project name or work order title
- A location for seals, stamps, and/or approval signatures
- A drawing number
- A project or work order number
- The author of the drawing and the name of any individual(s) who checked the drawing, if required
- The name of the AutoCAD drawing file
- The date that the drawing was printed or plotted
- A copyright notice, if required
- Additional general information, such as a project address, plant name, and owner's name
- Line work that organizes the title block information and its relationship to the drawing

The design of title blocks is often the source of great debate within a company. No perfect title block design exists, and your needs might include items not listed in the preceding guide. Generally, the more information (either critical or organizational in nature) that you can place in the lower-right corner of the sheet, the easier it will be for others to quickly find the desired drawing. The title block should provide the information legibly for all size plots, but it should not dominate the sheet. You also might need to develop a title block for multiple sheet sizes. Most likely, you will not be able to use the same title block for an 8 1/2×11 inch sheet as you can for a 34×44 inch sheet. You will need to experiment with different designs until you have a set of title blocks that works for all content possibilities and sizes.

Additionally, the title block can contain a grid design that promotes the modular development of your drawings. For example, if you typically develop details that can be printed on 8 1/2×11 inch paper, then you could develop a drawing module that enables you to piece together a number of small modular drawings into a larger drawing. In this case, you should be concerned with the drawing area within the title block for the module size rather than the sheet of paper size. This is because you will transfer the drawing area from one sheet to the next. Figure 2.12 shows one example of a modular approach to the drawing area.

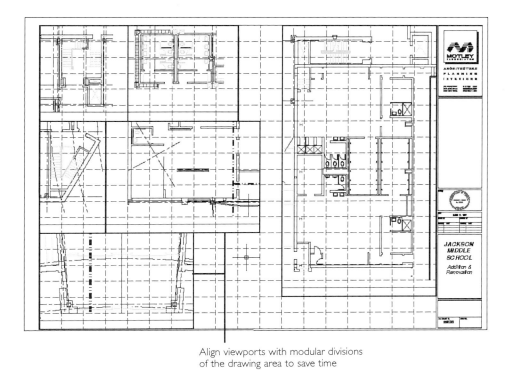

Align viewports with modular divisions
of the drawing area to save time

**Figure 2.12**    Using a modular grid for drawing development enables you to use modular drawings more effectively.

## Determining Units and Angles

The discipline and country in which you work determines whether you'll use fractional inches, feet and fractional inches, decimal feet, decimal inches, meters, or millimeters in the creation of drawings. Additionally, you must determine how accurately to display the dimensions. AutoCAD does not understand any specific system of the division of distance—the program simply draws using units. As a result, you must tell AutoCAD how you want those units displayed. You change the display of units and angles from the Drawing Units dialog box (shown in Figure 2.13), which is accessed by choosing Units from the Format pull-down menu.

**Figure 2.13**   The Drawing Units dialog box is used to set AutoCAD units and angles displayed to the user.

You should set up the default units that you will typically use in your template drawings. By doing so, all new drawings that use the template will automatically use the default units and angles settings. You should also note that you can select the precision of the display of your units and angles.

**I**NSIDER **TIP**

> Don't confuse the precision setting for units and angles with the precision setting for dimensions. You set the dimension precision independently when you define dimensioning defaults. Refer to Chapters 16 and 17 on dimensioning for more information.

When selecting the units' and angles' precision, your primary concern should be how much precision you need to see when you create your AutoCAD drawings. High-precision settings often cause AutoCAD to display the drawing coordinates using scientific notation, such as 1.07E+10, which usually isn't much help. On the other hand, if you're trying to track down a drafting error, high-precision settings can tell you that a line has been drawn at an angle of 179.91846 degrees rather than 180 degrees. The simple process of trial and error can help you determine the best settings for your needs.

**I**NSIDER  **N**OTE

> The units in AutoCAD actually have no bearing on how you draw. If you draw a line 4-7/32" long, it is exactly that long. But if you have your drawing UNITS set to 1/8", listing that line may state it is 4-1/4" long. You must pay careful attention when drawing so that you can trust the information provided by AutoCAD.

### *Converting Between Units*

If you need to convert your drawings from feet and inches to metric units, the units in which you create your drawing will not automatically convert. This is because you are drawing in units, not in real-world sizes. For example, when you create a drawing in feet and inches, one unit is an inch. When you convert to a metric drawing, you must change units to decimal units and convert the drawing to a metric drawing by scaling the drawing by the proper conversion factor. As a result of this component of AutoCAD's units architecture, you must determine what the drawing should represent before you start creating lines, circles, and arcs. You can instruct AutoCAD to dimension objects by scaling them between different units of measurement (accomplished by setting a linear scale factor for dimensioning), but the model will not be drawn true to size in the converted units. For more information, refer to Chapter 7, "Using Coordinate Systems."

# Summary

In this chapter, you learned about the components of an effective project-delivery system. You also learned the factors needed to get organized before creating a drawing, as well as how to use OLE to create a task list that is embedded in each drawing. Finally, you learned how to use a mock-up process to view your entire project as a whole for planning purposes based upon priorities, how much detail is necessary, how your drawings relate to other drawings and documents, and how to account for the people who work on the drawings.

Other issues that need to be considered before you start a project include the basic factors used in layers, linetypes, lineweights, text styles, blocks, and dimension styles. The following chapters deal more directly with the features of AutoCAD 2005 and how you can apply these features to aid in project delivery.

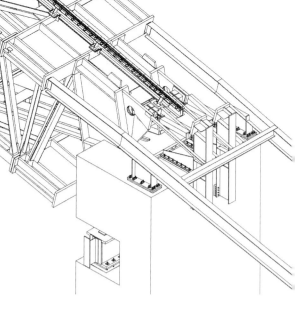

*Chapter 3*

# Starting a Drawing in AutoCAD

AutoCAD is a versatile drawing application that is used by many industries to draft and design a multitude of products. Because of the wide range of industries that use AutoCAD, the program is designed to enable users to easily customize AutoCAD's drafting settings to suit their unique needs. This chapter explains AutoCAD's drafting settings and looks at how AutoCAD simplifies setting up your drawing environment with the Startup dialog box.

This chapter covers the following topics:

- The Startup dialog box
- Creating and saving a template file
- Controlling drawing settings
- Understanding drawing limits
- Controlling drawing units
- Defining drafting settings

# The Startup Dialog Box

AutoCAD 2005 provides users with two primary schemes to begin work. The system you use is controlled by the Startup drop-down list within Options under the System tab, General Options area. How this option is set determines what happens when you open AutoCAD.

When the Startup option is set to Show the Startup dialog box, AutoCAD begins in a zero document state, meaning no drawing is open for editing. Instead, the Startup dialog box is presented within the graphics area, waiting for you to decide how you want to start work. The Startup dialog also automatically recalls the last option used in it.

## Startup Start From Scratch Option

The first option to start a new drawing within the Startup dialog box is the Start from Scratch option. As shown in Figure 3.1, the Default Settings area has but two options.

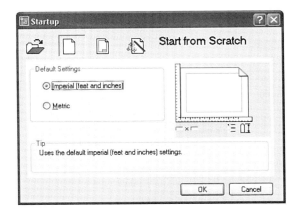

**Figure 3.1**   The Start from Scratch option displays only two types of default settings.

You can choose Imperial (feet and inches) or Metric. These relate to units of measurement, as shown in Figure 3.2. If you choose Imperial, AutoCAD creates a new drawing based on the Imperial measurement system, which uses the ACAD.DWT template file. If you choose Metric, AutoCAD creates a new drawing based on the Metric measurement system, which uses the ACADISO.DWT template file.

## *Understanding AutoCAD's Default Values*

When you choose Imperial or Metric settings, you are actually affecting two key system variables: MEASUREMENT and MEASUREINIT. The MEASUREMENT system variable sets the drawing units as either Imperial or Metric for the current drawing and is originally set in the template, whereas the MEASUREINIT system variable sets the drawing units as either Imperial or Metric for new drawings when they are created and is stored in the current profile.

Specifically, the MEASUREMENT system variable controls which hatch pattern and linetype files a drawing uses. When the system variable is set to 0, the Imperial units are set, and AutoCAD uses the hatch pattern file and linetype file designated by the ANSIHatch and ANSILinetype Registry settings. When the system variable is set to 1, the Metric units are set, and AutoCAD uses the hatch pattern file and linetype file designated by the ISOHatch and ISOLinetype Registry settings.

**I**NSIDER **N**OTE

Each time you launch AutoCAD and the Startup dialog appears, you can choose the Close button [X] instead of any specific option. The Close button cancels the Startup dialog and leaves you with a new drawing using the most recent template selected in the Start from Scratch option.

It is important to determine which system of measurement you will use before starting your drawing because the system of measurement you select influences how objects appear in your drawing. For example, Figure 3.2 shows two rectangles that contain a hatch pattern. Both hatch patterns are the same (ANSI31), and their rotation and scale are identical. However, it is obvious that the hatch pattern on the left displays lines much closer together than the hatch pattern on the right.

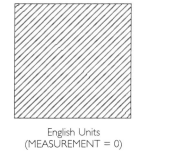
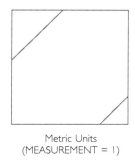

English Units
(MEASUREMENT = 0)

Metric Units
(MEASUREMENT = 1)

**Figure 3.2**    The MEASUREMENT system variable affects the appearance of hatch patterns when they are inserted in a drawing.

The difference between the two hatch patterns occurs because the hatch pattern on the left was drawn with the MEASUREMENT system variable set to 0 (Imperial units). Then the MEASUREMENT system variable was set to 1 (Metric units), and the same hatch pattern was drawn on the right. This example demonstrates that AutoCAD uses two different hatch pattern files based on the current value of MEASUREMENT. Be sure to choose the correct units of measurement to ensure that AutoCAD inserts the proper hatch patterns and linetypes into your drawing.

**INSIDER TIP**

To correct a hatch pattern inserted with the wrong units of measurement, change the MEASUREMENT system variable, select the hatch pattern, click the right mouse button, and then choose Hatch Edit. After AutoCAD displays the Hatch Edit dialog box, choose the same hatch pattern from the list and then click OK. AutoCAD updates the hatch pattern based on the current units of measurement.

**INSIDER CAUTION**

If you load linetypes while the drawing's MEASUREMENT system variable is incorrect, the linetypes don't automatically change when you modify the system variable. You must reload any loaded linetypes from the correct linetype file after changing the variable.

**INSIDER NOTE**

Something that should be understood about AutoCAD is that it is essentially unit-less—a unit of 1.0 is whatever you understand it to represent. It can be an inch, a meter, a mile, or a light-year. You generally rescale your objects so that your interpreted distance of a unit of 1.0 matches something you are creating. Unfortunately, there is no "switch" to change your drawings to another scale.

## Startup Use a Wizard Option

AutoCAD provides wizards to help you set up a new drawing. As you complete setting one value, the wizard takes you to the next, using the standard Windows wizard interface that enables you to go to the next default setting or back to edit previous settings. By using AutoCAD's wizards, you can quickly set certain default values and change them again if needed.

## Understanding the Wizard Selections

When you choose the Wizard option (the fourth option on the Startup dialog box), the Use a Wizard area offers two choices, the Advanced Setup or the Quick Setup, as shown in Figure 3.3. The Advanced Setup Wizard takes you through five dialog boxes, enabling you to set values for units, angle, angle measure, angle direction, and area. The Quick Setup Wizard offers a subset of these values, removing options for setting the various values related to angles and enabling you to set values for units and area only.

**Figure 3.3**    The Wizard option offers two methods from which to choose.

The following describes the various values you can set with the Advanced Setup Wizard:

- **Units.** The Units dialog box enables you to set the way linear units are displayed in your drawing.

- **Angle.** The Angle dialog box enables you to set the way angles are displayed in your drawing.

- **Angle Measure.** The Angle Measure dialog box enables you to set the base angle from which all angles are measured (it represents 0 degrees).

- **Angle Direction.** The Angle Direction dialog box enables you to set the direction all angles are measured from the base angle (clockwise or counterclockwise).

- **Area.** The Area dialog box enables you to set the drawing's limits, which represent the area in which your model should be drawn and contained.

The Units dialog box enables you to set how AutoCAD displays measured values, such
as the length of a line, the radius of a circle, or the area of a region. It also controls how
AutoCAD displays coordinate values. For example, if the units are set to Decimal, and
you list the values of a circle object in a drawing, AutoCAD displays values as shown:

```
center point, X=    5.8796  Y=    4.2286  Z=    0.0000
            radius         1.1396
     circumference         7.1601
              area         4.0797
```

However, if the units are set to Fractional, and you list the values of the same circle,
AutoCAD displays values as shown:

```
center point, X=    5 7/8  Y=    4 1/4  Z=         0
            radius         1 1/8
     circumference         7 3/16
              area         4 1/16
```

Notice the difference between the two formats. The Decimal format displays partial values as decimals. In contrast, the Fractional format displays partial values as fractions.
This is true even though the values for the exact same objects are listed.

The Units dialog box also enables you to control the displayed precision of the values. It
does not affect the actual value itself, only the display of the value. For instance, a line 7/8
of an inch long displays a length of 0.875 (assuming Decimal units) when precision is set
to at least 3 places but displays 0.9 when precision is set to a single place. The actual
length of the line is not affected.

When you select a Units value, you are actually setting the LUNITS system variable. The LUNITS system variable is based on an integer, with each value representing a units display mode, as shown in Table 3.1.

**Table 3.1    Units Display Mode Examples for the *LUNITS* Variable**

| Integer | Display Mode | Example |
| --- | --- | --- |
| 1 | Scientific | 1.1356E+00 |
| 2 | Decimal | 1.1356 |
| 3 | Engineering | 0'–1.1356" |
| 4 | Architectural | 0'–1 1/8" |
| 5 | Fractional | 1 1/8 |

When you select a Units precision, you are actually setting another system variable, LUPREC, which controls the displayed precision for units. Like the LUNITS system variable, LUPREC uses an integer to determine the number of decimal places (or the denominator) displayed with a value. The range of acceptable values is 0 through 8. In the case of values displayed in Architectural and Fractional mode, the integer value represents a fractional increment. Table 3.2 shows examples of the precision display for each value.

**Table 3.2    Units Precision Display Examples for the *LUPREC* Variable**

| Integer | Decimal | Architectural/ Fractional |
| --- | --- | --- |
| 0 | 0 | 0 |
| 1 | 0.0 | 1/2 |
| 2 | 0.00 | 1/4 |
| 3 | 0.000 | 1/8 |
| 4 | 0.0000 | 1/16 |
| 5 | 0.00000 | 1/32 |
| 6 | 0.000000 | 1/64 |
| 7 | 0.0000000 | 1/128 |
| 8 | 0.00000000 | 1/256 |

**I**NSIDER **TIP**

> You can adjust the value of a system variable by typing its name at the command prompt and then entering the desired value.

The Angle dialog box enables you to set how AutoCAD displays angle values, such as the angle of an arc or the angle between two lines. It also enables you to set the displayed precision of angles.

Like the Units dialog box, the Angle dialog box controls two system variables: AUNITS and AUPREC. When you select an angle value, you are setting the AUNITS system variable. The AUNITS system variable is based on an integer, with each value representing a units display mode, as shown in Table 3.3.

**Table 3.3   Angular Display Mode Examples for the *AUNITS* Variable**

| Integer | Display Mode | Example |
| --- | --- | --- |
| 0 | Decimal degrees | 23.9493 |
| 1 | Degrees/minutes/seconds | 23d56'57" |
| 2 | Grads | 26.6103g |
| 3 | Radians | 0.4180r |
| 4 | Surveyor's units | N 66d3'3" E |

The AUPREC system variable controls the displayed precision of angles and functions similarly to the LUPREC system variable, using an integer to determine the fractional places displayed with a value. The range of acceptable values is 0 through 8. In the case of values displayed in degrees/minutes/seconds or Surveyor's units, the integer values control the display of minutes and seconds. If the precision value defines the precision beyond minutes and seconds, the seconds are displayed in decimal format. Table 3.4 shows examples of the precision display for each value.

**Table 3.4   Angle Precision Display Examples for the *AUPREC* Variable**

| Integer | Decimal | Surveyor's Units |
| --- | --- | --- |
| 0 | 8 | N 82d E |
| 1 | 8.2 | N 81d46' E |
| 2 | 8.23 | N 81d46' E |
| 3 | 8.235 | N 81d45'55" E |
| 4 | 8.2347 | N 81d45'55" E |
| 5 | 8.23469 | N 81d45'55.1" E |
| 6 | 8.234689 | N 81d45'55.12" E |
| 7 | 8.2346894 | N 81d45'55.118" E |
| 8 | 8.23468944 | N 81d45'55.1180" E |

Notice that the Surveyor's units for values 1 and 2, and values 3 and 4, respectively, display the same level of precision. This occurs because minutes and seconds must be displayed as full values. This is true because there are 60 minutes of angular arc in one degree and 60 seconds of angular arc in one minute.

When displaying angles in degrees/minutes/seconds or Surveyor's units, the ' symbol stands for minutes, not feet, and the " symbol stands for seconds, not inches.

The Angle Measure dialog box enables you to set the base angle from which all angles are measured. AutoCAD uses the default value of 0 degrees being due East (or along the X-axis in the World Coordinate System, or WCS). See Chapter 7, "Using Coordinate Systems," for additional information on coordinate systems. The Angle Measure dialog box enables you to choose from four preset base angles (East, North, West, or South), and it also enables you to enter your own user-defined base angle. The value for the base angle is stored in the ANGBASE system variable and can represent any angle value.

The base angle is associated with the X-axis of the current User Coordinate System, or UCS. If you rotate the UCS, the base angle also rotates.

The Angle Direction dialog box works in conjunction with the Angle Measure dialog box and enables you to set the direction all angles are measured from. The only possible directions are counterclockwise or clockwise. The current direction value is held in the ANGDIR system variable, with 0 indicating a counterclockwise direction and 1 indicating a clockwise direction.

The Area dialog box enables you to set the drawing's limits, which generally represent the area in which your model is contained or the area within which you create your drawing. The limits are intended to help you manage your drawing.

When you set the width and length of the limits, AutoCAD defines the limits as a rectangle, with its lower-left corner located at coordinates 0,0, and its upper-right corner based on the values you enter for Width and Length. The Width and Length values are stored as a coordinate in the LIMMAX system variable. The lower-left coordinates are stored in the LIMMIN system variable.

You can instruct AutoCAD not to enable you to accidentally draw outside the drawing limits, although this concept is somewhat dated if you use layouts for plotting. This is called limits checking, and it is controlled with the LIMCHECK system variable. By setting the variable to 0, you turn off limits checking, and by setting it to 1, you turn on limits checking. The LIMCHECK variable only protects you against acquiring points outside the limits. You can copy objects outside limits and position other items as well.

The drawing area within the limits is also the area in which AutoCAD displays its grid. The *grid* is made up of a series of dots and is used as a frame of reference when creating objects. The grid is useful for quickly drawing objects based on grid locations. The grid's visibility is controlled from the Grid button located on the status bar at the bottom of AutoCAD's screen. You can also press the function key F7 to toggle the grid on and off.

Finally, you can use limits with the ZOOM command and when plotting. When zooming, you can select the All option to immediately display the entire Limits area on AutoCAD's screen. When plotting from model space, you can select the Limits option to plot the entire area defined by the Limits setting.

You have learned how AutoCAD can make starting a drawing easy by using its wizards to walk you through the setup process. Next, we cover the use of predefined template drawings.

## Startup Use a Template Option

A *template* is a drawing file that contains predefined drawing settings and/or geometry, such as a title block, and is used to begin a new drawing. Templates are intended to be a quick way to take advantage of an existing drawing that contains the proper drawing settings and base geometry you use in every drawing.

For example, suppose you are creating 10 drawings that use the same units and angle settings and title block. To minimize your work effort, you can create the drawing once, defining the proper units and angle settings and inserting the desired title block, and then save the drawing as a template. As you begin each new drawing, you select the template file you previously created, which contains the correct units, angle settings, and title block. The template acts as a base for your new drawing and thereby eliminates a lot of repetitious preparation and setup work.

When you choose the Template option, AutoCAD displays the list of available templates, as shown in Figure 3.4. AutoCAD 2005 comes with over 60 predefined template files, and you can add your own. You create a template file by defining the proper units and angle settings, creating any desired geometry, and saving the drawing as a DWT file.

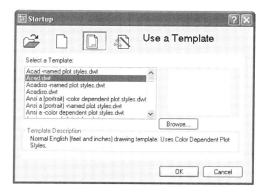

**Figure 3.4**    The Use a Template option offers quick access to your predefined templates.

As you generate more and more templates, storage of the files becomes important. Mixing your custom files with the default files that come with AutoCAD might not be efficient. On the Use a Template option is a Browse button. Clicking this button displays the Select template dialog box. This is covered in the "Creating and Saving a Template File" section.

## Startup Open a Drawing Option

The last option on the Startup dialog box to discuss is actually the first option available. However, this option is only available if you are first starting AutoCAD. Providing a familiar interface to the standard Select File dialogs, it maintains a history of the drawings you recently accessed. Interestingly, it does not matter if you saved a drawing you opened; it still is listed in the Select a File area. As shown in Figure 3.5, you can review a few properties about your highlighted drawing, including the file size, when it was last modified, and the thumbnail preview image of the drawing when it was last closed.

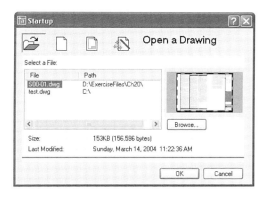

**Figure 3.5**    The Open a Drawing option provides a history of recently accessed drawing files.

Similar to the Use a Template option, the Open option has a Browse button that, when clicked, launches a Select File dialog where you can browse for a drawing to open.

The default installation of AutoCAD has the Startup dialog system turned off. As described earlier, it is easy to turn on and take advantage of after you realize the value of the mechanisms it provides to ease the tedious nature of drawing setup. However, if you prefer that this feature be disabled, many of the same features are still available in a similar form. The following sections discuss what happens after the Startup dialog closes or is bypassed.

## Creating and Saving a Template File

Although Autodesk has made a considerable effort to provide a broad array of templates, chances are you will want to customize your own templates at some point. You can do so by modifying one of the template files provided with AutoCAD or by creating a drawing from scratch.

In the following exercise, you begin with an existing default template file, modify a few of its drawing settings, and then save the drawing as a new template file.

### Exercise 3.1    Creating a Template Drawing

1.  If the Startup dialog is active, launch AutoCAD and choose the Use a Template option. Choose the Ansi b -color dependent plot styles.dwt template file, as shown in Figure 3.6, and click OK.

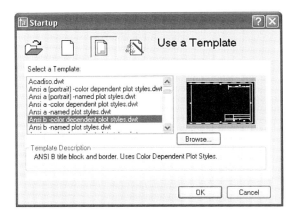

**Figure 3.6**    The Select a Template option used when the Startup dialog option is on.

2. If the Startup dialog is turned off, AutoCAD opens with a drawing. Choose New from the File pull-down menu and on the Select template dialog box, choose the ANSI B -Color Dependent Plot Styles.dwt template file, as shown in Figure 3.7, and click Open.

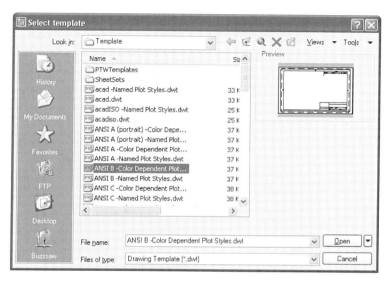

**Figure 3.7**    The Select template dialog provides quick access to your template directory as well as the capability to browse for other locations.

3. At the command prompt, type **UNITS** and then press Enter. The Drawing Units dialog box appears.

4. Verify that the Length Type unit is set to Decimal. Select the 0.00 option for the Length Precision. This sets the display of units to two decimal places.

5. Select Surveyor's Units for the Angle Type.

6. Select the N 0d00' E option for Angle Precision. This sets the angle display to degrees and minutes.

7. Select OK to close the dialog box.

8. From the File pull-down menu, choose Save As.

9. In the Save Drawing As dialog box, from the Files of Type drop-down list, choose AutoCAD Drawing Template File (.dwt).

   When you choose the AutoCAD Drawing Template File (*.dwt) option, AutoCAD automatically switches to the Template folder, as shown in Figure 3.7. Although you don't have to save your template in this folder, it is the default folder that AutoCAD looks in for template files. Therefore, it's a good place to store your custom template files, unless the files are specific to a project.

**10.** In the File Name edit box, type `ANSI B -Survey Units` and then click Save.

**11.** In the Template Description dialog box that appears, replace the contents with "Angles are measured in Survey Units," as shown in Figure 3.8, and then click OK to save the current drawing as a template file. Then close the new drawing template file.

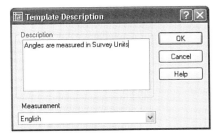

**Figure 3.8**   The Template Description dialog box enables you to enter a description for your template file.

**12.** To start a new drawing using the template you just created, choose New.

**13.** Your newly created template file should appear in the Template list, as shown in Figure 3.9.

You can close this drawing without saving.

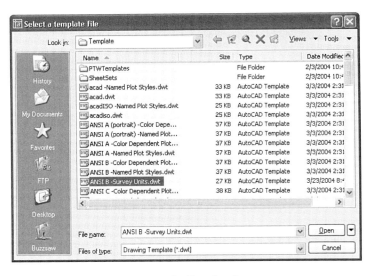

**Figure 3.9**   The new template appears in the Template list.

**I**NSIDER **T**IP

There is a really quick command for dismissing all open drawings. The CLOSEALL command queues all your open drawings, one after the other, prompting you to save changes and closing them for you.

The QNEW command in AutoCAD 2005 is similar in concept to the NEW command, but it enables you to start a new drawing based a single template you prefer to use. This template is defined in the Options dialog, as shown in Figure 3.10. You simply browse to the template of choice.

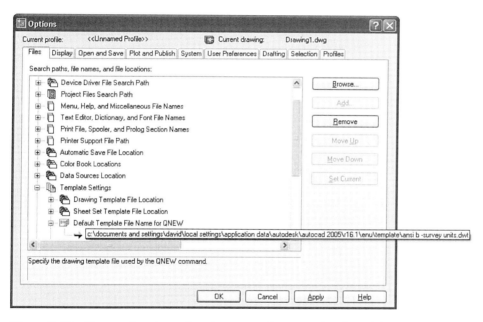

**Figure 3.10** Your preferred template drawing can be assigned and used through the QNEW command.

When you execute the QNEW command, AutoCAD immediately opens that template and names the new drawing Drawing#.dwg. This is a very fast method to start a preferred template file. The NEW command can still be used to locate a specific template file as needed.

**I**NSIDER **T**IP

The File pull-down command to start a fresh drawing runs the NEW command, whereas the toolbar icon to start a new drawing actually runs the QNEW command.

**I**NSIDER **NOTE**

If the Default Template File Name for QNEW entry is set to None, the command acts just like the NEW command.

Next, you learn how to control drawing settings during the current drawing session.

# Controlling Drawing Settings

AutoCAD provides the capability to modify drawing settings during the current drawing session. By changing these settings, you control how AutoCAD behaves. Therefore, you can modify the current session to optimize your productivity. In the next few sections, you learn how to control drawing settings for the current drawing session.

## Revisiting the Drawing Limits

Previously, you learned about setting the limits for a drawing using a wizard. Although this information is useful, it doesn't provide an easy method to modify the limits during the current drawing session.

So how do you easily change the limits during the current drawing session? The process is simple. To change the current drawing's limits, from the Format menu, choose Drawing Limits. When you choose Drawing Limits, AutoCAD starts the LIMITS command, which prompts you to enter new values for the lower-left and upper-right corners of the Limits rectangle. You can enter values by picking them on-screen using your pointing device, or you can enter the coordinates explicitly using your keyboard. After you enter the new Limits values, AutoCAD resets the drawing limits to the new values.

## Controlling Drawing Units

In the previous discussion about using the Startup Advanced Setup Wizard, you learned how to set various Unit and Angle values and how those values affect AutoCAD's display. You also learned how to set those values using the Drawing Units dialog box. In this section, you learn how to control a few other settings using this dialog box.

A Clockwise direction control is available in the Drawing Units dialog box, as shown in Figure 3.11. The direction positive angles are drawn in is controlled by toggling the Clockwise feature on or off.

**Figure 3.11**   The Clockwise direction control appears in the Drawing Units dialog box.

In addition, there is a feature that works in conjunction with AutoCAD DesignCenter and controls the unit of measure used for block insertions. This system automatically adjusts the size of blocks as they are inserted. If a block created in different units is inserted into the drawing, it is automatically scaled and inserted in the specified units of the current drawing.

This is a powerful tool, making the insertion of blocks with predefined units very simple. You no longer need to worry about properly scaling a block when it is inserted. On the other hand, if you don't want to automatically adjust the block, select the Unitless mode in the Insert dialog box to insert the drawing as a block without scaling the block to match the specified units. You learn more about how to use this feature in Chapter 12, "Applications for DesignCenter."

Unlike the Angle Measure section of the Advanced Setup Wizard, the Drawing Units dialog enables you to define a new base angle by picking points on-screen. By choosing Other, then the Angle button, shown in Figure 3.12, you can select two points on-screen using your pointing device.

**Figure 3.12**   The Pick an Angle button enables you to set the base angle by picking two points on-screen.

## Defining Drafting Settings

Drafting settings are tools you use as an aid when drawing. These features can increase accuracy, ease object editing through on-screen visual enhancements, and automate object creation and editing by providing a mouse-only interface. By controlling AutoCAD's drafting settings, you make working with AutoCAD easier, quicker, and more accurate.

The Drafting Settings dialog box is accessed from the Tools pull-down menu by choosing Drafting Settings. When the dialog box appears, you see three tabs, as shown in Figure 3.13. These tabs control features such as Snap and Grid, Polar Tracking, and Object Snap. Polar Tracking enables you to automate certain command processes, such as drawing lines from one point to another, by making the process more automatic. Object Snap is where you can set *running* (also called active) object snap (or osnap) modes. This tab also has a feature called Object Snap Tracking, which is a way to build snap points temporarily from actual geometry.

For detailed information on the functions and features of the Drafting Settings dialog box, including the Polar Tracking feature, refer to the AutoCAD online Help system.

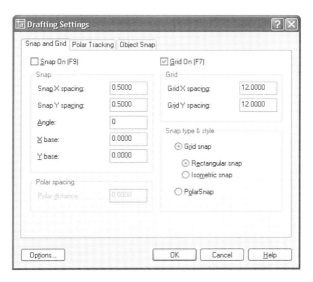

**Figure 3.13**   The Drafting Settings dialog box controls settings for Snap and Grid, Polar Tracking, and Object Snap features.

# Summary

In this chapter, you learned about controlling various AutoCAD settings both when creating a drawing with the Startup dialog and during the current drawing session through different menu commands and dialog boxes. By controlling AutoCAD's drafting settings and saving those environments in templates, you can start new drawings that match your needs more quickly.

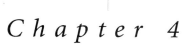

*C h a p t e r    4*

# Managing Your Drawing Projects

If you have used AutoCAD for any length of time, you probably have a good grasp of what it uses for file management because it uses *you*. Because AutoCAD has never had any formal file management system, you are the workhorse that keeps things organized. All of that changes, however, with the introduction of AutoCAD 2005 and its new Sheet Set Manager. This book by and large assumes you understand how to open and close drawings, create basic objects, and perform simple editing tasks. It also assumes that because AutoCAD has never had a file management system, you probably utilize a series of directories and subdirectories in which to store and access your drawings.

This style of file organization may seem straightforward and easy, and it is, but it falls short of the desires that many have had for AutoCAD. When AutoCAD was first released, it only had one space—model space. You did everything from there, from drawing the first line to the final plot. With the inclusion of paper space, the application was divided in two: one space (model) for drawing and one space (paper) for plotting. Now with AutoCAD 2005, you gain a way to organize your plots as a set without even opening the drawings! You can rename, renumber, and reorganize the sheets that make up a project from a single dialog. You can locate a particular view by name, preview it, renumber and rename it, and even open its drawing from the same interface.

This chapter discusses the new AutoCAD 2005 Sheet Set Manager. Topics to be discussed are:

- Creating a sheet set and importing sheets
- Creating new sheets and using fields
- Creating intelligent view labels and callouts
- Placing view labels and callouts
- Becoming a power user of the Sheet Set Manager

# Understanding Sheets

To appreciate the true simplicity of the Sheet Set Manager, you need clarity as to what exactly a *sheet* is. A sheet is a paper space layout, simple as that. Think of the Sheet Set Manager as a layout manager, where you can organize drawing layouts into groups. When ready, these layouts or sheets in a sheet set can be published, electronically transmitted, or archived in a single step.

**I**NSIDER  **C**AUTION

A given drawing cannot belong to more than one sheet set.

Ideally, the best time to begin utilizing the Sheet Set Manager is when a project starts. But AutoCAD and the Sheet Set Manager understand that might not always be possible, so there are mechanisms for bringing drawings for an existing project into the Sheet Set Manager. As shown in Figure 4.1, the Sheet Set Manager is composed of a three-tab palette dialog. Each of these tabs and how to apply them is covered in the following exercises.

You might think that there is a whole other series of files and data structures that the Sheet Set Manager uses to do its work. Not so; the Sheet Set Manager needs but one file, a DST file. A sheet set file contains all the project and relationship data about your job. This makes the process of sharing or storing a sheet set very simple.

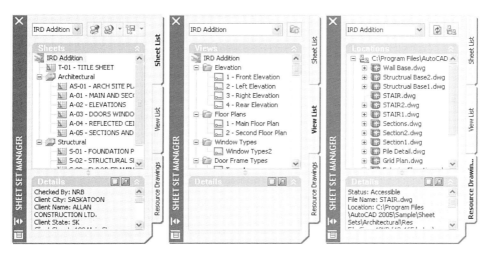

**Figure 4.1**   The Sheet Set Manager is a palette-based dialog interface with tabs used to access Sheets, Views, and Resource Drawings.

**I**NSIDER **N**OTE

> The Sheet Set Manager cannot create any folders on its own. It can only create drawing files and assign a layout as a new sheet.

# Creating a Sheet Set and Importing Sheets

Whether you are starting a new job or migrating an existing one, you begin by creating a sheet set. However, that makes the assumption that the files needed for the Sheet Set Manager already exist. If each and every job uses the same set of prototype files, simply firing up the Sheet Set Manager application would be step 1. But if your jobs have different title blocks or different standards, you need to do some work prior to creating the sheet set.

One of the key benefits with the Sheet Set Manager is that it takes advantage of the new Field feature in AutoCAD 2005. When implemented, fields display dynamic information within your drawings. This is a perfect application for the Sheet Set Manager where sheets can be renamed, renumbered, relocated, and so on without opening the drawing.

> **INSIDER NOTE**
>
> You can learn about the new Field feature in Chapter 21, "Using Fields and Tables."

As you begin to implement the Sheet Set Manager, you will discover areas of configuration that can set up at the beginning, speeding up their implementation later. The very nature of AutoCAD is its capability to create designs using different methods. Generally, no one method is always better than others. It is the goal of this chapter to expose you to a straightforward approach to make it easier to understand. Then you will be better informed for how to apply the Sheet Set Manager to your work process.

### Exercise 4.1    Creating a Sheet Set

1. Create a folder in your My Documents folder named **IAC2005**. Browse to the Ch04 folder on the accompanying CD-ROM. Copy all files and folders to the IAC2005 folder. This is where we will create and store all new project files.

> **INSIDER NOTE**
>
> Folder and file capitalization is not important. The files and folder structure you should have is as follows:
>
> My Documents\IAC2005\Border.dwt
> My Documents\IAC2005\Foundation Plan.dwg
> My Documents\IAC2005\Blocks\Detail Info Block.dwg
> My Documents\IAC2005\Blocks\Section Mark.dwg
> My Documents\IAC2005\Details\S02-01-01.dwg
> My Documents\IAC2005\Details\S02-01-02.dwg
> My Documents\IAC2005\Plans\S-FP-01.dwg
> My Documents\IAC2005\Plans\S-FP-02.dwg

> **INSIDER NOTE**
>
> Depending on your computer operating system and configuration, you might need to change the Read-Only attribute of the files after they are copied. The Read-Only file attribute needs to be off to enable the files to be changed during the exercises.

2.  Start a new session of AutoCAD, select the File pull-down menu, and choose New Sheet Set.

**I**NSIDER **N**OTE

The New Sheet Set option is only available if you are not in a zero document state. Therefore, you must have at least one drawing file open to use the option.

On the Create Sheet Set – Begin dialog box, you have two methods for creating a sheet set. You can use an example sheet set, perhaps one provided by Autodesk, or you can begin working with existing drawings. The tutorials that come with AutoCAD 2005 utilize the example sheet set option.

**I**NSIDER **N**OTE

You do not have to actually begin with existing drawings inasmuch as you have to begin with a folder structure, a place to put your new sheet set itself.

3.  Choose the Existing drawings option and click Next.

    On the Sheet Set Details dialog box, you name your new sheet set and provide description information.

4.  In the Name of new sheet set edit box, type **Bank Project**. Enter the information shown in Figure 4.2 for the description. Next to the Store sheet set data file here edit box is a [...] icon, which is a browse button. This unnamed button is used extensively throughout the Sheet Set Manager. Click it to begin browsing. In the Browse for Sheet Set Folder dialog, locate and select the IAC2005 folder. This is the folder you created earlier.

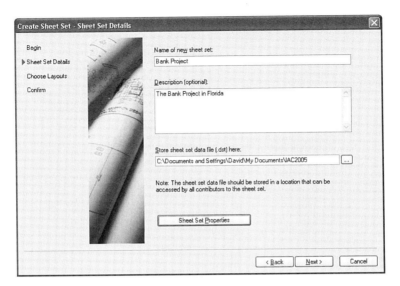

**Figure 4.2** You use the Sheet Set Details dialog to define basic information about your new sheet set.

5. We will skip using the Sheet Set Properties button. All the items within it are available later after we have the sheet set open. Click the Next button.

6. The Choose Layouts dialog appears. It is used to build sheets from layouts in existing drawings. Click the Import Options button.

   On the Import Options dialog exist a few controls. The Prefix sheet titles toggle does just that—in the Sheet Set Manager list, the sheets will be prefixed with their respective filenames.

   The Create subsets option causes the Sheet Set Manager to mimic the directory structure on disk. The Ignore top level control assumes that you don't need to index the top folder level.

7. As shown in Figure 4.3, you can toggle on all options on the dialog. We don't use this feature in the exercise, but you needed to see this. Click the Cancel button to close.

**Figure 4.3**   The Import Options dialog determines how your sheets are imported in the Sheet Set Manager.

8. You are back on the Choose Layouts dialog. Click the Next button to continue.

**I** NSIDER NOTE

In this exercise, we are going through the process as simply as possible. With that in mind, we don't actually import any drawings; rather, we use the features later to bring them in. When you understand the Sheet Set Manager system, you can take advantage of the Import process to speed up populating your new sheet set with as many sheets as you need.

9. As shown in Figure 4.4, the Confirm page shows the status of the sheet set you are about to create. A number of options are still blank; we complete them in the following exercises. Click the Finish button to continue.

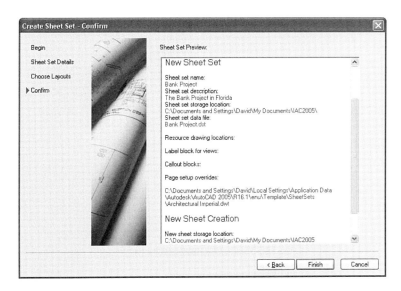

**Figure 4.4**   The Confirm dialog gives an overview of how your sheet set is configured and what sheets it will start with.

The new sheet set is created, the Sheet Set Manager is activated, and the sheet set is loaded. The appearance of the Bank Project loaded into the Sheet Set Manager is shown in Figure 4.5.

**Figure 4.5**   The Sheet Set Manager with your new sheet set open, listing nothing else but ready for use.

**I**NSIDER **N**OTE

> The Sheet Set Manager is a non-modal dialog, meaning it can exist outside of the AutoCAD application window. If you have a dual-monitor system, it can be located on the other display. It is also has the capability to be docked to the sides of the AutoCAD display, between the border and side-mounted toolbars. You can also have it "stuck" to the inside edge of the graphics window, where it also can be made to Auto-hide (collapse).

10. We need to adjust the properties of the sheet set so we can create new sheets. Using the Sheet List tab, right-click over the name of the Bank Project sheet set, displaying the shortcut menu, as shown in Figure 4.6. Choose Properties; the Sheet Set Properties dialog then appears.

**Figure 4.6** The right-click shortcut menu provides access to a number of management controls, such as Properties.

**I** NSIDER NOTE

The Sheet Set Properties dialog box is what was skipped previously in step 5.

Some of the Sheet Set Properties dialog is empty; we fill it as we go along. The Sheet creation template might have something already listed. This is controlled by the default Template for Sheet Creation and Page Setup Overrides feature under the Files tab within the Options dialog box.

11. Click the Sheet creation template line. Click the [...] button that appears. You use the Select Layout as Sheet Template dialog to define a layout within a template file as the prototype for a new sheet for this sheet set.

12. In the Select Layout as Sheet Template dialog box, again choose the [...] browse button and then locate and select the IAC2005\Border.dwt file. Click the Open button.

13. Back in the Select Layout as Sheet Template dialog, you specify what layout to use for new sheets. As shown in Figure 4.7, our template file has but one layout. Click OK to choose it.

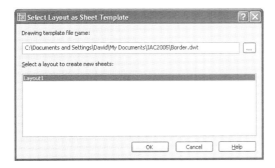

**Figure 4.7** Assigning the template and layout to be used for newly created sheets.

**I**NSIDER **N**OTE _____ —————

Projects that require multiple sheet styles, Arch D size and Tabloid for example, can use the Prompt for template option to allow for template and layout selection when you actually create the sheet.

**14.** The Sheet Set Properties dialog now should match Figure 4.8 (don't worry if you do or don't have an entry in the Page setup overrides file). There are items still to customize, but for now, we will make some sheets. Click the OK button to close the Properties dialog.

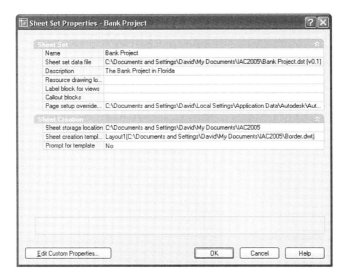

**Figure 4.8** The Sheet Set Properties dialog controls overall sheet set functionality and access to blocks, page setups, and default settings.

**15.** We can now create new sheets and import others. Right-click over the Bank Project title again and choose Import Layout as Sheet from the shortcut menu.

**16.** Using the Import Layouts as Sheets dialog, you can read in existing drawings and utilize their layouts to create sheets in the Sheet Set Manager. Click the [...] button and select drawing Foundation Plan that was copied to the IAC2005 directory.

**17.** Now, as shown in Figure 4.9, the Import Layouts as Sheets dialog contains one drawing and lists a single layout below. Here, you can select as many initialized layouts as exist in the drawing.

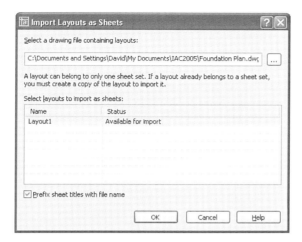

**Figure 4.9**   The Import Layouts as Sheets dialog is what you use to bring existing layouts into the sheet set.

**I**NSIDER **N**OTE

Layouts that have not been initialized (clicked on at least once) are not listed for Import Layout as Sheet.

**18.** Uncheck the Prefix sheet titles with file name option. Because we know what sheet we are bringing in, we don't need the extra editing. Click OK to continue.

**19.** We now have a sheet named after the layout name in the Foundation Plan drawing. Obviously, you want your sheet names to be more distinguishable. Right-click over the Layout1 sheet and choose Rename & Renumber.

**I**NSIDER **N**OTE

Everyone has his or her preferred way to name drawing files. Although the Sheet Set Manager accommodates any filename you want to use, the exercises in this chapter keeps the filenames very generic.

**I**NSIDER **T**IP

You might be tempted to use the sheet number as part of the drawing's filename. As you will see from the exercises in this chapter, you might find that this is undesirable.

**20.** Using the Rename & Renumber Sheet dialog, enter **S1.1** as the Number. Then enter **Foundation Plan** as the Sheet title. The dialog should now match Figure 4.10. Click OK to close the dialog.

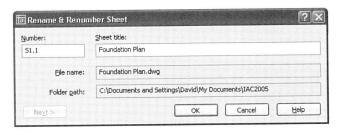

**Figure 4.10**   The Rename & Renumber Sheet dialog enables you to adjust how sheets are named, especially after importing.

**21.** Now the Sheet Set Manager shows the new sheet with a descriptive name. Double-click on the sheet to open it. As shown in Figure 4.11, you can use the Sheet Set Manager as a navigation tool to access your drawings.

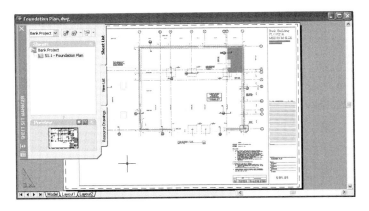

**Figure 4.11**   Using the Sheet Set Manager as a drawing navigation tool.

Notice the Details area at the bottom of the Sheet Set Manager. When you select the Preview button, you can see a preview of the selected sheet. Too small to read, but this can be helpful when trying to remember what was on a sheet.

Close the Foundation Plan drawing, saving changes. Leave the Sheet Set Manager and AutoCAD open for the following exercise.

You have successfully created a new sheet set. You also determined what template a new project sheet will use. Lastly, you imported an existing layout from a drawing, creating the first sheet in the Bank Project sheet set. You now have an intelligent management tool for AutoCAD drawings that belong together in a project. The Sheet Set Manager provides quick and easy access to your drawings that make up your project document set.

# Creating New Sheets and Using Fields

As you have just witnessed, the process of using the Sheet Set Manager to create a sheet set and then customize it is not difficult. In this book's exercise format, we approach the process in a step-by-step method. The neat part about the Sheet Set Manager is that at any time you can change settings or go back and finish areas that were bypassed originally.

The new AutoCAD 2005 Sheet Set Manager is a great organizational tool for drawings. With it, you can literally *see* what your project is composed of at any time. When you utilize Windows Explorer for this purpose, you have to wade through many other file types that often exist in the same directories, including backup files, scripts, images, and plot files, just to name a few. After you get rid of this clutter by implementing the Sheet Set Manager, you will truly appreciate what the Sheet Set Manager system can do for you.

But it doesn't stop there! By leveraging the more advanced features of the Sheet Set Manager, such as automatic sheet numbers, you can speed your way through mundane drawing tasks. In addition, these high-tech tools can empower your entire work team to become better organized and can aid in accessing your drawing data very quickly.

AutoCAD 2005 brings with it the new concept of fields. Fields are dynamic annotation content that can be placed into any text format object, such as mtext and attributes. When you begin to use fields and the Sheet Set Manager together, your productivity will really begin to accelerate.

**I**NSIDER NOTE

You can learn about the new Field feature in Chapter 21.

In the previous exercise, we assigned a template drawing (DWT) to the project sheet set. This was done so that we can create a new sheet with our project title block already placed. But because this template has never been used in a sheet set, it doesn't contain the intelligent links to make it work with the sheet set's properties. In the next exercise, we create a new sheet that is used as a framework to prepare the template's title block to use fields to read the data stored in the Sheet Set Manager's properties.

**I**NSIDER  **N**OTE

It is recommended that you review and complete the exercises in Chapter 21 prior to working on the following exercises. There is a general level of comprehension that can be beneficial from experiencing Chapter 21 first.

### Exercise 4.2   Developing a Border Template and Applying It

**I.** AutoCAD 2005 and the Sheet Set Manager should still be open. If not, start AutoCAD and the Sheet Set Manager and  then locate and open the IAC2005\Bank Project.dst sheet set that you created in the last exercise (note, this file was not provided on the CD; you must complete Exercise 4.1 before starting this exercise) using the Sheet Set Manager.

**I**NSIDER  **N**OTE

You might find yourself at times in a zero document state, meaning no drawing is open for editing. Most of the features within the Sheet Set Manager are disabled in a zero document state except the capability to create a new sheet or import one. Open an existing drawing or create a new drawing to restore all the disabled features.

**I**NSIDER  **N**OTE

The default AutoCAD installation stores DST files within your user profile under My Documents\AutoCAD Sheet Sets. Although this might be fine for single users, network users should always place project DST files on network drives where they can be shared and accessed by others.

**2.** On the Sheet List tab, right-click over the Bank Project name and, using the shortcut menu, choose New Sheet.

**3.** The New Sheet dialog then appears. In the Number box, type `TEMP Number`. In the Sheet title box, type `TEMP Sheet Title`.

**I**NSIDER  **T**IP

Did you notice how the File name edit box is filled in as you type? The Sheet Set Manager does this to speed up the file-naming process.

4. The File name edit box now has the number and the sheet title. Replace the content with **TEMP Setup**. We want no confusion as to the purpose of this sheet or our ability to recognize the field data later. When your settings match that of Figure 4.12, click OK to continue.

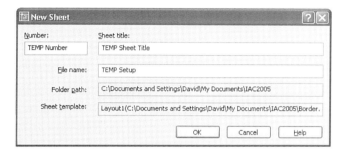

**Figure 4.12**   The New Sheet dialog with the temporary sheet information.

5. The new sheet is added to the sheet set list, as shown in Figure 4.13. Double-click it to open it for editing.

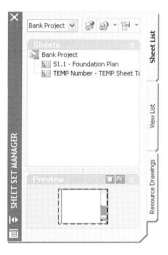

**Figure 4.13**   The Sheet Set Manager listing the new sheet, ready for use, and a basic-looking title block in a layout.

6. As shown in Figure 4.13, the drawing opens and contains a title block with normal sheet type information. Notice that the layout's name is the same as the filename. Zoom the window around the lower right of the title block so that you can read it clearly.

---

**I**NSIDER **N**OTE

Many standard work processes used to utilize blocks with attributes for their title borders. This was important in at least two ways—providing a set number of parameters for the user to fill in and keeping all these pieces of text as one unit. Now that data is stored in the Sheet Set Manager, it is very likely that you will begin to use mtext objects with fields grouped to the title block instead. The reason is that attributes do not support multiple lines of text, yet some of the data stored in the sheet set's properties will need to be wrapping as only mtext can provide.

---

Normally, the next step would be to edit the attributes. We would change the number and title to whatever we need; not a big deal. But we want to take advantage of the data already input by you in the Sheet Set Manager. We want to set up our title block to use fields to display sheet-related information automatically.

---

**I**NSIDER **T**IP

Fields display dynamic information. Because of that, some field data related to sheet sets doesn't show if the field used cannot locate the proper information. Therefore, so that you can witness the dynamic settings as they are applied, we insert fields into this new temporary sheet. Doing this makes the process easier to comprehend, and you will understand more as we go along.

---

As stated in the tip, we want to work with a temporary sheet to aid in the field placements. Many types of field data can be used with a template and the Sheet Set Manager. We focus on the most generic formats, but they all basically work the same way.

We have a title block here that users edit when they place it into a sheet. Some of the attributes have been filled in for the project already, such as the project number and "drawn by" name. Attributes that the user should change on each sheet are left with default values. Those attributes have the –ATT suffix to aid in identifying them.

7. Double-click on the SHEETNO-ATT value. The Enhanced Attribute Editor dialog then loads and makes that attribute active for editing. Right-click over the highlighted SHEETNO-ATT value, displaying the right-click shortcut menu, and select Insert Field (see Figure 4.14).

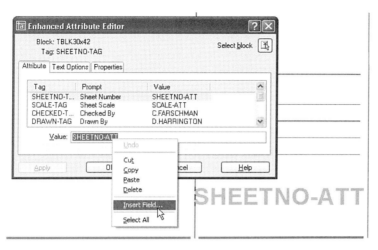

**Figure 4.14**    You can insert fields from the right-click shortcut menu available in the Enhanced Attribute Editor.

8. In the Field dialog box, change to the SheetSet category, select CurrentSheetNumber in the Field names box, and set the Format to Uppercase. Notice that the box labeled CurrentSheetNumber displays TEMP NUMBER; this matches what we assigned for the sheet number (see Figure 4.15). Click OK to close the dialog.

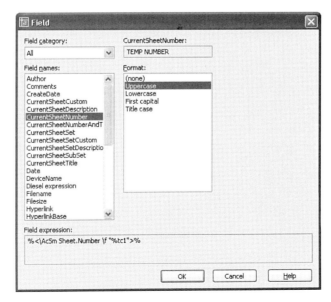

**Figure 4.15**    The Field dialog enables you to assign sheet set information to a text or attribute object.

**I** NSIDER **N** OTE

If you choose to edit your template file directly, it does not belong to the sheet set as a sheet, so the fields cannot determine CurrentSheet information and cannot display live information. In that condition, you would instead see #### values, which doesn't tell you very much and can lead to using incorrect field codes.

9. Again in the Enhanced Attribute Editor, scroll down to the SHEETNAME-TAG tag. Highlight the value content, right-click, and choose Insert Field again.

10. Within the Field dialog, select CurrentSheetTitle in the Field names list. Verify that the Format is Uppercase. Notice that TEMP SHEET TITLE shows in the box at the top. Click OK to accept.

11. Click OK in the Enhanced Attribute Editor dialog to close it. We have made all the changes needed. Now, as shown in Figure 4.16, the field is valid for the current sheet.

**I** NSIDER **N** OTE

A visual indicator that you have field code in a text-type object is the shaded background. This display option is controlled in the Fields area under the User Preferences tab on the Options dialog box.

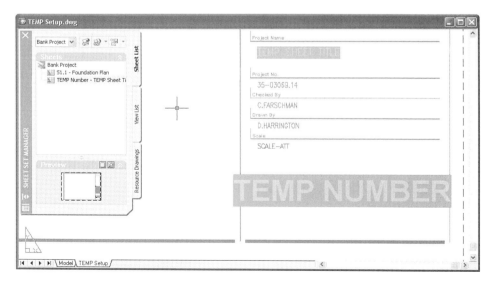

**Figure 4.16**    Fields, by default, have a shaded background.

**I**NSIDER **N**OTE

> You should always make backup copies of your template or prototype files in case you make a mistake.

**12.** Execute a ZOOM extents to return to the full sheet extents.

**13.** From the Edit pull-down menu, choose Copy, select the title block, and press Enter to end selection and store the block to the clipboard for use in a later step. We now need to save this drawing as our template, overwriting the previous one.

**14.** Using the File pull-down menu, choose Save As and then change the Files of type to AutoCAD Drawing Template. AutoCAD then switches you to your Options-controlled default Template directory.

**I**NSIDER **T**IP

> You can change the default template location under the Files tab in the Options dialog. Switching it to a server drive can be helpful if that is where you store your templates.

**15.** You can use the <- button to move back to your previous active directory structure, or you can browse and locate it yourself. Find and select the IAC2005\Border.dwt template file. Press the Save button, click Yes to overwrite, and click OK to accept the Template Description box, thereby overwriting the existing template. Close the Border template file.

**16.** Return your attention to the open Sheet Set Manager. Right-click over the TEMP Number sheet you made earlier and choose Remove Sheet. You are presented with an alert; it says that what you are doing only removes the sheet from the set—not the drawing file itself or its layout. Click OK to close the alert box.

**I**NSIDER **N**OTE

> You can use Windows Explorer or AutoCAD's File dialog boxes to remove files that are no longer needed.

The sheet is then removed from the Bank Project sheet set. Now we can test the revised sheet template to see it in action.

**17.** Use the Sheet Set Manager and double-click on S1.1 – Foundation Plan, opening the foundation plan drawing we imported in Exercise 4.1. Its title block needs to be updated.

**INSIDER NOTE**

For title blocks that use attributes, you must redefine the border block to use fields. Unfortunately, this requires that the existing block with attributes be replaced with a new one—the new one containing the fields.

**18.** Erase the title block in the layout. Then use the right-click shortcut menu and choose Paste to Original Coordinates.

**INSIDER TIP**

You can use the Windows clipboard as a location to hold blocks and other objects and then use the Paste feature in AutoCAD to retrieve and place them in a drawing.

Notice the number on the title block. It reads TEMP NUMBER, which is what the Border template had. How do we cause this to be updated? Just do a regen! Use the View pull-down menu and select Regen. The fields update to the current data.

**19.** Also, notice that the layout's name does not match the filename. If you want, you can rename it to match what occurs when you create new sheets. Right-click on the Layout1 tab, choose Rename, and then rename it to **Foundation Plan**. Close this drawing and save changes.

You might be in a zero document state, meaning no drawings are open, but the Sheet Set Manager is still active and can be used for organizing your sheets. If you find yourself in the zero document state during this exercise, simply use the New button in AutoCAD to open a blank drawing.

**20.** Once again, right-click over the Bank Project name and choose New Sheet.

**21.** On the New Sheet dialog box, type the number **S1.2**, followed by **Framing Plan** as the Sheet title. Then modify the File name to just be **Framing Plan**, with no number (see Figure 4.17). Click OK when ready. The sheet is created but not opened.

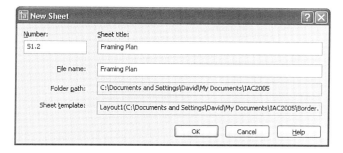

**Figure 4.17**   The New Sheet dialog box, properly filled in for our second sheet.

22. Double-click on the S1.2 – FRAMING PLAN listed on the Sheet Set Manager. The drawing opens.

23. Perform a ZOOM window and pick the area around the lower right so that you can read the information. It should appear as Figure 4.18, showing live data from the sheet set!

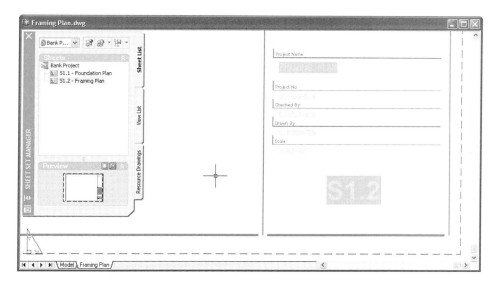

**Figure 4.18**   Live, dynamic sheet information displayed in title block attributes using fields.

**I**NSIDER **T**IP

> When you have more than one sheet listed in the Sheet Set Manager, you can con-
> trol the order in which they are listed. Just by clicking and dragging, you can move
> sheets up and down in the list. This order is used when they are published, archived,
> transmitted electronically, or shown in a Sheet List Table.

Suppose that we didn't provide the full sheet title. It's missing the word Roof. This is easy to fix!

**24.** Right-click on the open sheet listed in the Sheet List to display the shortcut menu and choose Rename & Renumber.

**25.** Within the Rename & Renumber Sheet dialog, click in front of the word Framing and type **Roof** with a space between Roof and Framing. Note that the filename does not change. Then click OK to close.

The display of the open sheet title in the Sheets list changed, but the title block itself didn't—not yet anyway.

**26.** Perform a REGEN on the open drawing. You should now see ROOF FRAMING PLAN listed in the title block. In this case, it is in all capital letters because we formatted the field to display its data in this manner. Perform a ZOOM Extents. Save the drawing but leave the Framing Plan drawing and Bank Project sheet set open for the following exercise.

You should now understand how the Sheet Set Manager can increase your productivity. You have a template associated with your sheet set that, when used to make a new sheet, displays the appropriate data from the Sheet Set Manager. When in the Sheet Set Manager, you can revise the number and title (indeed, other data as well) as needed and have that information dynamically updated in the drawing.

The previous exercise showed how you use the Sheet Set Manager to control sheet num-bers and titles. This information then is leveraged into the title block fields, automati-cally displaying the data keeping up-to-date with the sheet set. The productivity gains with this functionality are amazing. After you get the sheet set properties correct, you can create new sheets very quickly indeed.

# Assembling Sheet Content

Having the ability to create blank sheets is great, but you also need to be able to put drawing content on them. The content needs to be to scaled and located properly and still be accessible.

AutoCAD uses the external reference feature to aid this process. The concept is that a series of separate drawing files, called resource drawings, can be used to store the actual work, such as floor plans or elevations. These resource drawings are then used to display views on new sheets. These can also be standalone details. They can even be groups of details that make up an entire drawing. The common ground is that they are all used as xrefs in sheet drawings.

The Sheet Set Manager utilizes the VIEW command in AutoCAD in a new and exciting way. Now in AutoCAD 2005, a view can store the layers visible when the view is created. Somewhat similar to a layer state, this then provides the ability to use the stored view when xrefed into other drawings, such as sheets.

Within the Sheet Set Manager is the Resource Drawings tab. Whereas the Sheet List tab contains the sheets for plotting the set, the Resource Drawings tab is where you can locate drawings that store the work. From this tab, you then open resource drawings or place views onto sheets.

### Exercise 4.3    Placing Plan Views into a Sheet

1. Continuing from the previous exercise, AutoCAD should be active, with the Framing Plan drawing open as well as the Bank Project sheet set. The layout is blank except for the title block.

2. On the Sheet Set Manager, click on the Resource Drawings tab. It has nothing listed yet. Double-click on the Add New Location item.

3. Using the Browse for Folder dialog, locate and select the IAC2005\Plans folder you copied from the CD-ROM earlier. Select the Open button to close the Browse for Folder dialog box.

**I**NSIDER **T**IP

> Each directory added to the Resource Drawings tab can be expanded and collapsed as need.

4. Expand the `Plans` folder in the Locations list, if needed, and then select the S-FP-02 drawing file. When a drawing is selected, you can see Detail information or a Preview image at the bottom of the Sheet Set Manager (see Figure 4.19).

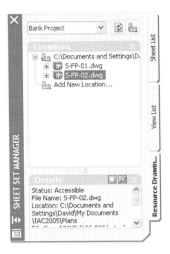

**Figure 4.19** The Resource Drawings tab of the Sheet Set Manager also provides detailed drawing information or a preview pane.

5. In order to place a resource drawing on a sheet and have it within a specific viewport size, you first make a view of the area to be shown. Double-click on S-FP-02 to open it for editing.

6. The drawing contains a large box around the perimeter; this is the area we want to the view. Use the View pull-down menu and select Named Views.

7. In the View dialog box, click New. Then in the New View dialog, type **Plan** for the name. In the View category entry, type **Plans**. Click the Define window button (see Figure 4.20) and use a Endpoint object snap to select two opposite corners of the large box. Click OK to close the dialog. Click OK to dismiss the View dialog as well.

8. Close the drawing, saving your changes.

9. Back in the Sheet Set Manager, click on the S-FP-02 item to reread the drawing. A [+] button appears next to the drawing; click the [+] to expand. The new Plan view is displayed.

**Figure 4.20**   The AutoCAD 2005 New View dialog lets you create specific views, categorize them, and control whether layers are stored with them.

10. Selecting the Plan item then enables you to see the view in the preview area, as shown in Figure 4.21.

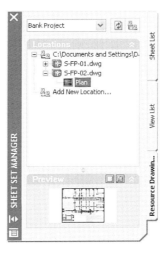

**Figure 4.21**   The Sheet Set Manager displays available views for placement from within the Resource Drawings tab.

**I**NSIDER **N**OTE

When you select the drawing name itself, you can use the Preview button to see the drawing as it was last saved. Each drawing contains a default area that can be placed onto a sheet. This area is not an AutoCAD view but rather the extents of all the objects in the drawing's model space, so it is possible that the Preview shown is not how it will be placed on a sheet. Placing drawings on sheets without a named view is similar to xrefing a drawing in, except that you can specify a scale, and a viewport is created to display the xref inserted in the sheet's model space.

**11.** After you have a view created, you can easily place it on a sheet. Right-click on the word Plan and, from the shortcut menu, choose Place on Sheet. AutoCAD then creates a viewport that displays that view, enabling you to drag it about on-screen (see Figure 4.22). In order to apply a specific scale, use the right-click shortcut menu *before selecting a point* and select 1/4"=1'. The viewport then updates to reflect the new scale.

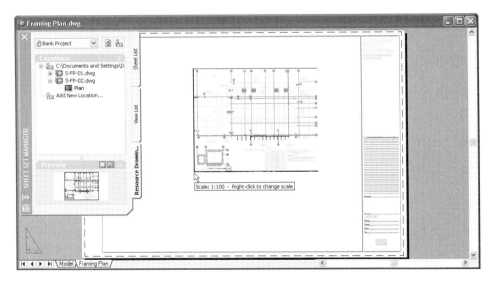

**Figure 4.22** Dynamic xref placement of the S-FP-02 drawing using its Plan view.

**12.** At the `Specify insertion point` prompt, use an endpoint object snap and pick the lower end of the red line on the left. It defines the left edge of the area where we can place content.

**I**NSIDER  **NOTE**

AutoCAD uses the current layer in which to create the viewport. We anticipated this in
the template drawing; it was saved with a $Viewport layer current and set to No Plot.
That way, no user intervention is required to modify the viewport for plotting needs.

The sheet is assembled, as shown in Figure 4.23. Save changes to the Framing
Plan drawing and close it, but leave the Sheet Set Manager open for the following
exercise.

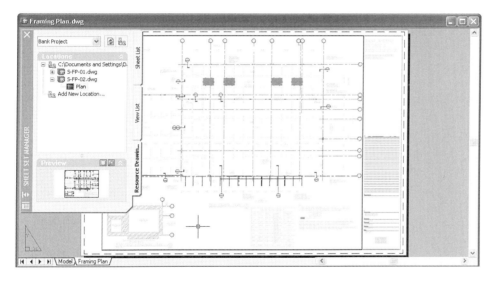

**Figure 4.23**   The view is placed, completing the sheet.

AutoCAD did a number of things here. It located the resource drawing, created a layer
matching the resource drawing name, xrefed it in on that layer as attached, and saved a
relative path for it. It placed the xref in model space at 0,0. It also made a new viewport
on the current layer, with a display scale set according to what we specified. It matched
the viewport's size and alignment to the Plan view that we made earlier. There is a lot of
productivity gain there.

When you placed that Plan view on the sheet, it was also added to the View List tab in
the Sheet Set Manager. As shown in Figure 4.24, this list contains references to placed
views. If you place the same view on multiple sheets, each placement generates another
item in the View List. This functionality makes it easy to locate where views are being

used. When you categorize the views as you create them, the categories are displayed here. When you double-click on the View List item, you open the sheet displaying the view, not the resource drawing containing the view.

**Figure 4.24**    The View List tab records all view placements in your sheets for coordination, such and naming and numbering, and provides automatic callouts.

The following exercises continue to explore additional areas of the Sheet Set Manager and how to apply them to help you label plans and details.

# Creating Intelligent View Labels and Callouts

Productivity is the primary factor in this fast-paced, production-driven design world. Everyone wants his or her drawings done tomorrow. But if you make a mistake because you worked too quickly, then you really didn't save any time or money because corrections must be made. Not to mention the time it takes to repair a relationship or trust level! Fast but accurate—that's the true key.

With that in mind, the Sheet Set Manager can place dynamic view labels and callouts. View labels identify areas of a sheet, such as a floor plan or a detail. Callout blocks are used to refer the reader to another drawing, such as a specific detail. In previous versions of AutoCAD, view labels and callout blocks in plan would have no connection to the details they referenced. In AutoCAD 2005, however, dynamic labels and callouts change all that, ensuring the accuracy of the elements to which you assign them. All you need to do is use blocks with fields—if you have them. In order to get them, we edit some existing blocks that were created before AutoCAD 2005 and sheet sets.

### Exercise 4.4   Assigning and Customizing a View Label Block

1. Continue from the previous exercise. The Bank Project sheet set should be loaded. Make the Sheet List tab is active, if needed. Right-click over the Bank Project title and then choose Properties from the shortcut menu.

2. Click the Label block for views line, activating the [...] button, and then click the [...] button. This opens the Select Block dialog box.

3. On the Select Block dialog box, select the [...] button and then browse and select this drawing:

   IAC2005\Blocks\Detail Info Block.dwg

4. Right-click on the filename and select Open. Click the Open button to close the Select Drawing dialog box. Select OK to close the Select Block dialog box. Select OK once more to close the Sheet Set Properties dialog box.

5. Open the Detail Info Block drawing for editing. We will edit this drawing to add fields to the attribute definitions. This gives the block the capability to be filled in from the Sheet Set Manager.

6. View label blocks should be defined so that they insert below the viewport, so we must move the block's objects below 0,0. Use the Modify menu to select the Move command. At the `Select objects` prompt, type **ALL** to select the entire drawing. Press Enter to exit the object selection prompt. At the `Specify base point or displacement` prompt, type **0,-1** and press Enter twice. The objects move down one unit.

7. The circle and attribute definitions located within the circle need to be moved to the left side of the block, for reasons you will see later on. Click on the circle, the DTLNO-TAG attribute, and DTLSHT-TAG attribute to select them. Right-click to display the shortcut menu and select the Move command. Use an Endpoint object snap to select the right end point of the blue line as the base point. Use an Endpoint object snap to select the left end point of the blue line as the second point. Move the blue line to the left by 0.6875 units so that the drawing matches Figure 4.25.

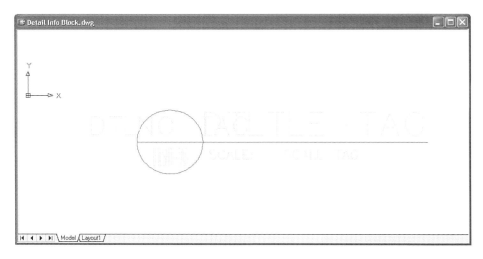

**Figure 4.25**   The revised Detail Info Block.

8. Double-click on the DTLTLE-TAG attribute definition. Select the Default item, DETAIL, and right-click to display the shortcut menu. Select the Insert Field item. The Field dialog box is displayed.

**9.** Select the SheetSet Field category. In the Field names list, select SheetSetPlaceholder. Select ViewTitle in the Placeholder type list. Verify that Uppercase is selected for the field's Format (see Figure 4.26). Select OK to close the Field dialog box.

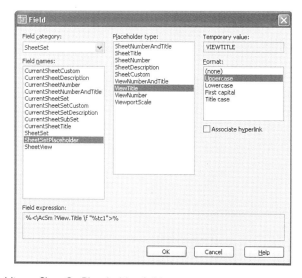

**Figure 4.26**   Adding a SheetSetPlaceholder field.

**10.** The Default value should now read VIEWTITLE, and if you deselect the value, it should have a gray background to indicate a field, as shown in Figure 4.27. Select OK to close the dialog box.

**Figure 4.27**   The attribute's value now uses a field as the default.

**11.** Click on the DTLTLE-TAG attribute definition to select it. Right-click to display the shortcut menu and select the Properties item. Change the Preset option to Yes in the Misc section. Click in the drawing editor and press Esc to unselect the attribute definition.

**I**NSIDER **N**OTE

> A View Label block's attributes that use fields should be set to Preset because these attributes are filled in automatically anyway. There is no need to make the user deal with the prompts for the attributes.

**12.** Repeat steps 8 through 11 for the remaining attribute definitions, using the Field and Format shown in Table 4.1. Be sure to make the attributes Preset.

**Table 4.1   Attribute Field Code Settings**

| Attribute | SheetSetPlaceholder Field | Format |
|---|---|---|
| DTLNO-TAG | ViewNumber | Uppercase |
| DTLSHT-TAG | SheetNumber | Uppercase |
| SCALE-TAG | ViewportScale | #" = 1' - 0" |

Close the drawing, saving the changes. Leave the Sheet Set Manager open for the next exercise.

Next, we perform nearly the same exercise on a callout block, with some key differences. Whereas you can specify only one label block, you can specify multiple callout blocks. For Exercise 4.5, we specify only one callout block. We also attach a hyperlink to the fields added to the callout block.

### Exercise 4.5    Assigning and Customizing a Callout Block

1. Continue from the previous exercise. The Bank Project sheet set should be loaded. Make the Sheet List tab active, if needed. Right-click over the Bank Project title and then choose Properties from the shortcut menu.

2. Click the Callout blocks line, activating the [...] button, and then click the [...] button. This opens the List of Blocks dialog box.

**I**NSIDER **N**OTE

> When choosing the Callout block, you can use a drawing that contains multiple blocks for different types of callouts. In that case, the Select Block dialog enables the Choose blocks option. You can then decide to use it and have the Sheet Set Manager offer the user a choice when placing a callout.

3. Select the Add... button. This opens the Select Block dialog box.

4. On the Select Block dialog box, select the [...] button and then browse and select this drawing:

   IAC2005\Blocks\Section Mark.dwg

5. Right-click on the filename and select Open. Click the Open button to close the Select Drawing dialog box. Select OK to close the Select Block dialog box. The List of Blocks dialog box now lists the drawing we just added.

6. Select OK to close the List of Blocks dialog box. Select OK once more to close the Sheet Set Properties dialog box.

7. Open the Section Mark drawing for editing. Double-click on the SECNO-TAG attribute definition. Select the Default item, SECNO-ATT, and right-click to display the shortcut menu. Select the Insert Field item. The Field dialog box is displayed.

8. Select the SheetSet Field category. In the Field names list, select SheetSetPlaceholder. Select ViewNumber in the Placeholder type list. Verify that Uppercase is selected for the field's Format. Select the Associate hyperlink option so that it is checked. Select OK to close the Field dialog box.

9. The default value should now be a field named VIEWNUMBER. Select OK to close the dialog box.

10. Click on the SECNO-TAG attribute definition to select it. Right-click to display the shortcut menu and select the Properties item. Change the Preset option to Yes in the Misc section. Click in the drawing editor and press Esc to unselect the attribute definition.

11. Repeat steps 7 through 10 on the SECSH-TAG, using the SheetSetPlaceholder Field SheetNumber. Be sure to select the Associate hyperlink option once again.

    Close the drawing, saving the changes. Leave the Sheet Set Manager open for the next exercise.

The two previous exercises modified existing blocks used in pre-2005 projects to prepare them for use with sheet sets. The next section shows you how these blocks are used.

# Placing View Labels and Callouts

A powerful feature of the Sheet Set Manager is dynamic view labels and callout blocks. They are dynamic because the data they display come from the Sheet Set Manager. Therefore, if you change the number of a view on a sheet, all callouts that refer to that view number are changed automatically. The following exercise demonstrates the power of this functionality.

### Exercise 4.6   Including View Labels in a Drawing

1. Continue from the previous exercise. The Bank Project sheet set should be loaded. Make the Sheet List tab active, if needed.

2. Right-click over the Bank Project title and then choose Properties from the shortcut menu.

3. Click on the Resource Drawing Locations line, activating a [...] button, and then click it.

4. On the Resource Drawing Locations dialog box, click the Add button. Browse for the Details folder copied from the CD-ROM earlier and click Open. This adds the directory to the location list. Your dialog should now look like Figure 4.28, showing two directory locations. Click OK to close.

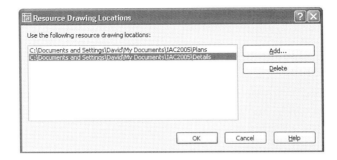

**Figure 4.28**    The Resource Drawing Locations dialog lists directories where you can access drawings within the Sheet Set Manager.

5. Click OK to close the Sheet Set Properties dialog. Time to place some details, but first we need a new sheet!

6. Right-click on the Bank Project title and choose New Sheet. As shown in Figure 4.29, fill in values for Number, Sheet title, and File name and click OK to create the sheet. Back in the Sheet Set Manager, double-click on the new sheet to open it for editing.

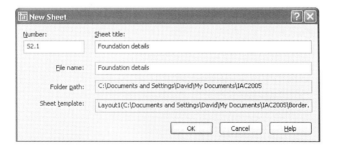

**Figure 4.29**    The New Sheet dialog with information for our detail sheet.

7. Zoom to the lower left of the sheet, showing about 1/4 of the detail area. This is where we place our details.

8. On the Sheet Set Manager, click the Resource Drawings tab to make it active. In the list, expand the Details folder, click on S02-01-01, and then right-click. Select Place on Sheet. The detail image is brought in, and you can drag it about on-screen.

9. Use the right-click menu and select the 1"=1' scale option. Pick a point near the inside lower-left corner of the sheet area.

   The detail is xrefed in, with a viewport around it. You also have an old detail title block that came in with the xref.

**INSIDER NOTE**

When you assigned the Detail Info Block.dwg to Label for views in the Sheet Set Properties dialog, you instructed the Sheet Set Manager system to insert this block after placing any view, which it did. The concept here is that the view's title block is inserted in your sheet, not the detail. But the S02-01-01 drawing has one already because it came from an existing job. All we need to do is edit that drawing and remove it.

10. Within the Resource Drawings tab on the Sheet Set Manager, double-click on the S02-01-01.dwg file, opening the detail drawing for editing.

11. Erase the detail title block at the bottom, perform a ZOOM extents, and save and close the drawing.

12. By default, AutoCAD displays a notification when an xref has been changed (see Figure 4.30). Select the link to run the XREF command and reload the detail drawing in order to update the appearance (see Figure 4.31). Now the detail has only one view label.

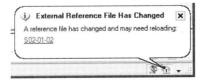

**Figure 4.30**    The External Reference File Has Changed notification.

**Figure 4.31** The newly placed detail on our sheet drawing.

13. Zoom in closer to the view label (see Figure 4.32). Notice that the sheet number and scale attributes have the correct data in them already. The detail number does not have data it can use yet, indicated by the "----". The detail's title itself is only the filename of the original detail at the moment.

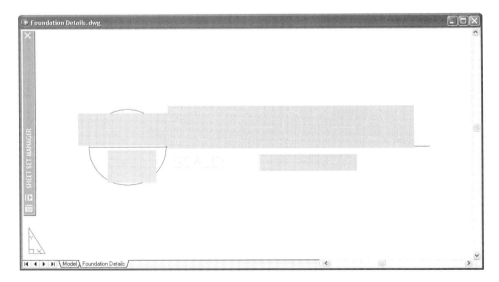

**Figure 4.32** The View Label immediately after insertion.

**14.** Select the View List tab in the Sheet Set Manager. Notice the new view listed, S02-01-01, as shown in Figure 4.33. Right-click on the view and select Rename & Renumber. The Rename & Renumber View dialog box appears. Specify 1 as the Number and change the View title to Detail. Select OK to close the dialog. The list updates to reflect the changes made.

**Figure 4.33**   Specifying the detail's number and name using the Sheet Set Manager.

**15.** Right-click on the Bank Project item in the Views list. Select the New View Category item. The View Category dialog box is displayed. Type **Details** in the Category name edit box and select OK to close the dialog.

**▌INSIDER TIP**

> View categories not only help you to organize the list of views but also enable you to define specific callout blocks to apply to each view category.

**16.** Click and drag the 1 - Detail item down into the Details category.

**17.** Activate the drawing and use the REGEN command to update the display of the view label block. Zoom to the previous display so that we can add another detail.

**▌INSIDER NOTE**

> This system creates two objects in the layout, the viewport object and view label. It places both on the current layer, which is $Viewport and was set to not plot in the template. So, after placement, you need to move the detail title block to a layer that does plot.

A programmatic alternative is to make sure layer 0 is current before placing a view and then, using a Visual LISP reactor or VBA event hander, to change the viewport to a layer that is set to No Plot.

**18.** In the Resource Drawings tab, click on the [+] icon next to S02-01-02.dwg, expanding it. It contains a view named Detail. Right-click on it and choose Place on Sheet.

**19.** Right-click to change the scale to 1"=1'. Place it adjacent to the previous detail.

The use of active object snaps and object tracking makes the chore of lining up viewports much easier.

**20.** Select the View List once again in the Sheet Set Manager. Right-click on the Detail view and select Rename & Renumber. The Rename & Renumber View dialog box appears. Specify **2** as the Number, yet leave the View title the same. Select OK to close the dialog. Drag-and-drop the view beneath the Details category.

Update the drawing using the REGEN command. Our sheet should look like Figure 4.34 now. Save the Foundation Details drawing and close it but leave the Bank Project sheet set open for the following exercise.

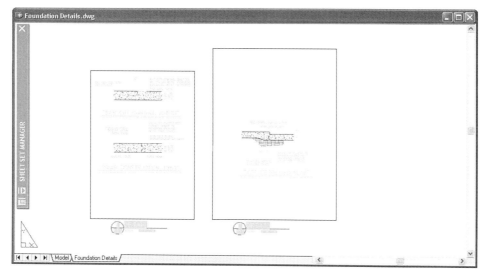

**Figure 4.34**   The second detail had a named view that was used to size the viewport properly.

# Becoming a Power User of the Sheet Set Manager

The new Sheet Set Manager is a huge addition to AutoCAD 2005. There are still features not covered that can reward you with added productivity. This section describes these additional accessories that you can put in your AutoCAD toolbox.

## Creating Sheet List Tables

In Chapter 21, you learn about the new table object in AutoCAD 2005. This new object type has been extended in the Sheet Set Manager. At any point during the documentation process, you can "export" the entire collection of sheets to a Sheet List Table and have it placed onto a sheet in your set. As shown in Figure 4.35, all that is needed is to open the sheet where you want the list. Right-click on the sheet set title, choose Insert Sheet List Table, select or create a Table Style to use, and adjust any content and data structure, and AutoCAD generates the table and populates it, enabling you to place it as needed.

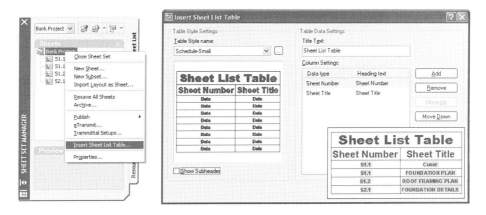

**Figure 4.35**   You can create a Sheet List Table object from within the Sheet Set Manager.

## Callout Connectivity

Earlier, we covered the functionality of the view label block. It comes in as you place a view onto a sheet—automatically filling in values from sheet set data. There is another mechanism that takes this to another level. The callout blocks, controlled by the Sheet Set Properties dialog, provide a way to connect a sheet set view to a callout block in a drawing. The View List tab in the Sheet Set Manager provides a middle manager, enabling you to select a view from another drawing and place a callout to that view in the current drawing. Figure 4.36 is a composite of the various elements that come into play in this process.

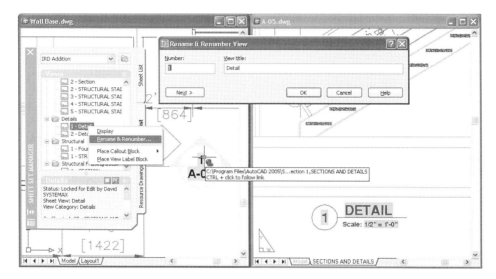

**Figure 4.36**    The various elements tying a callout to a view. The Sheet Set Manager View tab has the actual view reference. The dialog enables you to edit the name and number. The hyperlink indicates that you can open the drawing using the callout. The detail information block shows the latest information after a regen.

### Exercise 4.7    Including Callouts in a Drawing

1. Continue from the previous exercise. The Bank Project sheet set should be loaded. Make the Sheet List tab active, if needed.

2. Double-click on sheet S1.1 to open it. Zoom in on one of the foundation walls, near an existing section mark.

3. Click on the View List tab in the Sheet Set Manager. Right-click on 1 - Detail and select Place Callout Block, Section Mark. Place the block on the drawing near another section mark. Notice how the detail's number and sheet are automatically filled in.

   Suppose that the designer chooses to change the number of the sheet that the details are placed on, 15 minutes before the plots are due! Disaster? Not with Sheet Set Manager!

4.  Select the Sheet List tab in the Sheet Set Manager. Right-click on S2.1 and choose Rename & Renumber. Change the Number of the sheet to S3.1 and select OK to close the dialog.

**I**NSIDER **N**OTE

As you can see from this exercise, it is easy to change a sheet's number. If you used to use the sheet number as part of the drawing's filename, you might find it difficult to reconcile a changed sheet number in the Sheet Set Manager with the drawing's filename using the old sheet number. This is the reason why the drawing filenames in this chapter's exercises do not contain a reference to the sheet number.

5.  Activate the Foundation Plan drawing and use the REGEN command to update all fields. Notice how the sheet number changes on the callout block we just added.

6.  Double-click on sheet S3.1 in the Sheet Set Manager. The Foundation Details drawing opens. Zoom in on the details in the lower left. Notice how the sheet number has been updated here, too. Pan over to the title block. The sheet number has even been automatically fixed there!

Close AutoCAD, saving the drawings only if you choose to; they are no longer needed.

This short exercise demonstrates how the time you spend up front creating the sheet set and its supporting properties and files is well worth the investment. However, there are even more advantages.

## Page Setup Override and Subsets

Page setups are a great way to control how a given sheet plots. However, at times you might need to change a page setup or provide a new one to a sheet set. The Page Setup Override feature of the Sheet Set Manager, as shown in Figure 4.37, can help you quickly publish sheets that are missing the specific page setup.

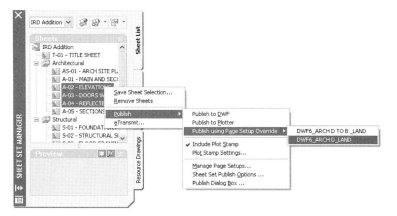

**Figure 4.37**   Publish multiple sheets using any predefined page setup from the Sheet Set Manager.

Also on Figure 4.37, notice in the sheet list a hierarchy of sheets. There is an Architectural section and a Structural section. These are just subsets within the primary sheet set. To create one, right-click on the sheet set name, choose New Subset, and then name it appropriately. After that, you simply drag your existing sheets in the order you need. Also, any new sheets started in a subset are created in that subset. Subsets can be published as a set or as part of the entire sheet set.

## Archiving Sheet Sets

At the end of specific milestones in a project, you will often need to create a snapshot of the design set of documents (the files). By using the Sheet Set Manager and its Archive tools, you can get this done in minutes instead of hours. If the files are part of your sheet set, as shown in Figure 4.38, the Archive A Sheet Set dialog packages it up, compresses it as needed, and saves it as the specified DWG format.

**I**NSIDER **N**OTE

The Etransmit portion of the Sheet Set Manager functions the same way as the Archive utility—except it is used to send the package electronically through email.

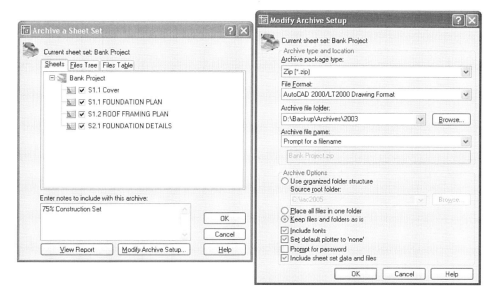

**Figure 4.38**   Archiving from within the Sheet Set Manager removes all the guesswork and file errors.

## Accessing Sheet Sets Through Programming

Finally, AutoCAD provides access to the sheet set and its data for programmers through VBA and Visual C++.NET. Unfortunately, you cannot use Visual LISP to access the Sheet Set Manager. That limitation aside, the possibilities are exciting. Imagine placing all the data stored in the Sheet Set Manager in an Excel spreadsheet or Access database. Programs can be created to easily renumber all the sheets without user input. More information can be found in the Developer's Help section.

# Summary

In this chapter, we covered many aspects of the new Sheet Set Manager. We learned how easily a sheet set can be created and how you can use it as a simple file management tool. From there, you explored using it to create new sheets and populating the new sheet data automatically from the Sheet Set Manager. Also, we covered placing plans and details on a sheet, as well as controlling their scale and position. We followed that up with automatic view labels using the current viewport and sheet. Lastly, we touched on even more really valuable aspects of the Sheet Set Manager that can be used to get the project out the door—faster than ever before!

As with any major enhancement to AutoCAD, the key to understanding is the trials that come from doing. Working through these exercises here, as well as testing on your own, will enable you to fully comprehend the possibilities that this new feature brings to the AutoCAD community. As more and more users adopt sheet sets, the requirement to follow along will increase. Learning about these new techniques now will put you in a position to guide your comrades.

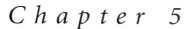

# Chapter 5

# Organizing a Drawing with Layers

Prior to the advent of Computer Aided Design (CAD), projects consisted of dozens of mylar and vellum drawings that were ultimately printed as bluelines and then taken into the field or the shop where they were used in the construction of buildings or the fabrication of parts. Although drawings are still necessary in the construction and fabrication process, today the person who initials the "Drawn by" box can more efficiently organize the information formerly drawn on those dozens of sheets by using AutoCAD's layers.

In AutoCAD, layers mimic the individual pin-registered mylar sheets, when layers of mylar sheets were stacked one on top of the other to create a composite drawing. By placing specific information on an AutoCAD layer, the former process of placing item-specific information on a mylar sheet is emulated. Because AutoCAD can contain an unlimited number of layers, you can expand upon the idea of composite sheets and include layers for the object geometry, dimensions, notes, and so on. When using layers to organize your drawings, you can create a single model that serves many purposes.

This chapter discusses using layers to organize your drawings and shows you how to use AutoCAD's Layer Properties Manager, improved for AutoCAD 2005. This chapter explores the following topics:

- Implementing layering standards
- Controlling the drawing's layer features
- Creating layers and assigning color to them
- Locking layers
- Setting a layer filter
- Using layer states

# The Layer Properties Manager

With the introduction of AutoCAD 2005, the Layer Properties Manager dialog was updated substantially from its predecessor. The dialog is larger than before and fully adjustable, enabling you to view more layers and layer status information than before, as shown in Figure 5.1. Plus, the dialog remembers your adjustments, even between AutoCAD sessions.

**INSIDER NOTE**

The Layer Properties Manager dialog box dedicates itself to dealing only with layers. Linetypes have their own dialog box, called the Linetype Manager, which is discussed in Chapter 6, "Effective Linetypes and Lineweights Use."

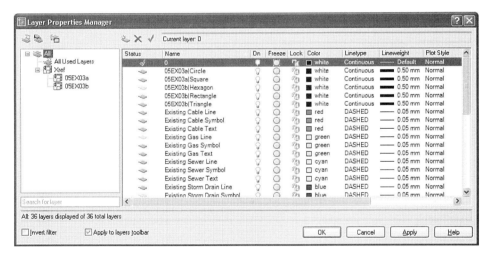

**Figure 5.1**    The Layer Properties Manager has been redesigned and improved in AutoCAD 2005.

**INSIDER TIP**

There is a new layer control column called Status. The blue, or darker, icons indicate that the layer is used (has something on it), the lighter gray icons are unused layers, and the layer with the green check is the current layer. You can double-click a layer to make it current or select a layer followed by the Set Current button at the top of the Layer Properties Manager dialog box.

The Layer Properties Manager's new features, as well as those features found in previous versions, are explored in this chapter. But before you learn how to use the Layer Properties Manager to its fullest potential, you need to learn about the importance of consistent layer names.

# Consistent Layer Names

Whether you're the only person working with AutoCAD in your company, or one of several dozen, establishing consistent layer names can increase the efficiency of layer management. You can simplify the process of displaying the desired elements by using layers to organize those elements in your drawing. This makes editing and plotting easier. For example, if your drawing has gas lines and sewer lines but you only want to edit the gas lines, you can make your drawing easier to work with visually by turning off the layer where the sewer lines are drawn.

## Layer Name Considerations

The process of defining standard layer names can be daunting. Because the drawing you are creating represents only one portion of the project's life cycle, you must consider not only the number of layers and their names necessary to fulfill your needs, but also how your drawing will be used by others.

For example, will half-scale versions of your drawing be inserted into reports? If so, it may be necessary to place duplicate text on two different layers: one to hold text that is easy to read at full scale, and the other layer to hold duplicate text that is easily read at half scale. Will other departments or companies incorporate your drawing into theirs, creating a composite drawing? If so, you must establish layering standards that you both find acceptable. What different objects must you display on the set of hardcopy plots provided to the contractor for construction?

Although a single model space drawing may contain both gas lines and sewer lines, your hardcopy plots may need to separate these two components, creating one set of plots showing only gas lines, and the other showing only sewer lines. Your understanding of the many ways your drawing will be used, and whether you properly develop and use layering standards, can make working on your project productive and easy or disastrously difficult.

> Another new feature in AutoCAD 2005 is the Description column in the Layer Properties Manager dialog. This provides a user-definable value for your layer-naming convention. If a given project requires a cryptic naming system, you can utilize the Description value to clarify a given layer's content.

## Predefined Standards

Although there are many things you must consider when developing layer standards, the good news is that in reality, you probably don't have to do too much. Because AutoCAD has been around for more than 20 years, many companies have established their own internal layering standards. As a consequence, when you work for a company, you are typically issued a CAD Standards Manual and are expected to read it and use it in your day-to-day drafting activities. In addition, many industries have adopted an agreed-upon standard that can simplify your standards development and decision-making process.

> For the latest information on AIA CAD layering guidelines, browse the National CAD Standards web site at www.nationalcadstandard.org.

In addition to a layering standard, many companies have created drawing template files that already contain the proper layers. By using template files when starting a drawing, you are guaranteed that your drawing file has all the layers you need, with each layer pre-set to the correct properties of Color, Linetype, and Lineweight. You can learn more about creating your own drawing templates in Chapter 3, "Starting a Drawing in AutoCAD."

## Extended Layer Names

Since AutoCAD 2000, AutoCAD has extended the allowable length of layer names substantially. Layer names can now be 255 characters long if needed. They can also include spaces, and AutoCAD preserves upper- or lowercasing of characters. With these enhancements, you can utilize very meaningful and descriptive layer names.

Although xref names are still appended to the beginning of xref-dependent layers, the xref's drawing name does not count toward the 255-character limit. You can learn about layering issues with regard to xrefs in Chapter 11, "Working with External References."

Although the extended features of layer names are good, you should use discretion when creating layering standards. For example, Figure 5.2 shows two different methods of using the extended layer name features. The layer name on the bottom of the list reads `This is the layer on which I placed all the existing sewer line text.`, and actually includes the period at the end. This layer name may be very descriptive, but it's not very practical in terms of layer name standards.

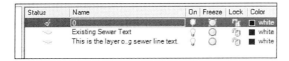

**Figure 5.2**   The Layer Properties Manager allows for long layer names.

For example, if your drawing contains dozens or even hundreds of layers, it is not easy to find the sewer text layer with the longer name in an extensive list. In contrast, the layer name in the middle of the list reads `Existing Sewer Text`. This much shorter name relates the same information and enables users to easily peruse the layer list and find the correct layer. Using concise layer names can make it easier to isolate and recognize specific layers, whether the layers are sorted alphabetically or filtered (a feature described later in this chapter).

# Controlling Object Properties

AutoCAD 2005 provides four object properties you can control through the Layer Properties Manager. The first three, Color, Linetype, and Lineweight, affect object appearance when displayed on the screen. All four properties control the appearance of objects when plotted for output.

Through the Layer Properties Manager, you can control the values of object properties. More importantly, the Layer Properties Manager provides a method of globally controlling properties. For example, by using the Layer Properties Manager to change a layer's color to red, you automatically change the color of all objects on that layer to red (provided they have their color value set to ByLayer). This global method of changing the color of all objects by changing only one value in the Layer Properties Manager is a tremendous timesaver, especially if there are dozens of objects on a layer. By using the Layer Properties Manager, you can simultaneously edit the Color, Linetype, Lineweight, and Plot Style properties of numerous objects.

**I**NSIDER **N**OTE

> The concept of ByLayer is sometimes overlooked. When any object has its Color, Linetype, or Lineweight property set to ByLayer, then that property finds its value from the layer on which the object resides. An object on a layer with a red color appears red, and when placed on a layer with a blue color, the same object appears blue.

Fortunately, AutoCAD provides a simple method for setting object properties to ByLayer. By understanding and controlling how AutoCAD assigns properties to objects, you can create objects whose property values are globally controlled through AutoCAD's 2005 Layer Properties Manager.

The following section discusses how AutoCAD assigns properties to an object when it is created and how to use the Layer Properties Manager to control the object's property values when they are set to ByLayer.

## Assigning Properties to New Objects: The Layers and Properties Toolbar

When you create a new object, AutoCAD automatically assigns the object to the current layer. Additionally, AutoCAD also assigns values of Color, Linetype, Lineweight, and if applicable, Plot Style. These four properties that AutoCAD assigns to an object are determined by the values displayed in the Properties toolbar. For example, to assign new objects the layer value of 0 and the color red, you select the desired values from the appropriate drop-down list in the Layers and Properties toolbar, as shown in Figure 5.3. After these values are set, when a new object is created, it is assigned to layer 0 and assigned the color red. To assign new objects to a different layer, simply choose the desired layer from the Layer drop-down list.

**Figure 5.3**   The Layers and Properties toolbar sets the Layer, Color, Linetype, Lineweight, and Plot Style properties for new objects.

AutoCAD's default layer is 0. Geometry created on layer 0 has unique and beneficial properties with respect to blocks. Consequently, when creating new geometry for your project, you should typically create a new layer for the geometry, reserving layer 0 to create blocks with special uses. For more information on the relationship between layers and blocks, refer to Chapter 10, "Creating and Using Blocks."

# The ByLayer Property Value

Notice that in Figure 5.3, the last three drop-down lists in the Properties toolbar all display the current property value as ByLayer. These last three lists are the object property values for Linetype, Lineweight, and Plot Style, respectively. When an object's property is set to ByLayer, it means those particular property values are controlled by the settings in the Layer Properties Manager. Therefore, with the property assignments shown in Figure 5.3, if you created a new object, its Linetype, Lineweight, and Plot Style values are controlled by the Linetype, Lineweight, and Plot Style values in the Layer Properties Manager. Consequently, to view the values for Linetype, Lineweight, and Plot Style, you must view the values for layer 0 in the Layer Properties Manager, as shown in Figure 5.4.

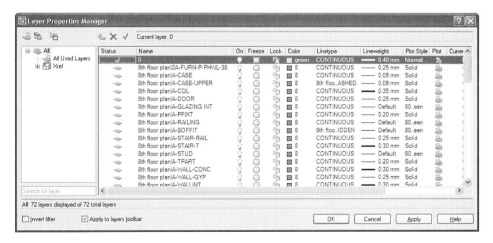

**Figure 5.4**    The Layer Properties Manager controls the Color, Linetype, Lineweight, and Plot Style settings for all objects whose property values are set to ByLayer.

Remember that because the Layers toolbar is set to layer 0, all new objects are created on layer 0 in this example. This means that any properties set to ByLayer when an object is created are controlled by the property values for layer 0. As shown in Figure 5.4, the property values for layer 0 are as follows:

- Color = Green
- Linetype = Continuous
- Lineweight = 0.40 mm
- Plot Style = Normal

**I**NSIDER **N**OTE

> If the lineweights in your drawing display in millimeters (mm), you can switch to an inches format by choosing Lineweight from the Format menu. Then, from the Lineweight Settings dialog box, select the Inches option in the Units for Listing area. For more information, refer to Chapter 6.

Once again, AutoCAD looks to the property values in the Layer Properties Manager only when an object's properties are assigned as ByLayer.

It is important to note that although Figure 5.4 shows the color value for layer 0 as green, newly created objects will be drawn in the color red. This is true because the Properties toolbar shown in Figure 5.3 is set to the color red, and therefore AutoCAD explicitly assigns the color red to newly created objects. AutoCAD displays any new object's color as red if a color is set explicitly in the Properties toolbar.

**I**NSIDER **T**IP

> It is generally a good concept to try to assign an object's property values as ByLayer. This provides you with the ability to globally change Color, Linetype, Lineweight, and Plot Style through the layer rather than the object. Some exceptions exist for objects needing a specific linetype, even though the layer linetype may be set to Continuous.

## The Color Property

One of the simplest properties to understand is the Color property. AutoCAD provides many colors from which to choose, but your color choice should be influenced by two factors:

- How objects appear on-screen
- How objects appear when plotted

For on-screen appearance, you should typically use colors to help you differentiate between objects. By using an assortment of colors, you make viewing easier for objects that are adjacent or that overlap. However, when it comes to plotting objects, there is more involved to an object's appearance than just color.

When plotting objects, AutoCAD enables you to assign lineweights by color or named plot style. The user determines the weight values at plot time by setting lineweight values in the plot style. For more detailed information on controlling lineweights when plotting, see Chapter 19, "Productive Plotting."

**INSIDER NOTE**

> Quite often, the colors you assign to objects are determined by layering standards. If your company or your client has defined color assignments in their layering standards, spending a small amount of research and documentation time will reap great rewards when you submit your work.

## The Linetype and Lineweight Properties

The Linetype property enables you to set the style of a linetype. A linetype style defines whether AutoCAD draws an object with a continuous, unbroken line, or with dashed or dotted lines. You can choose from a wide variety of non-continuous linetypes, and you can also select linetypes that have text in them. AutoCAD includes an assortment of linetypes, and you can create your own custom linetype patterns. Learn about lineweights and linetypes in Chapter 6, including how to create custom linetype patterns.

The Lineweight property, on the other hand, controls how heavy a line AutoCAD displays and possibly plots. In fact, the Lineweight property performs the same function as the Plot Style described previously. Instead of assigning lineweights by color, however, it assigns the lineweight as a property. Consequently, you can display the lineweight on-screen, as opposed to observing how wide a line is by plotting the objects. Therefore, you can make one object's lineweight very thin so that it appears subtle, set another's lineweight much wider to make it appear bold, and then view the results on-screen without plotting.

## The Plot Style Property

The Plot Style property affects how objects appear when plotted by enabling you to assign a Plot Style to an object and override its Color, Linetype, and Lineweight values. Additionally, Plot Styles enable you to specify end, join, and fill styles, as well as control output effects such as dithering, gray-scale, pen assignment, and screening.

Plot Styles are intended to enable you to plot the same drawing in many different ways without making elaborate changes to the original Color, Linetype, and Lineweight properties. By creating multiple Plot Style tables, you can create one plot of a drawing that displays objects with bold, heavy lines, and then plot the same drawing as a grayscale, all without making any changes to Layer, Color, Linetype, or Lineweight properties within the drawing. For more detailed information on Plot Styles, see Chapter 19.

# Controlling Object Behavior with the Layer Properties Manager

In the previous sections, you learned how to control object properties that determine how an object looks when AutoCAD draws it on-screen or plots it on paper. In this section, you learn how to control object behavior using the Layer Properties Manager. Specifically, you learn how to control object visibility and how to protect objects from being edited accidentally.

## Layer Visibility

One handy feature of using layers to organize objects into logical groups is that you can use the Layer Properties Manager to manipulate groups of objects by modifying layer settings. In addition to controlling object colors and linetypes as previously discussed, you can control object visibility. With a simple click of your pointing device, entire groups of objects become invisible on-screen and therefore non-plottable.

AutoCAD enables you to control object display on-screen with two features in the Layer Properties Manager. You can turn layers off and on, and you can freeze and thaw layers. In either case, objects that reside on a layer that's turned off or frozen become invisible and non-plottable. Additionally, a feature called Plot/No Plot enables you to control whether objects appear on a plot, even though the objects may be displayed.

In the next few sections, you learn about the important differences between turning layers off and on as opposed to freezing and thawing, and we'll explain the Plot/No Plot feature.

### Turning Off Layers Versus Freezing Layers

Although the end result of making objects invisible by turning layers off or by freezing layers may seem the same, there is a very important reason why AutoCAD makes both methods available. When a layer is turned off, even though the objects on the layer become invisible, AutoCAD still performs certain zoom and regeneration calculations on the invisible objects. In contrast, when a layer is frozen, AutoCAD does not include the objects on the frozen layer in zoom or regeneration calculations.

By freezing objects, you can dramatically reduce zoom and regeneration times. If you only need to edit objects that reside on one layer, then you can increase your productivity by freezing the layers on which all other unneeded objects reside.

So, if freezing layers improves productivity, why not always freeze layers instead of turning them off? Every time you thaw a layer that had been frozen, it causes AutoCAD to perform a regeneration, also called a *regen*. In contrast, turning layers off (or on) does not cause a regen. Therefore, turning layers off makes sense during typical editing sessions when you want to make objects only temporarily invisible. Freezing layers is the proper choice when there are objects you don't need to view during a lengthy editing session. By freezing them, AutoCAD visually removes the objects from the screen and no longer includes the objects on the frozen layers in future regens, which can dramatically reduce overall regen times.

In the following exercise, you experience the difference between turning layers off and freezing layers by seeing their effects on the ZOOM Extents command.

### Exercise 5.1    Turning Layers Off Versus Freezing Layers

1. Open the drawing 05EX01.dwg. The drawing displays a circle and a square side-by-side.

2. From the Layers toolbar, use the drop-down list to choose the light bulb symbol for the Circle layer, as shown in Figure 5.5, and then pick any spot in the drawing. The Circle layer turns off and removes the circle from the screen.

3. Using the Zoom fly-out found on the Standard toolbar, choose the Zoom Extents toolbar button, as shown in Figure 5.6.

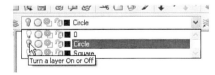

**Figure 5.5**
Choosing the light bulb symbol from the Layer drop-down list in the Layers toolbar turns off the Circle layer.

**Figure 5.6**
The Zoom fly-out contains shortcuts to the most commonly used zoom functions.

AutoCAD starts the ZOOM command and then executes the Extents option, resulting in the display shown in Figure 5.7.

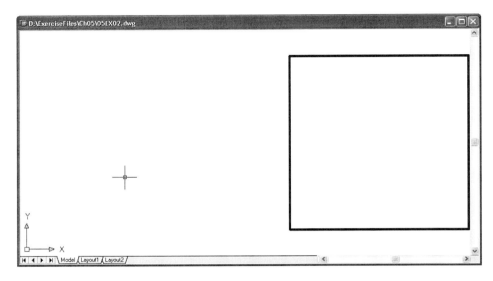

**Figure 5.7**    With the Circle layer turned off, AutoCAD calculates the position of the invisible circle when a ZOOM Extents is executed.

4. From the Layers toolbar, choose the sun symbol for the Circle layer in the drop-down list, as shown in Figure 5.8, and then pick any spot in the drawing. AutoCAD freezes the Circle layer.

**Figure 5.8**    Choosing the sun symbol from the Layer drop-down list in the Layers toolbar freezes the Circle layer.

5. Using the Zoom fly-out found on the Standard toolbar, choose the Zoom Extents toolbar button.

Notice now that after AutoCAD performs a ZOOM Extents, the rectangle displays in the center of the screen, as shown in Figure 5.9. By comparing Figures 5.7 and 5.9, you can see the difference between turning a layer off and freezing the same layer when performing a ZOOM Extents. When the layer is turned off, AutoCAD still takes the time to calculate the position of the circle. When the layer is frozen, AutoCAD ignores the circle and only calculates the position of the square.

**I**NSIDER **NOTE**

When you freeze a layer, the entities on that layer cannot be modified or deleted. However, when you turn off a layer, the entities on that layer are still subject to modification through global editing commands such as ERASE ALL, even though they are not visible.

Although the difference in regen time initiated by the ZOOM Extents was nearly imperceptible, the time difference becomes much more obvious when the frozen layer contains thousands of objects.

When finished, you may close the drawing without saving your changes.

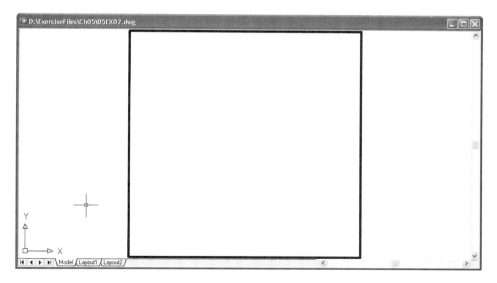

**Figure 5.9**   With the Circle layer frozen, AutoCAD does not calculate the position of the invisible circle when a ZOOM Extents is executed.

### *Freezing Globally Versus Freezing in the Active Viewport*

Although this exercise didn't discuss it, the methods used to turn off and freeze layers were global. In other words, they affect all objects in all viewports. Although turning off or freezing layers in all viewports is generally acceptable, there are circumstances when it is not. Specifically, when you are working with Paper Space layouts that have multiple viewports, you may want objects on a layer to be visible in one viewport but invisible in another. This effect is accomplished by freezing layers in the active viewport. For detailed information on freezing layers in the active viewport, see Chapter 18, "Paper Space Layouts."

### *The Plot/No Plot Feature*

The Plot/No Plot feature, introduced in AutoCAD 2000, controls whether objects on a layer are plotted by toggling the feature on or off. What makes this feature useful is that objects that are visible on-screen are prevented from plotting if the Plot option is toggled off. Therefore, you can display and use objects such as construction lines on-screen but prevent them from plotting.

**INSIDER TIP**

You can use AutoCAD's Plot Preview feature to view the results of layers set to No Plot. For more information, see Chapter 19.

**INSIDER NOTE**

In previous releases, you could simulate the Plot/No Plot option by creating a layer called DEFPOINTS and placing objects on it that you wanted to view and edit on-screen but did not want to plot. The problem with this technique was that you could only have one DEFPOINTS layer, and therefore the layer could become cluttered with an array of objects that you needed to use on-screen but did not want to plot.

The Plot/No Plot option affects blocks and external references (xrefs) in unique ways. For example, you can control which objects in a block don't plot by setting their layers to No Plot. Also, you can prevent an entire block from plotting by setting the layer on which the block is inserted to No Plot. This is true for xrefs as well.

## Locking Layers

When editing a drawing with multiple layers, you can control which objects are editable by locking and unlocking the layers on which they reside. The ability to lock layers enables you to display the objects on a given layer without selecting any objects on that layer. More importantly, although objects on a locked layer are not selectable for edit commands, you can snap to them using object snaps.

**INSIDER NOTE**

> You can place blocks on a layer that is locked, and even though they may contain data from other layers, you will not be able to erase the blocks.

**INSIDER CAUTION**

> You can create data on a locked layer and then be unable to modify the object you just created. This can often be a trap during LISP routines or scripts that create data on locked layers.

# Using Layer Filters

As discussed previously, organizing many objects into collections using layer names is very useful. Get too many layers, though, and the usefulness of layering degrades. It's cumbersome to use the Layer Properties Manager to locate a specific layer when there are too many of them.

More than likely, you will work on drawings that contain dozens, hundreds, or even thousands of layers. This is especially true when you attach xrefs to the current drawing, adding to its list of layers the layer lists of each xref.

Fortunately, AutoCAD's Layer Properties Manager provides a feature called Layer Filters, which enables you to control which layer names are displayed by defining certain parameters. By using Layer Filters, you can realize the benefit of organizing your drawing with layers and not be overwhelmed by viewing too many layer names in the Layer Properties Manager.

In this section, you explore how to create and apply Layer Filters to make working with layers easier.

## Applying Layer Filters

AutoCAD 2005 introduced a revamped Layer Properties Manager, and a major addition is the new Filter TreeView panel on the left side of the Layer Properties Manager dialog. In the previous release, filtering was done through a drop-down list after assigning it by using the Named Layers Filter dialog.

Now applying a layer filter is much simpler. By opening the Layer Properties Manager dialog box and then selecting a saved filter from the Filter TreeView panel, AutoCAD instantly adjusts the display of layers in the Layer Properties Manager's layer list.

Each AutoCAD drawing automatically includes two standard Layer Filters:

- Show All Layers
- Show All Used Layers

With just these two layer filters, you can make viewing layer lists much easier. Additionally, the Layer Properties Manager includes two controls that enable you to perform the following actions:

- Invert the current layer filter
- Apply the current layer filter to the Layer drop-down list in the Layers toolbar

In the next exercise, you learn how to use these standard layer filter features.

### Exercise 5.2    Layer Properties Manager's Standard Filter Features

1. Open the drawing 05EX02.dwg. The drawing displays a column of lines, symbols (block inserts), and text.

2. From the Layers toolbar, click the Layer Properties Manager button. AutoCAD then displays the Layer Properties Manager dialog box.

3. From the Filter TreeView panel on the left, choose the All Used Layers filter. AutoCAD then invokes the selected layer filter.

   The All Used Layers filter displays only layer names on which objects reside. This filter is useful in determining which layers have objects on them.

   Next, you apply the Invert Filter feature.

4. From the Filter TreeView panel, select the Invert Filter check box. AutoCAD inverts the current layer filter, displaying only those layers that do not have objects on them, as shown in Figure 5.10.

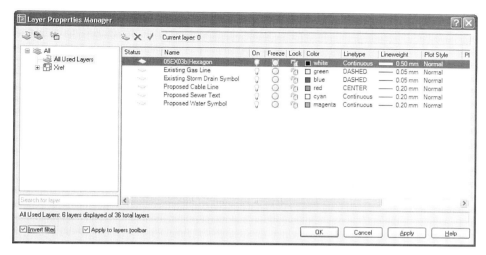

**Figure 5.10**   The current layer filter is inverted, and therefore, only layer names with no objects on them are displayed.

Notice in the lower-left corner of the Layer Properties Manager that AutoCAD indicates 36 total layers, but only six layers are displayed. You could delete these layers to reduce the number of layer names cluttering the layer list.

Next, you examine the Apply to layers toolbar feature.

5. From the Filter TreeView panel, verify the Apply to layers toolbar check box is checked, click the Apply button at the bottom right of the Layer Properties Manager dialog, and then click OK.

6. From the Layers toolbar, choose the down arrow to open the Layer drop-down list, as shown in Figure 5.11.

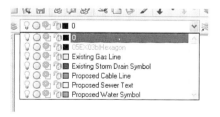

**Figure 5.11**   The current inverted layer filter is applied to the Layer drop-down list in the Layers toolbar.

Notice that the current inverted layer filter is applied to the Layer drop-down list in the Layers toolbar. This feature is very useful when you need to frequently switch between a few layers in a drawing that contains many layers.

This drawing is used in the next exercise. If you want to continue the next exercise at a later time, be sure to save the changes you made during this exercise to your hard drive.

Another layer filter mechanism that AutoCAD provides is showing all xref-dependent layers. By selecting the name Xref at the top of the xref tree, you can easily view all the layers of attached xrefs. By selecting the actual name of any given xref, you can then view only the layers in that xref. Figure 5.12 shows the tree-like nature of this automatic filtering system.

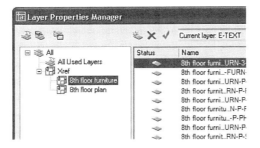

**Figure 5.12**    When you select a single xref layer filter, only those layers that exist in that xref are listed in the Layer Properties Manager.

By inverting the primary Xref filter, you can display all layers that do not reside in attached xrefs. This provides you with the ability to remove unwanted xref layer names from the layer list and the Layer drop-down list on the Layers toolbar.

## Creating Named Layer Filters

In the previous section, you learned how to use the standard layer filters provided with AutoCAD. Although these filters are useful, they probably will not fulfill all your filtering needs. To satisfy all your needs, the Layer Properties Manager enables you to create your own layer filters. In the next exercise, you learn how to create custom layer filters.

## Exercise 5.3    Creating Custom Layer Filters

1. Continue using the drawing from the previous exercise or open 05EX02.dwg from the accompanying CD. From the Layers toolbar, click the Layer Properties Manager button. AutoCAD then displays the Layer Properties Manager dialog box.

2. If the Invert Filter option at the lower left is checked, uncheck it so the dialog shows the results of any applied filter.

3. From the Filter TreeView panel, click the New Property Filter button. The button is at the top left of the Layer Properties Manager dialog. AutoCAD displays the Layer Filter Properties dialog box.

4. For the Filter Name value, type **Symbols Only**.

5. In the Filter definition table under the Name heading, type **\*symbol**. The asterisk (\*) is a wildcard character that tells AutoCAD to accept any characters in front of the word "symbol." Figure 5.13 shows the filter dialog at this point.

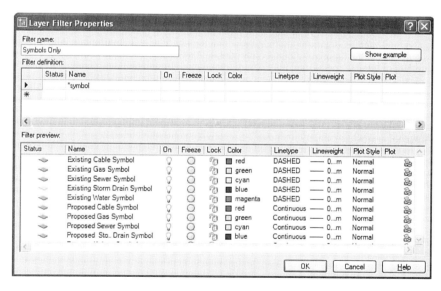

**Figure 5.13**   The Layer Filter Properties dialog box enables you to create custom layer filters.

6. Click the OK button. AutoCAD adds the new filter to the list of available filters and makes it active.

7. AutoCAD displays only those layer names that end with the word "symbol," as shown in Figure 5.14.

This drawing is used in the next exercise. If you want to continue the next exercise at a later time, be sure to save the drawing to your hard disk.

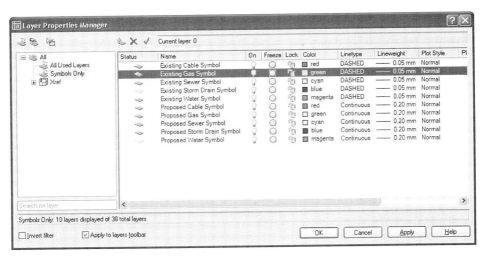

**Figure 5.14**    The custom layer filter Symbols Only displays layer names that end with the word "symbol."

**INSIDER TIP**

There is a new on-the-fly filter for layer names only. The Search for layer box at the bottom of the Filter TreeView area enables you to just type in a series of letters and/or wildcards, and the list area presents all layer names matching that criteria. This is very quick method; however, this "list" cannot be saved, although after you have a list together, you can group the items. Group Filters are explained later in this chapter.

By using the numerous fields available in the Layer Filter Properties dialog box, you can precisely identify the layers you want to display. Additionally, by inserting asterisks in the layer name, you can filter for layers whose differing names have only certain words in common.

Next, you learn how to more precisely identify layers.

## Exercise 5.4    Creating Precise Custom Layer Filters

1. Continue using the drawing from the previous exercise or open 05EX02.dwg from the accompanying CD. From the Filter TreeView panel, click the New Property Filter button. The button is at the top left of the Layer Properties Manager dialog.

2. For the Filter Name value, type **Green Symbol and red Text**.

3. Under the Name heading for the Filter definition table, type **\*symbol**. Be sure to include the asterisk.

4. For the Color value, type **green**.

5. In a blank Name value, type **\*text** and then type **red** for its color value.

    As you complete this task, the filter dynamically updates to show the results. The Layer Filter Properties dialog box appears as shown in Figure 5.15.

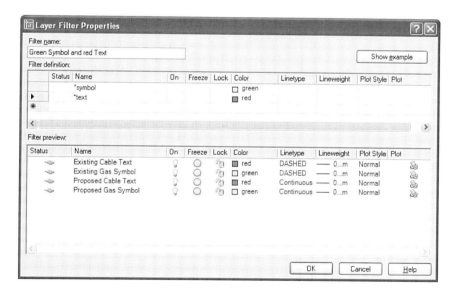

**Figure 5.15**  Custom layer filters can include multiple layer names and colors specific to those layers.

6. Click the OK button. AutoCAD adds the new filter to the list of available filters and makes it current.

    AutoCAD has invoked the selected layer filter. AutoCAD displays only those layer names that end with the word "symbol" and are green in color, and layers that end with word "text" and that are red in color.

    When finished, reset the Filter TreeView area to All and click OK to close the Layer Properties Dialog. Leave the drawing open for the following exercise.

# Using Wildcard Characters in Layer Filters

You can use wildcard characters such as the asterisk (*), comma (,), and tilde (~) to control which layers are displayed in the Layer Properties Manager's layer list. There are, in fact, 10 different wildcard characters you can use with layer filters, and these wildcard characters can be used in combination with each other. Table 5.1 lists the available wildcard characters and their purposes.

**Table 5.1    Wildcard Characters**

| Character | Description |
| --- | --- |
| # (Pound) | The # symbol matches any single numeric character. Suppose you have layer names that are labeled with numbers 1 through 400. You can filter for layer names 200 through 299 by typing **2##** as the layer name filter. |
| @ (At) | The @ symbol matches any single alpha character. Suppose you have two layers named NORTH and SOUTH. You can filter for both these layer names by typing **@O@TH** as the layer name filter. |
| . (Period) | The . symbol matches any single non-alphanumeric character. Suppose you have layers named GAS-TXT, GAS TXT, and GAS_TXT. Notice that the alpha characters are separated by a hyphen, a space, and an underscore character, respectively. You can filter for these three layer names by typing **GAS.TXT** as the layer name filter. |
| * (Asterisk) | The * symbol matches any character sequence and can be used at the beginning, middle, or end of the filter. Suppose you have layers whose names include the word LINE. You can filter for these layer names by typing ***LINE*** as the layer name filter. |
| ? (Question Mark) | The ? symbol matches any single character. Suppose you have layers named GAS-TXT, GAS2TXT, and GASeTXT. You can filter for these three layer names by typing **GAS?TXT** as the layer name filter. |
| ~ (Tilde) | If the ~ symbol is the first character in the filter, then it excludes the filter value. Suppose you have layers that include the name LINE. You can filter for layers that do not include the name LINE by typing **~*LINE*** as the layer name filter. |
| [  ] (Brackets) | The [  ] symbols match any one of the characters enclosed in the brackets. Suppose you have four layers whose names are 1LINE, 2LINE, 3LINE, and 4LINE. You can filter for the layers whose names begin with 1, 2, or 4 by typing **[124]*** as the layer name filter. |
| [~] (Tilde brackets) | The [~] symbol excludes each of the characters enclosed in the brackets that follow the tilde. Suppose you have four layers whose names are 1LINE, 2LINE, 3LINE, and 4LINE. You can exclude the layers whose names begin with 1, 2, or 4 by typing **[~124]*** as the layer name filter. |

| Character | Description |
|---|---|
| - (Hyphen) | The - symbol used inside brackets enables you to specify a single-character range of values. Suppose you have four layers whose names are 1LINE, 2LINE, 3LINE, and 4LINE. You can filter for the layers whose names begin with 1, 2, or 3 by typing **[1-3]*** as the layer name filter. |
| , (Comma) | The , symbol separates multiple filters, enabling you to enter more than one filter in a text box. Suppose you have four layers whose names are 1LINE, 2LINE, 3LINE, and 4LINE. You can filter for the layers whose names begin with 1 or 3 by typing **1*,3*** as the layer name filter. |

The wildcard characters listed in Table 5.1 can be used for several of the filters in the Named Layer Filter dialog box, including the following:

- Layer name
- Color
- Lineweight
- Linetype
- Plot Style

By using the wildcard characters, you can develop powerful layer filters that display only the matching layers you want to view in the Layer Properties Manager or the Layers toolbar.

# Grouping Your Layers

A new feature in AutoCAD 2005 is Layer Groups. It functions similarly to layer filters and is available through the TreeView panel icons, the second from the left. Whereas the Filter mechanism enables you to determine what parameters a layer must match in order to be shown in the Layer Properties Manager, the Group mechanism enables you to determine exactly which layers will be shown. Regardless of any new layers coming into existence and matching a given filter scheme, a group only shows those layers that are assigned to it.

## Layer Grouping

The Group feature is fairly simple to use. The following exercise will show the very basic application of this new and helpful feature.

**Exercise 5.5    Assigning a Layer Group**

1. Continue using the drawing from the previous exercise or open the drawing 05EX02.dwg found on the accompanying CD.

2. Open the Layer Properties Manager by clicking the Layer Properties Manager button on the Layers toolbar.

3. Click the New Group Filter icon, the second icon from the left at the top of the dialog.

4. When the default group name appears, type over it with **EXISTING**. This names the group for ease of use and ideally is descriptive in nature.

   After you create the group, it becomes active, and because no layers have yet been assigned, the Layer listing area is void of any layers.

5. Click on the All filter, bringing back all the layers in the drawing into the listing area.

6. Select a number of the layers with the word EXISTING in their name and drag them onto the group EXISTING. Nothing visibly happens, but you just added those layers to the EXISTING group.

**I**NSIDER **T**IP

You can use the right-click shortcut menu to remove layers from a named group. Select the layer(s) in the group list, right-click, and remove them. See Figure 5.16 for this and many other options on the Layer Properties Manager shortcut menu.

**Figure 5.16**    The Layer Properties Manager shortcut menu provides many editing functions and quick layer-management features.

7. To check your assignments, click on the group name EXISTING. You should then see in the list area those layers that you dragged over.

8. Click the Cancel button to not apply these changes and exit to the command line.

   You can leave this drawing open for the following exercise.

As you learned, using the new Group filters can be extremely helpful to organize layers into sets or collections. And because they only change through explicit action on your part, new layers that are created will not be included unless you want them to be. A typical application would be to invert the list, showing all the layers you don't want. Next, select them and freeze/turn off those non-desired layers. Then you could create a layer state of this visibility change and be able to recall it later when needed. You learn about useful Layer States in the following section.

# Using Layer States

A very useful feature is Layer States. This feature enables you to save and restore a "state of layers" as well as export a given state to a file that can be retrieved later or even imported into another drawing.

## Layer State Saving

Often while working with your drawings, you will need to go beyond the saved filters method of restoring a pattern of displayed layers. In this section, you discover the power of the Save State feature and its companion, the Layer States Manager. In the following exercise, you learn how to profit from this feature.

### Exercise 5.6    Saving a Layer State

1. Continue using the drawing from the previous exercise or open the drawing 05EX02.dwg found on the accompanying CD.

2. Open the Layer Properties Manager by clicking the Layer Properties Manager button on the Layers toolbar.

3. In the layer listing area, select all three Existing Cable layers. Then click on the Red color swatch and choose Yellow. Click OK to close the Select Color dialog.

4. Now select the Dashed linetype to change the linetype for all three layers. In the Select Linetype dialog, choose Continuous and click OK.

5. Now that some changes have been made but not applied, you can save these changes for use later. Use the Layer States Manager button near the top left of the Layer Properties Manager dialog box. It is the third from the left.

6. When the Layer States Manager dialog appears, click the New button at the top right. In the New layer state name text box, type **Revised**. There is no need for a description, so go ahead and click OK.

7. In the Layer States Manager, select the Clear All button. This unchecks all options. Check the options for Color and Linetype in the Layer settings to restore area. The current settings for both color and linetypes for all drawing layers are now recorded in the state. See Figure 5.17 for the dialog settings.

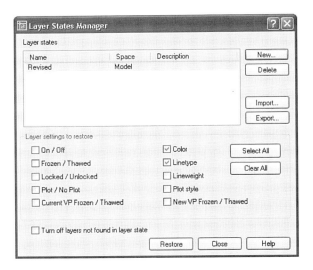

**Figure 5.17**    The Layer States Manager dialog enables specific layer settings to be saved for later use.

In the Layer States Manager dialog, you can save all visibility and usability settings as needed.

8. Click the Export button to save this state to a file for later retrieval. The location of the file in the Export Layer State dialog does not matter; use the default location, accept the default filename of Revised, and click the Save button.

9. Click the Close button to record this layer state named Revised. The Layer States Manager dialog closes, leaving the Layer Properties Manager dialog open.

10. The saved layer state is in this instance of the Layer Properties Manager dialog, but you need to see the power of this process, so click the Cancel button to close the Layer Properties Manager dialog without saving.

**11.** Press the spacebar to recall the Layer dialog. Note that the changes made to the layers in steps 3–4 are gone.

**12.** In the primary Layer listing area, right-click and select the Restore Layer State option. This activates the Layer States Manager dialog. It is currently blank, but this is quickly rectified.

**13.** Click the Import button. Select the Revised.las file and click the Open button.

---

**I**NSIDER **T**IP

> A LAS file is the file type extension for a saved layer state. This file is an ASCII file and can be viewed and edited with text editors such as Notepad. However, the information is quite lengthy, so using the Edit feature of the Layer States Manager is much more efficient.

---

**14.** AutoCAD thinks ahead and offers the opportunity to apply the newly imported layer state. Choose Yes because you just want to see it applied, and the dialog will close. Figure 5.18 shows that the Existing Cable layers have been modified by the content of the saved layer state.

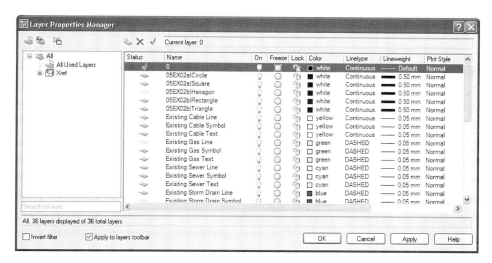

**Figure 5.18**    The Layer Properties Manager dialog showing the changes have been applied to the layers after importing a layer state.

**15.** Now in the Layer Properties Manager dialog, go ahead and click OK; the changes are now applied to the current drawing.

You can now close this drawing without saving.

**I**NSIDER **N**OTE

Applying a saved layer state cannot modify or create layers that do not exist in the current drawing. This only affects layers that match the saved layer names that are being applied.

**I**NSIDER **T**IP

AutoCAD 2005 introduces a new enhancement for users of the View command. It now has the capability to not only restore your display view but also all the layer visibility settings made at the time of the view creation. This means layer freeze/thaw and on/off status can be restored just by resetting a saved view. It also ignores any new layers and all other layer settings such as Color, Linetype, and Plot Style. If your layer state needs fit the capability of the View command, then this may be a great solution.

Even from this simple example, you can tell that this new layer state feature is powerful. A great application is setting up plans with specific layer patterns that can be shared between drawings and users. After a layer state is saved to a file, you can easily import it to "fix" a drawing that has been changed improperly.

**I**NSIDER **N**OTE

If you have a standardized set of layers that you use, you may consider applying AutoCAD CAD Standards to your work. This feature can aid in keeping you and your users on track with regard to layers. Learn more about this in Chapter 24, "Implementing CAD Standards."

## Layer Previous Tool

Another handy feature in AutoCAD 2005 is the Layer Previous tool. This is basically an "undo" for your current layer session, but it works without changing any objects. As you manipulate any layer's visibility property, such as color and on/off, the previous status of the entire layer setup in the drawing is stored temporarily. You could freeze a bunch of layers, do your work, and then click the Layer Previous icon on the toolbar (see Figure 5.19). All the previous layer settings are restored.

**Figure 5.19**

The Layer Previous icon in the Layers toolbar.

The layer properties restored by Layer Previous are

- On/Off
- Freeze/Thaw

- Freeze/Thaw in current viewport
- Lock/Unlock
- Color
- Linetype
- Lineweight
- Plot Style (if using a named plot style)

**INSIDER NOTE**

> There are few things that Layer Previous does not restore. If you rename a layer, it will not be restored to the previous name. Also, layers added or removed during an editing session cannot be removed or added back.

The Layer Previous command does not have a dialog interface but does have a command name, LAYERP, which just restores the previous layer condition. If you just opened a drawing and clicked the Layer Previous tool, it would report *No previous layer status* because nothing affecting a layer has been done. If you have made a layer change and restored it, the command would report Restored previous layer status.

Additionally, there is a system variable to turn off Layer Previous tracking, LAYERPMODE. Turning this off and on controls the storing of temporary layer states used the with LAYERP command. In some scripting or customization conditions, you might find the ability to limit what can be restored helpful.

# Summary

Managing objects through the new Layer Properties Manager improves your ability to organize your drawings. By using the Layer Properties Manager's features, you can control object properties such as Color, Linetype, and Lineweight, and you can control object behavior such as object visibility.

In this chapter, you learned about the importance of layer standards. You also learned about the difference between turning off layers versus freezing them. You worked with layer filters and discovered how you can use wildcard characters to create sophisticated layer filters. Finally, you touched on how to use saved layer states to increase your layer management proficiency.

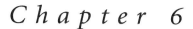

*Chapter 6*

# Effective Linetypes and Lineweights Use

By applying different linetypes and lineweights to different objects in your drawing, you can make individual objects more distinguishable. By using linetypes and lineweights effectively, you can create a drawing that more effectively visually transfers its meaning to the viewer.

But using linetypes and lineweights requires more than just knowing how to make a drawing look good. It requires an understanding of the features in AutoCAD 2005 that control the appearance of linetypes and lineweights. These features include setting defaults, controlling scale globally and individually, and customization. By learning about the range of features offered in AutoCAD, you can exploit the usefulness of linetypes and lineweights to the fullest.

This chapter covers the following subjects:

- Assigning linetypes
- Manipulating the linetype scale factor
- Creating simple and complex linetypes
- Assigning lineweights
- Understanding lineweight display behavior

# Working with Existing Linetypes

A *linetype* is a series of dashes and/or dots that have a specified spacing that you can apply to an object. Linetypes are one of the most useful tools in AutoCAD for getting your drawing's meaning across.

In this section, you learn about several features of linetypes that range from the simple, such as assigning linetypes to objects, to the advanced, such as creating your own custom complex linetypes.

# Assigning Linetypes

Assigning a linetype to an object is a straightforward process and can be accomplished by one of two methods. You can assign linetypes globally through the Layer Properties Manager, or you can assign linetypes individually at the object property level. Both methods are easy to use.

Although both methods accomplish the same thing, one method has a usability advantage over the other. By applying a linetype to a layer in the Layer Properties Manager dialog box, you control the appearance of all objects on that layer, provided that the objects are set to a ByLayer linetype setting. This means you can instantly change the linetype used by hundreds of objects with a few simple clicks.

In contrast, although assigning linetypes to objects individually does enable you to control their individual appearances, the process of individually changing the linetypes for dozens or even hundreds of objects can require tremendous amounts of editing time. Therefore, it is often best to avoid setting linetypes individually and instead use the Layer Properties Manager to control a layer's linetype assignment.

**INSIDER TIP**

It is good practice to set the object linetype creation mode to ByLayer in the Properties toolbar. This ensures that all new objects have their linetypes controlled by the layer they are placed on.

For more information on controlling linetypes globally through the Layer Properties Manager and individually through the Properties toolbar, refer to Chapter 5, "Organizing a Drawing with Layers."

## Loading Linetypes

In Chapter 5, in the section "The Linetype and Lineweight Properties," you learned how easy it is to assign linetypes to objects by using layer controls. You simply select the desired linetype from the Select Linetype dialog box, shown in Figure 6.1.

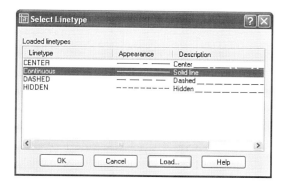

**Figure 6.1**    The Select Linetype dialog box enables you to choose a layer's linetype.

Notice that there are not a lot of linetypes to choose from in the Select Linetype dialog box. However, AutoCAD 2005 is installed with dozens of predefined linetypes that you can use. You simply need to load them into your drawing.

The Load or Reload Linetypes dialog box can be opened by clicking the Load button on the Select Linetype dialog box. From here, you can choose which linetypes to make available to your drawing. After you've made them available, you can assign a wide range of linetypes to layers or directly to objects. Assigning a linetype, however, is only half the solution to displaying objects with linetypes. The other half is to apply the proper line-type scale.

**INSIDER TIP**

If you constantly load the same linetypes over and over, you should consider placing them into your template drawing file. Refer to Chapter 3, "Starting a Drawing in AutoCAD," for more on using templates.

## Working with the Linetype Scale Factor

In general, a linetype is simply a series of repeated dashes and spaces. The lengths of the dashes and spaces in a specific linetype are defined by the linetype description, or its pattern. However, the pattern only specifies how many units long a dash or a space is.

Depending on the visual scale of your drawing, the linetype may not be visible because the dashes and spaces appear too close together or too far apart. To compensate, AutoCAD enables you to apply an overall linetype scale factor to your drawing.

The linetype scale factor multiplies a given linetype pattern by the desired scale factor. As with linetypes, linetype scale factors can be assigned globally or individually. Unlike linetypes, however, you cannot assign a global linetype scale factor when using `ByLayer` in the Layer Properties Manager. When you set the linetype scale factor, it immediately affects all objects with non-continuous linetypes, no matter what layer they are on.

You change the linetype scale factor globally using the Linetype Manager dialog box, accessed by choosing Linetype from the Format pull-down menu. If needed, clicking the Show Details button displays the Details area shown in Figure 6.2.

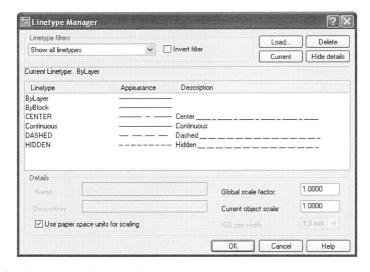

**Figure 6.2** The Linetype Manager dialog box enables you to change the linetype scale factor.

To change the current drawing's global linetype scale, enter a new value in the Global Scale Factor text box. After you click OK, AutoCAD immediately assigns the new global scale factor to the display of all linetypes.

To assign a linetype scale factor individually to all new objects, enter the desired linetype scale in the Current Object Scale text box. Don't be confused by the title of this particular option. When you use this edit box to define a linetype scale, you are setting a scale factor for all new objects, not any existing objects in your drawing.

Although it may be useful to assign an individual linetype scale to new objects, it is more probable that you will also want to edit the linetype scale of existing objects. To do so, click the Properties button on the Standard toolbar, shown in Figure 6.3. Next, select the object(s) whose linetype scale factor you want to change. Finally, click in the Linetype scale edit box, enter the new linetype scale factor in the Properties palette as shown in Figure 6.4, and then press Enter. AutoCAD assigns the new linetype scale factor individually to the selected objects. For more information about using the Properties palette to assign new values to selected objects, see Chapter 9, "Object Selection and Manipulation."

**Figure 6.3**
The Properties palette can be accessed from the Standard toolbar.

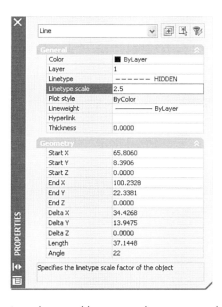

**Figure 6.4**   The Properties palette enables you to change many values for selected objects, including their individual linetype scale factor.

The final feature for controlling the linetype scale factor is PSLTSCLE system variable. It controls how linetypes appear in Layout viewports. This system variable is necessary because AutoCAD enables you to create as many viewports in your Layout tab as you need to display your drawing. More importantly, you can apply a different zoom factor to each viewport. As a result, if one viewport is zoomed in close to an object, and another is zoomed out, the linetype will display differently in each viewport. Figure 6.5 shows two viewports of the same object, but each viewport is zoomed at a different scale. Notice the object's dashed lines in the left viewport appear much tighter than in the viewport on the right. This is the effect when the Use paper space units for scaling feature is off. With this feature off, the dashed lines display proportionally to their zoom factor.

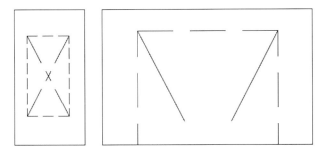

**Figure 6.5**    The dashed lines of the same object appear different when the Use paper space units for scaling feature is turned off (PSLTSCALE=0).

In contrast, review the same drawing with the Use paper space units for scaling feature selected, shown in Figure 6.6. Notice that the length of the dashes and the spaces are the same in both viewports. This is the effect the feature has on linetypes. Either method for scaling linetypes is acceptable; choose the one that suits your needs.

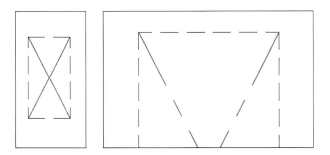

**Figure 6.6**    The dashed lines of the same object appear identical in each Paper Space viewport with the Use paper space units for scaling feature selected (PSLTSCALE=1).

There is one other property you should be aware of when dealing with linetypes and, specifically, polylines. It is called Linetype Generation. Polylines are made up of a series of lines and arcs segments, connected at their endpoints. When a linetype is assigned to a polyline, AutoCAD either generates the linetype as one continuous line or generates the linetype anew at each vertex. Figure 6.7 shows this option located at the bottom of the Properties palette; it can be enabled or disabled.

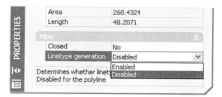

**Figure 6.7**   The Linetype generation option in Properties can change selected polyline line-type appearances.

---

**I**NSIDER **T**IP

You can change how all new polylines' linetypes are generated by using the system variable PLINEGEN. A setting of 0 is off; a setting of 1 is on.

---

In Figure 6.8, the objects at the left have their linetype generation turned off. This produces a desired look for the star, but not for the curved polyline. However, the objects at the right have their linetype generation turned on, but now the star vertices do not always have a ending segment, and the curved polyline looks more appropriate.

**Figure 6.8**   The Linetype Generation property affects how linetypes appear when assigned to polylines. The property is disabled for the objects to the left and enabled for the objects on the right.

Either method is acceptable, and the method you use depends on your needs. However, most users prefer to see their linetypes applied equally only along curved objects.

# Creating and Using Custom Linetypes

Earlier in this chapter, you learned about loading linetypes into the current drawing. Loading AutoCAD's provided linetypes presents you with a fairly large and diverse selection of linetypes to use in your drawing.

Occasionally, even though AutoCAD 2005 ships with a fairly large number of ready-to-use linetypes, you may come across situations in which the ready-made linetypes don't fit your needs.

To accommodate this situation, AutoCAD enables you to create your own linetypes. Additionally, there is no limit to the number of linetypes you can create to meet your needs.

This section discusses the two kinds of linetypes you can create in AutoCAD. Most of your needs can be met by creating the first type, called *simple linetypes*. For situations in which an annotated linetype is required, you can create the second type, called *complex linetypes*.

## Simple Linetype Definitions

As the name implies, *simple linetypes* are relatively simple to create. In fact, you can create a simple linetype during your current session of AutoCAD by starting the `-LINETYPE` command and typing in just a few values. More importantly, you can instantly use the new linetype and apply it to objects in your current drawing.

> **INSIDER NOTE**
>
> Both simple and complex linetypes are stored in ASCII text files that are appended with LIN. It is possible to create or edit linetypes directly in this file, as discussed later in the section, "Complex Linetype Definitions."

In the following exercise, you learn how to create simple linetypes during the current AutoCAD session.

## Exercise 6.1    Creating Simple Linetypes

1. Open the drawing 06EX01.dwg from the accompanying CD. The drawing displays a series of boxes and cross lines.

**INSIDER NOTE**

Only the command-line version of the LINETYPE (-LINETYPE) command provides the ability to create simple linetypes within AutoCAD. The Linetype Manager dialog box does not have this capability.

2. At the command line, type **-LINETYPE** (be sure to include the hyphen at the beginning). AutoCAD starts the command line version of the LINETYPE command and prompts you to create, load, or set a linetype.

3. At the Enter name of linetype to create prompt, type **C** to create a new linetype. AutoCAD prompts you to enter a name for the new linetype.

4. At the command prompt, type **Short Dash** for the new linetype name. AutoCAD then displays the Create or Append Linetype File dialog box.

   As mentioned in a previous Note, AutoCAD saves linetype definitions in ASCII text files appended with LIN. By default, AutoCAD lists its own standard linetype definition file, ACAD.LIN, as the file in which to save your new linetype definition. For this exercise, you will create a new linetype definition file.

**INSIDER TIP**

In practice, it is best to leave AutoCAD's standard files, such as ACAD.LIN, in their original condition. Customizations you make to AutoCAD should be stored in your own custom files.

5. In the Create or Append Linetype File dialog box, enter **MYLINES** in the File Name text box, as shown in Figure 6.9.

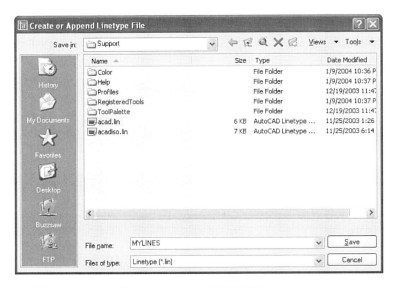

**Figure 6.9**    The new linetype file is to be named MYLINES.

6. Click Save. AutoCAD creates the new linetype definition file and then dismisses the dialog box.

7. At the `Descriptive text` prompt, type **This is a short dash** and then press Enter. AutoCAD then prompts you for the linetype definition code and begins the line of code for you.

   The linetype definition code always starts with the letter "A" followed by a comma (A,). Because this is how all lines of code begin when defining linetypes, AutoCAD automatically specifies it for you. AutoCAD now expects you to enter the series of real number values that represent the dashes and spaces you want to have in the linetype. All values must be entered as real numbers, with positive values defining dash lengths and negative numbers defining the length of gaps. A zero value represents a dot (a dash of zero length), and a comma separates each number.

8. After the `Enter linetype pattern` prompt and the following "A," prompt, type **0.25,-0.125** and then press Enter. AutoCAD creates the new linetype definition, adding it to the new MYLINES.LIN linetype definition file. It then prompts you again to create, load, or set additional linetypes.

9. Press Enter to exit the `-LINETYPE` command.

The series of command-line prompts and the appropriate responses are shown in Figure 6.10. Now that the new linetype is defined, the next step is to assign it to the line in the drawing and see what it looks like.

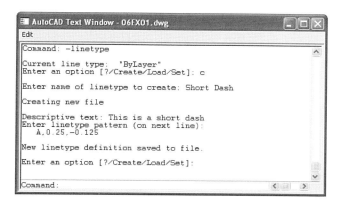

**Figure 6.10**    The series of command-line prompts and the appropriate responses to create a new linetype.

10. Click the Layer Properties Manager icon on the Layer toolbar. AutoCAD displays the Layer Properties Manager.

11. Choose the Continuous linetype in the Linetype column for layer 0. AutoCAD displays the Select Linetype dialog box.

12. Click the Load button. AutoCAD displays the Load or Reload Linetypes dialog box.

13. Click the File button. AutoCAD displays the Select Linetype File dialog box.

14. Choose the MYLINES.LIN file, as shown in Figure 6.11, and then click Open. AutoCAD displays the Short Dash linetype in the Load or Reload Linetypes dialog box, as shown in Figure 6.12.

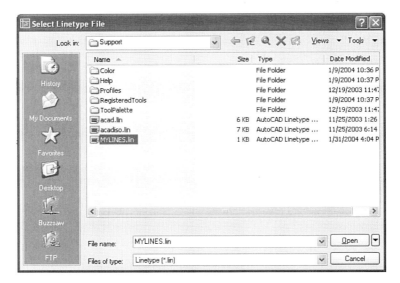

**Figure 6.11** Choose the MYLINES.LIN file to display the newly created linetype.

**Figure 6.12** The newly created Short Dash linetype appears.

15. Choose the Short Dash linetype and then click OK. AutoCAD loads the new linetype into the current drawing and displays it in the Select Linetype dialog box, as shown in Figure 6.13.

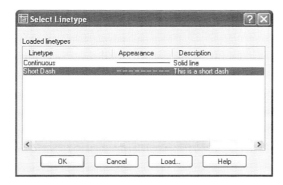

**Figure 6.13**   The newly created Short Dash linetype is loaded into the current drawing.

**16.** Choose the Short Dash linetype and then click OK. AutoCAD assigns the new linetype to layer 0.

**17.** Click OK to dismiss the Layer Properties Manager dialog box. AutoCAD regenerates the objects with the new linetype, as shown in Figure 6.14.

Leave this drawing open if continuing; it is used in the next exercise.

**Figure 6.14**   The newly created Short Dash linetype is assigned to the objects in the drawing.

As you just experienced, creating a simple linetype during an AutoCAD session is truly simple. Keep in mind that you can create as many simple linetypes as you need, and if you want, you can save new linetype definitions in the MYLINES.LIN file. You can also create new linetype definition files to help you organize your linetypes. For example, you can create a UTILITY.LIN linetype definition file to store all utility-related linetypes.

Now that you know how to create simple linetypes, it's time to move on to the next level: creating complex linetypes.

## Complex Linetype Definitions

As the name implies, creating a *complex linetype* is a little bit more difficult than creating *simple linetypes*. But don't let its name intimidate you. The fact is that creating complex linetypes is almost the same as creating simple linetypes. The main difference is that complex linetypes can not be created using the -LINETYPE command. Instead, you create them by entering linetype parameter values directly into a linetype definition file.

In the next exercise, you learn how to create complex linetypes using an ASCII text editor.

### Exercise 6.2    Creating Complex Linetypes

1. Continue using the drawing from the previous exercise, or open the drawing 06EX02.dwg from the accompanying CD. The first step in creating a complex linetype is to open the MYLINES.LIN file in an ASCII text editor.

> **INSIDER NOTE**
>
> The default location for your AutoCAD support files was changed in AutoCAD 2004. AutoCAD is now Windows XP-certified and dictates that your user-specific support files are stored under your C:\Documents and Settings directory tree. Mine as an example is:
>
> C:\Documents and Settings\David\Application Data\Autodesk\AutoCAD 2005\R16.1\enu\support
>
> Browsing to this from outside applications like Notepad is tedious at best. If you know the name of the file, you can use a little AutoLISP code to ease your pain. It is shown in step 2.

2. At the command prompt, type **(startapp "notepad" (FINDFILE "MYLINES.lin"))**. If Notepad finds and opens MYLINES.LIN, skip to step 5.

> **INSIDER NOTE**
>
> If the AutoCAD returns a prompt of "nil," then perhaps you misspelled the filename or didn't save the file from the previous exercise. Use steps 3 and 4 to get the file you need for the rest of the exercise.

3. A copy of the LIN file is on the CD, named MYEXLINES.LIN. Browse to it using Notepad and open it. You may need to change the file type to open to *.*. (Notepad can usually be found in the Start Menu in Windows 2000 or Windows XP, under Programs > Accessories.)

4. Now use the File pull-down menu and save the file to your profile \Support directory as MYLINES.LIN. Close Notepad, return to AutoCAD, and repeat step 2.

5. Notepad opens the linetype definition file.

   For this exercise, you will modify the Short Dash simple linetype already created. Complex linetypes contain two main elements. The first element is the same definition as a simple linetype, which describes the dashes and gaps in the linetype. The second is the text or shape that also displays in the linetype.

6. Change the first real number to 1.25 and the second one to –0.5. This increases the length of the dashes and the length of the spaces.

7. Add the following text to the end of the Short Dash linetype values (there should be no spaces between the values):

   ```
   ,["<>,"STANDARD,S=0.2,R=0.0,X=-0.1,Y=-0.1],-0.5
   ```

   The Short Dash linetype values should now read as follows:

   ```
   A,1.25,-0.5,["<>,"STANDARD,S=0.2,R=0.0,X=-0.1,Y=-0.1],-0.5
   ```

   Recall that the first two real numbers define the length of the dash and the length of the gap, respectively. Next is the code within the brackets, which defines the various parameters of the text to display within the complex linetype. After the closing bracket, another space is added, and in this case, its value is set to –0.5. Notice that commas separate all values. For a detailed description of the values within the brackets, see Table 6.1.

8. In Notepad, choose File, Save. Notepad saves the modified linetype definition file. Leave Notepad open.

9. Back in AutoCAD, click the Layer Properties Manager icon on the Layers toolbar. AutoCAD displays the Layer Properties Manager.

10. Choose the Short Dash linetype in the Linetype column. AutoCAD displays the Select Linetype dialog box.

11. Click the Load button. AutoCAD displays the Load or Reload Linetypes dialog box.

12. Click the File button. AutoCAD displays the Select Linetype File dialog box.

13. Find and choose the MYLINES.LIN file and then click Open. AutoCAD displays the Load or Reload Linetypes dialog box.

14. Choose Short Dash and then click OK. AutoCAD displays the Reload Linetype dialog box, verifying if you want to reload the linetype.

    Because the previous exercise used this same linetype, you must reload the linetype to use it.

15. Click Yes. AutoCAD reloads the linetype into the current drawing.

**16.** Choose the Short Dash linetype, then click OK. AutoCAD assigns the modified linetype to layer 0.

**17.** Click OK to dismiss the Layer Properties Manager dialog box. No change has occurred; you need to type **REGEN** and press Enter. AutoCAD now displays the objects with the new complex linetype, as shown in Figure 6.15. If your display appears to be different, go back to step 5 and double-check the values in Notepad.

You may close Notepad and the drawing without saving your changes.

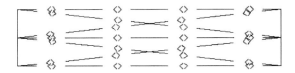

**Figure 6.15** The newly modified Short Dash linetype is assigned to the horizontal line.

**Table 6.1    Complex Linetype Text Values**

| Value | Description |
|---|---|
| <> | The first value is the text string that is displayed in the linetype—in this case, <>. Notice that the text value is enclosed in quotes. |
| STANDARD | The next value is the text style. You may enter any text style. Just be sure the one you name is loaded in the current drawing in which you want to use the linetype; otherwise, the load will fail with a "Bad definition" error. For this exercise, AutoCAD's default STANDARD text style is used. |
| S=0.2 | The next value is the text's scale. This value is multiplied by the selected text's height value. Because the height value of the STANDARD text style is set to 0, AutoCAD interprets the S value as the height literally; in this case, 0.2. |
| R=0.0 | Next is the rotation value, the amount that the text is rotated relative to the line; in this case, 0. By setting the value to 0, as the line changes direction (including through curves), the text aligns itself parallel to the line. If the value is set to any other angle, the text is rotated at each point along the line where it occurs by the specified angle. |
| | Although R= indicates rotation relative to the line, you can define a rotation value with A=, which signifies absolute rotation of the text with respect to the origin. In other words, all text occurrences along the line point in the same direction, regardless of their position relative to the line. Additionally, the value can be appended with a d for degrees (if omitted, degree is the default), r for radians, or g for grads. If A= rotation is omitted, 0 relative rotation is used. |
| X=-0.1,Y=-0.1 | The X and Y values represent the offset of the text relative to the line. Typically, you will set both these values as negative real numbers and at half the complex text's scale. |

In the previous exercise, you actually accomplished two things. First, you edited an existing simple linetype. Second, you created a complex linetype. When creating both simple and complex linetypes, a little trial and error is usually necessary to achieve the desired results. Notice that after you saved the edited ASCII text file, you left Notepad running with the linetype definition file still open. Even so, you were able to reload the Short Dash linetype in AutoCAD to view it. The ability to leave a file open in Notepad while loading it in AutoCAD to view the results is very useful.

### Using Shape Files in Complex Linetype Definitions

In the previous exercise, you learned how to create a complex linetype with text. You can also create complex linetypes with shape files. A shape file contains code that defines shapes that you can use over and over. For example, many of AutoCAD's text fonts are actually shape files. (They're the files that end with SHX.) In addition to the text fonts, AutoCAD also ships with a shape file called LTYPESHP.SHP, which you can review and edit in an ASCII text editor. You can also create your own shape files and use them to store your custom shape definitions.

**I**NSIDER **N**OTE

> Shape files are saved as ASCII text files with a .SHP extension and can be viewed and edited in an ASCII text editor. However, for AutoCAD to use the shape definitions in the shape file, you must compile the shape file. Compiled shape files end with .SHX and cannot be edited or viewed by an ASCII text editor.

You define a complex linetype that uses shape files in much the same way as you did with text in the last exercise. You begin the definition with any dash and space code you may desire, and then you add the complex linetype code. The code for the shape is almost exactly the same as the code for text.

The following text string defines a complex linetype using a shape named CIRC1 from the LTYPESHP.SHX file:

```
A,1.25,-0.5,[CIRC1,LTYPESHP.SHX,S=0.2,R=0.0,X=-0.2,Y=0.0],-0.5
```

Notice that the preceding complex linetype definition is almost identical to the one in the previous exercise. The major differences are that the text name and the text style are replaced. Table 6.2 defines the two major differences.

### Table 6.2   Complex Linetype Shape Values

| Value | Description |
|---|---|
| CIRC1 | The first value that is displayed is the shape definition's name, in this case, CIRC1. The shape definition resides in a shape definition file. A single shape definition file can contain many shape definitions. Notice that in the case of shapes, their names are not enclosed in quotes. |
| LTYPESHP.SHX | The next value is the compiled shape definition filename. The file must be in AutoCAD's search path. A good location to save this file is in AutoCAD's Support folder. A copy is provided on the CD along with this chapter's exercise files. |

The previous complex linetype definition creates a linetype as shown in Figure 6.16.

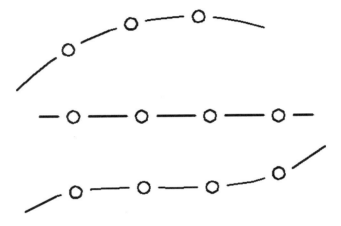

**Figure 6.16**   The CIRC1 shape definition is used to create a new complex linetype.

**INSIDER TIP**

Shape files involve the creation of complex, cryptic code and are beyond the scope of this book. You can read about creating shape files in AutoCAD's online Customization Guide, under Shapes and Shape Fonts.

In the first portion of this chapter, you learned about working with linetypes. Next, you learn about a feature first seen in AutoCAD 2000—lineweights.

# Working with Lineweights

AutoCAD 2005 has a feature called lineweights, which enables you to affect the appearance of objects. Just as linetypes make similar objects, such as lines and polylines, stand apart from each other, lineweights too can make individual objects more easily identifiable.

In previous releases of AutoCAD, you could assign widths to polylines, which perform a function similar to that of lineweights. The problem was that you could assign widths only to polylines, not lines, arcs, or circles, and certainly not text. Another problem with assigning widths to polylines was how difficult it was to change them. If a polyline was already created with the wrong width, you had to edit it to change the width. More importantly, unless you had access to specialized AutoLISP routines, you could only edit the width of polylines one at a time. In contrast, lineweights enable you to assign widths to a wide range of objects, including text, and assign the widths individually, globally, and even by layer using AutoCAD's Layer Properties Manager.

In this section, you learn about assigning lineweights to objects. More importantly, you learn how the appearance of lineweights is affected under different circumstances.

## Assigning Lineweights

Assigning lineweights is very similar to assigning linetypes: You can do it either globally through the Layer Properties Manager or individually through the Properties palette. In addition, as in the argument presented in the "Assigning Linetypes" section, it is strongly suggested that you avoid assigning lineweights individually because doing so makes changing the lineweights of many objects a daunting, unproductive task.

If you are new to AutoCAD, you will probably find yourself tempted to pick just a single object and reassign its lineweight individually. After all, it is a very easy thing to do. You just pick the object, choose the desired lineweight from the pull-down list on the Properties toolbar, and you're done. But chances are, you will regret setting that lineweight individually as your drawing becomes more and more complex, containing hundreds, or perhaps thousands, of objects. It is much better in the long run to consistently assign a lineweight globally using the Layer Properties Manager, even if it means creating a new layer for just that one object and assigning that layer the desired lineweight. By doing so, you create an understanding not only with yourself but also with anyone else who may work on your drawing that lineweights are always edited using the Layer Properties Manager. This understanding provides a consistent pattern for everyone to use when editing objects.

For more information on controlling lineweights globally through the Layer Properties Manager and individually through the Properties toolbar, refer to Chapter 5.

## Understanding Lineweight Behavior

Lineweights are displayed differently under different circumstances. For example, while working in model space, lineweights are displayed by a certain number of pixels. Consequently, as you zoom in closer to a line, the width of pixels displaying the lineweight does not change. If a lineweight in model space is displayed as four pixels, it's always displayed as four pixels, no matter how far you zoom out or how close you zoom in. Therefore, the lineweight always appears as the same width.

In contrast, while working in a layout, lineweights are displayed at their true width. If a lineweight of 0.25 mm is assigned, AutoCAD displays the line as 0.25 mm wide in the layout. Therefore, as you zoom in closer, the line appears wider. In other words, the lineweights of objects drawn in a layout are displayed in real-world units.

There is another feature of lineweights that you can control. When in model space, if you assign lineweights to objects, you can alter their apparent scale so they appear thinner or thicker. This apparent scale does not affect lineweight widths when viewed in a layout or when plotted and has no plotting impact in either space. Therefore, you can dynamically alter lineweights in model space to make viewing objects easier without adversely affecting how they plot.

In the next exercise, you learn how lineweights act in model space and in a layout and how to alter their apparent scale in model space.

### Exercise 6.3    Understanding Lineweight Behavior

1. Open the drawing 06EX03.dwg from the accompanying CD. The drawing opens a layout that displays objects drawn in both model space and paper space, as shown in Figure 6.17. The circle, triangle, line, and the text "Model Space" are drawn in model space. The text "Paper Space" is drawn in paper space in the Layout tab. The solid rectangle is the edge of the floating viewport, and the dashed rectangle represents the plotting limits.

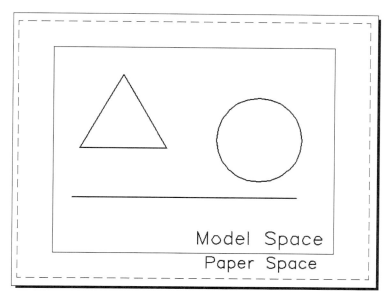

**Figure 6.17**   The drawing in a layout view has several objects drawn in model space, including the text Model Space. The text Paper Space is drawn in paper space.

**2.** From the View pull-down menu, choose Zoom, Window, and then pick a zoom window that surrounds the two text objects, as shown in Figure 6.18. Notice that the lineweights of both text strings appear equal in width. More importantly, they also appear wider. This occurs because you are viewing the layout in Paper Space mode. Therefore, AutoCAD displays the lineweights at their real-world size. As you zoom in closer, the lines appear wider.

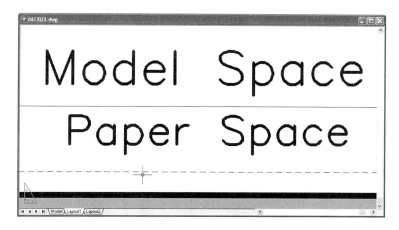

**Figure 6.18**   In paper space, the lineweights of the two text objects appear wider as you zoom in closer.

3. From the View pull-down menu, choose Zoom, Previous. The view again appears as shown in Figure 6.17.

4. Choose the Model tab. AutoCAD switches to model space, and the model space objects are displayed as shown in Figure 6.19. (Although the objects in the figure appear with a heavy lineweight, your drawing may look different because of your on-screen lineweight width setting.)

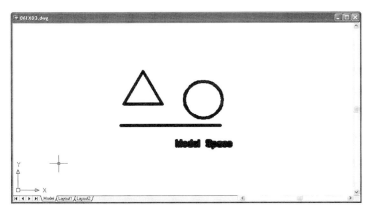

**Figure 6.19**   The model space view of the objects.

5. Again, from the View pull-down menu, choose Zoom, Extents. AutoCAD zooms in closer to the objects, as shown in Figure 6.20. Notice that the lineweights of the objects did not get wider as you zoomed in. This occurs because in model space, the number of pixels that are used to display a lineweight does not change as you zoom in closer.

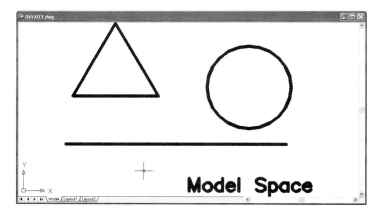

**Figure 6.20**   Notice that lineweights of the model space objects do not get wider as you zoom in closer.

**6.** From the Format pull-down menu, choose Lineweight. The Lineweight Settings dialog box appears, as shown in Figure 6.21.

**I** NSIDER TIP

You can also access the Lineweight Settings dialog box through the Status bar LWT icon. Just right-click over it and choose Settings.

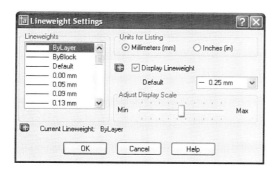

**Figure 6.21**    The Lineweights Settings dialog box enables you to control various features of lineweights.

**7.** Pick and drag the Adjust Display Scale button along its slide bar all the way to the left and then click OK. The lineweights change to appear thinner, as shown in Figure 6.22.

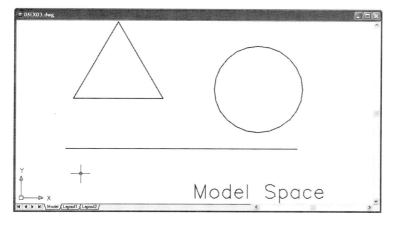

**Figure 6.22**    The Adjust Display Scale feature affects how wide lineweights appear in model space.

8. Choose the Layout1 tab. AutoCAD switches to Layout1 and displays the objects in paper space, as shown in Figure 6.17. Notice that the lineweights were not changed because they were in model space. Once again, this occurs because objects in the layout appear at their real-world scale. AutoCAD therefore ignores the Adjust Display Scale setting when in Paper Space and when plotting.

You may close the drawing without saving any changes.

One last feature you should be aware of is how to control whether lineweights display on-screen. You can turn off lineweight display by clicking the LWT button in the AutoCAD 2005 Status bar. By clicking this button, you toggle lineweights off and on. Again, however, this button does not affect how lineweights plot.

# Summary

In this chapter, you learned about working with linetypes and lineweights effectively. You reviewed assigning linetypes to objects, and you worked through an exercise on how to create and load custom linetypes, both simple and complex. You also reviewed how to control the linetype scale factor, both globally and individually.

In the section discussing lineweights, you learned how to control the width of lines that AutoCAD uses to draw objects. You learned that you can assign lineweights by layer or individually. You learned that lineweights behave differently in model space and paper space. You also worked with controlling how lineweights appear on-screen in model space, by adjusting their apparent scale without affecting their width in paper space or when plotted.

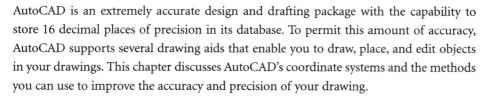

# Chapter 7

# Using Coordinate Systems

AutoCAD is an extremely accurate design and drafting package with the capability to store 16 decimal places of precision in its database. To permit this amount of accuracy, AutoCAD supports several drawing aids that enable you to draw, place, and edit objects in your drawings. This chapter discusses AutoCAD's coordinate systems and the methods you can use to improve the accuracy and precision of your drawing.

This chapter discusses the following subjects:

- World Coordinate Systems
- User Coordinate Systems
- Using the USC command
- Controlling the UCSICON

The most basic concept that you should know already is the application of *object snaps*. Object snaps, or OSNAP, as they are accessed, enable the user to use existing geometry as a foundation for generating additional geometry. Osnaps are just one (but the most popular) method of creating geometry, and they can be used even when you don't know the absolute coordinates needed.

For most of your work, you will be able to use the basic OSNAP mechanism and leave it at that. For those special conditions, however, you will need something that enables accuracy with other *planes* of work, 2D and/or 3D. Often, users have several orientations in which to create their work. Being able to quickly move from one plane to another and maintain a level of accuracy is the focus of this chapter.

# Understanding Coordinate Systems

When you create a new AutoCAD drawing from scratch, you are by default using a Cartesian coordinate system that is called the *World Coordinate System*, or *WCS*. In addition to the WCS, you can create other planes of work or coordinate systems called *User Coordinate Systems*, or *UCSs*. They are called UCSs because you, the user, define them in order to facilitate the creation of your drawings.

The beginning and intermediate users of AutoCAD probably are only familiar with drawing in X and Y coordinates. But even in the World Coordinate System, you can draw in three dimensions, and even while drawing in 2D, if you ID a point, it reports three coordinates (X, Y, and Z).

**INSIDER TIP**

When entering the angle portion of polar coordinates, you can specify the angle as either positive (counterclockwise) or negative (clockwise). Thus, 37<90 is equivalent to 37<–270. This applies to both absolute and relative coordinate entries.

**INSIDER TIP**

If you have the Status bar active and click a grip to make it hot, the bar displays the coordinate of the grip location. This is a very quick alternative to using the ID command.

AutoCAD enables you to create your own UCS because this ability often makes defining points for your model easier. For example, suppose you are creating a model of a 3D pyramid, and you need to define points along the surface of one of the pyramid's faces. This is easily accomplished by aligning a UCS with the face. By doing so, you define an XY plane coincident with the face. After the UCS is properly aligned, it's just a matter of using the Cartesian coordinate system to create the points along the pyramid's face, as shown in Figure 7.1. Also, Chapter 25, "Introduction to 3D," presents additional UCS concepts for use when creating 3D geometry.

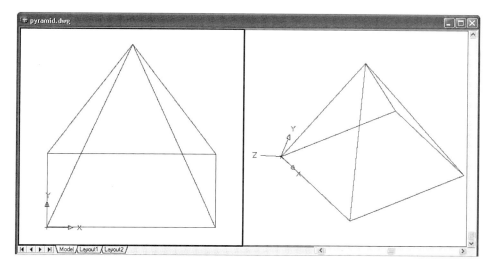

**Figure 7.1**    By properly aligning a User Coordinate System (UCS), developing complex 2D and 3D models becomes easier.

The following section helps you learn about various UCS commands and features you can use to make creating detailed drawings of complex models easier.

# The World Coordinate System

The World Coordinate System is nothing more than a fixed rectangular coordinate system with the origin defined as 0,0,0, a horizontal X-axis running left to right, and a Y-axis extending vertically from the bottom to the top of the screen. The Z-axis is perpendicular to both the X- and Y-axes and is considered to extend out toward you in a direction perpendicular to the screen. To identify the WCS and establish its orientation, AutoCAD by default places the WCS icon at or near the origin. The two different styles of the WCS icon are shown in Figure 7.2. The defining characteristic of the original WCS symbol on the left is the "W" appearing on the icon; this tells you that you are in the World Coordinate System. The default style in AutoCAD 2005, the one on the right, indicates the World Coordinate System by the box at the symbol corner.

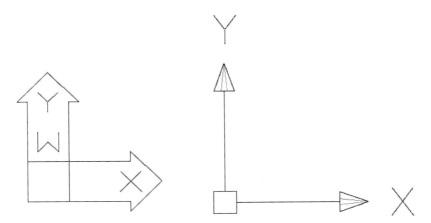

**Figure 7.2**   The two variations of the World Coordinate System (WCS) icon.

Ever since the introduction of the UCSICON, it has been plagued with complaints about its functionality and its appearance. With AutoCAD 2000, the pesky little icon was given a control dialog to help users manipulate it (see Figure 7.3). The control dialog is accessible through the UCSICON command under the Properties option. Within the dialog are controls for displaying the traditional icon or the new 3D appearance. If you choose the 3D version, you also can control cone or arrow points and the line width of the icon itself. Other options include a size control for the icon and display colors for its use in model space or paper space layouts.

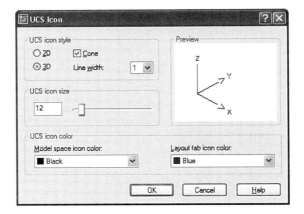

**Figure 7.3**   The UCS Icon properties dialog enables users to enter their preferences for its display.

# User Coordinate Systems

As mentioned earlier, you can create your own coordinate systems called User Coordinate Systems, or UCSs. In a UCS, the origin and the direction of the X-, Y-, and Z-axes can be made to move or rotate relative to the WCS. A USC can also align with drawing objects. Although the three axes in a UCS remain mutually perpendicular, a great deal of flexibility can be achieved in placing and orienting your UCS. Figure 7.4 shows two original UCS icons representing two different coordinate systems; one is the WCS, indicated by the "W" on the UCS icon; the other is a UCS defining a User Coordinate System. User Coordinate Systems are indispensable for working in 3D space.

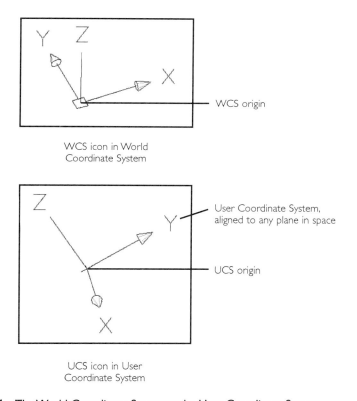

**Figure 7.4**   The World Coordinate System and a User Coordinate System.

The following exercise demonstrates how to create a User Coordinate System by aligning the UCS with two points.

### Exercise 7.1    Aligning a UCS with a 2D Object

1. Open the drawing named 07EX01.dwg from the accompanying CD. Your drawing should resemble Figure 7.5, showing components of a screw.

**I**NSIDER **N**OTE _____

> We are using the 3D style UCS icon symbol. If you have set AutoCAD to the original
> 2D style UCSICON style, you may want to set it to match in order to follow along.

2. Select the Tools pull-down menu, New UCS, 3 Point. The following prompt
   appears:

   ```
   Specify new origin point <0,0,0>
   ```

3. Press Shift plus right-click at the same time to display the Cursor shortcut menu
   and select Endpoint. Then pick ❶ shown in Figure 7.5. The following prompt
   appears (the points given as a default may differ in your drawing):

   ```
   Specify point on positive portion of the X-axis <6.58,2.04,0.00>
   ```

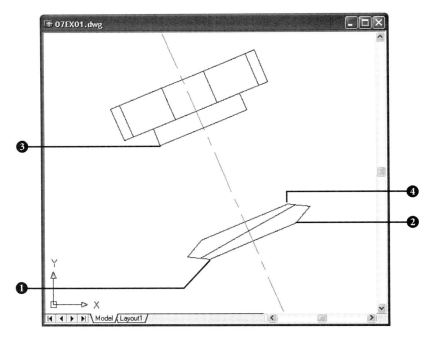

**Figure 7.5**    The pick points used to change the UCS.

**4.** Shift+right-click to display the Cursor menu, choose Endpoint, and pick ❷. The following prompt appears:

```
Specify point on positive-Y portion of the UCS XY plane
➥<5.19,2.96,0.00>
```

**5.** Pick anywhere near ❸. Note that the UCS icon changes orientation to align with the new UCS plane and that the box at the corner of the icon disappears, indicating that you are no longer in the WCS (see Figure 7.6).

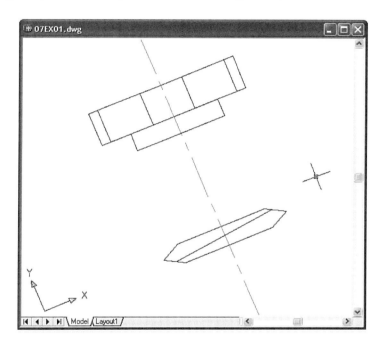

**Figure 7.6**   The UCS rotates to match the model orientation.

**6.** Select the Array button found on the Modify toolbar. The Array dialog appears.

**7.** Verify that the new array will be rectangular and then enter **6** for the number of rows and **1** for the number of columns. See Figure 7.7 for an example.

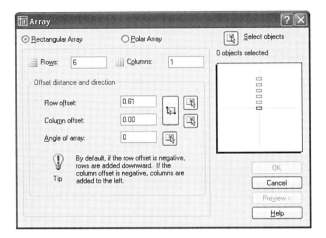

**Figure 7.7**    The Array dialog box greatly simplifies the ARRAY command.

8.  Click the Pick Row offset button to the right of the Row offset edit box. This enables you to pick an on-screen distance for the row distance. The dialog disappears and prompts with `Specify the distance between rows`.

9.  Activate the Cursor menu (Shift+right-click) and select Intersection. Refer to Figure 7.5; click at ❷. Again, activate the shortcut menu, select Intersection, and click at ❹. The dialog then reappears.

10. Click the Select Objects button in the top right of the Array dialog. The dialog then disappears and prompts with `Select objects`. Select just the thread object because it is only one single block and then press Enter. Now click OK.

**I**NSIDER **N**OTE

The Array dialog does not allow you to click the OK button until you have provided it with enough information to create the array of objects.

11. The array is carried out in a direction perpendicular to the X-axis of the new UCS. Your drawing should resemble Figure 7.8.

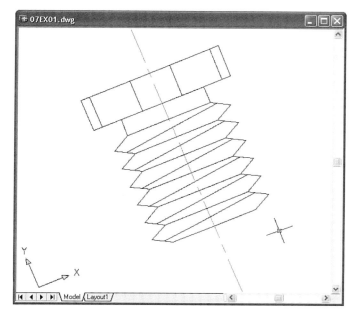

**Figure 7.8**   The completed array.

Now return the UCS to the WCS by using the UCS command.

12. Type **UCS** and press Enter. When the Enter an option prompt appears, accept the default, World, by pressing Enter.

Leave this drawing open for Exercise 7.2.

Although defining new UCSs is most frequently used in 3D drafting, the preceding exercise demonstrated that the capability to change the UCS is helpful in 2D work as well. By aligning the UCS with the horizontal axis of the thread object in the drawing, a simple 6-row array could be quickly carried out with the "axis" of the array perpendicular to the horizontal axis of the object. This procedure is often done for projects that have varying site orientations because after the drawings are turned (via UCS), drawing becomes much easier.

The following exercise demonstrates two more options of the UCS command, reestablishing the most previous UCS and controlling the display of the UCS icon.

**INSIDER TIP**

It is possible to change the UCS to the position and orientation you want in more than one way. In the preceding exercise, for example, you could have rotated the UCS about its Z-axis instead of using the 3-Point option. You may prefer to use the 3-Point option because it's more intuitive and easier to use.

### Exercise 7.2    Displaying the Previous UCS and Controlling the Position of the UCS Icon

1. Continue using the drawing from the previous exercise. The drawing will resemble Figure 7.8.

2. At the command prompt, type **UCS** and then press Enter. The following prompt appears:

```
Enter an option
[New/Move/orthoGraphic/Prev/Restore/Save/Del/Apply/?/World] <World>
```

3. Type **P** (for Previous) and then press Enter. Note that the UCS reverts to the UCS defined in the previous exercise.

4. Select View pull-down menu, Display, UCS Icon, Origin. Note that the UCS icon moves to the origin point of the currently defined UCS, as shown in Figure 7.9. This is the origin point you defined in step 3 of Exercise 7.1.

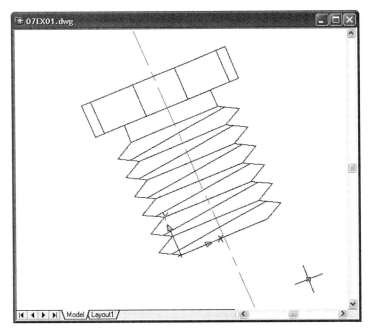

**Figure 7.9**   Placing the UCS icon at the current UCS origin.

5. Again, select the View pull-down menu, Display, UCS Icon, and notice that a check mark appears beside the Origin selection. Click on Origin to toggle off the feature, which moves the icon back to its default position at the lower-left corner of the screen.

**6.** Lastly, select the View pull-down, Display, UCS Icon, and notice that a check mark appears beside the On selection. Click On to remove the check mark. The UCS icon is no longer visible.

You can close the drawing without saving changes.

---

**I**NSIDER **T**IP

Although the preceding exercise uses shortcuts from the pull-down menus, some users prefer to turn the UCS icon on and off by typing **UCSICON** at the command prompt and then typing either **On** or **Off**. You can also move the UCS icon to and from the current origin with the UCSICON command by typing **OR** for origin or **N** for no origin. Both methods are faster than traversing across three levels of cascading pull-down menus.

---

**I**NSIDER **T**IP

If the UCSICON command is something that you find yourself using frequently, you should consider adding the UCSICON command to your ACAD.PGP file, perhaps as a "UI" shortcut. Learn more about the ACAD.PGP file in Chapter 22, "Customizing Without Programming."

---

# The *UCS* Command

The UCS command is the key to placing, moving, rotating, and displaying User Coordinate Systems. This command enables you to correctly position UCSs to draw the elements necessary to properly define your 2D or 3D model. By understanding the various options available through the UCS command, you ease the task of defining your model.

Most of your 2D work can be accomplished with the following subset of UCS options (which are actually available at the root-level of the command):

- **Origin.** Specifies a new origin point relative to the current origin.
- **3 Point.** Enables you to set the X- and Y-axes by specifying the origin and a point on both the X- and Y-axes.
- **Object.** Defines a new coordinate system based on a selected object.
- **Z.** Rotates the X- and Y-axes about the Z-axis.
- **Previous.** Reverts to the previous UCS. You can recall as many as 10 previous UCSs.
- **Restore.** Sets the UCS to a previously named UCS.

- **Save.** Enables you to store the current UCS with a name you specify.
- **Delete.** Removes a stored UCS.
- **?/Named UCSs.** Lists saved UCSs by name.
- **World.** Displays the WCS.

The Restore, Save, Delete, and ?/Named UCSs options are tools that enable you to manage UCS configurations. By using these tools, you can save defined UCS configurations and then restore them for later use. One feature that makes these options very useful is that named UCSs are saved with the current drawing. Therefore, as you develop a series of different UCS configurations, you can save the configurations with the drawing, knowing that you can recall them later during another editing session.

**INSIDER TIP**

> You can use the new AutoCAD DesignCenter (ADC) to import saved UCS configurations from other drawings into the current drawing. For more information, see Chapter 12, "Applications for DesignCenter."

## The *UCS* Command Features

The UCS command in AutoCAD 2005 has many features. These features enhance the usefulness of UCSs by making them easier to manipulate. By using these features, you can make defining and controlling UCSs simpler. The features are described as follows:

- **Multiple UCSs.** This feature enables you to set a different UCS for each viewport you have open.
- **UCS Face Align.** This option enables you to quickly configure a new UCS by aligning it to the selected Face object. Face objects are discussed in Chapter 27, "Surfacing in 3D."
- **UCS Apply.** This option enables you to apply the UCS configuration of one viewport to another by simply selecting the viewport.
- **UCS Move.** This option enables you to move the origin of a UCS without the need to redefine or rename the UCS. For example, if you move the origin point of a named UCS, AutoCAD simply applies the new origin point to the named UCS.
- **UCS Manager.** Displays the UCS Manager dialog box.

The following exercise demonstrates the new features and options.

## Exercise 7.3    AutoCAD's UCS Features and Options

1. Open the drawing 07EX03.dwg from the accompanying CD. The drawing appears, showing four different viewports, all viewing the same cube object and all having identical UCSs, as shown in Figure 7.10.

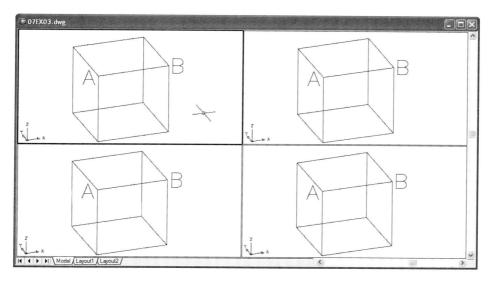

**Figure 7.10**   The UCS is identical in each viewport.

2. Pick anywhere inside the lower-left viewport. The lower-left viewport becomes active.

3. From the Tools pull-down menu, select New UCS, Face. AutoCAD prompts you to select the face of a solid object.

4. In the lower-left viewport, pick the edge between AB, near A. AutoCAD highlights the front face of the cube. (If AutoCAD highlights the top face of the cube, choose N to switch to the adjoining face, and then press Enter to select to the front face.)

5. Press Enter to accept the front face selection. Notice that AutoCAD rotated the lower-left viewport's UCS, as shown in Figure 7.11. Also notice that no other UCS rotated in any of the other viewports.

6. From the Tools pull-down menu, select New UCS, Apply. AutoCAD prompts you to pick a viewport to apply the current UCS.

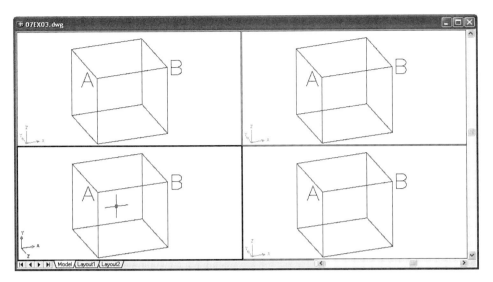

**Figure 7.11**   The UCS Face option aligns the lower-left viewport's UCS with the selected front face of the cube. Notice that all other UCSs remained unchanged.

7. Choose the upper-right viewport and then press Enter. AutoCAD updates the upper-right viewport's UCS to match the lower-left viewport's UCS.

8. Again, from the Tools pull-down menu, select Move UCS. AutoCAD prompts you to specify the new origin point for the current UCS.

9. In the upper-right viewport, pick a point in the approximate center of the front face. AutoCAD redefines the UCS's origin point, but nothing has visibly changed.

10. From the View pull-down menu, select Display followed by UCS Icon, and then Origin. The UCS icon moves to the new origin point.

11. On the Tools pull-down menu, select Named UCS. AutoCAD displays the UCS dialog box with the Named UCSs tab displayed. Notice that the current UCS is Unnamed.

12. Right-click on the highlighted Unnamed UCS. AutoCAD displays the shortcut menu.

13. Select Rename, type **My Front**, and press Enter. AutoCAD renames the UCS, as shown in Figure 7.12.

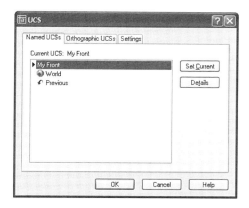

**Figure 7.12**    The current UCS is renamed My Front.

14. Click OK. AutoCAD closes the UCS dialog box.

15. Select the lower-right viewport, and then select Tools pull-down menu, Named UCS. AutoCAD displays the UCS dialog box.

16. Select My Front, click Set Current (or double-click on My Front), and click OK. AutoCAD redefines the UCS's origin point. But, we also need the icon to move to the origin point.

17. From the View pull-down menu, select Display, followed by UCS Icon, and then Origin. The icon then moves to the origin point previously defined in the top right viewport.

18. Select Tools pull-down menu, Named UCS. AutoCAD displays the UCS dialog box.

19. Select the Orthographic UCSs tab. AutoCAD displays six predefined UCSs, as shown in Figure 7.13.

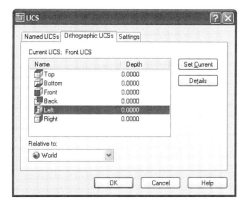

**Figure 7.13**    AutoCAD provides six predefined orthographic UCSs.

**20.** Select the orthographic UCS named Left, and then Set Current, and click OK. AutoCAD aligns the lower-right viewport's UCS with the left face of the cube, as shown in Figure 7.14.

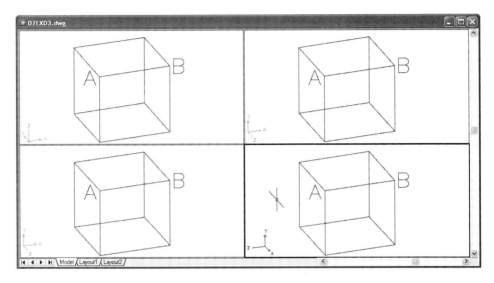

**Figure 7.14**    AutoCAD applies the orthographic UCS named Left to the lower-right viewport.

You can close the drawing without saving changes.

AutoCAD's UCS features and options make using a UCS easier than before. By applying these tools, you can simplify object editing and increase your productivity.

## The *UCSICON* Command

In an earlier exercise, you saw how the UCSICON command can be used to control the placement and visibility of the UCS icon. To round out the discussion of User Coordinate Systems, here is an explanation of the options for the UCSICON command. First, the UCSICON command displays the following prompt:

```
Enter an option [ON/OFF/All/Noorigin/ORigin/Properties] <ON>
```

- **ON** and **OFF.** Turns visibility of the UCS on and off, respectively.

- **All.** Applies changes to the UCS icon in all displayed viewports; otherwise, changes affect only the current viewport.

- **Noorigin.** Displays the UCS icon at the lower-left corner of viewports.

- **Origin.** Displays the UCS icon at the 0,0,0 origin of the current UCS if possible. Otherwise, it displays the UCS icon at the lower-left corner of viewports.

- **Properties.** Displays the UCS Icon control dialog, where the user can define the style, size, and application for the UCS Icon.

**I**NSIDER **T**IP

> Another capability of the UCS icon that you should know about is the system variable UCSFOLLOW. This variable controls whether a plan view is automatically generated whenever you change the UCS. Setting this variable to 0 does not affect the view; setting it to 1, however, causes the plan view to be immediately generated. For 2D drafting, you may find the automatic plan view setting to be helpful.

The UCS icon options just described can be set from the command prompt or from the UCS dialog box. By selecting Tools, Named UCS, and then selecting the Settings tab, AutoCAD displays the UCS icon options shown in Figure 7.15. By selecting or clearing the options, you toggle on or off the options, described as follows:

- **On.** When selected, it turns on the UCS icon. When cleared, it turns off the UCS icon.

- **Display at UCS Origin Point.** When selected, it displays the UCS icon at the origin of the current UCS if possible. When cleared, it displays the UCS icon at the lower-left corner of the viewport.

- **Apply to All Active Viewports.** When selected, AutoCAD applies changes to the UCS icon in all displayed viewports. When cleared, it changes to the UCS icon only affecting the current viewport.

In addition to the UCS icon settings, you can also control two UCS settings, described as follows:

- **Save UCS with Viewport.** When selected, this option enables you to set and retain a different UCS for each viewport. When cleared, the viewport reflects the current UCS each time the UCS is changed, even if the viewport is not the current viewport.

- **Update View to Plan When UCS Is Changed.** When selected, the plan view is automatically applied when the UCS is changed. When cleared, the plan view is not invoked when the UCS changes. (This is the same as setting the UCSFOLLOW system variable, described in the previous tip.)

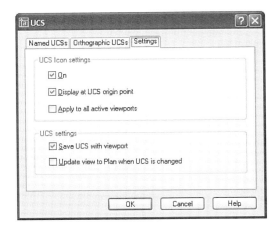

**Figure 7.15**    The new UCS manager enables you to set options for the UCS icon.

The plan view described here refers to rotating the view of the model in the current viewport so that the Z-axis of the UCS appears normal (perpendicular) to the screen. For example, in Figure 7.16, the image on the left has its view rotated normally with respect to the screen, whereas the image on the right does not. You can invoke a plan view by using the PLAN command.

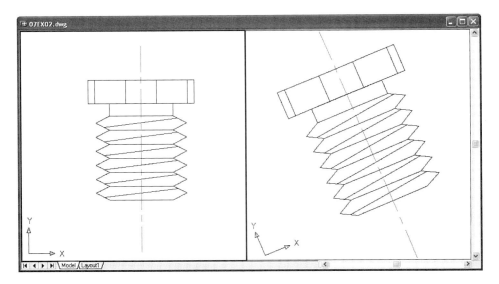

**Figure 7.16**    The view of the image on the left is automatically rotated by using the PLAN command.

# Summary

In this chapter, you learned about the methods you can use to manipulate a User Coordinate System (UCS) and how they can aid in general drawing activities. You also learned how to create custom coordinate systems by creating your own UCS. Additionally, you applied default UCS orientations and learned how you can carry an active UCS from one viewport to another.

By utilizing the basic tool of a UCS and its icon, you can maintain complex 2D and 3D working environments, helping you to generate drawings that have absolute accuracy and thereby reducing your drawing creation and editing time.

# Part III

# Creating and Editing Drawings

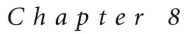

*Chapter 8*

# Obtaining
# Object
# Information

To get the most power out of AutoCAD, sometimes you must gain information from AutoCAD objects. When an object is created, AutoCAD does more than just draw the object on the screen. It creates a list of object data and stores this data in the drawing's database. This data includes not only the layer, color, and linetype of an object, but also the X,Y,Z coordinate values of an object's critical elements, such as the center of a circle or the endpoints of a line. The data can include the names of blocks, as well as their X,Y,Z scale and rotation angles. Information about block attributes and their text values can be extracted from the drawing into a text file. The area of closed polygons and the volume of objects can be determined. By querying AutoCAD's objects, you can extract a wealth of information pertinent to your work, and you can query important data that AutoCAD creates automatically.

This chapter discusses the following topics:

- Gaining entity information
- Using Inquiry tools
- Using Object Selection Filters
- Querying for areas in blocks and xrefs
- Extracting block and attribute data

# Gaining Entity Information

The capability to query for object and drawing data is a valuable feature. With AutoCAD 2005, querying tools are conveniently grouped in the pull-down menus for easy, intuitive access. Additionally, the Properties, Layers, and Styles toolbars make identifying the most common properties of an object as easy as selecting the object itself.

## Properties Toolbar

In AutoCAD 2005, the Properties toolbar automatically displays the selected object's color, linetype, lineweight, and plot style. When you select multiple objects that have different properties, such as different colors, the non-unique property values are left blank.

The following exercise demonstrates the querying capabilities of the Properties toolbar.

### Exercise 8.1    Querying Objects with the Toolbars

1. Open the 08EX01.dwg drawing file found on the accompanying CD. Notice that the Properties toolbar lists the current layer 0, the default color ByLayer, the default linetype ByLayer, and the default lineweight ByLayer. This represents the current object-creation mode. If an object were to be created now, it would be assigned these properties.

2. Choose the blue dashed contour line. AutoCAD displays the grips along the polyline (see Figure 8.1). Notice that the properties displayed in the Layers and Properties toolbars now reflect the properties of the selected object.

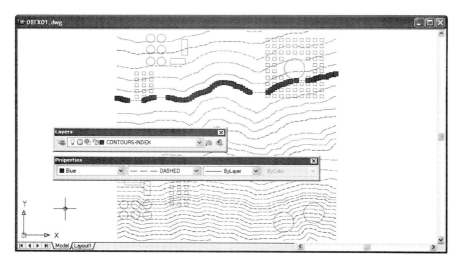

**Figure 8.1**   The selected object's properties are displayed in the Layers and Properties toolbar.

3. Choose the dashed contour line above the one you just selected. AutoCAD displays grips along this polyline (see Figure 8.2). Notice that AutoCAD no longer displays any values on the Layers or Properties toolbars. This occurs because the two objects reside on different layers and have different color and linetype settings.

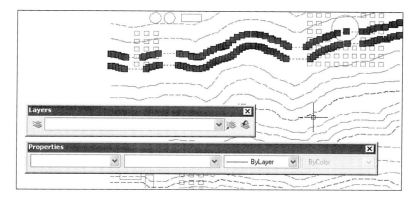

**Figure 8.2**   No values are displayed in the Layers and Properties toolbars unless the objects have common properties.

Close this drawing; there is no need to save.

**INSIDER TIP**

There is a matching feature that shows all the same information as the Properties and Layers toolbars; it is called PROPERTIES naturally. Start the command by choosing the Modify pull-down menu and then select Properties. The Properties palette is a non-modal dialog box, so you can select different objects while it is open and still see the properties. You can also launch the command using just PR, a shortcut defined in the default ACAD.PGP file. Learn more about the ACAD.PGP file in Chapter 22, "Customizing Without Programming."

## Layers Toolbar

The Layers toolbar's primary purpose is to provide quick access to change layer visibility or to make a given layer current. However, it also displays any currently selected object's layer. However, when you select multiple objects that have different layers, the value is again shown blank.

## Styles Toolbar

AutoCAD 2005 has a Styles toolbar that displays any selected annotative-type object's name. If you select a mixture of objects, the list is blank, but you can use it to change all matching text objects to another style. The other two style controls on the Styles toolbar, Dimension Styles and Table Styles, act the same way. They are blank when non-matching objects are selected, but they show any that match, and they can then be selected to set to a new style.

As you can see, you can gain a lot of information just from the standard user interface that comes with AutoCAD. Proper understanding of these existing features can save on the time it takes to inquire about objects. However, you will often need to know data that is a bit more in-depth. The following section explores more intelligence-gathering features.

# Using Inquiry Tools

The standard inquiry tools enable you to retrieve information about objects in your drawing. In AutoCAD 2005, the querying tools are conveniently grouped in a single location: the Tools, Inquiry pull-down menu (see Figure 8.3).

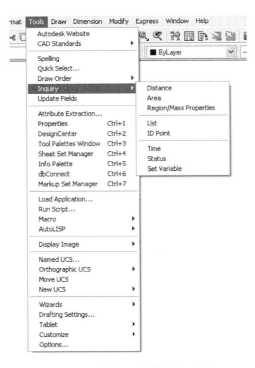

**Figure 8.3**   Accessing the querying tools from the Tools pull-down menu, Inquiry option.

# Distance

The DIST command is used to measure the distance between two points in a drawing. When you use the DIST command to query lengths, it's important to realize that this command measures points three-dimensionally. If you pick two points that are not on the same plane, the overall distance will be based on a 3D vector. To ensure that the distance is based on the current two-dimensional UCS, use X,Y,Z point filters when you query distance from 3D objects.

**I**NSIDER **N**OTE

> The last distance queried by using the DIST command is saved as a system variable. To view the value, type **DISTANCE** at the command prompt. The value format is controlled by the current drawing Units settings.

# List

The LIST command provides a way to view a lot of entity data on the text screen. When you use the LIST command on a object, the text screen pops in front of the graphics screen, reporting information about your object(s). Depending on the number of objects you selected, the feature may pause, enabling you to read the contents before scrolling on and showing more data. If the information you are trying to obtain is fairly basic but beyond the Layers and Properties toolbars, then using LIST is a quick solution.

**I**NSIDER **T**IP

> You can use the Properties palette to view list-type information from objects. For example, if you select a polyline, both the length and area values are shown in the Geometry section of the Properties palette. Keeping the Properties palette open and available for this type of work can really help your productivity.

# Area

The AREA command enables you to select an object—circles, ellipses, splines, regions, or closed polyline objects—and report back the area and perimeter. You can pick points and build an *imaginary* boundary for the AREA command to cover in its report. It permits you to select several objects in series, increasing the report data as you select each object. It also can quickly find the length of an open polyline. Using the AREA command's Object option, AutoCAD calculates and lists the object's area and perimeter length.

## ID

Whenever you need simple location data, the ID command may fit the bill nicely. The ID command reports the coordinate of a point you select, using the current drawing units and accuracy setting. This is often used just to verify that geometry is set properly, such as an insertion point for an xref.

As you can see, the basic tools for gaining object information are simple enough. Now the key to success is actually selecting the objects you want in the first place. Your drawings can contain hundreds, if not thousands, of objects with many different properties. You can use these different properties as a means to separate and/or select them. The following sections explore the tools that facilitate this activity.

# Using Quick Select

When editing a drawing, often the task of selecting the objects to change is more work than the actual change itself. This is where object filtering becomes crucial to your work. Imagine having a drawing of a convention center where you need to change the layer and color of a circle with a radius of 12". Now compound the problem by increasing the number of circles to be changed to hundreds and the layers they reside on to include nearly all layers in the drawing. Zooming and panning around and selecting these circles among other circles and layers would be a huge task.

This could be done with one visit to the Quick Select dialog box, where you can set the proper parameters. In Figure 8.4, you see the standard settings for the QSELECT command dialog box.

The first thing to understand about the Quick Select dialog box is where it can be used. It is not a transparent command, so it cannot be used at any Select objects prompt. It works with the Properties palette box because it is non-modal, meaning that the Properties command can be active all the time. So to utilize the QSELECT command, you must initiate it before the command that will use its selection is started.

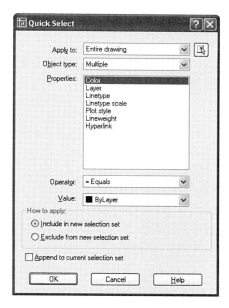

**Figure 8.4**    The Quick Select dialog box contains controls for many basic object properties in which you can filter to a new selection.

When the QSELECT command is executed, your first task is to define the parameters of the filter selection. As you modify the settings in the dialog box, you build the criteria that objects must meet in order to be selected. When you're finished, exit the dialog box; the drawing database is filtered to match those parameters. These controls are covered in the following sections.

## Specifying Objects to Be Filtered with Apply To

The Apply To control is very simple to understand. By default, the Apply To drop-down list is set to Entire Drawing. If you click the Select Objects tool to its right, you can choose a set of objects using standard selection techniques. AutoCAD then filters against this selection set. If you do select a group of objects, or if you have selected objects prior to opening the Properties dialog box, the drop-down list for Apply To displays Current Selection. You may then switch between that selection and the entire drawing at your leisure.

## The Object Type Drop-Down List

The Object Type control enables you to specify which object types are to be considered when filtering through the selection made in the Apply To drop-down list. If only one type of object exists in the drawing, that single object is your only choice. But if other object types exist, each type is displayed in the drop-down list, from which you can choose one. This control determines which properties to list in the Properties area.

## The Properties Area

This area displays a categorized listing of the properties of the object(s) currently being filtered. For example, if a line is the current object type, this control shows all the properties that lines have. If you change the object type to circle, then Properties shows all settings unique to circles, such as a radius. This is where you get specific beyond simple object type filtering.

## The Operator Option

With this control, you can create conditional statements that the objects must meet in order to be selected. Table 8.1 outlines these conditions.

**Table 8.1    Quick Select Conditional Operands**

| Operand | Definition |
| --- | --- |
| = | **Equal To.** With this operand, the data in the field must be matched perfectly to be valid. |
| <> | **Not Equal To.** With this operand, the data in the field must not match to be valid. |
| > | **Greater Than.** With this operand, the data in the field must be greater in value to be valid. |
| < | **Less Than.** With this operand, the data in the field must be smaller in value to be valid. |
| * | **Wildcard Match.** This is used only with text fields that can be edited by the user. |

**INSIDER NOTE**

Not all operands are available with all objects. As you define different object types, the Operator list changes automatically to the available options for that type of object.

## Using the Options in How to Apply

This option box control is where you add and remove objects from the current selection set. Its two settings, Include or Exclude, specify what AutoCAD should do with the objects that meet the filter criteria.

The Include option adds all matching objects to the selection set when the user exits QSELECT. By choosing Exclude, you can then select all non-matching objects and apply them to the current selection set.

## The Append to Current Selection Set Control

The last item in the Quick Select dialog box is the Append to Current Selection Set toggle. This toggle determines if the selection set created from the QSELECT command adds to the current drawing selection set or if it simply replaces it. After you have completed the QSELECT command, the objects are selected and the grips are displayed (if grips are on) and ready for immediate use. You then can proceed with editing or, if needed, use QSELECT again to further filter your object selection set.

The QSELECT command is a very easy-to-use filtering method for building selection sets. Another method that has been in AutoCAD for several versions is the FILTER command. The following section examines the use of this feature.

# Using Object Selection Filters

*Object filtering* enables you to search for objects based on certain attributes. For example, you could use object filtering to select all circles in a drawing with a specific radius. To invoke object filtering, type the command 'FILTER at the Select objects prompt. This displays the Object Selection Filters dialog box (see Figure 8.5).

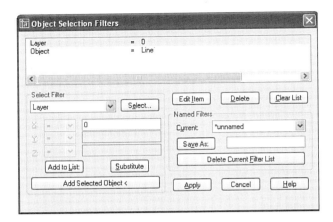

**Figure 8.5**   The Object Selection Filters dialog box is a robust filtering system with the added capability to save filter lists for later use.

You can assemble a list of the properties, also known as *filter criteria*, with which you want to conduct the search. Then, by clicking the Apply button, you can select a group of objects within which you want to find those objects that meet your list of characteristics. The following sections discuss how to define your list of filters.

## Defining Simple Selection Criteria for Filters

The list of available filters is extensive and is displayed in the Filters drop-down list. A filter can be a type of object or a property, or it can be defined from a specific object's property. For example, you can search for arcs in general or arcs that have a specific radius. If you choose a property, you also must supply the specific value of that property that you want within the X: edit box, located below the filter list. For some filter selections, you can click the Select button to choose the specific value from a list of existing or valid values. For other properties, you must type that value in the edit box.

After you select the filter and its associated value (if any), click the Add to List button to add the selected filter to the list at the top of the dialog box. To select the objects to which your filter criteria will be applied, click the Apply button.

To remove a filter from the list, choose the filter and click Delete. To edit the specific value of a filter in the list, select the filter and click Edit Item. After changing the value of the property, click Substitute to replace the old property with the revised property.

## Defining Complex Selection Criteria for Filters

The search criteria employed can be a complex set consisting of multiple filters. By default, when you assemble a list of filters, only objects that meet all the individual filters in the list are selected. For example, you could choose to select only arcs that reside on the layer CURVES by choosing the Arc and Layer filters. In doing so, you assemble a list of properties that must be met; this is referred to as an AND conditional. When you assemble a list of properties, the system assumes that you are assembling an AND conditional filter list. Other options do exist, however.

The most common option is to create an OR conditional filter list. In an OR conditional, the objects must meet only one of the conditions, not all of them. For example, you could assemble a list of properties such that any object that is an arc *or* that resides on the CURVES layer is selected. You begin an OR conditional by choosing the **Begin OR filter. Then you assemble the various properties in which you are interested. You end the list of properties with the **End OR filter.

The list of filters can consist of AND and OR conditionals nested within each other, but for most users, a simple search criterion consisting of a single conditional filter is enough.

**I**NSIDER **T**IP

> To gain an idea of the properties that are available for a particular object, click the Add Selected Object button and select an object in your drawing. All the relevant filters and their specific values for the selected object automatically are assembled into a list. You then can delete the filters you do not need, leaving only the properties for which you want to search.

## Saving and Restoring the Criteria for Filters

To save a list of filters you have assembled so that the list can be reused at a later date or in another drawing, type a name in the Save As edit box and click Save As. The next time you want to use that filter, simply select its name from the Current drop-down list. To delete a named filter, select the name from the Current drop-down list and click Delete Current Filter List. Named filter lists are saved in the file FILTER.NFL, which is created in the current working directory when you initially click the Save As button.

### Exercise 8.2 Using the Filters to Assemble Selection Sets

1. Open the 08EX02.dwg file from the CD that accompanies this book. This office plan includes many object types for using filters.

2. From the Tools pull-down menu, choose the Quick Select menu option. The Quick Select dialog box appears.

3. From the Object type list box, choose Line and click OK to close the dialog. AutoCAD then highlights 336 line objects in the drawing. Now we need to refine this selection to fewer objects.

4. Press Enter to restart the QSELECT command. From the Properties list box, choose Layer. Then, in the Value list box, choose 1FL_WALL. Click OK to close the dialog box.

**INSIDER TIP**

> The previous QSELECT setting of Line is still set. Repeated executions of the command can therefore build on the previous assignments.

5. AutoCAD then replaces the 336 object selection set with a 274 object selection set and highlights it for you. We are not done, so press Enter to restart the QSELECT command.

6. From the Properties list box, choose Start Y. Change the Operand to > Greater than. In the Value edit box, type **77'3"**, as shown in Figure 8.6. Then click OK to close the dialog box.

**Figure 8.6** QSELECT understands input values that match your current UNITS settings.

You can get odd selection results when inputting distance values that do not match your current UNITS settings. Units set to Decimal and inputting Architectural values may not work properly. Your input values should match your UNITS format.

7. AutoCAD then selects and highlights all the line objects on layer 1FL-WALL with a Y start point greater than 77'-3". These 123 objects are now available for general editing, such as a COPY or MOVE command. Press the ESC key to clear the selection.

   If you want to save and restore a selection set, you must use the FILTER command. The rest of the exercise demonstrates this method.

Although you cannot save a Quick Select setting, you can save the results of a QSE-LECT procedure into a GROUP. A group can be any set of objects saved by a name to be utilized at a later time. Refer to Chapter 9, "Object Selection and Manipulation," for how to use the GROUP feature.

8. Type **Filter** at the command line and press Enter.

9. In the Select Filter area, choose Line from the list box and click the Add to List button. This adds a filter for line objects only.

10. From the Select Filter area, choose Line Start. Change the X and Z operands to *
    from their list box and verify 0.000 is in each of the edit boxes. Change the Y
    operand to > and in its edit box, type **927**. Then click the Add to List button.
    This adds a filter for coordinates in any X and Z location but only points greater
    than 77'-3" in the Y direction.

The FILTER command requires input data to be in decimal format. Other units such as Architectural are not permitted.

11. From the Select Filter area, choose Layer. Click the Select button and choose
    1FL_WALL from the listing; then click OK. Click Add to List to add this required
    layer name to match against. In the Named Filters area, locate the edit box to the
    right of the Save As button. Type **North Walls** and click the Save As button, as
    shown in Figure 8.7. The current filter name then changes from *unnamed to
    North Walls.

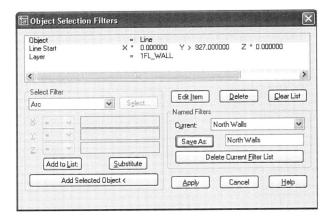

**Figure 8.7** The Object Selection Filters dialog box enables you to define and save a filter for later use.

12. Click the Apply button at the bottom of the Object Selection Filters dialog box. This closes the dialog box and prompts you to select objects. Type **ALL** and press Enter. Then press Enter again to end the Select Objects request. This applies the filters to all the objects in the drawing and prepares a specific selection set matching your North Walls filter criteria.

13. Press Enter to restart the FILTER command. You will notice that your filter parameters are still available and the name set. Click the Clear List button, and the filter parameters disappear.

14. Now choose North Walls from the Current name list. Notice that the filter criteria reappear in the list area. Click the Delete Current Filter List button to remove the saved list and clear the filter area. Then click Cancel to exit the dialog box.

You may close this drawing. There is no need to save it.

While most of the time you will be searching for objects that share certain properties within the current drawing, on occasion, you will need to get information from within blocks and xrefs. The next section explains this process in detail.

# Querying for Areas in Blocks and Xrefs

If you use the AREA command and select an object that is a block or xref, AutoCAD warns that the selected object does not have an area. How can you calculate the area of objects inserted as blocks or xrefs? The answer is to use the BOUNDARY command. You can use this command to create a temporary region or polyline boundary from which you can then quickly determine the area of the xref objects. Otherwise, you would have to bind the xref objects and then explode the resulting block to accomplish this, which defeats the purpose of using either xrefs or blocks.

Another viable and useful option is to use REFEDIT. This feature works with both blocks and external references in the current drawing. Normally, this tool is used to actually modify the content of the block/xref, but it can also be used to query objects when they exist outside of their block parent. After the block objects are available, treat them as single objects and use the AREA command as you normally would. Refer to Chapter 11, "Working with External References," for more information about the REFEDIT command.

**I**NSIDER **N**OTE

> The REFEDIT command requires that any external reference you want to edit be available and not open by any other user. If someone has the drawing open for editing, you will be unable to use REFEDIT on the xref.

**I**NSIDER **C**AUTION

> When editing an external reference drawing, the REFEDIT command updates the drawing format to AutoCAD 2004 when the changes are saved. Even though you may have a different setting in the Options dialog for the Save As format, because the drawing is not actually opened in the drawing editor, AutoCAD creates a file using the latest version format. Unless you made edits you need to keep, get in the habit of discarding changes when closing the REFEDIT command.

Another useful aspect of AutoCAD 2005 is the capability to extract attribute information to outside files for use with other programs. The following section covers these commands and their use.

# Extracting Block and Attribute Data

Blocks and attribute object definitions contain a great deal of data. AutoCAD automatically creates some of the data, including data that defines the block, such as the block's name, its insertion coordinates, its insertion layer's name, its X,Y,Z scale factors, and its X,Y,Z direction. This wealth of information can easily be extracted into a text file.

Attribute data is user-defined. The data that AutoCAD extracts consists of one element, which is either a character string or a numeric value. The attribute value can be anything the user wants it to be, and the number of attributes that can be attached to a block is unlimited.

By choosing the particular data records of blocks and the attributes you need, you can easily extract an abundance of important information from your drawing.

## Using the *ATTEXT* Command

The ATTEXT command displays the Attribute Extraction dialog box and is shown in Figure 8.8. The Attribute Extraction dialog box creates an ASCII text file (by default, a TXT file) containing the extracted information.

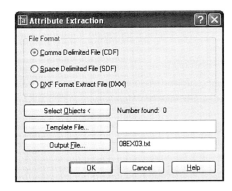

**Figure 8.8**   The Attribute Extraction dialog box.

This command tells AutoCAD which block and attribute information to extract and how the extracted information should be arranged. The arrangement of the information is determined by a template file and the file format you select, as discussed in the following section.

## Extraction Formats

The first item AutoCAD requests in the Attribute Extraction dialog box controls the extraction file format. The selected format determines the way each field within each record is separated and stored in the ASCII text file. AutoCAD provides three types of extraction file formats:

- **Comma Delimited File (CDF).** The file format writes one record for each block on a separate line. Each data value in a record is separated from the next by a comma, with text strings enclosed in apostrophes, as follows:

  ```
  'Sewer','Manhole', 36

  'Storm Drain','Manhole', 48

  'Storm Drain','Manhole', 36
  ```

- **Space Delimited File (SDF).** The SDF file format also writes one record for each block on a separate line, and each data value in a record occupies a predefined field width. If the string or numeric value does not use the entire space allotted, AutoCAD fills the remainder of the field with spaces, as follows:

```
Sewer            Manhole      36

Storm Drain      Manhole      48

Storm Drain      Manhole      36
```

- **Drawing Interchange File (DXF).** The DXF file format writes block data in AutoCAD's standard drawing interchange file format. The following is an excerpt from a DXF file created with the ATTEXT command:

```
  0
INSERT
  2
MANHOLE
 10
5.115973
 20
5.442408
 30
0.0
  0
ATTRIB
  1
Sewer
  2
OBJECT_CATEGORY
  0
ATTRIB
  1
Manhole
  2
```

As you can see, the format options are somewhat cryptic and limited. In order to use the ATTEXT command, you must have a good grasp of your data types, and you must predefine a template matching your data. The following section describes an alternative to the ATTEXT command.

## Using the *EATTEXT* Command

The EATTEXT feature makes the process of extracting data from your drawing much easier. The EATTEXT command has a step-by-step dialog interface that walks you through the process. Each insertion has three attributes.

In the following exercise, the attribute data is extracted and saved to a file.

### Exercise 8.3    Extracting Attribute Data

1. Open the drawing 08EX03.dwg from the accompanying CD. Save the file on your local disk to anywhere you choose.

2. From the Tools pull-down menu, select Attribute Extraction. The Attribute Extraction dialog appears.

3. In the Select drawing dialog, be sure the Current Drawing is selected, and then click Next.

4. In the Settings dialog, you have the options to not include external reference files or nested blocks. For this exercise it does not matter, so click the Next button.

5. In the Use Template dialog, you import a template file to help in the data query process. You don't need one, so just click the Next button.

6. The Select Attributes dialog enables you to specify which attribute values you want to export. In this exercise file, you only have one type of block, but this page can often be cluttered. Under the Attributes for Block <MANHOLE> area, click the Uncheck All button at the bottom and then check the OBJECT_CATEGORY, OBJECT_TYPE, and OBJECT_SIZE toggles (see Figure 8.9). Then click the Next button.

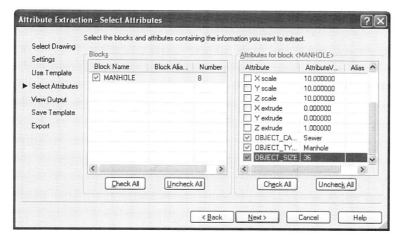

**Figure 8.9**   The EATTEXT command Select Attributes dialog enables you to choose which attributes to export.

7. The next panel is the View Output dialog. Here, you can specify the type of view in which you want the data to appear. Click the Alternate View button to show the longer data format. Then click the Next button.

8. In the Save Template dialog, you can save out the query filter you determined in step 6 into a Block Template File (BLK). Click the Next button to continue.

**NOTE**

> Saving to a Block Template File is highly recommended if you repeat the same attribute filtering often. If you always extract information for title blocks, and your blocks have the same formatting each time, loading a saved template can speed up the extraction process.

9. The Export dialog enables you to write the attribute data out to a file. With the EATTEXT command, you have four file output types from which to choose. Pick the Tab Delimited File (*.txt). Then in the File Name box, type a directory path and \08EX04 and then click the Finish button.

10. If you receive an Enhanced Attribute Extract Alert, click Yes and AutoCAD then creates the file and closes the dialog.

11. This command created a file with a TXT extension. Using Windows Notepad, browse to where you saved the file and open it (see Figure 8.10). Note that it only has the attribute settings you selected.

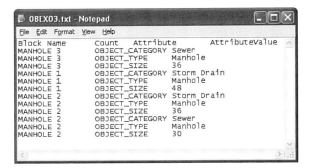

**Figure 8.10**    Using Notepad to view the saved TXT extraction file.

You may close this drawing without saving.

As you can see from this section, extracting attribute and block data from AutoCAD drawings is not overly difficult with the extraction tools. You now know what can be extracted and how to format that information.

# Summary

In this chapter, you learned how to quickly query for object data from the Properties toolbar and how to query properly for 2D distances, points, and areas in blocks and xrefs. Quickly querying objects for data that AutoCAD automatically creates, such as layer, color, and linetype, increases your productivity by providing information you frequently need during an editing session. By querying data that users assign, such as attribute data, you can increase your productivity by automatically extracting large amounts of information required to complete your work, such as when you need to create a bill of materials.

You also learned how to handle additional data that is associated with AutoCAD objects, whether that data consists of block attributes or general data. You learned about using AutoCAD 2005 commands for block and attribute extraction and about the different extraction formats. By understanding how blocks and attributes work and how to properly manage blocks and extract their data, you have learned how to make AutoCAD do tedious, repetitious drafting work automatically, thereby increasing your productivity.

*C h a p t e r   9*

# Object Selection and Manipulation

In your everyday work, you will be creating objects of varying types. This is easy to do. What can be a headache is the process of changing these objects later. The basic commands and tools used to make changes to objects are simple enough, but many additional tools and procedures exist that can vastly improve your productivity when doing this type of work. In this chapter, we build on your existing knowledge and discuss the following topics:

- Using cut and paste
- Using drag and drop
- Using grip editing commands
- Understanding the Properties palette
- Using the Matchprop tool
- Creating and editing groups
- Exploding objects
- Using specialized object editing
- Lengthening and shortening objects
- Aligning objects
- Renaming and purging named objects

# Windows Functionality

There are many advantages to opening several drawings in a single session of AutoCAD, including two that relate to blocks. Along with the Multiple Document Editor (MDE), AutoCAD 2005 also has two features that take advantage of multiple open drawings. These features enable you to either cut and paste or drag and drop objects from one drawing to another. Additionally, you have the option to insert the objects as a block.

## Copying with the Clipboard

To copy using the clipboard, choose Copy (COPYCLIP) from the Edit pull-down menu. This copies selected objects to the clipboard. Choose Copy Link to copy the current view to the clipboard. Copy Link copies all objects in the drawing and preserves the current view of the drawing. As an alternative, you can use the Cut (CUTCLIP) feature to copy objects to the clipboard and remove them from the drawing.

**I**NSIDER **T**IP

> A great feature of the Copy options is *Copy with Base Point*. This option enables you to define a coordinate and save it with the copy stored in the clipboard. This is then matched with a *Paste to Original Coordinates* option that enables you to paste this data using the recorded base point. This is very useful for transferring data from drawing to drawing while maintaining a specific location. You can also maintain relative locations by using *Copy with Base Point* and pasting using object snaps.

## Cut and Paste Block Insertion

The phrase "cut and paste" refers to the process of selecting an object or group of objects and cutting (or copying) them to the Windows clipboard. When objects are cut, they are copied to the clipboard and erased from the original document. In contrast, when you copy objects, they are copied to the clipboard, and the selected objects are left untouched in the original document.

If you choose Paste (PASTECLIP) from the Edit pull-down menu in an AutoCAD drawing, the contents of the clipboard are inserted as individual objects.

Another great feature is Paste as Block. When this feature is used, the items are placed within a block that you can later explode to remove the arbitrary block name assigned by the PASTEBLOCK command.

You also can paste an entire drawing into the current drawing by dragging the icon of the file from within Windows Explorer into the current drawing.

┃ **NSIDER NOTE**

You cannot use Paste Special when the contents you want to paste are taken from another AutoCAD drawing.

┃ **NSIDER NOTE**

To use the Copy with Base Point feature, you must be in MDE mode. If you only use the Single Drawing Interface, the Titlecase option will be unavailable.

## Drag and Drop Block Insertion

When you drag and drop objects, you are moving them from one place to another. When you drag and drop objects within the same AutoCAD drawing, the result is the same as using the MOVE command to move the object. When you drag and drop from one drawing to another, the result is similar to copying the object from the original drawing to the target drawing.

**Figure 9.1**
The shortcut menu has many copy/paste options on it, which are available from a simple right-click of the mouse.

Being able to use the drag and drop feature takes some getting used to because most editing commands focus on using the available grips. To use drag and drop, you specifically must not pick on a grip. Picking on the object by left-clicking and dragging provides a single drop option. Right-clicking to select the object (again, not on a grip, though) offers more options when you release in the current drawing or another drawing.

Another variation of the drag and drop concept is the i-drop feature in AutoCAD 2005. Based on XML technology, it enables you to "drop" drawing data from web pages. Refer to AutoCAD online Help for more information.

The following is a list of the options available on the shortcut list when right-clicking on a selection set and dragging and dropping into either the same drawing or a different drawing:

- **Move Here.** This option appears when the selected objects are dragged and dropped within the same drawing.

- **Copy Here.** This option appears when objects are dragged and dropped within the same drawing or between two drawings.

- **Paste as Block.** This option appears when objects are dragged and dropped within the same drawing or between two drawings.

- **Paste to Original Coordinates.** This option appears only when objects are dragged and dropped between two drawings.

- **Cancel.** This option appears when objects are dragged and dropped within the same drawing or between two drawings.

**INSIDER NOTE**

You can also drag and drop files from Windows Explorer into a drawing.

The drag and drop feature is useful for quickly moving or copying objects. However, this method does not provide a way to accurately select the base point for pasting the objects as a block. Consequently, to select objects in one drawing and paste them as a block in another while controlling the new block's base point, use the Copy with Base Point and Paste feature described in the previous section.

# Grip Editing

The usage of grips at first can be confusing because the grips appear so often, but after grips are understood and utilized, they can be extremely helpful and efficient for editing existing geometry.

## Implied Windowing

In order to fully comprehend proper grip operation, you need to have an understanding of Implied Windowing and how it affects grip usage. When you position the pickbox over an empty portion of the drawing and left-click, the system assumes you want to place the first corner of a rectangular selection window at that point. You determine its size by moving the cursor to the opposite corner and then picking a second point (the opposing diagonal corner point relative to the initial point).

When the window is defined from left to right, all objects completely enclosed in the window are selected. When the "window" is defined right to left, it is referred to as a "crossing window." In a crossing window, all objects that are completely enclosed in the window or that merely cross the boundaries of the crossing window are selected. A crossing window is shown with a dotted line, whereas a normal window is drawn with a continuous line. You can enable or disable this feature with the Implied Windowing setting in the Selection tab of the Options dialog box.

**I**NSIDER **NOTE**

By default, the Implied Windowing selection option on the Selection tab of the Options dialog box is enabled. If it's disabled, the only way you can define a window or a crossing window is to use the Window or Crossing Window options explicitly. This feature is disabled for backward-compatibility with previous versions of AutoCAD. Rarely, if ever, will you need to turn off Implied Windowing.

**I**NSIDER **NOTE**

With the Implied Window setting disabled, you will still be able to directly select objects at the command prompt for use with the grip commands.

# Enabling Grips

*Grip editing* is a facility that integrates object property points with the most commonly used editing commands and then places the combined capabilities literally at your fingertips. With grips, it is possible to edit objects and select specific object snap points without ever having to pick a tool, use a menu command, or type a command. In the following sections, you will learn how to enable the grips function, activate grips, and make use of the various options available with grips.

Grips are an optional facility that you can choose to use. By default, grips are enabled. You can disable grips with the Enable Grips toggle on the Selection tab of the Options dialog box (see Figure 9.2), which is displayed by choosing Options from the Tools pull-down menu.

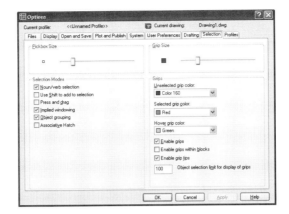

**Figure 9.2**   The Grip options is found on the Selection tab in the Options dialog box.

**I**NSIDER **T**IP

A new feature introduced in AutoCAD 2004 is the Grip Object Limit system variable. Controlled in the Grips options shown in Figure 9.2, it defaults to 100, and it enables you to determine how many objects may be selected at one time while still displaying their grips. This is helpful in case you ever accidentally select too many objects at one time, which can degrade performance. Be aware, however, that no grips are shown if the object selection limit is exceeded. If Enable grips within blocks is enabled, the block insertion counts as only one object; therefore, you may potentially have more objects displaying grips than the limit supposedly allows.

With grips enabled, you start the process of using the grip editing modes by selecting the objects you want to edit at the command prompt. In other words, you do not initiate any commands. Instead, you simply select the objects by picking them or by using implied windowing. After you have selected the objects, the object's grips are displayed as blue squares by default. The color and size of these *unselected* grips are set with the Unselected grip color control. The displayed grips correspond to the control points of the objects, and for the most part, the grip locations are the same as some object snap points for the various types of objects. The major exceptions to this rule are presented in Table 9.1.

## Table 9.1    Specific Grip and Object Snap Discrepancies

| Object | Description |
| --- | --- |
| Arc | Only three grips exist for an arc: its two endpoints and its midpoint. In contrast, object snap points include the center point and any valid quadrant points. Grip editing on an arc can be used to lengthen or change its radius. |
| | Note: When moving a grip on an arc, it changes the geometry unless the new point placement results in the same radius and center coordinate. |
| Block Insertion | By default, only one grip is displayed at the insertion point of each block insertion. However, if you enable the Enable grips within blocks setting from the Selection tab in the Options dialog box, then the grips of all the component objects are also displayed. Grip editing a block relocates the block. |
| Elliptical arc | Grips correspond to the arc's endpoints, midpoint, and center points but not to its visible quadrant points. Grip editing an ellipse relocates it or resizes it about its center. |
| Mline | Grips exist at the end points used to locate the mline object. However, endpoint, intersection, and midpoint object snap points can occur on each visible segment. Grip editing an mline changes the vertex points. |
| Mtext | Up to five grips can exist on an mtext object—one at each corner of the imaginary box that surrounds an mtext object and one at the insertion point. Grip editing an mtext object can be used to relocate or resize the bounding box, affecting the paragraph appearance. |
| Spline | A grip exists at every point used to define the spline, known as the spline's control points. Object snap points include only the endpoints and, obviously, the nearest osnap mode. Grip editing can be used to redefine the curves as well as the start and end points of the spline. |

Grips enable you to easily choose a provided point on an object. After the grips are displayed, you can choose one grip to activate the grip editing modes.

## Activating the Grip Editing Modes

When you select one or more objects, unselected grips are displayed. By default, the unselected grip box color is blue. You may then select any grip or multiple grips by holding down the Shift key while selecting grips, which initiates the grip edit mode for the selection set. Selecting a grip affects the cursor much like osnaps do—the grip acts as a magnet and pulls the cursor to the grip. After a grip is selected, by default it is displayed as a red box and is referred to as a hot or selected grip. The color used to fill in the grip box is set from the Selection tab of the Options dialog box. The selected grip subsequently is used as the base point for the various grip editing modes: Stretch, Move, Rotate, Scale, and Mirror. Initially, the Stretch grip mode is activated, but you can press Enter or the spacebar to cycle through the other grip commands. Alternatively, right-click and pick the desired grip mode from the shortcut menu that appears (see Figure 9.3). The various editing mode options are discussed in the following sections.

## Deactivating the Grips

When you select objects at the command prompt, the grips of the objects are displayed, and the objects are highlighted. The highlighting indicates the objects that have been selected. In AutoCAD 2005, it only takes a single Esc key press to both un-highlight and un-grip the gripped objects.

**Figure 9.3**
The shortcut menu presented when a hot grip is used with a right-click.

You can also selectively deselect highlighted objects by pressing the Shift key and selecting the highlighted objects (not on a grip), thereby leaving the grips displayed.

Another common problem that users experience when using grips is that they accidentally select objects and activate a grip editing mode by selecting one of the grips. To exit a grip editing mode, just press the Esc key. Remember that in AutoCAD 2005, pressing the Esc key cancels the active command. To deselect the objects and clear the display of the grips, press the Esc key again.

The first grip edit mode to discuss is the Stretch mode. The next section covers this valuable grip editing feature.

# Using the Stretch Mode

The default edit mode when working with grips is *Stretch*, which enables you to relocate the selected grip. This in turn affects only the object or objects defined by the selected grip(s). For example, if the selected grip is the endpoint of two lines, then the endpoint of both lines can be stretched to the new position.

If the selected grip is the endpoint at which multiple lines meet (as shown in Figure 9.4), all lines are stretched to the new endpoint location. As you decide on the new location of the selected grip, notice that the rubber band line is anchored at the selected grip. Thus, the selected grip is referred to as the base point of the stretch.

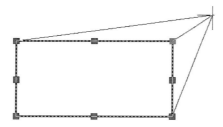

**Figure 9.4**   Using a selected grip to stretch the endpoint of multiple objects.

**INSIDER TIP**

> The Stretch grip editing mode offers two advantages over the STRETCH command. The Copy option of the Stretch grip mode enables you to scale and make copies of the selected objects simultaneously. In addition, STRETCH cannot be used to stretch circles or ellipses, whereas the Stretch grip mode can.

## Stretching Multiple Points at the Same Time

If you want to stretch more than one point on the selected object(s) at a time, you must initiate a modified procedure to activate grips. First, you must hold down the Shift key while selecting all the grips you want to edit during the stretching procedure. Then, after releasing Shift, pick the grip that you want to use as the base point (the hot grip) of the stretch. This activates the grip edit modes on the prompt line.

**INSIDER TIP**

> The grips are now planar to the object's UCS. When a 2D object lies on a plane other than the current UCS, the object is stretched on the plane on which it was created, not on the plane of the current UCS.

**INSIDER NOTE**

When using the grip Stretch and Move modes and/or their Copy option, if you know the exact delta-X, delta-Y, delta-Z, or distance and angle you want to apply to the selected grip, you can specify relative or polar coordinates rather than picking the new location for the edit. You also can define the distance and direction of the stretch with direct distance entry.

## Using the Move Mode

Use the Move grip mode to move the selected objects to the new location. Unlike the Stretch grip editing mode, in which only the selected objects controlled by the selected grip(s) are affected, all selected objects, with hot grips or not, are moved by the grip's Move editing mode (see Figure 9.5).

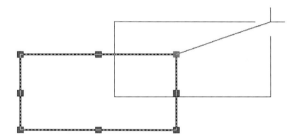

**Figure 9.5** The Move grip edit mode relocates selected objects.

## Using the Rotate Mode

The Rotate grip editing mode enables you to rotate the selected objects about the selected grip (see Figure 9.6).

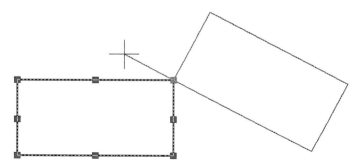

**Figure 9.6** The Rotate grip mode rotates all selected objects.

You can specify the amount of rotation to apply to the selected objects graphically with the "rubber band" line or by typing the specific value. The angle entered is relative to the drawing's 0 degree angle set in Units. Alternatively, you can specify the Reference option.

To use the Reference option, you first specify a reference angle by picking two points that define that angle or by typing an angular value. Then you specify the desired angle the reference line is to be rotated around by dragging or typing the angle.

**I**NSIDER **TIP**

The Reference option is useful when you know the desired angle for the object(s) but do not know the exact amount of rotation needed.

## Using the Scale Mode

The Scale grip mode enables you to scale the selected objects using the selected grip as the scale from point. You can either type the scale factor or pick a point using the rubber-band line. Picking a point is subsequently used as the graphic specification of the scale factor. The grip point is the static point about which the objects expand or contract. Similar to the Rotate grip mode, the Scale grip mode has a Reference option.

To use the Reference option, you specify a reference length by picking two points to define that length or by typing a known length value. Then you specify the desired length to which you want the reference line to be scaled. The second length can be defined by entering the desired length or by picking two points to define that length.

**I**NSIDER **TIP**

One advantage that Scale grip edit mode has over the SCALE command is that grip edit mode enables you to use the Copy option to scale and make copies of the selected objects simultaneously.

## Using the Mirror Mode

The Mirror grip edit mode enables you to mirror the selected objects about the mirror line that is anchored at the selected grip (see Figure 9.7).

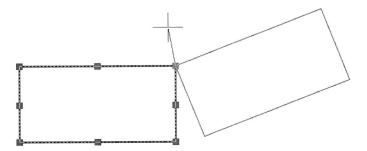

**Figure 9.7**   The Mirror grip mode mirrors all selected objects about the axis specified. Note the cursor difference from Figure 9.6.

The mirror line is the imaginary line about which all the selected objects are flipped. Text and mtext objects can also be flipped so that they appear backward. By default, the MIRRTEXT system variable is set to 0, which produces normal-reading text objects during mirroring. If you want the text and mtext objects to actually be mirrored, type **MIRRTEXT** at the command prompt, and type **1** to turn on the mirroring of text objects. Prior to AutoCAD 2004, the default for this system variable was On. This new change in AutoCAD functionality is a welcome refinement.

## Invoking the Grip Editing Base Point Option

The base point option of the grip edit modes enables you to relocate the anchor point of the rubber band line. In the Stretch grip edit mode, relocating the base point does not affect the grip that is stretched. A base point option exists in each grip edit mode. This option is very useful in the Mirror grip edit mode when either of the mirror line points do not coincide with a grip location.

## Invoking the Grip Editing Copy Option

A Copy option also exists in each of the five grip editing modes. When this option is invoked, the original objects are left unchanged, and any changes are made to copies of the original. An alternative when using the Copy option is to hold down the Shift key after you have placed the first copy. Be aware, however, that if you continue to press the Shift key, AutoCAD uses the distance and direction between the original object and the first copy point to create a set of invisible snap points. For the STRETCH, MOVE, and SCALE commands, the snap points are arranged into a grid, with one of the grid axes running from the base point to the first selected point (see Figure 9.8).

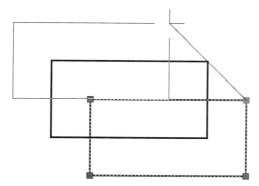

**Figure 9.8**   The Shift key can be used to place copies with temporary invisible snap points that are arranged into a grid.

For the Rotate and Mirror grip modes, the snap points are arranged into a circular arrangement such that the angular displacement between adjacent snap points is equal (see Figure 9.9). When used with the Shift key, this process presets the available angles in increments equal to the first angle selected.

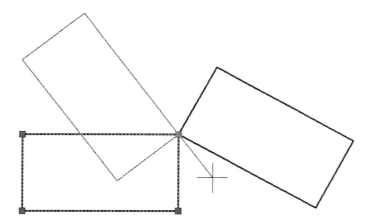

**Figure 9.9**   The Shift key can be used to place copies with temporary snap angles that are arranged into a polar configuration during Rotate and Mirror.

In the following exercise, you use grips to make changes and additions to an office layout. These changes include rotating and duplicating a chair and stretching a cabinet.

### Exercise 9.1    Using Grips to Make Changes and Additions

1. Open the drawing 09EX01.dwg from the accompanying CD.

2. Choose Named Views from the View pull-down menu and select the view named OFFICE-A. Click the Set Current button in the View dialog box and click OK.

3. At the command prompt, pick the chair located below the desk (see Figure 9.10). The chair is a block, which explains why only one grip is displayed.

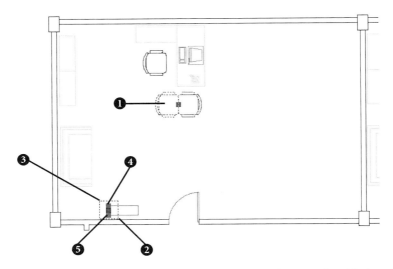

**Figure 9.10**    In this drawing, grips are used to relocate and copy a chair block and to resize a file cabinet.

4. Select the grip at ❶. You have just activated the grip editing modes; Stretch is the default mode. Right-click and choose Rotate from the shortcut menu. Type **180** to rotate the chair 180 degrees.

5. Select the same grip and press the spacebar once to cycle to the Move grip mode.

6. Type **C** to specify the Copy option and then type **@3'<270**. Press Enter to exit the Move grip mode. Press Esc to remove the selected grips on the screen.

7. At the command prompt, use Implied Windowing to pick ❷ and ❸ to select the cabinet. Because the cabinet was drawn with four lines, it displays grips at the endpoints and midpoints.

**8.** While holding down the Shift key, pick ❹ and ❺ to select the multiple grips to stretch.

**9.** Release the Shift key and pick ❹ again to activate the editing modes. Type **@2'<0** to stretch the rectangle 2' to the right and exit the command.

**10.** Press the Esc key once to clear the selection and the grips.

**11.** Refer to step 1 and restore the view OFFICE-B. Select the single chair (notice the highlighted chair in Figure 9.11) and pick the grip to enable the grip editing modes.

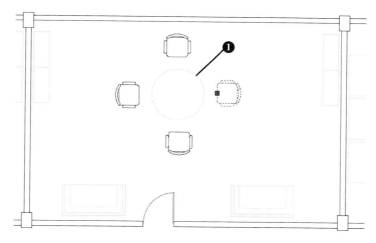

**Figure 9.11**   In this drawing, grips are used to "array" copies of the chair around the table.

**12.** Right-click and choose Rotate, then right-click again and choose Base Point.

**13.** Move your cursor to a point that's not on a grip, hold the Shift key and right-click the mouse, then select Center from the Object Snap shortcut menu. Then pick the desk at ❶.

**14.** Right-click and choose Copy. Then type **90**, **180**, and **270** to make three copies at the three respective angle positions. Press the Enter key to exit the Rotate grip mode.

**15.** Restore the view OFFICE-E, then select the office cubicles on the left side of the room with an implied crossing window by picking ❶ and ❷ (see Figure 9.12).

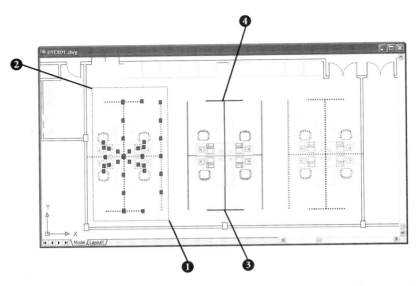

**Figure 9.12**   In this drawing, grips are used to mirror a set of room objects about an axis line.

**16.** Pick one of the displayed grips, then right-click and pick Mirror, then right-click and pick Copy. Now right-click and choose Base Point.

**17.** Use the Shift+right-click shortcut menu and pick the Midpoint object snap and then pick ❸. Turn on Ortho and pick up near ❹. By turning on Ortho, you ensure that you create a horizontal or vertical mirror line. Press Enter to exit Mirror grip edit mode.

The collection of objects is now mirrored, leaving the originals in place. Note the high level of editing you were able to do without accessing any pull-down menus or toolbars.

You do not need to save the changes.

So far, this chapter has discussed how to use grips to modify and create duplicate objects. The following section covers AutoCAD 2005's object modification tools.

# Changing an Object's Properties

The properties of an object are defined as its layer, color, and linetype and, for most objects, also include its object linetype scale and/or thickness. You can use the Layers and Properties toolbars, the Properties icon on the Standard toolbar, or the Match Properties icon also on the Standard toolbar to change an object's properties (see Figure 9.13).

**Figure 9.13**    The Standard, Layers, Properties, and Styles toolbars.

## Understanding the Properties Palette

The Properties palette is the next generation of a properties editor (see Figure 9.14). With it comes everything from the power to change a simple layer setting to manipulating individual dimension variables of a selected set of dimensions. The Properties palette can either be accessed from within the Tools pull-down menu under Properties, by selecting the Properties toolbar button, by pressing Ctrl+1 on the keyboard, by selecting an object and using the right-click shortcut menu item Properties, or by typing **PR** at the command prompt.

**Figure 9.14**    The Properties palette has controls for many object properties.

**I**NSIDER **TIP**

> A feature in AutoCAD 2005 is double-click editing of objects. If you quickly double-click on an object, the most typical editing mechanism is opened on that object. In the case of a line and other typical geometry objects, the Properties palette automatically appears with the object already listed in the dialog. With other objects like text, mtext, and blocks with attributes, their respective editor appears and is populated with the text values. Even when an image is double-clicked, it loads the IMAGEADJUST dialog, ready to adjust.

The Properties palette is structured into categories. It essentially breaks the information into groups, typically General and Geometry for a single or like objects.

When you select multiple objects, the Properties palette filters the available options down to those that are shared. For instance, selecting two circles enables editing of the radius, but selecting a line and a circle limits you to standard appearance settings, such as layer and color.

At the top of the Properties palette is a drop-down list that provides a listing of the type of object(s) selected. The listing allows you to modify similar objects when multiple object types are selected. For example, if you select a circle and two lines, this list allows you to change all general properties but also to choose to modify the circle properties independently from the whole selection. You could then choose to change the two lines and have the edited values shown accordingly.

**I**NSIDER **NOTE**

> In the Properties palette, if the value in an edit box is blank, you can simply type in new values. Some edit boxes expand to a list box for their value options, and some edit boxes are unavailable. Edit boxes that are blank generally indicate that the objects selected do not share identical values for that property.

The Properties palette can be docked, which enables the user to place it permanently on-screen. In Figure 9.15, you can see the many different user settings also found in the pull-downs and toolbars. Additionally, you have multiple UCS control options that can come in handy.

**Figure 9.15**   The Properties palette in a "no selection" state.

There are a few remaining items in the Properties palette. First is the Quick Select icon (the filter + lightning icon) in the upper-right corner. Quick Select is covered in Chapter 8, "Obtaining Object Information." To the left of that is a Select Objects tool. This tool enables you to build a selection set just like many other editing commands, and when you press Enter, the selection is then added to the Properties palette. Next to that button is a toggle button for the PICKADD system variable. This controls whether subsequent selections replace the current selection set or just add to it.

## Properties Palette Display Controls

Depending on your display area, you may choose to leave the Properties palette docked at all times. Even then, though, its mere presence can become bothersome. However, there are additional steps you can use to help keep it active and yet out of your way.

The first option is found by right-clicking over the vertical Properties title bar. In the shortcut menu that appears, you will find an option to Auto-hide. When this is enabled, the palette collapses to the just the vertical bar when you move outside of the palette area. As you return the cursor over the bar, the palette appears and is ready for action, including anything you may have selected.

**INSIDER TIP**

You also can toggle Auto-hide by using the small arrows near the lower left of the palette.

The other option is less of a space-saving method as it is just a way to avoid dealing with the problem of objects appearing beneath the palette. You can dock the palette to the left or right side, outside of the drawing area and toolbars. If you have a large monitor, or multiple monitors, you may opt to try it out; perhaps you will find it more productive than closing or hiding it because it will be on 100% of the time, just like normal toolbars.

By using Properties, you can very quickly edit multiple objects to share command settings. In those cases where the editing is more specific, you may find the Match Properties tool more applicable.

## The Match Properties Tool

The MATCHPROP command is a great feature in AutoCAD and is very dynamic and customizable. Accessed from the Match Properties tool on the Standard toolbar or from the Modify pull-down menu, this command enables the user to copy the properties of one object (the source) and then paste any similar parameters to selected objects (the destination objects). When selecting the destination objects, you can use any of the object selection methods available. Table 9.2 outlines the properties that can be pasted and which objects will accept the change.

**Table 9.2     Object Properties Changed by *MATCHPROP***

| General Property | Application |
| --- | --- |
| Color | Matches the color of the destination object(s) to that of the source object. This applies to all objects except OLE objects. |
| Layer | Matches the layer of the destination object(s) to that of the source object. This applies to all objects except OLE objects. |
| Linetype | Matches the linetype of the destination object(s) to that of the source object. This can applied to all objects except for attribute, hatch, mtext, OLE, point, and viewport objects. |

| General Property | Application |
|---|---|
| Linetype Scale | Matches the linetype scale factor of the destination object(s) to that of the source object. This applies to all objects except attribute, hatch, mtext, OLE, point, and viewport objects. |
| Lineweight | Matches the lineweight of the destination object(s) to that of the source object. Available for all objects. |
| Plot Style | Matches the plot style of the destination object(s) to that of the source object. However, if color-dependent plot style mode is active (PSTYLEPOLICY is set to 1), this control is not applicable. This applies to all objects except OLE objects. |
| Thickness | Matches the thickness of the destination object(s) to that of the source object. This applies only to arc, attribute, circle, line, point, 2D polyline, region, text, and trace objects. |

| Object Property | Application |
|---|---|
| Dimension | Matches the dimension style of the destination object to that of the source object. Available only for dimension, leader, and tolerance objects. |
| Hatch | Matches the hatch pattern of the destination object(s) to that of the source object. This applies only to hatch objects (both associative and non-associative). |
| Polyline | Matches a constant width setting from an existing 2D polyline to another 2D polyline. It does not match or accept widths that have a width setting that varies. This applies only to 2D polyline objects. |
| Table | Matches the table style of the destination table to that of the source table. This only applies to table objects. |
| Text | Matches the text style of the destination object(s) to that of the source object. This applies only to attribute, field, mtext, and text objects. |
| Viewport | Matches many of the viewport settings from an existing viewport to another viewport. The properties copied are on/off, display locking, scale, shading, snap, grid, and the UCSICON visibility and location. This applies only to viewport objects. |

In the following exercise, you will experience firsthand the power of the MATCHPROP command.

### Exercise 9.2    Using the *MATCHPROP* Command

1. Open the drawing 09EX02.dwg from the CD that accompanies this book. This drawing contains a variety of object types that you might use every day (see Figure 9.16).

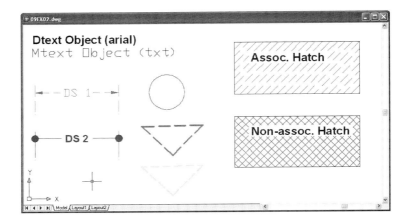

**Figure 9.16**    The drawing used for the MATCHPROP exercise.

2. Locate and choose the Match Properties icon found on the Standard toolbar; it looks like a paintbrush.

3. At the Select Source object prompt, choose the Dtext Object (arial) text object in the top left of your drawing.

    Let's pause for a moment to examine the Settings options found in the MATCHPROP command.

4. Type s to display the Property Settings dialog box shown in Figure 9.17.

5. AutoCAD users prefer the default settings because they speed up the process of using the MATCHPROP command. In some cases, you may need to change one or more of these options. However, for this exercise, click OK to close the dialog box.

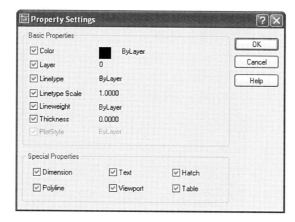

**Figure 9.17** The Property Settings dialog box for the MATCHPROP command controls the variety of object types and how their properties can be "painted" onto others.

6. When the paintbrush pickbox is active, it indicates that you will be "painting" properties to any objects you select. Pick the object mtext object (txt); doing so paints the dtext properties onto it.

    After pasting, you could continue to paste properties to any additional objects. For this exercise, however, stop and restart the command.

7. Press Enter twice to exit and restart the MATCHPROP command.

8. Select the dimension DS 2 to establish a dimension as the source object and then choose the dimension DS 1. The DS 2 dimension properties are then applied to the DS 1 dimension as well as the DS 2 layer setting.

9. Press Enter twice to exit and restart the command.

10. Select the associative hatching in the top right of the display and then choose the non-associative hatch object at the lower right in the drawing to paste the hatch and layer settings from the top hatch to the bottom.

11. Press Enter twice to exit and restart the command.

12. Select the green dashed polygon at the bottom of the display as the source object. Property values garnished from this object include color, layer, linetype, linetype scale, and lineweight.

13. Now, instead of choosing one by one, use implied windowing by picking a point at the bottom left of the green polygon, then use the window to enclose all three polygons. The upper two then inherit the original polygon's properties, including layer and color.

Press Enter to exit the command and then close the drawing without saving changes.

Using the MATCHPROP command is highly recommended over other methods of general object editing. When you need to select objects on a broader scale, using Quick Select in combination with the Properties palette can more helpful.

In addition to searching for objects that share certain properties, you can also gather up objects and place them in named groups for later retrieval. The next section explains this process in detail.

# Creating and Editing Groups

You can link disparate objects on different layers into what is referred to as a group. After a group is created, all the member objects of the group can be selected by selecting one member of the group or by using the group name. Assembling the objects into a group, however, does not prevent you from editing the member objects individually. To create and edit a group, you use the GROUP command (see Figure 9.18). The following sections discuss how to use the GROUP command for specific tasks.

**Figure 9.18**   The Object Grouping dialog box of the GROUP command enables you to create and edit a group.

## Creating a Group

Groups may be named or unnamed. To create a named group, you first type a name in the Group Name edit box. Then click New and select the objects you want to include in the group. To complete the creation of the group within the drawing, you must click OK in the Object Grouping dialog box. If you do not want to name the group, enable the Unnamed option, and AutoCAD gives the group an arbitrary name that begins with an asterisk. Unnamed groups also are created when you duplicate a group using commands such as COPY or ARRAY. By default, unnamed groups are not displayed in the list of groups. To include unnamed groups in the list of groups displayed in the dialog box, enable the Include Unnamed option.

By default, any group you create is selectable. This means that the group of objects can be selected by name or by selecting a member. If you turn off the Selectable option before you create a group, the group will not be selectable. The individual group members still will be listed as members of the group, but they will be selectable only as individual objects. You might want to create a non-selectable group, for example, if you want to associate various objects together for use with custom programs (created by you or a third-party developer) that interact with the drawing database but are not for use with AutoCAD editing commands. The typical user does not have an application for non-selectable groups, so as a rule, always make your groups selectable.

A group can have as many members as you desire, and an individual object can be a member of more than one group. The group description is an optional piece of information that you can use to better describe the contents of the group or the relationship between the member objects.

## Selecting a Group to Edit

After you create a selectable group, you can select all members of the group simply by selecting one group member or by using the group name at a selection prompt with the Group option. The Object Grouping setting controls the selection of all members of a group when one member is selected. This setting is found in the Settings tab of the Options dialog box. The Object Grouping setting can also be enabled or disabled with the Ctrl+Shift+A key sequence. Even with the Object Grouping setting disabled, the members of a selectable group can be selected by typing **G** at the Select objects prompt and then entering the group name.

## Inquiring About a Group's Membership

If you ever forget whether an object is a member of a group or which objects are members of a particular group, you can use the following two buttons to find this information when in the Object Grouping dialog box:

- **Find Name.** Use the Find Name button to determine the group, if any, to which a selected object belongs. This enables you to select an object within a group and thereby learn the group name.

- **Highlight.** Select a group name from the list of group names and click the Highlight button to highlight all the members of the selected group on-screen.

**I**NSIDER **N**OTE

You also can use the LIST command to see the contents of a group. When listing a group, all the group objects are highlighted, and descriptions of the objects contained within are listed.

## Modifying an Existing Group

To modify the makeup of a particular group, first select the group name from the list of groups. The following list shows the buttons you use to modify the group you select (refer to Figure 9.18):

- **Remove** and **Add.** You can use these buttons to remove an object from or add an object to an existing group.

- **Rename** and **Description.** You can rename a group or change the group's description by selecting the group name, typing in the new name or description, and then selecting the corresponding button.

- **Selectable.** Use this button to change the selectable status of the selected group.

- **Re-Order.** Selecting this button displays the Order Group dialog box, which enables you to change the order in which the member objects are arranged in a group. You can use this option to visually control how the objects in the group are ordered internally.

## Deleting a Group

To remove or undefine a group, click Explode in the Object Grouping dialog box (refer to Figure 9.18). Exploding a group dissolves the associations between the member objects but does not erase or explode (see the next section) the member objects.

The previous sections have discussed the various ways to select an object or objects for editing. After you have selected the object(s), you can edit the properties or even explode a complex object into basic objects, as discussed in the following section.

# Exploding Compound Objects

Several objects are considered *compound objects*—meaning the objects themselves are composed of other AutoCAD objects, such as a block insertion. Other objects are complex—meaning the object is of one type but can be reduced to a number of other simpler objects. These objects can be *exploded*, or broken down, into their constituent parts with the EXPLODE command. You usually explode such an object to modify one or more of its constituent objects in a way that you cannot do with the original object.

EXPLODE is issued by choosing Explode from the Modify pull-down menu or toolbar. Table 9.3 lists the types of 2D objects covered in this book (with appropriate chapter references) that can be exploded. It also describes briefly how EXPLODE affects the objects and some reasons why you should examine your reasons for exploding the object.

### Table 9.3    2D Objects That May Be Exploded

| Object Type | Result of Explode |
| --- | --- |
| Block insertions | An insertion of a block is replaced with duplicates of the block's component objects. Component objects originally drawn on Layer 0 are re-created onto Layer 0. |
| | When a block has attributes and is exploded, those attributes are returned into Attribute Definitions and left where the attributes were formally located. |
| | A block insertion is usually exploded because you want to modify the component objects themselves. This is usually, but not always, done in the context of redefining the block definition. See Chapter 10, "Creating and Using Blocks," for more information. |

*continues* ▶

**Table 9.3   Continued**

| Object Type | Result of Explode |
|---|---|
| Dimensions | A dimension is replaced by a combination of lines, mtext, points, solids, and block insertions. Dimensions usually are exploded so that you can further manipulate their component objects. Generally, because exploded dimensions are no longer associative, you should avoid exploding dimensions. For information about dimensions, see Chapter 16, "Quick Dimensioning," and Chapter 17, "Intelligent Dimensions." |
| Hatch | A hatch is replaced by its component lines or objects. An exploded hatch is no longer associative. Again, because of the loss of associativity, exploding a hatch is normally not a good idea. Hatching is covered in Chapter 13, "Drawing Hatch Patterns." |
| Mline | An mline (multiline) is replaced by its component lines. In this way, you can work around editing commands, such as EXTEND and TRIM, that don't work with mlines. By exploding the mline object into its component lines, you then can trim or extend normal lines. |
| Mtext | Exploding an mtext object converts each line of text into a text object. If the mtext object also contains fields, the fields are converted into static text. Refer to Chapter 21, "Using Fields and Tables," for more on fields. |
| Polylines | A polyline is replaced by a series of lines and arcs. If the polyline has a width, the replacement lines and arcs will have no width. Polylines are drawn with the PLINE, POLYGON, RECTANG, and DONUT commands. |
| Region | A region is replaced by the edge objects (such as lines and circles) that define the loops (closed shapes) in the region. Regions are covered in Chapter 26, "Drawing in 3D." |
| Table | New in AutoCAD 2005, a table is a spreadsheet-like element that leaves behind mtext objects and lines when exploded. Learn more about tables in Chapter 21. |

**INSIDER TIP**

An exploded object can only be returned to its original unexploded form by using the U or UNDO command.

An additional alternative to the standard EXPLODE command is XPLODE. This command enables the user to control what happens to the objects after they are exploded. You can opt to apply the changes individually or globally. Properties that can be controlled are color, layer, lineweight, and linetype. These properties can also be gathered from the object being exploded.

Common components of the block insertion object are attributes. The next section discusses the tools used to modify and control these objects.

# Specialized Editing Commands

Numerous commands exist within AutoCAD that have been provided to edit very specific object types. These unique objects have characteristics that can be exposed through specialized commands made just for them.

## Editing Attribute Values

There are two editing commands available that are used specifically on attributes contained within an attributed block insertion. The commands are DDATTE and ATTEDIT, both of which are discussed in Chapter 10 for complete coverage of attributes and their use with inserted blocks.

## Editing External References

Editing commands are available that are used specifically on external references: REFEDIT, XBIND, and XCLIP, which are discussed in Chapter 11, "Working with External References."

## Editing Raster Images

Three editing commands are available that are to be used specifically on raster images: IMAGECLIP, IMAGEADJUST, and TRANSPARENCY. In addition to the commands, the system variables IMAGEFRAME and IMAGEQUALITY affect the way images are displayed. The commands and system variables are discussed in the following sections.

### Clipping Images

You can clip portions of an image just as you can clip the display of an external reference. The equivalent of XCLIP (used for xrefs) is IMAGECLIP, which is designed for use on images. To issue the IMAGECLIP command, choose Clip from the Clip submenu of the

Modify menu. With IMAGECLIP, you can define a new rectangular or irregular polyline clipping boundary. You can also use the command to turn on or off the clipping boundary. To display the clipping frame of all images, turn on the system variable IMAGEFRAME by choosing Frame from the Image submenu. If the frame is not displayed, you cannot select the boundary object.

### Adjusting the Image

Several additional editing commands are available in the Image submenu. Choosing Adjust issues the IMAGEADJUST command and displays the Image Adjust dialog box (see Figure 9.19), in which you can adjust the Brightness, Contrast, and Fade settings of the selected image.

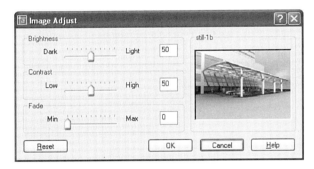

**Figure 9.19**    The Image Adjust dialog box is used to modify the appearance of raster images inside AutoCAD.

You can accelerate the display of images by setting the system variable IMAGEQUALITY to the Draft setting. IMAGEQUALITY, accessed by choosing Quality from the Image submenu, affects only the display of raster images, not the plotting of images; raster images are always plotted at the High quality setting.

### Controlling Transparency

Some raster image file formats support a transparency setting for pixels. When transparency is enabled, the graphics on the display show through the transparent pixels of the overlaid raster image. By default, images are inserted with transparency off. You can turn this setting on or off for the selected images by using the TRANSPARENCY command, issued by choosing Transparency from the Image submenu.

# Using Wipeouts

There are times when you need to edit your drawing objects but can't or really don't want to do it permanently. WIPEOUT comes to the rescue! Whereas most editing procedures actually modify the objects they manipulate, the WIPEOUT command prides itself on leaving your objects totally unharmed.

Formally, WIPEOUT was an Express Tool; however, in AutoCAD 2004, it was assimilated into the core program. The object uses a basic "white" raster object to literally *hide* the drawing space behind it.

The concept of a WIPEOUT is as simple as creating a boundary outline around the space that you want to hide. When complete, AutoCAD replaces your boundary with a WIPEOUT object that hides all objects behind it.

You can witness the simplicity of the command sequence for a 3-sided WIPEOUT:

```
Command: WIPEOUT
Specify first point or [Frames/Polyline] <Polyline>: 0,0
Specify next point: 1,0
Specify next point or [Undo]: 0.5,1
Specify next point or [Close/Undo]: CLOSE
```

AutoCAD then creates a triangular-shaped WIPEOUT. Now you should notice the Frames option at the first prompt. Normally when one makes a WIPEOUT, the purpose is to hide the area behind it AND not show the perimeter as well. Obviously, though, if you can't see the perimeter, you can't manipulate or grab the WIPEOUT object to erase it, and that can be a problem. The Frames option enables you to turn off and on the display of WIPE-OUT boundaries so that WIPEOUT objects can be selected or viewed.

Now an alternative method that many will try is to put the WIPEOUT on the Defpoints layer or a layer with the No Plot option turned on. Nice idea with most items, but not with a WIPEOUT object. This method omits the WIPEOUT from the Plot process, which is probably not what you wanted. The best solution is to use the Frames option to turn them off at the source.

**I**NSIDER **N**OTE

> When you use the Properties palette or Quick Select on a WIPEOUT, it lists as a raster image (which is what the object really is, after all). However, if you use the LIST command, it shows it as a WIPEOUT object.

The last item of note is the Polyline option. Similar to other commands such as XCLIP, you can create a closed polyline and then use it to determine the boundary for the future use of the WIPEOUT command. When you use the option, you can choose to erase the polyline or leave it.

## Editing Multilines

The MLEDIT command is designed specifically to enable you to perform specialized editing operations on mline objects. To issue the MLEDIT command, choose Multiline from the Objects submenu. Figure 9.20 shows the Multiline Edit Tools dialog box.

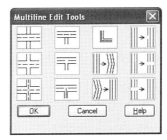

**Figure 9.20**   The Multiline Edit Tools dialog box is used to trim mlines in various configurations.

With MLEDIT, you can clean up various types of intersections of two mlines, remove or add a vertex point in an mline, and insert or heal breaks in an mline.

## Editing Polylines

The PEDIT command is designed for the editing of polylines and is issued by choosing Polyline from the Object submenu on the Modify pull-down menu. With PEDIT, you can accomplish the following tasks:

- Create a polyline from a selected line or arc.
- Close an open polyline (Close option) or open a closed polyline (Open option).
- Join additional segments to the selected polyline (Join option).
- Change the polyline's width (Width option).
- Set the polyline's Ltype generation setting (Ltype gen option).
- Fit a curve to the polyline (Fit option).
- Fit a spline to the polyline (Spline option).

- Delete the curve- or spline-fitted polyline (Decurve option).

- Move, delete, add, or change the width of individual vertex points in the polyline (Vertex option).

**INSIDER TIP**

The new PEDITACCEPT system variable enables you to preset the option for whether to convert non-polyline objects to polylines that then can be edited. This removes the prompt "Do you want to turn it into one? <Y>" when you select a non-polyline object to PEDIT. A very handy and time-saving feature!

## Editing Splines

The SPLINEDIT command is designed for the editing of splines and is issued by choosing Spline from the Objects submenu. With SPLINEDIT, you can accomplish the following tasks:

- Edit the fit points of the spline (Fit Data option).

- Open or close a spline (Open and Close options).

- Move the vertex points of the spline (Move option).

- Control the number or weighting of the control points (Refine option).

- Reverse the direction of the spline (Reverse option).

## Editing Text and Mtext

The DDEDIT command enables you to edit text and mtext objects (as well as the value of associative dimensions). The DDEDIT command is issued by choosing Edit Text from the Objects submenu on the Modify pull-down menu. If a text object is selected, a single-line text editor dialog box is displayed. If an mtext object is selected, the new Text Formatting dialog box is displayed. The drawing and editing of text is covered in detail in Chapter 14, "Text and Mtext Annotation."

# Lengthening and Shortening Objects

Any open object, such as a line or an arc, can be lengthened or shortened with the LENGTHEN command. The following listing details the options available at the initial prompt:

- **Select Object.** The default option involves selecting an object. When an object is selected, its length is displayed, and the initial prompt is redisplayed. The length value is shown using the current units setting for both style and precision. However, this value can contain round-off error.

- **DElta.** Use this option to specify the length by which the object is to be lengthened or shortened. Enter a positive value to lengthen the object or a negative value to shorten the object. If the object to be affected is an arc, you have the option of entering a change in the arc length (the default) or a change in the included angle.

- **Percent.** Use this option to define the change as a percentage, where 100 percent is the original length. Enter a percentage greater than 100 percent to lengthen the object or a percentage less than 100 percent to shorten the object.

- **Total.** Use this option when you know the final length you want the object to have.

- **DYnamic.** Use this option to dynamically drag the endpoint to the desired location. In dragging the endpoint of the object, the alignment of the object cannot change.

  After defining the amount of change to be applied, pick the object to be affected. The endpoint nearest the point used to select the object is the endpoint that is moved, so pick closer to the endpoint that you want to affect when selecting.

As a general rule, when using the DElta, Percent, or Total option, pick a point on the portion of the line to which the edit is to be applied.

# Aligning Objects

The ALIGN command initially was conceived as a 3D editing command, which explains why it is found in the 3D Operation submenu of the Modify pull-down menu. In 2D work, however, ALIGN can also be very helpful. In effect, it is a combination of the MOVE, ROTATE, and SCALE commands. ALIGN typically is used to align one object with another object (see Figure 9.21).

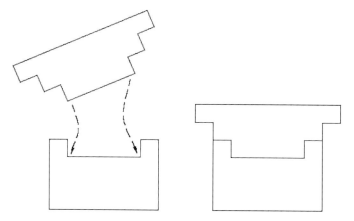

**Figure 9.21**   The ALIGN command is very useful for moving and rotating objects in one command.

After selecting the objects to be aligned, you are prompted to specify up to three pairs of points. Each pair consists of a source point and a destination point. The source point is a point on the object to be aligned, and the destination point is the corresponding point on the object to which you want to align.

As you can see in Figure 9.21, you must specify only two pairs of points in 2D work—simply press Enter when prompted for the third pair. The selected objects are moved from the first source point to the first destination point. Then the objects are rotated such that the edge defined by the first and second source points is aligned with the edge defined by the first and second destination points.

Finally, you have the option to scale the objects such that the length defined by the first and second source points is adjusted to be equal to the length defined by the first and second destination points. In effect, this scaling option serves the same function as the Reference option of the SCALE command.

### Exercise 9.3    Editing with *LENGTHEN* and *ALIGN*

1. Open drawing 09EX03.dwg that accompanies the CD with this book.

2. By using the VIEW command, choose the view OFFICE-E and make it current.

3. From the Modify pull-down menu, choose 3D Operation, Align. This initiates the ALIGN command for use.

4. At the Select objects prompt, type **c** and press Enter. At the Specify first corner prompt, type point **98',65'** and press Enter. At the Specify opposite corner prompt, type **79',67'** and press Enter. Then press Enter to end selection of objects. This selects the first series of five file drawers in the upper part of the room (see Figure 9.22).

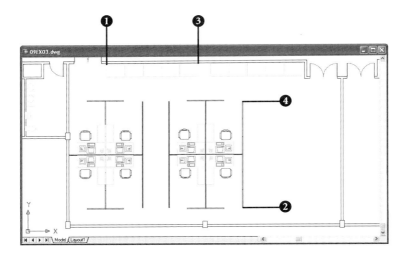

**Figure 9.22**    The office room used for the ALIGN and LENGTHEN exercise.

5. Turn on a running Osnap Endpoint if it is not active. At the Specify first source point prompt, pick at ❶. At the Specify first destination point prompt, pick at ❷. This establishes the first set of transformation points.

6. At the Specify second source point prompt, pick at ❸. At the Specify second destination point prompt, pick at ❹. This establishes the second set of transformation points.

7. At the Specify third source point or <continue> prompt, press Enter to accept the default. Do the same at the Scale objects based on alignment points prompt (press Enter to accept the default).

8. The file drawers then align with the workstation panels starting at ❷ with an angle through ❹.

9. Now start the COPY command, then select the two vertical wall lines on the right side of the room and press Enter to end the selection. At the Specify Base point prompt, type **-10',0** and press Enter twice. See Figure 9.23.

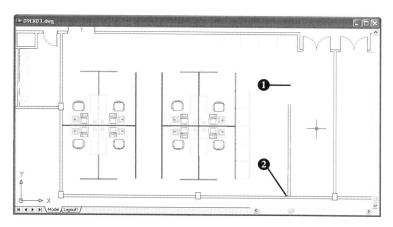

**Figure 9.23**   The modified file drawers and new interior wall.

10. Now use LENGTHEN to adjust the wall. From the Modify pull-down menu, choose Lengthen. At the Select an object or [DElta/Percent/Total/DYnamic] prompt, type **T** and press Enter. At the Specify total length or [Angle] prompt, type **20'** and press Enter.

11. At the Select an object to change or [Undo] prompt, pick a point at the top of each of the two new lines near ❶ in Figure 9.23. Press Enter to exit the command. As you select each line, it shortens to a total length of 20' from the opposite end selected.

12. Press Enter to restart the LENGTHEN command. At the Select an object or [DElta/Percent/Total/DYnamic] prompt, type **DE** for a delta distance. At the Enter delta length or [Angle] prompt, type **9"** and press Enter. Now pick a point on each of the two new lines near ❷. Press Enter to exit the command. Because this value is positive, the lines grow in length. If you had typed a negative number, the lines would shorten in length.

You may now close the drawing; it is not necessary to save.

As you work in your drawings, you may want to cleanse your drawing of unneeded data. In the following sections, you will be exposed to renaming and purging objects from the current drawing.

# Renaming Named Objects

AutoCAD objects fall into two inclusive categories: named and unnamed objects. *Named objects* are items that you name when you create them and are referred to by their assigned names. Examples of named objects include layers, block definitions, and text styles. *Unnamed objects* are objects such as lines, circles, and arcs and cannot be assigned individual names.

Sometimes, you need to rename a layer or a block because of changing conditions or simple typographic errors committed when you initially created the objects. To rename a named object, you can use the Rename dialog box (see Figure 9.24), which is invoked by choosing Rename from the Format pull-down menu.

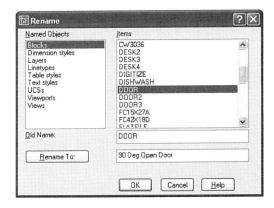

**Figure 9.24**   The Rename dialog box is used to rename named objects such as Blocks.

After you choose the type of object to be renamed, a list of the existing objects of that type is displayed. To change a name in the Items list, you first select the specific object to be renamed, and its name appears in the Old Name edit box. Type the new name in the edit box to the right of the Rename To button, then click Rename To: in order to queue the name change.

**INSIDER NOTE**

> Layer 0 is the only layer that cannot be renamed, which accounts for why this layer is never displayed as part of the list of layers that can be renamed. Layers may be deleted from the Layer Properties Manager in addition to being purged by the PURGE command.

**I**NSIDER **C**AUTION

> You have the ability to rename default objects named Standard. However, I have per-
> sonally experienced some level of drawing corruption due to a drawing missing those
> default named objects. If at all possible, it is recommended that you leave both the
> Standard dimension style and Standard text style as-is and create your own new
> named objects.

Any changes entered into the Rename dialog box will not actually be processed until you click OK and the dialog box closes. Every valid modification you make changes visually in the dialog box, but they don't actually occur if you exit the dialog box by clicking the Cancel button. Consequently, you cannot rename one item to the name of a previously renamed item because it would not be unique to the RENAME command session.

# Deleting Named Objects

Often, you will find unneeded layers or linetypes; you should delete these objects from the drawing to clean up the drawing database.

The act of removing a named object from the database is referred to as *purging* the object. This action is performed with the PURGE dialog box, which is invoked by choosing Purge from the Drawing Utilities submenu of the File menu (see Figure 9.25). From the dialog box, you can choose to purge all named objects or limit the command to a specific type of named object, such as text styles.

**Figure 9.25**   The Purge dialog box provides an intuitive interface.

**I**NSIDER **T**IP

> The traditional method of purging is still available by the use of the -PURGE command, if so desired.

Named objects that are not used, such as a layer with no objects drawn on it, are referred to as unreferenced objects. Only unreferenced objects can be purged from a drawing. Whenever PURGE finds a named object suitable for removal, you are prompted to confirm the removal prior to the object being deleted.

**I**NSIDER **N**OTE

> Layer 0 can never be purged, even if it is unreferenced and unused.

Although saved User Coordinate Systems, views, and viewport configurations are named objects and can be renamed with the RENAME command, PURGE does not give you the option of deleting these types of objects. Instead, if you want to remove these objects, you must use the command that manages them. For example, you must use the right-click shortcut menu item Delete or the Delete button in the View dialog box to delete a named view. Use UCSMAN to delete a named UCS and use the VPORTS right-click menu to delete named viewport configurations.

As seen in this section, renaming and purging objects in your drawings is an easy task. Regular usage of these commands keeps drawings clean and maintains minimal file sizes.

# Summary

This completes the discussion of the advanced editing commands. This chapter introduced you to grip editing and the available object-specific editing commands. To learn more about how and when to create and edit the objects discussed with the object-specific editing commands, please refer to the chapters cited in the text. In the next chapter, you learn how to create and use blocks, a very important productivity tool.

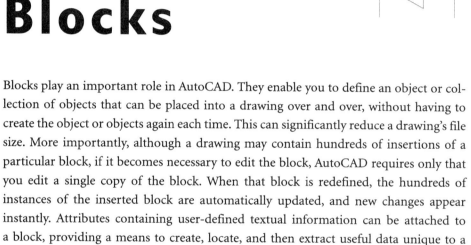

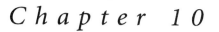
*C h a p t e r   1 0*

# Creating and Using Blocks

Blocks play an important role in AutoCAD. They enable you to define an object or collection of objects that can be placed into a drawing over and over, without having to create the object or objects again each time. This can significantly reduce a drawing's file size. More importantly, although a drawing may contain hundreds of insertions of a particular block, if it becomes necessary to edit the block, AutoCAD requires only that you edit a single copy of the block. When that block is redefined, the hundreds of instances of the inserted block are automatically updated, and new changes appear instantly. Attributes containing user-defined textual information can be attached to a block, providing a means to create, locate, and then extract useful data unique to a particular block insertion.

This chapter discusses the following subjects:

- Defining and inserting blocks
- Creating and incorporating attributes
- Modifying blocks with the in-place reference editing feature
- Using nested blocks
- Attribute editing commands
- Attribute management tools
- Managing blocks effectively

# Understanding Blocks

A block is a collection of individual objects combined into a larger single object. Think of the block as the parent of a family, and think of the individual objects as the parent's children. Although the children have identities of their own (color, layer, lineweight, and linetype), they are also under the control of their parent, which has its own color, layer, lineweight, and linetype properties.

The fact that both the block (parent) and its individual objects (children) have their own properties makes it important to understand how these properties are affected by certain conditions. For example, assume that a block has been created from several objects and that each object was originally created on its own layer. The layers on which the objects were created can be frozen individually. If one of these layers is frozen, the corresponding object that resides on that layer gets frozen and becomes invisible. However, the other objects in the block remain visible because the layers they are on are still thawed. In contrast, if the parent block is inserted on a layer and that layer is then frozen, all its objects become frozen. This is true even when the layers on which the child objects reside are on and thawed.

## The Block Definition Dialog Box

The Block Definition dialog box is the most common method used to create new blocks. You can access "Make Block" from the Draw toolbar or the Draw pull-down menu by choosing Block, Make. The command dialog is shown in Figure 10.1.

**Figure 10.1** The Block Definition dialog box.

The following list describes the dialog box's features:

- **Name.** This is where you specify the name of the block. This task is streamlined by use of the drop-down list. The list displays the names of all currently defined blocks. In addition to displaying block names, by selecting a name, you can display all its current settings and then redefine any or all of its values.

- **Base point.** This enables you to define the X,Y,Z insertion coordinates for the block. You can enter the coordinate values in the appropriate edit boxes, or you can click the Pick Point button and specify the insertion base point by selecting a point on the screen.

  The base point value is saved with the block and represents the point in the block that AutoCAD uses to define the block's position when it's inserted in the drawing. This point is also used by the object snap Insert when elements of blocks are selected.

- **Objects.** This area controls various options when selecting objects that define a new block, and it displays the number of objects selected.

  If you click the Select Objects button, you can then choose the objects that make up the block definition on-screen.

  Clicking the Quick Select button (the funnel/lightning bolt icon at the upper right) displays the Quick Select dialog box, which enables you to select objects based on filter criteria. For example, you can select all CIRCLE objects whose color is blue.

  Refer to Chapter 8, "Obtaining Object Information," for more information on using the Quick Select command.

  The Retain, Convert to Block, and Delete option buttons tell AutoCAD what to do with the selected objects after the block is defined. When you retain the objects, they are left in the drawing and are not converted to a block after AutoCAD defines the new block. When you convert the objects to a block, the original objects are erased and then the block is inserted as a single block using the original location. When you delete the objects, AutoCAD erases them from the drawing after the new block is defined.

- **Preview icon.** This controls whether AutoCAD creates an image of the new block and saves it with the block definition. You can display the image when viewing blocks by selecting a block name, using the AutoCAD DesignCenter (discussed in Chapter 12, "Applications for DesignCenter"), or by using the latest version of Windows Explorer.

- **Drag-and-drop units.** This feature specifies the units to which the block is scaled when it's inserted from the AutoCAD DesignCenter. You can choose from numerous unit types including feet, inches, or millimeters. This feature is also discussed in Chapter 12.

- **Description.** This feature enables you to provide a detailed description of the block definition. The description is displayed when it's selected in the BLOCK command and when blocks are viewed using the AutoCAD DesignCenter.

- **Hyperlink.** This button enables you to associate a hyperlink with the new block. When the block is inserted, the hyperlink is already there for use as needed and can be activated from any object within the block.

## Defining Blocks

What happens inside a drawing when a new block is defined? If you have created blocks before, you know that when you finish the BLOCK command, all your objects disappear from the screen (if you choose the Delete option). This happens because AutoCAD can automatically erase them after they have been used to define a block.

**I**NSIDER **T**IP

> Use the OOPS command to un-erase the objects. The OOPS command can always be used to un-erase the most recently erased selection set. This is true even if several other commands have been executed since the object(s) were erased.

It can seem silly that AutoCAD erases a block's originating objects. After all, one typically creates the objects where they are needed in the first place. However, there is a logical reason why AutoCAD erases the objects.

The BLOCK command is more than another type of COPY command; it enables you to place duplicates of your collection of child objects, and that uses less file space. It minimizes the file size of an AutoCAD drawing by storing each child object's property data in a place AutoCAD calls the *Block Table*. It stores this information under the name of the parent block. When you insert a block into AutoCAD, instead of duplicating the property data of each child object (as the COPY command does), AutoCAD simply refers to the property data stored in the Block Table. It then graphically draws the child objects based upon this data. This enables AutoCAD to store each child object's property data in just one place, the Block Table. You can, therefore, insert multiple instances of a block, duplicating the child objects where needed. In each case, AutoCAD refers back to the

Block Table for the data it needs to show the child objects. Consequently, you would typically erase the original objects after they are used to define a block because you would probably want to reinsert those objects as a block in order to reduce the file size of your drawing.

## The Effect of the Current UCS on Block Definitions

When you create a block, you must define its insertion base point. This point's coordinates are relative to the block object and are set to its 0,0,0. Consequently, when you define a block's insertion base point, even though the current UCS (User-defined Coordinate System) coordinates may be 43.5,71.3,22.5 when you pick them, AutoCAD ignores these values and stores the block's insertion base point as 0,0,0. This is true in both paper space and model space. If you were then to export this block out as its own drawing using the WBLOCK command, the insertion base point would be at 0,0,0 of the WCS (World Coordinate System) in the new drawing. This feature enables predictable insertion of blocks.

**I**NSIDER **T**IP

> AutoCAD remembers the series of commands you enter at the command prompt. Therefore, you can recall the previously entered commands by pressing the up arrow on your keyboard. Each time you press the up arrow, you move back through the previous commands. You can also press the down arrow to move forward through the previous commands. When the desired command is displayed, press Enter to execute the command.
>
> You can also use the right-click shortcut menu, either for the most recently used command by right-clicking in the drawing area, or for a list of recent commands by right-clicking over the command-line area.

**I**NSIDER **N**OTE

> AutoCAD ignores the current UCS coordinate values in paper space and model space when defining a block's insertion base point.

**I**NSIDER **T**IP

> When you're defining the insertion base point of a new block, simply understand that AutoCAD is temporarily redefining the UCS origin to the point you pick.

In addition to understanding how AutoCAD deals with the current UCS's coordinates when defining a block, you must also understand the effect the current UCS's X-axis orientation has on the angle a block assumes when it is inserted into a drawing.

> **I**NSIDER **TIP**
>
> You can use the BASE command to change the insertion point for a drawing file that will be used for a block via the INSERT command or by a external reference via the XREF command.

When creating a block, AutoCAD uses the current UCS to determine its insertion angle. This angle is oriented relative to the current UCS's X-axis.

To demonstrate the effect of the current UCS orientation, the following exercise walks you through inserting two different arrowhead blocks into an existing drawing.

### Exercise 10.1 Examining the Effect of the Current UCS's Orientation

1. Open the 10EX01.dwg drawing file on the accompanying CD.

    The drawing contains two sets of objects that appear on the right side of your screen. Both sets are made up of a closed polygon in the shape of an arrowhead with a text object inside. The first set was used to create a block definition called AR1. The second set was used to create a block definition called AR2.

    It is important to note the X-axis orientation relative to the two arrowheads. Both arrowheads were defined as blocks with the same UCS orientation. As a consequence, when you insert each block during this exercise, you will see the effect the current UCS orientation has on the inserted objects.

    Now you will insert the AR1 block.

2. From the Insert pull-down menu, choose Block. The Insert dialog box opens.

3. Choose AR1 from the Name drop-down list if it is not already displayed.

4. In the Insertion point area, be sure the Specify On-screen option is selected. In the Scale and Rotation areas, make sure the Specify On-screen option is cleared.

5. Click OK to close the Insert dialog box. The dialog box closes, and the AR1 block object appears. Notice that the arrowhead is oriented in the same direction as the original AR1 objects that appears on the lower-right side of your screen.

6. Choose a location in the lower-left portion of the drawing to insert the arrowhead.

    Now you will insert the AR2 block.

**7.** From the Insert pull-down menu, choose Block to open the Insert dialog box.

**8.** Choose AR2 from the Name drop-down list.

**9.** Click OK to close the Insert dialog box. The dialog box closes, and the AR2 block object appears. Notice that the arrowhead is oriented in the same direction as the original AR2 objects that appears on the upper-right side of your screen.

**10.** Choose a location in the upper-left portion of the drawing to insert the arrowhead. Your drawing should look similar to Figure 10.2.

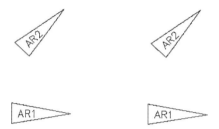

**Figure 10.2**    The two arrowhead blocks are inserted along with their original block objects.

Next, you change the rotation of the WCS about its Z-axis. Then you redefine the AR2 block to see the effect the revised UCS has on the block's rotation.

**11.** From the Tools pull-down menu, choose New UCS, and then choose Z.

**12.** At the `Specify rotation angle about Z axis <90>` prompt, type **45**.

Notice that the UCS's X-axis arrow is now rotated parallel to the AR2 objects in the upper-right corner.

**13.** From the Draw pull-down menu, choose Block, Make. The Block Definition dialog box opens.

**14.** From the Name drop-down list, choose AR2.

**15.** In the Base Point area, click the Pick Point button. The Block Definition dialog box temporarily disappears, enabling you to pick an insertion point for the block.

**16.** Using an Endpoint snap, select the tip of the AR2 arrowhead object in the upper-right corner. AutoCAD captures the coordinates for the pick point and displays the values in the Block Definition dialog box.

**17.** In the Object area, choose the Select Objects button. The Block Definition dialog box temporarily disappears, enabling you to select the objects.

18. Select the two AR2 objects in the upper-right corner and press Enter. AutoCAD displays the Block Definition dialog box, noting that two objects are selected. Make sure to set the Retain objects option.

19. Click OK. AutoCAD displays a message noting that the AR2 block is already defined and asks if you want to redefine it.

20. Choose Yes to redefine the AR2 block and close the warning dialog box.

    AutoCAD redefines the AR2 block definition using the current UCS's X-axis orientation and regenerates the drawing. Note the change in orientation of the AR2 block in the upper-left corner.

    Next, you will set the UCS back to the World Coordinate System and insert the AR2 block.

21. From the Tools pull-down menu, choose New UCS, World.

22. From the Insert pull-down menu, choose Block to open the Insert dialog box.

23. Choose AR2 from the Name drop-down list.

24. Click OK to close the Insert dialog box. The dialog box closes, and the AR2 Insert object appears. Notice that the arrowhead is now oriented in the same direction as the World Coordinate System X-axis.

25. Choose a location near the center of the drawing to insert the arrowhead. Your drawing should look similar to Figure 10.3. Notice that both AR2 block insertions align parallel to the World Coordinate System X-axis.

    Close the drawing without saving.

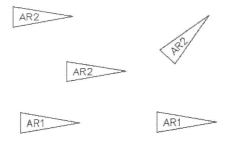

**Figure 10.3**   The redefined AR2 block is inserted.

This exercise shows how the current UCS affects a block's orientation when it is created and then inserted into a drawing. By understanding this behavior, you can better control how blocks are inserted into drawings and thereby maintain a higher level of productivity.

# Inserting Blocks

Several commands can be used to insert blocks. Understanding the unique features of these commands is important in selecting the right tool for a particular task.

> **INSIDER NOTE**
>
> You can browse web sites for blocks to insert into your drawing.

## INSERT *and* -INSERT

The INSERT and -INSERT commands are used to insert blocks. The INSERT command gets insertion information using the Insert dialog box, whereas -INSERT prompts for the information at AutoCAD's command prompt. The Insert dialog box interface makes it easy to select blocks already stored in the current drawing's Block Table. The Insert dialog box also makes it easy to search for blocks stored outside the current drawing by choosing the Browse button.

> **INSIDER TIP**
>
> When you use script files to perform repetitious commands, AutoCAD automatically uses the command-line version of the commands. Therefore, you can use the -INSERT command to understand the series of options the script file will need to address to ensure that the script functions correctly.

> **INSIDER NOTE**
>
> To use the standard command ACAD.PGP alias of the INSERT command, at the command prompt, simply type **I** to open the Insert dialog box, or type **-I** at the command prompt to start the command line version of the INSERT command.
>
> Learn more about the ACAD.PGP and other customization in Chapter 22, "Customizing Without Programming."

## MINSERT *Versus* ARRAY

Sometimes, it may be necessary to insert a block as a rectangular array. Two options exist to accomplish this—MINSERT and ARRAY.

### The *MINSERT* Command

First, the MINSERT command is a combination of the INSERT and ARRAY commands. When executed, the first command line prompts are the typical ones for inserting a block. After that, the typical command line prompts for creating an array appear. The exception is that MINSERT can only create rectangular arrays. Therefore, no option is available for selecting a polar array.

One drawback to this command is that the MINSERT object cannot be exploded, nor can its individual objects be moved or edited. The advantage to using this command, however, is that less file space is required to define the MINSERT object, which reduces the file size of your drawing. It is important to note that the reduction in file size can be dramatic. For example, a simple block inserted as an array of 100×100 using the MINSERT command will have little, if any, impact on the file's size. In contrast, the same number of blocks inserted using the ARRAY command can increase the file's size by 500k or more.

If you need to insert an array of blocks and you will not need to explode or edit the objects, then use the MINSERT command. Otherwise, use the ARRAY command discussed in the next section.

### The *ARRAY* Command

The ARRAY command accomplishes the same thing as the MINSERT command, but it affords you more control over the inserted objects. With the ARRAY command, you can choose between rectangular and polar arrays. Also, after the array is created, you can explode the inserted objects individually or move them independently of the other Insert objects. To use the ARRAY command with a block, however, you must first use the INSERT command to create the first block object; then you can use the ARRAY command to create the desired array.

The disadvantage of using the ARRAY command is that multiple insertions of the block object are made, which therefore increases your drawing's complexity and file size to a degree. However, this is still a much smaller increase than if the arrayed objects were not contained in a block.

## *MEASURE and DIVIDE*

The MEASURE and DIVIDE commands provide two methods of inserting a block along a path. This can be very helpful when laying out regularly spaced objects like street lights.

## The *MEASURE* Command

The MEASURE command enables you to insert a block in multiple places along a line, arc, or polyline at a given distance. To demonstrate, the next exercise shows you how to create a series of rectangles along the centerline of a street design. By creating a block of a rectangle and inserting it at the appropriate distances along a centerline path, you can quickly create a series of viewport guides. For this particular drawing, the guides can be used to define the various plan view sections for street improvement plans.

### Exercise 10.2    Using *MEASURE* to Set a Series of Blocks Along a Path

1.  Open the 10EX02.dwg drawing file on the accompanying CD. This file contains a typical street centerline with right-of-way lines. A block called Viewport exists in the Block Table. This block consists of a rectangle with an insertion base point located in the center of the rectangle. The rectangle is 400 units wide by 1,000 units long.

    You will use the MEASURE command to insert this block every 800 units along the centerline.

2.  From the Draw pull-down menu, select Point, Measure. AutoCAD prompts for the object to measure.

3.  Select near the left end of the red centerline.

4.  At the Specify length of segment or [Block] prompt, type **B** to select block and then press Enter.

5.  At the Enter name of block to insert prompt, type the block name **Viewport** and then press Enter.

6.  At the Align block with object? [Yes/No] <Y> prompt, type **Y** and then press Enter.

7.  At the Specify length of segment prompt, type a segment length of **800** and then press Enter. AutoCAD creates many Viewport blocks along the centerline path, placing one every 800 units, as shown in Figure 10.4.

    Leave this drawing open for the following exercise.

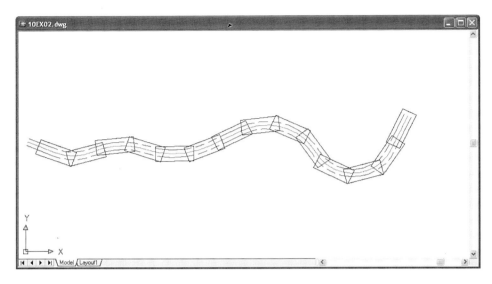

**Figure 10.4**    The MEASURE command places the Viewport blocks along a path.

## The *DIVIDE* Command

The DIVIDE command enables you to insert a block along a line, arc, or polyline any given number of times. Suppose you must draw a series of manholes along the street centerline in the previous example. In order to place the Manhole block, you can use the DIVIDE command to insert 30 copies of it along the centerline path.

### Exercise 10.3    Using *DIVIDE* to Insert 30 Manhole Blocks Along a Path

1.  Continue with the previous drawing, or open the 10EX03.dwg drawing file on the accompanying CD.

2.  From the Draw pull-down menu, select Point, Divide. AutoCAD prompts for the object to divide.

3.  Select near the left end of the red centerline.

4.  At the Enter the number of segments or [Block] prompt, type **B** to select block and then press Enter.

5. At the `Enter name of block to insert` prompt, type the block name **Manhole** and then press Enter.

6. At the `Align block with object? [Yes/No] <Y>` prompt, type **Y** to align the block with the selected object and then press Enter.

7. At the `Enter the number of segments` prompt, type a segment number of **30** and then press Enter. AutoCAD draws 30 evenly spaced Manhole blocks along the centerline path, as shown in Figure 10.5. Note, however, that the Manhole blocks are not placed at either end of the polyline.

You can now close the drawing without saving.

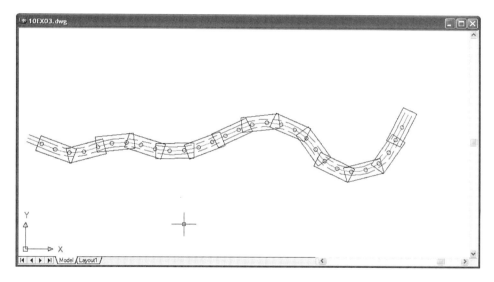

**Figure 10.5**   The `DIVIDE` command evenly spaces the Manhole blocks along a path.

---

**INSIDER NOTE**

When you're inserting blocks into a drawing, it is important for you to remember that AutoCAD aligns the block's coordinate system parallel to the current UCS. This feature not only affects the insertion angle of the block, but it also affects the rotation angle. If the rotation angle is assigned when a block is inserted, the rotation angle is relative to the current UCS. This is true in both paper space and model space.

## *Windows-Based Insertion Features*

AutoCAD 2005 utilizes a Multiple Document Environment (MDE), which enables you to open multiple drawings in a single AutoCAD session. This feature works in the same fashion as other Windows applications, such as Microsoft Word.

There are many advantages to opening several drawings in a session of AutoCAD, and two of them relate to blocks. Along with the other benefits of MDE, these new features enable you to either cut and paste or drag and drop objects from one drawing to another. Additionally, you are given the option of inserting the objects as a block.

### Cut and Paste Block Insertion

The phrase "cut and paste" refers to the process of selecting an object or group of objects and cutting or copying them to the Windows clipboard. When you cut selected objects, they are copied to the clipboard and erased from the original document. In contrast, when you copy objects, they are copied to the clipboard, but the selected objects are left untouched in the original document.

AutoCAD 2005 enables you to identify the base point of an object when copying it to the clipboard. This very powerful feature provides you with the control to specifically identify the new insertion point of the selected object.

When you insert the block from the clipboard, you can paste it using either a selected base point or the block's original coordinates. The Paste to Original Coordinates option, found on the shortcut menu and on the Edit pull-down menu, copies the coordinate location of the objects in the original drawing and then pastes the objects in the new drawing using those same coordinates. This option is useful for copying objects from one drawing to another when both drawings use the same coordinate system. You must have previously saved a base point to have access to the Paste to Original Coordinates option.

### Drag and Drop Block Insertion

When you drag and drop objects, you are moving or copying them from one place to another. When you drag and drop objects within the same AutoCAD drawing, the result is the same as using the MOVE command to move the object. When you drag and drop from one drawing to another, the result is similar to copying the object from the original drawing to the target drawing.

The drag and drop feature is useful for quickly moving or copying objects. However, this method does not provide a method for accurately selecting the base point for pasting the objects as a block. Consequently, to select objects in one drawing and paste them as a block in another while controlling the new block's base point, use the copy and paste feature described in the previous section.

**I**NSIDER **N**OTE

> You can also drag and drop drawing files from Windows Explorer into a drawing. When you utilize a right-click drag method, you get additional features: Insert Here, Open, Create Xref, and Create Hyperlink Here. A great timesaver method to take advantage of!

# Block Reference

When you insert a block, you are actually creating an Insert object. The Insert object references a particular set of block data in the Block Table. This is called a Block reference. AutoCAD uses the Block reference to find the data stored in the Block Table. It uses this data to draw the child objects that make up the Insert object.

Although only one set of data in the Block Table is used to define a block, multiple block references can refer to that data. In fact, there is no limit to the number of Insert objects you can create. In each case, AutoCAD uses the Block reference to find the data it needs to draw the Insert object.

## Behavior of Block Properties

There are three properties of blocks that behave in different ways depending on their settings when the block is defined. The color, linetype, and lineweight properties can behave in different but predictable ways when defined on the 0 layer as opposed to other layers. In addition, you can define these properties explicitly by selecting particular values, or you can define them implicitly as ByLayer or ByBlock.

## The Effect of Creating Blocks on Layers Other Than 0

The simplest way to control the appearance of a block is to define it on a particular layer and thereby explicitly define child objects' color, linetype, and lineweight. For example, suppose you have created a circle object on a layer called Circles. To explicitly define its color, open the Modify menu and choose Properties. When AutoCAD displays the Properties palette, select the circle. When the palette displays the circle's properties, select a color from the Color property drop-down list, or choose the Select color option from the list to display the Select Color dialog box. The Properties palette now lists the color you chose as the property of the circle and changes the circle object's color to reflect the modified property. You have just defined the color value explicitly. As a consequence, if you use the circle object to define a block and the block is inserted into the drawing, its color will be constant. It will always be the color you explicitly defined.

In contrast, if you implicitly define an object's color, linetype, and lineweight by choosing ByLayer, altering the layer properties the original object existed on when it was defined as a block changes the object's appearance in the block. For example, suppose the circle object in the previous example is used to define a block. Also suppose the circle's color, linetype, and lineweight are defined as ByLayer, and the circle object is on a layer called Circle. When the block containing the circle object is inserted into the drawing, altering the color, linetype, or lineweight of the Circle layer changes the circle object's color, linetype, or lineweight. This is true no matter what layer the block is inserted on. When a child object's color, linetype, and lineweight properties are set to ByLayer, those properties are determined by the values of the child object's original layer.

## The Effect of Creating Blocks on Layer 0

Layer 0 has a unique feature. When a block is defined from child objects created on the 0 layer, AutoCAD assigns special properties to that block if its color, linetype, and lineweight properties are set to ByLayer or ByBlock. This feature can be very powerful.

**INSIDER NOTE**

Another property that may be set to ByLayer or ByBlock is the Plot Style property. The Plot Style property is discussed in Chapter 19, "Productive Plotting."

If ByLayer is used to define a child object's color, linetype, lineweight, and, if applicable, the plot style, the layer on which the block is inserted controls the child object's appearance properties.

The following exercise demonstrates the effects of inserting a block whose color, linetype, and lineweight properties have been set to ByLayer.

### Exercise 10.4   Inserting a Block with ByLayer Properties

1. Open the 10EX04.dwg file on the accompanying CD. The screen is blank, containing no objects. In this drawing file, two blocks are already defined. The block C1 is a circle created on layer 0 with its color, linetype, and lineweight properties set to ByLayer. The block C2 is a circle created on layer 0 with its color, linetype, and lineweight properties set to ByBlock.

   Note that on the Layers and Properties toolbars, the current layer is BLUE, and the layer's color, linetype, and lineweight properties are set to ByLayer.

2. From the Insert pull-down menu, choose Block. The Insert dialog box appears.

3. From the Name drop-down list, choose the C1 block.

4. In the Insertion Point area, be sure the Specify On-Screen option is selected. In the Scale and Rotation areas, make sure the Specify On-Screen option is cleared.

5. Click OK to close the Insert dialog box.

6. Choose a location on the left side of the screen where you want to insert the block. The C1 block is inserted and assumes the color, linetype, and lineweight of the BLUE layer's property values. Remember, this occurs because the block's child objects were created on layer 0, and their property values for color, linetype, and lineweight were set to ByLayer.

   Leave this drawing open for the following exercise.

In contrast, if ByBlock is used to define a child object's color, linetype, and lineweight, the current Object Creation values control the child object's color, linetype, and lineweight values. This is true no matter which layer the block is inserted on. These values are controlled from the Properties toolbars.

The following exercise demonstrates the effect of inserting the C2 block whose color, linetype, and lineweight properties have been set to ByBlock.

### Exercise 10.5   Inserting a Block with ByBlock Properties

1. Continue from the previous exercise or if needed open 10EX04.dwg. Using the Properties toolbar, change the Color property to Magenta, change the Linetype property to Hidden2, and change the Lineweight property to 0.50mm.

2. From the Insert menu, choose Block. The Insert dialog box appears.

3. From the Name drop-down list, choose the C2 block. Click OK to close the Insert dialog box.

4. Choose a location on the right side of the screen to insert the block.

Now if you show lineweights on-screen by using the LWT button on the status bar, your screen should look similar to Figure 10.6. Notice that the C1 block acquired the Color, Linetype, and Lineweight property values based on the layer's values, whereas the C2 block acquired the Color, Linetype, and Lineweight property values set in the Properties toolbar.

You can now close this drawing without saving.

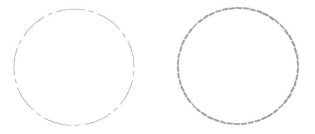

**Figure 10.6** The effects of ByLayer and ByBlock on inserted blocks.

**I**NSIDER **N**OTE

DEFPOINTS is another layer that AutoCAD deals with uniquely. AutoCAD automatically creates this layer any time you draw associative dimensions. The unique property of this layer is that objects residing on this layer are not be plotted. Also, point objects placed on this layer only ever appear as a single pixel dot.

**I**NSIDER **C**AUTION

Autodesk formally does not recommend that users place objects on the DEFPOINTS layer. Instead, utilize a layer with the No Plot option activated to ensure items won't plot.

**I**NSIDER **C**AUTION

Objects that didn't plot have occasionally frustrated users because they could see them on-screen. Often the problem was that the objects, including blocks, were accidentally placed on the DEFPOINTS layer.

# Creating Attributes in Blocks

When you begin utilizing blocks for their repetitive application benefits, you will soon want to extend that usage to include text. Now as you have experienced in earlier chapters, you can easily place text objects in a block definition. But what if you need text objects that can change content value *and* be in a block? You then need to utilize attributes.

## The Attribute Definition

When you create an attribute object within a drawing (outside of a block), it is known as an *attribute definition*. This object is created using the ATTDEF command, and the attribution definition contains three primary properties: a tag, a prompt, and a value (see Figure 10.7).

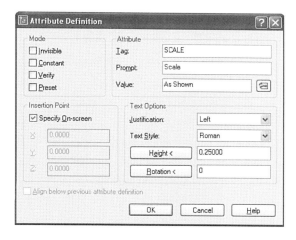

**Figure 10.7**   You create attribute definitions by using the ATTDEF dialog box.

The Tag value is a simple code word (spaces are not permitted) that will appear in AutoCAD when the object exists as an attribute definition. When it is contained within a block, it becomes an *attribute*. The Tag value also changes to full uppercase text no matter what you type during its naming.

Next is the Prompt value. This is the prompt that is shown when the block is inserted in which to populate the attribute value. Here, you can use any text style, lettering case, or special characters as well as spaces. Later on, we will discuss how this prompting can be suppressed if needed.

Last is the default value. Here, you can provide for the user a default starting value that can be accepted or replaced. This is used when the block is inserted and AutoCAD prompts for an attribute value. If your attributes tend to contain the same value, then setting a default can be a timesaver.

### The ATTDEF Modes

Within the Attribute Definitions dialog box is a Modes area that contains four control options:

- **Invisible.** Enabling this option makes your attribute value invisible when inserted as part of a block. This can be helpful for tracking information that has no viewing or plotting purpose. However, this can be disabled using the ATTDISP system variable as needed for viewing.

- **Constant.** This enables you to create an attribute that has a constant value. This may seem redundant, but having an attribute that can't change can be helpful, for instance, when exporting information to a data file.

- **Verify.** Perhaps you might want to double-check your attribute values after inserting a block. This feature prompts you to verify everything you just entered again. Not used much, obviously.

- **Preset.** If you are fairly confident the value does not need to be changed often, consider the Present option. It ignores the option of prompting for a value, using the default value instead. You can edit it later as needed.

### Insertion and Text Options

These are fairly self-explanatory. The Insertion point is where you want to place the Attribute Definition when done. Most use the Specify On-screen option and place as needed. The Text Options are similar to other text controls; you need to define a justification, style, height, and rotation in which to create the Attribute Definition. Of course, after you create the object, if you need to adjust something, you can use the Properties palette to change various characteristics.

The Align below previous attribute definitions toggle is something you need occasionally. Attributes by their very nature are single-line text entities. So when multiple lines of "text" attributes need to be aligned, you can use this toggle to get them to line up one after another as you create them. You could, of course, move them to align later anyway.

# Creating Attribute Definitions for Blocks

Attributes are very powerful and simple elements that have proven to be easy to create and include in block objects. The following exercise walks you through a typical use.

### Exercise 10.6    Developing and Utilizing Block Attributes

1. Open the file 10EX06.dwg from the accompanying CD. The drawing contains the various objects needed to create a basic detail title block. We already have the circle and line, along with the number and scale info. The last attribute needed for this block is the title itself.

2. Using the Draw pull-down, choose Block, Define Attributes. The Attribute Definition dialog box appears. Figure 10.8 shows the values we need.

3. Using the Attribute Definition dialog box, fill in the various settings to "build" our attribute. Enter the settings as shown in Figure 10.8.

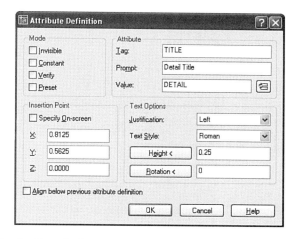

**Figure 10.8**    The Attribute Definition dialog box values to create a detail title.

4. Now adjust the text options. We want Roman and 0.25" text.

5. As for the insertion point, we know exactly where it needs to go so it can be entered here in Figure 10.8. Input the X and Y values as shown.

6. After your dialog matches Figure 10.8, press the OK button. AutoCAD immediately creates the Attribute Definition and places it accordingly.

    Now this will look a bit messy, as shown at the top in Figure 10.9, but as soon as these items get incorporated into a block, it will clean up nicely. Often using overly lengthy attribute tags can help you identify these unique objects within a drawing because the drawing may get crowded.

**Figure 10.9**    The before and after appearance of the detail title.

You can use the Properties palette to adjust attribute definition settings as well attribute values for an inserted block.

7.  We are now ready to build the block. Using the Draw pull-down menu, select Block, then Make. The Block Definition dialog box appears.

8.  For the Block name, enter **DTLBLK**.

9.  Click the Select Objects button. The Block Definition dialog disappears temporarily.

10. Select the objects in this order. First pick the circle and line. Then pick the NUMBER attribute followed by the TITLE attribute. Lastly, select the two SCALE objects.

    The SCALE object is just a piece of text; the other is another Attribute Definition. Press Enter to return to the Block Definition dialog.

The order in which you select your attribute definitions will be the order in which you will be prompted when the block is inserted. However, you can use the BATTMAN command to reorganize your attribute order within a block if needed. This command is discussed later in this chapter.

As you can see, just a few attributes can become tedious to create. Often in revision lists, users will place repetitive attributes in a column format. It can be more productive to simply create one row (block) with attributes and then copy that for each following row forming the column of text needed.

11. Under the Select Objects button, toggle the Delete option; this provides a clean drawing in the next step. Then click the OK button to finish.

    All the objects vanish and are now stored in the Block Table database within this drawing.

12. Choose the Insert pull-down menu, Block, thereby implementing the `INSERT` command. It should already have the block name you entered because there are no other blocks in this drawing. Make sure the Insertion point select on-screen option is toggled and press the OK button. The dialog disappears.

13. You now have the block "attached" to your cursor, enabling you to visualize where to place it. Pick somewhere on-screen to insert it.

14. AutoCAD prompts you to fill in the attribute data as determined when they were defined.

    ```
    Detail Number <#>:3
    Detail Title <DETAIL>:<PRESS ENTER>
    Detail Scale <As Shown>:3/4"=1'-0"
    ```

15. As shown at the bottom of Figure 10.9, the block is placed and the attribute values have now been updated to match the data you just provided.

    You may now close the drawing without saving.

This exercise has shown that creating attributes and then incorporating them into a block is a simple process. This simplicity by no means displays the level of productiveness that a block with attributes can provide.

**INSIDER NOTE**

> A new feature in AutoCAD 2005 is Fields. This feature is really an extension of the various annotation object types in AutoCAD, such as attribute definitions and mtext. See Chapter 21, "Using Fields and Tables," for information on how to utilize them within an attribute definition.

As with many objects in AutoCAD, there will come a time when you need to edit your attribute values or manipulate their settings. The following sections expose many editing options that can be used to further your attribute prowess.

# Redefining Blocks with In-Place Reference Editing

You have a great tool to redefine blocks with in-place reference editing. This feature enables you to edit an inserted block, altering its child objects and automatically redefining all block insertions. Although this feature enables you to edit inserted blocks, its real power is its capability to edit attached external references in the current drawing and save the changes to the original drawing (for more information, see Chapter 11, "Working with External References"). Nonetheless, you can use it to quickly edit an inserted block without having to explode the block. The following exercise shows you how.

---

**INSIDER NOTE**

Two editing commands are available to be used specifically on external references: XBIND and XCLIP, both of which are discussed in later chapters. For additional information about external references, see Chapter 11.

---

### Exercise 10.7    Editing a Block with In-Place Reference Editing

1. Open the 10EX07.dwg file on the accompanying CD. The drawing opens and displays four insertions of the same block.

2. From the Modify menu, choose Xref and Block Editing, Edit Reference In-Place. AutoCAD prompts you to select the reference to edit.

3. Choose the block in the upper-left corner named Kara. AutoCAD displays the Reference Edit dialog box.

   Figure 10.10 shows two tabs within the Reference Edit dialog box. Notice that within the Identity Reference tab, the block's name is listed as Circle in a Square.

4. In the Identify Reference tab area, make sure that the Prompt to select nested objects option is chosen.

5. Select the Settings tab to gain access to other editing options.

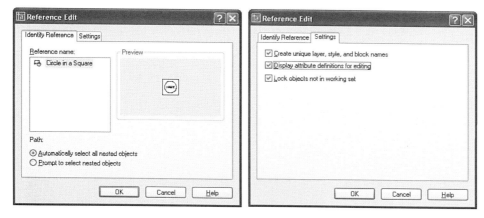

**Figure 10.10**   The Reference Edit dialog box enables you to edit inserted blocks. The Settings tab allows for unique object editing.

6. Select the Display Attribute Definitions for Editing option, as shown to the right in Figure 10.10, because the name in the center of the block insertion is an attribute. Selecting this option enables you to edit the block's attribute.

7. Click OK. AutoCAD prompts you to select nested objects.

8. Select the circle in the block named Kara and then press Enter. The circle is added to the list of objects to edit. You should notice the circle was removed from the other inserted blocks. This is another example of what you have available to edit at the moment.

AutoCAD then displays the Refedit toolbar, as shown in Figure 10.11. There is no need to try to select the attribute.

**Figure 10.11**   The Refedit toolbar.

9. Choose the circle. AutoCAD highlights the circle and displays its grips.

10. Choose the grip in the bottom quadrant of the circle and then drag the grip down to the bottom line in the square. Use the midpoint snap to snap the circle to the midpoint of the line. The circle's radius increases.

11. Right-click anywhere in the drawing area and choose Deselect All from the shortcut menu. The highlighted circle is unselected.

12. Choose the attribute and then drag and drop it toward the lower half of the circle.

13. Click the Save Back Changes button on the Refedit toolbar. It's the far right icon. Click OK to verify to save changes.

    Notice the enlarged circle object appears in all the blocks. However, the attribute you moved toward the lower half of the circle appears to not have changed, as shown in Figure 10.12. This occurs because changes in edited attributes do not change in previously inserted blocks, but only relocate in new block insertions.

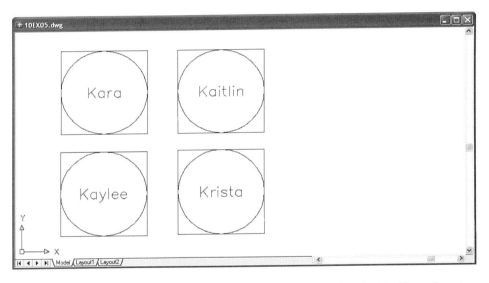

**Figure 10.12** The circle object is updated in all inserted blocks, but the block's attribute is not updated.

14. From the Insert menu, choose Block. The Insert dialog box displays.

15. Make sure the `Circle in a Square` block is selected in the Name drop-down list, click OK, and insert the block on the right side of the drawing. Then enter your name when prompted. AutoCAD inserts the revised block. Note that the attribute appears in its modified position in the lower half of the circle, as shown in Figure 10.13.

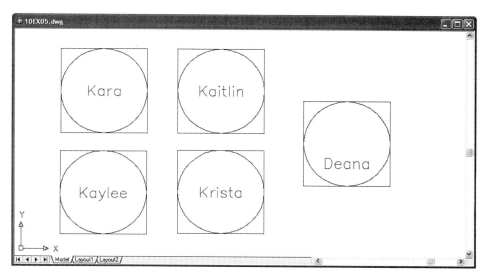

**Figure 10.13**    The redefined block attribute appears in its new position, but with new block insertions.

You may now close this drawing without saving.

**INSIDER NOTE**

> With AutoCAD 2005, another feature does enable you to force existing blocks to take on changes to attribute properties. The Block Attribute Manager (BATTMAN) Sync option "pushes" attribute changes into already inserted blocks. This and other tools for blocks and attributes are discussed later in this chapter.

# Using Nested Blocks

As indicated earlier in this chapter, two significant reasons exist for using blocks. The first is to reduce a drawing's file size. The second is to quickly update all the insertions of a particular block. For example, suppose you have a block that is made up of a circle with a text object in its center, and you have inserted this particular block hundreds of times. If the text value is currently the letter M but needs to be changed to S, you can simply redefine the block with the correct letter. After you redefine it, the hundreds of block insertions are instantly updated with the S text value. This is a very valuable feature that can save you hours of editing time.

The previous example demonstrates a powerful feature of blocks. This power can be expanded through the use of nested blocks. A nested block is simply a block that contains other blocks and objects.

Nested blocks increase the power of blocks by making it easier for you to redefine blocks. For example, suppose you have a large block made up of numerous objects. Also suppose that one object in the large block occasionally changes color. Instead of redefining the large block and all its objects every time the object changes color, you can create a small block consisting of the one object and insert it as a nested block in the large block. Then, when it becomes necessary to change the object's color, you can redefine it in the small block. When you redefine it, the small block is automatically updated in the large block. The important point in this example is that the large block reflects the new color of the nested block object, but the large block does not have to be redefined.

**I**NSIDER **C**AUTION

One problem exists that you must be aware of when you redefine nested blocks. To redefine a nested block, you must redefine it explicitly in the current drawing. If you redefine a nested block in its parent block outside of the current drawing and then use the -INSERT command to redefine the parent block in the current drawing, the nested blocks won't be updated. AutoCAD redefines only the parent block when you use the -INSERT command. The nested block definitions in the current drawing always take precedence over nested block definitions inserted from another drawing. The nomenclature for this –INSERT process is blockname=filename.

**I**NSIDER **T**IP

Using the -INSERT command with = is a technique that enables you to redefine a nested block. Simply WBLOCK the updated nested block to its own drawing and then use the -INSERT command to redefine the nested block in the necessary drawing.

# Understanding Block Attributes

Block attributes are an additional feature of blocks that are very useful. Block attributes store informational data. This data can be defined as a constant value, input by a user at the moment the block is inserted, or edited afterward.

**I**NSIDER **T**IP

> There is no limit to the number of attributes that can be associated with a block. Some have 20 or 30 attributes attached to title sheets, for example. When the title sheet block is inserted into the current drawing, the user is then prompted for various values: the sheet number, title, project engineer's name, CAD technician's name, and so on. This is useful for guaranteeing that appropriate data is added to a drawing and not accidentally overlooked.

When creating attributes for a block, it is important to control the sequence by which a user is prompted for data. For example, if a block will prompt for a series of data, and this data appears on-screen in alphabetical order, it makes sense to prompt the user for the data in the same order in which it appears on-screen.

To demonstrate how to control the sequence that AutoCAD prompts for attribute values, the following exercise creates two block definitions from a circle object that has five attributes. For the first block, the attributes are selected from top to bottom. For the second, the attributes are selected from bottom to top. Finally, the two blocks are inserted so that you can observe the order in which you are prompted to define values for the attributes.

### Exercise 10.8   Determining the Order Attributes Prompt for Values

1. Open the 10EX08.dwg drawing file on the accompanying CD. The drawing already contains the circle and five attributes you will use to define the two blocks, as shown in Figure 10.14.

   ONE
   TWO
   THREE
   FOUR
   FIVE

2. From the Draw pull-down menu, choose Block, Make. The Block Definition dialog box appears.

**Figure 10.14**
An example drawing with a basic entity and a number of attribute definitions.

3. In the Name list box, type **C1**.

**I**NSIDER **T**IP

> AutoCAD 2005 enables you to use extended symbol names when naming blocks. This feature provides the capability to use upper and lowercase characters as well as spaces in block names.

4. Click the Pick Point button. The Block Definition dialog box is temporarily dismissed.

5. Using Center Osnap, select the circle. AutoCAD assigns the circle's center as the block's base (insertion) point. The dialog box reappears.

6. Click the Select Objects button. The Block Definition dialog box is again temporarily dismissed.

7. Select the circle object first, then select each attribute from the top down, and then press Enter. Once again, the dialog box appears.

8. In the Objects area, click the Retain option button and then click OK.

   This completes the first block. Next, you create the second block.

9. From Draw, choose Block, Make. The Block Definition dialog box appears.

10. In the Name list box, type **C2**.

11. Click the Pick Point button. The Block Definition dialog box is temporarily dismissed.

12. Using Center Osnap, select the circle. AutoCAD picks the circle's center as the block's base point, and the dialog box returns.

13. Click the Select Objects button. The Block Definition dialog box is temporarily dismissed.

14. Select the circle object first, then select each attribute from the bottom up, and then press Enter. The dialog box reappears.

15. In the Objects area, ensure that the Retain option button is still selected and then click OK.

    AutoCAD creates the second block and leaves the objects used to define the blocks. Next, you insert the two blocks to observe the order AutoCAD prompts to fill in the attributes.

16. From the Insert pull-down menu, choose Block. The Insert dialog box opens.

17. Choose C1 from the Name drop-down list, if it is not already displayed.

18. In the Insertion Point area, be sure the Specify On-Screen option is selected. In the Scale and Rotation areas, be sure the Specify On-Screen option is cleared. Click OK to close the Insert dialog box.

19. Choose a location adjacent to the original objects to insert the block. AutoCAD prompts for the attribute values at the command line.

**20.** When AutoCAD prompts for the first attribute value, type **1**. At each subsequent prompt, type the numbers **2**, **3**, **4**, and **5**, respectively.

AutoCAD inserts the block and its attributes. The numbers 1, 2, 3, 4, and 5 appear in numerical order from top to bottom. Next, you insert the second block.

**21.** From the Insert pull-down menu, choose Block. The Insert dialog box opens. Click on the Block button. Choose C2 from the Name drop-down list. Click OK to close the Insert dialog box.

**22.** Choose a location on the right side of the screen to insert the block.

**23.** When AutoCAD prompts for the first attribute value, type **1**. At each subsequent prompt, type the numbers **2**, **3**, **4**, and **5**, respectively.

AutoCAD inserts the block. Notice this time, however, that the numbers 1, 2, 3, 4, and 5 appear in reverse order, as shown in Figure 10.15. This occurs because you selected the attributes in reverse order when you defined the second block.

You can close this drawing without saving.

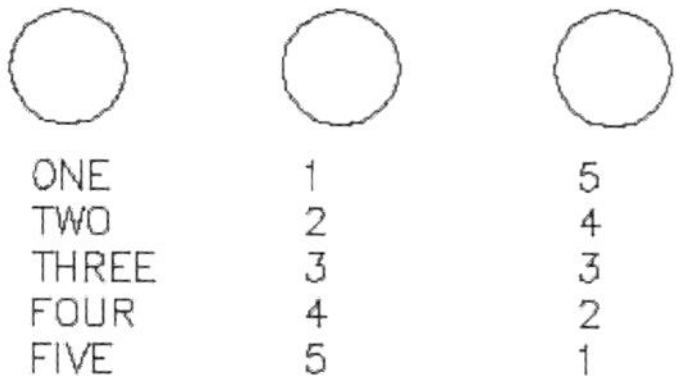

```
 ◯       ◯       ◯

ONE      1       5
TWO      2       4
THREE    3       3
FOUR     4       2
FIVE     5       1
```

**Figure 10.15**   The resulting effect of the order in which attributes are selected.

**I**NSIDER **NOTE**

The order in which attributes prompt for data is affected by the order in which they are selected when being defined. Therefore, their originally defined order is important when using the ATTREDEF command to redefine blocks with attributes.

**I**NSIDER **TIP**

To determine the proper order to select attributes when redefining a block, use the LIST command to list one of the block insertions. When redefining the block, the attributes should be selected in the order in which they appear because this is the order in which they were originally defined.

There are two editing commands available that are used specifically on attributes contained within a block. The commands are ATTEDIT and -ATTEDIT, both of which are discussed in the following sections.

## Using *ATTEDIT* on Attributes

If you want to change the text values of a variable attribute that is part of an inserted block, use ATTEDIT. This command is started by typing ATTEDIT or ATE at the command prompt. After selecting the block, the Edit Attributes dialog box is displayed. It shows the attribute prompts and the current text values of the attributes (see Figure 10.16).

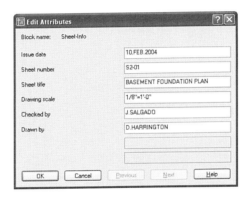

**Figure 10.16**    The Edit Attributes dialog box is displayed as a result of the ATTEDIT command.

If more attributes exist than can be displayed in the dialog box, use the Next and Previous buttons to display the additional sets of attributes.

## Using *-ATTEDIT* on Attributes

Whereas ATTEDIT enables you to change the text values of attributes, the -ATTEDIT command enables you to change other properties of inserted attributes. -ATTEDIT is issued by selecting Global from the Attribute submenu under Modify, Object. You are prompted whether you want to edit attributes one at a time. If you answer No, you can perform a text search-and-replace on the text string of the selected attributes. If you answer Yes to editing attributes one at a time, you can change the value, position, height, rotation angle, style, and color of the selected attributes.

Whether you answer Yes or No, you also have the option of filtering the selected attributes by block name, attribute tag name, or attribute value. The default value for all three filters is an asterisk (*), which indicates that no filters should be used and that the attributes the user selects are to be accepted.

There are a number of commands for dealing with existing Attribute data. The Enhanced Attribute Editor and the Block Attribute Manager both extend new functionality that greatly increases the potential for modification of attributes.

## Finding and Replacing Attributes

AutoCAD 2005 has a tool that enables you to find and replace attribute text values in a drawing. To use this helpful feature, from the Edit pull-down menu, choose Find to display the Find and Replace dialog box. To locate a text value, enter the value in the Find Text String list box. If you want AutoCAD to replace the found text string with a new one, enter the new text value in the Replace With list box; otherwise, leave it blank.

To specify that AutoCAD should search only block attributes for a listed text value, click the Options button to display the Find and Replace Options dialog box, then clear all options except for Block Attribute Value, as shown in Figure 10.17. From the Find and Replace Options dialog box, you can also tell AutoCAD to match the upper or lowercase spelling of the search word. Additionally, you can instruct AutoCAD to find the whole word, not compound words that are partially composed of the search word.

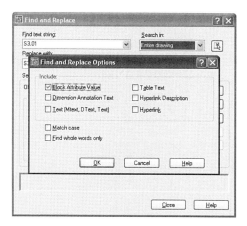

**Figure 10.17**   The Find and Replace Options dialog box enables searching for text values in block attributes only.

After the find and replace words are indicated and the options selected, to find the listed word or phrase, click the Find Next button in the Find and Replace dialog box. To replace the found word with the listed replacement word or phrase, click the Replace or Replace All button. When AutoCAD finds an occurrence of the listed search word, it displays the listed word and the phrase in which it's embedded in the Context area. When a word is found, you can zoom to its location by clicking the Zoom To button.

# Attribute Tools

Attribute tags within AutoCAD blocks are an extremely powerful entity type but can be extremely difficult to work with. They look like normal text, but they have a wealth of configuration and application issues that you need to understand. In this section, we look at the more powerful Attribute tools provided with AutoCAD 2005 and how to use them. Now with these tools, the process of managing and extracting information is much easier than before.

## The Block Attribute Manager

Affectionately known as BATTMAN, the Block Attribute Manager enables you to modify block attributes without having to explode and redefine the block. Also, as you make changes to a block with BATTMAN, they are immediately reflected in the objects in AutoCAD 2005. The following exercise shows the power of this attribute tool.

### Exercise 10.9   Managing Attributes

1. Open the 10EX09.dwg file from the accompanying CD. This drawing is an array of MANHOLE blocks inserted with varying attribute data values.

2. From the Modify pull-down menu, choose Object, Attribute, then Block Attribute Manager. This starts the BATTMAN command dialog box (see Figure 10.18).

**Figure 10.18**   The BATTMAN dialog and its multitude of attribute controls.

At first look, this dialog seems to have many controls, and it does. It is powerful, but a little "walk around the dialog" will enlighten you.

At the top of the dialog, you have a Select Block button and Block drop-down list. Both enable you to get your block name into the BATTMAN dialog. Because just one block exists in this drawing, the list only shows the MANHOLE block.

The main area of the dialog shows which attributes are defined in the MANHOLE block. It shows the tag names, their prompts, and any default values that exist.

The series of buttons on the right provide controls for the attributes. The Sync button is somewhat redundant because the system automatically shows your changes as you do them, but it does provide a method to verify that changes are applied. However, the Sync button can also be used to push changes into other matching block insertions.

The Move Up and Move Down buttons can be used to change the order of attributes appearing in the block. This can be helpful if you selected an attribute in the wrong sequence.

The Edit button launches the Edit Attribute dialog, covered later in this exercise.

The last button on the right is Remove and is used to delete an attribute from your block. After you press Remove and close the BATTMAN dialog, those deleted attributes are removed from all block insertions.

The final item to cover is the Settings button in the lower left. This provides a fil-tering, if you will, of which attribute properties to show in the main area of the dialog (see Figure 10.19). It has a control to highlight duplicate tags in a block, and it also has a control to "push" your changes into existing blocks by using the Apply button to change existing references.

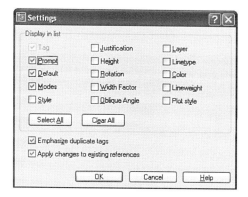

**Figure 10.19**   The Settings dialog of the BATTMAN command enables filtering for attribute properties.

3. Now that you know the sections of the BATTMAN dialog, let's do some work. We need to make a few changes to attribute values, so with the OBJECT_CATEGORY tag selected, click the Edit button. This opens the Edit Attribute dialog (see Figure 10.20).

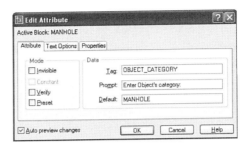

**Figure 10.20**   The Edit Attribute dialog accesses all attribute properties.

4. In the Attribute tab panel, verify MANHOLE is the default value. Note the controls for the attribute modes on the left. These can be used to make attributes invisible and other action properties.

5. Click the Text Options tab. Change the height to 0.30 and then put your cursor in the Width Factor edit box. Note in the drawing that the text heights just changed automatically!

6. Change the width value to 0.80 and press Enter. The blocks change the moment you do this.

**I**NSIDER **T**IP

If you were to uncheck the Auto Preview Changes toggle in the lower left, all these changes would only be seen when you close the BATTMAN command.

7. Click the Properties tab. Change the color to red. This also is immediately seen in the drawing as you click a color. Click the OK to close the Edit Attribute dialog.

8. Click OK to close the BATTMAN dialog.

Leave this drawing open for the following exercise.

As you have discovered, the new BATTMAN command makes updating blocks very easy. Next, we will cover more specific attribute commands.

# The Enhanced Attribute Editor

Often in your work, you will need to change attribute properties, but just on one block, not all of them. The new Enhanced Attribute Editor is used to adjust single block instances rather than wholesale global changes.

### Exercise 10.10    Using the Enhanced Attribute Editor

1. Continue with the previous exercise or open 10EX10.dwg from the accompanying CD.

2. From the Modify pull-down menu, select Object, Attribute, then Single. This opens the Enhanced Attribute Editor after the object has been selected (the EATTEDIT command).

3. Select the top-left MANHOLE block; that way you can see the block and the dialog.

4. From the Attribute tab panel, select the Sewer value in the main area, and then in the Value box, type **Subway** (see Figure 10.21). You may notice that the dialog value changes as you type.

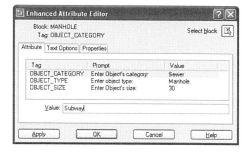

**Figure 10.21**    The Enhanced Attribute Editor enables individual block modifications.

5. Click the Text Options tab, and in the Height edit box, change the value to 2.0.

**I**NSIDER NOTE

> If you completed Exercise 10.9, you may remember that the height value was changed to 0.3, but here it reads 3.0. This is because the BATTMAN works with native block values (before scaling), and the Enhanced Attribute Editor reports the values as they really are (after scaling).

6. Click the Properties tab and change the color red to blue.

7. Click OK to close the dialog.

You may now close the drawing without saving.

The `EATTEDIT` command is very useful for modifying individual block instances. It supplements the `ATTEDIT` and `-ATTEDIT` commands with a more powerful and complete dialog. Not too long ago, there were text options that could not be changed easily. Now with the `BATTMAN` and `EATTEDIT` commands, you are free to adjust your attributes as needed.

# Managing Blocks Effectively

As you learn how to take advantage of the power of blocks, you will eventually develop hundreds of blocks, possibly more. You can further enhance the power of blocks by managing those blocks in a fashion that enables you and other users to quickly find the desired block definition. If you do not do this, productivity will be lost in one of two ways. First, it will take significant time to simply find the appropriate block. Second, if the block can't be found, it will take time to re-create the block from scratch. It is therefore necessary to establish criteria that everyone must follow to properly create and store blocks for future use.

## *WBLOCK* Command

When you're creating a block library, the most important component is the block itself. Chances are you probably already have a wealth of predefined blocks residing in existing drawing files. These existing files are the first place you should go to when developing your block library because they probably contain blocks your organization frequently uses.

After you find useful predefined blocks in an existing drawing, you generally export them as individual drawings. The `WBLOCK` command is a convenient way to quickly extract blocks from the current drawing.

When you type `WBLOCK` at the command prompt, the Write Block dialog box appears (see Figure 10.22). This dialog box makes the process of exporting a block very intuitive. You can export an existing block by selecting the Block option, exporting the entire drawing, or by selecting a group of objects and exporting them as a new block. When you have identified the desired block or objects, you can assign a new filename, determine the location in which to save the new block, and select its Insert Units. After selecting the desired options, you click the OK button, and AutoCAD exports the data and creates the new drawing. The new drawing file can then be inserted as a block into any drawing.

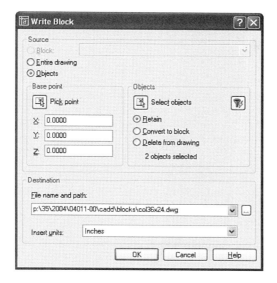

**Figure 10.22**   The Write Block dialog box.

## Organizing Blocks

The key to managing your block library is to organize the block locations using a well-designed storage structure. Store blocks in a standard location on each computer or on a network server. You can further organize blocks into classes and subclasses. The organizational structure should reflect a class structure used in your industry. For example, in civil engineering, it may be useful to organize standard storm drain junction structures using the following path structure:

```
p:\documents\cadd\blocks\stormdrains\junstr\201a.dwg
```

With this type of structure, a AutoCAD user could easily follow the path to find a particular block. If the block cannot be found in this path structure, the block probably has not been created yet. In such a case, it could be created in the current drawing and then Write Blocked out to the appropriate path location.

## AutoCAD DesignCenter

AutoCAD 2005 has a very powerful drawing content management tool, DesignCenter. The ADC helps you manage drawing content by providing tools for searching for, locating, and viewing blocks created in other drawings. For information on ADC's features, refer to Chapter 12.

# Summary

Blocks are a very powerful feature of AutoCAD. This chapter has shown you how to extract the power of blocks by explaining the nature of blocks. You learned what happens to AutoCAD's database when a block is defined and how the current UCS affects a block when it's being defined or inserted. You learned how AutoCAD stores a block definition in the Block Table and how it references the Block Table to create the Insert object. You saw the effects of defining blocks on a normal layer and on layer 0 and the difference between explicitly and implicitly defining the color, linetype, and lineweight properties of a block. This chapter also outlined the advantages of creating complex blocks from simpler blocks and the steps for redefining nested blocks with the -INSERT command. In addition, it presented several techniques for managing block libraries.

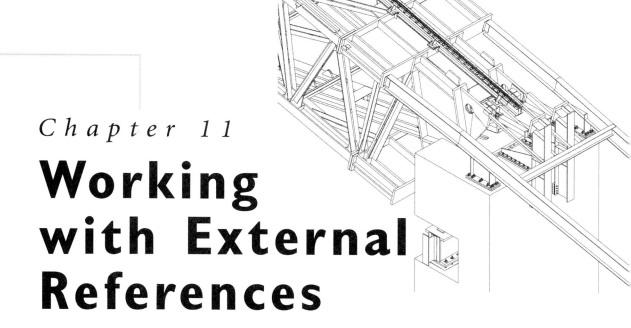

*C h a p t e r   1 1*

# Working with External References

AutoCAD 2005 has several features that enhance how you work with drawings and external references (xrefs). The Partial Open and Partial Load commands give you the ability to load only the portions of a drawing you need to edit. In addition, features that enable you to insert and edit external references in the current drawing can greatly increase your productivity.

This chapter discusses the following subjects:

- Partial Open and Partial Load features
- When you should use xrefs rather than blocks
- Attaching versus overlaying xrefs
- Permanently binding xrefs to the current drawing
- Clipping xref boundaries
- Demand Loading and layer and spatial indexes
- Managing xrefs
- AutoCAD's Reference Editing
- Xref notifications

# Working with Drawings Productively

Throughout AutoCAD's history, to edit a drawing, you simply opened it. Although this technique works fine in many situations, it can be a slow, tedious process if you're working with large drawing files. To solve this problem, we must somehow decrease the drawing's file size and thereby increase productivity through faster response by AutoCAD.

Although the majority of this chapter deals with external references, a few commands exist that can be utilized as a method to work with large drawing files. The Partial Open and Partial Load features simulate the advantages achieved when separating a drawing into smaller files without the need to divide the original drawing into groups of smaller drawings. These features enable you to open only a portion of a drawing, thereby loading only the elements you need to edit. Objects can be loaded based on selected layers by choosing a predefined view or by windowing in on an area. When you're finished, simply save the drawing normally. This feature enables you to maintain a high level of productivity even while working on large drawings, and it avoids the management problems encountered by separating a single drawing into many smaller drawings.

## AutoCAD 2005's Partial Open Feature

The Partial Open feature enables you to open a portion of a drawing either by selecting the drawing's extents or the last view when the drawing was saved or by selecting a predefined view if one exists. After you select the desired view option, you identify the object geometry you want to load by selecting the layer(s) on which they reside.

The following exercise demonstrates how to use AutoCAD's Partial Open feature.

### Exercise 11.1   Using the Partial Open Feature

1. Open the file 11EX01.dwg from the accompanying CD. The drawing appears in the Preview window, as shown in Figure 11.1. Next, you load only a portion of the object geometry from the drawing.

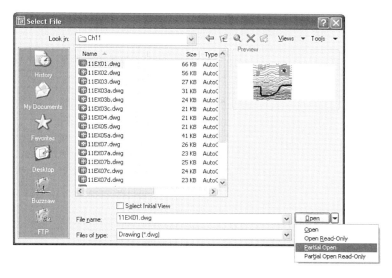

**Figure 11.1**   The Partial Open feature is accessed from the Select File dialog box.

2. Click the down arrow next to the Open button and then choose the Partial Open option. AutoCAD then displays the Partial Open dialog box.

3. In the View Geometry to Load area, choose Area 1. This instructs AutoCAD to load objects that lie within or pass through the predefined view named Area 1.

4. In the Layer Geometry to Load area, select the check boxes next to layer names BUILDINGS, CONTOURS-INDEX, and CONTOURS-NORMAL, as shown in Figure 11.2. This instructs AutoCAD to load objects on the selected layers.

5. Click Open to complete the process and load the drawing partially in AutoCAD. Then close the drawing; do not save your changes.

AutoCAD opens the drawing, loading only the objects that lie within or pass through the view and that reside on the selected layers, as shown in Figure 11.3. At this point, you can edit the loaded geometry, create new objects, and zoom or pan the drawing. You can also create and modify data outside the area you opened. You are not limited by the initial view when working with partially opened drawings.

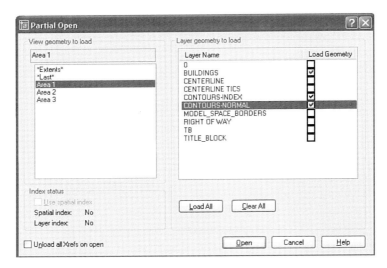

**Figure 11.2** The Partial Open dialog box enables you to identify the object geometry to load by selecting the view and the layers in which the objects reside.

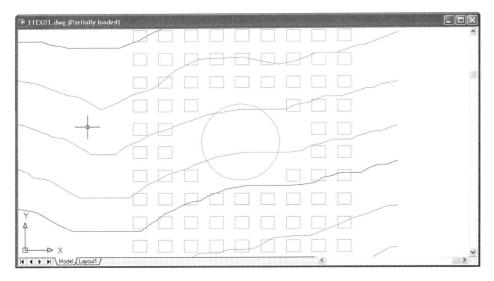

**Figure 11.3** The Partial Open feature loads only the objects that lie within or pass through the selected view and that reside on the selected layers.

When you used the Partial Open feature in the previous exercise, you selected a view and three layers. However, it is not necessary to select layers. You can select a view but leave all the check boxes next to the layer names cleared. If you do, when you click Open, AutoCAD issues a warning that no objects will be loaded. However, AutoCAD does load all the layer names and also loads all the other named objects such as blocks, text styles, dimension styles, and linetypes. When the drawing is partially opened, it is possible to use these named objects to create new object geometry in the drawing without actually loading any existing geometry.

Another behavior unique to the Partial Open feature occurs when you save and then reopen a drawing that was partially opened. When you reopen the drawing, AutoCAD displays a warning noting that the drawing was partially opened when last saved. This warning, and the options it presents, is described in the next section.

# AutoCAD 2005's Partial Load Feature

The Partial Load feature enables you to load additional geometry into a drawing that is already partially opened. By using this feature, you can further refine the selection set of objects you load into the current editing session.

The following exercise demonstrates how to use AutoCAD's Partial Load feature.

### Exercise 11.2   Using the Partial Load Feature

1. From the accompanying CD, select the 11EX02.dwg file. The drawing was created at the end of the previous exercise by saving the partially opened 11EX01.dwg file. Notice that the drawing's image does not appear in the Preview window. This is because the drawing was saved while only partially opened.

2. Click the Open button. AutoCAD displays a warning noting that the drawing was partially opened when last saved, as shown in Figure 11.4.

   AutoCAD presents three options for handling the file. By clicking the Fully Open button, you load all the drawing's object geometry. This is how AutoCAD normally opens a drawing. By clicking the Restore button, you partially open the drawing using the previous Partial Open settings. By clicking the Cancel button, you stop AutoCAD from loading the drawing and abandon the "open a drawing" effort altogether.

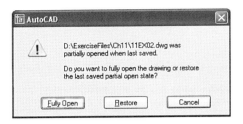

**Figure 11.4**   AutoCAD displays a warning when you select a file that was partially opened when last saved.

3. Click the Restore button. AutoCAD partially opens the drawing using the previous Partial Open settings that were saved with the drawing.

4. From the File pull-down menu, choose Partial Load. AutoCAD displays the Partial Load dialog box.

   This dialog box is almost identical to the Partial Open dialog box. The main difference is that the Partial Load dialog box includes the Pick a Window button, which enables you to drag a selection window around the area from which to load objects.

5. In the Layer Geometry to Load area, select the check box next to the CENTER-LINE layer name. This instructs AutoCAD to load objects on the selected layer.

6. Click the Pick a window button, as shown in Figure 11.5. When AutoCAD temporarily removes the dialog box, create a window selection around the circle, after which AutoCAD redisplays the Partial Load dialog box.

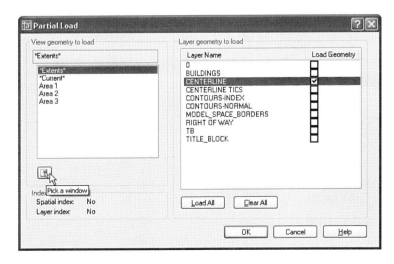

**Figure 11.5**   The Partial Load dialog box enables you to pick an area from which to load windowed objects.

**7.** Click OK. AutoCAD loads the objects within the defined area and on the CENTERLINE layer, as shown in Figure 11.6.

Close the drawing and do not save changes.

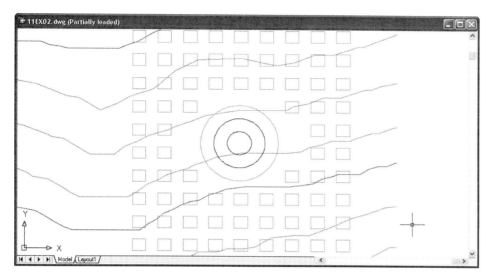

**Figure 11.6**   The objects within the defined area and on the CENTERLINE layer are partially loaded.

AutoCAD's Partial Open and Partial Load features enable you to load specific objects into the current editing session. By using these features, you can reduce the time it takes to open a large drawing and thereby increase productivity.

# Working with External References Productively

External references, or xrefs, represent a powerful feature of AutoCAD. They provide the capability to create a composite drawing using other saved drawings, even while those other drawings are being edited. In a multidisciplinary work environment, you can attach another discipline's drawings to see the impact their design will have on your design. The drawings can be attached temporarily or inserted permanently as a block. You can permanently insert the entire xref or just its named objects, such as text styles or dimension styles. You can attach an entire xref or just the portions you need to review. You can even define an irregularly shaped polygon as the clipping boundary for the portion of the xref you want to attach. By attaching small clipped portions of an xref, you can dramatically reduce regen times.

Additionally, AutoCAD has a feature called Reference Editing, which enables you to change an attached xref from within the current drawing and save the changes back to the original drawing file. These versatile features make AutoCAD's xrefs a very powerful tool.

## Using Xrefs Versus Blocks

External references have behavior that is similar to blocks. They can be inserted or "xrefed" into a drawing and used to display many objects as a single object. They can be copied multiple times, and all the insertions of that xref can be changed by editing the original reference file. The only real difference between the two is that blocks are inserted permanently into the current drawing as a part of the drawing, whereas xrefs exist externally in independent drawing files that are only attached to the current drawing.

So, if xrefs behave like blocks, then when should you use xrefs rather than blocks? One situation in which you should use xrefs is when the objects in external drawings that you need to view are undergoing change. When edits are made to an externally referenced file, you can reload the xref to update it to reflect the most recent condition of the xref. Additionally, AutoCAD automatically loads the latest version of an xrefed drawing when you open your drawing. This is not true with blocks.

**I**NSIDER TIP

> When a loaded xref is changed by you or someone else, AutoCAD alerts you to this through a "balloon" notice that pops up in the Status bar. This notice can simply be ignored or used to reload the xrefs.

Another reason to use xrefs instead of blocks is when the xrefed drawing is large. Not only can you keep the current drawing's file size low by attaching large drawings as xrefs, you can also instruct AutoCAD to only load a small portion of an xref instead of the entire xrefed drawing. This reduces the number of objects in the current drawing and therefore reduces file size and regen times.

Lastly, a great benefit of xrefs is the capability to "insert" them into multiple drawing files. An example of this is a grid drawing for a building being attached to multiple floor plans. If the grid changes, all levels instantly reference the updated file.

## Inserting an Xref: Attach Versus Overlay

You can link an xref to the current drawing in two different ways—you can either attach it or overlay it. Both methods enable you to turn layers on and off or to freeze and thaw layers. Both enable you to change the color, linetypes, and lineweights of layers of xrefed drawings. Both methods are virtually identical, with one exception: Attached xrefs appear when nested in other xrefed drawings, whereas overlays do not.

The following exercise demonstrates the difference between attaching and overlaying an xref.

### Exercise 11.3    Attaching Versus Overlaying an Xref

1. Open the 11EX03.dwg file on the accompanying CD to display a Tentative Tract Map consisting of right-of-way lines, property lines, street centerlines, and proposed building pads.

   Next, you insert two xrefs: one attached, and the other overlaid.

2. From the Insert pull-down menu, choose Xref Manager and then click the Attach button. The Select Reference File dialog box opens.

3. From the Select Reference File dialog box, open the 11EX03a.dwg drawing file. AutoCAD displays the External Reference dialog box.

4. In the External Reference dialog box, under Reference Type, choose Overlay.

5. In the Insertion Point area, Scale area, and Rotation area, clear any checked Specify On-Screen check boxes, as shown in Figure 11.7.

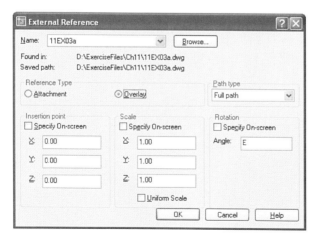

**Figure 11.7**   The Overlay option is selected in the External Reference dialog box.

6. Click OK. AutoCAD overlays the drawing and displays its existing contours.

7. From the Insert pull-down menu, choose External Reference. The Select Reference File dialog box opens.

The action in step 7 launches the XATTACH command, not the XREF command. This command can be used to streamline the process of selecting a drawing to xref.

8. From the Select Reference File dialog box, open the 11EX03b.dwg drawing file. AutoCAD displays the External Reference dialog box.

You can xref multiple drawings in one step if they exist in the same directory. By using the Shift+left-click process in the Select Reference File dialog, you can select as many drawing files as needed and then click Open. The following External Reference dialog then enables you to set the same attachment and options for all the new xrefs. When done, they all are inserted as if you had repeated the process over and over.

9. In the External Reference dialog box, under Reference Type, choose Attachment.

10. In the Insertion Point area, Scale area, and Rotation area, clear any checked Specify On-Screen check boxes.

11. Click OK. AutoCAD attaches the drawing and displays its existing trees, as shown in Figure 11.8.

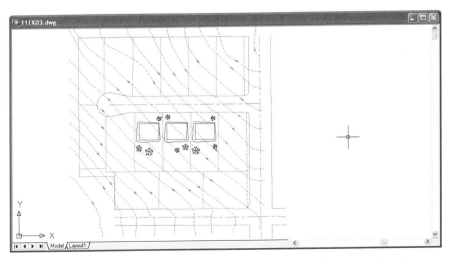

**Figure 11.8**   One xref is attached, and the other is overlaid in the current drawing.

**12.** Create a directory on your C:\ hard disk named IAC2005. Then save the current drawing to that directory.

**13.** Close the newly created 11EX03.dwg drawing file.

**14.** Open the 11EX03c.dwg drawing file on the accompanying CD. AutoCAD displays the drawing, which displays the building plans.

Next, you xref the Tentative Tract Map drawing, with its two xrefs.

**15.** From the Insert pull-down menu, choose External Reference. The Select Reference File dialog box opens.

**16.** From the Select Reference File dialog box, open the 11EX03.dwg drawing file from the C:\IA2005 directory. AutoCAD displays the External Reference dialog box.

**17.** In the External Reference dialog box, under Reference Type, choose Attachment.

**18.** In the Insertion Point area, Scale area, and Rotation area, clear any checked Specify On-Screen check boxes.

**19.** Click OK. The xref then appears.

AutoCAD attaches the drawing, as shown in Figure 11.9. It's important to realize that the existing Contours and the existing Trees drawings are already referenced in the Tentative Tract Map drawing and are therefore nested xrefs. Note that the Trees xref appears, but the Contours xref does not. This occurs because the Contours drawing was overlaid, whereas the Trees drawing was attached to the Tentative Tract Map drawing.

You may now exit the drawing without saving your changes.

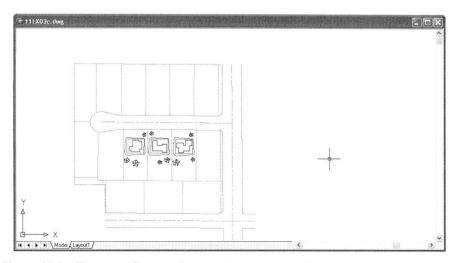

**Figure 11.9**   The nested Trees xref appears, but the nested Contours xref does not.

By using the attach and overlay features as shown in the preceding exercise, you can more easily manage the visibility of xrefed drawings.

> **INSIDER NOTE**
>
> In AutoCAD 2005, if the xref drawing you attach or overlay has objects organized with the AutoCAD 2005 DRAWORDER command, the objects appear in that drawing order. This is because the DRAWORDER command has been updated to preserve the organization you apply throughout the chain of usage.

## Unloading and Reloading Xrefs

After you have placed xrefs, the xrefs can be unloaded and then reloaded as desired. This capability enables you to temporarily unload xrefs from a drawing so that AutoCAD does not spend time calculating the positions of xref objects during regens. When you unload an xref, AutoCAD leaves its path and insertion properties. To display the xref in the drawing again, you can reload the xref.

In addition to reloading xrefs that have been unloaded, you can also reload xrefs that are already loaded. This is useful when you know that an xrefed drawing has been edited, and you want to refresh the drawing's display to see any new changes that have taken place since you originally loaded the xref.

> **INSIDER TIP**
>
> Loaded xrefs can significantly increase regen times. If you are editing a drawing and do not need to see a loaded xref, use the XREF Unload option to remove it temporarily from the drawing. Also selecting xref objects when editing other objects can be very bothersome. If needed you can unload the xref to clear up the area on which you are working. This will increase your productivity.

## Permanently Inserting an Xref: Bind Versus Xbind

Occasionally, you might need to make an xref drawing a permanent part of the current drawing. When archiving files for permanent storage, for example, or when submitting a file to another technician, you might find it useful to make xrefs a part of the drawing to which they are attached, thereby combining all the drawings into a single DWG file. By combining the xrefs into a single drawing, you ensure that all the drawing data exists in a single file. You can make an xref a permanent part of another drawing by binding it to the drawing, which inserts the entire xref into the drawing as a block.

When you choose to bind an xref to the current drawing, AutoCAD prompts you to select the type of bind to use: Bind or Insert. When the Bind option is selected, AutoCAD inserts the xref into the current drawing and prefixes all named objects with the xref's drawing name. Therefore, named objects such as layers, blocks, and text styles are prefixed by the xref's drawing name and then inserted into the current drawing. However, if you choose the Insert option, AutoCAD inserts the drawing as a normal block and does not prefix named objects with the xref's drawing name. Consequently, any duplicate named objects in the xref are ignored, and the named objects from the current drawing hold precedence.

This means, for example, that if a block in the xref has the same name as a block in the current drawing, the block in the current drawing takes precedence and is used in place of all same-name block insertions in the xref. Although this feature eliminates the redundancy of duplicate layer names, it can give unexpected results if you are not aware of duplicate named objects.

**I**NSIDER **NOTE**

> When you attach an xref to a drawing, the xref's drawing name is prefixed to its named objects, such as layers and blocks, which are separated by the pipe "|" symbol. When you bind the xref to the drawing, the pipe symbol is replaced by $0$, where the zero represents the first instance of a bound xref. If another xref with the same name as the first is also bound to the drawing, the zero increments to one and appears as $1$. This feature avoids potential problems when binding xrefs from different departments or companies that might coincidentally use the same xref name.

Although binding an xref into the current drawing is useful, there are occasions when it is more useful to only bind an xref's named objects. You can accomplish this with the XBIND command.

Suppose, for example, that you have attached an xref to the current drawing. You intend to leave the xref attached for a short time only and then detach it. After the xref is attached, you notice that some of its text objects are using a text style that you want to use in the current drawing. You can easily insert the text style in the current drawing with the XBIND command.

An alternative to the XBIND command is to use AutoCAD DesignCenter. This feature enables you to drag and drop named objects from one drawing into another. You can move items from drawings that are open or drawings that are on a network or even on the Internet. Learn more about the aspects of this feature in Chapter 12, "Applications for DesignCenter."

# Clipping Boundaries

The XCLIP command enables you to use rectangles or irregularly shaped closed polygons to define clipping boundaries for xrefs. The polygons can be created on-the-fly or by selecting an existing 2D polyline. After the clipping boundary has been chosen, AutoCAD removes from display any portion of the xref that lies outside the clipping boundary.

The following exercise demonstrates how to use the Select Polyline feature of the XCLIP command to define the xref clipping boundaries with an irregular polygon.

### Exercise 11.4    Using the Select Polyline Feature of the *XCLIP* Command

1. Open the 11EX04.dwg drawing file on the accompanying CD. The 11EX04a.dwg drawing file is attached as an xref.

2. From the Modify pull-down menu, choose Clip, Xref.

3. Select the contour xref and press Enter.

4. Press Enter again to accept the default for a new boundary.

5. Type **s** to choose Select Polyline.

> **INSIDER TIP**
>
> Don't forget, you can also use the right-click shortcut menu to select XCLIP command options.

6. Select the large, green polyline.

    AutoCAD determines the limits of the clipping boundary and redisplays only the portion of the xref that is inside the clipping boundary, as shown in Figure 11.10.

    You can close the drawing without saving.

The preceding exercise demonstrated how to use the Select Polyline feature of the XCLIP command. In some cases, however, defining only one clipping boundary for the xref might not be enough.

A limitation of the XCLIP feature is that an xref can have only one clipping boundary. But what if you want to clip the same xref with more than one polygon? How do you create multiple clipping boundaries? The answer is to insert the same xref more than once.

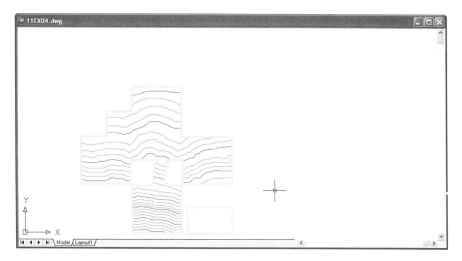

**Figure 11.10**   The xref is clipped using the polyline.

---

**I**NSIDER **T**IP

> As an alternative method of inserting a copy of an xref, you could rename the original xref insertion with the RENAME command, insert the xref again, and then use XCLIP on the new insertion. This method would create two uniquely named xrefs, which can be useful for modifying different xref layer properties.

---

**I**NSIDER **T**IP

> An xref can also be renamed from the Xref Manager dialog box. Simply highlight the xref to be renamed and then press F2. After you change the name, press Enter.

---

**I**NSIDER **T**IP

> When creating similar drawings, each with a different xref, it can save you time to set up the first one by attaching, scaling, and placing the xref drawing, followed by saving. Then from within the saved drawing, use the SAVEAS command for your next drawing and modify the path for the next xref. This effectively swaps one xref for another but preserves placement and scale settings. When swapped, rename the xref to match that of the new xref drawing. Continue for all drawings as needed. This technique is a big timesaver!

# Demand Loading

Demand Loading works in conjunction with layer and spatial indexes and reduces regen times. By enabling Demand Loading when using xrefs, AutoCAD loads only specific objects from the xref into the current drawing. By loading only a portion of the xref's objects, the number of objects in the current editing session is minimized, thereby increasing AutoCAD's performance.

Demand Loading is controlled by a system variable named XLOADCTL, which controls how AutoCAD uses layer and spatial indexes that might exist in xrefs. By enabling Demand Loading (setting XLOADCTL to either 1 or 2), AutoCAD loads only objects on layers that are thawed when the xref has layer indexes and loads only objects within the clipping boundary when the xref has spatial indexes. Table 11.1 shows the variable's three settings and their effects.

**Table 11.1   The Demand Loading Settings**

| Setting | Effect |
| --- | --- |
| 0—Disabled | Turns off Demand Loading. The xref cannot be opened by anyone while someone has a drawing opened with that xref. |
| 1—Enabled | Turns on Demand Loading and prevents other users from editing the drawing file while it is xrefed. The xref cannot be opened by anyone while someone has a drawing opened with that xref. |
| 2—Enabled with Copy | Turns on Demand Loading and creates a copy of the drawing that it xrefs. This enables other users to edit the xref's original drawing and actually helps xrefs load faster across a network. |

In most networked environments, a setting of 0 is preferred so that duplicate files do not exist whatsoever and so that you always load the latest files. With today's newer systems, the time saved with setting 1 is negated by the problems with xrefing drawings that others have opened or xrefed. Setting 2 can be useful because of its time savings, but it can result in increased hard disk activity by the duplication of the drawing file.

**I**NSIDER **N**OTE

The XLOADCTL system variable's settings can be controlled through the Options dialog box from the Open and Save tab.

## Layer and Spatial Indexes

In the previous section, you learned about the system variable that controls Demand Loading. AutoCAD has another system variable, called INDEXCTL, that controls layer and spatial indexing and that works in conjunction with the Demand Loading system variable, XLOADCTL.

When layer indexing is enabled, AutoCAD does not load xref objects residing on layers that are frozen in the external reference drawing. When spatial indexing is enabled, AutoCAD does not load xref objects that reside outside the clip boundary. In both cases, fewer objects are brought into the current drawing, and regen times are reduced.

By enabling the INDEXCTL system variable, AutoCAD's performance can be enhanced by reducing the regen times of drawings with xrefs. Table 11.2 shows the variable's four settings and their effects.

### Table 11.2   The Layer and Spatial Index Settings

| Setting | Effect |
| --- | --- |
| 0—None | Both layer and spatial indexing are disabled. |
| 1—Layer | Only layer indexing is enabled. |
| 2—Spatial | Only spatial indexing is enabled. |
| 3—Layer & Spatial | Both layer and spatial indexing are enabled. |

**I**NSIDER **N**OTE

> Setting the INDEXCTL system variable to a value other than 0 enables layer or spatial indexing (or both). Consequently, when the drawing is saved, AutoCAD adds to it the additional layer and spatial index data, thereby increasing the drawing's file size.

Spatial indexes work in three dimensions by defining a front and back clipping plane. The front and back clipping planes are defined by the XCLIP command's Clipdepth option. By creating a clipping boundary and specifying the Clipdepth, you can greatly limit the xref objects that AutoCAD loads into the current drawing session.

Layer and spatial indexes are created in a drawing when the INDEXCTL system variable is set to the desired value and the drawing is then saved. If INDEXCTL is set to 3, for example, both layer and spatial indexes are created when the current drawing is saved. The indexes are saved with the drawing file. Consequently, if you attach the drawing as an xref to a new drawing that has Demand Loading enabled, AutoCAD uses the xref's layer and spatial indexes to load only those objects that are on thawed layers and that lie within the clipping boundary.

**I**NSIDER **TIP**

> Leave the INDEXCTL system variable set to its default value of 0 to help keep the drawing's file size minimal. Only set the variable to a value other than 0 when the file you are saving is to be used as an xref, and the layer and spatial indexes will be used by the Demand Loading feature.

# Managing Xrefs

The advantage of using xrefs is that they provide the capability to create composite drawings that have relatively small file sizes and are easily updated. Unfortunately, on large projects involving multiple disciplines, keeping track of xref drawings can be difficult. Proper xref management is critical to ensure that composite drawings can find the latest versions of xrefs on standalone stations or over networks. Features available in AutoCAD can make managing xrefs easier.

The Xref Manager dialog box makes the task of managing xrefs easier. The dialog box's diagrams and intuitive button commands are great visual aids, as is the dialog's display of such pertinent data as the xref's name and path, current load status, whether the xref is attached or overlaid, and the xref's file size and last modification date.

## Displaying Xrefs with Tree View Versus List View

When the Tree View feature is selected, it displays any nested xrefs that might exist in a diagram of the hierarchy of the xrefs. This feature makes it easy to see which xrefs have been attached and how they relate to one another.

**I**NSIDER **NOTE**

> The Tree View feature instantly displays a visual diagram of xrefs and any nested xrefs. More importantly, the nested xrefs are actually shown attached to their parent xref.

The following exercise demonstrates the Tree View feature.

### Exercise 11.5    Accessing Tree View Display

1. Open the 11EX05.dwg file on the accompanying CD. The drawing contains two xrefs, each of which also contains two xrefs. When the drawing opens, the hierarchy of the xrefs and nested xrefs appears on-screen, as shown in Figure 11.11.

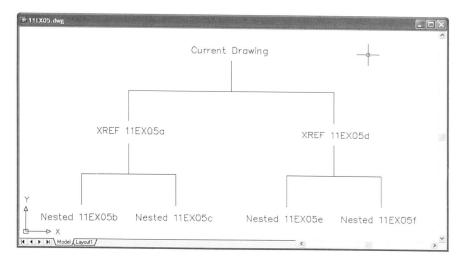

**Figure 11.11**   The hierarchy of the xrefs and nested xrefs.

2. From the Insert pull-down menu, choose Xref Manager. The Xref Manager dialog box opens. Initially, it opens in List View mode. Two buttons appear in the upper-left corner of the dialog box. The one on the left, the List View button, is active. The one on the right is the Tree View button.

**I**NSIDER **T**IP

In List View mode, you can sort the xrefs in the display box in ascending or descending order. This is true for any of the displayed data. To sort, choose a column's title bar. AutoCAD sorts the data in ascending order based on the selected column. Select the column's bar again to sort the data in descending order.

3. Click on the Tree View button.

   The text box below the buttons changes and now displays the hierarchy of the xrefs, as shown in Figure 11.12. From this display, you can easily manage the xrefs. For example, you can unload a nested xref that is no longer needed.

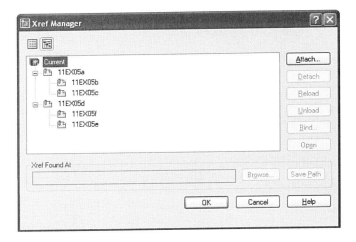

**Figure 11.12**   The Xref Manager in Tree View mode.

4. In the Xref Manager, choose 11EX05b.dwg. Several buttons in the Xref Manager become active, and the xref's path and drawing filename appear, as shown in Figure 11.13.

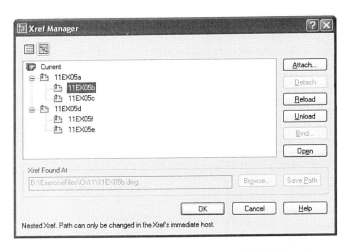

**Figure 11.13**   The Xref Manager's buttons activate when 11EX05b is selected.

5. Click the Unload button and then click OK.

**I**NSIDER **T**IP

Notice the Open button in Figure 11.13. It enables you to open a given xref in its own drawing editing window. You can also select more than one xref to open by using the Shift-pick method. After the Xref Manager dialog is closed, each xref is opened immediately into its own window. The current drawing becomes active again after the xref(s) are opened. This is another great reason to use the Multiple Document Environment.

AutoCAD unloads the nested xref 11EX05b and redisplays the drawing, as shown in Figure 11.14.

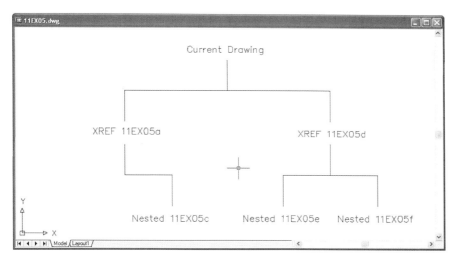

**Figure 11.14**   The Xref Tree View illustrating the condition after 11EX05b is unloaded.

You can now close the drawing. Do not save changes.

Depending on the structure of your xref drawings, an unloaded xref in a drawing might reload when you reopen the drawing. In the previous exercise, you unloaded an xref that was attached in another xref. This nested xref reloads when this drawing is reopened, regardless of its state when you saved the drawing. This functionality therefore can be used to maintain a certain level of expected tree structure because you cannot "mess" it up unless you unload the top-level xref.

▌**NSIDER TIP**

> The best way to eliminate the display of unwanted nested xrefs is to overlay them, but you can achieve the same effect—reducing regen time—by unloading an unwanted nested xref.

▌**NSIDER CAUTION**

> It is not recommended that you use long layer names if the data is to be used by R14 or earlier. Even though AutoCAD now supports long names, these names cannot be read properly by older versions.

## Pathing Your Xrefs

An xref's path can be defined as Full path, Relative path, or No path. Full paths include the entire directory path and end with the xref's filename. Relative paths contain only a partial subdirectory path and the xref's filename. AutoCAD saves both Full and Relative path data with the drawing. As for the No path option, all AutoCAD saves is the drawing filename.

There is an advantage to saving the xref paths relatively. If the drawing is opened on another workstation, AutoCAD successfully resolves the xref as long as the relative path hierarchy exists at the new workstation. In contrast, if the path is fully defined, AutoCAD might not find the xref file.

For example, suppose that a drawing lies in the following directory:

`C:\WORK\JOB-ONE\11EX06a.dwg`

Also, suppose that this drawing has an xref attached that lies in the following directory:

`C:\WORK\JOB-ONE\XREFS\11EX06b.dwg`

The xref path is fully defined. Notice that the entire drawing's path is shown, including its root directory. This means that while you edit the 11EX06a.dwg file at the workstation on which it resides, AutoCAD can successfully resolve the xref because it will find it in the full path. In other words, the xref file is still located on the `C:` drive in the subdirectory shown.

But what happens if the drawing and xref are moved to another workstation? Suppose that the files are moved to the following hard drive and directory:

```
C:\WORK\CLOSED-JOB-ONE\11EX06a.dwg
C:\WORK\CLOSED-JOB-ONE\XREFS\11EX06b.dwg
```

The 11EX07a.dwg file can still be opened in AutoCAD on the new workstation after it is located, but if the xref's path is not in the fully defined path, AutoCAD issues the following error message:

```
Resolve Xref "11EX06B": C:\WORK\JOB-ONE\XREFS\11EX06b.dwg
"C:\WORK\JOB-ONE\XREFS\11EX06b.dwg" cannot be found.
```

AutoCAD indicates that it can't find the xref indicated by the fully defined path. Consequently, AutoCAD opens the 11EX06a.dwg file without resolving the attachment of the xref that it could not find. To avoid the problem of unresolved xrefs, you can redefine the xref's path relatively, as described in the following exercise.

### Exercise 11.6    Implicitly Defining an Xref's Path

1. Create a new directory folder on your C: hard disk called **IAC2005**. Create a subdirectory in this directory named **XREFS**.

2. Copy the 11EX06.dwg drawing file on the accompanying CD into the C:\IA2005 subdirectory.

3. Copy the 11EX06a.dwg drawing file on the accompanying CD into the C:\IA2005\XREFS subdirectory.

4. Open the 11EX06.dwg drawing file from the C:\IAC2005 directory.

   The drawing opens and then issues the warning that it can't find the xref. (By pressing F2, you can toggle on the AutoCAD Text Window and view this warning.)

5. From the Insert pull-down menu, choose Xref Manager. The Xref Manager appears, as shown in Figure 11.15. Notice that the 11EX06a drawing file's status is Not Found. Also notice that AutoCAD looked for the xref in the explicitly defined path location listed in the Saved Path column.

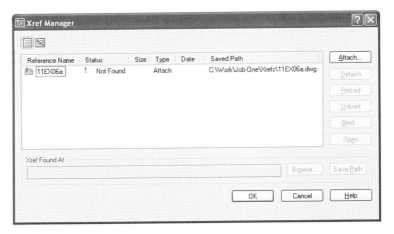

**Figure 11.15**    AutoCAD cannot find the xref using its explicitly defined path.

6. Select the reference name 11EX06a. The Xref Found At text box becomes active.

7. Click the Browse button. The Select New Path dialog box opens.

8. Open the 11EX06a.dwg drawing file from the C:\IA2005\XREFS directory.

   The display returns to the Xref Manager. The xref's path is now displayed in the Xref Found At text box, as shown in Figure 11.16. Notice that the 11EX06a status is now Reload.

**Figure 11.16**    The 11EX06a file's location is displayed in the Xref Found At text box.

**I**NSIDER NOTE

A new path assignment to an xref changes its status to Reload. This xref then automatically reloads upon exiting the Xref Manager dialog.

Next, you redefine the xref's path to be relative.

**9.** In the Xref Found At edit box, highlight the beginning portion of the path, from the root directory listing up to the Xrefs folder, as shown in Figure 11.17.

**Figure 11.17**    The beginning portion of the 11EX06a file's path is selected for deletion.

**10.** Press the Delete key. AutoCAD deletes the highlighted portion of the path.

**11.** Press Enter to save the modified path as the relative path. AutoCAD redefines the path as given and displays it in the Saved Path column, as shown in Figure 11.18.

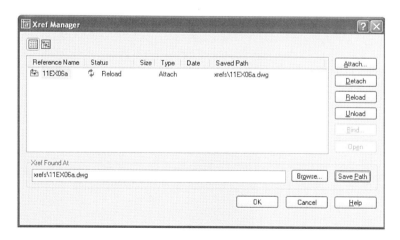

**Figure 11.18**    The 11EX06a file's path is redefined as relative.

**12.** Click OK.

You may close the drawing without saving your changes.

AutoCAD resolves the xref and loads it into the current drawing. AutoCAD was able to resolve 11EX06a using the relative path because the 11EX06.dwg file and the XREFS folder were in the same folder. In the exercise, both were in the C:\IAC2005 folder.

With the xref's path now relatively defined and saved with the drawing, if the 11EX06.dwg is moved to a different folder, and the 11EX06a.dwg is moved and placed in a subfolder named XREFS, AutoCAD resolves the xref when the 11EX06.dwg is opened. This is true as long as the 11EX06.dwg file and the XREFS subfolder are placed in the same folder.

By using the preceding technique to define xref paths relatively, you can avoid the problem of unresolved xrefs when transferring drawing files from one workstation to another.

### Relative Path Methods

A relative path is a partially provided folder path. This method is the most flexible, and it enables you to move drawings from one place to another, provided you maintain the original folder structure.

**I**NSIDER **N**OTE

> When the drawing that is xrefed is on a different drive or network server than the current drawing, the relative path option is not available. Because it is impossible to establish a relative path if the drive is different, you must use the full path method in this case.

Table 11.3 shows the various path conventions that can be used when specifying relative paths.

**Table 11.3    Relative Path Conventions**

| Option | Target |
| --- | --- |
| \ | Start at the root of the current drawing's drive. |
| path | From the folder of the current drawing, use this specific path. |
| \path | From the root folder, follow this specific path. |
| .\path | From the folder of the current drawing, follow this specific path. |
| ..\path | From the folder of the current drawing, go up one folder level and follow this specific path. |
| ..\..\path | From the folder of the current drawing, go up two folder levels and follow this specific path. |

**I**NSIDER **N**OTE

> If a drawing or series of drawings is moved or has its path information invalidated, you can use the Reference Manager application that comes with AutoCAD 2005 to correct the path problems. You can find the Reference Manager application on the Windows Start menu where the AutoCAD link is stored.

## *No Path Option*

If you choose to use the No path option when inserting xref drawings, you do not totally lose all path abilities. In reality, the path controls move from the drawing to how AutoCAD is configured. If no path information is stored in an xref, a series of other path controls begins the hunt for your xref in this order:

- The folder of the current drawing.

- A defined Project search path from the Files tab in the Options dialog box and a matching PROJECTNAME system variable.

- All the Support search paths listed under the Files tab in the Options dialog box.

- The Start In folder specified in the Microsoft Windows AutoCAD 2005 shortcut.

- If the Start In box is blank in the shortcut, the actual directory location of the shortcut link.

**I**NSIDER **T**IP

> You can use the PROJECTNAME system variable to assign xref search paths for your workstation. By assigning the search paths to a project name, you can resolve xrefs even when their paths are defined fully or relatively. In conditions where the drawings are shared or on a network, this can be a complicated process because each system would require set up prior to accessing the drawings.

**I**NSIDER **N**OTE

> AutoCAD 2005 introduced a new feature called Sheet Sets. This system of drawing management can greatly improve your ability to manage your drawings, much more than simply adjusting xref paths and using the PROJECTNAME system variable. You can learn more about this powerful new feature in Chapter 4, "Managing Your Drawing Projects."

## Circular Xrefs

Circular xrefs occur when two drawings are inserted as xrefs into each other. For example, suppose you have drawing A and drawing B. A circular xref occurs when drawing A is attached as an xref into drawing B, and then drawing B is attached as an xref into drawing A.

> **INSIDER NOTE**
>
> Circular xrefs will not occur if the xrefs are overlaid instead of being attached.

In releases prior to Release 14, AutoCAD would issue a warning about the circular reference and abort the XREF command. Now, AutoCAD loads the xref up to the point where the circularity exists. It stops at the point of circularity because a drawing cannot load itself as an xref.

> **INSIDER CAUTION**
>
> A circularity anomaly introduced into AutoCAD 2000 can cause problems in certain file-naming techniques. If a drawing has a period in its name other than the one separating the name and dwg suffix (filename.dwg), attaching xrefs will be halted if they share the same name up to the first period. For example: A2.10.dwg could not attach xref A2.10-2.dwg because AutoCAD 2000 would assume circularity at the A2. and halt attachment. With AutoCAD 2002, this problem was resolved, but it might be a good idea to avoid that naming practice if you need backward compatibility.

## Using *PROJECTNAME* to Specify Xref Search Paths

The PROJECTNAME system variable enables you to assign a project name to a drawing. The project name would also need to be declared in AutoCAD on each workstation and assigned search paths for xrefs. By assigning xref search paths to a project name on a workstation, you can load a drawing that has the same project name assigned to its PROJECTNAME variable and thereby use the workstation's search paths to resolve xrefs.

AutoCAD saves the project name in the workstation's system Registry and includes the search paths assigned to the project name. AutoCAD also saves the project name to the current drawing but does not save the search paths in the drawing. This means a particular project name can be assigned to a drawing that has xrefs attached, and each CAD technician can assign different xref paths to the same project name on his workstation.

When the drawing is opened, no matter what xref paths are defined in the drawing, each workstation resolves the drawing's xrefs. This feature avoids the problem of managing xref paths, either Full, Relative, or No path, in order to resolve xrefs.

This feature also enables you to create multiple project names on your workstation, each of which can contain a specific set of xref search paths. This means you can have many project names defined for your workstation, each with its own set of xref search paths.

**I**NSIDER **NOTE** _____

When AutoCAD searches for xrefs, it searches first for xrefs in the current drawing's folder, and then it searches using Full and Relative defined paths. Next, it searches using the current PROJECTNAME search paths, and finally, it uses AutoCAD's default search paths.

**I**NSIDER **NOTE** _____

It is recommended that you compare the speed of the loading xrefs through the PROJECTNAME variable and the Support File Search path from the Files tab in the Options dialog box. Some conditions can result in slower load times either way.

You can add as many paths as necessary to each project name, and you can create as many project names as you need. When a project name is highlighted by clicking the Set Current button, as shown in Figure 11.19, you set the current drawing's PROJECTNAME variable to the highlighted project name. The highlighted project's search paths then become the current paths that AutoCAD uses to find xrefs.

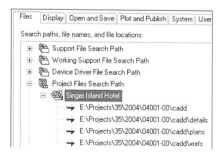

**Figure 11.19**   Highlighting the project name and clicking the Set Current button located to the right of the Options dialog, sets the drawing's PROJECTNAME system variable.

# Xref Layers and Their Properties

When an xref is attached to the current drawing, AutoCAD adds the xref's layer names to the current drawing. AutoCAD prefixes the layer names with the xref's name, followed by the pipe symbol (|). These layers initially have the same properties as the layers in the xref drawing. The exceptions to this are layers 0 and Defpoints.

Just like blocks, objects in the xref on layer 0 have special properties. If the object's properties are set to ByLayer, it assumes the properties of the layer on which the xref itself is inserted. If the object's properties are set to ByBlock, it assumes the properties that are currently defined for the creation of new objects in the current drawing, as displayed in the Object Properties toolbar. Finally, if the object's properties are explicitly defined in the xref, those properties remain fixed.

Except for properties assigned explicitly in the xref, you can change the properties of any xref's layers from the Layer Properties Manager. These changes appear in the current drawing and do not affect the properties in the original xref file. After you exit the drawing, however, any changes to the properties are lost. When the drawing is opened again, the properties assume the settings in the original xref.

**I**NSIDER **T**IP

> To save changes you make to an xref layer's properties with the current drawing, set the system variable VISRETAIN to 1. When you close the drawing, the changes you made to the xref layer's properties in a previous editing session are saved.

# The Reference Editing Feature

AutoCAD 2005's most powerful editing feature is called Reference Editing. This feature enables you to edit objects in an inserted xref file from the current drawing and save the changes back to the xref file. You can use Reference Editing to quickly edit an inserted xref without the need to open the xref file.

Reference Editing is intended to enable you to make modest edits to an xref file from the current drawing. Although you can make significant changes to the xref file from the current drawing, it is more efficient to open the xref file to directly perform significant edits. Using Reference Editing to make significant changes to xref files can temporarily increase the current drawing's file size, thereby increasing regen times and slowing productivity. Therefore, use this feature only to quickly make modest edits to xrefs.

**I**NSIDER **T**IP

When you need to edit an xref, you have two options. The REFEDIT command loads objects into the current drawing so they can be changed. Depending on the volume of work you want to do, you may also use the XOPEN command. This feature simply opens the problem xref into a new AutoCAD drawing session, ready for changing.

After you select the xref, you specify the objects you want to edit. AutoCAD temporarily brings the selected objects into the current drawing for modification and makes them part of a working set. After the objects are modified, the working set of objects is saved back to the xref file.

The following exercise demonstrates how to use Reference Editing.

### Exercise 11.7    Changing an Xref with Reference Editing

1. Copy the files 11EX07.dwg and 11EX07a.dwg from the accompanying CD to the C:\IAC2005 subdirectory. Before you continue with the exercise, you might need to clear the read-only attribute on drawing files.

2. From Windows Explorer, select the C:\IAC2005 copies of the 11EX07.dwg and 11EX07a.dwg files and then right-click to display the shortcut menu.

3. From the right-click shortcut menu, choose Properties. The Properties dialog box appears.

4. From the Properties dialog box, clear the Read-Only check box and then click OK. The read-only attribute is cleared from the files.

   Next, you start a new drawing and xref the 11EX07.dwg file.

5. In AutoCAD 2005, start a new drawing from scratch.

6. From the File pull-down menu, choose Save. AutoCAD displays the Save Drawing As dialog box.

7. Name the file **MYFILE** and save it to the C:\IAC2005 subdirectory.

8. From the Insert pull-down menu, choose External Reference. The Select Reference File dialog box appears.

9. Open the 11EX07.dwg drawing file from the C:\IAC2005 directory. AutoCAD displays the External Reference dialog box.

10. In the External Reference dialog box, under Reference Type, choose Attachment.

11. In the Insertion Point area, Scale area, and Rotation area, clear any checked Specify On-Screen check boxes. The Path type can be whatever you want.

12. Click OK. AutoCAD attaches the drawing and displays two text objects inside a rectangle object.

    The upper text object is located in the 11EX07.dwg xref file. The lower text object is located in the 11EX07a.dwg file and is a nested xref.

13. Perform a ZOOM extents to view the xref better.

14. From the Modify pull-down menu, choose Xref and Block Editing, Edit Reference In-Place. AutoCAD prompts you to select a reference.

15. Select the lower text object. AutoCAD displays the Reference Edit dialog box, which shows the two xref filenames, as shown in Figure 11.20.

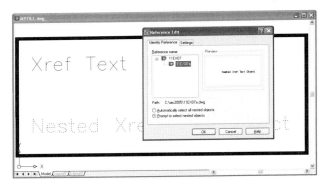

**Figure 11.20** The Reference Edit dialog box enables you to select the xref to edit.

Because the 11EX07a.dwg file is nested within the 11EX07.dwg file and you selected the text object that's in the nested xref, AutoCAD displays both names. At this point, you select the file whose objects you want to edit.

16. In the Reference Name area, be sure to choose the 11EX07a.dwg file. Also select the Prompt to select nested objects option as shown in Figure 11.20.

17. Click the Settings tab at the top of the Reference Edit dialog box. As shown in Figure 11.21, this tab has more controls that can be used when editing xrefs.

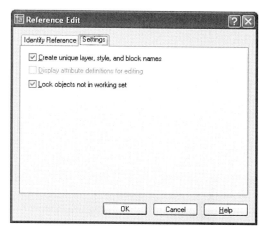

**Figure 11.21**    The Settings tab of the Reference Edit dialog has several controls for the data within an xref.

**I**NSIDER **N**OTE

The three options on the Settings tabs perform different tasks. The first enables AutoCAD to create unique named objects for use during the editing period. This cuts down on conflicts during the process such as frozen layers. The Display attribute definitions during edit control is needed when accessing blocks with attributes. More information on this is found in Chapter 10, "Creating and Using Blocks." The last option, Lock objects not in working set, locks down all other objects not selected so that you cannot accidentally modify them.

**18.** Be sure the Create unique layer, style, and block names control is checked and that the Lock objects not in working set control is checked as well.

**I**NSIDER **N**OTE

AutoCAD creates temporary layer names in the current drawing when the Create unique layer, style, and block names check box is selected.

**19.** Click OK. AutoCAD prompts you to select the nested objects.

**20.** Choose the lower text object and then press Enter to end object selection. AutoCAD relocates the selected object into the current drawing and displays the Refedit toolbar.

Notice that AutoCAD fades objects that are not being edited, as shown in Figure 11.22. This makes it easier to identify the objects you selected for editing.

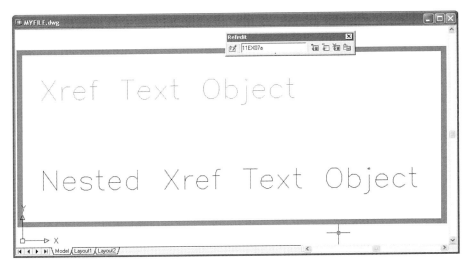

**Figure 11.22**   AutoCAD fades objects that are not being edited.

Next, you edit the lower text object and save the changes back to its xref.

**21.** Select the lower text object. AutoCAD highlights the object.

**22.** Right-click to display the shortcut menu and then choose Text Edit. AutoCAD displays the Edit Text dialog box.

**23.** In the text box, replace the highlighted text with the word MODIFIED.

**24.** Click OK and then press Enter to end object selection. AutoCAD modifies the text object.

**25.** Click the Save back changes to reference button. AutoCAD issues a warning noting that all reference edits will be saved.

**26.** Click OK. AutoCAD saves the changes back to the xref file and then exits the reference edit mode.

You may close the drawing without saving your changes.

At this point, if you open the 11EX07a.dwg drawing from the C:\IAC2005 directory, you will see that the text object has changed to MODIFIED.

**I**NSIDER **T**IP

> There is a command-line method to open an external reference from within a given drawing. With the XOPEN command, you can simply select an xref to open, and AutoCAD immediately opens the selected xref in another drawing window. This command can also be reached from the right-click menu after selecting an xref.

AutoCAD enables you to add or remove additional objects to the working set. This is done by clicking the Add or Remove Objects from the Working Set buttons, located on the Refedit toolbar. If you decide you don't want to save edits back to the original xref, you can click the Discard Changes button.

While in the Reference Edit mode, if you create new objects, they are almost always added to the working set. In some situations, this is not true, such as when AutoCAD generates an arc object during the FILLET command.

Although AutoCAD fades objects that are not part of the working set, the objects can still be edited if the Lock objects not in working set option is off. In those cases, caution should be taken when editing. For example, if the MYFILE drawing contained another text object, you could edit its text string.

## Xref Update Communications

A helpful management tool in AutoCAD 2005 is the Communication Center. This area is located in the lower right of the AutoCAD application dialog. Aside from the various icons that appear in this area, when you have an xref inserted into the current drawing, a specific icon becomes available to help with xref management.

The primary component of this is the Manage Xrefs icon, as shown in Figure 11.23. When you simply click this icon, the Xref Manager dialog becomes active. Then you can perform any xref-related task you need, such as attaching or reloading an xref.

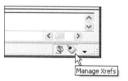

**Figure 11.23**
The Manage Xrefs icon provides quick access to several xref activities.

Additional ability is gained through its right-click shortcut menu. If you right-click above the icon, you also gain the option to simply reload all xrefs. Another benefit of the Communication Center area is that when an attached xref changes, you get a balloon notification.

If, in the previous exercise, you used XOPEN command, edited the text from within the xref drawing itself, and then saved and closed the drawing, when you returned to the MYFILE drawing, a notification as shown in Figure 11.24 would be in the lower right of the AutoCAD window. Additionally, when an attached xref in your drawing changes, you get a balloon notice to reload, even if someone else changed the xref.

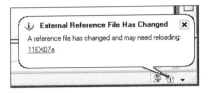

**Figure 11.24**    The balloon notification that appears when an attached xref changes.

Within the balloon itself, you have two action options. When you click the xref name link, the Xref Manager opens, enabling you to reload an xref or do some other xref management activity. You also have the option to do nothing by clicking the [X] button on the balloon notification.

**INSIDER TIP**

Often, when you are working in a network environment, you might need to open drawings that others might have open. When you do this through the Open command, AutoCAD notifies you of who has it open if it is actually open by someone else. But perhaps you don't want to open it and just want to know who has it open. Then you can use the WHOHAS command. This lets you browse to a given directory and drawing file and then report who has the file open for editing. This can be very helpful in wide-area networks because you can't just walk around and see who has what open.

In addition, as long as you have xrefs that need to be reloaded, the Manage Xrefs icon is enhanced with a exclamation mark. This visual clue can be very helpful because your xrefs might change frequently, and you might want to keep the latest versions loaded. This system works for xrefs that you have changed in another drawing window or xrefs that others have changed within your network.

There are also visual clues within the Xref Manager dialog box under the Status column. When a loaded xref changes while attached in the current drawing, as shown in Figure 11.25, the Status column provides visual indicators.

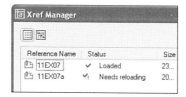

**Figure 11.25**   The Status column within the Xref Manager dialog changes if attached xrefs change during the current drawing session.

The Status column also provides other information about your xrefs. A good understanding of these terms will aid in your quick repair of situations that might occur as you use xrefs with your drawings.

- **Loaded.** Xref is current and attached.

- **Unloaded.** Will be unloaded after the Xref Manager dialog closes.

- **Unreferenced.** Xref is attached to the drawing database but not inserted, as if it were erased.

- **Not Found.** Does not exist in any valid search path.

- **Unresolved.** Not compatible with AutoCAD; possibly corrupt.

- **Orphaned.** Attached to another xref that is unreferenced, unresolved, or not found.

As you see, many different situations can exist for your xrefs. Understanding these conditions and how to resolve them is crucial to using xrefs successfully.

# Summary

In this chapter, you learned about the Partial Open and Partial Load features and about the Reference Editing feature. You also learned about the differences between attaching and overlaying xrefs, and about the differences between binding and xbinding xrefs. You reviewed how to create clipping boundaries, and you learned how to increase productivity with Demand Loading and spatial and layer indexes. The way AutoCAD deals with circular xrefs was covered, as was the PROJECTNAME system variable and the way it stores xrefs' paths. You learned about the Xref Manager and how it is used to manage xrefs and nested xrefs. You also learned about new methods for understanding the status of your xrefs.

AutoCAD's xref capabilities are powerful. You can save regen time and increase your productivity by using these xref features to better manage xrefs.

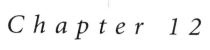

# Chapter 12

# Applications for DesignCenter

The power of AutoCAD lies in its capability to reuse existing data. Objects such as blocks and xrefs, as well as layers, text styles, and linetypes, can be used repeatedly after they are defined. By reusing existing data in your drawing, you avoid duplicating tasks, which saves time and increases productivity.

AutoCAD 2005 contains a powerful feature called AutoCAD DesignCenter, which enables you to quickly locate, view, and import a variety of existing AutoCAD objects into the current drawing. In essence, you can peek inside a drawing to see the blocks it contains and even identify its xrefs. You can view its defined text styles, dimension styles, and linetypes. You can also identify its layers and layouts. After the desired objects are located, DesignCenter enables you to place duplicates of the objects into the current drawing, thereby instantly populating your drawing with valuable data from other drawings. By using AutoCAD DesignCenter, you take advantage of AutoCAD's real power—the power to reuse existing, valuable data.

In this chapter, you learn about the following subjects:

- Understanding the AutoCAD DesignCenter interface
- Loading content into DesignCenter
- Adding content to drawings

# Understanding the AutoCAD DesignCenter Interface

AutoCAD DesignCenter is primarily composed of two windowpanes, as shown in Figure 12.1. The pane on the left is the navigation pane or Tree View interface, and the pane on the right is the content pane or palette interface. The Tree View enables you to locate source objects, and the palette enables you to view the content of the source objects. For example, in Figure 12.1, the Tree View is used to navigate to the My Computer folder, and the folder's contents are displayed in the palette. In the following two sections, we explore the Tree View and the palette interfaces.

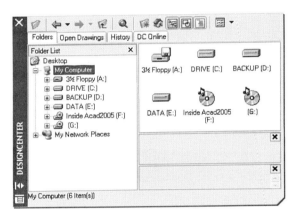

**Figure 12.1**   DesignCenter is composed of the Tree View and palette windowpanes.

## Exploring the DesignCenter Tree View

DesignCenter's Tree View enables you to easily navigate through a directory structure. It works similarly to Windows Explorer, enabling you to expand or collapse folders to control the display of subfolders. By using the Tree View, you can navigate to the desired location.

Although the Tree View enables you to easily view and navigate a directory structure, you are not required to use it. You can turn off the Tree View display by clicking the Tree View Toggle button, as shown in Figure 12.2. Toggling off the Tree View display is useful after you have located the desired folder and no longer need the Tree View. By toggling off the Tree View, the palette automatically expands, making the viewing of source objects easier.

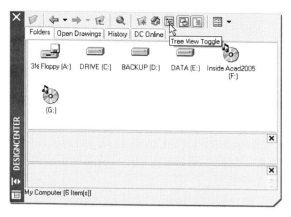

**Figure 12.2**   You can toggle off the Tree View display.

> Although you can use the palette to navigate through a directory, it's better to use the Tree View because it makes it easier to identify your location in a directory structure.

Tree View can display views in four different modes. Using a particular mode can assist you in locating the desired content source more quickly. The four modes are as follows:

- **Folders.** Enables you to locate source data on local or network drives.
- **Open Drawings.** Lists all opened drawings in the current AutoCAD session.
- **History.** Displays the last 20 locations of source objects accessed through DesignCenter.
- **DC Online.** Opens the DesignCenter Online web page. When you get a web connection, the left pane displays folders containing symbol libraries, manufacturer sites, and additional content libraries. The right side shows more information and symbols enabling you to insert a web-located drawing into your current drawing.

> A fifth mode, called Custom Content, is displayed only when there are applications currently registered with your AutoCAD 2005 application. When applications that contain custom content are registered with AutoCAD, such as Object ARX applications, DesignCenter displays the Custom Content tab, allowing you to locate and view the registered application's content.

You can switch to the desired tab by clicking the appropriate tab button. The current tab in Figure 12.3 is Open Drawings, which lists all open drawings from which source objects can be accessed.

---

**I**NSIDER **T**IP

You can use the ADCNAVIGATE command to navigate to a specific filename, directory location, or network path in the DesignCenter Tree View. Simply type **ADCNAVIGATE** at the command prompt and enter a folder path, a folder path and drawing filename, or a UNC equivalent.

---

In the History tab, DesignCenter automatically turns off the palette. This mode is intended to enable you to quickly locate the most recent locations from which you copied source objects. To redisplay the palette, click one of the other tabs in DesignCenter. You can refresh the Tree View and palette display by right-clicking in the palette and then selecting Refresh from the shortcut menu.

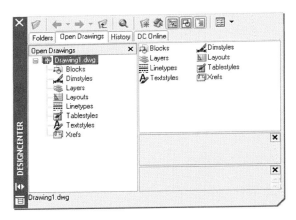

**Figure 12.3**    Tree View's different display modes are accessed from the various tabs that line its top edge.

By using DesignCenter's Tree View, you can easily navigate through a directory structure to the desired location of source data. In the next section, you learn about DesignCenter's palette interface, which enables you to view source objects.

# Exploring the DesignCenter Palette

DesignCenter's palette displays the source objects found in a particular location. For example, when a location is selected using the Tree View, the location's source objects are displayed in the palette, as shown in Figure 12.4.

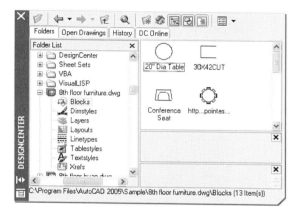

**Figure 12.4**   The palette displays the source objects using the Large Icons view.

The palette can display source objects in one of four views. The view you select largely depends on the source objects you want to view. For example, when viewing blocks in a drawing, it is appropriate to use the Large Icons view to better see each block's thumbnail image, as shown in Figure 12.4. However, when viewing drawing files in a folder, choosing the Details view may be more desirable, as shown in Figure 12.5. The four available views are as follows:

- **Large Icons.** Displays source objects using large object icons and uses thumbnail images, if available.

- **Small Icons.** Displays source objects using small object icons and does not use thumbnail images, even if they are available.

- **List.** Displays source objects as a simple list, without file detail information.

- **Details.** Displays source objects as a list and includes file information such as each file's size and type, if available.

By selecting the desired view, you can preview the source objects in an appropriate format.

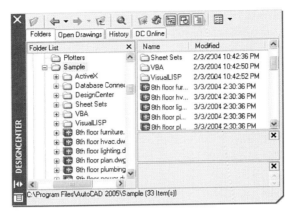

**Figure 12.5**    The palette displays source objects using Details view.

INSIDER TIP

> By right-clicking in the palette, you can select the desired view display by selecting View from the shortcut menu.

By using the DesignCenter's palette, you can easily view source objects in a format that you find useful. In the next section, you are introduced to two additional panes that provide additional information about the selected source object.

INSIDER TIP

> You can control the sort order of objects displayed in the Details view by clicking the button at the top of each column. For example, in Figure 12.5, if you click the Modified button at the top of the palette, you can sort the objects in the list by date in ascending order. By clicking the button a second time, you can re-sort the objects by date in descending order.

# Viewing Images and Descriptions of Source Objects

There are two additional windowpanes you can open in DesignCenter. These panes display an image of the selected source object and its description, if such information was saved with the source object. By using these preview and description panes, you can better identify the contents of a source object before its contents are copied to the current drawing.

The preview pane enables you to display an image of the selected object, and it is activated by clicking the Preview button, as shown in Figure 12.6. The preview pane is resizable, and it can be expanded to better view the source object's image.

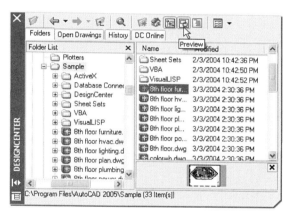

**Figure 12.6**   The palette displays source objects with a preview window.

**I**NSIDER **T**IP

> You can automatically generate preview images for blocks that do not have preview images by using the BLOCKICON command, which generates preview images for block references defined in the current drawing.

The description pane displays text that describes the selected source object. When you click the Description button, if a description was provided, the description pane displays the description below the palette, as shown in Figure 12.7. By using the DesignCenter's Description feature, you can better determine whether the selected source object is the one you need to copy into the current drawing. Description data can be placed in a drawing by using Drawing Properties and in blocks by using the Block Definition dialog box.

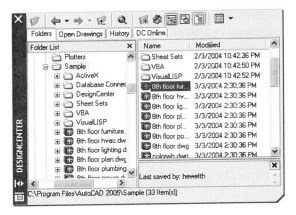

**Figure 12.7**   The palette can display source object descriptions such as who saved it last.

By using the preview and description features provided in DesignCenter, you can better identify the contents of a source object before its contents are copied to the current drawing. In the next section, you learn about other techniques for displaying source objects in the DesignCenter's palette.

# Loading Content into DesignCenter

When you use the Tree View to locate source objects and then display those objects in the palette, you are actually loading content into the palette. Although the Tree View's simple interface can load content into the palette, its capabilities are limited. For example, the Tree View does not enable you to define the file type you want to locate when browsing for source objects. Additionally, Tree View does not provide an automated find feature that locates content based on a keyword search.

To compensate, DesignCenter has additional, powerful methods for loading content. For example, you can locate drawings using a feature similar to AutoCAD's Select File dialog box, which enables you to browse for files. The Load feature enables you to indicate the file type for which you are searching, and it displays a preview image of the selected file.

You can also use the powerful Search feature, which can look through local and network drives for files, as well as source objects within files, using search criteria. By using these features, you can more easily locate the desired source objects, especially when you're not sure where to look.

In the following two sections, you learn how to use the Load and Search feature to more easily locate the desired source objects.

# Using the Load Feature

By using the Load dialog box, you can browse for files on local and network drives, in your Favorites folder, or over the Internet. You can also use this feature to automate searching for a particular file based on its name or its file type. By using the Load dialog box, you can use specific tools to locate, preview, and load content into the palette.

The Load dialog box is opened by clicking the Load button located at the top of DesignCenter, as shown in Figure 12.8. After you click the Load button, the Load dialog box appears, as shown in Figure 12.9. After you've opened this dialog box, you can use the various features of the Load dialog box to locate files.

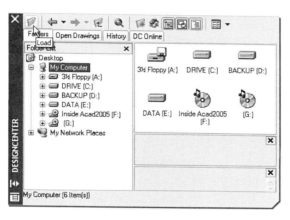

**Figure 12.8**    DesignCenter's Load button.

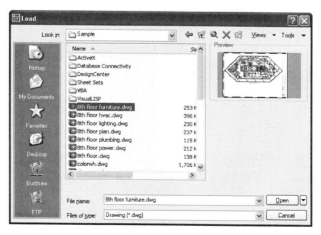

**Figure 12.9**    The Load dialog box locates source files. This is similar to a standard Open dialog.

In the following exercise, you use the Search feature.

### Exercise 12.1   Locating Files with DesignCenter

1. Create a new folder on your computer hard disk off C:\ called Find Files.

2. Copy the 12EX01.dwg, 12EX01A.dwg, and 12EX01B.dwg files from the accompanying CD to the Find Files folder.

3. After copying the files, right-click on the DWG files and select Properties, then clear the Read-only attribute if it is active.

   Next, you use the Locate feature to find the files.

4. Start a new drawing in AutoCAD.

5. From the Standard toolbar, select AutoCAD DesignCenter. AutoCAD opens DesignCenter.

6. From DesignCenter, select Search (the icon with the magnifying glass). AutoCAD displays the Search dialog box (see Figure 12.10).

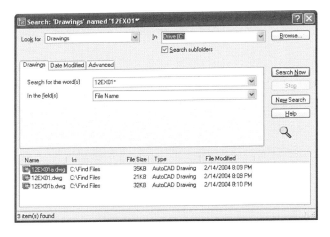

**Figure 12.10**   The Browse/Search feature of the Search dialog box locates files based on patterns.

7. In the Look for drop-down list, make sure Drawings is selected. Select the Drawings tab if needed.

8. In the Search for word(s) text box, type **12EX01\***. (Be sure to include the asterisk at the end of the text string and not the period ending the sentence.)

9. At the In drop-down list, select the drive on which you created the Find Files folder. Also make sure the option to search subfolders is checked.

**10.** Click Search Now. AutoCAD searches the selected drive using the `12EX01*` search filter and displays the results in the results area, as shown in Figure 12.10.

**11.** From the results area, double-click the 12EX01.dwg file, returning you to the DesignCenter dialog box. AutoCAD displays the file's location in the Tree View and displays its content in the palette, as shown in Figure 12.11.

**INSIDER NOTE**

The Search dialog is put behind AutoCAD but remains open. You can close this by making it active and then selecting the [X] in the top right of the dialog.

You may close DesignCenter and close the drawing without saving changes.

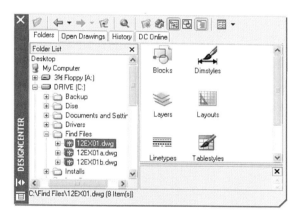

**Figure 12.11**    The found files' locations are displayed in the Tree View, and their contents are displayed in the palette.

**INSIDER NOTE**

You can also load content into the palette using Windows Explorer by dragging a file from Explorer to DesignCenter's palette.

In the next section, you use the Search feature to locate content within files.

# Searching for Content Using the Find Feature

DesignCenter has a very powerful search feature that enables you to locate the source objects you need. For example, you can search for drawing files by name, keyword, or description. You can also search inside drawings for a variety of source objects including blocks, layers, linetypes, and text styles. By using DesignCenter's Search feature, you can locate the source objects you need, even if they reside within a drawing.

**I**NSIDER **T**IP

> To make drawings easier to find, add keywords to the current drawing by using the Drawing Properties dialog box, which appears when you select Drawing Properties from the File pull-down menu. To make blocks easier to find, AutoCAD enables you to add a description to the block in the Block Definition dialog box. By adding keywords and descriptions to drawings and blocks, you can use DesignCenter's Search feature to quickly locate the desired source object.

In the following exercise, you use DesignCenter's Search feature to locate a specific block that resides inside a drawing.

### Exercise 12.2   Locating Blocks with DesignCenter's Search Feature

This exercise uses drawing files previously copied to the C:\Find Files folder, as instructed in steps 1 and 2 of Exercise 12.1.

1. Start a new drawing in AutoCAD.

2. From the Standard toolbar, select AutoCAD DesignCenter. AutoCAD opens DesignCenter.

3. From DesignCenter, click the Search button. AutoCAD displays the Search dialog box.

4. From the Look For list, select Blocks.

5. From the In list, select the drive on which you created the Find Files folder.

6. From the Blocks tab, in the Search for the name box, type **alarm**. This instructs AutoCAD to search for blocks that are named alarm.

7. Click Search Now. AutoCAD searches the selected drive for any drawing files that contain a block named alarm and displays the results, as shown in Figure 12.12.

**Figure 12.12**    The Search dialog box locates source objects, such as blocks, within drawing files.

8. In the list of found files, double-click the Alarm name; AutoCAD then loads its related drawing into the DesignCenter panel. AutoCAD displays the file's location in the Tree View and its content in the palette.

**I**NSIDER **TIP**

> You can quickly place blocks and other objects onto Tool Palettes by selecting an object and using the right-click menu. See Chapter 22, "Customizing Without Programming," for how to create and customize Tool Palettes.

You may close DesignCenter, close the Search dialog box, and close the drawing without saving changes.

The Search dialog box enables you to locate files and source objects within files by entering search criteria. You can use its three tabs to locate files by type, by date modified, or by specific text. You can search for a variety of object types, such as blocks, layers, layouts, and xrefs, and you can search for objects based on text values for block names, drawing and block descriptions, and attribute tags and values.

**I**NSIDER **T**IP

> You can avoid searching for frequently accessed source objects by right-clicking the source object and selecting Add to Favorites from the shortcut menu, which adds a shortcut to the source object in the Autodesk Favorites folder. The source object can then be loaded into the palette by clicking the Favorites button in DesignCenter and then selecting the source object's shortcut icon. The Favorites listing in DesignCenter is different from Windows Favorites.

In the previous sections, you learned how to use DesignCenter's various tools for locating content. In the next section, you learn how to load content into the current drawing.

# Adding Content to Drawings

The purpose of DesignCenter is to make locating existing AutoCAD objects easy. Consequently, DesignCenter provides several methods for locating and identifying premade source objects.

After you have located a desired source object, you must copy it into the current drawing. After it is copied into the current drawing, the object becomes a part of the current drawing and can be used just as if it were originally created in the current drawing. Therefore, objects such as blocks, xrefs, layers, layouts, text styles, and dimensions styles can be copied into the current drawing from DesignCenter's palette.

Typically, after you've identified a source object and displayed it in DesignCenter's palette, you can copy the object to the current drawing by simply dragging it from the palette into the current drawing's window. This works for the following objects:

- Blocks
- Dimstyles
- Layers
- Layouts
- Linetypes
- Tablestyles
- Textstyles
- Xrefs

You can select multiple source objects of the types shown in this list. By dragging the desired source object(s) from the palette into the current drawing, you can quickly add content to the current drawing.

But not all individual objects can be simply dragged into the current drawing. Primary file type objects such as drawings, blocks, images, and xrefs can be only copied one at a time. Additionally, you can define their scale, rotation, and insertion point.

In the following exercise, you use DesignCenter to locate source objects and insert them into the current drawing.

### Exercise 12.3   Loading Content into the Palette

This exercise uses drawing files copied to the `C:\Find Files` folder, as instructed in steps 1 and 2 of Exercise 12.1.

1. Start a new drawing in AutoCAD.

2. From the Standard toolbar, select AutoCAD DesignCenter. AutoCAD opens DesignCenter.

3. In Tree View, navigate to the `C:\Find Files` folder, then click the plus sign to expand the folder. The three drawing files in the `Find Files` folder appear in the Tree View.

   Next, you use DesignCenter to attach an xref to the current drawing.

4. In Tree View, click the plus sign next to the 12EX01.dwg file to display its source objects.

5. In Tree View, select the Xrefs source object. The palette displays the two xrefs that are attached to the 12EX01.dwg drawing, as shown in Figure 12.13.

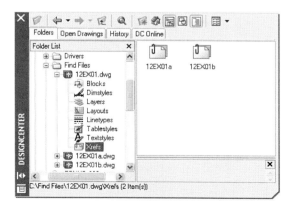

**Figure 12.13**   The attached xrefs are displayed in the palette.

6.  In the palette, right-click the 12EX01a xref.

7.  From the shortcut menu, select Attach Xref. AutoCAD displays the External Reference dialog box.

8.  In the Insertion Point area, clear the Specify On-Screen check box, then click OK. AutoCAD attaches the xref to the current drawing.

---

**I**NSIDER **CAUTION**

DesignCenter will not copy an object if an object with an identical name already exists in the current drawing. To copy the object using DesignCenter, you must change the name of the object that already resides in the current drawing.

---

Next, you use DesignCenter to copy a block definition into the current drawing.

9.  In Tree View, click the minus sign next to the 12EX01.dwg file to collapse the display of its source objects.

10.  In Tree View, click the plus sign next to the 12EX01A.dwg file to display its source objects.

11.  In Tree View, select the Blocks source object. The palette displays the block definitions that are stored in the 12EX01A.dwg drawing, as shown in Figure 12.14.

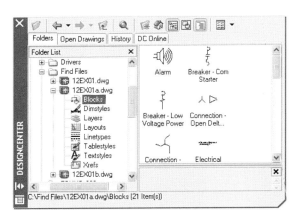

**Figure 12.14**   The selected drawing's block definitions are displayed in the palette.

12.  In the palette, right-click the Alarm block definition.

13.  From the shortcut menu, select Insert Block. AutoCAD displays the Insert dialog box.

At this point, you could specify the insertion values to use to insert the block into the current drawing's model space. For this exercise, though, just click Cancel to close the Insert dialog box without inserting a block reference.

**14.** Click Cancel. AutoCAD saves the block definition in the current drawing, then closes the Insert dialog box.

**I**NSIDER  **N**OTE

> By clicking Cancel to close the Insert dialog box, you insert a block definition into the current drawing without actually inserting a block reference into the current drawing's model space. The block definition can then be used at a later time to insert a block reference using the INSERT command.

Next, you use DesignCenter to copy layers into the current drawing.

**15.** In Tree View, select the Layers source object. The palette displays the layers that are stored in the 12EX01A.dwg drawing, as shown in Figure 12.15 in List view.

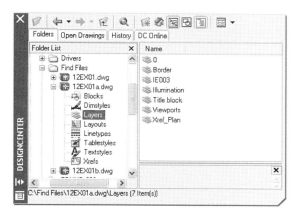

**Figure 12.15**    The selected drawing's layers are displayed in the palette.

**16.** In the palette, starting in the upper-left corner, drag a window around all the layers to select them. DesignCenter highlights all the layers.

**17.** Right-click over one of the highlighted layers, then select Add Layer(s) from the shortcut menu. DesignCenter adds the highlighted layers to the current drawing.

You may close DesignCenter and the drawing without saving changes.

By using DesignCenter, you can easily locate source objects and copy their content into the current drawing. When copying objects such as blocks and xrefs, you can only copy the objects one at a time. When copying objects such as layers, linetypes, and textstyles, however, you can select multiple objects and copy them simultaneously.

## DesignCenter Online

A new mechanism you can leverage to find and use data is the DC Online tab panel. This feature can be a real time-saver because there is a continually growing library of web resources. Figure 12.16 shows a sample area that is accessible from within the DC Online panel.

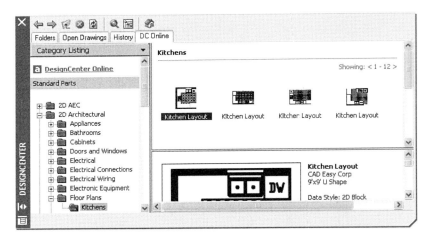

**Figure 12.16**   The DC Online panel shows Internet-served resources that are simple to utilize.

The basis of this technology is *i-drop*. Although this subject is outside the scope of this book, the Internet is made CAD-ready through i-drop technology. It provides a way to store, review, and insert drawings from Internet sites.

# Summary

In this chapter, you learned how to use DesignCenter to locate source objects and copy their content into the current drawing. You used DesignCenter's Load and Search features to acquire source objects. You also learned how to use the Tree View to locate source objects and how to display the content of source objects in the palette. You experienced dragging different types of content from the palette and copying them into the current drawing. In this chapter, you learned how to use DesignCenter to find and use existing data, which enables you to work more productively by reusing existing AutoCAD objects located in other drawings.

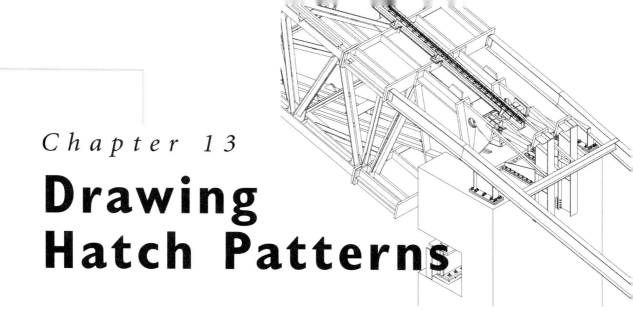

# Chapter 13

# Drawing Hatch Patterns

Hatching is one of the most time-consuming processes in AutoCAD. You often will need to fill an area with a repetitive pattern or a solid fill, in which case you use the BHATCH command to create the required hatch object. In this chapter, you will learn to do the following:

- Specify the pattern to be used and the parameters governing the generation of the hatch
- Define the boundaries of the area to be filled
- Create gradient hatching
- Edit a hatch pattern
- Control the visibility of hatch objects
- Create your own custom hatch pattern
- Use the BOUNDARY command to create outlines of complex areas
- Deal with gaps in geometry

# Creating Hatch Patterns Using *BHATCH*

Hatch patterns, including solid fills, are used to highlight an area of your drawing, to visually separate areas of your drawing that share common boundaries, or to convey information about an area of your drawing. Figure 13.1 shows several examples of using hatch patterns.

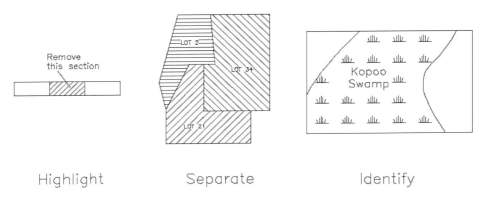

**Figure 13.1**   Examples of the use of hatch objects.

To issue the BHATCH command, from the Draw toolbar, choose Hatch. The Boundary Hatch and Fill dialog box appears (see Figure 13.2).

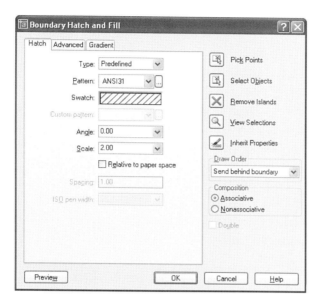

**Figure 13.2**   The BHATCH command's Boundary Hatch and Fill dialog box.

## Specifying a Pattern

When selecting a hatch pattern, you have several choices. First, you can choose from any of the predefined patterns that come with AutoCAD. Second, you can make a basic line pattern on-the-fly using the current linetype. Last, you can select a pattern that is defined in any custom PAT file that you have added to the AutoCAD search path. All these methods are discussed in the following sections.

### Predefined Patterns

AutoCAD comes with a large number of predefined patterns. A number of these are standard patterns established by the American National Standards Institute (ANSI) and are used widely in North America. Another group of predefined patterns is derived from patterns established by the International Standards Organization (ISO), the organization that sets international drafting standards in all fields except electrical and electronic. Yet a third group of predefined patterns includes many useful and traditional patterns used worldwide. Figure 13.3 shows a sampling of these patterns.

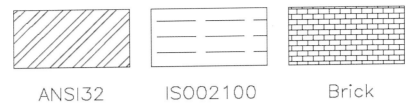

ANSI32          ISO02100          Brick

**Figure 13.3**   Some sample predefined hatch patterns supplied with AutoCAD.

To select a predefined hatch pattern, in the Hatch tab of the Boundary Hatch and Fill dialog box, make sure that Predefined is selected from the Type drop-down list (refer to Figure 13.2). In the Pattern drop-down list, select a pattern name. Notice that a representation of the selected pattern is displayed in the Swatch display box. You can also select a pattern by type (ISO, ANSI, and so on) by clicking the [...] button next to the Pattern drop-down list. This displays the Hatch Pattern Palette dialog box (see Figure 13.4). You can select a pattern from any of the tabs either by double-clicking on the pattern or by selecting the pattern and closing the dialog box by clicking OK.

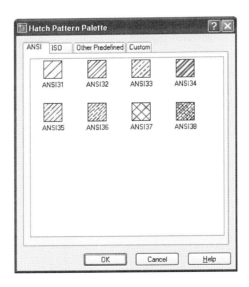

**Figure 13.4**   The Hatch Pattern Palette dialog box of the BHATCH command.

## Choosing Scale and Angle Settings

After you choose a pattern, you can also adjust the Angle and Scale settings as desired in the Boundary Hatch and Fill dialog box. Figure 13.5 shows the effects of changing scale and rotation.

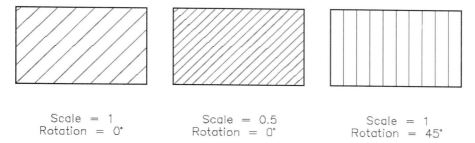

**Figure 13.5**   The effects of changing hatch pattern scale and rotation.

Some of the predefined patterns are intended to represent real-world materials and are defined with appropriate dimensions. Drawing these patterns at a scale factor at or near 1.0 yields realistic results in full-scale drawings. The pattern AR-B88, for example, represents 8"×8" building blocks; when drawn at a scale of 1.0, the blocks measure 8 inches by 8 inches. Other patterns, such as ANSI31, are simply standard drafting hatching symbols and can be scaled to give the best visual results that are consistent with the plot or dimension scale factor for which the drawing is set up.

**I**NSIDER **T**IP

> If you set the scale of a pattern too small, it will take an inordinate amount of time to generate and may plot unsatisfactorily. If you set the scale to an overly large value, the pattern may be so large that it doesn't appear in the area being hatched. Use the Preview feature of the Boundary Hatch and Fill dialog box to visually fine-tune the pattern's usable scale.

**I**NSIDER **N**OTE

> AutoCAD by default does not create a hatch object that has more than 10,000 "pieces." However, this is controllable through the MAXHATCH environment variable. If you really must generate a very large hatch pattern with over 10,000 hatch elements, at the command prompt, type **(setenv "MaxHatch" "50000")**. This sets your hatch limit to 5 times the default. Then try to create your hatch again. If it still fails, consider breaking it up into smaller areas. The absolute range for the MAXHATCH setting is from 100 to 10,000,000. Please note that the environment name "MaxHatch" is case sensitive—it must be provided in this format.

### ISO (Metric) Patterns

The ISO hatch patterns are designed to be used with metric drawings. These patterns begin with the prefix ISO. They appear alphabetically in the drop-down list of pre-defined patterns and can be viewed on the ISO tab of the Hatch Pattern Palette dialog. These patterns are defined with the millimeter as the unit of measure. Choosing an ISO pattern enables the ISO pen width input box and drop-down list on the Hatch tab of the Boundary Hatch and Fill dialog box. Choosing a pen width sets the initial value for the pattern's scale setting equal to the pen width. You can, of course, override this initial scale setting.

### *User-Defined Patterns*

You can define a simple line hatch pattern on-the-fly by choosing the User-Defined option from the Type drop-down list in the Boundary Hatch and Fill dialog box. This disables the Pattern and Scale input boxes and enables the Spacing input box and the Double check box. User-defined patterns are simple and consist of either one or two sets of parallel lines. The spacing and angle of the lines are set in the Spacing and Angle input boxes, respectively. If you check the Double check box near the lower-right side of the Boundary Hatch and Fill dialog box, a second set of parallel lines perpendicular to the first is generated. The spacing of the second set is the same as the first set.

Although user-defined patterns lack a great deal of variety, their simplicity and the speed with which they can be drawn make them useful for quickly hatching an area.

### *Custom Patterns*

You can define additional patterns similar to the patterns supplied with AutoCAD. You can add these additional pattern definitions to the ACAD.pat file (or ACADISO.PAT file for metric patterns), or you can save each definition as an individual PAT file. These individual hatch pattern files are referred to as custom pattern files. To access one of these custom pattern files, choose Custom from the Type drop-down list on the Hatch tab of the Boundary Hatch and Fill dialog box. This enables the Custom pattern input box, where you enter the name of the custom pattern you want to use. The Scale and Angle parameters for a custom pattern function as they do for a standard predefined pattern.

Procedures for creating your own custom hatch pattern are discussed in the section "Customizing Hatch Patterns," near the end of this chapter.

### *Inherit Properties Button*

By clicking the Inherit Properties button on the right side of the Boundary Hatch and Fill dialog box, you can copy the parameters of an existing hatch object to other objects in the drawing. After clicking this button, the dialog box is temporarily dismissed, and a special "inherit" pick box and icon appear in the drawing, as shown at left in Figure 13.6. Select the hatch pattern whose properties you want to duplicate. Another special "painter" crosshair and icon appear. Use these crosshairs to select an internal point of the area to which you want to apply the hatch pattern (see the right side of Figure 13.6).

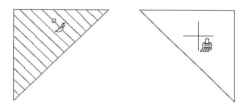

**Figure 13.6**   Two distinctive inherit hatch properties and fill with hatch icons.

---

**I**NSIDER TIP

> After selecting the hatch object whose properties you want the new hatch object to inherit, you can right-click and use the shortcut menu to toggle between the Select Objects and Pick Internal Point options to create boundaries.

## Associative Versus Non-Associative Hatch Objects

By default, the BHATCH command generates an associative hatch object. An associative hatch object is one that conforms to its boundary object(s) such that modifying the boundary objects automatically adjusts the hatch. If, for example, the boundary object's defining an associative hatch are edited, the hatch object's size is automatically adjusted to fill the new boundary area.

---

**I**NSIDER TIP

> Unless there is a compelling reason to generate a non-associative hatch object, use the default associative hatch generation method. Associative hatch objects offer the significant advantage of enabling you to edit the boundary object without having to reselect the boundary and re-create the hatch.

# Defining Hatch Boundaries

After selecting a hatch pattern and specifying its parameters, you need to define the area or areas you want to fill with the pattern. The area must be completely enclosed by one or more objects.

In Figure 13.7, a single closed object—a circle—defines the boundary of area A. A series of lines and curves that meet end-to-end defines the boundary for area B. Two lines and two arcs define the boundary for area C. The lines and arcs of area C overlap and do not meet end-to-end, but together they define an enclosed area. Objects that define the area to be filled are called boundary objects.

**Figure 13.7**   Closed areas that define permissible areas to hatch.

With the BHATCH command, you can define the boundaries of the area you want to hatch either by choosing a point or points within the desired boundary or by selecting an object or objects that defines an outer boundary.

## Using Pick Points

When you click the Pick Points button in the Boundary Hatch and Fill dialog box, the overall hatch boundary can be calculated automatically by the BHATCH command. You merely pick a point that lies within the area that you want filled. This point is referred to as an internal point. Using this method of establishing a hatch boundary offers a major advantage: If multiple objects are involved in establishing the boundary, the boundary objects do not have to meet end-to-end (recall area C in Figure 13.7).

## Selecting Objects

Another method for indicating the boundary of an area you want to hatch is provided by clicking the Select Objects button in the Boundary Hatch and Fill dialog box. With this method, you select the individual boundary objects that define the area to be hatched. This method is adequate for simple areas bounded by a single closed object, such as a circle, but if more than one object makes up the boundary, this method requires that the objects meet end-to-end, as shown in area B of Figure 13.7. Using the Select Objects method with an intended boundary such as area C in Figure 13.7 yields erroneous results because the boundary objects do not meet end-to-end.

**INSIDER TIP**

> If the area you want to hatch is enclosed by a single boundary object and no areas within the boundary need to be excluded from hatching, the Select Objects method may be faster than picking an internal point. In all but the simplest situations, however, picking an internal point and letting the BHATCH command calculate the boundary generally yields the best results.

## Dealing with Islands

It is not uncommon to have enclosed areas within the overall hatching area. These areas are referred to as islands. Islands can even exist within other islands. Text and mtext objects lying within an area to be hatched can behave like islands.

If you use the Pick Points method of defining the hatch boundary, AutoCAD automatically detects islands. This is one of the advantages of using the Pick Points method. On the other hand, if you use the Select Objects method, you must explicitly indicate those internal boundary objects that you want to be considered islands—otherwise, the BHATCH command does not recognize their presence. One or more objects can define islands in the same way that boundary objects define the overall hatch area.

The methods islands are detected and treated by the BHATCH command are controlled by settings found on the Advanced tab of the Boundary Hatch and Fill dialog (see Figure 13.8).

**Figure 13.8**   The Advanced tab of the Boundary Hatch and Fill dialog box.

On the Advanced tab, under Island Detection Style, you can control the way the BHATCH command treats successive levels of nested islands. The three styles are Normal, Outer, and Ignore. Figure 13.9 shows how the same outer boundary and inner islands are treated using these three detection styles.

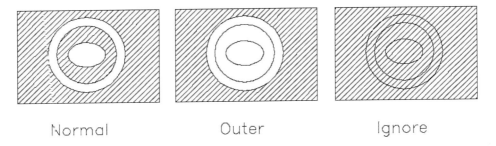

Normal                    Outer                    Ignore

**Figure 13.9**   The three styles of island detection.

- **Normal.** Hatches inward from the outermost boundary. Hatching is turned off at the first internal island then turned on at the next detected island, hatching alternate areas.

- **Outer.** Hatches inward from the outermost boundary. Hatching is turned off and remains off at the first detected island.

- **Ignore.** Hatches all of the area within outermost boundary, ignoring all internal islands.

The default style is Normal and is applicable in most situations. The Outer detection style is useful if you want to hatch overlapping islands with different patterns. Figure 13.10 shows how this can be done. Using the Outer style, pick in area 1 and apply a pattern. Next, repeat the BHATCH command, again using the Outer style, pick island 2, and apply a different pattern. Continue with this method until all islands are hatched. In Figure 13.10, islands 2 and 3 have different patterns applied; the outer area and island 4 have the same pattern with a different angle value applied.

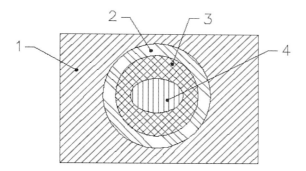

**Figure 13.10**   Use the Outer style to hatch overlapping areas.

The BHATCH command can also be used on regions. Islands within a region are detected by the BHATCH command and treated according to the current setting of the island detection style. A benefit of using a single region is that it effectively saves the boundary set into an object that can be selected quickly for later use. Regions are discussed in Chapter 28, "Solid Modeling in 3D."

**INSIDER TIP**

> The Normal, Outer, and Ignore options are also available from a shortcut menu by right-clicking in the drawing area after you specify points or select objects to define your boundaries.

### Defining the Boundary Set

Normally, the Pick Points method of defining the boundary set of an area to be hatched examines all the objects in the current viewport. You can, however, click the New button under Boundary Set on the Advanced tab of the Boundary Hatch and Fill dialog box and explicitly select a smaller set of objects to be examined for valid hatch boundaries. This option is useful when you have a crowded drawing and want to speed up the search mechanism by restricting the number of objects examined.

If you use the New button to create a new set of objects to be examined, the drop-down list under Boundary Set lists an existing set in addition to Viewport. There can be a maximum of two search sets at any time: the entire viewport, which is the default set and is always available, and an existing set, if you have defined one. Defining a new set replaces any preexisting set.

### *Retaining Boundaries*

When hatch area boundaries and internal islands are defined, AutoCAD uses temporary polylines to delineate these areas. These polylines are normally removed after the hatch object is generated. By checking Retain Boundaries under Object Type on the Advanced tab of the Boundary Hatch dialog box, the temporary polylines instead are retained on the current layer. You can save them either as closed polylines or as regions, depending on the option you select from the drop-down list.

Enabling the Retain Boundaries option is useful when the hatching area is delineated by multiple objects and you want polylines or regions to represent the hatch area. If you subsequently use the AREA command on the resulting polylines or the MASSPROP command on the resulting region, you can easily measure the hatched area.

### *Detecting Islands*

The controls located under Island Detection Method on the Advanced tab of the Boundary Hatch and Fill dialog box enable you to turn island detection on or off. There are two choices:

- **Flood.** Includes islands as boundary objects.
- **Ray Casting.** Runs a line from the point you specify to the nearest object, then traces the boundary in a clockwise direction, excluding islands as potential boundary objects.

If you use the Ray Casting method, you must be careful where you pick because AutoCAD casts a ray to the nearest object. In Figure 13.11, for example, point A is a valid point, whereas point B is not. The object nearest point A is a line that qualifies as part of a potential boundary of which point A is inside. Point B, however, is closest to a line that qualifies as a part of a potential boundary of which B is outside. Point B causes the BHATCH command to issue an error message, as shown in Figure 13.11.

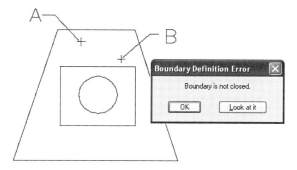

**Figure 13.11**   Selecting valid points with the Ray Casting option.

## Other Boundary Hatch Controls

There are several other buttons shared by both the Hatch and Advanced tabs of the Boundary Hatch and Fill dialog box:

- **Remove Islands.** Enables you to remove individual islands from the boundary set when you use Pick an Internal Point. You can also remove an island by pressing the Ctrl key and picking inside the selecting island.

- **View Selections.** Displays the currently defined boundaries with highlighted boundary objects. This option is unavailable when you have not yet specified points or selected objects.

- **Preview.** Displays the currently defined boundaries with the current hatch settings. This option is not available when you have not yet specified points or selected objects to define your boundaries.

### Exercise 13.1   Hatching Areas with *BHATCH*

1. Open 13EX01.dwg from the accompanying CD. Start the BHATCH command by opening the Draw pull-down menu and choosing Hatch. On the Hatch tab of the Boundary Hatch and Fill dialog box, select pattern ANSI33. Check that the angle is set to 0 and the scale is set to 1.000.

2. Click the Select Objects button. The lock screw is drawn on its own layer and is composed of a pair of mirrored polylines with ends meeting, forming an enclosed space. Pick the two polylines at ❶ and ❷ of Figure 13.12. Press Enter to return to the dialog.

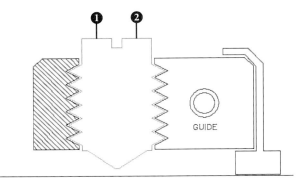

**Figure 13.12**   Select the two polylines that compose the lock screw.

3. Click the Preview button in the lower-left corner to review the hatch. Then click or press the Esc key to return to the Boundary Hatch and Fill dialog box and change to a scale of 0.75. Click Preview again. Notice the new scale is a bit tighter. Right-click to apply the hatch object. Notice that the new hatch is drawn on the current layer. Your drawing should resemble Figure 13.13.

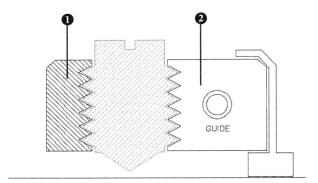

**Figure 13.13**   Hatching the lock screw.

4. Set the layer BODY current. Restart the BHATCH command, and at the right side of the dialog box, click Inherit Properties. In the drawing, place the "inherit" cursor in the area at ❶ and pick this hatch (refer to Figure 13.13).

5. Right-click and select Pick Internal Point from the shortcut menu. Place the "transfer to" cursor in the area to the right of the lock screw at ❷ and pick. BHATCH calculates and highlights the boundary and internal islands. Right-click and choose Preview. Notice that the text object is treated as an island and is excluded from hatching.

6. Next, we assume that we do not want the inner circle representing a guide bar to be hatched. Pick somewhere on-screen or press the Esc key to return to the dialog box and then click Remove Islands. In the drawing, select the inner circle to remove it from the boundary set. Right-click and choose Preview. Right-click to accept the hatch.

7. Right-click and choose Repeat Hatch from the shortcut menu. In the Boundary Hatch and Fill dialog box, under Type, select User-defined from the drop-down list. In the Spacing input box, type **0.1**. Select the Double option check box.

8. Click Pick Points, and in the drawing, pick inside the inner circle. Right-click and choose Preview. Right-click to accept the new hatch. Your drawing should resemble Figure 13.14.

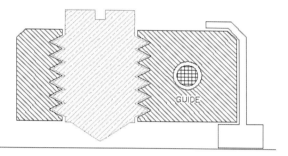

**Figure 13.14**   Hatching the guide bar with a user-defined pattern.

9. Right-click and repeat the BHATCH command. In the Type drop-down list, select Predefined. In the Pattern drop-down list, select the Solid pattern. Notice that there are no Angle or Scale parameters available with the Solid pattern.

10. Click Pick Points, and in the drawing, pick inside the bracket on the right of the assembly. Right-click and Preview the boundary set. Right-click to accept the solid hatch. Your drawing should now resemble Figure 13.15.

   If you plan to continue immediately with the next section, go ahead and leave this drawing open. Otherwise, you may close it without saving.

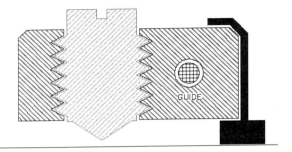

**Figure 13.15**   Hatching the mounting bracket with a solid pattern.

---

**I**NSIDER **N**OTE

The BHATCH command is also available on the Draw toolbar or by typing **BHATCH** at the command line.

---

# Editing Hatch Patterns

The HATCHEDIT command lets you modify hatch patterns or replace an existing pattern with a different one. Hatch objects drawn as associative hatch objects (the default type) automatically adjust to modifications in the boundary that defines them.

---

**I**NSIDER **T**IP

In AutoCAD 2005, the Properties palette provides a comprehensive interface for all adjustable settings of an associative hatch pattern and can be accessed easily through the highlight and right-click shortcut menu under Properties.

---

## Using *HATCHEDIT*

With the HATCHEDIT command, you can change the pattern of a hatch object or the parameters that control the generation of the pattern. To issue the HATCHEDIT command, choose Object, Hatch from the Modify pull-down menu. Although this method works well, the fastest method is to double-click on the hatch object itself. The Hatch Edit dialog box is identical to the Boundary Hatch and Fill dialog box with several settings disabled (see Figure 13.16).

In the following exercises, you perform an edit on a previously drawn hatch object and investigate the behavior of associative hatches.

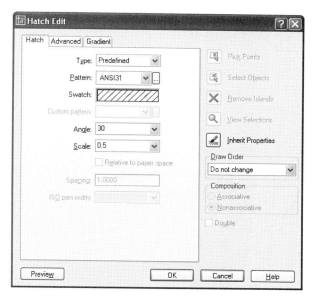

**Figure 13.16**   The Hatch Edit dialog box.

### Exercise 13.2   Editing a Hatch Pattern

1. Continue from the previous exercise or open 13EX02.dwg from the accompanying CD. Start the HATCHEDIT command through the Modify pull-down menu by selecting Object, Hatch. Select the solid hatch pattern by picking anywhere inside the hatch object.

2. In the Hatch Edit dialog box, notice that the name and parameters of the pattern you just selected are now displayed in the appropriate edit and drop-down boxes.

3. In the Pattern drop-down list, select ANSI31. Click the Preview button.

4. To further modify the pattern, left-click to return to the dialog box. Set the Angle to 30 and the Scale to 0.500. Click Preview. Right-click to accept the edits. Your drawing should resemble Figure 13.17.

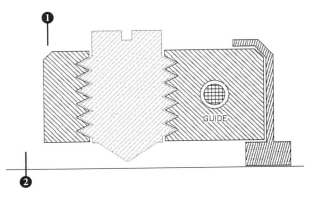

**Figure 13.17** Modifying a hatch pattern with HATCHEDIT.

Leave this drawing open if you are doing the next exercise; otherwise, close it without saving.

## Editing Hatch Boundaries

If you stretch or otherwise modify the scale or shape of the boundary objects defining the overall area of an associative hatch object, the hatch object automatically adjusts to fit the modified boundaries. If you move, delete, or stretch any of the islands within the overall hatch boundary, the hatch object is also adjusted.

If you delete any of the boundary objects defining the overall hatch area or islands (resulting in an open rather than a closed area), however, the associative property is removed from the hatch object, and the hatch loses the capability to adjust to modifications to the boundary. In the following exercise, you see how associative hatch objects automatically adjust to changes in their boundaries.

It is impossible to "repair" an associative hatch pattern after editing removes the associative property. However, you can use the Undo command (U) to correct a drafting mistake immediately afterward.

### Exercise 13.3    Understanding Hatch Associativity

1. You can continue from the preceding exercise, or you can open 13EX03.dwg from the accompanying CD. From the Modify pull-down menu, choose Stretch and pick first at ❶, then ❷ (refer to Figure 13.17). Right-click to end the object selection process.

2. Type in the displacement -1,0 and press Enter twice to carry out the stretch. Notice that the hatch pattern automatically adjusts to fill the new boundary geometry.

Next, we look at the new trim functionality for associative hatches.

**3.** Draw a line starting at 1.5,1.5 and ending at 1.5,5.5. Then, using the Modify pull-down menu or toolbar, select Trim.

**4.** At the `Select Cutting Edges and Select objects` prompt, pick the line just created and press Enter to end selection.

**5.** At the `Select objects to trim` prompt, pick the hatch on the left side of the vertical line. The hatch object then adjusts itself to the new "boundary" made by the line and previous polyline perimeter. Press Enter to end the `TRIM` command.

Next, we look at how a hatch adjusts as boundary edges changes.

**6.** Using the `MOVE` command, relocate the line. At the `Select objects` prompt, choose the line and press Enter. Then type `-0.5,0` and press Enter twice.

The hatch again adjusts itself to fill in along the line object and polyline perimeter. There are a few more ways for a hatch to repair itself after its boundary is changed.

**7.** Using the `MOVE` command, select the larger circle on the right side of the drawing. Then just move it to the outside of the series of objects.

When you finish, the hatch fills in the space left by moving the circle out and then fills in the circle with the hatch. This then generates one hatch object that occupies two separate areas.

**8.** Using the `COPY` command, copy the smaller circle 4.4 units to the left. This places a duplicate within the hatch area on the left side of the drawing. We want to "add" this circle to the boundary of the hatch that we trimmed in steps 4-5.

**9.** Use the `TRIM` command and select the new circle as the cutting object. Then select the hatch object that resides within the circle as the object to be trimmed.

The hatch inside the circle trims out, generating a hole in an existing hatch that was created long ago. The key to success with this type of action is the use of associative hatching. We mentioned it already, but always use this feature unless you have a good reason not to.

Leave this drawing open if you are continuing with the next exercise. Otherwise, close it without saving.

# Other Hatching Considerations

There are several other considerations to keep in mind when creating and working with hatch objects. These include hiding, or turning hatching off, exploding hatch objects into their constituent lines, and controlling whether associative hatch objects include their boundaries when selected for an editing operation.

## Aligning Hatch Objects

Areas hatched with the same pattern and scale and angle parameters have the corresponding elements in the pattern lined up in adjacent areas. All hatch patterns are referenced to the snap origin, which usually coincides with the drawing's 0,0. If you want to realign a hatch pattern, change the snap origin before drawing the hatch. The snap origin is controlled by the system variable SNAPBASE, which stores the value of a point. Set the system variable SNAPBASE to a point other than 0,0 by picking a point such as the corner of a rectangular area to cause the next hatch object drawn to align with the current snap origin.

This stems from the fact that families of lines in the pattern were defined with the same base point and angle, and this is true no matter where the patterns appear in the drawing. This causes the "hatching lines" to line up in adjacent areas. All hatch patterns are referenced to the snap origin, which by default is the drawing's 0,0 origin.

**I**NSIDER **T**IP

> AutoCAD 2005 introduces a new feature to enable you to not select osnap points on hatch objects if you don't want them. By setting the OSNAPHATCH system variable to 0, the OSNAP modes ignore any hatch objects when targeting points. This can be very helpful when using dotted patterns because often a dot exists near the edges and can be "osnapped" accidentally.

## Exploding Hatch Objects

You can explode a hatch object into its constituent lines with the EXPLODE command. Exploding a hatch object removes any associativity. Additionally, the grouped set of line objects that make up the pattern replaces the single hatch object. Although exploding a hatch object does enable you to edit the individual lines of the hatch, in most cases you lose more productivity than you gain.

**I**NSIDER **N**OTE

> Because a hatch object is composed of lines, you can use the same object snap modes (such as endpoint and midpoint) on the individual lines in hatch objects (associative or exploded) as you use on line objects if the system variable OSNAPHATCH is set to 1.

# Controlling Visibility with *FILLMODE*

You can control the visibility of all hatch objects in a drawing by setting the FILLMODE system variable to 0. With FILLMODE off (set to 0), all hatch objects become invisible, regardless of the status of the layers on which the hatch objects reside. You must issue the REGEN or REGENALL command after changing FILLMODE for the change in visibility to take effect.

The disadvantage of using FILLMODE to control hatch object visibility is that FILLMODE also controls the fill of other objects such as wide polylines and mlines. If you want to hide hatching more selectively, place hatching objects on separate layers so that the layers can be turned on and off without affecting other elements of the drawing.

# Selecting Hatch Objects and Their Boundaries

Usually, you want to select both an associative hatch and its boundary for editing operations such as moving, mirroring, or copying. By default, however, AutoCAD treats the two elements separately during the object selection process. To speed hatch and boundary selection, you can change the PICKSTYLE system variable from its default value of 1 to a value of 3. The PICKSTYLE system variable controls the selection of groups and hatch elements. A setting of 0 or 1 disables simultaneous hatch and boundary element selection. A value of 2 or 3 enables simultaneous hatch and boundary selection.

# Using Point Acquisition with the *HATCH* Command

The older version of the BHATCH command is the HATCH command. Although BHATCH replaced HATCH in functionality and especially the capability to calculate boundaries, HATCH is still supported. The principle disadvantage of the HATCH command is that it can create only non-associative hatch objects.

Despite its drawbacks, the HATCH command does have an option that you may find useful: the Direct Hatch option. The Direct Hatch option enables you to define an area to be hatched on-the-fly, negating the necessity to draw boundary objects before drawing the hatch object. The Direct Hatch option, or point acquisition method, is useful when you want to "suggest" large hatch areas by hatching only a few representative patches. This method is shown in the following exercise.

### Exercise 13.4    Direct Hatching Using *HATCH*

1. Continue from the previous exercise or open 13EX04.dwg from the accompanying CD. Start by typing **HATCH** at the command prompt. Press Enter to accept the default ANSI31 hatch pattern.

2. At the next two command-line prompts, type **0.75** for the pattern scale and accept the default of 0 for the pattern angle.

3. At the Select objects prompt, press Enter to indicate that you will be specifying points instead of objects.

4. Type **N** to indicate that you want to discard the polyline boundary after the hatch is completed. Turn the Ortho drafting aid off if it is on.

5. Referring to the top portion of Figure 13.18, use an endpoint osnap to pick point 1, and then pick points 2 through 9. Use an endpoint osnap to pick point 10, then type **C** and press Enter to create and close the polyline boundary on-the-fly.

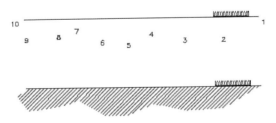

**Figure 13.18**    Using the HATCH command and direct hatching.

The hatching is completed. Your drawing should resemble the bottom portion of Figure 13.18.

If you are continuing with the next exercise, leave this drawing open. Otherwise, you may close the drawing without saving.

# Gradient Hatch Patterns

On occasion during your hatching work, you may be asked to produce toning in your hatching. Typical hatch objects are generally defined as a series of lines and/or dots arranged in a pattern and applied to an area. A gradient hatch is similar to a solid hatch, but with the added benefit of a density change across the volume of the hatch. This typically produces a pleasing appearance on presentation drawings but would work in many mainstream applications.

A gradient hatch is still a hatch object, with all the normal modification methods, but it presents itself as a graphic tone with varying alignments and effects. The following exercise quickly touches on this new hatching style.

### Exercise 13.5    Using a Gradient Hatch Pattern

1. Continue from the previous exercise or open 13EX05.dwg from the accompanying CD. Double-click on the hatch object at the bottom of the part. The HATCHEDIT dialog box appears.

2. Select the Gradient tab across the top of the dialog.

   Gradient hatching can be blended from one or two colors, depending on your needs.

3. Select the One color toggle. Then click the [...] button to open the Select Color dialog box. Gradient hatching can use standard colors, True Color, or Color Books matching color.

4. Select the Index Color tab and then select color 7 (white) followed by the OK button. The Select Color dialog disappears.

5. The main part of the Gradient tab consists of a series of sample fills with different directions and fill formats. Pick the upper-left swatch and then drag the Shade/Tint bar to near the middle.

6. Under the Angle option, select 90 degrees. The dialog now should resemble Figure 13.19.

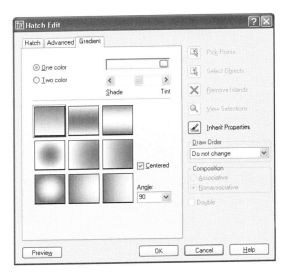

**Figure 13.19**    The Gradient tab of the Hatch Edit dialog is the same as in the Boundary Hatch and Fill dialog.

7.  Click the OK button to close the Hatch Edit dialog box. The hatch should update, as shown in Figure 13.20. As you can see, providing hatch tones in your drawings can be very stylish.

    You may now close the drawing without saving.

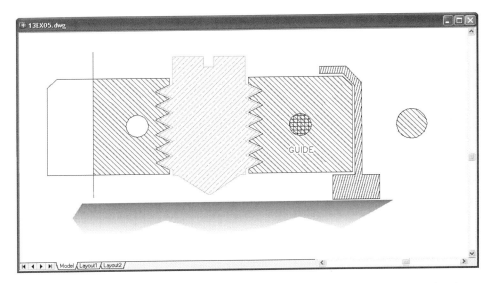

**Figure 13.20**    The Gradient hatching at the bottom provides unique opportunities for clarity and quality beyond typical lines and dots.

**I**NSIDER **NOTE** _____

> A new feature of the BHATCH and HATCHEDIT commands is direct access to the DRAWORDER feature for overlaying objects graphically in your drawing. This feature really comes into play on solid or gradient hatching because those objects can interfere with your ability to "see" the drawing in AutoCAD. The DRAWORDER feature can also solve plotting problems that can occur with certain print drivers and solid type objects.

# Customizing Hatch Patterns

It is possible to add new patterns to the ones supplied with AutoCAD. You can add these new patterns (called custom hatch patterns) to the file ACAD.PAT (or ACADISO.PAT for metric patterns), or you can define each new pattern and assign it to its own PAT file. ACAD.PAT and ACADISO.PAT are found in the \AutoCAD 2005\UserDataCache\Support folder of a standard AutoCAD installation. If you choose to store each custom pattern in its own PAT file, the file must have the same name as the pattern. The new custom pattern files should be placed in one of the directories/folders defined in your installation's support file search path (see the OPTIONS command dialog). Because hatch pattern files are ASCII files, a text editor is all you need to create custom pattern files and add them to the ACAD.pat file.

**I**NSIDER **NOTE** _____

> If you choose to add custom hatch patterns to the ACAD.pat file, you should first make a backup copy of this file. This enables you to revert to a functional file, should ACAD.pat become corrupted. Creating a folder under your AutoCAD 2005 installation called \BACKUP, for example, provides a convenient place to locate such backup files.

A hatch pattern consists of one or more segments of pattern lines. Even though some hatch patterns look like points or dots, they are in fact very short lines. The rules for defining a pattern line are the same as those for defining a new linetype, except that no text or shapes can be included in the definition of a hatch pattern line. (Refer to Chapter 6, "Effective Linetypes and Lineweights Use," for information on linetypes.) A pattern definition can be broken down into two components: the header and the definition body. These are explained in the next section.

## Defining the Header Line

The first line in any pattern definition is called the header line. The format for the header line is as follows:

```
*Pattern-name [, description]
```

The pattern name cannot contain any blank spaces. As shown, the description and the preceding comma are optional and are used only by the HATCH command.

The header line is followed by one or more pattern line descriptors, one for each family of lines. A pattern line has the following syntax:

```
Angle, x-origin, y-origin, delta-x, delta-y [,dash-1, dash-2, ...]
```

The following line descriptor, for example, results in the hatch shown on the left in Figure 13.21:

```
*L45, 45 degree lines @0.25 units
45,0,0,0,0.25
```

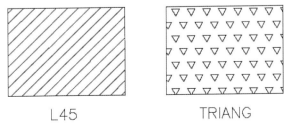

L45                    TRIANG

**Figure 13.21**    The L45 and TRIANG patterns.

Each family of lines starts with one line, and the line's angle and origin are specified by the first three numbers of the line descriptor. In the L45 example, the first line is drawn at a 45-degree angle through the point 0,0. The family of lines is generated by offsetting each successive line by delta-x and delta-y offsets, with delta-x measured along the line and delta-y measured perpendicular to the lines. In L45, each succeeding line is offset 0 in the x direction and 0.25 in the y direction. With no other dash specifications included in the definition, AutoCAD draws the lines with the current linetype.

The pattern shown on the right in Figure 13.21 is found in AutoCAD's ACAD.PAT file. It has the following definition:

```
*TRIANG, Equilateral triangles
60, 0,0, .1875,.324759526, .1875,-.1875
120, 0,0, .1875,.324759526, .1875,-.1875
0, -.09375,.162379763, .1875,.324759526, .1875,-.1875
```

In this example, the pattern consists of three families of lines: one family drawn at 60 degrees, another drawn at 120 degrees, and a third drawn at 0 degrees. The dash specifications (the last two numbers of each line) indicate that each line is to consist of a 0.1875 dash and a 0.1875 space repetitive pattern.

# Using *BOUNDARY* to Delineate Areas and Islands

As you saw earlier in this chapter, when calculating the boundary for a hatch object using the Pick internal point(s) method, the BHATCH command constructs a polyline or region to delineate the boundary set. The BOUNDARY command is a variation of the BHATCH command and creates objects delineating an overall area and the islands, if any, within that area. BOUNDARY also offers the choice of creating region objects from the calculated polylines. The Boundary Creation dialog box is nothing more than the Advanced tab of the Boundary Hatch and Fill dialog box (see Figure 13.22). You use the BOUNDARY command when you want to delineate an area and its internal islands without applying hatch objects.

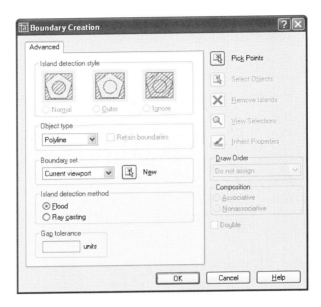

**Figure 13.22** The Boundary Creation dialog box of the BOUNDARY command.

# Closing Gaps in Boundaries

A new feature in AutoCAD is the HPGAPTOL system variable. With this mechanism, it becomes possible for AutoCAD to determine a boundary in spite of less-than-precise geometry. So even if the area you want to hatch has "holes," by assigning an appropriate value, you can bridge these gaps to build a boundary in which to hatch. This feature can be found on the Boundary Hatch and Fill dialog box under the Advanced tab. The usage is simple—assign a value equal to just larger than the largest gap you may have in your geometry. If you don't really know, start with something reasonable but smaller and then bump it up after each boundary failure.

**I**NSIDER **N**OTE

Depending on the geometry being hatched, if you assign too large of a gap value, you can bridge geometry you might otherwise want to exclude. Applying the proper HPGAPTOL value is important when using this feature.

When you first apply this feature and bridge your first gap, AutoCAD notifies you with a dialog like the one shown in Figure 13.23. This dialog can be turned off, but you may want to keep it around so you know what AutoCAD is doing. Because your drawing has holes, AutoCAD has to fill them in what it judges is the right way. In most cases, it probably won't matter, but if it does, consider fixing your geometry rather than using the HPGAPTOL system variable.

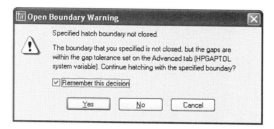

**Figure 13.23**    The Open Boundary Warning dialog can be permanently dismissed if needed.

# Summary

Hatching is a powerful tool for clarifying the meaning of your drawing or for conveying information to the reader. Effective use of hatching is one of the more powerful features of computer-aided design. Hatching is easy to apply using the BHATCH command and just as easy to edit with the HATCHEDIT command. Creating associative hatch objects lets you modify the hatched area easily after its creation. You can even design your own hatch patterns and add them to those that are supplied with AutoCAD.

# Part IV

# Annotating, Dimensioning, and Plotting

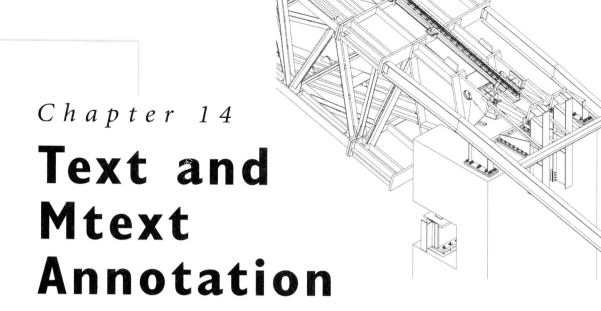

*Chapter 14*

# Text and Mtext Annotation

Annotation is a very important component of any document. On any given drawing, annotation can range from a single word to a column of paragraphed text. Being able to efficiently create and edit text directly affects your productivity. In this chapter, you learn how to do the following:

- Determine your text height
- Define a text style
- Use single-line text
- Create and modify mtext
- Perform a spelling check
- Look at additional text options
- Perform text property modification
- Invoke Quick Text mode, mapping fonts, and the Windows clipboard

# Choosing the Correct Text Height

The hardest part of adding text is deciding on the correct text height for the scale for which the drawing is set up. Use Tables 14.1 and 14.2 to help you determine the correct text height. To use these tables, go to the row associated with your drawing scale, and then move along the row to the column associated with the height you want your text to have on your plot.

**Table 14.1    Text Heights for Architectural Scales**

| Drawing Scale | Plotted Text Heights | | | | |
| --- | --- | --- | --- | --- | --- |
| | 3/32" | 1/8" | 3/16" | 1/4" | 3/8" |
| 1/16"=1' | 18" | 24" | 36" | 48" | 72" |
| 3/32"=1' | 12" | 16" | 24" | 32" | 48" |
| 1/8"=1' | 9" | 12" | 18" | 24" | 36" |
| 3/16"=1' | 6" | 8" | 12" | 16" | 24" |
| 1/4"=1' | 4.5" | 6" | 9" | 12" | 18" |
| 1/2"=1' | 2.25" | 3" | 4.5" | 6" | 9" |

**Table 14.2    Text Heights for Decimal Scales***

| Drawing Scale | Plotted Text Heights | | | | |
| --- | --- | --- | --- | --- | --- |
| | 3/32" | 1/8" | 3/16" | 1/4" | 3/8" |
| 1:10 | 0.9375 | 1.25 | 1.875 | 2.5 | 3.75 |
| 1:20 | 1.8750 | 2.50 | 3.750 | 5.0 | 7.5 |
| 1:50 | 4.6875 | 6.25 | 9.375 | 12.5 | 18.75 |
| 1:100 | 9.3750 | 12.50 | 18.750 | 25.0 | 37.5 |

*All values in basic drafting units

**I**NSIDER **T**IP

The simple equation to determine the size to make your text is the plotted scale multiplied by the desired text height. For example, at the scale 1/4"=1'-0", divide 12" by 1/4", or 12.0/0.25, which equals 48.0. Then multiply by the desired text height, 1/8", or 48.0×0.125, which equals 6.0. This calculation can be done directly in AutoCAD using the CAL command >> Expression: 12/(1/4)*0.125.

# Choosing a Text Style

The appearance of text is controlled through a drawing named object know as a text style. The default text style supplied in a blank drawing is STANDARD, whereas in other template drawings, several text styles can be predefined for you. Although the default text style STANDARD is available, most users will generally want to customize the appearance. You use the STYLE command to create a new text style definition prior to creating new text objects.

## Defining Text Styles

You can define as many text styles as you need in a drawing. You can access the STYLE command by choosing Text Style from the Format menu. Figure 14.1 shows the Text Style dialog box. The various settings within the Text Style dialog box are explained in more detail later in the chapter.

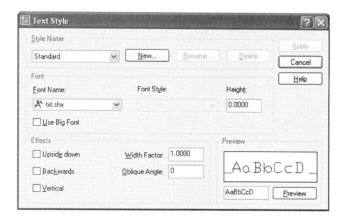

**Figure 14.1**   The Text Style dialog box.

To create a new style, click the New button. It uses the current style as a prototype for the new one. If the current style is not the style you want to begin with, select the desired style from the list of existing styles (thereby making it the current style).

After clicking the New button, you type a name in the New Text Style dialog box. A duplicate style is then created from the selected style and assigned the name you provided. To rename an existing style, select the style from the list of existing styles, click the Rename button, and enter a new name. To delete an existing style, highlight the name from the list of existing styles and click the Delete button. The STANDARD text style cannot be deleted or renamed. The current text style cannot be deleted either.

**INSIDER NOTE**

When a text object is created, the style with which it is created is stored as a property of the object. A text style can be deleted only if no existing text objects reference the style.

**INSIDER CAUTION**

The STANDARD text style cannot be renamed using the STYLE command but can be renamed using the RENAME command. However, doing so has been known to cause AutoCAD instability—it is suggested you avoid renaming it.

Text styles are stored in the drawing in which they are defined. If you want multiple styles to be available in a new drawing immediately, define the styles in your template drawings. If you want to import a style from another drawing, use AutoCAD's DesignCenter. For more information on importing text styles into the current drawing, refer to Chapter 12, "Applications for DesignCenter."

When defining a new style or modifying an existing style, you must choose a font file, a text height, a width factor, an oblique angle, and the special effects you want enabled. Choosing these settings and previewing the results of these settings are covered in the following sections.

## Choosing a Font and Style

The font file is the file that contains the information that determines the look of each character. Table 14.3 lists the various types of font files supplied with AutoCAD.

**Table 14.3    Font Files Types**

| Filename Extension | Font Type |
| --- | --- |
| SHX | AutoCAD's native fonts, known as an SHX font file. |
| TTF | TrueType font file or TTF. |

TrueType fonts are supplied with Windows or other Windows applications.

**INSIDER NOTE**

An SHX file may also be a Big Font file. Big Fonts are used to support text shapes that are non-ASCII. For instance, you can create symbols to use as text in a Big Font file without affecting a text style's normal ASCII characters. Big Fonts are also used to support other languages, such as providing the Kanji character set.

You can use PostScript files in AutoCAD. To do so, you must first use the COMPILE command to compile the PostScript (PFB) font file into a shape (SHX) file.

AutoCAD supports TrueType font families, which means that for some TrueType fonts, you can choose a font style such as regular, italic, bold, or bold italic. Note that not all TrueType fonts have more than the regular style defined.

Two system variables affect the plotting of text using TrueType fonts: TEXTFILL and TEXTQLTY. When TEXTFILL is disabled, the characters are plotted in outline form only. If TEXTFILL is enabled, the characters are filled in. The value of TEXTQLTY affects the smoothness of the characters at plot time. The value of TEXTQLTY can be set from 0 to 100, with the default value set to 50. The higher the value, the better the resolution of the characters, but the longer it takes to process the drawing for plotting. Both system variables can be typed at the command prompt and then set to the desired value.

**I**NSIDER **TIP**

> Using the simplest-shaped characters minimizes the drawing size and speeds up opening and working with the drawing file. Simpler-shaped characters are those that use very few elements, or line segments, to define a character's shape. The characters in the Simplex and Romans SHX files are quite simple in appearance and are similar to the Leroy characters used previously in manual drafting. Some shape files contain the alphabet of foreign languages, such as GREEKS.SHX, or even symbols, such as SYMUSIC.SHX.

After you change the font file associated with an existing style and apply the change, all text that has already been created with the modified style is updated to reflect the change.

**I**NSIDER **NOTE**

> The density of the fill of a given text font, including solid fill TrueType fonts, can increase the size of a plot file dramatically. It has no effect on the drawing file size itself, however.

### *Setting a Height*

Also found in the Font area of the Text Style dialog box is the text height setting. The default height of 0 dictates that the user is allowed to set the text height at the time the text is created. A height other than 0 forces the text height for that particular style to that height. The style is then referred to as a fixed height style, and any text command height prompts are suppressed.

Changing the text height setting of an existing style does not affect the appearance of existing text objects.

### Previewing the Text Style Settings

The character Preview area enables you to view a sample of the selected style and the results of changing the various settings. To view your own sample text, type your sample text in the text edit box and click the Preview button.

## Specifying Special Effects

The Effects section of the Text Style dialog box contains the Upside Down, Backwards, Vertical, Width Factor, and Oblique Angle settings. These settings are covered in detail in the following sections.

### Upside Down, Backwards, and Vertical Text

In the Effects area, you can enable the Upside Down, Backwards, and Vertical settings. See Figure 14.2 for an example of how these settings affect the appearance of text.

**Figure 14.2**    The effects of Upside Down, Backwards, and Vertical text settings.

**I**NSIDER **N**OTE

> Although the Upside Down and Backwards options work with all font files, the Vertical setting works only with specific SHX files.

Unlike the font file setting, the Upside Down and Backwards settings for an existing style can be changed without affecting text that has already been typed in that style; the text is not automatically updated to reflect setting changes. Changing the Vertical setting, however, does affect existing text objects, so you may want to create a new style before changing the Vertical setting.

**I**NSIDER **T**IP

> The Backwards option is useful if you want to plot text on the back side of a transparent plot sheet so that the text is readable when viewed from the front.
>
> The Vertical option is useful when you need to add text in a column format like a schedule heading.

## Setting a Width Factor

The Width Factor determines the width of the characters. A factor of 1 results in the characters being displayed with the width as defined in the chosen font file. A factor greater than 1 results in wider characters; a factor less than 1 results in thinner characters. Figure 14.3 illustrates the effects of using different width factors. All three text objects were added with the same text height.

Skinny Letters With Width Factor of 0.5
Normal Letters With Width Factor of 1
Fat Letters With Width Factor of 1.5

**Figure 14.3**    The effects of the Width Factor setting on text objects.

**I**NSIDER **T**IP

> Adding text with a width factor that is less than 1 may make it easier to squeeze text into an already crowded drawing while still keeping the text readable.

### *Setting an Oblique Angle*

The Oblique Angle setting affects the slant of the characters. It is often used to add italic text when the characters in the font file being used are not naturally italic. Unlike the text rotation angle, the oblique angle of 0 refers to a vertical direction (see Figure 14.4). A positive angle value makes the letters lean to the right, and a negative value makes the letters lean to the left.

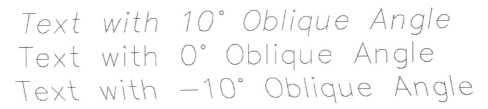

**Figure 14.4**   The effects of the Oblique Angle setting on text objects.

Now you have an understanding of the STYLE command and how to define a new text style and adjust the properties. Next, you learn about the various types of text objects.

## Single-Line Text

A single line of text can consist of a single character, a word, or a complete sentence. The simplest form of text is created by using the TEXT command. To insert a single line of text, use the Draw pull-down menu and choose Text, Single Line Text. The initial prompt displayed in the command window presents a few options:

```
Specify start point of text or [Justify/Style]
```

**I**NSIDER **N**OTE

> A non-dynamic version of the TEXT command is available by typing **-TEXT**. This other command version can be used to create text by using AutoLISP or scripts.

**I**NSIDER **T**IP

> When you enter text, you can take advantage of the command history to repeat previously entered text. You use the up and down arrow keys to scroll through the command history.

The default option is to specify the lower-left corner, otherwise known as the start point, of the new line of text. After picking the start point, you are prompted to supply the height (unless the height is defined in the style being used), the rotation angle of the text, and the actual text to be created. As you type the text, it is displayed on your drawing. If you make a typographical error, you can use the Backspace key to delete the error and retype the text. You signify the end of the line of text by pressing the Enter key, at which point you can begin a new line of text immediately below the text object just created. To stop adding lines of text, press the Enter key without typing any new text. You can also relocate the next line of text by picking a point with the cursor. You may skip a line of text by pressing the spacebar and then pressing Enter. Note that this does not create a text object for the blank line.

**I**NSIDER **T**IP

> The spacing between successive lines of text is fixed by the font used for the text style. In many cases, this spacing is at a factor of approximately 1.666 of the text height. Each line of text created with the TEXT command is a separate object and can be moved independently.

If, after you end the TEXT command, you want to add an additional line of text below the last line created, you can easily do so by issuing the command again and pressing the Enter key instead of picking a new start point. TEXT then adds the new line of text right below the last one, using the style, height, and rotation angle of the previous line. You can also do other activities, such as drawing lines, erasing objects, and placing dimensions, and still continue with a new line of text below the last one.

**I**NSIDER **T**IP

> To help you spot the last line of text created, that line is highlighted when you begin TEXT. The highlighting, however, may not be apparent if the text is too small or off the screen.

Typing the text you want to create is the easy part. It is also important to know how to format the text according to your needs. The following sections discuss how to choose the correct text height, justification, and text style.

## Choosing a Justification

The default option of TEXT is to specify the left endpoint, or the start point, of the line of text. Specifying the Justify option at the initial prompt displays the following prompt:

```
Enter an option [Align/Fit/Center/Middle/Right/TL/TC/TR/ML/MC/MR/BL/BC/BR]
```

Figure 14.5 shows the various TEXT justification options and their corresponding locations.

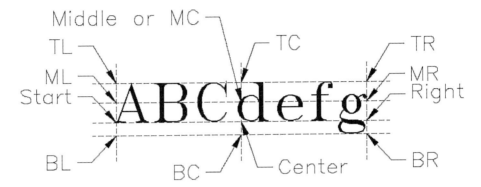

**Figure 14.5**   Justification points for a standard piece of text.

Unlike the justification options illustrated in Figure 14.5, the Align and Fit options require you to define two points.

Use the Align option when you want to specify the left and right endpoints of the text and do not care about the resulting height. The text height is automatically set to make the text fit between the specified points. Also, the angle from the first point to the second point is used as the rotation angle of the text.

Use the Fit option when you want to specify the left and right endpoints and the height of the text. To make the text fit between the specified points, AutoCAD varies the width of the text characters. Therefore, you may end up with skinny-looking characters on one line and very fat-looking characters on the next.

**I**NSIDER TIP

You can enter the required text justification option when the TEXT command prompts for the start point, which eliminates the need for first selecting the Justify option.

When the text is initially added with one of the alternate justification options specified, it is displayed left-justified, as if the default justification were being used. When the TEXT command ends, the text is relocated and set with the correct justification.

**INSIDER NOTE**

> You can snap to the justification point of a text object by using the Insert object snap mode.

## Editing Single-Line Text

Two commands are of particular use for editing existing text: DDEDIT and PROPERTIES. DDEDIT is easier to use than PROPERTIES when all you want to do is change the text string. PROPERTIES is more powerful than DDEDIT in that it displays the Properties dialog box, which enables you to change all the properties of the selected text.

### *Using* DDEDIT

From the Modify menu, click Object, choose Text, Edit to issue the DDEDIT command. Select the text object to be changed, and the Edit Text dialog box appears, displaying the selected text (see Figure 14.6).

**Figure 14.6**   The Edit Text dialog box.

**INSIDER TIP**

> If you double-click on a text object, it opens up in the appropriate text editor—a handy thing to use when you need edit your text objects.

Initially, the entire line of text is highlighted and is replaced by whatever you type. If you want to edit a specific portion of the text, position the cursor at the desired point in the text and pick it. You also use the Insert, Delete, and Backspace keys to add and delete characters.

If you want to replace a portion of the text displayed in the Edit Text dialog box, highlight the portion to be replaced and then type the new text.

### *Using Special Formatting Codes and Symbols*

You can do a limited amount of formatting with the TEXT command. For instance, you can add a line under or above the text simply by adding the codes %%u (for underlining) and %%o (for overlining) to the text as you enter it. The codes act as toggle switches; the first time you include the code in a text object, it turns that effect on and is applied to the successive text characters. The second time you enter the code in the same text object, the effect is turned off. If you do not enter the code a second time in the text object, the effect is continued to the end of the text object but is not continued to the next text object. For example, to add the text shown in Figure 14.7, you would type this line of text: `%%uUnderlining%%u and %%oOverlining%%o can be used separately or %%o%%utogether.`

Underlining and Overlining can be used separately or together

**Figure 14.7**   Using underline and overline formatting codes.

### *Using Properties*

Choose Properties from the Standard toolbar or the Modify pull-down menu to launch the Properties palette, as shown in Figure 14.8. The Properties palette enables you to change the text contents, style, justification point, and various settings that control the appearance of the text object.

**Figure 14.8**   The Properties palette.

As you can see, the Properties palette provides an edit area for changing the text value, although it is generally used only for manipulating the format of text objects. The next section delves into the mainstream annotation type, MTEXT.

# Multiline Text

The TEXT command can be used to add multiple lines of text, yet each text object is added as a separate object. Often, you want to add multiple lines of text as a single object. In such cases, you need the MTEXT command, issued by choosing Multiline Text from the Draw toolbar or from the Text submenu of the Draw pull-down menu.

After you start the MTEXT command, you are prompted to select the first corner point of a window. This window is used to determine the point where the mtext object will exist. By default, the mtext object is created with a top-left justification. If you want, you can change the justification type to one of eight others: TC (Top Center), TR (Top Right), ML (Middle Left), MC (Middle Center), MR (Middle Right), BL (Bottom Left), BC (Bottom Center), or BR (Bottom Right). These justification types are similar to those available with the TEXT command (refer to Figure 14.5), except that they apply to the whole mtext object and not just a single line of text.

You then indicate the desired width of the mtext window. A width of zero disables the automatic word wrap feature of the Text Formatting dialog box. With that setting, you must press the Enter key when you want to start a new line of text.

Several other command line options appear, but many of these are easier to set through the Text Formatting dialog box (see Figure 14.9). The Text Formatting interface is divided into two parts. The bottom part is the editor, and the top part controls the properties, which are described in detail in later sections.

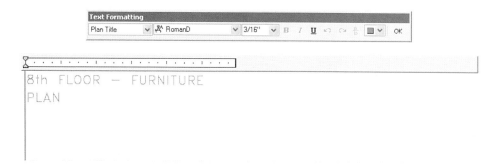

**Figure 14.9**   The Text Formatting dialog box.

## Creating Mtext Objects

Previous versions of the Text Formatting editor were somewhat crowded with icons and tabs. It was revamped in AutoCAD 2004 and reduced to the bare essentials needed to produce text. The plethora of options still exists, however, and the options are now located in the right-click shortcut menu. As shown in Figure 14.10, there are many options related to creating mtext that can be taken advantage of.

**I**NSIDER **N**OTE

Several options, Line spacing and Rotation, are still only available at the command line before the dialog box appears.

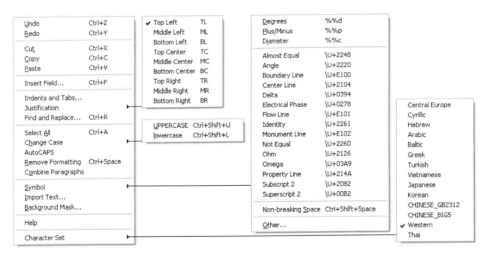

**Figure 14.10**   The right-click shortcut menu has many features, as well as several submenus.

In the following exercise, you learn about the various aspects of creating and editing mtext objects.

### Exercise 14.1   Using *MTEXT* to Create Paragraphs of Text

1. Open the drawing 14EX01.dwg from the accompanying CD. It contains several predefined text styles that we will utilize.

2. Start the MTEXT command by choosing the Multiline Text tool from the Draw toolbar. AutoCAD reports at the command line:

```
Current text style:  "Standard"  Text height:  0.2000
```

This indicates which text style is current and what height will be active in the editing dialog.

3. At the `Specify first corner` prompt, go ahead and pick the upper-left corner mark.

The little text sample attached to the cursor is adjustable. Normally it reads abc, but you can change the `MTJIGSTRING` system variable to whatever you would like it to read.

After you pick the first corner, you then are permitted to make changes to the current mtext settings, as shown in the prompt:

`Specify opposite corner or [Height/Justify/Line spacing/Rotation/Style/Width]`

4. Similar in nature to the `TEXT` command, you adjust the size of the text, its justification, and other properties prior to entering the editor. We pass on this now; go ahead and specify the opposite corner by using the lower-right corner mark. The Text Formatting dialog then appears.

The `AutoCAPS` item on the right-click menu permits you to leave Caps Lock off, yet type text in the editor window in uppercase letters.

5. Within the editor window, type the following note:
   `6"x1/2" CONT. EMBED PLATE WITH 3/4" DIA. x 5" LONG H.S. @ 24"`
   `➥O.C. (STAGGER LOCATIONS OF STUDS WITH BRIDGING ANCHORS)`

Depending on how your system is configured, as you typed the note, you may have gotten the AutoStack Properties dialog, as shown in Figure 14.11. This dialog enables you to control how your fractions should appear and enables you to "set it and forget it." Select your preference; the examples used here are similar to the Architectural style of drafting.

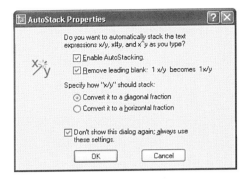

**Figure 14.11**    The AutoStack Properties dialog box is where you can tweak your fraction's appearances.

**INSIDER TIP**

If you need to adjust the AutoStack Properties dialog settings and have instructed it to not show again, you can still get to it. Highlight an existing stacked fraction and, using the right-click shortcut menu, choose Properties. Then on the Stack Properties dialog box, as shown in Figure 14.12, choose the AutoStack button to gain access once again.

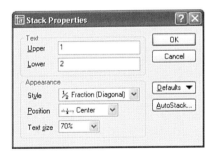

**Figure 14.12**    The Stack Properties dialog box enables custom stacking styles to be applied to an individual fraction.

6. After typing the note, it is obvious that the current font is rather unappealing. Use the Style drop-down list and select Romans. Instantly, the text within the editor changes appearance to that of the Romans font.

**INSIDER NOTE**

The other drop-down list to the right of the Style drop-down is Font. It is not related to the Style control; in reality, it is similar to a dimension override, enabling specific portions of the mtext object to use another font. It should only be used if you must have a differing font embedded within the rest of the text.

Your multiline text is now complete. Press the OK button to close the Text Formatting dialog box. You should now have a text object that looks like Figure 14.13.

Leave this drawing open for the following exercise.

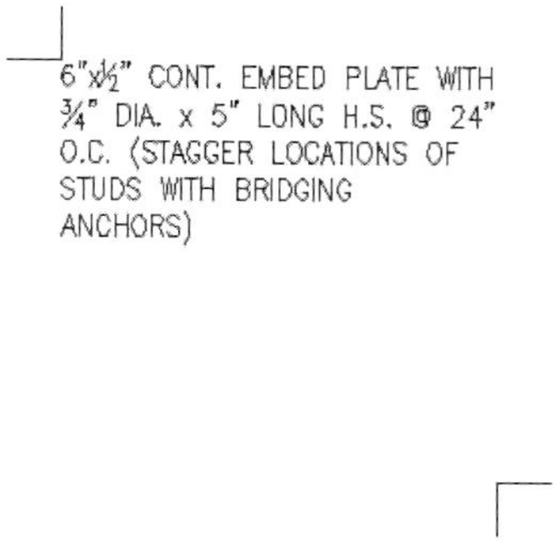

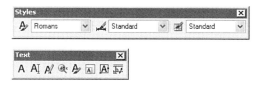

**Figure 14.13**  A typical mtext object.

This short exercise exemplifies the ease of use of the Text Formatting interface. Although the control area of the dialog is available, facilitating immediate changes to text properties, productivity can be gained by presetting the various properties prior to actually showing the interface. Some of the controls are also available through toolbars and system variables.

## Customizing for Text Styles

AutoCAD 2005 comes with two toolbars for creating and manipulating text objects. Shown in Figure 14.14, the Styles toolbar contains a drop-down list for setting the current text style. Also shown in Figure 14.14 is the Text toolbar, which has tools to create single and multiline text as well as other editing features.

**Figure 14.14**  Toolbars available to control, create, and edit text and mtext objects.

System variables affect the creation of text objects and their preset properties (see Table 14.4). These can be used in your customization methods to speed setting up your environment.

**Table 14.4    Text Formatting System Variables**

| System Variable | Description |
| --- | --- |
| TEXTSIZE | Sets the text height for all new text-based objects created. |
| TEXTSTYLE | Sets the current text style. |

After you begin to customize your AutoCAD environment, you can take advantage of ways to set to specific properties and start the MTEXT command in one click. The following menu macro is an example:

```
^C^C_.-style;romans;romans.shx;;0.8;;;;;
```

When executed, this creates the text style Romans, assigning ROMANS.SHX to it and leaving all properties except for width set to 0 or off. The width factor is set to 0.8, providing a slightly narrower text style:

```
^C^C(setvar "TEXTSIZE" (* (getvar "DIMSCALE") (getvar "DIMTXT")))
```

This short AutoLISP code first retrieves the current DIMSCALE value, which is used to control how large the parts in a dimension object appear. The code then gets the current dimension style text height, multiplies these two together, and applies that size to the system variable TEXTSIZE. Click this button, and the next time you create text, it will match your current dimension style appearance.

Customization such as this can be placed within your Custom menu, on a Tool palette, or on a toolbar, or it can even be coded as small AutoLISP programs. As you develop the formatting specifics, you will learn where best to house them for the greatest effectiveness.

## Editing Multiline Text

Very often, you will have to change the content in a mtext object. Early versions of AutoCAD required the user to erase the text and re-create it. Luckily for you, editing isn't that bad now. Just as easily as you create the content, you can later edit it as needed.

## Exercise 14.2    Editing Mtext Objects

1. Continue from the previous exercise. If needed you can open the drawing 14EX02.dwg from the accompanying CD. It contains a single mtext object and some reference polylines.

2. Double-click on the mtext object, utilizing AutoCAD's double-click editing feature. The MTEDIT command starts, and the Text Formatting dialog box appears.

3. Locate on the top line CONT. and highlight the period. Then type **INUOUS**, eliminating the abbreviation. You probably noticed that a few words moved down to the next line. That's a key feature of mtext—word wrapping.

4. Now highlight the word PLATE. Using the right-click shortcut menu, choose Symbol and select Property Line. The word PLATE is then replaced with a new AutoCAD 2005 PL symbol.

**I** NSIDER TIP

As you work with the MTEDIT dialog, you may notice it moves around to located itself over the text being edited. If this functionality is bothersome, you can use the MTEXTFIXED system variable to eliminate that activity. When turned on (1), the dialog enables you to place it on-screen wherever you want, and it displays there until moved. Additionally, turning this system variable on makes the editor background match the display background color. When off, the dialog background is translucent to show objects behind it.

5. Next, locate the word DIA. and highlight it. Use the right-click shortcut menu and select Symbol. At the top of the Symbol submenu, select Diameter %%c. It doesn't look like much now; you will have to wait until the command ends.

6. Locate the O.C. and highlight it. Again use the right-click shortcut menu and select Change Case. Select lower case to change the case for the ON CENTER reference.

**I** NSIDER TIP

You can also use Ctrl+Shift+U or Ctrl+Shift+L to change selected text case to upper or lower, respectively.

7. Click the OK button to close the editor. You can also click outside of the editing window to end the command.

You have edited the mtext object. You should also notice that the %%c now represents a diameter (Ø) symbol, as shown in Figure 14.15.

Leave this drawing open for the following exercise.

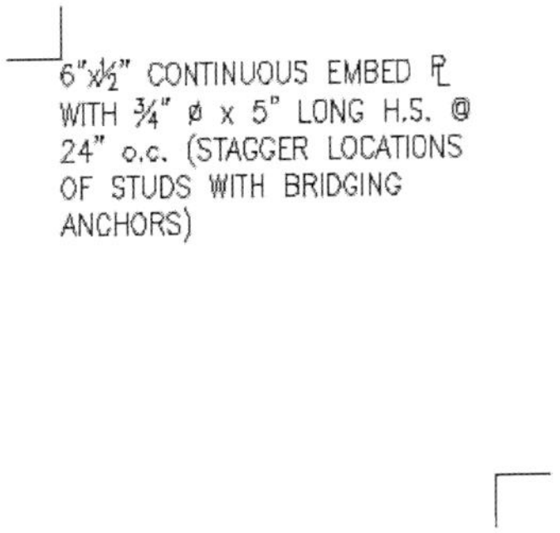

6"x½" CONTINUOUS EMBED ℙ
WITH ¾" Ø x 5" LONG H.S. @
24" o.c. (STAGGER LOCATIONS
OF STUDS WITH BRIDGING
ANCHORS)

**Figure 14.15**    The edited mtext object with new text content and symbols.

There are a few specialty character combinations used by AutoCAD, as described in the following section.

### Specialty AutoCAD Symbols

You can add symbols that are in the font file but that are not on the keyboard. Table 14.5 shows several formatting codes and the resulting symbols.

**Table 14.5    Additional Formatting Codes**

| Formatting Code | Symbol | Meaning |
| --- | --- | --- |
| %%c | Ø | Diameter |
| %%d | ° | Degree |
| %%p | ± | Plus/minus |

The codes are not case-sensitive. In addition to the codes in Table 14.5, you can enter the code %%nnn, where nnn is a three-digit integer, to add any character in a font file.

AutoCAD 2005 comes with a series of new symbols. Shown previously in Figure 14.10, these new symbols require that you use new AutoCAD 2005 versions of SIMPLEX and ROMANS files as well new ISOCP and ISOCT series files.

**I**NSIDER  **C**AUTION

> In the previous exercise, if you change the font file to Arial, for example, the PL sym-
> bol becomes undefined and represents itself as small square. Due to this characteris-
> tic, caution should be taken when using new AutoCAD 2005 symbols with drawings
> that will be used by others who may not be on the same release.

A much easier way to add a symbol is to use the Windows Character Map program. To
use the Character Map program in place of the %%nnn code, simply start the Character
Map program by selecting Other on the Symbols submenu and select the TrueType font
file you have specified in the current text style. Then select the character you want to add
and copy it to the clipboard. You can then paste the character into the text you are typing.

**I**NSIDER  **C**AUTION

> Not all font files contain the same characters, which is why it is important that the
> font file you choose to copy from in the Character Map program is the same font
> file specified in the text style you are drawing with in AutoCAD. What the Character
> Map program actually copies when you copy a character to the clipboard is the
> character's position number in the font chart. When you paste that character into
> AutoCAD, the character corresponding to the position number recorded in the clip-
> board is drawn. Therefore, if you are using a different font file in AutoCAD, you may
> end up with a different character altogether.

## *MTEDIT* Right-Click Shortcut Features

As you have discovered, there are many options available on the MTEDIT right-click
shortcut menu. The following sections discuss some of these features in detail.

### Insert Field

Fields are a new AutoCAD 2005 feature for embedding dynamic text values within text-
type objects such as mtext. Refer to Chapter 21, "Using Fields and Tables," for more
information.

### Indents and Tabs

With the addition of indentation and tab stops, using AutoCAD as a limited word
processor is easier than before.

As shown in Figure 14.16, the highlighted row of text in these notes is utilizing both features. It has an tab stop to push the 2. text over. It has another tab stop to push start of the REDUCTION text over. It then has an indent for all lines after the first one, helping it line up with the previous line.

---

**I**NSIDER **N**OTE

There is a dialog specifically for setting indents and tabs. Accessed from the Text Formatting right-click shortcut menu, choose Indents and Tabs, showing the Indents and Tab dialog.

---

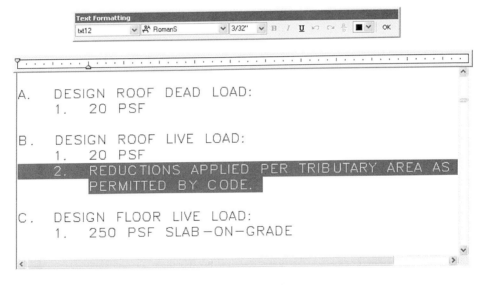

**Figure 14.16**   Indents and tab stops in mtext aid in alignment.

---

**I**NSIDER **T**IP

You can adjust your indents within the editor window; just grab the appropriate indent marker and slide as desired. The top marker sets the first line indent; the bottom marker sets the indent for the rest of the paragraph. You can also place new tab stops by clicking on the ruler. Remove tabs by clicking on one and dragging it off the ruler.

## *Justification*

After you are in the Text Formatting dialog, you can still change text justification if needed. The Justification submenu contains all available alignments for mtext objects. Just click the placement type you need, and the content of the editor instantly updates.

## *Find and Replace*

Use the Find and Replace feature to search for a specific combination of characters and even to replace the text found with different text. If the Match Case setting is enabled, AutoCAD finds only text that exactly matches the case of the search string. If the Whole Word setting is enabled, AutoCAD finds only words that fully match the search string; otherwise, other words that contain the search string are located. After you specify the settings you want, use the Find button to start the search.

## *Stack and Unstack*

The Stack/Unstack option is an slick feature in AutoCAD 2005 that is used to stack or unstack selected text. For example, you can designate selected text to be stacked by using special characters between the characters you want stacked. The text to the left of the character is placed on top of the text to the right of the character. To unstack stacked text, select it and then click the Unstack option.

AutoCAD 2005 provides for three stacked text types based on which of the following characters is used:

- **Carat (^).** Converts selected text to left-justified tolerance-style stacking.
- **Forward slash (/).** Converts selected text to center-justified text separated by a horizontal bar.
- **Pound sign (#).** Converts selected text to a fraction-style stack separated by a diagonal bar.

You can edit stacked text and change the stack type, its alignment, or the size of stacked text in the Stack Properties dialog box, shown previously in Figure 14.12.

## *Import Text*

If you have text in an existing TXT or RTF file, you can use the Import Text button to import the file into the editor, and then you can edit the text as needed. Click this option and then simply locate the text file to bring in. The content is read and placed within the editor at the current cursor location.

### *Background Mask*

A great new feature in AutoCAD 2005 is text masking. Basically, this provides the capability have a colored background property applied to your mtext object. In addition, this mask can display the background of your screen—essentially blanking out other drawing content that may exist within the mtext object boundary.

### *Setting the Bold, Italic, and Underline Text Properties*

The Bold and Italic buttons enable you to bold or italicize the text, but only if the chosen font file is a TrueType font. You can use the Underline button to underline any selected text, regardless of the font file used. All three buttons act as toggles, and you can turn their properties on or off by simply selecting the desired text and clicking the appropriate button.

**INSIDER TIP**

If you are using an SHX-based font, you can use the oblique angle to achieve the appearance of italics.

### *Color Settings*

The Text Color list enables you to set the color for selected text. You can set the color to ByLayer, ByBlock, one of AutoCAD's 255 colors, or a True Color or Color Book setting.

## **Secondary Editing of Mtext Objects**

You can use grips to move or change the width of the mtext object. When you select the grip point that corresponds to the justification point, you can move the mtext object. If you select any other grip point, you stretch the width of the mtext object. The following exercise shows the ease with which other mtext properties can be changed.

**INSIDER TIP**

A new object snap opportunity exists in AutoCAD 2005. Now the corners (same locations as the grips) can be targeted using the Node osnap mode. Primarily used to align the corners or edges with other objects, this feature can be controlled through the OSNAPNODELEGACY system variable. When set to 0, it is active; when set to 1, AutoCAD does not provide nodes for an mtext object.

### Exercise 14.3   Modifying Mtext Objects

1. Continue from the previous exercise. If needed you can open the drawing 14EX03.dwg from the accompanying CD. It contains a single mtext object and two reference polylines made in the previous exercise.

2. Double-click on the mtext object, invoking the MTEDIT command.

3. Press Enter to create a new line. Then move the cursor back up to the top line and type **NOTE:**. Then select that new text and then press the U (underline) button.

   Notice that the Bold font property is unavailable. The current style's font does not include a bold component.

4. Highlight (if needed) the NOTE: text and, using the Font drop-down list, select Arial. It is near the top of the list. Choosing it changes just the selected text to that font.

5. Now the Bond font property is available. Select it to make the NOTE: bold.

6. Select the NOTE: text (if needed). In the size list, type in **0.25**, making the text noticeably bigger than the rest of the text.

7. Again, with the NOTE: text selected, use the Color drop-down list and pick red. Now the added text is bigger and more distinctive.

8. Use the right-click shortcut menu and select Background Mask. The Background Mask dialog box is presented. Turn on the Use background mask option, and leave the other settings as shown in Figure 14.17. Close the dialog. Press OK to close the Text Formatting dialog box.

**Figure 14.17**   You can set an mtext background color with the new Background Mask feature.

   You didn't see a visible change to the background of the mtext object. This is partly due to the fact that the background color and the mask are identical. To truly appreciate this feature, you need something to hide.

9. Draw a line from one corner mark to the other mark.

   Again, no change. This is because the last object drawn is on top of previous items drawn. But that is easily corrected.

**10.** Select the mtext object so that its grips are activated. Then use the right-click shortcut menu and choose the Draw Order submenu, Bring to Front option.

Instantly, the line is now hidden by the area of the mtext object, plus a little bit more. Notice in Figure 14.18 that the corner mark is also being clipped. This clipping is handled by the border offset factor, as shown in Figure 14.17.

You can close this drawing without saving.

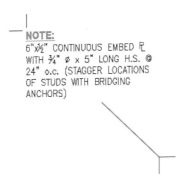

NOTE:
6"x½" CONTINUOUS EMBED ℄
WITH ¾" ⌀ x 5" LONG H.S. @
24" o.c. (STAGGER LOCATIONS
OF STUDS WITH BRIDGING
ANCHORS)

**Figure 14.18**    The revised mtext object, hiding all objects behind it.

**INSIDER NOTE**

It should be noted that the entire mtext boundary box is the space that gets filled with the mask. As the bottom line content shows, even though the text doesn't extend very far, the boundary masks that area. Also note that the Draw Order command is crucial to implementing this feature well. A given mtext object can mask all other things, including other mtext objects and dimensions that are below it in the draw order.

**INSIDER TIP**

Even geometry that is masked is still there, selectable and available.

## *Line Spacing Controls*

Shown in Figure 14.19 is a portion of the Properties palette with the mtext object from the previous exercise selected. Most text properties can now be managed through the right-click shortcut menu found within the Text Formatting dialog box. A few exceptions exist, including the line spacing properties.

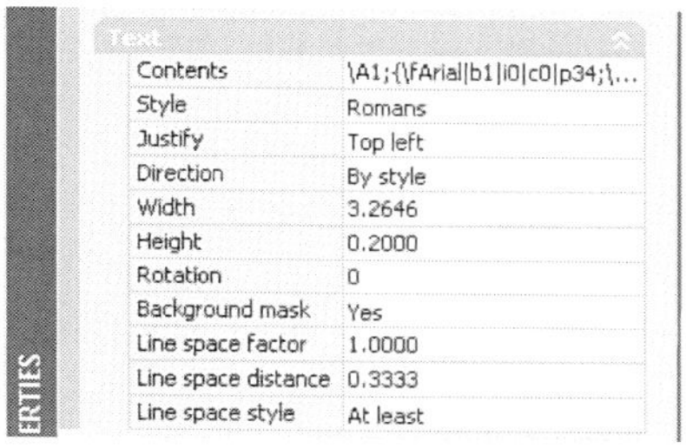

| Text | |
| --- | --- |
| Contents | \A1;{\fArial\|b1\|i0\|c0\|p34;\... |
| Style | Romans |
| Justify | Top left |
| Direction | By style |
| Width | 3.2646 |
| Height | 0.2000 |
| Rotation | 0 |
| Background mask | Yes |
| Line space factor | 1.0000 |
| Line space distance | 0.3333 |
| Line space style | At least |

**Figure 14.19**   Mtext-related spacing features on the Properties palette.

The default Spacing Factor is 1.0, which sets the line spacing as a multiple of the single line spacing. Single spacing is 1.666 times the text height in most cases. The Space Distance value follows the factor value, but it shows the value as a true distance. For example, text with a height of 0.20 has a default distance of 0.333 (0.20 × 1.666).

The combination of these two settings enables the mtext object to have a minimum spacing while the Line Spacing Style is set to "At least." If characters go above or below the line, such as a [ or /, the lines adjust to maintain proper clearance. However, if you need a specific line spacing, for a schedule perhaps, you can set the Style to Exact and then the Spacing Distance to your desired setting.

# Performing a Spelling Check

To check spelling within all your text-based objects, including attributes, issue the SPELL command by choosing Spelling from the Tools pull-down menu. When you start the command, AutoCAD prompts you to select the objects to check. If the SPELL command encounters an unknown word, the Check Spelling dialog box appears, and you must choose to replace the word, ignore the discrepancy, or add the word to your supplemental dictionary. If no errors are found, a message box appears, informing you that the spell check is complete.

## Specifying the Dictionaries

The SPELL command looks up words in two dictionaries at any given time: a main dictionary and a supplemental dictionary. Several main dictionaries are supplied with AutoCAD; the default is the American English Dictionary. The default supplemental dictionary is SAMPLE.CUS (it contains a number of AutoCAD command words and terms). To change the dictionaries used by SPELL, issue the OPTIONS command. In the Options dialog box, select the Files tab, then change the Main Dictionary and Custom Dictionary File settings located under Text Editor, Dictionary, and Font File Names.

Unlike the supplemental dictionary, the main dictionary file cannot be modified or added to. You can, however, add words to update the current supplemental dictionary.

> **I**NSIDER **N**OTE
>
> The SPELL command within AutoCAD 2005 can delve into all forms of annotation, including blocks, to locate misspelled text-type items. It also displays misspellings in xrefs but cannot correct them.

## Creating a Supplemental Dictionary

A supplemental dictionary file is an ASCII-based text file that contains the additional words you want SPELL to use when checking for correct spelling. The supplemental dictionary contains one word per line. You can create as many supplemental dictionaries as you want, but you can use only one at time. When you create a supplemental dictionary, be sure to use a CUS filename extension.

# Looking at Additional Text Options

This section covers several optional text handling features that may prove useful to you. These features enable you to speed up the display of text, handle missing font files, and insert text files into the current drawing.

## Enabling the Quick Text Display

When AutoCAD opens or regenerates a drawing, if the drawing contains numerous text objects, it can take quite some time to complete a selection process, especially if the text uses complex fonts. If you want to speed up the process and do not need to actually see the existing text, enable the Quick Text mode (QTEXT). To enable the Quick Text mode, access the Display tab of the Options dialog box and select the Show Text Boundary

Frame Only check box. When Quick Text is enabled, text-based objects are displayed as simple rectangles that contain no characters. When you enable Quick Text mode, you need issue a REGEN command to redisplay the text as simple rectangles.

> **I**NSIDER  **N**OTE
>
> When Quick Text is enabled, new text objects are displayed as text characters while the TEXT and MTEXT commands are active, which makes it easier to read what you are typing.

## Specifying an Alternate Font File

Font files are not stored with the drawing file. If a font file that is referenced in the drawing is not available when the drawing is opened, an error message is displayed. You are then prompted to choose a replacement font file. If you want to bypass all such error messages, you can specify a font file that is automatically used whenever a needed font file cannot be found. You specify this alternate font file in the Alternate Font File setting under Text Editor, Dictionary, Font File Names in the Files tab of the Options dialog box. The default alternate font is SIMPLEX.SHX.

> **I**NSIDER  **C**AUTION
>
> A couple of problems can occur when you use an alternate font. If the missing font file contains special characters that the alternate font file does not have, the text on the drawing may end up incomplete. Furthermore, because the space that a line of text occupies depends on the font file used to generate the text, you may find that when the alternate font is applied, the text on the drawing looks out of place or does not fit properly. The best solution is to obtain the correct font files and use them unless you are sure you have a suitable alternative font file.

## Mapping Fonts

If you need to specify more than one alternate font file, use a font mapping file. A font mapping file is an ASCII-based text file in which each line in the file specifies the font filename to be replaced and its substitute font filename (separated by a semicolon). Note that you should include the extension if there could be any ambiguity. The default font map file is ACAD.FMP. You can identify a different font map file by changing the Font Mapping File setting under Text Editor, Dictionary, Font File Names in the Files tab of the Options dialog box.

## Adding Text as Attributes

An alternate method to adding text objects that are to be incorporated into block definitions is to create attributes. Attributes behave much like text objects but have additional functions beyond displaying text. Attributes are discussed in more detail in Chapter 10, "Creating and Using Blocks."

## Dragging and Dropping Text Files

In Windows, you can drag a text file from the desktop or from Windows Explorer and drop it into your drawing. AutoCAD automatically inserts the file as an mtext object, using the current text settings for the text height, rotation angle, and text style.

## Copying Text Using the Clipboard

You also can copy text from any application to your clipboard and paste the contents into your drawing. If you use the PASTE command, the contents are dropped into your drawing as an embedded object. If you use the PASTESPEC command, you can choose to paste the clipboard contents as text, in which case the text is an mtext object.

The clipboard operations depend on OLE (Object Linking and Embedding). For more information on AutoCAD's OLE features, refer to Chapter 15, "Applications for OLE Objects."

# Text Property Modification

AutoCAD 2005 includes a few commands to aid the process of changing text properties such as height and justification. These new tools can help tasks that take hours to complete finish in mere seconds. Learning these features and how to leverage them in your everyday work is key to high productivity.

## Scaling Text

Accessed through the Modify pull-down menu, Object, Text, the SCALETEXT command enables you to select as many text objects as needed to modify. After selecting your objects, you get a prompt

```
[Existing/Left/Center/Middle/Right/TL/TC/TR/ML/MC/MR/BL/BC/BR] <Existing>
```

where you can choose any number of methods to change the size of the text objects.

If you choose the default `<Existing>` option, the base point for the scaling procedure is based on the existing text insertion point. If you choose any other option, the scaling process is relative to that justification type. For example, `TC` would change the scale of the text relative to the Top Center of the text.

Following the choice of from where to scale the text, you get another prompt:

```
Specify new height or [Match object/Scale factor] <0.1000>
```

Here you decide how to change the size of the text. You can specify a literal size, pick an object on-screen to get a distance, or just provide a scale factor such as 1.5. This changes your text heights by 1.5 times. After that, the various text objects change.

**I**NSIDER **NOTE**

> The SCALETEXT command has no dialog interface.

## Changing Text Justifications

Also accessed in the Modify pull-down menu under Object, Text, the new JUSTIFYTEXT command enables you to change the justification of multiple text objects very easily. You could of course use the Properties palette, but that adjusts the justification only about the insertion point. What this means is a piece of text that is left-justified at 0,0 when switched to right justification will graphically move to a -X value but keep the insertion at 0,0.

However, using the JUSTIFYTEXT command preserves all graphic locations of text and relocates the insertion points. If you have ever had this problem, you will recognize what a timesaver this is.

At the `Select Objects` prompt, gather all your text objects to change justification. Then another prompt appears:

```
[Left/Align/Fit/Center/Middle/Right/TL/TC/TR/ML/MC/MR/BL/BC/BR] <TC>
```

Choose which justification type you want and then press Enter. AutoCAD then changes the justification but doesn't move the text's first line visually. Of course, when you change the justification on mtext objects, the subsequent lines of text in the mtext object alter to honor the new justification.

> **INSIDER NOTE**
>
> The JUSTIFYTEXT command has no dialog interface.

## Space Translation

SPACETRANS is a transparent command available in AutoCAD 2005. This command converts distances from space, such as model space, to an equivalent distance in paper space. This is typically needed for determining text heights between spaces. The program is transparent-capable, so it can provide the data to other commands.

> **INSIDER NOTE**
>
> A transparent command is any program that can be used while running another command. An example of this is the ZOOM command; you can zoom while drawing lines in the LINE command. To use a transparent-aware command, prefix it with a (') sign and press Enter.

# Summary

AutoCAD provides a variety of tools that deal with adding and editing text. This chapter covered the various steps for creating and working with single lines of text in your drawings, as well as how to add multiple paragraphs of text using the MTEXT command. The chapter also provided detailed information on editing mtext and defining and changing text styles to control the appearance of text.

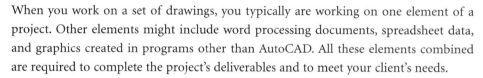

*Chapter 15*

# Applications for OLE Objects

When you work on a set of drawings, you typically are working on one element of a project. Other elements might include word processing documents, spreadsheet data, and graphics created in programs other than AutoCAD. All these elements combined are required to complete the project's deliverables and to meet your client's needs.

Often, data created in other applications must be duplicated in your AutoCAD drawing. Elements such as General Notes created in a word-processing program or a Bill of Materials created in a spreadsheet application must be duplicated in your drawing to satisfy the project's final delivery requirements. By inserting documents created from other applications into your AutoCAD drawing, you create a compound document and take advantage of data already created in other applications. By simply dragging existing files into your drawing, you can insert data, such as word processing information from Word and tabular spreadsheet data from Excel, directly into your AutoCAD drawing. By using OLE, you make the process of completing a set of drawings easier by using existing data in its native format.

This chapter reviews AutoCAD OLE capabilities and covers the following subjects:

- Understanding Object Linking and Embedding
- Importing objects into AutoCAD using OLE
- Exporting AutoCAD objects using OLE

# Understanding Object Linking and Embedding

Object Linking and Embedding (OLE) is a feature provided by the Windows operating system. Whether an application takes advantage of OLE is up to its developers. In the case of AutoCAD, the application is designed to take advantage of OLE technology, enabling you to interact with other OLE-compliant applications. By using OLE, you can insert files from other applications directly into AutoCAD drawings, and you can insert AutoCAD views and AutoCAD objects into other OLE-compliant applications.

OLE refers to two different ways you can insert a file from another application into your drawing. You can either insert an OLE object as a linked object or as an embedded object. A linked object inserts a copy of a file that references the original source file. A linked OLE object behaves similarly to xrefs in that any modifications made to the source file are reflected in the linked OLE object when the link is updated in your drawing.

In contrast, although an embedded object also inserts a copy of a file into your drawing, it does not maintain a link to the source file. An embedded OLE object behaves similarly to a block inserted from another drawing in that the inserted file exists independently of the source from which it was copied and can be edited independently without affecting the source file. More importantly, any edits made to the source file are not reflected in the embedded OLE object. Use linked objects when you want modifications to the source file to appear in your drawing, and use embedded objects when you want to insert a copy of a file but don't want edits to the source file to appear in your drawing.

OLE objects inserted into AutoCAD drawings have certain limitations. A main limitation is that OLE objects cannot easily be rotated in your drawing. Even with that limitation, you will find OLE to be a useful feature.

**INSIDER NOTE**

> You can use the OLESTARTUP system variable to improve the quality of plotted OLE objects. The variable controls whether the source application of an inserted OLE object loads when plotting. Setting the value to 1 instructs AutoCAD to load the OLE source application when plotting. Setting the value to 0 instructs AutoCAD to not load the OLE source application when plotting. This system variable is stored with the drawing.

# Importing Objects into AutoCAD Using OLE

You can create compound documents in AutoCAD by linking or embedding objects from other applications. For example, you can insert content from a spreadsheet application, a set of notes from a word-processing application, and a graphic image from a paint program. By inserting the desired objects into your AutoCAD drawing, you create a compound document.

**I**NSIDER **N**OTE

A functional limitation exists when dealing with many Microsoft Windows application files such as Word .doc files. Documents bigger than a single 8"×11" page are truncated to that size in spite of how much you select to paste into AutoCAD. Due to the Windows Metafile format, long Word documents cannot show more than the first whole page. Your options at this point are to tile multiple "Copy-Paste" objects or to try to compress the font and spacing to get more in one 8"×11" page.

**I**NSIDER **T**IP

The problem mentioned in the previous note also existed for Excel. But beginning with Microsoft Office XP, the problem was corrected for Excel spreadsheets. You can now paste in a 256 column by 10,000 row spreadsheet—if your system can handle it, of course.

AutoCAD provides several options for linking and embedding objects in drawings, as described in the following sections.

## Using the Insert Object Dialog Box

You can insert OLE objects into AutoCAD using the Insert Objects dialog box. This procedure enables you to insert linked or embedded objects from within AutoCAD by executing an AutoCAD command. From the Insert Objects dialog box, you can insert an object from an existing file or create a new OLE object that exists only in the current drawing.

The Insert Object dialog box is opened from the Insert menu by choosing OLE Object. When opened, the Insert Object dialog box presents a list of object types it can link or embed, as shown in Figure 15.1.

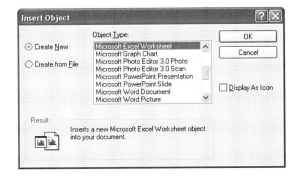

**Figure 15.1**    The Insert Object dialog box enables you to insert OLE objects from within AutoCAD.

From the Insert Object dialog box, you select whether you want to create a new OLE object or insert an OLE object from an existing file. The Create New option opens the selected application so you can create the object. Then, when the object is saved, the selected application is closed, and AutoCAD embeds the new OLE object in the current drawing.

In contrast, by choosing the Create from File option, the Insert Object dialog box changes its display, enabling you to browse for an object to link or embed, as shown in Figure 15.2. By selecting the Link check box, the selected object is inserted into AutoCAD and linked back to the original file.

The Insert Object dialog box provides a straightforward method for inserting OLE objects. By giving you the option of browsing for existing OLE object files to insert or creating new OLE objects by selecting the desired application, you can easily insert the needed OLE object into your AutoCAD drawing.

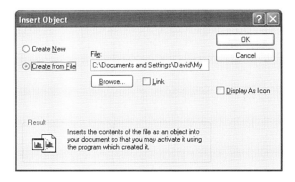

**Figure 15.2**    The Insert Object dialog box enables you to browse for existing OLE object files to insert in AutoCAD.

In the following exercise, you embed an OLE object you create into an AutoCAD drawing.

### Exercise 15.1    Embedding an OLE Object

1.  Start a new drawing in AutoCAD.

2.  From the Insert pull-down menu, choose OLE Object. The Insert Object dialog box appears.

3.  Check the Create New option button if needed.

4.  From the Object Type list, choose a word-processing object type to insert into AutoCAD. The exercise in this book uses Microsoft Word Document, as shown in Figure 15.3; click OK.

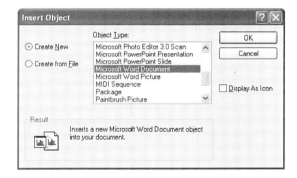

**Figure 15.3**   The Microsoft Word Document is selected as the type of object to insert.

5.  The source application launches, enabling you to create a new document.

6.  In the source application, type **My Word Text**.

7.  From the source application's File pull-down menu, choose Close & Return to Drawing…. The source file is then saved, and the application closes.

    The OLE object should now exist in the AutoCAD drawing. You may close the drawing without saving.

Because AutoCAD launches the source application, the application might stay open even after you close the file and return to the AutoCAD drawing. Just close the source application if needed.

## Pasting OLE Objects into AutoCAD

You can insert OLE objects into AutoCAD by pasting them from the Windows clipboard. This procedure is a very common way to insert OLE objects from one application to another. Using this feature, you can copy an object directly from its application to the clipboard and then paste the clipboard's contents into AutoCAD.

You paste objects from the clipboard with either the PASTE command or the PASTESPEC command. These commands are accessed from AutoCAD's Edit pull-down menu. The PASTE command also can be accessed from the shortcut menu, which is displayed by right-clicking in the drawing area. These commands are only available when the clipboard contains objects.

Although both commands paste objects into the current drawing from the clipboard, they differ in one important way. The PASTE command only embeds objects. The PASTE-SPEC command enables you to either embed objects or insert them as linked objects.

When you choose the PASTE command, the object is immediately embedded into AutoCAD. Additionally, the OLE Properties dialog box appears if the Display Dialog Box When Pasting New OLE Objects check box is selected. The OLE Properties dialog box enables you to control the size of the OLE object and is discussed in detail later in this chapter.

When you choose the PASTESPEC command, AutoCAD displays the Paste Special dialog box. From this dialog box, you can choose either the Paste option or the Paste Link option.

When you use the Paste option, the OLE object is embedded into the drawing. The difference between pasting an object from the Paste Special dialog box and pasting it directly from the Edit or shortcut menu is that by using the Paste Special dialog box, you have more control over the OLE object type you are embedding.

When you choose the Paste option in the Paste Special dialog box, the available object types appear in the As list. The object types listed depend on the OLE object you are pasting from the clipboard.

For example, if the clipboard contains a Microsoft Word document, you can embed the clipboard's contents as one of several object types shown in Figure 15.4. The list only displays acceptable types for the particular object. Several other object types are described as follows:

- **Picture (Metafile).** Inserts the contents of the clipboard into your drawing as a vector-based picture.

- **AutoCAD Entities.** Inserts the contents of the clipboard into your drawing as circles, arcs, lines, and polylines. Text is inserted as text objects, with each line of text located in a paragraph in the source file being converted to individual AutoCAD text objects.

- **Image Entity.** Inserts the contents of the clipboard into your drawing as an AutoCAD raster image object.

- **Text.** Inserts the contents of the clipboard into your drawing as an AutoCAD mtext object. Any line objects are ignored.

- **Package.** Inserts the contents of the clipboard into your drawing as a Windows Package object. A package is an icon that represents embedded or linked information. The information may consist of a complete document, such as a Paint bitmap, or part of a document, such as a spreadsheet cell. You create packages using the Windows Object Packager, which is accessed from the Taskbar by choosing Start, Programs, Accessories, Object Packager.

- **Bitmap Image.** Inserts the contents of the clipboard into your drawing as a bitmap image object.

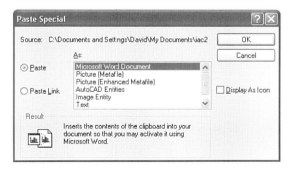

**Figure 15.4**   The PASTESPEC command enables you to select an object's type when it is embedded.

When you choose the Paste Link option, you can insert the OLE object only as its original object type. For example, if you choose the Paste Link option to insert a Microsoft Word document, you can insert it only as a Microsoft Word document. This ensures that you can open and edit the source Word document to which the OLE object is linked.

**INSIDER TIP**

If you work with a black background in AutoCAD and paste an image from a word-processing or spreadsheet application, the pasted image appears with a white background in the drawing. If this is undesirable, change your background in either program to match the other.

**INSIDER TIP**

The background color of an OLE object is reversed when plotting if needed. The actual content in the OLE object is what shows when it is plotted from within AutoCAD.

By using the PASTE and PASTESPEC commands, you can embed or link OLE objects in your AutoCAD drawing from the clipboard. Next, you learn about another method for inserting OLE objects.

## Using Drag and Drop to Insert OLE Objects

The Windows operating system provides the capability to drag selected objects from another application into an AutoCAD drawing. By selecting objects in an open application and then dragging the selected objects into AutoCAD, you in effect cut the objects from the application and embed them in the AutoCAD drawing. To copy the objects from the open application instead of cutting, hold down the Ctrl key while dragging the objects into the drawing.

**INSIDER TIP**

After you select objects in an application, drag them into AutoCAD by right-clicking with your pointing device. When you release, AutoCAD displays the shortcut menu and enables you to either move the objects (Move here), copy the objects (Copy here), or insert the objects (Paste as block) into the AutoCAD drawing. You can also cancel the operation from the shortcut menu.

Additionally, you can drag objects from Windows Explorer. If AutoCAD recognizes the object type, it embeds it into the drawing. If AutoCAD does not recognize the file type, or if the object type cannot be inserted as an OLE object, AutoCAD issues an error and cancels the function.

# Controlling OLE Object Properties

AutoCAD provides specific tools for manipulating an OLE object because some AutoCAD commands can be problematic when editing OLE objects. By using specific tools designed for manipulating OLE objects, you can control an OLE object's appearance in AutoCAD.

**I**NSIDER **T**IP

> When you select an OLE object in AutoCAD to display its grips, you can press the Delete key to delete the object.

## Controlling OLE Object Size

AutoCAD provides you with the ability to manipulate an OLE object's size in a drawing through the Properties palette. The palette enables you to control an object's size any one of three ways: by size, scale, or text size (see Figure 15.5). You access the dialog box by selecting an OLE object, right-clicking, and selecting Properties from the shortcut menu.

You control an OLE object's size by entering values in the height and width fields. If the Lock Aspect entry is set to Yes, when one field value is changed, the other updates automatically, proportionally maintaining the OLE object's aspect ratio size. The units entered in the field are based on the drawing's current units setting.

**Figure 15.5**
The Properties palette enables you to control various settings of an OLE object.

**I**NSIDER **T**IP

If you need to change an OLE object back to its original placement scale, choose OLE, Reset from the right-click shortcut menu.

You can also control the OLE object's size by entering a percentage of the object's dimensions. As with the values in the size area, if the Lock Aspect entry is set to Yes, when one field value is changed in the height and width fields, the other value updates automatically.

A third method for controlling an OLE object's size is available in the OLE Text Size dialog box. If the OLE object contains text, you can enter a new text size value to adjust the object's size. The first field displays the list of fonts in the OLE object, and the second field contains a list of the selected font's used point sizes. Points are a typographical measurement; there are 72 points in an inch. By choosing the desired font and size in the first two fields, you can control the object's overall size by entering the desired height of the text in the third field. For example, in Figure 15.6, the OLE object will be resized based on the 10-point Arial font being set to 1.0 drawing units.

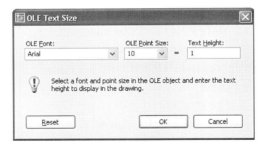

**Figure 15.6**    Use the OLE Text Size dialog box to adjust the size of OLE objects based on text content.

**I**NSIDER **N**OTE

It's important to understand that the three areas provided for controlling an OLE object's size work in unison. When one set of values is changed in one area, the values are automatically changed in the other two areas. The values in the three areas cannot be set independently of one another.

In the following exercise, you resize an OLE object for a specific font size.

### Exercise 15.2   Resizing an OLE Object

1. Open the drawing 15EX02.dwg from the accompanying CD. The drawing displays an embedded OLE object that consists of a small single line of text and a 4.8"-tall text object.

2. Select the OLE object to highlight and display object grips.

3. Using the right-click shortcut menu, choose the OLE option followed by Text Size. AutoCAD then displays the OLE Text Size dialog box. There is only one font in this OLE object, Arial, and only one size for that font, 10 points.

   You will resize the object using this dialog. For this exercise, assume we need a text height of 4.8.

4. In the Text Height text box on the right, type **4.8** and then click OK.

   AutoCAD resizes the OLE object based on the current text's size equaling 4.8. You might need to execute a ZOOM Extents to see the OLE object.

**I**NSIDER **C**AUTION

> OLE Text Scaling is still not an exacting procedure. As you can see in the exercise, the OLE text is much bigger, but not quite the same size as the single text object. This is partially due to fonts having characters that extend above and below the line; whether they show is irrelevant. Also, the font you use can appear as a different size, even though the text scaling might be the same. If your size needs are absolute, then further scaling and experiments will be needed to determine the exact values to use.

You can close the drawing without saving your changes.

In this exercise, the calculations determined that the OLE object's text height must be converted to 4.8. This means that when the drawing is plotted at 1:48, the text's height will plot at 0.10 units high.

In addition to controlling an OLE object's size, the Properties palette provides you with the ability to control the plot quality of an OLE object. From the Plot Quality control, you can choose one of the following three plot quality styles:

- **Monochrome.** Intended for plotting objects such as a spreadsheet.
- **Low Graphics.** Intended for plotting color text and pie charts.
- **High Graphics.** Intended for plotting objects that are color images.

The plot quality options are applied specifically to the selected OLE object. Therefore, you can insert a Word document that contains only text and set the plot quality to Monochrome. Then you can insert a true-color image and set its plot quality to High Graphics. By applying the desired plot quality to each OLE object, you can control an object's appearance when plotted.

## Controlling OLE Objects Using the Shortcut Menu

After an OLE object is inserted into a drawing, you can control several object properties and perform edits through commands accessed from the shortcut menu. By using these commands, you can delete the OLE object and copy it to the clipboard. You can determine whether the object appears on top or below other objects in the drawing, and you can control whether it can be selected for editing. The shortcut menu offers these commands and more, providing useful control over OLE objects.

### Cutting and Copying OLE Objects

When you right-click over an OLE object, AutoCAD displays the available OLE shortcut commands, as shown in Figure 15.7. The first two commands do the following:

- **Cut.** Erases the selected object from the drawing and places a copy on the clipboard. You can also accomplish the same procedure by pressing Ctrl+X.

- **Copy.** Leaves the selected object in the drawing and places a copy on the clipboard. You can also accomplish the same procedure by pressing Ctrl+C.

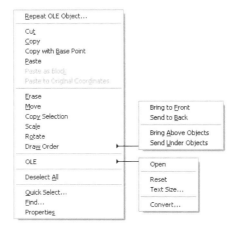

**Figure 15.7**   Right-click on a selected OLE object to display the shortcut menu commands.

When you use the Cut and Copy OLE options on an object, the object is placed on the clipboard in its original object format, not as an AutoCAD object. For example, suppose a Word document resides in your drawing as an OLE object. If you use the Copy OLE option to copy the Word document object from your drawing to the clipboard, when you paste the object into another application, it is pasted as a Word document object.

### Undoing OLE Object Edits

A very powerful command in AutoCAD is UNDO, which can undo edits made to the OLE object while in your drawing. For example, if you move or resize the object in your drawing, you can undo the edit by selecting Undo from the shortcut menu. By using the UNDO command specifically, you can undo a series of edits made to the object.

The UNDO command has one important limitation: It does not undo edits made to the OLE object in the object's source application. For example, if you paste a Word document object into your drawing and then edit the document object in Word by adding additional text, when you save your edits and return to your drawing, the edits made in Word cannot be undone in AutoCAD. In other words, the text added to the document from the Word application cannot be undone by using the UNDO command in AutoCAD.

### Controlling OLE Object Placement

An item of concern for most AutoCAD users is placement. Fortunately, with AutoCAD 2005, you can use object snaps (osnaps) to aid in aligning OLE objects. Additionally, when you click on an OLE object, AutoCAD creates grips at the four corners of the object.

As with other AutoCAD object types, grips can be used to move and scale the OLE object. When you pick on a grip, it becomes hot, and becomes the base point for the scale, move, and mirror commands available in the shortcut menu. As shown in Figure 15.8, a typical OLE objects presents useful grip points at its corners. If needed, you can always fall back on osnaps such as Intersection, Endpoint, and Midpoint to get the right points to grab the OLE object.

| METAL STUD DESIGNATIONS | |
|---|---|
| THICKNESS (MILS) | CORRESPONDING GAUGE (REFERENCE ONLY) |
| 18 | 25 |
| 27 | 22 |
| 33 | 20 |
| 43 | 18 |
| 54 | 16 |
| 68 | 14 |
| 97 | 12 |

**Figure 15.8**   Excel spreadsheets can be manipulated through the grips on the OLE object.

The grip options just discussed use the hot grip location as the base point for the action requested. However, for the Stretch option, the hot grip location is the corner that the OLE object will expand/contract to match. The functionality can be a little odd at first because of this difference.

**INSIDER TIP**

The sizing or hot grip color is controlled by the selected grip color. This can be changed in the Grips area of the Selection tab of the Options dialog box.

The three objects in Figure 15.9 are OLE objects inserted from a Word document, and they provide an example of how stretching and resizing affects an object. The top object shows how all three objects appeared at original placement. The middle object is a copy of the top object and was stretched by adjusting its width to 200%, leaving the height of the text the same as in the original. The bottom object is also a copy of the top object and was resized by using a corner grip. Notice that although the text's height and width are larger than the original, its aspect ratio is maintained and its overall size is correctly proportioned.

This is the original size.

T h i s   i s   t h e   s t r e t c h e d   s i z e .

# This is the resized size.

**Figure 15.9**   The original object is at the top, the stretched object is in the middle, and the resized object is at the bottom.

**I**NSIDER **TIP**

> To quickly duplicate an OLE object inserted in AutoCAD, select the object and then drag it while pressing the Ctrl key.

### OLE Frames

When you first begin using OLE objects in your drawings, depending on the OLE object type, the frame that borders your object can present some problems. Aside from Excel spreadsheets, just the visual presence of this box can be bothersome. Luckily, this can be handled through use of the OLEFRAME system variable.

The OLEFRAME system variable has three possible integer values you can set, described as follows:

- **0.** The frame is not displayed and not plotted.
- **1.** The frame is displayed and plotted.
- **2.** The frame is displayed but not plotted.

It is very likely that your drawings will end up utilizing each of these settings as you work with OLE objects. When the OLEFRAME variable is set to 0, you cannot select the object at all. This option is useful to maintain an object's size and position in your drawing after it is set as desired. By having OLEFRAME set to 0, you ensure that the OLE objects will not be moved or resized in your drawing.

If your OLE objects are of the type that visually benefit from the frames, then set OLEFRAME to 1. This is usually for images such as pictures or aerials because they typically would have a border shown. When the OLEFRAME system variable is set to 1, the frame is displayed, and it plots according to the layer it resides on or the color property assigned to it.

Last, if your OLE objects benefit from not changing the value all the time, then try the setting of 2, which shows the frame but doesn't plot it. This setting does not affect the actual OLE content, just the plotting of the frame around it.

> **INSIDER NOTE**
>
> The OLEFRAME system variable is saved in the drawing, so it can be different on a per-drawing basis. It, however, cannot be specific at the OLE object level. How it is set within a drawing affects all OLE objects in that drawing.

### Controlling OLE Object Display Order

A constant problem with OLE objects has been getting them to display properly in a drawing. Many times, the object needs to be on a certain level with regard to other objects. Because an OLE object is "solid," it can block items behind it. By using the DRAWORDER command, you can stack your objects in the preferred display sequence.

The two primary commands are Bring to Front and Send to Back. These two options control an object's position in the drawing relative to other objects. By selecting Bring to Front or Send to Back from the Tools pull-down menu, Draw Order or from the right-click shortcut menu, you can place the object above or below other objects, as shown in Figure 15.10.

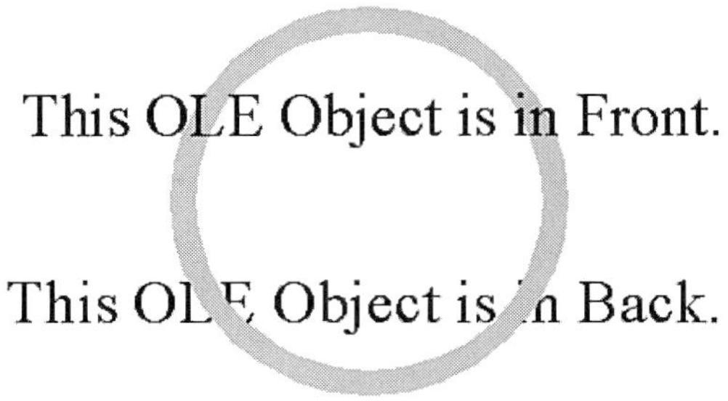

This OLE Object is in Front.

This OLE Object is in Back.

**Figure 15.10** The OLE object at the top has been sent to the front, whereas the object at the bottom has been sent to the back.

> **INSIDER NOTE**
>
> Clicking inside an OLE object always selects it, even though it might be behind other AutoCAD objects. To select AutoCAD objects that lie within an OLE object's frame, be sure to pick directly on them.

Another component of the DRAWORDER command is the capability to adjust objects as they relate to other specific objects. By using the Above objects or Under objects, you can more easily make the special adjustments required to get the exact look you need.

## Converting OLE Objects

The OLECONVERT command opens the Convert dialog box, which enables you to specify a different source application for an embedded object. By selecting the desired source application and then clicking OK, the object's source application type is changed to the new application type.

The different object types to which you can convert an object depend on the object selected. For example, when you select an embedded Word document object and then choose the OLECONVERT command, you are enabled to convert the document object to a Word picture object, as shown in Figure 15.11. The object types listed are those supported by the source application.

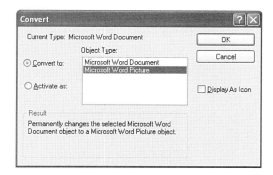

**Figure 15.11**   The Convert dialog box enables you to convert the selected object to a different object type.

When you convert an object, you can choose from one of two options: Convert To or Activate As. The Convert To option converts an embedded object to the type specified under Object Type. This means the object is actually converted to the new selected object type. For example, if you converted a Word document object into a Word picture object and then right-clicked over the object, the shortcut menu would list the object as a picture object. This means that when you edit the object, you would edit it as a Word picture, not a Word document.

The Activate As option acts similarly to the Convert To option, except that it only temporarily converts the object during the editing process to the selected object type. After the editing is complete, the object returns to its original type. For example, you can edit a Word document object by temporarily activating it as a Word picture object. This means the document object opens as a picture object in the Word application, which enables you to modify the object using Word's picture editing tools. After you finish modifying the picture and close and save the file, the modified object appears in AutoCAD in its original format as a Word document object.

Referring to Figure 15.11, you will notice that you can also convert the Word document object to a Word document object. This option is intended to maintain an object in its current type while working in conjunction with the Display as Icon check box. For example, by choosing to convert the Word document object into a Word document object and choosing the Display as Icon option, the document object maintains its current type and changes its appearance to a Word document icon, as shown in Figure 15.12. To return the document object back to its original display, convert the Word document object into a Word document object and then clear the check box.

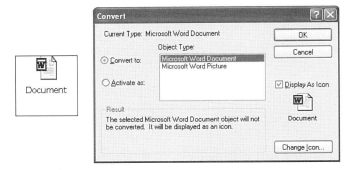

**Figure 15.12**   The Convert dialog box enables you to display an OLE object as an icon.

**INSIDER TIP**

Double-clicking the object icon launches the object's source application and enables you to modify the file.

**INSIDER NOTE**

When you select the Display as Icon option, the Change Icon button activates. When selected, this button displays the Change Icon dialog box, which enables you to select a new icon to appear as the object icon.

**I**NSIDER **N**OTE

> If you convert an OLE object to an icon and it appears stretched beyond reason, to the point where you can't make out the icon at all, just change the width and height values to something more reasonable, such as a value of 1 × your DIMSCALE value.

Next, you learn about two features that enable you to control an OLE object's visibility.

# Controlling OLE Object Visibility

When you insert OLE objects into your drawing, you probably will want to control their visibility. Whether objects are inserted temporarily or are used for drawing construction purposes the way you might use construction lines or rays, you might want the visibility of OLE objects turned off in your drawing or on plotted sheets. By controlling OLE object visibility, you can use the objects to assist you in your work by displaying reference information, and you are not forced to delete them to control their display.

AutoCAD enables you to control the visibility of OLE objects through two features. The first is to simply insert the OLE object on a layer that you turn off or on, or that you freeze or thaw. The second is to use a special command that enables you to globally control the visibility of all OLE objects. By using these two features, you can easily control the visibility of OLE objects inserted in your drawing.

## Controlling OLE Object Layer Properties

Controlling object visibility from the layer on which it is inserted is a very common method for controlling whether an object appears in your drawing. One of the chief reasons for using layers to organize the objects in your drawing is to control the visibility of groups of objects that reside on a common layer. By inserting OLE objects on their own layers, you can easily control their visibility from the Layer Properties Manager.

**I**NSIDER **C**AUTION

> When you cut or copy an OLE object from an AutoCAD drawing and then paste it back into the drawing, the object reverts to its original size, and any modifications to the object are lost. Therefore, the OLE object's size must be reset to the desired value after it is pasted back into the drawing. You can resize the OLE object using the Properties palette.

The Layer Properties Manager enables you to control more than just an OLE object's visibility. Specifically, OLE objects react to the following layer properties:

- **On/Off and Freeze/Thaw.** The On/Off and Freeze/Thaw layer properties control an OLE object's visibility, both on-screen and when plotted. By turning off or freezing the layer on which an OLE object resides, the object is no longer displayed in your drawing, either on-screen or when plotted. To restore the object's visibility, turn on or thaw the layer. To learn about the differences between the On/Off and Freeze/Thaw layer properties, refer to Chapter 5, "Organizing a Drawing with Layers," in the section "Turning Layers Off Versus Freezing Layers."

- **Lock.** The Lock property prevents the OLE object from being selected. It functions similarly to the OLEFRAME system variable, except that it does not allow any type of edits from the OLE object shortcut menu. When the layer on which an OLE object is inserted is locked, the OLE changes cannot be applied. The Lock property absolutely prevents the OLE object from being edited.

- **Plot.** The Plot property enables an object to remain visible on-screen but prevents it from plotting. This feature is useful if you need to display an OLE object during an editing session for reference information only and do not want the object to appear when plotted. By turning off the Plot property, you ensure that the OLE object will not appear on plotted drawings.

By using the layer properties discussed in this section, you can control the behavior of an OLE object from the layer on which it resides. In the next section, you learn how to globally control OLE object visibility.

### Globally Controlling OLE Object Visibility

AutoCAD provides a method to globally control OLE object visibility. The OLEHIDE system variable enables you to determine if OLE objects are visible in paper space and model space. By using the OLEHIDE command, you control the visibility of all OLE objects and whether they appear in paper space and model space.

The OLEHIDE command is a system variable whose current setting is stored in your computer's system registry. This means that when you set a value for OLEHIDE, the setting affects all drawings in the current editing session and future sessions. To control the display of all OLE objects in all drawings, set the desired display value for the OLEHIDE system variable.

Typing OLEHIDE at the command prompt enables you to set the current OLEHIDE system variable value. There are four possible integer values you can set, described as follows:

- **0.** Makes all OLE objects visible, both in paper space and model space.
- **1.** Makes OLE objects visible only in paper space.
- **2.** Makes OLE objects visible only in model space.
- **3.** Makes all OLE objects invisible, both in paper space and model space.

By setting these values, you can control the appearance of all OLE objects, both in paper space and model space.

**I**NSIDER **N**OTE

> If the OLEHIDE system variable is set to 1 or 2 when you insert a new OLE object, AutoCAD automatically changes the OLEHIDE system variable value to enable the new OLE object to appear in the current space. This also causes all OLE objects in the current space to appear.

In the next section, you learn how to work with OLE objects that are linked to their original file.

# Working with Linked OLE Objects

When you insert an OLE object and link it to its original file, the file can be edited in its source application, and the linked object automatically updates. This means that when a linked object is inserted into a drawing, and the object's original file is modified, the linked OLE object in AutoCAD automatically updates to reflect the modifications. This feature is very useful for ensuring that the latest version of an inserted OLE object appears in an AutoCAD drawing.

Although the ability to automatically update and display the latest version of a linked file is very useful, there will probably be occasions when you don't want the linked object to automatically update. For example, if you want to permanently save a set of drawings that represents a 50% completion set, then you do not want OLE objects to automatically update when the 50% completion set of drawings is reopened for reference in the future. You need the ability to control whether linked OLE objects automatically update.

AutoCAD provides a tool that enables you to control whether linked OLE objects automatically update. By choosing the OLE Links command from the Edit pull-down menu, the Links dialog box appears, as shown in Figure 15.13. From the Links dialog box, you can choose either the Automatic or Manual update option, which controls whether linked objects are automatically or manually updated. Additionally, from the Link dialog box, you can restore links lost when the original file can't be found, and you can associate the link to a different file. You can also break the link connection between the OLE object and the original file, which converts the linked object to an embedded object.

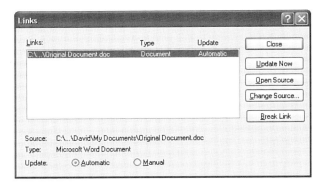

**Figure 15.13**    The Links dialog box enables you to control the link between an OLE object and its source file.

In the following exercise, you restore a lost link using the OLELINKS command.

### Exercise 15.3    Restoring Lost Links to OLE Objects

1. Create a new folder on your C:\ disk called IA2005.

2. Copy the Replacement Document.doc file from the accompanying CD to the C:\IA2005 folder.

3. Open the drawing 15EX03.dwg from the accompanying CD. The drawing displays a linked OLE object that consists of a single line of text.

   At this point, the OLE object is a linked object whose linked file is unavailable for update. Next, you restore the link between the OLE object and its original file.

4. From the Edit pull-down menu, select OLE Links. The Links dialog box appears.

5. Select the Original Document.doc file from the Links list. The link highlights, and the buttons on the Links dialog box activate, as shown in Figure 15.13.

6. From the Links dialog box, click the Change Source button. The Change Source dialog box appears.

7. From the Change Source dialog box, browse your C:\ drive for the IA2005 directory, select the Replacement Document.doc file, and then click Open Source. The
link for the OLE object is replaced, and the new link path is displayed, as shown
in Figure 15.14.

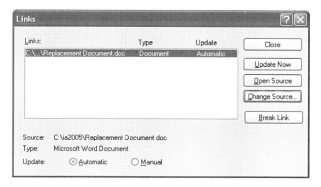

**Figure 15.14**   The updated link path is displayed.

8. Close the Links dialog box. AutoCAD updates the link to the source file.

   You may exit the drawing without saving your changes.

The Links dialog box enables you to select either an automatic or manual link update.
If you choose to manually update, the link can be updated by clicking the Update Now
button on the Links dialog box. The Open Source button opens the linked file's source
application, enabling you to edit the source file. The Change Source button enables you
to either locate a missing source file or select a new file. The Break Link button termi-
nates the link between the OLE object and the source file, and it cannot be reestablished.
After the link is broken, the OLE object permanently becomes an embedded object.

# Exporting AutoCAD Objects by Using OLE

Just as you can insert files from other applications into AutoCAD, you can also insert
AutoCAD drawings into other application files. By using certain commands created
specifically for AutoCAD drawings and AutoCAD objects, you can either insert linked
or embedded AutoCAD files into other application files. The OLE features in AutoCAD
work both for inserting other application files into AutoCAD and for inserting
AutoCAD files into other applications.

Exporting AutoCAD objects into other application files as OLE objects involves determining whether the AutoCAD objects will be linked or embedded. Linked objects are based on a named view in AutoCAD. When the view is updated in the AutoCAD drawing, the link is updated, and the modified view appears in the application's file. In contrast, embedded objects are AutoCAD objects that are selected in the drawing and then copied to the clipboard. After they are pasted from the clipboard, the objects are inserted as independent objects with no association to the original AutoCAD objects. Therefore, if the original AutoCAD objects are edited in the drawing from which they were copied, the objects embedded in the application are not updated.

AutoCAD provides three commands (each of which can be found on the Edit menu) for exporting AutoCAD information into other applications for linking and embedding, described as follows:

- **Cut.** Executes the CUTCLIP command, which copies AutoCAD objects to the clipboard, erasing the selected objects from the drawing.
- **Copy.** Executes the COPYCLIP command, which copies AutoCAD objects to the clipboard.
- **Copy Link.** Executes the COPYLINK command, which copies the current AutoCAD view to the clipboard.

When you use the CUTCLIP or COPYCLIP commands, AutoCAD prompts you to select objects if no objects are currently selected. After the objects are selected, AutoCAD copies the selected objects to the clipboard. If objects are selected prior to executing the commands, the selected objects are immediately copied to the clipboard, and the command ends. If the COPYLINK command is selected, AutoCAD copies all objects in the current view to the clipboard without prompting for object selection. Therefore, the main difference between the CUTCLIP and COPYCLIP commands and the COPYLINK command is that the CUTCLIP and COPCLIP commands prompt you to select objects; the COPYLINK command does not.

When the AutoCAD objects are pasted into the target application, an object frame surrounds the objects that represents the drawing's viewport display at the time the objects were copied. This is true for all three commands. Therefore, whether you use the CUTCLIP, COPYCLIP, or COPYLINK commands to select an object, the AutoCAD OLE object pasted into the target application includes the visible area displayed in the current viewport.

When you paste an AutoCAD OLE object that was copied using the COPYLINK command, AutoCAD creates a named view representing the current viewport display. This is necessary to maintain the link and accurately update the OLE object when the drawing file is modified. By associating the OLE object with a named view, modifications to AutoCAD objects in the area of the drawing defined by the named view can be accurately updated to the AutoCAD OLE object and correctly displayed in the target application.

**I**NSIDER **TIP**

> You can use the COPYLINK command to paste an existing named view to the clipboard by making the named view current immediately before executing the COPY-LINK command.

In the following exercise, you use the COPYLINK command to copy AutoCAD objects and paste them into a target application.

### Exercise 15.4    Inserting AutoCAD Objects into Other Applications

1. Open the drawing 15EX04.dwg from the accompanying CD. The drawing displays two objects. Execute a SAVEAS command and save the drawing to the C:\IA2005 directory you made earlier.

   Next, you launch the target application.

2. From the Windows taskbar, choose Start, Programs, Accessories, WordPad. The WordPad application launches. Return application focus to AutoCAD.

3. From the View pull-down menu, select Named Views. Then from the View dialog box Named Views tab, in the View list, choose the view named OLE Object Area, then click the Set Current button, as shown in Figure 15.15.

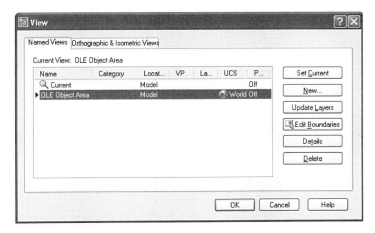

**Figure 15.15**   A named view is used to set the display for the AutoCAD objects to be copied to the clipboard.

4. Click OK. AutoCAD restores the named view.

5. From the AutoCAD Edit pull-down menu, select Copy Link. AutoCAD copies the objects in the current view to the clipboard.

   Next, you paste the AutoCAD objects in the target application.

6. From WordPad's Edit menu, select Paste Special. WordPad displays the Paste Special dialog box.

7. From the Paste Special dialog box, click the Paste Link option button and then click OK. WordPad pastes the AutoCAD OLE object into the current file and links it to the named view in the AutoCAD drawing.

   After the OLE object is inserted in the WordPad file, you may need to resize the object to view it, as shown in Figure 15.16. You can resize the object using the object frame's sizing handles.

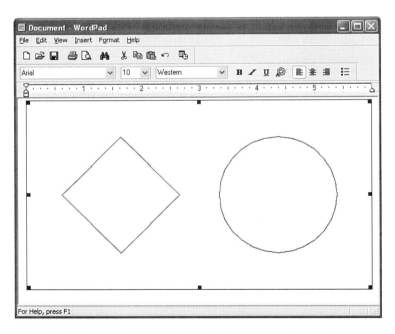

**Figure 15.16**    The linked AutoCAD OLE object in the WordPad application.

Now let's see it change. Back in AutoCAD, stretch the diamond's right corner to the center of circle. Then click back to Wordpad. No change. Back in AutoCAD, click the Save button on the Standard toolbar. Now pop back to Wordpad; you should now see the change in the link drawing file. The link only updates to match the current drawing on disk.

You may close the AutoCAD drawing and the WordPad file without saving changes.

**I**NSIDER **TIP**

> Often, the main complaint with importing drawings into other applications is the lineweight control. In prior releases, it was difficult to have weights that reflect an AutoCAD plot. However, in AutoCAD 2005, you can create drawings that provide their own means for showing wide lineweights for both line objects and text.

By using AutoCAD's commands for exporting AutoCAD drawing information to target applications, you can create compound documents in other applications using AutoCAD drawings.

# Summary

In this chapter, you reviewed how to insert OLE objects from within AutoCAD, how to paste OLE objects into AutoCAD from the clipboard, and how to drag and drop OLE objects into AutoCAD drawings. You learned how to control various OLE object properties, including how to resize an OLE object and control its visibility. You also reviewed how to edit OLE objects and how the Layer Properties Manager can affect certain OLE object properties. Finally, you learned how to export objects from AutoCAD into other applications, thereby creating AutoCAD OLE objects.

By using the techniques discussed in this chapter, you can create compound documents by inserting OLE objects into AutoCAD. You can also create compound documents in other applications by pasting AutoCAD OLE objects.

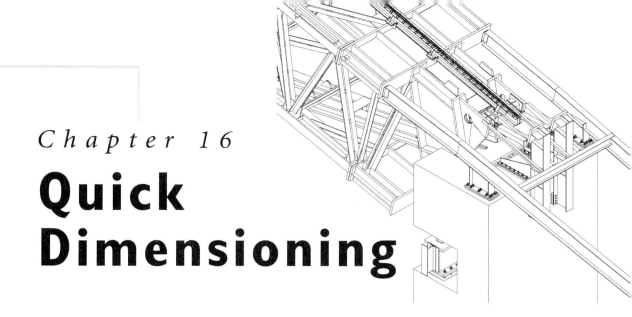

*Chapter 16*

# Quick Dimensioning

When working in a production environment, one of the more time-consuming and critical challenges is the need to dimension a drawing quickly and accurately. Then, if necessary, you must also be able to modify and correct existing dimensions just as quickly and accurately.

This chapter and Chapter 17, "Intelligent Dimensions," introduce you to various techniques necessary to dimension a drawing quickly and easily. The techniques are the same, regardless of the type of drawing. In particular, this chapter focuses on how to become more productive when dimensioning by using AutoCAD's basic dimensioning tools and covers the following:

- Linear dimensions
- Other dimension types
- Leaders
- Comparing dimensioning in model space to dimensioning in a layout

# Becoming Proficient at Dimensioning

To become proficient at dimensioning a drawing, you need practice and understanding about some of the various options made available to you by AutoCAD. The most commonly used dimensioning type is linear dimensioning.

## Linear Dimensioning

*Linear* dimensions, of course, define a specific length, whether it is horizontal, vertical, or aligned to the object you are dimensioning. AutoCAD provides you with five different linear dimensioning commands, including DIMLINEAR, DIMCONTINUE, DIMBASELINE, DIMALIGNED, and DIMROTATED. Each command can be accessed through the command prompt. With the exception of DIMROTATED, they can also be accessed through the Dimension pull-down menu (see Figure 16.1) or the Dimensioning toolbar (see Figure 16.2). You should access these commands using the method with which you are most comfortable and productive.

The typical dimension command, DIMLINEAR, is fairly straightforward and easy to use. But there are other options that you may not be aware of.

**Figure 16.1**
The Dimension pull-down menu, where you can access the dimension- and leader-creating commands in AutoCAD 2005.

**Figure 16.2**   The Dimension toolbar houses the most command dimension command icons for quick user access.

### *Linear Options*

The DIMLINEAR command is based on selecting three points to create a dimension. These points are the starting and ending points, or nodes, of the dimension, and the location of the dimension line. When choosing the first two points for the linear dimension, you are prompted to select the first and second extension line origin points.

An alternative method is to press Enter when prompted to select the first extension line origin. At that point, you can select an object to dimension. Then all you have to do is place the dimension line. When selecting an object using this method, the endpoints of the dimension are automatically determined. This alternate method works well when you are dimensioning a single line, arc, circle, or polyline segment that is precisely the length you need it to be. When this method is applied to a multi-segmented polyline, only the segment you select is dimensioned. If you use this method with a circle, you can dimension the diameter of the circle with a linear dimension. DIMLINEAR recognizes objects that it cannot dimension and prompts the following message: `Object selected is not a line, arc, or circle`. Figure 16.3 shows you some example dimensions created with two clicks.

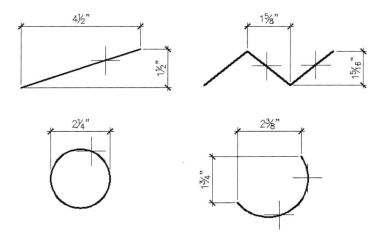

**Figure 16.3**   Examples of using DIMLINEAR with selected objects on various types of geometry.

The DIMLINEAR by selection option, however, does not solve every situation for linear dimensions. You may still need to resort to using construction lines in conjunction with object snap modes. In these cases, AutoCAD 2005's tracking feature can very helpful. You should also see Chapter 7, "Using Coordinate Systems," for more information on other methods of drawing with accuracy.

Ultimately, to get more productivity when creating linear dimensions, you need to explore a few more commands—in particular, DIMBASELINE and DIMCONTINUE. Both commands are used after creating an initial linear dimension to quickly create additional dimensions.

## Baseline Dimensions

*Baseline* dimensions quickly and easily create a series of dimensions from a single base point. If you want to dimension various objects along a wall but want all the dimensions to measure from one end of the wall, for example, baseline is the method to use.

To make use of the baseline feature, you must create a linear, aligned, or rotated dimension before using the baseline option. After you have the initial dimension, choose Baseline from the Dimension pull-down menu or the Dimension toolbar. When inside the command, select the endpoint of the next dimension. Each dimension is then automatically placed next to or above the previous dimension with a user-specified spacing, using the first node of the initial dimension as the "baseline." When using DIMBASELINE and DIMCONTINUE, AutoCAD remembers the position of the last dimension placed.

**I** NSIDER **N** OTE

> You can perform any non-dimensioning command between the use of DIMLINEAR and DIMBASELINE and not lose the last dimension for use by the command.

**I** NSIDER **T** IP

> If you want to baseline a dimension that was not the most recently based dimension, you can press the Enter key at the Specify a second extension line origin or (<select>/Undo) prompt. This enables you to select the dimension you want to baseline. This works with the continuous dimension type as well.

Figure 16.4 shows the click points necessary to create a series of dimensions using the baseline command.

The following exercise shows you how to dimension a steel plate quickly and efficiently using baseline dimensions.

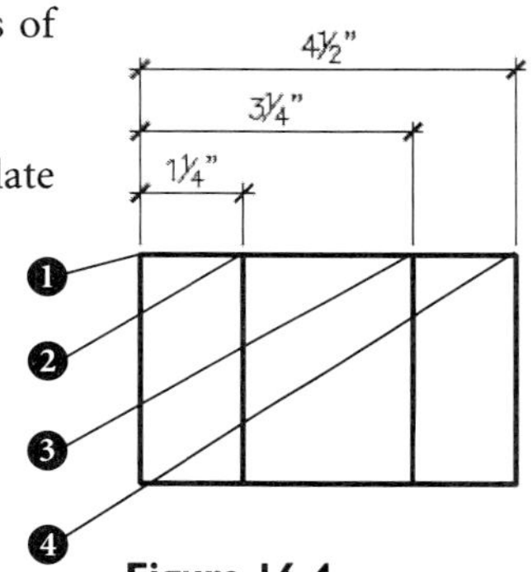

**Figure 16.4**
A set of baseline dimensions and the mouse clicks that created them.

### Exercise 16.1    Creating Linear Dimensions by Using Baselines

1.  Load the drawing 16EX01.dwg from the accompanying CD.

2.  Create a linear dimension by using the DIMLINEAR command from the left end of the block to the center point of the first circle, as shown in Figure 16.5.

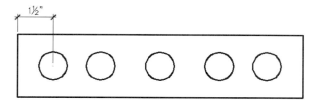

**Figure 16.5**   The block with the first linear dimension applied.

3.  Choose Dimension, Baseline from the pull-down menu or the Dimension toolbar.

4.  When prompted for the second extension line, select a Center object snap mode and select the center of the second circle.

5.  Continue using Center snap modes and select the center of the rest of the circles, moving from left to right.

6.  When you are finished with the circles, select the endpoint of the upper-right corner of the block. Figure 16.6 shows the block with all the dimensions applied.

    Close this drawing without saving, or undo these dimensions and leave it open for the following exercise.

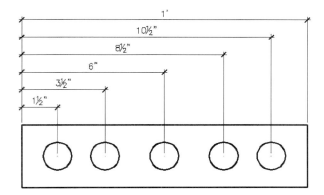

**Figure 16.6**   The block dimensioned using the DIMBASELINE command.

As you can see from this exercise, after you have created the first linear dimension, regardless of whether the dimension was created using DIMLINEAR, DIMALIGNED, or other commands, the block is dimensioned quickly with a minimal amount of mouse operations.

To further test the baseline command, try rotating the plate 45 degrees before you create the first dimension. Then create a DIMALIGNED dimension for the first dimension. When you use the baseline command again, you can see that it works perfectly.

## Quick Dimensions

*Quick* dimensions, or QDIM, is an automated system for quickly dimensioning a series of objects. It works by selecting the objects you want to dimension and then placing the dimension line. To illustrate this, let's run through the previous exercise again, but this time, let's use QDIM to create the dimensions.

### Exercise 16.2    Dimensioning a Block with *QDIM*

1. Continue from Exercise 16.1 or reload the file 16EX01.dwg from the accompanying CD.

2. Choose the Dimension pull-down menu, Quick Dimension. It is also found on the Dimension toolbar (the little dimension icon with the lightning bolt).

3. Select all the objects in the scene and press Enter.

4. Click above the block to place the dimensions, and you're done. Figure 16.7 shows you the block.

   Close the drawing—there is no need to save.

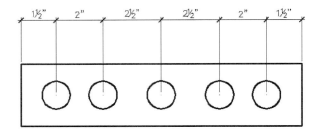

**Figure 16.7**    The block after using the QDIM command to create the dimensions.

As you can see from this exercise, QDIM is very quick and easy to use to create a set of linear dimensions. As you work with AutoCAD 2005, you can find that this command is a great time-saver.

## Continued Dimensions

*Continued* dimensions are very similar to baseline dimensions with one exception: Instead of basing all the dimensions off a single point, they are based off the endpoint of the previous dimension created. Continued dimensions automatically line up the dimension lines to create crisp, clean strings of dimensions. For example, a wall is generally dimensioned from centerline to centerline of the components of the wall, such as doors and windows. Using the continued dimension makes this very easy.

If you have to create a series of dimensions, one after the other on a single dimension line, use the DIMCONTINUE command, because it automates the placement of additional dimensions, much like the DIMBASELINE command did. Figure 16.8 shows you an example of a continued dimension.

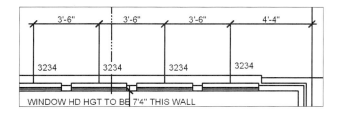

**Figure 16.8**   A set of dimensions showing the use of the DIMCONTINUE command.

Like baseline dimensions, continued dimensions rely on having one linear dimension type already created, followed by the DIMCONTINUE command.

For an exercise on how to use this command, repeat the baseline exercise but use the DIMCONTINUE command instead. Both commands work the same way but produce different results. As you may have guessed, in a lot of ways QDIM can replace continued dimensions, but you might find instances in which it is easier to use DIMCONTINUE.

## Aligned and Rotated Dimensions

The last two linear dimension types are aligned and rotated. Both types are similar to each other in the fact that they are not horizontal or vertical dimensions. Aligned and rotated dimensions are the only linear dimensions in which the dimension line is not horizontal or vertical.

*Aligned* dimensions arrange the dimension line to match the angle produced between the start and endpoints of the dimension. *Rotated* dimensions have the dimension line rotated a specific angle amount that is different from the angle between the start and end points. Figure 16.9 shows an example of both types of dimensions.

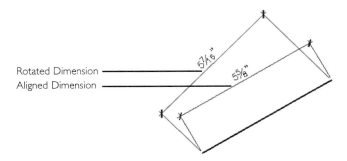

**Figure 16.9**    Two dimensions, showing the difference between an aligned and a rotated dimension.

As you can see in Figure 16.9, you can use the rotated feature to create linear dimensions with any orientation. The aligned feature, however, is forced to align itself along the start and endpoints of the dimension. Also note that a different dimension is determined because of the dimension angle, even though both dimensions use the same endpoints.

The aligned dimension command can be accessed through the pull-down menu or toolbar or entered at the command prompt.

The following exercise shows how to create a few non-vertical or horizontal dimensions. The exercise also shows why you need to be careful when using this dimension type—because an aligned or rotated linear dimension can end up with a different measured length than what is intended by the design.

### Exercise 16.3    Creating a Rotated Dimension

1. Load the file 16EX03.dwg from the accompanying CD. This drawing shows three circles that you are going to dimension from center point to center point.

2. From the Dimension pull-down menu, choose Linear.

3. Select the center of the left circle as the start point. Select the center of the middle circle as the end point.

4. At the `Specify dimension line location or [Mtext/Text/Angle/Horizontal/Vertical/Rotated]` prompt, type **R** and press Enter. You can also use the right-click shortcut menu and choose Rotated.

5. When prompted for an angle, type **38**. This sets the angle of the dimension line.

6. Pick a point above and to the left to position the rotated dimension. The distance between the left and middle circles should measure out to 4".

7. Press Enter to bring up the DIMLINEAR command again.

8. Select the center point of the middle circle as the start point. Select the center point of the circle on the right.

9. Type **R** again, and this time, enter an angle of **315** (45 degrees down and to the right).

   Figure 16.10 shows the three circles dimensioned. Note the inaccurate value on the second dimension; this is something to keep in mind when dimensioning.

   Close the drawing without saving.

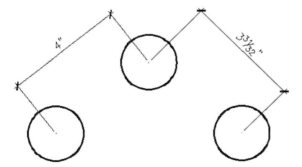

**Figure 16.10**   A 38-degree and a 45-degree rotated dimension showing what happens when you use a rotated linear dimension. Because the 45-degree angle dimension does not match the angle of the circles, the value presented is inaccurate and has a rounding error.

> **INSIDER TIP**
>
> Using aligned dimensions can be problematic because when the dimension nodes change, the angle and therefore the dimension length can change. Unless specifically needed, use rotated dimensions because they are much more predictable.

# Other Dimensions

Several other dimensioning types are worth mentioning. These dimension types are not linear and serve specific purposes. Depending on your discipline, you may have a use for some of these types. For example, a mechanical part designer can make heavy use of radius and diameter dimension types, whereas a civil engineer can make use of datum dimension types.

## Radius and Diameter Dimensions

*Radius* and *diameter* dimensions are used to dimension the size of an arc or circle. If you create a polyline with an arc in it, for example, you can use either dimension type to dimension the arc. If you select the Center Mark check box in the Dimension Styles dialog box, the center mark is automatically used with radius and diameter dimensions when the dimension text is placed outside the circle or arc. Other than that, the placement of radius and diameter dimensions is relatively straightforward. With these dimension types, you simply pick the arc or circle to dimension and then the dimension line location. Features of the Dimension Style dialog box are presented in Chapter 17.

## Angular Dimensions

*Angular* dimensions are used to dimension the angle between two non-parallel lines. Of course, when you dimension angles between two lines, two angles are possible: the oblique or the acute angle. Each angular dimension has two possible positions, for a total of four choices. Where you place the dimension line determines which angle is measured. Like radius and diameter dimensions, angular dimensions are straightforward.

> **INSIDER NOTE**
>
> Angular dimensions cannot use arcs or dimensions to develop the boundary edges for the angle. You may on occasion need to create construction objects to draw the angular dimension and then dispose of them.

The following exercise demonstrates how to make use of the DIMANGULAR and DIMRADIUS commands.

### Exercise 16.4    Dimensioning Angles and Radii

1. Load the file 16EX04.dwg from the accompanying CD. This file contains a simple filleted triangular object that you can dimension.

2. To start, choose the Dimension pull-down menu, Radius to activate the DIMRADIUS command.

3. You are prompted to select a circle or an arc. Select one of the filleted corners of the object.

4. You immediately see the dimension appear. By moving the mouse around, you can see different looks for the dimension. Place the dimension outside the triangular area.

5. Now, again from the Dimension pull-down menu, choose Angular to start the DIMANGULAR command.

6. You are prompted to select a line, arc, or circle or a first vertex. Click on the left vertical line of the shape.

7. You are then prompted to select a second line. Click on the angled line on the top of the shape.

8. Now, move the mouse in a circle around the upper-left corner of the shape. You can see that you have four possible locations for the angular dimension, two of which are the acute angle, and the opposite two are the oblique angle. Place the dimension inside the shape so it measures the angle as 57 degrees.

   Close this drawing without saving.

## Ordinate Dimensions

*Ordinate* dimensions are used to dimension a specific coordinate location, such as a point from a civil survey. For example, a civil survey relies on a set of three-dimensional data points on which to base a topography. These coordinates are labeled using an ordinate dimension type, which labels the point's exact X and Y coordinates.

When using ordinate dimensions, you may dimension the X- or Y-axis points, called *datums*. You also have the option to create a leader-like ordinate dimension that has text before or after the coordinate. Figure 16.11 shows an ordinate dimension.

The Ordinate dimension feature can be accessed from the Dimension pull-down menu, the Dimension toolbar, or by typing **DIMORD** at the command prompt. When you select this command, you are prompted to select the feature, or the coordinate, to dimension. After you select the coordinate, you can select the type of ordinate dimension you want to use.

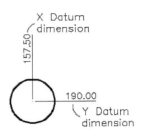

**Figure 16.11**
An ordinate dimension showing both X and Y datums.

The four types of ordinate dimensions are X datum, Y datum, mtext, and Text. The X and Y datum points produce the corresponding coordinate. Mtext pops up the Text Formatting dialog box so you can add text before and after the datum dimension. The datum dimension appears as <> in the editor. In fact, the first set of <> are used by all dimensions to produce the default dimension value. Figure 16.12 shows the Text Formatting dialog box when used with the ordinate mtext option. The Text option enables you to modify the text of the datum dimension without having to use the Text Formatting editor.

**INSIDER NOTE**

If you delete the <> marker, the coordinate value will not appear in the final dimension text.

Exercise 16.5 shows how to use ordinate dimensions to dimension several survey points. In this exercise, the PDMODE system variable has been set so that points appear as crosses.

**Figure 16.12**    The Text Formatting dialog box showing the text before and after the ordinate dimension.

### Exercise 16.5    Using Ordinate Dimensions

1. Load the file 16EX05.dwg from the accompanying CD.

2. Choose Ordinate from the Dimension pull-down menu or toolbar if it is open.

3. Using a Node osnap mode, click on one of the crosses and place the dimension to the right of the point.

4. Repeat steps 2 and 3, but place the dimension above the cross this time.

5. Repeat steps 2 and 3 for several other crosses so you get a little practice. Figure 16.13 shows this drawing with a few ordinate dimensions added.

   Close the drawing without saving it.

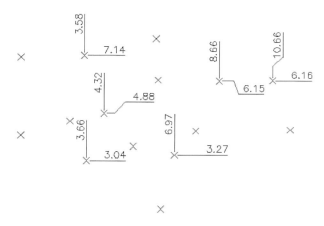

**Figure 16.13**    The points dimensioned with ordinate dimensions.

## Tolerance Dimensions

Another dimension type is the tolerance dimension. *Tolerances* are used to provide constraints within which you can construct the drawn object. For example, you might construct a mechanical part and specify that its length may be 2.0 cm ±0.001 cm.

AutoCAD provides you with two methods of creating tolerance dimensions. One method is to specify the tolerances in the Dimension Styles dialog box. The tolerances are then automatically added to the dimension text as you place dimensions. The second method is to use the tolerance command and place tolerance symbols on the drawing. The second method is discussed in the following section. Figure 16.14 shows a standard tolerance symbol inside of AutoCAD.

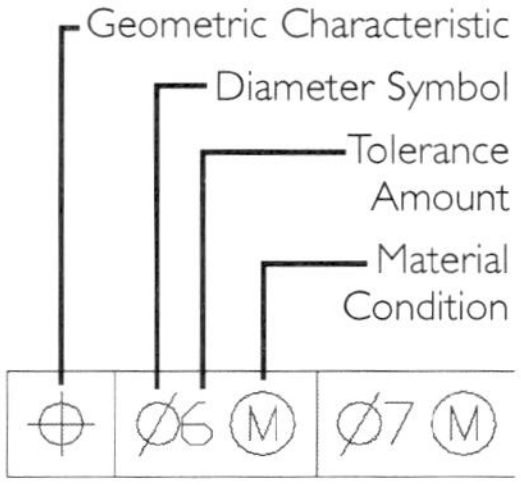

**Figure 16.14**
The tolerance dimension and its parts.

### Placing Tolerance Symbols in a Drawing

Under the Dimension pull-down menu and toolbars, you can find a Tolerance option. Choosing this option displays the Geometric Tolerance dialog box, shown in Figure 16.15. The Geometric Tolerance dialog box is used to select the appropriate type of tolerance you want to use, through the use of industry-standard tolerance symbols.

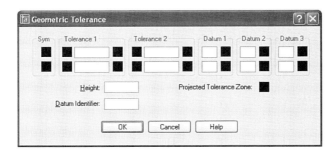

**Figure 16.15**    The Geometric Tolerance dialog box enables you to specify tolerances.

In the Geometric Tolerance dialog box, you can specify values for tolerances 1 and 2, as well as round symbols. You can also specify up to three datums, such as a material condition and a value for that condition. You can also specify height, projected tolerance zones, and datum identifiers.

**INSIDER TIP**

Even though your field of work may not utilize tolerances in any form, you can still benefit from their simple use. If you ever need a piece of text inside a rectangle, try using a `tolerance` object. The value is easy to edit, and you can type dozens of characters in one box. You can also stack a few boxes or place boxes with text next to each other.

At the far left of the Geometric Tolerances dialog box, you can find two black boxes for symbols. If you click on one, you see the Symbol dialog box (see Figure 16.16). In this dialog box, notice the many different symbols, each representing a different geometric characteristic. When you choose one of the symbols, the selected tolerance method is placed in the tolerance dimension itself. After you click on a geometric tolerance type, you are transferred back to the Geometric Tolerance dialog box where you may then enter the values for the tolerances.

**Figure 16.16**
The Symbol dialog box, in which you can select the type of tolerance you want to use.

# Creating Annotation with a Leader

Leaders are the most popular method of adding notes and pointing out specific aspects of a drawing. A leader is a line with an arrowhead pointing to a specific feature with some sort of text or graphics at the end of the line. For example, you might create a wall section of a house and use leaders to point out specific materials in the section.

**I**NSIDER **N**OTE

> AutoCAD now has a QLEADER command that makes the traditional LEADER command somewhat obsolete. With QLEADER, many of the options are streamlined for you. You simply place the arrow point and second point and then enter the text to complete the command. It saves you time by controlling the various options, unlike the older LEADER command. Also, all AutoCAD menu LEADER command access has been replaced with QLEADER. If possible, you should try to use the QLEADER command.

A leader is easily created by selecting the QLEADER command from the Dimension pull-down menu. When prompted for the first point, select the point where you want the arrowhead of the leader to appear. Then you simply draw as many straight leader segments as you determine based on its settings. When you are done, enter your text and press Enter to exit the command. This chapter focuses on several more advanced features of leaders, such as using the Text Formatting dialog box to enter multiple line text and using splines instead of straight line segments in your leaders.

## *Leader Options*

When you select the QLEADER command, you are prompted for a point. This point is, of course, the location of the arrowhead. But this is also when you would set your options for leaders and related objects. At the Specify first leader point, or [Settings] <Settings> prompt, you would press **S** followed by Enter. This opens the Leader Settings dialog box, as shown in Figure 16.17.

Under the first tab, Annotation, you can determine what AutoCAD places when you finish generating the leader object. In the Annotation Type area, you can choose to place an mtext, block, or tolerance object at the end. You can choose the Copy option, which enables you to copy what was created on an existing leader and apply it to your new one. This is very handy when placing similar notes. The last option is None. Sometimes all you need is a leader without any annotation.

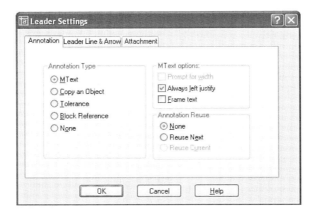

**Figure 16.17**    The Annotation tab of the Leader Settings dialog enables you to control what is placed after the leader tail.

Over in the mtext options area, you can choose to have your text always left justified or enclose it in a box. If you turn off left justified text, you can also choose to set the width of the mtext object at time of placement. Below that area is the Annotation Reuse section. Here you can choose to copy the text content from the current or next leader placed.

As shown in Figure 16.18, the next tab over is the Leader Line & Arrow control panel. If you prefer splined leaders, you set that here. If you want to limit the segments of your leaders, that is controlled in the Number of Points area. Under the Arrowhead list box, you can determine what block to use at the start point.

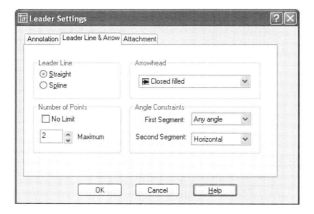

**Figure 16.18**    The Leader Line & Arrow tab controls how your leader and arrowhead look when placed.

**I**NSIDER **N**OTE

The Arrowhead list box provides access to a dimension style override on the DIMLDRBLK dimension variable. The default is as set in the current active DIMSTYLE. It is recommended that you control your arrowhead style through a dimension style child property, as opposed to applying a DIMLDRBLK override so that updating is streamlined. Learn more about dimension styles in Chapter 17.

The last area is the Angle Constraints section. Here you can determine to force the first or second (and all following) segments to be specific angles. This can aid in producing matching leaders if your standards require that.

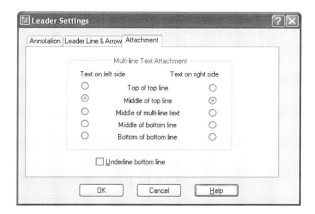

**Figure 16.19**   The Attachment tab controls how your mtext object relates to the leader tail.

Depending on your drafting standards, you might need to always place text with a specific attachment point to the leader. Under the Attachment tab, you decide where the mtext object appears when left or right of the leader tail. These are pretty straightforward to understand; choose the format that you prefer. The Underline bottom line toggle is used if you prefer the leader tail to fully cover the width of the mtext object and be below the bottom line of text.

Exercise 16.6 shows how to create leaders on a simple architectural wall section.

### Exercise 16.6    Creating Leaders in AutoCAD

1. Load the file 16EX06.dwg from the accompanying CD. Figure 16.20 shows how the drawing should appear by the end of this exercise.

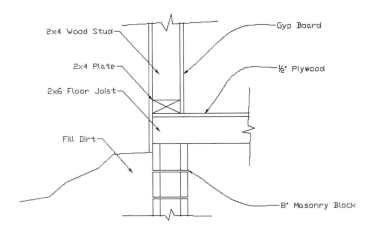

**Figure 16.20**    The wall section as it will appear at the end of this exercise.

2. On the left side of the wall, you create straight leaders by choosing the QLEADER command from the Dimension pull-down menu or toolbar.

---

**INSIDER TIP**

Your preferred settings for QLEADER can be saved in a drawing, and you can then use this drawing as a template for new drawings. If your QLEADER preferences are far from the QLEADER defaults then you would be wise to take advantage of this feature.

---

3. At the Specify first leader point, or [Settings] <Settings> prompt, select a point close to the arrowhead location of the 2x4 Wood Stud leader.

4. Select the second point of the leader, as shown in Figure 16.20.

5. Type **2x4 Wood Stud** and press Enter twice to complete the leader.

6. Repeat steps 3 through 5 for the rest of the straight leaders on the left, as shown in Figure 16.20.

7. For the spline leaders shown in Figure 16.20, again enter the QLEADER command.

8. At the Specify first leader point, or [Settings] <Settings> prompt, type **S** and press Enter.

You can call up the Leader Settings dialog box by using the right-click shortcut menu and choosing Settings.

**9.** The Leader Settings dialog box appears. Click the Leader Line & Arrow tab.

**10.** Change the Leader type from Straight to Spline. Then set the number of points to 3. Also change the First Segment from 45 degrees to Any Angle. Press the OK button to close the dialog.

**11.** Select your start point for the top splined leader on the right of Figure 16.20. Then pick two more points, creating a smooth spline look for the leader.

**12.** At the `Enter first line of annotation text <Mtext>` prompt, instead of typing your text in, press Enter. This opens the Text Formatting dialog box. Type **Gyp Board** in it and then click OK.

AutoCAD then places your mtext object adjacent to the splined leader using your preferred attachment method.

**13.** Start the `QLEADER` command again, repeat step 11 for the middle right leader, and press Enter to show the Text Formatting dialog.

**14.** Begin typing the **1/2" Plywood** text.

**15.** Close the AutoStack Properties dialog if open and continue the rest of the text. Repeat the `QLEADER` command one more time to finish the last note on the right.

The detail is now complete. Close the drawing without saving it.

Depending on your AutoCAD installation, the AutoStack Properties dialog box may appear, as shown in Figure 16.21. With this dialog, you can determine how, if at all, stacked fractions should be shown within mtext objects. If you use this style in your dimensions, you should probably match the look for your mtext notes as well. Learn more about this feature applied in dimension objects in Chapter 17. Learn about the mtext controls in Chapter 14, "Text and Mtext Annotation."

**Figure 16.21**
The AutoStack Properties dialog controls how your fractions will appear within multiline text objects.

# Dimension Placement in the Drawing

When looking at productivity in terms of dimensioning a drawing, one other factor to consider is where you are placing your dimensions. You have two choices in AutoCAD: model space and paper space. Each space has its own pros and cons.

## Pros and Cons of Dimensioning in Model Space

Most users today dimension their drawings in model space as opposed to placing dimensions in a paper space layout. The concept and features involved with layouts is covered in Chapter 18, "Paper Space Layouts." Dimensioning in model space comes naturally because the drawing is actually created in model space.

The following are some advantages of creating dimensions in model space rather than in the layout window:

- You can use quick intuitive dimensioning directly on the drawing.
- When using associative dimensioning, you can stretch both the geometry and dimensions at the same time, enabling both the geometry and the dimensions to update at the same time.

The following are some disadvantages of creating dimensions in model space rather than in the layout window:

- If you have a sheet with drawings created at different scales, you must use different scale dimensions and perhaps use different layers.
- For dimensions to plot correctly, all dimension elements must be scaled by a DIMSCALE factor that is matched to the output plot scale.

Overall, the biggest reason to place your dimensions in model space is if you do not understand the layout window and how it works. Until you feel comfortable working in the layout window, create your dimensions in model space.

**INSIDER TIP**

If you work in an environment in which you constantly create drawing sheets with varying drawing scales, you should strongly consider using the layout window and its associated dimensioning methods.

## Pros and Cons of Layout Dimensioning

When dimensioning in the layout environment, you are separating them from the drawing objects being dimensioned. Like model space, dimensioning in a paper space layout also has advantages and disadvantages.

The following are some advantages of creating dimensions in the layout window rather than using model space:

- Layout dimensions are separate from the drawing, which makes it easy to switch over to model space and view a clean drawing or xref it into another drawing as a base.

- All layout dimensions make use of the same dimension scale factor: 1.

- Dimensions can be placed on sheets more easily with multiple scales.

The following disadvantages occur only if you are NOT using AutoCAD's Associative Dimensioning feature. This feature is covered in more detail in Chapter 17:

- You cannot stretch layout dimensions and model space geometry at the same time.

- You cannot use the object selection dimensioning method.

- You must adjust linear scaling factors to show the true model space dimension distance.

Ultimately, the decision of whether to use layout window dimensioning depends on your comfort with and understanding of the layout window itself. If you are not comfortable with it, continue to place dimensions in model space.

# Improving Productivity: Tips and Techniques

The following are a few techniques to help you increase your dimensioning speed when you create dimensions. Editing dimensions is covered in Chapter 17:

- Use ACAD.PGP keyboard shortcuts for the dimension commands. For example, DIMLINEAR can be shortened to DLI, which obviously is quick to type. See Chapter 23, "Menu Customization," for more information about keyboard shortcuts and the ACAD.PGP file.

- Create a chart of dimension scales for standard plot scales. That way, you create consistency in your drawing throughout your drafting operations.

- Create a variety of dimension styles and save them to a AutoCAD template file. Then all you have to do is assign the appropriate style as the current one and begin dimensioning.

- Whenever possible, use QDIM (quick dimension) for dimensioning because you can simply select the objects to be dimensioned.

- If you are going to create a series of dimensions, consider using baseline or continue dimensions to help automate and speed up the process.

- If you have a third-party program, consider using that program's dimensioning routines if it has any. These routines are probably quicker than the standard AutoCAD commands.

# Increasing Productivity with Third-Party Programs

At this point, you have seen most of the options available for creating standard AutoCAD dimensions. By practicing and using the options that are available to you, you can increase your productivity to some degree when dimensioning. The standard AutoCAD dimensioning commands are by no means slow, but you can increase your speed with a little help.

Many users today make use of third-party programs to help increase productivity in their respective professions. Many of these programs provide automated methods for creating these same dimensions.

An architectural modeling program, for example, enables you to create with one click all the necessary dimensions for a wall, including intersecting wall, door, and window locations, as well as overall dimensions. Then all you have to do is correct any errors, if they exist. Autodesk Architectural Desktop is an excellent example of a program that automates the dimensioning process.

Other disciplines, such as civil engineering, may make use of programs such as Autodesk Land Desktop as well as their Civil and Survey packages for this specific application.

In some programs, such as Mechanical Desktop, dimensions are a critical aspect of using the program correctly. In Mechanical Desktop, you must add enough dimensions to the object to fully constrain (define) it. After the object is constrained, the dimensions are parametric, meaning if you change the value of the dimension, the geometry also changes.

# Summary

Overall, AutoCAD 2005's dimension commands are fairly productive, and they are much quicker than dimensioning by hand. Be familiar with all of your dimensioning options. Many times, using a different command such as `DIMCONTINUE` is quicker that using `DIMLINEAR`. When possible, use the object selection dimensioning method. Otherwise, you must pick the start, end, and dimension line points. In many cases, you may need to create temporary construction lines for dimensioning purposes.

The next chapter delves further into the world of dimensions and covers topics such as dimension styles and editing existing dimensions, where AutoCAD is extremely fast.

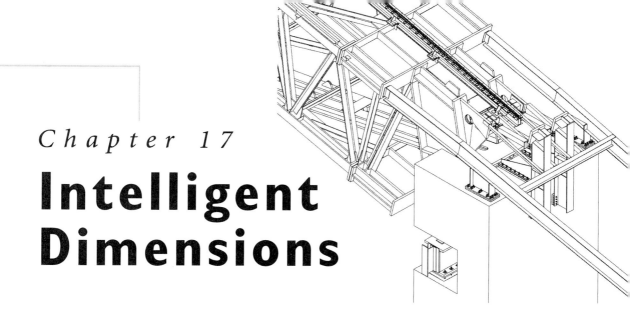

# Chapter 17

# Intelligent Dimensions

One of AutoCAD's best features is its capability to create and control dimensions in a drawing. AutoCAD 2005 provides you with several tools for editing dimensions and controlling how a dimension appears in the drawing. This chapter focuses on the following topics:

- Dimension styles
- Style options
- Modifying dimensions
- Associative dimensioning

# Defining Dimension Styles

Dimension styles are your primary methods for controlling how a dimension appears. By creating a dimension style, you define exactly how that dimension is going to appear in the drawing. This includes the dimension scale, the types of arrowheads, and whether the dimension lines appear (and if so, what color the dimension lines are).

AutoCAD enables you to control dimension styles through the use of dimension variables (DIMVARS). You can control these variables in two different ways. You can use the Dimension Style Manager dialog box to access many of the variables using a graphical interface, or you can type the variable name at the command prompt and assign it a new value. There are 70 dimension variables in AutoCAD 2005, but don't let that discourage you. However, most of the time, adjusting the dimension variables through the Dimension Style Manager is the best method to use (see Figure 17.1). You can access this dialog by choosing Dimension Style from the Dimension toolbar or by choosing Style from the Dimension pull-down menu.

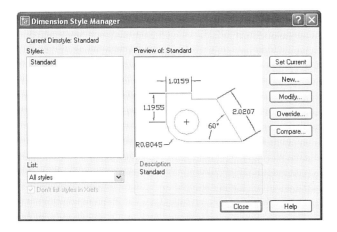

**Figure 17.1**   The Dimension Style Manager dialog box enables you to control how a dimension is drawn.

The Dimension Style Manager enables you to set the current dimension style, create a new style, modify an existing style, override part of the current style, or even compare two existing styles in the same drawing. To make it even easier for you to make changes, the Style Manager gives you a graphical preview of what the currently selected dimension style will look like when used in the drawing.

# Dimension Style Options

Dimension styles provide you with a method for saving different sets of dimension variables for the various types of drawings you might create. You have many options for defining how a dimension looks. To help you understand some of these options, Figure 17.2 shows a default linear dimension with the components of the dimension labeled.

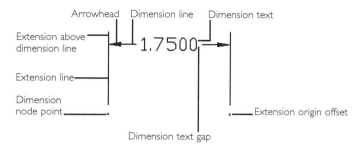

**Figure 17.2**   A typical dimension and all its parts.

To edit a dimension style, you simply open the Dimension Style Manager, select the style you want to edit, and click the Modify button. To create a new style, you can choose New in the Dimension Style Manager. In the dialog box that appears (see Figure 17.3), you can name the style and base it on an existing style.

**Figure 17.3**   In the Create New Dimension Style dialog box, you can give the style a name, select the base style, and specify how the dimension style will be used.

Regardless of whether you choose to modify an existing dimension style or create a new one, the New Dimension Style dialog box shown in Figure 17.4 appears, in which you can edit the individual parts of the style.

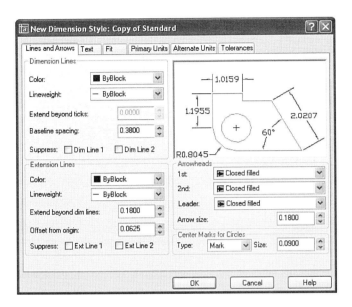

**Figure 17.4** The New Dimension Style dialog box enables you to change the settings for each individual part of the dimension.

The following exercise shows how to create and edit dimension styles.

### Exercise 17.1 Creating a New Dimension Style

1. Start a new drawing in AutoCAD from scratch.

2. From the Dimension pull-down menu, select Style. This launches the Dimension Style Manager dialog box, in which you can create, edit, and even compare dimension styles.

3. All drawings come with the Standard dimension style, on which you can base new dimension styles. To create a new style, click on the New button. This opens the Create New Dimension Style dialog box.

4. Under New Style Name, enter a name for the style using a name that you will recognize easily. This can be any name you like.

5. Under Start With, select the dimension style you want to base the new style on. The Standard style already exists in this drawing, so you can create another style based on it.

Although you have the ability to rename the Standard dimension style, it is highly suggested that you leave it as-is. I have witnessed corrupt drawings due to renaming the Standard dimstyle to some other name. There are evidently components in AutoCAD that expect it to exist. I suggest you let it exist in your drawings.

6.  In the Use For drop-down list, select the types of dimensions you want to use the style for. If you select an option other than All, the new dimension style can be used with only the type of dimension object you choose.

7.  Click Continue, and the Dimension Style Manager dialog box appears. You can make any changes you need to the style.

8.  In the Arrowheads area, click in the drop-down list for 1st Arrowhead and choose Closed Blank. Then click OK to return to the Dimension Style Manager dialog box.

9.  In the list on the left, you now see the name of the new style you just created. To edit the dimension style, make sure it is highlighted and click on the Modify button. This returns you to the Modify Dimension Style dialog box, where you can make further changes. If you picked Modify, pick OK to return to the Dimension Style Manager.

10.  To compare two dimension styles, click the Compare button. This launches the Compare Dimension Style Manager dialog box.

11.  At the top of this dialog box, you will see two drop-down lists. In the Compare drop-down list, select the first dimension style.

12.  In the With drop-down list, select the second style. You immediately see a list of variables that differ between the styles (if there are any).

13.  Click Close in each dialog box to return to the drawing.

    You may close this drawing without saving.

After you begin using dimension styles, you will likely find yourself with a number to choose from. You can of course use the Dimension Style Manager to make a specific DIMSTYLE current. But you can also use the Styles toolbar and its Dimension Style Control list box. This toolbar contains other style-related controls and provides the quickest access to change the current dimension style.

The New Dimension Style dialog box contains a tabbed interface for each set of controls for the style. A preview window accompanies each tabbed page to show you exactly what the dimension style looks like based on the current settings. This preview window enables you to make a change to the style so you can immediately see the effect of that change. The tabs in this dialog box are listed here and explained in the following sections.

### Lines and Arrows Tab

The selections found on the Lines and Arrows tab (refer to Figure 17.4) enable you to control all the dimension system variables related to the geometry of the dimension except for the text. This tab is broken down into four distinct areas: Dimension Lines, Arrowheads, Extension Lines, and Center Marks for Circles.

The Dimension Lines section controls the appearance of the dimension line. In a linear dimension, this is the line beside or below the dimension text. In certain circumstances, you might want to create a dimension without the dimension line. For example, you might have a short dimension with large text centered inside of the dimension line. In this situation, you can suppress the first or second dimension line or both. When the dimension text is above the dimension line, the suppression options have no effect. The location of the dimension text is controlled by the Format options, which are covered in the next section.

The Extend beyond ticks option, which is grayed out by default, is used in conjunction with certain arrowhead types. In particular, the oblique and architectural tick arrowheads make use of this option. When one of these two arrowheads is active, you can adjust the extension of the dimension line beyond the extension lines.

A commonly used dimension line option is Color. The default color of the dimension line is ByBlock, which means the line will take on the color of the dimension as a whole. The only reason to change this color is if you are using CTB plot styles and you want a different line width for the dimension line. For example, you could have a thinner line for the dimension line versus the extension lines. Note that this does not work for name-based plot styles.

Another way to control the thickness of the plotted lines is to use lineweights. You can control extension or dimension lineweights in the Dimension Style Manager to apply to all same-name dimension styles. Additionally, it should be noted that lineweights set at the dimension level override any settings to the layers or object directly. Refer to Chapter 6, "Effective Linetypes and Lineweights Use," for more information about using lineweights.

The options in the Extension Lines area of the dialog box perform the same functions as those under Dimension Lines. The notable exception is the Offset from origin option. When you create a dimension, such as a linear dimension, you select two points for the dimension. These points are considered the extension line origin points. The origin offset defines the distance from these points that the extension line is started.

The Arrowheads section of the Lines and Arrows tab provides you with complete control over the arrows. AutoCAD provides you with standard arrowheads, including closed filled, open 30, dot blanked, box filled, and many others. Even with all these arrowheads, you might want to create your own. To create your own arrowheads, in the 1st and 2nd drop-down lists, select the User Arrow option. This option enables you to select any block for use as an arrow, as long as that block is already defined in the current drawing. The arrowhead block should be created with an overall size of one unit so it will be correctly scaled when used in the dimension. It also should be created for use at the right-hand end of a horizontal linear dimension. The insertion point of the block should be the tip of the arrowhead. The block will be rotated for the opposite end. See Figure 17.5.

**I**NSIDER **TIP**

When you create a custom arrowhead, you should save the arrowhead as a block in a template file so that it is available to all drawings based on that template.

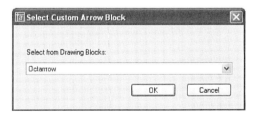

**Figure 17.5**    In the Select Custom Arrow Block dialog box, you can select any block for use as the arrowhead in your dimensions.

The following exercise shows how to create your own arrowheads.

### Exercise 17.2   Creating Your Own Arrowheads

1. Start a new drawing from scratch.

2. Create an octagon using the POLYGON command. Specify 0,0 as the center of the polygon. Use the Inscribed option. Make the radius of the polygon one unit (1.0).

3. Make a block of the polygon with an insertion point of 0,0 at the center of the polygon. Name the block Octarrow.

4. From the Dimension pull-down menu, choose Style.

5. In the Dimension Style Manager dialog box, select the Standard style and click on the Modify button.

6. In the Lines and Arrows tab, select User Arrow from the 1st drop-down list.

7. In the User Arrow dialog box, if needed, enter **Octarrow** as the arrow name.

8. Click OK to close the Select Custom Arrow Block dialog box.

9. Click OK to close the Geometry dialog box and return to the Modify Dimension Styles dialog box.

10. Click Close to save the dimension style changes to Standard and exit the dialog box.

11. Create a linear dimension. Figure 17.6 shows a linear dimension created with your new custom arrowhead.

    You can now close the drawing without saving it.

**Figure 17.6**   A linear dimension with a custom arrowhead.

The last section of the Lines and Arrows tab controls center marks and scaling. The Center options define how center marks appear when used with radius and diameter dimensions.

## Text Tab

The Text tab, shown in Figure 17.7, enables you to control how the text is displayed in your dimensions. In the Text style drop-down list, you can select any previously defined text style. (See Chapter 14, "Text and Mtext Annotation," for more on how to define a text style.) You could also create a new text style by clicking on the button to the right of the Text Style drop-down list. This launches the Text Style dialog box, where you can create the new style.

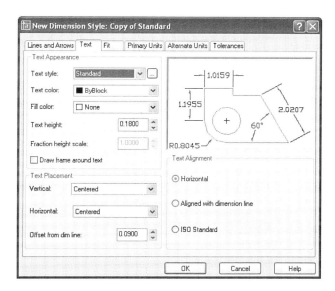

**Figure 17.7**    The Text tab of the New Dimension Style dialog box. Here, you can control how and where the text appears in your dimensions.

After you select a text style, you can apply other properties, such as height and color. The Text Height option, in particular, depends on how the text style is defined. If the text style is defined with a fixed height, that height is used. If the originating text style's height is set to 0, the height specified in the Text tab is used instead.

In addition to selecting the text style, you can control the placement of the text around the dimension line, as well as the alignment of the text in the drawing.

## Fit Tab

The Fit tab of the Modify Dimension Style dialog box (see Figure 17.8) enables you to control how the text is placed when the dimension is too small for the text to fit between the extension lines.

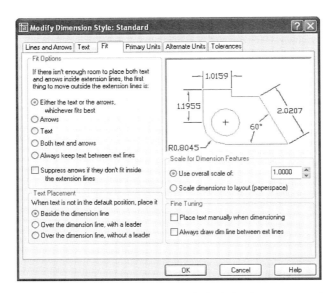

**Figure 17.8** The Fit tab of the Modify Dimension Style dialog box is primarily used to control what happens to text when there isn't room for it.

The Fit Options section contains the following six options:

- **Either the text or the arrows, whichever fits best.** When this option is selected, AutoCAD tries to determine the best method to use to create the most readable dimension. This is the default option.

- **Arrows.** When this option is selected, only the arrows are forced inside of the extension lines. Text may appear outside the extension lines when the distance between the lines is too small for the text to fit otherwise.

- **Text.** When this option is selected, only text is forced inside the extension lines. Arrows can be pushed outside the extension lines when the distance between the lines is small enough.

- **Both text and arrows.** When this option is selected, both the text and arrows are forced inside the extension lines, even when there is not enough room for them.

- **Always keep text between ext lines.** When this option is selected, the text is always placed between the extension lines of the dimension, regardless of whether it fits.

- **Suppress arrows if they don't fit inside the extension lines.** This option enables you to suppress the drawing of the arrows on a dimension when the text is forced inside of the extension lines.

The Text Placement options enable you to control where the text is placed in relation to the dimension line when the text is not in the default position. You can choose from three ways of handling this: You can place the text beside the line, over the line with a leader, or over the line without a leader.

**I**NSIDER **T**IP

> In the architectural field, dimension text is typically above the dimension line. If you adjust an existing dimension with this property by using the grip feature and drag the dimension to the side, a leader appears underneath the text. This is usually undesirable and annoying. A quick fix to this is to use the DIMOVERRIDE command. When you use this command, the system asks you for a dimension variable to override. Type **DIMTAD** (DIMension Text Above Dimension), set it to **0**, and then select the newly moved dimension with the incorrect leader format. When you finish, the dimension settings are returned to normal.

Probably the most important options in the Fit tab of the Modify Dimension Style dialog box are the Scale options. There are two scale options: Use overall scale of and Scale dimensions to layout (paperspace). Overall scale controls how large all the features of the dimension (such as arrowheads) appear in the drawing. This scale is directly related to the final plot scale for the drawing. For example, if you are plotting at an architectural scale of 1/4 inch = 1'–0", your Overall Scale factor should be 48. You obtain this value by inverting the desired plot scale. In another instance, a scale such as 1":50' equates to 50'/1", so the overall scale factor is 600.

When you set the scale factor, you define a scale multiplier by which all dimension size variables are multiplied. For example, arrowheads default to 0.18 units in size. If you have a scale factor of 48, the 0.18 is multiplied by 48 to arrive at the current size, correctly scaled for plotting.

If you are going to dimension in a paper space layout, you can leave the Use overall scale of factor set to 1, or you can turn on the Scale dimensions to layout option. The Scale dimensions to layout option sets the dimension variable DIMSCALE to 0. In a layout, a default value of 1.0 is used. In this situation, when you are working with a layout viewport, you can create a dimension in either space, and it will be scaled correctly. This assumes that you have set the layout viewport's scale correctly. See Chapter 18, "Paper Space Layouts," for more information about layouts and working with layout viewports.

## Primary Units Tab

The Primary Units tab (shown in Figure 17.9) is used to define the units that dimensions will use in their text. AutoCAD does not automatically set the dimension units to match your Units setting. Therefore, you must correctly define the units for your dimensions separately.

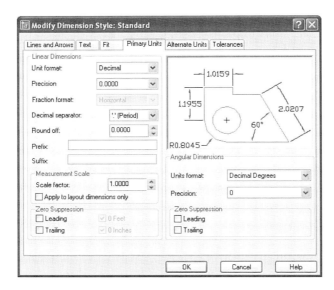

**Figure 17.9** In the Primary Units tab, you can define the units that are displayed in your dimensions. This enables you to match industry-specific unit standards.

> **INSIDER NOTE**
>
> One reason AutoCAD does not automatically use the Units setting from the drawing is because additional unit types are available to you in the dimensions that are not supported in the Units setting.

In the Linear Dimensions section of the tab, you can select the type of units, the precision of the display, and even prefixes and suffixes. For example, if you select architectural units, you can select the precision with which the units are displayed, how fractions are drawn (horizontal, slanted, or not stacked), and whether you want to append FT or IN to the dimension as a suffix. One important option in this section of the dialog box is the Round Off option, which enables you to define the increment to which the dimension measurements are rounded off.

The Measurement Scale option is used to adjust how the distance between the start and end points of the dimension is measured. Most of the time, this option is used when dimensions are drawn in a layout. When you place a dimension in a layout, it measures the dimension in layout units, not model space units.

In a layout viewport that is scaled to 1/4" = 1'–0", for example, a 4-foot line measures 1 inch in the layout itself. This is because the underlying scale factor differs 1/48 between the layout and model space. Just as you must adjust the overall scale factor of a dimension style for model space, you must adjust the linear scale to match the layout. It is calculated in the same way as the overall scale factor. In the previous example, a linear scale of 48 is correct.

Zero Suppression is used to control when a 0 appears in a dimension. For example, 6' is a valid dimension in architectural units. However, 6' is easily confused with 6", especially if the blueprint of the drawing is not very good. In both cases, the leading or trailing zeros have been suppressed. These dimensions read much easier as 6'-0" and 0'-6". You can set this up by disabling zero suppression for feet and inches. You can also control zero suppression for leading and trailing zeros such as 0.6 and 6.000.

Lastly, you can set the options for angular dimensions. Here, you can define the unit format for angles and the precision of the angle measurements. Like linear dimensions, angles also have a setting for zero suppression.

### Alternate Units Tab

The Alternate Units tab enables you to display alternate units in your drawing. For example, you might have drawings with architectural units and metric units as alternate units. Figure 17.10 shows an example of alternate units used in a dimension.

**Figure 17.10**   A dimension showing alternate units.

When alternate units are enabled, the controls for this tab of the Modify Dimension Style dialog box are the same as those found in the Primary Units tab.

### Tolerances Tab

The Tolerances tab (shown in Figure 17.11) of the Modify Dimension Style dialog box enables you to add tolerances to the end of the dimension text. These tolerances are different from those related to the Tolerance command discussed in Chapter 16, "Quick Dimensioning."

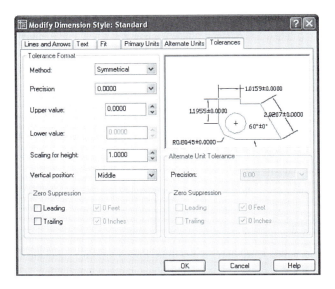

**Figure 17.11**    In the Tolerances tab of the Modify Dimension Style dialog box, you can set up dimensional tolerances to be displayed with your dimensions.

Actually, there are five different types of tolerances, each of which is briefly described in the following list:

- **None.** No tolerances are used in the dimension.

- **Symmetrical.** The tolerance is applied with a high and low limit that are the same. For example, 1.00 ±0.1 is a symmetrical tolerance.

- **Deviation.** The tolerance is applied with a high and low limit that can differ. As long as the object is manufactured within the limit, it is acceptable.

- **Limits.** The tolerance completely replaces the dimension. As long as the object is manufactured within the tolerances, it is acceptable.

- **Basic.** No tolerance is used, but a box is drawn around the dimension to help emphasize it.

After you select the tolerance method, you can apply an upper and lower value and justification of the text in the dimension line. Figure 17.12 shows a dimension with a symmetrical tolerance applied.

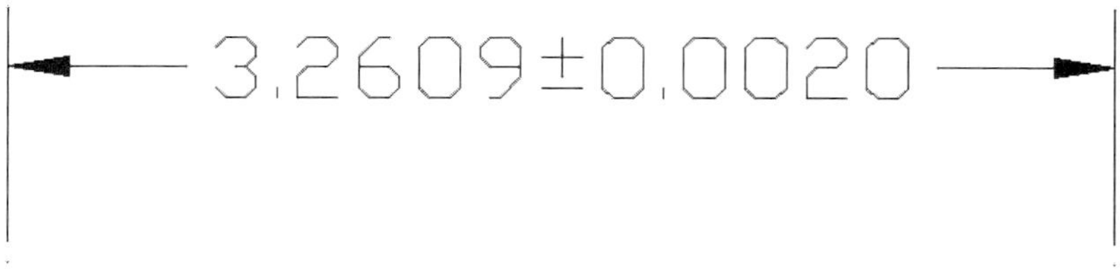

$$3.2609 \pm 0.0020$$

**Figure 17.12** A dimension showing the use of symmetrical tolerances.

The following exercise ties together all the information you have learned in this chapter so far. It shows how to quickly and easily set up a complete dimension style.

### Exercise 17.3   Creating a Dimension Style for a Mechanical Drawing

1. Start a new drawing from scratch.
2. From the Dimension pull-down menu, choose Style.
3. In the Dimension Style Manager dialog box, click on New and give the new style the name **MECH1**. Click on Continue.
4. Using the Lines and Arrows tab first, in the Center Marks for Circles area of the Lines and Arrows tab, select Line.
5. In the Arrowheads area, select Dot for 1st arrowhead. The 2nd arrowhead automatically changes to match the 1st.
6. In the Extension Lines area, select red as the color.
7. Click on the Text tab. In the Text Placement section, set the Vertical option to Above.
8. In the Text Alignment area, turn on Aligned with Dimension Line.
9. Under the Text tab panel, set the Text color to green.
10. Click on the Primary Units tab and, in the Linear Dimensions area, set the Precision to 0.00 (2 decimal places).
11. In the Angular Dimensions area, set the Precision to 0.0 (1 decimal place).
12. Click on the Tolerances tab and in the Tolerance Format area set the Method option to Symmetrical. Set the Upper value to 0.2. Click on OK to close the New Dimension Style dialog box.

13. Click on the MECH1 style and then click the Set Current button in the upper-right portion of the dialog box.

14. Click Close to save and exit the Dimension Style Manager dialog box.

15. Go ahead and create a couple of linear dimensions in this style. Figure 17.13 shows a few possibilities you could create using the MECH1 dimension types.

    After this, you can close the drawing without saving.

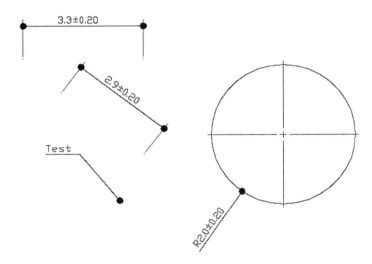

**Figure 17.13** A few dimensions created with the MECH1 dimension style.

Now you know about the processes and steps for working with dimension styles. The following section introduces some important tips that will help you optimize your dimension styles.

## Tips for Creating Effective Dimension Styles

The following list offers a few tips and techniques concerning dimension styles:

- Create all necessary styles and save them in a drawing template. That way, you never have to re-create the same styles and can easily load them into new drawings.

- Give your styles names that make sense to you and to others. For example, ARCH48 is more easily recognized as an Architectural dimension style for a 1/4" drawing than is a name such as STYLE1.

- An alternative to creating a dimension style for each and every `Dimscale` is to create a single dimension style based on a `Dimscale` of 1 and then to apply a `Dimscale` override for each dimension. This approach works well when dimensioning is controlled through programming.

- Make use of families when you need your dimension styles to change slightly when you're using different dimension types. This saves you from having to set dimension styles every time you change dimension types such as linear or angular.

**I**NSIDER **T**IP

> Most customized dimension styles have three primary format differences. Linear dimensions are primarily what gets changed (to ticks), and then, on occasion, leaders might have custom arrowheads. The other dimension types for angles and such usually would have closed filled arrows. So the simplest dimension style would only create children types for linear and leader and have a parent that provides the look for angular and radial dimensions. The productivity goal is to have one style that handles every object type and condition.

# Modifying Dimensions

After you have created your dimension styles and created a variety of dimensions in your drawing, eventually you will need to modify the dimensions. Some reasons you might need to modify existing dimensions include the following:

- The drawing plot scale changes.
- You make a change to dimensioned geometry.
- You want to override the AutoCAD measurement for the dimension.
- You want to reposition the dimension text for the purpose of clarity.
- You want to change the settings for some elements of a dimension without having to re-create the dimension.

The sections that follow discuss the various techniques for modifying existing dimensions.

**INSIDER NOTE**

The rest of this chapter assumes that Associative Dimensioning is active. This is controlled through the DIMASSOC dimension variable, which should be set to 1 or 2. When set to 0, you cannot update or modify your dimensions because they are exploded into individual objects and are not considered an single dimension object after they are created. To check the DIMASSOC setting, type **DIMASSOC** at the command prompt. DIMASSOC is set to 2 by default.

**INSIDER TIP**

AutoCAD used to employ a dimension variable named DIMASO, which performed the same function as DIMASSOC but only had 0 and 1. The setting of DIMASSOC to 2 was added to associate dimensions to objects, even from a layout to model space. The feature is covered in the following exercises.

Leaders, of course, are not dimensions and do not make use of associative dimensioning and, therefore, are slightly different when it comes to dimension editing. In most cases, you simply edit leaders as normal AutoCAD objects.

## Grip Editing

One of the most powerful methods of editing is grip editing. Just as you can grip edit most objects in AutoCAD, you can grip edit dimensions as well. However, you can use grip editing only if the variables PICKFIRST and GRIPS are enabled and set to a value of 1.

To grip edit a dimension, click on the dimension to highlight it. If the dimension is associative, the five grip boxes appear on a linear dimension, as shown in Figure 17.14. Of course, the exact location and the effect of each grip differs from dimension type to dimension type. Figure 17.15 shows the grip layout for a radius dimension.

**Figure 17.14**   You can use grips to edit a dimension.

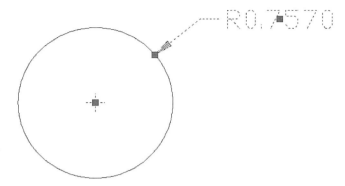

**Figure 17.15**   The dimension grips for a radial dimension.

When a dimension is selected with no hot grips, a right-click on a grip displays the pop-up menu shown in Figure 17.16. This enables you to control options such as the placement of the dimension text, the precision of the measurement, and even the dimension style itself.

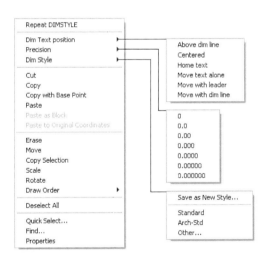

**Figure 17.16**   The menu that appears when you right-click on a selected dimension.

With the right-click capabilities in AutoCAD 2005, you will find that not only can you choose options for working with the selected grip, you can also find options for editing the dimension itself.

Most of the time, you directly use the grips to reposition the dimension text, the dimension line, or the start or end points of the dimension. See Chapter 9, "Object Selection and Manipulation," for more information on grip editing.

You might encounter a couple of problems when editing dimensions with grips:

- If you select the grip that is within the dimension text and select Rotate, the dimension rotates around the text. The text itself does not rotate. You must use a special dimension editing command (DIMEDIT) if you want to rotate the text and not the dimension line.

- If you are working with a radius or diameter dimension, you can grip edit the center point of the dimension. If you reposition the center point, the leader and arrow point change, but leave the same dimension value.

**I**NSIDER **N**OTE

> PICKFIRST and GRIPS must both be enabled. They are enabled by default in AutoCAD; if you have disabled them, please reenable them for this exercise.

The following exercise shows how to make use of grip editing with dimensions.

### Exercise 17.4    Grip Editing a Dimension

1. Load the file 17EX04.dwg from the accompanying CD-ROM and then turn on a running object snap mode of Endpoint.

2. Click on the dimension to highlight it and show the grips. Click on the lower-right grip to highlight it.

3. Right-click and choose Copy from the shortcut menu.

4. Select each corner going to the right to create three more dimensions. Then press Enter once.

5. Click on the dimension farthest to the right.

6. Select the grip at the intersection of the dimension and extension lines and move the dimension up into position, as shown in Figure 17.17.

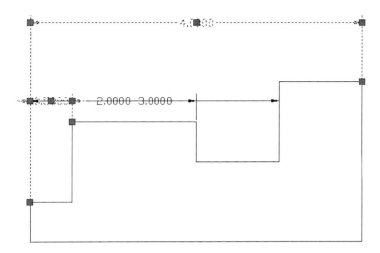

**Figure 17.17**    The first dimension is in position, but the copies overlay it.

7. Repeat steps 5-6 for the other two dimensions. Figure 17.18 shows the final dimensioned drawing.

Close the drawing without saving.

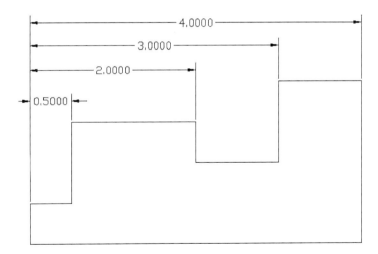

**Figure 17.18**    All dimensions are now correctly positioned in the drawing.

## Editing Dimension Text

One of the most common editing tasks for a dimension is changing the dimension text after the dimension has been created. The easiest way to edit the value is to choose Edit Text from the Text toolbar. This executes the DDEDIT command. When you select the dimension object, the Text Formatting interface appears, as shown in Figure 17.19.

**Figure 17.19**    The Text Formatting interface when used with a dimension.

The only thing that appears in the dialog box is <>. These symbols indicate the measured AutoCAD value. To replace the measured value, delete the <> and replace them with the value you want. Otherwise, add the text before and/or after the symbols as you see fit. Pay attention to the amount and size of the text for the dimension. You don't want to put in more information than there is room for.

**INSIDER CAUTION**

> It is generally considered poor practice to change the default value to a specific value because it might not update as the geometry updates. Only change the <> value if changing the geometry to be accurate is too time intensive.

**INSIDER TIP**

> If you delete the <> and add no other text, AutoCAD automatically reestablishes the <> when the Text Formatting dialog is closed. If you truly want no information to appear for the dimension, replace the <> with a single space.

When it comes to leaders, the DDEDIT command works just well for editing the text.

In addition to changing the value of the text in a dimension, you can also rotate and reposition the text. The fastest and easiest way to reposition text is to simply grip edit the dimension. Alternatively, you can use the DIMTEDIT command, which you access by clicking on the Dimension Text Edit button on the Dimension toolbar or by choosing Align Text from the Dimension pull-down menu. For the pull-down menu version, each DIMTEDIT option is listed individually on the Align Text cascade menu.

DIMTEDIT enables you to reposition the text and to align it to the left or right side of the dimension. If you make a mistake, DIMTEDIT also has a Home option you can use to move the text back to its original position. The last DIMTEDIT option is Angle, which enables you to rotate the text of a dimension without rotating the dimension itself.

The following exercise shows how to edit the text of a dimension.

### Exercise 17.5   Editing the Dimension Text

1. Load the file 17EX05.dwg from the accompanying CD.

2. Choose Object, Text, Edit from the Modify pull-down menu and click on the 4.000 dimension. AutoCAD displays the Text Formatting dialog box.

3. After the <> symbol, place a space and then the text **Overall Length**.

4. Click OK and then press Enter to exit the command. Figure 17.20 shows the resulting dimension.

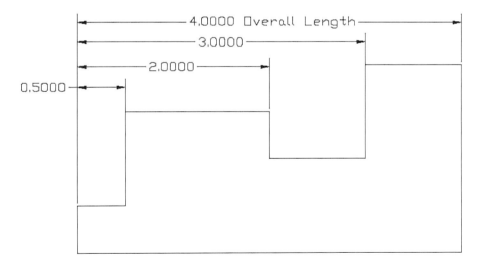

**Figure 17.20**   The dimension with the modified text.

> **INSIDER TIP**
>
> It is possible to have text both above and below the dimension line. By typing \X between strings of text, you could put the dimension value on top and the Overall Length text below the line. Go back and try this feature on the text you just entered.

5. Now suppose you want to rotate the text of the dimension 15 degrees. You can accomplish this with the DIMTEDIT command.

6. From the Dimension pull-down menu, select Align Text and then select the Angle option.

7. Select the dimension you just modified. Enter a value of **15** to rotate the text and then press Enter.

> **INSIDER TIP**
>
> If you make a mistake when editing the position and rotation of the dimension text with DIMTEDIT, or if you simply want to return the dimension to its original condition, you can use the Home option to restore it.

8. Choose Dimension, Align Text, Home.

9. Select the dimension and press Enter. The text is returned to its original position. You can close the drawing without saving it.

## Updating Dimensions

Another popular dimension editing task is updating an existing dimension to the current dimension style. This is often necessary when a user creates drawings with many different dimension styles. When you use many dimension styles in a drawing, it is easy to create a dimension in the wrong style by accident. AutoCAD offers three ways to update the style of a dimension:

- Modify the dimension style.
- Update the dimension object with DIMSTYLE.
- Revise the dimension with Update.

If you modify a dimension style that is currently in use in the drawing, when you save the style and exit the Dimension Style Manager dialog box, all dimensions using that style are automatically updated with the new settings.

If you want to change a dimension to a different named style, you must first set the active current style to the desired dimension style. You can do this in the Dimension Style Manager dialog box. After changing the current dimension style, you can choose Dimension, Update or use the Dimension Update icon on the Dimension toolbar. Then select the dimension, and it is updated to match the current style.

## Using *DIMEDIT*

DIMEDIT is another AutoCAD dimension editing tool. To use this command, select the Dimension Edit icon from the Dimension toolbar.

DIMEDIT enables you to reposition the dimension text back to the home position, rotate the text, and replace the dimension text, just as DIMTEDIT does. What is unique about DIMEDIT is its capability to add an obliquing angle setting to a dimension. An obliquing angle forces the extension lines off by the angle specified. This is more of a cosmetic adjustment you might use to make a dimension look more interesting. Obliquing a dimension does not affect the text, dimension line, arrowheads, or origin points. It affects only the extension lines.

## Overriding Dimension Variables

A lesser-known method of modifying a dimension is to override a dimension variable. When you are creating a dimension in a specific style, it is possible to override one or more dimension variables in the current style. For example, you might want to change the color of the dimension text for a couple of dimensions and then revert back to the original.

There are several ways to implement a dimension variable override. The easiest way is to override the dimension variable when you are creating the dimension. Unfortunately, to do this, you must know the name of the dimension variable you want to override. When you start the dimension command, such as DIMLINEAR, enter the name of the dimension variable you want to override. Give it the new value, and that value is used until you clear the override. For example, DIMASZ controls the size of the arrowheads. You can override this variable with a larger or smaller value than that found in the dimension style.

To clear a dimension override, you can use the DIMOVERRIDE command, which is available on the Dimension pull-down menu as Override. At the command prompt, you are asked for the dimension variable to override. You can type **c** at this prompt to clear all overrides and revert to the original style definition. Alternatively, you can enter any dimension variable, setting an active override, and apply it to existing dimensions.

Alternately, and probably more conveniently, you can override dimension style variables from the Dimension Style Manager dialog box. To do so, select the style you want to override and click on the Override button. The Override Current Style dialog box appears. Override any variables you like. Then click OK to return to the Dimension Style Manager dialog box, and you will see the dimension style listed in an outline format with a Style Overrides listing below it. To remove the overrides, right-click on the listing and choose Delete. You can also choose to rename those overrides or to incorporate them into the style permanently.

Overrides stay valid until you execute the CLEAR command, change to a new current style, or change the override to another value.

To help you make effective use of the OVERRIDE command, we have provided a ASCII text file, Dimvars.txt, on the CD where the exercise files for this chapter are located. Printing this document and posting it near your computer station provides quick reference to these valuable but seldom-used methods.

For most dimension variables, you might need to look up exactly what values can be used. Many are simply 1 or 0 (on and off); others, such as DIMSTYLE, accept text values. If you are going to use overrides, you need to know which variables you want to override and how you want to override them.

The following exercise shows how to make use of dimension overrides.

### Exercise 17.6    Overriding Dimension Variables

1. Load the drawing 17EX06.dwg from the accompanying CD.

2. Turn on the endpoint osnap if it's not already active.

3. Choose Linear from the Dimension pull-down menu and create an overall horizontal dimension near the top.

4. Select DIMLINEAR again by pressing Enter.

5. At the First Extension line prompt, type **DIMBLK** and press Enter.

6. Enter the string value of ARCHTEXT to set a new arrowhead format.

7. Dimension the smaller horizontal lengths of the block, as shown in Figure 17.21.

8. Start DIMLINEAR once again. Enter DIMBLK again and set it back to Closed Filled by entering just a period (.). That is a quick way to revert to a standard filled arrowhead.

9. Dimension the right vertical edge of the block. Figure 17.21 shows the final drawing.

   Close this drawing without saving.

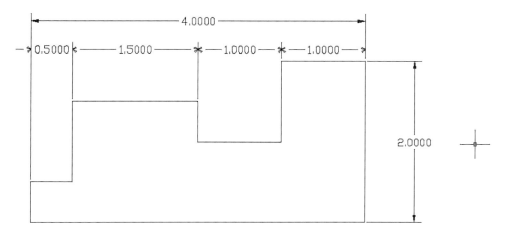

**Figure 17.21**   The drawing with overridden dimensions.

# Associative Dimensioning

Ever since the development of paper space, users have been torn between which "space" to create dimensions in. Another common problem is automatic updating of dimensions as the objects they dimension change. With AutoCAD 2005, great strides in answering these problems have been made with the Associative Dimensioning mechanism.

The following sections explores possible uses for this functionality and how it can benefit you in your everyday work.

## Controlling Associativity

With older versions of AutoCAD, you had two types of dimensions: Associative and Exploded. This basically meant you could make a smart dimension object or just "dimension" objects made up of lines and a piece of text. Most users would use associative dimensions, enabled them to edit the dimension object later. This option was controlled through the DIMASO dimension variable, which was stored within the currently defined DIMSTYLE.

But now, the DIMASO variable has been replaced with the DIMASSOC variable. So with AutoCAD 2005, a new definition is used to describe an Associative Dimension. Now that term really refers to a dimension that is linked to a object.

This system variable is controlled through a toggle in the Options dialog box in the User Preferences tab panel (see Figure 17.22). The small DWG logo next to the control indicates that it only affects the current drawing.

If this toggle is checked, any new dimensions you create "link" to the object that is used to define its node points. If it is unchecked, then typical non-linked associative dimensions are created.

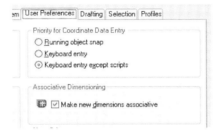

**Figure 17.22**    The Options dialog provides the control for Associative Dimensioning.

**I**NSIDER **T**IP

> The Associative Dimensioning system relies on the use of osnaps in order to "select" the point to link to. As you use an osnap, the system is also able to record the object that the osnap actually snapped to, thereby providing the object link. Obviously, if you do not use osnaps to define the node points, then you will not create a truly associative dimension. Another great reason to use osnaps.

## Using Associative Dimensioning

Until now, you have been able to modify dimensions using grips, and you can of course use the STRETCH command. Both of these methods provide a good level of productivity, but neither can compare to the enhanced productivity with "linked" Associative Dimensioning. In most circumstances, your first task of modification is to change the dimensioned object. Then you would have to modify the dimensions that define to that object. With AutoCAD 2005 and Associative Dimensioning, your task would end after the first step because the dimension would "fix" itself after you modified the object. The following exercise examines this process.

### Exercise 17.7    Applying Associative Dimensioning

1. Load the 17EX07.dwg from the accompanying CD.

2. Be sure that osnaps are turned on and Endpoint or Intersection is one of your options. You can right-click the Osnaps button on the status bar and choose Settings to check.

3. From the Dimension pull-down menu, choose Linear, press Enter and then select the object on the second horizontal top segment from the left.

4. Drag the cursor toward the top of the display to create a horizontal dimension.

5. From the Tools pull-down menu, choose Options. Click the User Preferences tab and then toggle on the Associative Dimensioning option (refer to Figure 17.22). Click Apply and then close the dialog.

6. Create another linear dimension using the two node points shown in Figure 17.23 but drag toward the bottom of the display. Now you have two dimensions for one segment of the object.

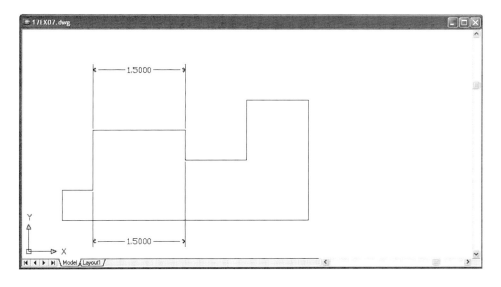

**Figure 17.23**   The drawing with two seemingly identical dimensions.

7. From the Modify pull-down menu, choose Move, select the object, and press Enter. At the `Specify base point or displacement` prompt, pick anywhere on the drawing.

8. At the `Specify second point of displacement or <use first point as displacement>` prompt, type `@1<0` to move the object 1 unit to the right.

Notice that the object moved as well as the last dimension you made, but not the first dimension—it got left behind. The first dimension was made with the Associative Dimensioning toggle (`DIMASSOC`) turned off. But there is something you can do about that to fix it.

9. From the Dimension pull-down menu, scroll all the way to the bottom and select Reassociate Dimensions.

10. At the `Select dimensions to reassociate` prompt, select the top dimension object. Press Enter to stop selecting dimensions.

11. At the `Specify first extension line origin or [Select object] <next>` prompt, type **S** and then press Enter. Select the same object line segment used originally.

The dimension then reassociates itself with the object geometry, keeping the same length extensions as well.

Keep this drawing open for the following exercise.

## Associative Dimensioning and Layouts

As discussed earlier in this chapter, placing dimensions in layouts does offer advantages in some cases. Until now, the biggest drawback was that the dimension text value had to be changed so that it reflected the true model space distance. Another big drawback was the inability to link to objects in model space from the dimension in the layout. This required multiple editing sequences to get the dimension to line up with the new locations of objects in model space.

Now with AutoCAD 2005, you can create dimensions in a layout and, due to the Associative Dimensioning feature, actually link them to their model space objects.

The following exercise shows the power of this new feature.

### Exercise 17.8   Associative Dimensioning in a Layout

1. Continue with the drawing from the previous exercise or, if needed, load the 17EX08.dwg from the accompanying CD.

2. Click on the Layout1 tab to open paper space.

3. This drawing has the Associative Dimensioning option set to On, so from the Dimension pull-down menu, choose Linear and place a dimension across the entire width of the object at the top (see Figure 17.24).

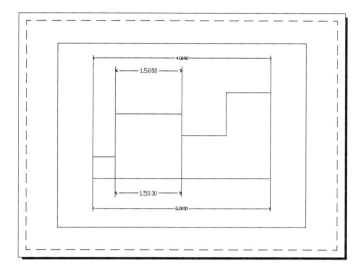

**Figure 17.24**   The drawing with one overall associative dimension.

4. Now using DIMASSOC, turn off Associative Dimensioning and set it to 1.

5. Create another dimension using the entire width of the object and place this one at the bottom of the display (see Figure 17.24).

   Note that one dimension shows 4.00 and one shows 6.00. The one with the 4.00 value is actually "linked" to the object in model space and is extracting its distance value and modifying its DIMLFAC value to factor it to read 4.00. This is done through an automatic dimension override that is being applied by AutoCAD.

6. Double-click in the viewport to move to model space.

7. Using the MOVE command, select the object and press Enter. At the Specify base point or displacement prompt, pick any point.

8. At the Specify second point of displacement or <use first point as displacement prompt, type @1<180 to move the object one unit to the left.

   Note that the object moved along with its two model space associative dimensions and the one paper space associative dimension that read 4.00.

   You can now close this drawing without saving the changes.

The final issue when using this feature is getting the dimension styles to match when it comes to size. This example had a zoom factor for the viewport of 1.5xp. This was done to show that the scale of a dimension object respects the current space it is in. One would need to adjust DIMSCALE values to match dimensions between spaces. Generally, layout dimensions would have a DIMSCALE value of 1, and then model space dimensions would use a scale factor such as a 48.0 for 1/4" scale DIMSCALE setting with a corresponding 1/48xp viewport scale factor.

With Associative Dimensioning, your decision about where to place dimensions becomes that much more complicated. Through proper planning before you start placing dimensions, you can determine the best method to fully recognize the potential with this new feature.

## Fields Within Dimensions

Often, when one thinks of associative dimensions, the key element is the dimensions' capability to adjust the value at a later time as needed and, in some cases, automatically. AutoCAD 2005 introduces a new mechanism that can be used wherever text type objects are used, and they are known as Fields. Typically, a field object is applied to an mtext object and can display data from a variety of drawing database subjects or objects. This new feature is explained in Chapter 21, "Using Fields and Tables."

# Summary

AutoCAD provides you with a fair amount of control over dimensions through dimension styles. By making good use of templates, you can save your dimension styles so that you don't have to re-create them.

After you create dimensions, of course, you need to be able to edit them. The primary methods for editing dimensions are grip editing, DDEDIT, and DIMTEDIT. Each method gives you various ways of editing the dimension, from editing text to positioning text. By taking advantage of new features such as layout-to-model space associativity, you can reduce your overall need to modify dimensions entirely.

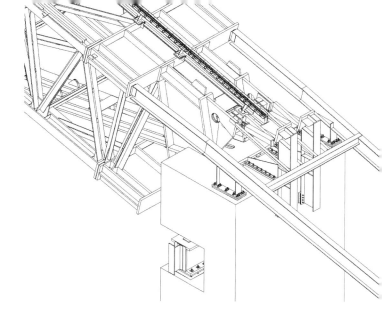

*C h a p t e r   1 8*

# Paper Space Layouts

Paper space layouts provide the capability to plot a drawing without cluttering the model with objects that are needed only for plotting purposes, such as title block borders. This is because layouts access an area called paper space. You can create a standard size sheet border in a layout, place a view of your model, and plot it at a 1:1 scale. By creating multiple viewports of a model space object, you can view the single object from different angles. After establishing the views, you can move and arrange the viewports in the layout area to any position inside the sheet border. You can accomplish all this without compromising the purity of model space by enabling the project's design model to exist separately from objects needed only for plotting sheets. By using layouts actively, you can quickly and easily design the sheets you need to plot model space objects.

This chapter discusses the following subjects:

- Using layouts
- Special paper space features and commands

# Using Layouts

Layouts make working in paper space easy to understand. Layouts provide a preview of what your plotted sheet will look like, and they make working with paper space intuitive. Layouts simulate the piece of paper your model will be plotted on and accurately reflect the plotted sheet's scale factor, the paper orientation and margins, the current lineweight setting of objects, and the layout's current plot style settings.

Layouts help prevent the confusion many users experience when dealing with model space and paper space. Because of the layout's "what you see is what you get" approach, it is easy to visualize what it is designed to do. Specifically, as shown in Figure 18.1, layouts make it easy to visualize how your model space objects are plotted on a sheet of paper.

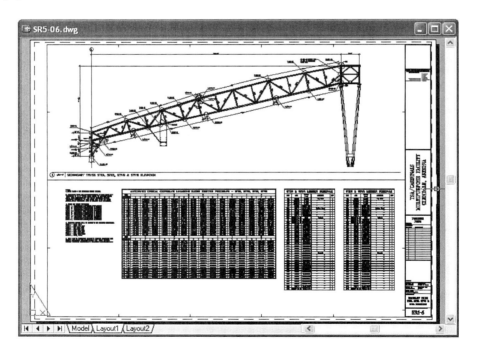

**Figure 18.1**    Layouts make paper plots easier to visualize.

**I**NSIDER **N**OTE

> Layouts also enable you to work in not just one paper space, but as many paper spaces as you desire, and they are named intelligently. The term *paper space* refers to the environment where multiple layouts can be created and used.

# Creating Layouts

When you start a new drawing from scratch, AutoCAD automatically creates a single Model tab and two Layout tabs, as shown in Figure 18.2. The Model tab is where your model, be it a floor plan, diagram, or 3D model, is created and edited. The Model tab itself cannot be renamed or deleted. Having more than one Layout tab, however, is not a requirement, and they can be renamed or deleted entirely. They are simply available to enable you to easily assemble several layout "sheets" you use to plot your drawing. One Layout tab always exists.

**Figure 18.2**    When you start a new drawing from scratch, AutoCAD automatically creates a single Model tab and two Layout tabs.

**INSIDER NOTE**

AutoCAD does not require plotting from a layout. You can plot your drawing from model space, but some plot features are not supported in that space. It is also easier to visually create a plot through the layouts' WYSIWYG display, so layouts are usually preferred for sheet plotting.

Although the number of layouts initially depends on the template used to create the drawing, you can create more. AutoCAD provides the following four methods for creating layouts:

- Create layouts manually
- Create layouts from templates
- Create layouts using a wizard
- Import a layout from DesignCenter

In the following exercises, you create a layout from scratch and save it as a layout template.

### Exercise 18.1 Creating a Layout Manually

1. Start AutoCAD and create a new drawing without using any template. If AutoCAD displays the Select template dialog, simply select the drop-down arrow next to the Open button and select one of the Open with no Template options. If AutoCAD displays the Create New Drawing dialog, select the Start from scratch option and then click OK. AutoCAD creates a new drawing with a single Model tab and two Layout tabs.

**INSIDER NOTE**

When you select a Layout tab for the first time, AutoCAD's default settings instruct it to not automatically show the Page Setup Manager dialog. The Page Setup Manager is where you configure your paper and plotting preferences. Learn more about page setups and plotting in Chapter 19, "Productive Plotting."

2. From the Tools pull-down menu, choose Options, then choose the Display tab.

3. In the Layout elements area, notice the Show Page Setup Manager for new layouts option. It should be off for this exercise. Notice also the Create viewport in new layouts option. If it is on, please turn it off, as shown in Figure 18.3.

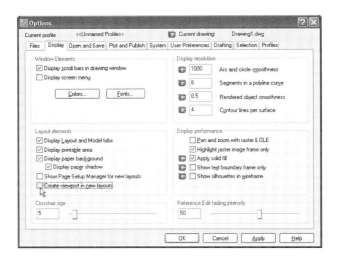

**Figure 18.3** When you first click on a new layout, AutoCAD creates a viewport and then opens the Page Setup Manager. You can stop this action by turning off those options in the Options dialog box.

**4.** Click OK to apply and close the dialog. Next, you create three additional layouts.

**I**NSIDER **T**IP

> You can step through the Model and Layout tabs by pressing Ctrl+PageUp or Ctrl+PageDown.

**5.** Move the cursor over the Layout2 tab and right-click. AutoCAD displays the Layout shortcut menu.

**6.** From the shortcut menu, select New Layout. AutoCAD creates a new layout, automatically naming it Layout3.

**I**NSIDER **T**IP

> The LAYOUT WIZARD is a helpful tool for making layouts. This application, found on the Insert pull-down menu under Layout, walks the user through the steps required to name a layout and assign a plotter, paper size, orientation, template for a title block, viewport configuration, and location. After you understand the mechanics of making them manually, using the wizard can help speed you through the process.

**7.** Repeat step 6 two more times until you have five Layout tabs in total.

**I**NSIDER **T**IP

> Layouts can be created manually, imported from a template, deleted, renamed, moved, copied, selected, configured for a page setup, or plotted using the right-click shortcut menu.

**8.** Rename the Layout3 tab. Position the cursor over the tab and right-click. AutoCAD displays the Layout shortcut menu again.

**9.** From the shortcut menu, choose Rename. The Rename Layout dialog box appears.

**10.** Type **First Layout** in the dialog box and click OK. AutoCAD renames the layout.

> **I** N S I D E R   N O T E _____
>
> You can name layouts using most keyboard characters except the following:
>
> < > / \ " : ; ? * | , = ' `

**11.** Repeat step 10 two more times, renaming Layout4 and Layout5 to Second
   Layout and Third Layout, respectively (see Figure 18.4).

**Figure 18.4**    The last three tabs have now been renamed.

**12.** To delete the two original Layout tabs supplied by AutoCAD, choose the
   Layout1 tab, hold the Shift key, and then choose the Layout2 tab. Both tabs
   are highlighted.

**13.** Move the cursor over either highlighted Layout tab and right-click. AutoCAD
   displays the shortcut menu.

**14.** From the shortcut menu, select Delete, as shown in Figure 18.5. AutoCAD issues
   a warning noting that the selected layouts will be deleted permanently.

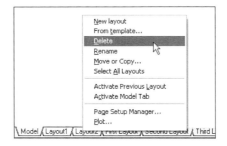

**Figure 18.5**    The first two layout tabs are selected for deletion.

**15.** Click OK to permanently delete the two Layout tabs. Only the three new layout
   tabs you created remain.

   Keep this drawing file open for the following exercise.

As you can see, creating layouts from scratch is simple. After you create a layout, you can save it in a template file and insert it into new drawings as needed. This is a useful method for sharing a set of standard layouts and enabling others to include them into their drawings.

In the following exercise, you save the layouts you created to a template and then insert them into a new drawing.

### Exercise 18.2   Saving a Drawing with a Layout as a Template

1. Continuing from the previous exercise, open the File pull-down menu and choose Save As. If needed, you can also open 18EX02.dwg from the accompanying CD and then choose Save As.

2. In the Save Drawing As dialog box, choose the Save As Type drop-down list and select AutoCAD Drawing Template (*.dwt). AutoCAD switches your active directory to the default template directory as determined in your Options dialog.

3. Name the drawing **Layouts**, then save it to the default Template subdirectory, as shown in Figure 18.6. AutoCAD then displays the Template Description dialog box.

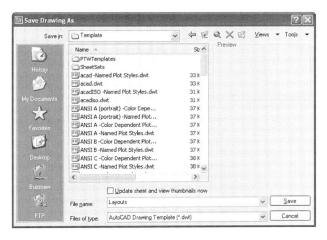

**Figure 18.6**   Save the drawing with the new layouts as a template file that you can insert into other drawings.

4. In the Description text box, type **My Layouts**. Note that the Measurement setting can be set to English or Metric; verify English is selected and click OK. AutoCAD then saves the drawing as an AutoCAD template file available for your use. You may close the saved template.

**INSIDER NOTE**

In AutoCAD 2005, the default location for saving templates is under your Windows profile, typically:

```
C:\Document and Settings\LoginName\Local Settings\Application Data\...
```

You can opt to change the setting using the Options dialog, under the Files tab, Template Settings. Changing it to a server directory can be more efficient to move from and to.

Next, you use the new template to insert a new layout from a template into another drawing.

5. From the File pull-down menu, choose New and create a new drawing from scratch.

6. Move the cursor over the Layout2 tab and right-click.

7. From the shortcut menu, select From Template. AutoCAD displays the Select File dialog box.

8. From the Select File dialog box, choose the Layouts template file you saved in step 4 from the Template folder, then click Open. AutoCAD displays the Insert Layout(s) dialog box.

**INSIDER TIP**

You can use AutoCAD DesignCenter to browse drawing files and to drag and drop layouts from these outside files directly into the current drawing. For more information on AutoCAD DesignCenter, refer to Chapter 12, "Applications for DesignCenter."

9. From the Insert Layout(s) dialog box, choose Third Layout from the Layout Names list (as shown in Figure 18.7) and click OK. AutoCAD inserts the Third Layout from the template you created in the previous exercise.

You may now close this drawing, there is no need to save.

**Figure 18.7**
You can insert predefined layouts from template files.

You cannot replace an existing layout with another of the same name from a template. If you attempt such a task, AutoCAD prefixes the inserted layout with Layout# - when it's created. If you want to replace an existing layout, you should delete the existing layout before inserting another layout of the same name.

To use the technique demonstrated in this exercise, you spend a little time at the beginning of a project setting up all the project's needed layouts and saving them to a template file. Then you can insert the layouts into new project drawings on-the-fly as needed. This approach is also similar to that performed when setting up a new sheet set.

## Understanding the Limitations of Layouts

It's important that you understand the limitations of working in a layout. Because layouts are intended to make creating plots easier, certain commands that are available in model space do not work when you are in a layout.

For example, the Layout tabs are intended to display the contents of two-dimensional environments. In model space, however, not only can you create three-dimensional objects, but you also can modify the model space view to look at these objects from different perspectives. Consequently, model space is where your project design work should be created. Therefore, use model space to design your project and use the Layout tab(s) to define your project's plots.

## Controlling Output Through a Page Setup

The Page Setup feature is a powerful tool that controls certain paper and plotter configuration information and links it to the current Model or Layout tab. By using Page Setup, you can define certain characteristics of the sheet of paper on which you plot your drawing. You can also associate a specific plotter configuration, which indicates the printer or plotter that plots your drawing. With Page Setup, you control values that define such things as the plot device, paper size, scale factor, plot orientation, XY offset values, and more.

A single drawing can contain many layouts, and each layout can be assigned a different page setup. Within a single layout, you can switch between numerous page setups. When a page setup is applied, AutoCAD redefines the paper size, scale factor, and all other page setup properties and shows this visually on-screen. You can also plot using a defined page setup without affecting the current page setup.

For example, if you need to plot a full-scale drawing to a large format plotter, you can set up a named page setup defined for the large format plotter. Then, in the same layout, you can create a second named page setup to plot the same drawing to a laser printer on an 8-1/2×11 sheet of paper. Because named page setups are available to all layouts simultaneously, you can quickly switch between the two to plot to the desired device. Additionally, when you choose the appropriate page setup, your drawing is plotted to the desired paper size at the proper scale using the appropriate lineweights, and you never have to redefine the plot parameters. This is a huge timesaver.

**I**NSIDER **N**OTE

> A page setup defined for model space cannot be applied to a layout, and vice versa.

Not only does the ability to associate a named page setup with a specific layout save you time when creating plots of your drawing, but also it saves you time by enabling you to use that named page setup configuration in another layout. You learned in the previous exercise how to save time when creating new drawings by inserting predefined layouts from a template file; in the same way, you can save time by importing named page setups into the current drawing.

The Page Setup dialog box is just a single dialog, as shown in Figure 18.8. On it, you select the plotter device to send plots. You also assign a plot style table, which defines the pen assignments and controls lineweights and line colors. In the lower half of the dialog, you define settings such as paper size, plot area, drawing orientation, and plot scale. If you are familiar with AutoCAD's Plot dialog box, you might notice that the Page Setup dialog box is very similar. This emphasizes that a page setup enables you to predefine plot settings, which means you do not have to make any adjustments to the plot settings if you already selected the appropriate page setup. For detailed information on using a page setup to control plot parameters, refer to Chapter 19.

When you select a layout in the Page Setup Manager, the title bar of the Page Setup dialog box indicates the current layout's name (FOUNDATION PLAN). When you select a page setup in the Page Setup Manager, the title bar indicates the page setup's name. Just below the title bar is the specific page setup name (42x30 Monochrome). Prior to this dialog, on the Page Setup Manager dialog box, you can choose to create additional page setups by clicking the New button. When you click the New button, the New Page Setup dialog box is displayed (see Figure 18.9). In that dialog box, you can name a new page setup and determine which existing page setup it should copy as a starting point.

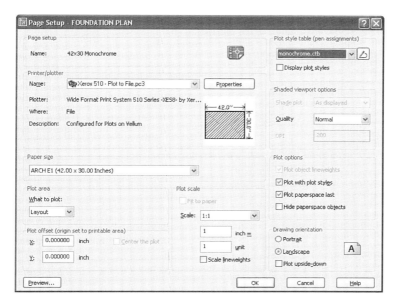

**Figure 18.8**   The Page Setup dialog box enables you to define paper and plotter settings and link them to the current Layout tab.

---

**I**NSIDER **NOTE**

When you save a page setup, it is saved in the current drawing only; it cannot be saved as a unique file type all by itself. Therefore, if you want to import a saved page setup, you must locate the drawing that contains the desired page setup and use the Import option in the Page Setup Manager dialog box or use PSETUPIN at the command line. Page setups can be created in drawing template files as well.

---

**Figure 18.9**   From the New Page Setup dialog box, you can create a new page setup and specify its prototype.

**I**NSIDER **N**OTE

The PSETUPIN command enables you to insert page setups from other drawings, templates, and DXF files.

Also, when PSETUPIN is called from AutoLISP, you can insert as many page setups as desired from external files. For example, by entering the following AutoLISP code, you can access MYPAGESETUPS.dwg and load in saved page setups named Fullsize and Halfsize:

```
(command "_.psetupin" "mypagesetups" "Fullsize,Halfsize")
```

This code can also be placed in a menu file for quick and easy access.

# Working with Viewports in a Layout

Viewports created in a layout, also called floating viewports, have unique settings for controlling the appearance of your project's model. When you control layer visibility, hidden line removal, model-to-paper space scale, and even rendering, your finished plot can display objects as precisely as needed. More importantly, you can control these properties on a viewport-by-viewport basis, even when you have several viewports on a single layout. The capability to control how your model appears through these viewports is a powerful feature.

Floating viewports in paper space have been around for a number of AutoCAD versions, but you can enhance their usefulness by creating non-rectangular viewports. You can also adjust a viewport and resize it to any shape by using grips. Additionally, you can lock the display scale of a viewport so it is not accidentally modified when you zoom or pan in the viewport.

This section discusses the differences between tiled viewports in model space and floating viewports in layouts.

## Tiled Viewports Versus Floating Viewports

Tiled viewports are created when you are working in model space. Floating viewports are created when you are working in paper space. When you create a viewport, AutoCAD automatically determines the type of viewport to create based on which space you are currently working in. Therefore, tiled viewports are automatically created when the Model tab is active, and floating viewports are automatically created when a Layout tab is active.

Tiled viewports, as the name implies, appear as tiles on the screen. They subdivide the original model space viewport (which is a single tiled viewport) into multiple viewports, as shown in Figure 18.10. They are fixed and cannot be moved. They never overlap, and their edges always lie adjacent to the surrounding viewports. Their usage is primarily for helping to view the model during its creation. The currently selected tile can be further divided into more tiles or joined with another tiled viewport to create a new larger one.

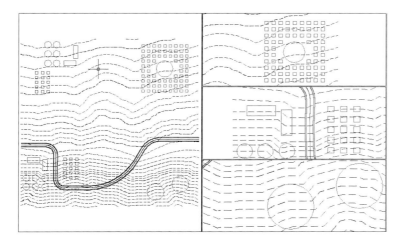

**Figure 18.10**   Model space viewports subdivide the screen into smaller tiled viewports that cannot overlap.

In contrast, floating viewports neither subdivide the screen nor remain fixed. Additionally, they can be copied, resized, and moved, just like any other AutoCAD object. They can even overlap each other, as shown in Figure 18.11.

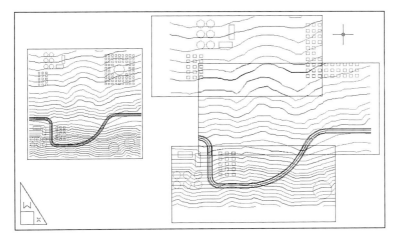

**Figure 18.11**   Paper space viewports can be copied and resized and can overlap.

## The Viewports Toolbar

AutoCAD 2005 provides a toolbar that makes creating viewports very easy. The Viewports toolbar, shown in Figure 18.12, enables you to insert a single viewport, define a polygonal- or non-rectangular viewport, and clip an existing viewport. Additionally, you can set the scale for a viewport, and you can display the new Viewports dialog box, which enables you to create multiple viewports by selecting the desired predefined viewport configuration.

**Figure 18.12**
The Viewports toolbar makes creating viewports very easy.

**I**NSIDER **T**IP

> To display the Viewports toolbar, right-click over any toolbar button. Then, from the shortcut menu, choose Viewports.

### Creating Non-Rectangular Floating Viewports

The Polygonal Viewport button enables you to create irregularly shaped viewports like the one shown in Figure 18.13.

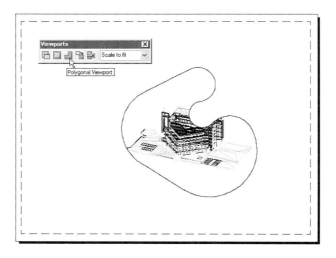

**Figure 18.13**    The Polygonal Viewport button enables you to create very curved viewports.

When you choose the Polygonal Viewport button from the Viewports toolbar, AutoCAD prompts you to specify the start point. Then the feature works much like the PLINE command, continuing to prompt for additional points to define the polygonal viewport's vertices. Also similar to the PLINE command, you can switch between a line segment and an arc segment, as well as close the polygon or undo the last point selected. After creating the polygonal viewport, you can even edit the viewport with several options from the PEDIT command.

**I**NSIDER **T**IP

> After you create a floating viewport, you can modify its shape by selecting the edge of the viewport to display its grips, selecting the grips, and then moving them to new positions.

**I**NSIDER **T**IP

> If you want to hide the display of a viewport's boundary, either freeze or turn off the layer on which the viewport is created. However, this can make it more difficult to work with your viewports. It is recommended that you create specific layers on which to place your viewports and then use the No Plot option for those layers to keep them from plotting.

### Converting Objects to Floating Viewports

Another handy feature enables you to convert an existing AutoCAD object into a floating viewport. Any closed object such as a circle or a closed polyline can easily be converted to a floating viewport. For example, if you click the Convert Object to Viewport button shown in Figure 18.14, a circle object can be selected and converted into a viewport, as shown in Figure 18.15.

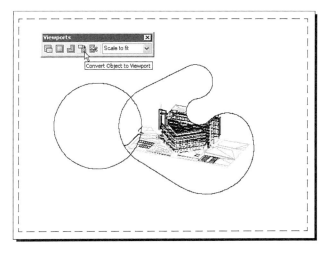

**Figure 18.14**  The Convert Object to Viewport button enables you to select a closed object and convert it into a floating viewport.

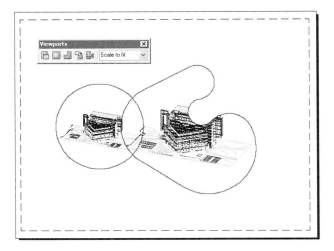

**Figure 18.15** This circle has been converted into a floating viewport.

You can convert a region object to a clipped viewport. By creating composite regions, you can define a region object with holes or voids, which can be used to blank model space areas in the viewport, as shown in Figure 18.16. This is a great way to show notes on top of a viewport. Simply create the composite region in the desired shape and then convert it to a viewport.

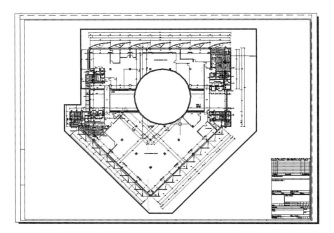

**Figure 18.16** The viewport, shown in bold, was created from a composite region object, which consists of the irregularly shaped polygon and the circle.

**I**NSIDER **T**IP

You can copy a floating viewport object just as you can any other AutoCAD object. This is especially useful for duplicating properties such as the viewport's scale factor and display area.

You can also use the MATCHPROP command to paste the viewport properties such as layer visibility from one viewport to another viewport.

## Clipping Existing Floating Viewports

There is a feature in AutoCAD 2005 that seemingly clips an existing floating viewport. Although the phrase "clip" might conjure visions of AutoCAD's TRIM command, this feature does not actually clip or trim an existing viewport. Instead, it replaces an existing viewport with a new viewport.

What makes this feature useful is that you can replace an existing viewport with a new closed object that assumes the current properties of the existing viewport. So, to quickly revise an existing viewport's shape while retaining its properties (such as the model's view position and scale in the viewport), use the new viewport clip feature.

To clip a viewport, click the Clip Existing Viewport button on the Viewports toolbar. AutoCAD then prompts you to select the viewport you want to clip. Next, AutoCAD prompts you to select the clipping object, or you may draw a new polygonal object on-the-fly. When you do, AutoCAD converts the clipping object into a viewport and deletes the existing viewport.

The following exercise demonstrates how to create a composite region object and use it to clip an existing viewport.

### Exercise 18.3   Clipping Floating Viewports

1. Open the 18EX03.dwg file on the accompanying CD. When the drawing opens, it displays a single floating viewport (as shown in Figure 18.17), as well as a polyline and a circle object, both of which are in paper space.

   Next, you convert the polyline and the circle into regions.

2. From the Draw pull-down menu, select Region. AutoCAD prompts you to select the objects to convert into regions.

3. Select the polyline and the circle and then press Enter. AutoCAD converts the two objects into region objects.

   Next, you convert the two region objects into a single composite region.

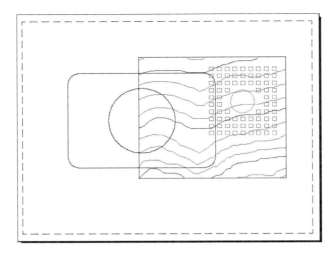

**Figure 18.17**    The existing viewport, along with the polyline and circle objects.

4. From the Modify pull-down menu, choose Solids Editing, Subtract. AutoCAD prompts you to select the regions to subtract from.

5. Select the region created from the polyline and press Enter. AutoCAD prompts you to select the regions to subtract.

6. Select the region created from the circle and press Enter. AutoCAD subtracts the circle region from the polyline region and creates a single composite region in their place.

   Next, you use the composite region object to clip the existing viewport.

7. If the Viewports toolbar is not visible, right-click over any toolbar button to display the shortcut menu and select the Viewports toolbar.

8. On the Viewports toolbar, click the Clip Existing Viewport button. AutoCAD prompts you to pick the viewport you want to clip.

9. Choose the existing viewport, and AutoCAD prompts you to select the clipping object.

10. Select the composite region. AutoCAD clips the existing boundary, replacing it with the composite region, as shown in Figure 18.18. Notice that the model space view does not display through the circle. This effect is achieved by using composite regions.

    Close this drawing; there is no need to save.

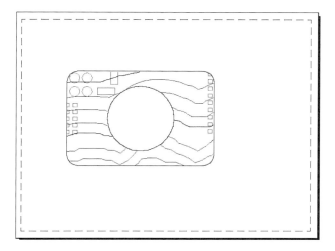

**Figure 18.18**    The new viewport created by clipping with the composite region object.

## Controlling a Viewport's Scale

Another welcome feature is the capability to easily scale your model in a floating viewport. You can quickly select the desired scale from the Viewports toolbar.

For example, suppose you are plotting your drawing from a layout, and you are displaying your model in a single floating viewport. If your plotted sheet's scale must be 1" = 4'-0", you would choose the 1/4"=1' option from the Viewport Scale Control.

The Viewport Scale Control comes with more than 30 predefined scales, as shown in Figure 18.19. To change an existing viewport's scale, select the viewport and then choose the desired scale from the drop-down list. To set the desired scale for new viewports as you create them, choose the desired scale without selecting any objects.

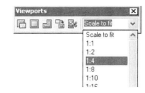

**Figure 18.19**
The Viewport Scale Control enables you to quickly set the scale for a floating viewport.

---

**I** NSIDER   **N** OTE

The list of predefined scales is not customizable. To set the viewport's scale to a scale that is not on the predefined list, you must change the Custom Scale property.

**I**NSIDER **T**IP

> You can double-click inside or outside a viewport to switch between the layout environment and model space.

## The Viewports Dialog Box

In the previous section, you learned about the various features of the Viewports toolbar. The only feature not discussed was the Display Viewports Dialog button, shown in Figure 18.20. When you click this button, AutoCAD displays the Viewports dialog box shown in Figure 18.21.

**Figure 18.20**
Clicking the Display Viewports Dialog button displays the Viewports dialog box.

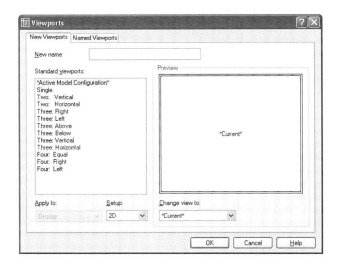

**Figure 18.21** The Viewports dialog box.

The Viewports dialog box enables you to create and edit both tiled and floating viewports. You can select from a list of standard viewport configurations, define new configurations, and assign saved views to each viewport in a configuration. If you are in the Model tab, you can name a defined configuration and save it for later use.

The Viewports dialog box contains two tabs: the New Viewports tab and the Named Viewports tab. The options displayed in each tab vary depending on whether the Model tab or a Layout tab is current. The New Viewports tab (shown in Figure 18.21) shows the options available when the Model tab is current.

When the Model tab is current, the New Viewports tab enables you to select a viewport configuration from the Standard Viewports list and apply it to the display or insert it into an existing viewport. If you apply the configuration to the display, the Model tab's current viewport configuration is replaced by the new configuration. If you insert the configuration into an existing viewport, the original viewport configuration is retained, and the new configuration is inserted into the Model tab's current viewport. You can also indicate whether the configuration is a 2D or 3D setup. A 2D setup enables you to define each viewport's view by selecting defined views from the Change View To drop-down list. In contrast, when you select a 3D setup, AutoCAD enables you to define each viewport's view by selecting from a set of standard orthogonal 3D views in the Change View To drop-down list. After you create the desired viewport configuration, you can name the configuration and save it for later use.

In contrast, when a Layout tab is current, the options available in the New Viewports tab (see Figure 18.22) are slightly different from those available in model space. For example, although you can select a viewport configuration from the Standard viewports list, you can only apply it to the display. You cannot insert it into an existing viewport. However, unlike with tiled viewports created in the Model tab, you can indicate the viewport spacing, which defines the amount of space to apply between viewports when they are created. Additionally, when you insert a new configuration in a layout, AutoCAD enables you to select the location to insert the viewports.

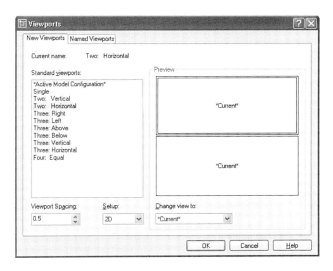

**Figure 18.22**   Viewport spacing is only available when a Layout tab is active.

The Named Viewports tab, shown in Figure 18.23, enables you to select a named model space viewport configuration to insert. Although named model space viewport configurations must be created in the Model tab, they can be inserted in either the model space or a Layout tab. The options available in the Named Viewports tab are the same for both model space and layouts.

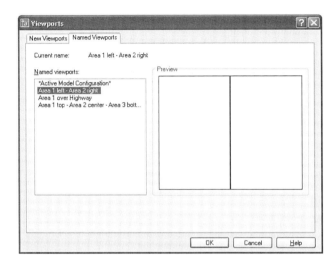

**Figure 18.23**     The Named Viewports tab enables you to select a named model space viewport configuration to insert.

## Accessing Viewport Commands Through the Shortcut Menu

AutoCAD 2005 enables you to access many commands through the shortcut menu. You access these commands with a right-click, and they are context-sensitive. The options displayed on the shortcut menu vary depending on the cursor's position in the drawing, whether objects are selected, and whether a command is currently in progress. For example, if you are in a Layout tab and a floating viewport is selected, a right-click of your mouse provides the wide selection of options shown in Figure 18.24.

Among these options, the following three are related to floating viewports:

- **Display Viewport Objects.** This option enables you to turn on or off the visibility of objects in a viewport. When turned off, the objects in the viewport are not displayed or regenerated and will not be plotted.

- **Display Locked.** This option enables you to lock the viewport so that its scale cannot be altered during zooms and pans. When you turn this option on, any zooms or pans occur in paper space and not in the viewport, thereby ensuring that the proper scale is maintained.

- **Shade Plot.** This option enables you to control the appearance of 3D models in the viewports when they're plotted from paper space. This feature is matched with features of the SHADEMODE command. Your model space environment could be in wireframe style, while your viewport could be rendered.

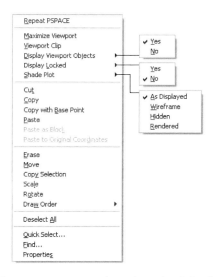

**Figure 18.24**   When a floating viewport is selected, a right-click of your mouse displays many options, several of which are related to floating viewports.

**I**NSIDER **T**IP

Using multiple viewports in paper space can aid in developing interesting and informative drawings. Because the property is at the viewport level and not the plot level, you can have one viewport remove hidden lines while another is rendered, and another could even be in wireframe style.

# Aligning Objects in Floating Viewports

Floating viewports can be edited in several ways. You can use grips to scale, move, or resize viewports. Viewports can be copied or erased. You can even create an array of viewports.

Although creating multiple viewports is easy, aligning objects in different viewports can be difficult unless you take advantage of the MVSETUP command.

The following exercise demonstrates how to use the MVSETUP command to align objects in two different viewports.

### Exercise 18.4    Aligning Objects in Two Different Floating Viewports

1. Open the 18EX04.dwg file on the accompanying CD.

   When the drawing opens, it displays two floating viewports in a layout. Each viewport shows a different view of the same model space objects. It is important to note that both viewports have the same scale.

2. Type **MVSETUP** at the command prompt, and AutoCAD initializes the MVSETUP routine.

---

**I**NSIDER NOTE _____

> The MVSETUP command is not available on the pull-down menus or the toolbars. If this is something you use often, it is suggested you create a toolbar or palette icon for the command.

---

3. At the option prompt, type **A** to start the Align feature.

4. Then type **H** to start the Horizontal feature. AutoCAD enables the lower-right viewport and then prompts for the basepoint. The view in the other viewport will be aligned with this point. If the lower-right viewport is not already highlighted, pick inside it to make it current.

5. With the lower-right viewport current, use endpoint osnap to snap the small rectangle (as shown in Figure 18.25).

6. When AutoCAD prompts for the other point, pick inside the upper-left viewport to make it current.

7. With the upper-left viewport current, use endpoint osnap to snap the small rectangle, as shown in Figure 18.26. AutoCAD moves the view in the upper-left viewport down and aligns the two small rectangles.

8. Type **V** to start the Vertical feature. Once again, AutoCAD prompts for the basepoint. Pick inside the lower-right viewport to make it current.

9. With the lower-right viewport current, use endpoint osnap to snap the same small rectangle shown previously in Figure 18.25.

10. When AutoCAD prompts for the other point, pick inside the upper-left viewport to make it current.

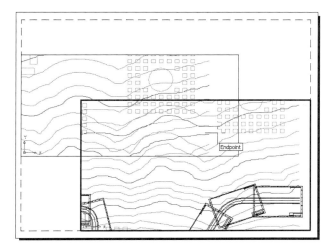

**Figure 18.25** Align objects in two different viewports using the MVSETUP command. First, snap to the endpoint of an object that appears in both viewports.

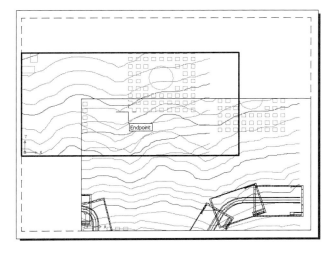

**Figure 18.26** Continue the MVSETUP command by snapping to the same endpoint of the same object in the other viewport.

11. With the upper-left viewport current, use endpoint osnap to snap the same small rectangle shown previously in Figure 18.26. AutoCAD moves the view in the upper-left viewport to the right and aligns the two small rectangles, as shown in Figure 18.27.

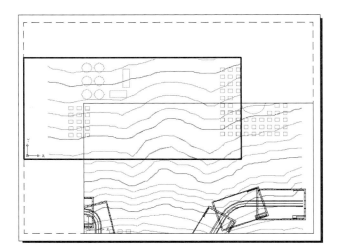

**Figure 18.27**    The MVSETUP command aligns the objects in the two viewports.

**12.** Press Enter twice to end the command.

Close the drawing; there is no need to save.

Notice that the MVSETUP command was started in paper space but exited in a model space viewport. Also note that the objects in these two viewports aligned perfectly because the two viewports have the same scale.

## Controlling Layer Visibility in Floating Viewports

With floating viewports, you can freeze and thaw layers individually, independent of other viewports. This means you can make a given object in model space invisible in one viewport by freezing its layer, but that object can remain visible in another viewport where its layer is thawed. You can accomplish this within the Layer Properties Manager or by using the VPLAYER command.

The advantage of using the Layer Properties Manager is that you can simply choose the Freeze/Thaw in Current Viewport icon to toggle the layer visibility. The disadvantage to using the Layer Properties Manager is that the settings affect only the current viewport or future viewports. Consequently, to apply the same layer freeze/thaw properties to multiple viewports, you must select each viewport individually to make it current and choose the desired settings. The advantage of using the VPLAYER command is that you can apply the desired freeze/thaw settings to multiple viewports simultaneously. However, because VPLAYER does not have a dialog box interface, you must type in the layer names manually.

Although you can control a layer's freeze/thaw property in the current viewport, the global freeze/thaw value can override a specified viewport's setting. If a particular layer is thawed in a viewport but frozen globally, for example, the model space objects on the frozen layer will not appear in any viewport.

The following exercise demonstrates the usefulness of the Layer Properties Manager and the VPLAYER command.

### Exercise 18.5   Viewport Layer Visibility and Maximizing for Editing

1. Open the 18EX05.dwg drawing file on the accompanying CD. The drawing opens in Layout1 and displays two floating viewports. At this point, it is obvious that some layers are not visible in the viewport on the right.

   Next, you determine which layers are frozen in the viewport on the right.

2. Click the Layer Properties Manager button on the Layers toolbar. The Layer Properties Manager opens, displaying the current list of layers (see Figure 18.28). Notice that the icons in the Current VP Freeze column indicate that all layers are thawed, which is no surprise, as a viewport isn't even active yet. If some right-side columns are not visible, simply widen the dialog or shorten the column fields to show items to the right.

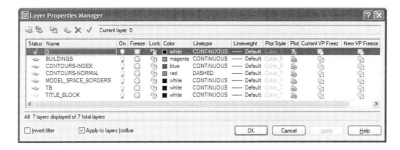

**Figure 18.28**   The Current VP Freeze column indicates all layers are thawed.

3. Click OK to close the dialog box.

4. Double-click in the right viewport. AutoCAD switches from paper space to model space, and the right viewport becomes active.

5. Click the Layers Properties Manager button on the Layers toolbar. The Layer Properties Manager again opens, displaying the list of layers (see Figure 18.29). Notice that the icons in the Current VP Freeze column indicate that three layers are frozen in the current viewport.

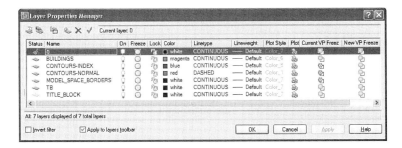

**Figure 18.29**    The Current VP Freeze column indicates that three layers are frozen in the current viewport.

6. Click OK to close the dialog box.

7. Double-click outside of the floating viewports, and AutoCAD switches from model space to paper space.

---

**INSIDER NOTE**

You can use the VPLAYER command to get a report of what layers are frozen in a viewport. By simply typing in the command name and a ? and then selecting a viewport, the following layer visibility information is then provided on the text screen:

```
Layers currently frozen in viewport 3:
"CONTOURS-INDEX"
"CONTOURS-NORMAL"
"MODEL_SPACE_BORDERS"
```

---

The next steps use the global freeze/thaw layer settings to set both viewports' current freeze/thaw layer settings.

8. Open the Layers Properties Manager dialog again from the Layers toolbar.

9. In the dialog, freeze all the layers except layer 0 in the New VP Freeze column, as shown in Figure 18.30. Click OK to close the dialog.

10. Time to create a new viewport. From the Viewports toolbar, click the Single Viewport button. This starts the -VPORTS command, also known as the MVIEW command.

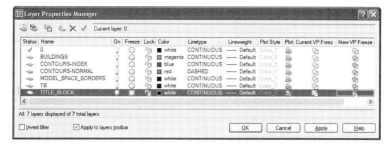

**Figure 18.30**    Controlling how new viewports display existing layers through the New VP Freeze column.

**INSIDER TIP**

> To view a column's entire heading, click and drag the line separating column titles to the right until the heading is visible. You can also stretch the dialog box wider to display more information.

11. Create a rectangular floating viewport across the top of the page, as shown in Figure 18.31. As you can see, the changes in the Layer Properties Manager controlled what layers were visible when a new viewport was created. Next, we match the viewports layer visibility.

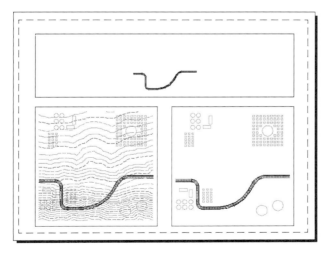

**Figure 18.31**    When new viewports are created, they accept the New VP Freeze setting in the Layers Properties Manager.

**12.** Using the Match Properties tool found on the Standard toolbar, select the lower-left viewport as the source object. Then paste onto the lower-right viewport.

The two large viewports now have matching layer visibility.

**13.** Again, use the Match Properties tool found on the Standard toolbar and select the top viewport as the source object. Then paste onto the lower-left viewport. Figure 18.32 shows what your viewports should look like now.

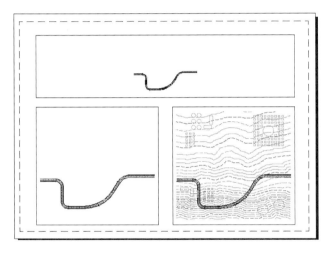

**Figure 18.32**   Matching layer settings from one viewport to another is as easy as using the Match Properties tool.

Next we use some new features of AutoCAD 2005. Notice the buttons at the bottom of the screen. As shown in Figure 18.33, this new button enables you to enlarge the viewport while still in paper space.

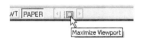

**Figure 18.33**
The new Maximize Viewport button and navigation controls.

**14.** Click the center button, Maximize Viewport. AutoCAD immediately changes the visible display, as shown in Figure 18.34.

As you can see from the UCS icon in the corner, you are in model space within a larger viewport.

**15.** It is possible that the viewport that AutoCAD determined you wanted to maximize isn't the desired one. In that case, you can use the navigation buttons on either side of the Minimize Viewport icon to step forward or backward through all your viewports. Try it a few times to see that AutoCAD maintains the initial view of each viewport.

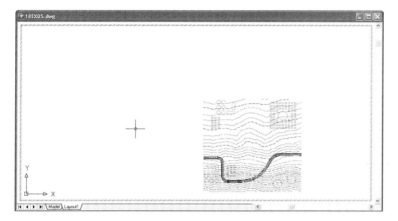

**Figure 18.34**   When employed, the Maximize Viewport button enables you to work in a larger viewport temporarily. The hatched style perimeter is a visual aid to let you know you are in a temporary state.

16. Utilize the ZOOM window feature to increase the size of the items in the display. The PAN command also works, as does the mouse wheel zoom and pan.

**INSIDER TIP**

When you navigate to another viewport, it is presented in the paper space scale and location. Any display changes are discarded after navigation to another viewport or out of the temporary state.

17. Click the Minimize Viewport button to return to paper space. AutoCAD restores the previous display appearance.

You can now close the drawing without saving.

**INSIDER TIP**

The commands attached to those buttons are VPMAX and VPMIN. You can type those at the command prompt if so desired. The navigation buttons, however, have no command prompt alternative.

**INSIDER NOTE**

You might have experienced a problem with retaining changes you made to layer values for xref objects after you closed the drawing and reopened it. If you make changes to the layer values of xrefs and you want those values to be saved with the drawing, set the VISRETAIN system variable to 1. This instructs AutoCAD to save any changes you make to xref-dependent layers with the drawing. This feature is also controlled from the Options dialog box's Open and Save tab; in the External References area, toggle the Retain Changes to Xref Layers check box.

**INSIDER CAUTION**

Although the VISRETAIN system variable can be very useful for tweaking a particular xref's layering appearance, that very capability can lead to problems when you try to update or change a layer property in the xref itself and expect to see that change across many drawings.

# Summary

This chapter covered layout basics and why you should use layouts to plot your drawings. You learned about the difference between tiled and floating viewports. You compared the differences between model space and paper space. You also learned about layout features in AutoCAD and how to use the MVSETUP command to align viewports to each other using model space objects common to each viewport. Finally, you learned how to quickly change the Current VP Freeze values in multiple viewports simultaneously and about the new Maximize/Minimize Viewport tools in AutoCAD 2005.

This chapter showed you how to productively use the layouts in AutoCAD 2005. By using the techniques discussed, you can easily control the appearance of your final drawings and ease the time-consuming process of plotting your drawings, thereby increasing your productivity.

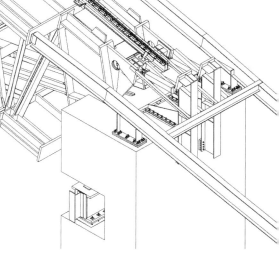

# Productive Plotting

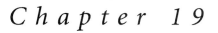

The ultimate goal of most AutoCAD drawings is the final plot because the piece of paper is what your end user reads to actually build the model you created virtually in AutoCAD. Consequently, when beginning a project, it is important to consider the form your final output must take to meet the needs of your client. By considering the form of the final output at the beginning of a project, you take an important step toward minimizing the amount of time spent editing a nearly complete project just so the final output meets your client's needs.

AutoCAD 2005 has features that make the process of creating output very easy. You can assign page setups to paper space layouts, which determines the printer or plotter the layout is sent to and how it will appear. You can control plot-specific information at the layout level, the layer level, or the object level by assigning the layouts unique page setups. Plots can even be created as DWF or PDF files, digital "what you see is what you get" plot files. These types of plot files require other applications to both view and plot them.

By understanding the plotting features available in AutoCAD 2005, you can ensure a high level of productivity and provide a final product that is useful to the end user.

This chapter discusses the following subjects:

- Configuring a plotter
- Defining plot styles
- Creating page setups
- Plotting from AutoCAD
- Plot stamping

The following sections first walk you through the process of configuring a printer and a plotter, then proceed to defining plot styles and page setups, and then finish up with plotting a drawing. The exercises do not require you to have access to a printer or plotter.

# Configuring a Plotter

The first step in plotting drawings from AutoCAD is configuring the plot devices intended for plotting. By configuring the printers and plotters to which AutoCAD will plot, you can predefine certain output properties and later refine them with plot styles and page setups.

AutoCAD supports many printers and plotters and ships with a variety of drivers. The drivers enable AutoCAD to communicate with the printers and plotters, including those that support raster and PostScript file formats. The device drivers support many plotting devices, including Hewlett-Packard, Océ, and Xerox plotters. Additionally, AutoCAD can plot to Windows system printers, including Adobe Acrobat PDF Writer, which enables you to create PDF files.

**INSIDER NOTE**

> The Windows System Printers can be accessed from the Windows Control Panel under Printers and Faxes.

## The Autodesk Plotter Manager

The Autodesk Plotter Manager enables you to easily configure non-system and Windows system plotter and printer devices. You can use it to configure AutoCAD to use local and network plotters and printers, and you can use it to predefine non-default output settings for Windows system devices.

AutoCAD 2005 stores information about media and plotting devices in plot configuration files, called PC3 files. If you have used older releases of AutoCAD, you are probably familiar with PCP and PC2 files. The PC3 files are similar to the earlier versions, except they do not store any pen setting information. The Autodesk Plotter Manager walks you through the process of creating PC3 files, as shown in the following exercise.

**I**NSIDER  **N**OTE

Pen setting information exists separately from PC3 files in CTB or STB plot style files.

### Exercise 19.1    Configuring Printers and Plotters

1. In AutoCAD, select the File pull-down menu, then Plotter Manager. AutoCAD displays the Plotters folder, similar to Figure 19.1.

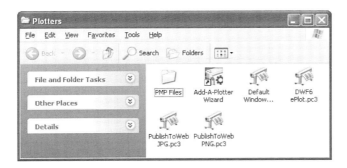

**Figure 19.1**   The Autodesk Plotter Manager stores PC3 files and is where you access the Add-A-Plotter Wizard.

2. Double-click the Add-A-Plotter Wizard. The wizard displays the Add Plotter - Introduction page.

3. Click the Next button. The wizard displays the Add Plotter - Begin page.

   The Begin page is where you indicate whether you want to use a local, network, or system printer. There are three choices:

   - **My Computer.** Configures plotter driver settings to be managed by your computer.

   - **Network Plotter Server.** Configures plotter driver settings to be managed by the network plotter server.

- **System Printer.** Configures a Windows system driver that already resides in your computer's operating system. It enables you to set default print/plot parameters that apply only when plotting from AutoCAD.

4. Select the My Computer option button and then click Next. The wizard displays the Add Plotter – Plotter Model page. The Plotter Model page is where you select the printer/plotter manufacturer and model type.

5. From the Manufacturers list, select Xerox.

6. From the Models list, scroll down and select Wide Format Print System 510 Series, as shown in Figure 19.2, and then click Next.

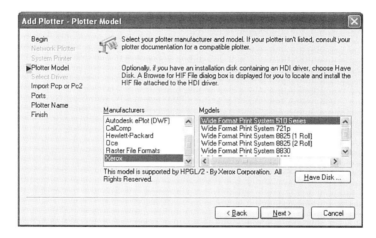

**Figure 19.2**    The Plotter Model page is where you select your plotter's manufacturer and model.

**I**NSIDER **N**OTE

Many companies use the Hewlett-Packard brand of plot devices, so much so that HP actively updates its drivers for the best possible performance. When you select a specific HP plotter, the wizard may issue a warning suggesting to install the HP DesignJet Windows system printer supplied on the AutoCAD 2005 installation CD. This Windows system printer driver is developed by Hewlett-Packard and is optimized for use with AutoCAD.

The wizard displays the Add Plotter – Import Pcp or Pc2 page. This page enables you to import certain PCP and Pc2 file information into the PC3 file.

**I**NSIDER  **N**OTE

AutoCAD enables PC3 files to import certain PCP and PC2 information such as pen optimization, plot to file configurations, paper size and orientation, resolution, device name, and plot destination.

7.  Click Next. The wizard displays the Add Plotter – Ports page. This page is where you indicate whether you want your plot to be sent to a port (serial, parallel, or network), to a file (PLT), or to AutoCAD's AutoSpool directory.

**I**NSIDER  **N**OTE

Some networks utilize AutoSpool for plotting. Basically, rather than AutoCAD sending the plot data to a port and queuing it, it creates a file of a certain naming convention in a certain network directory. This directory is essentially being watched by a supplemental program that then reroutes the plot file to the required device.

8.  Click the Plot to File option button and then click Next. The wizard displays the Add Plotter – Plotter Name page. This page is where you indicate the name to assign the PC3 file.

9.  In the Plotter Name text box, type **Xerox 510 - Plot to File**, as shown in Figure 19.3, and then click Next.

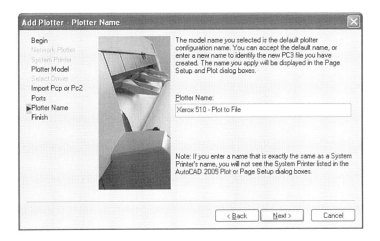

**Figure 19.3**   The Plotter Name page is where you assign a name to the PC3 file.

The wizard displays the Add Plotter – Finish page. This page notes that the PC3 file is installed and enables you to edit the PC3 file settings and to calibrate your file for the plotter.

**10.** Click Finish. The PC3 file is created and saved in the Plotters folder and is now available for use as a plotter configuration.

**I**NSIDER **TIP**

AutoCAD 2005 introduced a new Default Windows System Printer.pc3, which is a great new addition that points to your default Windows system printer.

Next, you create another PC3 file configured for a LaserJet printer.

**11.** If the Plotters folder is not visible, select Plotter Manager from the File pull-down menu. AutoCAD displays the Plotters folder.

**I**NSIDER **NOTE**

The Plotters folder display is independent from AutoCAD. Consequently, you can leave it open on your desktop, even after you end your AutoCAD session.

**12.** Double-click the Add-A-Plotter Wizard. The wizard displays the Add Plotter - Introduction page.

**I**NSIDER **TIP**

You can also open the Plotters folder and the Plot Styles folder by using the Windows Control Panel.

**13.** Click Next. The wizard displays the Add Plotter - Begin page.

**14.** Select the My Computer option button and then click Next. The wizard displays the Add Plotter – Plotter Model page.

**15.** From the Manufacturers list, select Hewlett-Packard.

**16.** From the Models list, select LaserJet 4MV, as shown in Figure 19.4.

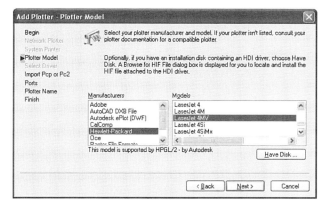

**Figure 19.4**   The Hewlett-Packard LaserJet 4MV is selected.

**I**NSIDER **N**OTE

> The Add Plotter – Plotter Model page enables you to install drivers not found in the
> list. If needed, click the Have Disk button, and the wizard prompts you to identify
> the driver to install.

17. Click Next. The wizard displays the Add Plotter – Import Pcp or Pc2 page.

18. Click Next. The wizard displays the Add Plotter – Ports page.

19. Click the Plot to File option button, then click Next. The wizard displays the
    Add Plotter – Plotter Name page.

20. In the Plotter Name text box, type **HP4MV - Plot to File**, as shown in Figure
    19.5, and then click Next. The wizard displays the Add Plotter – Finish page.

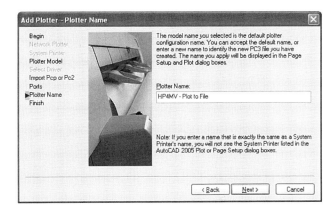

**Figure 19.5**   The new PC3 file is named HP4MV – Plot to File.

**21.** Click Finish to complete the plotter addition.

Leave AutoCAD open for Exercise 19.2.

The second PC3 file is created and saved in the Plotters folder and is now available for use as a plotter configuration.

**I**NSIDER **T**IP

> You can set a PC3 file as the default output device for new drawings and for Release 14 or earlier version drawings first opened in AutoCAD 2005. From the Options dialog box, in the Plot and Publish tab, select the desired PC3 file from the Use as Default Output Device list.

You can display the Plotters folder in any of the following four ways:

- From AutoCAD's File menu, select Plotter Manager.
- From AutoCAD's Options dialog box, in the Plotting tab, click the Add or Configure Plotters button.
- At AutoCAD's command line, type **PLOTTERMANAGER**.
- From the Windows Control Panel, double-click the Autodesk Plotter Manager.

Creating PC3 files is easy with the Add-A-Plotter Wizard. You can create as many PC3 files as you need and share them with others. Later in this chapter, you use the PC3 files you created and apply them to page setups.

Next, you use the Plotter Configuration Editor to modify one of the PC3 files.

## The Plotter Configuration Editor

You use PC3 files to predefine the print device to which your plot is sent. It is not necessary to create PC3 files using the Add-A-Plotter Wizard. For example, you can create a new PC3 file by copying an existing file and then modifying its settings. In this manner, you can quickly define a new PC3 file.

The Plotter Configuration Editor enables you to modify your PC3 files. It has options that enable you to provide a description of the PC3 file, switch the port to which drawings are plotted, and control device and document settings, such as the media source and custom paper sizes. By using the Plotter Configuration Editor, you can quickly edit your PC3 files, as shown in Exercise 19.2.

This exercise uses a PC3 file created in the previous exercise. Alternatively, you can copy the Xerox 510 - Plot to File.pc3 file from the accompanying CD to the Plotters folder. After copying the file, you might need to then clear the Read-only attribute.

**I**NSIDER  **N**OTE

> When copying PC3 Plotter files, be sure to copy any attached PMP files from the \Plotters\PMP Files directory. A PMP file is where AutoCAD stores any changes or additions to the paper sizes for a given plotter. A PMP file can be reattached to the PC3 files after they have been copied to the new location.

### Exercise 19.2   Editing AutoCAD Plotter Configuration (*PC3*) Files

1. Continuing from the previous exercise, using the File pull-down menu, select Plotter Manager. AutoCAD displays the Plotters folder.

2. Double-click the Xerox 510 - Plot to File.pc3 file. The Plotter Configuration Editor appears.

3. From the General tab, in the Description box, type **Configured for Plots on Vellum**, as shown in Figure 19.6.

**Figure 19.6**   The PC3 file's description is given.

The Ports tab enables you to select the port to send your plot. The Xerox 510 - Plot to File.pc3 file is currently set to Plot to File. This instructs AutoCAD to create a plot file of the drawing instead of sending the drawing to a network device or computer port.

4. Select the Device and Document Settings tab.

The Device and Document Settings tab enables you to define many of the PC3 file's settings. These include the paper source and size, custom properties settings for the device if available, and plotter calibration files. You can also define custom paper sizes, adjust the paper's printable area, and identify the type of media to use, such as opaque bond or high-gloss photo.

5. In the tree view window, under the Media branch, select Media Type. The Media Type list appears.

6. From the Media Type list, select Vellum, as shown in Figure 19.7.

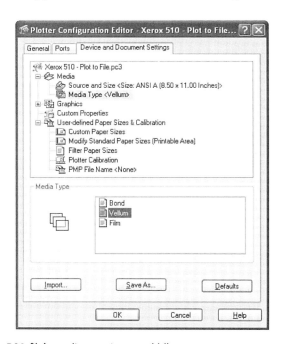

**Figure 19.7** The PC3 file's media type is set to Vellum.

7. Click OK. The Plotter Configuration Editor modifies the PC3 file and saves the changes.

8. Close the Plotters folder.

Leave AutoCAD open for the following exercise.

The Plotter Configuration Editor makes modifying PC3 files very easy. This is especially useful when you want to create several nearly identical PC3 files whose settings vary slightly. For example, by creating a single PC3 file using the Autodesk Plotter Manager and then copying the PC3 file, you can use the Plotter Configuration Editor to quickly make minor changes to the PC3 file copy. This saves time by duplicating all the settings from the original PC3 file and enables you to change the one or two settings necessary to customize the file.

In the next section, you continue the process of creating a plot by defining plot styles.

# Defining Plot Styles

When AutoCAD 2000 was introduced, it contained a new pen concept called plot styles, which enable you to control how objects in drawings appear when plotted. Through a plot style, you can easily vary the way objects look when plotted, no matter how they look in the drawing.

Plot styles enable you to control several object properties when you plot a drawing. You can control the object's color, linetype, and lineweight. You can also control values for dithering, gray scale, and screening. You can set pen assignments and define object fill styles. You can also control how line endpoints appear, as well as how they appear at joint points. With plot styles, you can create from a single drawing many plots that appear different without actually modifying any objects in the drawing.

If you have used prior releases of AutoCAD, you might be familiar with controlling linetypes and lineweights by assigning pen settings in the Print/Plot Configuration dialog box. The limitation with this approach is that you can only assign linetypes and lineweights globally, to all objects in the plotted drawing. With plot styles, however, the pen settings are assigned by layer or by object. This means you can control linetypes and lineweights by groups of layers or groups of objects. More importantly, you can also control other properties, such as object screening and fill styles, as noted earlier.

Plot styles are saved in a plot style table, and a plot style table can have as many individual plot styles as needed. To assign a plot style to a layer or object, you must attach a plot style table to the Model or Layout tab. Additionally, you can assign different plot style tables to the Model and Layout tabs. The capability to assign different plot styles to layers and objects and to then attach different plot style tables to the Model and Layout tabs provides you with a tremendous amount of flexibility on how your plotted drawings appear.

## The Plot Style Manager

The Plot Style Manager provides access to a location where you store your plot style tables. Similar in design to the Autodesk Plotter Manager, the Plot Style Manager contains the Add-A-Plot Style Table Wizard, which walks you through the process of creating plot style tables, as demonstrated in the following exercise.

### Exercise 19.3   Creating a Plot Style Table

1. Continuing from the previous exercise, using the File pull-down menu, select Plot Style Manager.

   AutoCAD displays the Plot Styles folder, similar to Figure 19.8.

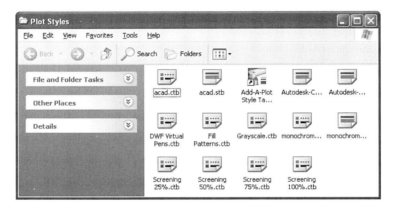

**Figure 19.8**   The Plot Styles folder stores color-dependent and named plot style tables and is where you access the Add-A-Plot Style Table Wizard.

2. Double-click the Add-A-Plot Style Table Wizard. The wizard displays the first page of the Add Plot Style Table dialog.

3. Click Next. The wizard displays the Add Plot Style Table - Begin page.

   The Begin page is where you indicate whether you want to create a plot style table from scratch or from an existing file. There are four choices:

   - **Start from scratch.** Creates a new plot style table.

   - **Use an existing plot style table.** Creates a new plot style table from an existing plot style table, duplicating all the defined plot styles.

   - **Use my R14 plotter configuration (CFG).** Creates a new plot style table by importing pen assignments stored in the acadr14.cfg file.

   - **Use a PCP or PC2 file.** Creates a new plot style table by importing pen assignments stored in a PCP or PC2 file.

4. Click the Start from scratch option button and then click Next. The wizard displays the Add Plot Style Table – Pick Plot Style Table page.

   The Plot Style Table page is where you select the type of plot style table to create: either color-dependent or named. These two types of plot style tables are discussed in the section following this exercise.

5. Click the Named Plot Style Table option button and then click Next. The wizard displays the Add Plot Style Table – File Name page. This page is where you indicate the name to assign the plot style table file.

6. In the File Name text box, type **Default**, as shown in Figure 19.9, and then click Next.

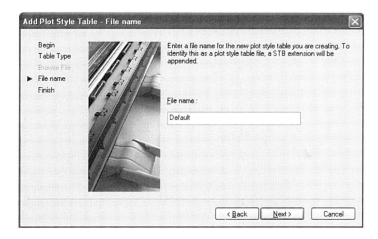

**Figure 19.9**    The File Name page is where you assign a name to the plot style table file.

   The wizard displays the Add Plot Style Table – Finish page. This page notes that the plot style table is created and enables you to edit the file settings.

7. Click Finish.

8. Close the Plot Styles folder.

   Leave AutoCAD open for the following exercise.

The plot style table is then saved in the Plot Styles folder. With the plot style table created, you can now define plot styles within the table and save it to a specific name. Then, the plot style table can be attached to the Model or Layout tab, and its plot styles can be assigned to layers or objects in the drawing.

Before you proceed to defining plot styles in the plot style table, it is important to understand the differences between color-dependent and named plot style tables. The next section reviews the differences between these two types of tables.

## Choosing the Plot Style Table Type

AutoCAD provides two types of plot style tables: color-dependent and named, and both types behave similarly. For example, both types enable you to control the appearance of objects when plotted, including controlling the object's color, linetype, and lineweight. Both types can be attached to the Model and Layout tabs, and both can assign plot styles by layer or by object. So, if both types are so similar, why have two?

Although similar, there are two important differences between the plot style table types. One difference is the number of plot styles each table type can hold. A color-dependent plot style table has a maximum of 255 color designations, which means you can define only 255 different "pens" per table. In contrast, a named plot style table can have an unlimited number of "pens" because the plot styles in each table are assigned unique names.

The other, perhaps more important, difference is how each type assigns plot styles to objects. As the name implies, color-dependent plot styles are based on the color of the object or the color of the layer on which the object resides. Consequently, you must be careful when selecting an object's color to ensure that it appears as desired when plotted.

If you have plotted drawings from prior releases of AutoCAD, then you are familiar with using colors to define an object's lineweight or linetype. When you plotted in prior releases of AutoCAD, you used color-dependent plot styles, whether you realized it or not.

Named plot styles, however, are not based on object color. Named plot styles assign properties by name. Therefore, you can assign objects any color and control properties such as lineweight and linetype, regardless of their color. This provides a new flexibility when creating objects because you no longer need to use colors to control an object's linetype or lineweight. With named plot styles, color is just another independent property like lineweight and linetype. A basic example of this use is a drawing in which all content is red in color, but because of name plot style usage, each object and layer could be plotted differently.

There is one very important feature to understand about color-dependent and named plot styles. A drawing can use only one type and cannot easily switch between the two types. When you create a drawing, the plot style table type is automatically assigned to the drawing and is somewhat permanent. Therefore, you must determine which type you will use before you create your drawing.

> **INSIDER NOTE**
>
> The default plot style table type is set in the Options dialog box's Plot and Publish tab by clicking the Plot Style Table Settings button. Within this dialog, choose either the Use Color Dependent Plot Styles option button or the Use Named Plot Styles option button. When changed, the new default plot style table type takes effect on new drawings or drawings created in R14 or earlier versions of AutoCAD that are opened.

> **INSIDER TIP**
>
> Although a drawing's plot style table type is permanently set to color-dependent or named, you can simulate changing a drawing from one type to the other. To do so, copy all the objects in the current drawing into a new, blank drawing whose plot style table is set to the type you want to use. A better option is to use the CONVERTPSTYLES command that comes with AutoCAD 2005. It enables you to switch a drawing between the two types of plot styles.

In the next section, you use the Plot Style Table Editor to add two plot styles to an existing plot style table.

## Adding Plot Styles to Plot Style Tables

After a named plot style table is created, you can add new plot styles, and you can edit or delete existing plot styles by using the Plot Style Table Editor. After you add plot styles to a plot style table, the table can be attached to the Model or Layout tab, and its plot styles can be assigned to layers or objects.

> **INSIDER NOTE**
>
> Plot styles can be added to or deleted from named plot style tables only. Color-dependent plot style tables have 255 predefined plot styles whose "names" are based on colors and whose values can only be edited.

The following exercise shows how to add and edit plot styles in a named plot style table. The exercise uses the named plot style table file created in the previous exercise. Alternatively, you can copy the Default.stb file from the accompanying CD to the \Plot Styles folder. After copying the file, you may need to clear the Read-only attribute.

### Exercise 19.4    Adding Plot Styles to a Named Plot Style Table

1. Continuing from the previous exercise, using the File menu, select Plot Style Manager. AutoCAD displays the `Plot Styles` folder.

2. Double-click the Default.stb file. The Plot Style Table Editor appears.

   The Plot Style Table Editor has three tabs. The General tab enables you to provide a description for the table. The Table View and Form View tabs display property information for the selected plot style. They display the same information but in different formats.

3. From the General tab, in the Description box, type **Plot styles configured for D Size sheets**, as shown in Figure 19.10.

**Figure 19.10**    The plot style table's description is set.

4. Select the Form View tab.

   The Form View tab displays the property information for the Normal plot style, as shown in Figure 19.11. Notice that only the Normal plot style is displayed in the Plot Styles list. The Normal plot style is automatically created as the default plot style in a table and cannot be edited or deleted.

**Figure 19.11**   Every named plot style table has the default Normal plot style.

5. To add a plot style to the table, click Add Style. The Add Plot Style dialog box appears.

6. In the Plot Style text box, type **Contours - Normal** and then click OK. The Contours - Normal plot style is created and added to the Plot Styles list.

   The Properties area displays the properties you can edit for the selected plot style. When you assign the Contours - Normal plot style to an object's plot style property, the Contours - Normal plot style's property values will override the object's properties when plotted.

   Next, you edit several properties of the Contours - Normal plot style.

7. From the Color list, select Black. The selected color is the color the plotter will use to draw the object.

**I**NSIDER **N**OTE

AutoCAD 2005 features a huge increase in plot color options over older versions. Previously, the 256-color limit meant that you had to accept less-than-stellar color matching. Now, through the True Color and Color Books tabs, accessed through the Select Color option, your color variation palette is in the millions.

8. In the Screening scroll box, type **30**.

    The screening value specifies a color intensity setting, which controls the amount of ink the plotter uses to draw a color. The lower the screening value, the less ink is used to draw the object, and the lighter—or less intense—the object appears when plotted. The range of screening values is 0 through 100. Selecting 100 displays the color at its full intensity.

9. From the Lineweight list, select 0.3500 mm.

10. In the Description text box, type **Objects are screened to 30%**, as shown in Figure 19.12. The new plot style is complete.

**Figure 19.12**    The Contours - Normal plot style is defined.

11. Select the Table View tab. Notice that the plot style properties are the same as those displayed in the Form View tab. They are simply arranged differently. Both forms enable you to control identical properties, and the form you use is up to you.

12. Click Add Style. A new plot style column is created and assigned the default name Style 2.

13. In the name row, type **Contours - Index** to rename the plot style.

**14.** Select the Description box in the Contours - Index column. The description box is highlighted.

**15.** In the Description box, type `Objects are screened to 70%`.

**16.** From the Color list, select Black.

**17.** In the Screening scroll box, type `70`.

**18.** From the Lineweight list, select 0.2000 mm, as shown in Figure 19.13. The new plot style is now complete.

**Figure 19.13**    The Contours - Index plot style is defined.

**19.** Click Add Style. A new plot style column is created and assigned the default name Style 3.

**20.** In the name row, type `Buildings` to rename the plot style.

**21.** Select the Description box in the Buildings column. The description box is highlighted.

**22.** In the description box, type `New fill style applied to objects`.

**23.** From the Color list, select Black.

**24.** From the Fill Style list, select Solid, as shown in Figure 19.14. The new plot style is complete.

**Figure 19.14**    The Buildings plot style is defined.

25. Select Save As to save the new plot styles to a new plot style table. The Save As dialog box appears.

26. Name the table **D Size Sheets** and then click Save. The plot style table is saved using the new name.

    Next, you complete the exercise by modifying the current plot style table and saving it as a new table.

27. From the General tab's Description box, change the description to Plot styles configured for A Size sheets.

28. From the Form View tab, select the Buildings plot style.

29. From the Fill Style list, select Horizontal Bars.

30. Click Save As to save the plot styles to a new plot style table.

31. Name the table **A Size Sheets** and then click Save. The plot style table is saved using the new name.

32. Click Save & Close to save the new plot style table and close the Plot Style Table Editor.

    Leave AutoCAD open for the following exercise.

The two new plot style tables are saved to the Plot Styles folder. The tables are now available for use with drawings and can be attached to the Model or Layout tab. Then their plot styles can be assigned to layers and objects.

**I**NSIDER **T**IP

> We started this exercise by creating a Default.stb plot style. This concept can be helpful if you have specific changes that are consistent to all your plot styles. You could make the changes once and then use that as a prototype for future tables.

As you just experienced, creating and editing plot styles is very easy. By using the various properties provided, you can alter the appearance of plotted objects, creating numerous versions of your drawing when plotted without actually changing any object properties in the drawing.

In the next section, you create page setups that use the plot style table you created.

# Creating Page Setups

Page setups were originally introduced in AutoCAD 2000, and they provide the ability to control certain paper and plotter configuration information. Page setups work similarly to PC2 files in that they enable you to store certain plot settings and restore them when needed. Plot settings such as plot device, paper size, scale factor, and plot orientation may be saved, as well as a plot style table that contains plot styles used in the current drawing.

What makes page setups especially powerful is the capability to assign different page setups to the Model and Layout tabs in your drawing. Consequently, a single drawing can have numerous page setups, with a particular page setup recalled and assigned to the current Model or Layout tab, which can then produce the desired results when plotted. Ultimately, this means you no longer have to worry about restoring prior plot and pen settings to duplicate a previous plot. All plot settings are saved with the drawing and are instantly recalled by selecting the desired Model or Layout tab and assigning the appropriate page setup. For more information on the versatility of page setups, refer to Chapter 18, "Paper Space Layouts."

The following exercise shows how to create page setups. This exercise uses the Plotter Configuration (PC3) files and named plot style tables created in previous exercises in this chapter. Alternatively, you can copy the following files from the accompanying CD to the designated folders:

- Xerox 510 - Plot to File.pc3 to the \Plotters folder
- HP4MV - Plot to File.pc3 to the \Plotters folder
- A Size Sheets.stb to the \Plot Styles folder
- D Size Sheets.stb to the \Plot Styles folder

After copying the files to their folders, if needed, be sure to right-click on each one and select Properties, then clear the Read-only attribute.

### Exercise 19.5    Creating Page Setups

1. Open the 19EX05.dwg drawing file, found on the accompanying CD. The drawing opens, displaying a D size sheet border and a single viewport that displays model space objects.

2. Right-click over the Layout1 tab and then select Page Setup Manager. The Page Setup Manager dialog box displays, as shown in Figure 19.15. Select the New button to create a new page setup for this drawing.

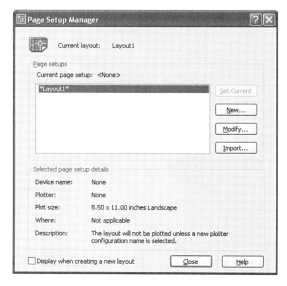

**Figure 19.15**    The Page Setup Manager provides a one-stop shop for managing your page setups.

**I**NSIDER **T**IP

You can see at the bottom of the Page Setup Manager that the selected layout is not configured. This helps you determine if any problems exist with existing layouts so that you can correct them.

3. On the New Page Setup dialog box, type **D Size Plots** as the name for the new page setup. The Start with option is *Layout1* because we have no other page setups. Click the OK button to continue. The Page Setup dialog box then appears.

4. From the Printer/plotter area of the dialog, use the list box and select Xerox 510 - Plot to File.pc3. This is the PC3 created in a previous exercise in this chapter, and it indicates the device to which AutoCAD plots.

5. In the Plot style table (pen assignments) area, use the list box and select D Size Sheets.stb. This is the plot style table that contains the plot styles created in a previous exercise in this chapter, and it controls the appearance of objects when plotted.

6. From Paper size area, select the ANSI expand D (34.00 x 22.00 Inches) paper size.

7. In the Drawing Orientation area, click the Landscape option button if needed. This instructs AutoCAD to use the long edge of the paper as the top of the page.

8. Notice that in the Plot area, the What to plot option is set to Layout. That is what we want, so leave it as is.

**I**NSIDER **N**OTE

Other Plot area options include Extents, Window, and View. Whichever you use will not include the layout's paper image and shadow, which appears in the background and is provided for appearance only.

**I**NSIDER **T**IP

Using the Layout option can greatly reduce page size errors but requires exacting paper sizes. If you use plot files extensively and create custom paper sizes, you should consider using custom paper sizes with margins set to 0. This exactly matches a Layout & Paper Size assignment. Depending on your plot device, normal paper size definitions contain margins and require adjusting of your title block size or using offset values to accomplish the same thing.

9. In the Plot Scale area, be sure the Scale is set to 1:1. Typically, in the case of layouts, the paper background represents your drawing's paper sheet and is set at the sheet's actual size. In this case, the sheet size is 34.00 x 22.00 inches. Therefore, the scale is set to 1:1—1 unit equals 1 inch.

10. In the Plot scale area, be sure the Scale lineweights check box is selected.

    Lineweights specify the line width of plotted objects and are normally plotted using the lineweight's value, regardless of the plot scale. This means that if an object's lineweight is set to 0.1000 inches, the object's lineweight is always plotted at 0.1000 inches. This is true even if the plot scale is set to 1:2. By selecting Scale Lineweights, if the drawings scale is set to a value other than 1:1, the lineweights are proportionally scaled based on the scale factor. In the case of a 1:2 plot scale, for example, if the lineweight is set to 0.1000 inches, AutoCAD rescales the plotted object's lineweight to 0.0500 inches.

**INSIDER NOTE**

The Scale lineweights option is only available in a paper space layout. This is another compelling reason to do all sheet plotting from paper space rather than model space.

Because we are using a layout to define our plot area, adjusting the Plot Offset is typically not required. If you were plotting by another means, you would also have the ability to center the output on the paper.

11. In the Plot Options area, be sure the Plot with plot styles check box is selected. This instructs AutoCAD to use the plot styles in the D Size Sheets.stb plot style table attached to the page setup. All your settings should now match Figure 19.16.

**INSIDER TIP**

The Display plot styles toggle at the upper right of the Page Setup dialog controls the display of the plot table effect within the layout. After you configure a page setup and make it current (and turn this toggle on), your layout appearance will then be as shown in a Plot preview.

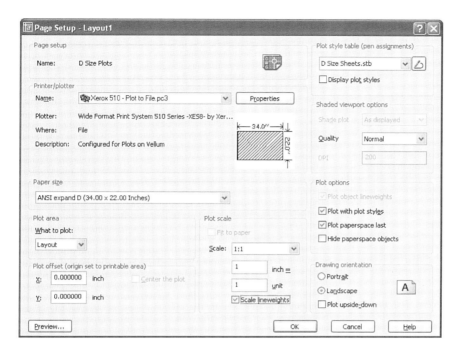

**Figure 19.16**    The current settings are stored in the D Size Plots page setup.

Next, you save the settings of the page setup.

12.  Click the OK button to dismiss the Page Setup dialog box.

    The current settings are saved as a named page setup called D Size Plots.
    The settings are saved in the current drawing and can be recalled anytime by
    selecting D Size Plots from the Page Setup name list.

**I**NSIDER **TIP**

You can insert named page setups from other drawings by clicking Import in the Page
Setup Manager dialog box. This is also available by typing **PSETUPIN** at the command
prompt.

Next, you define another page setup.

**13.** From the Page Setup Manager dialog box, click New, select the previous page setup, and then in the Name box, type **A Size Plots** and click OK.

**14.** In the Printer/plotter area, choose the HP4MV – Plot to File.pc3 file from the list. This is the second PC3 file created in a previous exercise in this chapter.

AutoCAD displays a warning that the paper size in the layout is not supported by the selected plot device and that the layout will use the paper size specified by the plot device.

**15.** Click OK to dismiss the warning message.

**16.** In the Plot style table (pen assignments) area, select A Size Sheets.stb.

This is the second plot style table that contains the plot styles created in a previous exercise in this chapter. The only difference between the two plot style tables is that the Buildings plot style in the A Size Sheets.stb displays fills using the Horizontal Bars fill style, whereas the Buildings plot style in the D Size Sheets.stb displays fills using the Solid fill style.

**17.** From the Paper Size area, notice that the ANSI A (8.50 x 11.00 inches) paper size is selected.

**18.** In the Plot area, select the Extents option from the list.

**19.** In the Plot Scale area, select Fit to paper.

**I** NSIDER  CAUTION

> You cannot utilize the Fit to paper option if the Layout option is selected in the Plot area. Therefore, if you need the Fit to paper option, you must select the Extents, View, or Window option.

**20.** In the Plot scale area, be sure the Scale lineweights check box is selected.

**21.** In the Plot Offset area, be sure the Center the plot check box is selected.

**22.** In the Plot options area, be sure the Plot with plot styles check box is selected. The page setup should now be as shown in Figure 19.17.

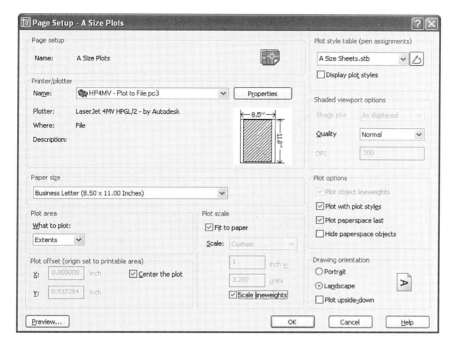

**Figure 19.17**   The current settings are stored in the A Size Plots page setup.

23. Click OK to accept the page setup changes. Double click on the A Size Plots page setup, and AutoCAD applies it to the current layout. Click Close to dismiss the Page Setup Manager dialog box.

Leave AutoCAD open for the following exercise.

AutoCAD saves the page setups to the current drawing, where they can be assigned to the Model or Layout tab or to any new Layout tabs. By right-clicking the Model or Layout tab and then selecting Page Setup Manager, you can assign the tab a given saved page setup or create a new page setup.

Recall that when you double-clicked on the A Size Plots page setup, it redefined the drawing's paper size and scale. This is one of the big benefits of page setups. Without the need to reset any scale values, you can instantly change the plot device, pen assignments, sheet size, and scale of the current tab by selecting the desired page setup.

Now that the plot style tables are assigned to the page setups, the only step remaining is to take advantage of the plot styles pen settings by assigning them to layers in the drawing, as demonstrated in the next exercise.

### Exercise 19.6    Creating Page Setups

1. Continue from the previous exercise. (It is required to complete the following exercise.)

2. Select the Layers icon on the Layers toolbar. AutoCAD displays the Layer Properties Manager.

3. Select the Normal plot style for the BUILDINGS layer. AutoCAD displays the Select Plot Style dialog box.

4. Select the Buildings plot style and then click OK. AutoCAD assigns the Buildings plot style to the BUILDINGS layer.

5. Select the Normal plot style for the CONTOURS-INDEX layer. AutoCAD displays the Select Plot Style dialog box.

6. Select the Contours - Index plot style and then click OK. AutoCAD assigns the Contours - Index plot style to the CONTOURS-INDEX layer.

7. Select the Normal plot style for the CONTOURS-NORMAL layer. AutoCAD displays the Select Plot Style dialog box.

8. Select the Contours - Normal plot style and then click OK. AutoCAD assigns the Contours - Normal plot style to the CONTOURS-NORMAL layer, as shown in Figure 19.18.

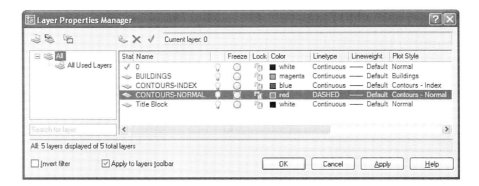

**Figure 19.18**    The layers have been assigned specific plot styles.

9. Click OK to close the dialog box and keep the assignments.

   With the plot styles now assigned to the appropriate layers, you can preview the effect a page setup will have on a plotted drawing.

**10.** From the File pull-down menu, select Plot Preview.

The plot preview of the A Size Plots page setup is shown in Figure 19.19. Notice that the contours (the jagged polylines) are displayed in shades of gray, and the fill style of the buildings is horizontal bars. In the drawing, the colors used to depict the polylines are red and blue, and the fill is solid and magenta. This demonstrates the effect plot styles have on the current Model or Layout tab.

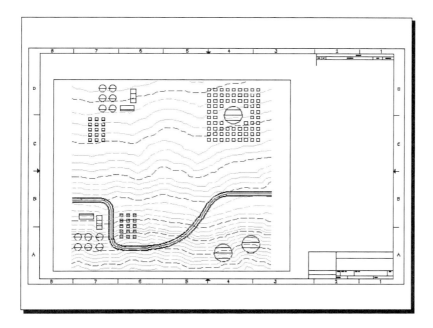

**Figure 19.19**    The effect of the A Size Plots page setup is previewed.

Next, you preview the D Size Plots page setup.

**11.** Right-click in the plot preview and then click Exit. AutoCAD closes the plot preview.

**12.** Right-click the Layout1 tab and then select Page Setup Manager. The Page Setup Manager dialog box appears.

**13.** Double-click on D Size Plots from the Page Setups list and then click Close. AutoCAD automatically switched to the D size sheet size and rescales the drawing to the correct size.

**14.** From the File pull-down menu, select Plot Preview. AutoCAD displays a preview of the drawing, as shown in Figure 19.20.

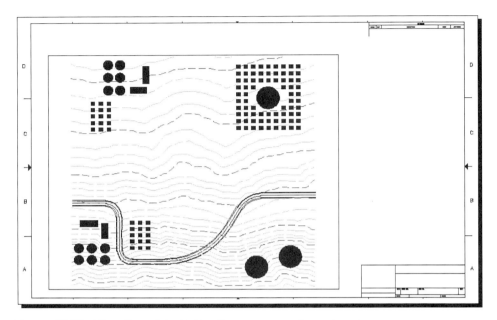

**Figure 19.20**    The effect of the D Size Plots page setup is previewed.

Notice that the contours are displayed in shades of gray, just as they were in the A Size Plots preview. However, the fill style of the buildings is now solid. This occurs because the two plot style tables use the same plot style names. In other words, when the A Size Plots page setup is selected, the A Size Sheets plot style table is used, whose Buildings plot style uses the Horizontal Bars fill style. In contrast, when the D Size Plots page setup is selected, the D Size Sheets plot style table is used, whose Buildings plot style uses the Solid fill style.

**15.** Exit the Plot Preview, and you can close the drawing.

By defining multiple page setups and assigning the desired PC3 files and plot style tables to each one, you can quickly switch a drawing's plot settings and achieve different output results when the drawing is plotted.

An easy way to access stored page setups is to create one drawing that contains all your standard page setup combinations and then save as pagesetups.dwg. Then create a custom toolbar button that executes the following string:

```
^C^C(command "psetupin" "pagesetups.dwg" "D Size Plots")
```

When you click the new toolbar button, AutoCAD automatically locates the drawing, enabling you to select the page setups you want to load from that drawing.

# Plotting from AutoCAD 2005

AutoCAD 2005 provides several methods for plotting drawings, with the most traditional method being the Plot dialog box. Additionally, there is also the capability to produce WYSIWYG digital plot files using a DWF plotter.

These methods of producing plotted drawings, combined with the page setup and plot style features, present a broad variety of options that ensures your ability to produce output that meets your needs.

## Features of the Plot Dialog Box

The totally new user interface for AutoCAD 2005 Plot dialog box is set to take advantage of the Plot Configuration (PC3) files, plot styles stored in plot style tables, and page setups as discussed previously in this chapter.

Additionally, there are several other improvements of which you should be aware.

When you execute the PLOT command, AutoCAD displays the Plot dialog box. Notice in Figure 19.21 that the Plot dialog box resembles the Page Setup dialog box (refer to Figure 19.16); the differences are highlighted.

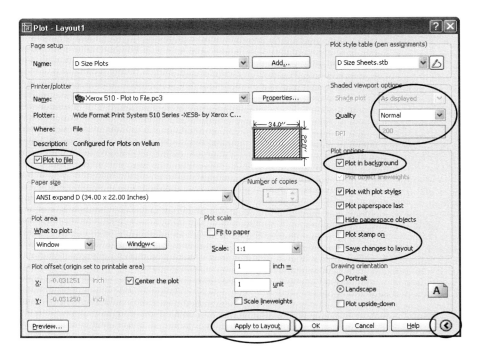

**Figure 19.21**    The Plot dialog box is similar to the Page Setup dialog box, with a few highlighted differences.

**I**NSIDER **T**IP

It is good practice to define the page setups required for a given layout when that layout is created. Doing this later can be time-consuming and potentially error-prone.

A useful feature of the Plot dialog is the Number of copies control. This feature enables you to define the number of copies AutoCAD should produce in the next plot sequence.

The Plot in Background option is new to AutoCAD 2005. When enabled, AutoCAD returns you to the drawing window while it works on making your plot and sending it. When complete, it can issue a balloon alert in the Communication Center at the far right of the Status bar. This functionality is also controlled by the BACKGROUNDPLOT system variable.

There are two Apply changes to layout options, but they are not exactly the same. The larger Apply to Layout button enables you to make adjustments to the plot settings and then apply them to the current layout prior to plotting. Then you can cancel the command and retain those adjustments.

The other option, Save changes to layout, enables you to save changes made to the plot settings to the layout after you dismiss the dialog and proceed with plotting. This is a subtle difference.

If you generate 3D models, you have options for how to show those models in a plot. Generally, the output is determined by the viewport itself, through properties you can utilize such as wireframe, hidden, rendered, or how the SHADEMODE command is configured, and the Plot dialog offers options for further refinement with regard to quality.

At the bottom right of the Plot dialog is a button that collapses the option column on the right, hiding it from view and from being changed. If you plot with page setups and have regular success, you might consider this option because it reduces the Plot dialog box size considerably.

**I**NSIDER TIP

> You can reduce the number of plot devices shown in the Printer/plotter list by eliminating the display of Windows system printers. By using the Options dialog box, Plot and Publish tab, you can uncheck the Hide system printers checkbox at the bottom of the General plot options area.

Another great feature is Plot Stamping. For years users have created various methods to stamp their plots with information to assist in tracking. AutoCAD 2005's Plot Stamp feature enables highly customized plot-time data to be added to your plots automatically (see Figure 19.22). After exploring the various options and turning the option on, the system is mostly "set-it-and-forget-it." Nothing is ever actually added to your drawing, just your plot output.

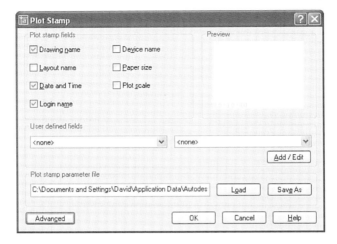

**Figure 19.22**    The Plot Stamp dialog controls what drawing information is added to your plots.

# Summary

In this chapter, you learned about configuring a plotter, the Autodesk Plotter Manager, and the Plotter Configuration Editor. You created plot styles and saved them in plot style tables and reviewed the difference between color-dependent and named plot style tables. You also learned how to create page setups and apply them and apply named plot style table to individual layers. Lastly, you learned about the new AutoCAD plotting features as part of the new plot interface.

# Part V

# Customizing and Advanced Concepts

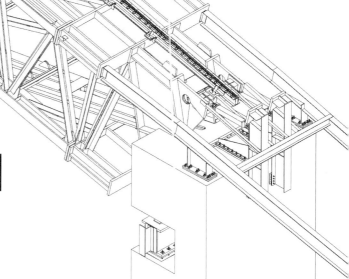

# Advanced Plotting

AutoCAD provides two useful features that enhance your plotting ability. The first is AutoCAD's DWF feature, which enables you to create plots that display within Internet browsers and specialty viewers. The other is AutoCAD 2005's Publish command, which enables you to identify a group of drawings and then plot them all automatically, using a single command. By using these two features, you can enhance your productivity either by sharing drawings over the Internet with clients and colleagues or by automatically plotting dozens or even hundreds of drawings with a single button click.

This chapter discusses the following subjects:

- Using DWF files
- DWF file formats and DWF-based PC3 files
- Understanding the PUBLISH command
- Creating Drawing Set Description (DSD) files
- Loading and changing a DSD file
- Plotting using the PUBLISH command
- Background plotting and plot logging

# Using *DWF* Files

AutoCAD 2005 extends the usefulness of the Internet by helping you meet certain plotting demands. Through AutoCAD's DWF plot files, you can create electronic plots of drawings and publish them to the web. With DWF files, you can distribute and share plots of your drawings over the Internet with anyone, anywhere in the world.

What makes DWF files so powerful is their capability to enable users to not only view drawings through their Internet browser, but also to create hardcopy plots of the drawings using their own plotter. This means that if you must deliver a set of hardcopy plots to your colleagues, you can do so by using DWF files to provide your drawings on the Internet and then instruct your colleagues to create hardcopy plots of your drawings at their location through their Internet browser.

**I**NSIDER **T**IP

> Aside from the high level of plot accuracy attained in using DWF files, you also do not need an AutoCAD license in order to view and plot the DWF file. Making a DWF viewer available to non-AutoCAD staff can save thousands on AutoCAD software used for viewing and plotting only.

In the following section, you learn about the relationship between the Plot command and AutoCAD's DWF file format.

## *DWF* File Formats

If you create a plot to DWF (Design Web Format), you are actually creating a vector-based plot file. The DWF format was first introduced with Release 13 and, in AutoCAD 2005, provides various DWF formats. All formats use the DWF6 ePlot plotter configuration driver. This one driver can be optimized for plotting purposes. It can provide less vector depth but higher-quality embedded raster image storage. It can provide less quality for online viewing purposes. It can provide a much higher vector depth for large zoom capability. And all these DWF file types require a compatible viewer, such as the Autodesk DWF Viewer, in order to see them.

**I**NSIDER **N**OTE

> The original version WHIP! plug-in cannot read the new DWF6 format.

To create a DWF file using the Plot command, you must use a DWF plot configuration file, as demonstrated in the following section.

# Creating a *DWF* Plot Configuration File

To create a DWF file, you must use a plot configuration (PC3) file configured for the DWF file format. AutoCAD 2005 provides a PC3 file that is already configured for the new DWF6 file format, and you can use this PC3 to create newer DWF files.

AutoCAD 2005 also enables you to set certain values in the PC3 file that affect the appearance of the final DWF file; you can set these values by configuring your own PC3 files. By creating your own PC3 files, you control how your DWF files appear when shared.

You create PC3 files by using the Add-A-Plotter Wizard, which is accessed from the Plotter Manager. The Add-A-Plotter Wizard steps you through the process of creating PC3 files. By using the Add-A-Plotter Wizard, you can easily create a PC3 file that is configured for your specific DWF file needs.

**I** NSIDER NOTE

> For detailed information on the Plotter Manager, see Chapter 19, "Productive Plotting."

In the following exercise, you use the Add-A-Plotter Wizard to create a PC3 file configured for the DWF6 file format.

### Exercise 20.1    Creating a *DWF*-Based Plot Configuration File

1. From within AutoCAD, use the File pull-down menu and select Plotter Manager.

   AutoCAD displays the Plotters folder, as shown in Figure 20.1. This folder is where AutoCAD stores PC3 files and where you access the Add-A-Plotter Wizard.

**Figure 20.1**   The Plotters folder stores PC3 files in the same directory in which you access the Add-A-Plotter Wizard.

2. Double-click the Add-A-Plotter Wizard. The Wizard displays the Add Plotter - Introduction page.

3. Click the Next button. The Wizard displays the Add Plotter - Begin page. You indicate the print device that you want to use on the Begin page.

4. Select the My Computer radio button and then click the Next button. The Wizard displays the Add Plotter - Plotter Model page.

   You select the printer/plotter manufacturer and model type on the Plotter Model page.

5. From the Manufacturers list, select Autodesk ePlot (DWF).

6. From the Models list, select DWF6 ePlot (shown in Figure 20.2) and then click the Next button.

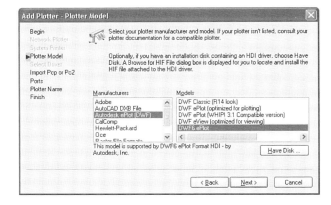

**Figure 20.2**   Select the Autodesk ePlot (DWF) plot device on the Plotter Model page.

The Wizard displays the Add Plotter - Import PCP or PC2 page. This page enables you to import certain PCP and PC2 file information into the PC3 file.

> ▌NSIDER NOTE _____
>
> AutoCAD enables PC3 files to import certain PCP and PC2 information, such as pen optimization, plot-to-file configurations, paper size and orientation, resolution, device name, and plot destination.

7. Click the Next button. The Wizard displays the Add Plotter - Ports page. This page is where you indicate that you want to plot to a file.

8. Be sure the Plot to File radio button is selected and then click the Next button. The Wizard displays the Add Plotter - Plotter Name page. This page is where you assign a descriptive name to the PC3 file. Because you are defining a PC3 file that stores layer information, you should choose an appropriate name.

9. In the Plotter Name text box, type **DWF6 ePlot (with Layers)**, as shown in Figure 20.3, and then click Next.

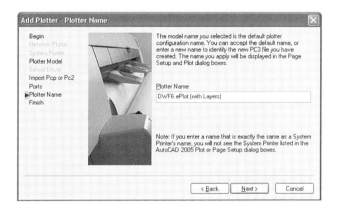

**Figure 20.3**   Assign a descriptive name to the PC3 file at the Plotter Name page.

The Wizard displays the Add Plotter - Finish page. This page notes that the PC3 file is installed, and it enables you to edit the PC3 file settings. You will edit the PC3 file settings in the following exercise.

10. Click the Finish button.

Leave AutoCAD open for the following exercise.

The PC3 file is created and saved in the Plotters folder and is now available for use as a plotter configuration.

Creating PC3 files is easy with the new Add-A-Plotter Wizard. Next, you use the Plotter Configuration Editor to edit the DWF6 ePlot (with Layers) PC3 file and modify a few of its settings.

### Exercise 20.2    Editing a *DWF*-Based Plot Configuration File

1. From the File pull-down menu, select Plotter Manager. AutoCAD displays the Plotters folder.

   This exercise uses a PC3 file created in the previous exercise. Alternatively, you can copy the DWF6 ePlot (with Layers).pc3 file from the accompanying CD to the Plotters folder. After copying the file, you might need to clear the Read-only attribute.

2. Double-click the DWF6 ePlot (with Layers).pc3 file. The Plotter Configuration Editor appears.

3. From the General tab, type **Configured to store layering information** in the Description box, as shown in Figure 20.4.

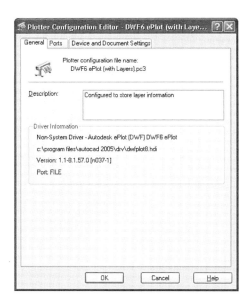

**Figure 20.4**    The PC3 file's description is set.

   The Ports tab enables you to select a port to which to send your plot. Because DWF files are by their very nature "files," the DWF6 ePlot (with Layers).pc3 file is set to Plot to File. Other plotter types can instruct AutoCAD to send the file to an actual plotter through a port.

4. Select the Device and Document Settings tab.

   The Device and Document Settings tab enables you to define many of the PC3 file's settings. These include the paper source and size and custom property settings for the device.

5. In the Tree View window, expand the Graphics branch and select the Vector Graphics options. The Resolution and Color Depths area displays in the lower half of the dialog box. Change the Color Depth to Monochrome.

**I**NSIDER **T**IP

Although you can control the color of your plots through the CTB or STB files, changing this option always forces your DWF files to be black and white—regardless of the Plot Style Table used.

6. Select the Merge Control option and then change the Merge control setting to Lines Merge, as shown in Figure 20.5.

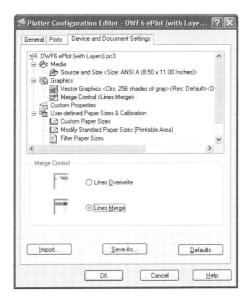

**Figure 20.5**   You can change how lines merge with solids from within the Plotter Configuration Editor.

**I**NSIDER **T**IP

Although you can control the draw order of objects in AutoCAD, changing this option always forces your screened solid areas to enable lines to show through and not be hidden by the solid.

7. In the tree view area, click the Custom Properties option followed by the Custom Properties button. The DWF6 ePlot Properties dialog box appears (see Figure 20.6).

**Figure 20.6** The DWF6 ePlot Properties dialog box enables you to control the appearance of plotted DWF files.

The DWF Properties dialog box enables you to control several values for the DWF file, including the file's resolution. By setting the file's resolution higher, you increase the precision at which the DWF file displays in an Internet browser. This means as you zoom in closer to small objects using your browser, those small objects display their true shape more accurately than they would at lower resolution settings. However, by setting the resolution higher, you also increase the DWF file's size, which makes for longer download times over the Internet. Autodesk suggests that a resolution setting of 400 is best for most DWF files.

An example of resolution can be seen in Figure 20.7. The sample image is of a 30"×42" plot with a 1/2" dia. section mark bubble. As you can see, the differences between the left, middle, and right are minimal at best. The top was created at 150 dpi, the middle at 400 dpi, and the bottom at 1200 dpi. The file sizes for the entire drawing were 60k, 64k, and 67k, respectively. Not something that most users need to worry about. Only extremely large and dense drawings would ever have a serious need to adjust from a 400 dpi setting.

**Figure 20.7**   Adjusting the DWF6 dpi settings can have a slightly perceivable difference.

The Background color setting controls the background color of the DWF file as it is viewed in an viewer. The White background is usually best if you are producing monochrome DWF files. If you are using color DWF files, you might consider switching to a black background to mimic the AutoCAD screen area.

  8. In the DWF6 ePlot Properties dialog box, at the bottom of the dialog, turn on the Include layer information and Save preview in DWF options.

     The first option specifies whether to include layer information in plotted DWF files. If this option is selected, any layers that are turned on and thawed when the DWF is created become available for manipulation in the plotted DWF file. This means layer visibility can be controlled through a DWF viewer. If this option is cleared, no layer information is available when the DWF file is viewed.

  9. Click the OK button. The modifications are saved, and the DWF6 ePlot Properties dialog box is closed.

 10. Click the OK button. The Plotter Configuration Editor modifies the DWF6 ePlot (with Layers).pc3 file and saves the changes.

     You can close the Plotters folder and AutoCAD if so desired.

The default DWF6 ePlot.pc3 that comes with AutoCAD is a great way to make color DWF files. But now after the previous exercise, you have another DWF plot configuration that you can use to make monochrome DWF files and to store layering information. With that option enabled, you can store various levels or stages of your drawing in one DWF file.

By using the Autodesk Plotter Manager and the Plotter Configuration Editor, you can easily create and edit PC3 files that are configured for DWF files. After a PC3 file is configured for DWF files, you can use it with AutoCAD's Plot command to create electronic plot files that you can share with others over the Internet and email.

Another feature of DWF files is the capability to store multiple sheets within one DWF file. This output type is a feature of the PUBLISH command, which is covered in the following section.

# Understanding the *PUBLISH* Command

AutoCAD is designed to enable you to plot one drawing at a time. Although plotting only one drawing at a time should satisfy most of your needs, there probably are occasions in which you want to plot multiple drawings by executing a single command. To meet the demands of plotting multiple drawings from a single command, AutoCAD provides a specially designed command called PUBLISH.

This section introduces the PUBLISH command and explains how to use its features.

## Reviewing the *PUBLISH* Command

The PUBLISH command is an application that runs within AutoCAD. By using the command, you can create a list of drawings to plot and then plot all the drawings by clicking a single button. After you click the Publish button, to begin plotting, the command fades to the background of AutoCAD, virtually loads each drawing, and then sends the drawing to the chosen plotter using an internal plot command.

The PUBLISH command enables you to easily create a list of drawings to plot. As you add a drawing to the list, you can select a different layout and named page setup file to use when plotting the drawing. After you finish creating the list of drawings, you can save the list as a Drawing Set Description (DSD) file that can be recalled later. By creating a DSD file, you can plot entire sets of drawings by simply loading the list into the PUBLISH command and running it.

The following section explains how to use the PUBLISH command to create a list of drawings to plot and how to save the list as a DSD file.

# Creating a Drawing Set Description File

The process of creating a DSD file is straightforward. From the PUBLISH command, create a list by selecting the drawings you want to plot. Then make any page setup changes you need. Next, save the list and its plot parameters as a DSD file. The saved DSD file can be recalled at any time to plot all the drawings in the file's list.

In the following exercise, you use the PUBLISH command to create and then save a DSD file. This exercise requires several AutoCAD drawings from the accompanying CD.

### Exercise 20.3   Creating and Saving a *DSD* File

1. Create a directory on your C:\ drive, IAC2005, and then copy all the drawings and SHX files from the Chapter 20 exercise files on the accompanying CD to this C:\IAC2005 location. You may need to change the read-only file attribute. In Windows Explorer, right-click on the copies, choose Properties, and clear the read-only option.

2. From within AutoCAD, start a new drawing and then select the File pull-down menu, followed by Publish. The PUBLISH command dialog box opens.

**I**NSIDER **N**OTE

> Don't confuse the PUBLISH command with the Publish to Web utility—they are not the same. The Publish to Web feature is used to create web pages that include your drawings as images and can provide references to your original drawings so they can be accessed through the web. You can learn more about this utility by accessing AutoCAD's online Help User's guide.

3. In the Publish dialog box, click the Add Sheets button, as shown in Figure 20.8.

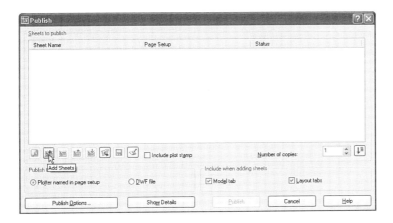

**Figure 20.8**   The Publish dialog and Add Sheets button location.

4.  From the Select Drawings dialog box, browse to the C:\IAC2005 directory and highlight all S-series drawings. Then click the Select button to dismiss the dialog.

    The 10 drawings appear in the list, but there are extraneous entries. When you use the PUBLISH command, you need to be somewhat specific about what you want to publish to avoid extra work getting your list correct. Notice in the list that you have a model entry for each drawing. Most users today do not plot model space, at least not for sheets anyway, and neither does this exercise.

5.  Right-click anywhere in the Sheets to publish area and, using the shortcut menu, select Remove All.

6.  In the Publish dialog box, toggle off the Model tab option in the Include when adding sheets area. This ensures that only paper space layout tabs are imported.

7.  Click the Add Sheets button again. Using the Select Drawings dialog box, again highlight all S-series drawings and then dismiss the dialog.

    Now, as shown in Figure 20.9, all the drawings and all their paper space layouts are listed in the Publish dialog box.

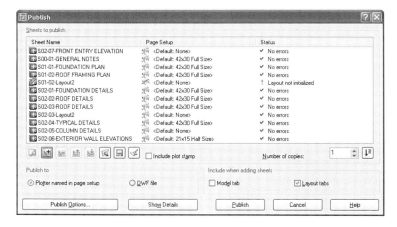

**Figure 20.9**    All 10 S-series sheet layouts are now listed in the Publish dialog box.

**I**NSIDER **T**IP

A convenient feature of the Publish dialog box is how it lists the actual layout name along with the drawing filename. This combination aids in knowing what your final output is set to be, as well what filename will be used if you save to a PLT or DWF file.

After you work with drawings for any amount of time, and as you share this work with others, you undoubtedly will encounter drawings with some warts—and our sample project is no exception. In order to have the best success when using the PUBLISH command, you need to free your drawing list of bad data.

Notice in the Sheet Name list that we have one different-looking icon. It has a red / on top of the typical icon. Now if you follow this row to the right, the page setup also has a red slash, and at the end in the Status column, we finally learn the cause: The layout has not been initialized.

When you create a new drawing without using a template, you are provided by default one model space and two layouts in paper space. However, unless you place more than one sheet in a drawing, this extra layout can be a problem.

**I**NSIDER **NOTE**

> It can be a real time-saver to develop templates that match your output needs. A template is just a drawing saved with a different file extension. But in this template, you can set up your layouts and page setups and place title blocks and viewports. So then when you start a new drawing and choose this template as a starting point, many of the repetitive tasks are already done, and you are ready to begin customizing the sheet.

8.  Click on the S01-02-Layout2 sheet and then press the Remove Sheets button (to the right of the Add Sheets) to delete it from the list.

    Looking through the list, you will see another stray layout on sheet S02-03-Layout2. Although this layout has no red /, meaning it has been initialized, we know we are not using unnamed layouts.

9.  Highlight the S02-03-Layout2 sheet and, using the right-click shortcut menu, select Remove.

**I**NSIDER **TIP**

> You can also press the Delete key on your keyboard to remove selected sheets from the list.

OK, now the list contains only the sheets we need, but we still have problems to resolve. First is sheet order. When you mass-select drawings in the Select Drawings dialog box, the order in which they come in is nearly always off—at least by one.

10. Click and hold to drag a sheet up or down the list. Do this as often as needed to get a list in numerical order. Continue to the next step when complete.

> **INSIDER TIP**
>
> The right-click shortcut menu also has options to move all selected sheets up or down one row at time.

11. When using the PUBLISH command, you can create two types of output: You can publish using the plotter defined in your page setups or to DWF. In the Publish to area, be sure the Plotter named in page setup is selected.

> **INSIDER NOTE**
>
> A given page setup can also be set to output to DWF, which then provides better control on plot styles and any specific DWF requirements. So even if you just want DWF files, you would be using a configured DWF-based PC3 rather than the simple DWF option.

Now that our list is in the correct order and we are set to the right form of output, we can save this sheet list to a Drawing Set Description file (DSD).

12. Click on the floppy disk icon, the Save Sheet List button. In the Save List As dialog box, type the name **Bank Project** and save it to local hard drive in the C:\IAC2005 directory made earlier.

13. After saving, you are returned to the Publish dialog; press the Cancel button to close the command.

    Leave AutoCAD open for the following exercise.

As this exercise has just shown, building your initial sheet list is easy. Getting the sheets into the proper order is also pain-free. Saving your sheet list for later use is as simple as any other file-saving procedure.

## Plotting with the *PUBLISH* Command

The next step is to load your DSD file and then make sure that every sheet plots properly. Notice in Figure 20.10 that the last three sheets have odd information in the Page Setup column. These sheets were probably made most recently and missed getting set up properly.

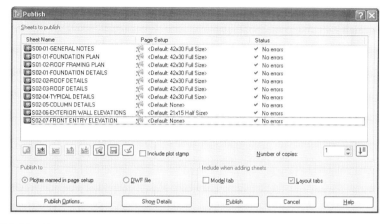

**Figure 20.10** The last three sheets are not set correctly for plotting.

### Exercise 20.4 Publishing and Background Plotting

1. Continuing from the previous exercise, use the File pull-down menu and select Publish. The dialog appears. It is clear of any sheet entries, so we need to load a DSD file.

2. Click the Load Sheet Set button, the folder icon, and browse to the C:\IAC2005 directory. Select the Bank Project.dsd file and click Load. If needed, you can load the matching DSD file from the accompanying CD.

   The Publish dialog box then is populated with the series of drawings from the previous exercise.

**I**NSIDER **N**OTE

A Drawing Set Description (DSD) file stores the entire drive and directory path to each drawing file. If you relocate the sheet drawings after creating the DSD, the PUBLISH command will be unable to locate the sheet drawings when you actually publish or plot them. It also will not report any errors that it was unable to find a DWG. Only after you publish will you know that a drawing was missing.

**I**NSIDER **T**IP

However easy it may be to re-create a sheet list, it is also easy to edit one with a text-based editor, such as Notepad. You can open the DSD file and revise the drawing locations as needed, save them, and then reuse them later. Be careful to not change anything else, though, because you might corrupt the file.

3. Select the S02-05-COLUMN DETAILS sheet and, using the Page Setup list box, change it from None to the 42×30-Full Size page setup. Now this drawing will plot properly.

   The next one has a page setup assigned, but it is the wrong one for our sheet set.

4. Select the S02-06-EXTERIOR WALL ELEVATIONS sheet and, using the list box, change to the 42×30-Full Size page setup. Evidently, the last time someone plotted this sheet, they used a half-size page setup and applied it to the layout. But now this drawing will plot properly.

   The last one is also incorrect for our needs.

5. Select the S02-07-FRONT ENTRY ELEVATION sheet and then use the Page Setup list box. All that is listed is None and Import, but we can still fix this for our needs.

6. Select the Import option, initiating the Import Page Setups for Publishing dialog box. As shown in Figure 20.11, browse to the C:\IAC2005 directory and select the pagesetups.dwg file. Click the Import button when you have it selected.

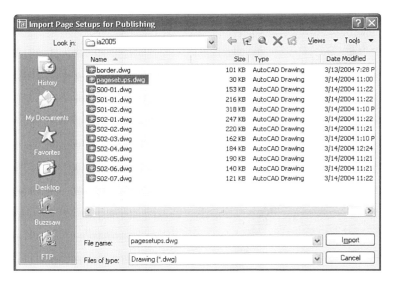

**Figure 20.11**    The Import Page Setups for Publishing dialog enables you to utilize saved page setups from external drawing files.

**I**NSIDER **T**IP

> Generally, it is better in real work conditions to stop at this point and actually correct the problem files by assigning or loading the right page setups. Realize that you can work around bad files by using the features of the PUBLISH command, but these "corrections" might have to be made again if you don't actively share or reuse a specific DSD file.

The page setup now assigned for the S02-07 sheet now reads Imported: 42×30 Full Size. This does actually change the sheet drawing to include this page setup. It will just use it when it goes to plot it.

**I**NSIDER **C**AUTION

> In order to publish properly, your system must have access to the same plotter names defined in the chosen page setups. The list of plot devices displayed in the Plotters folder indicates the plot devices that you have access to on your system.

Next to the Save Sheet List button is the control for utilizing Plot Stamps. You have both a Settings dialog for determining what the stamp should look like and a simple toggle to turn on and off the feature. Chapter 19 touched on this feature. We don't need it now, so leave it off.

There are number of other options available in the PUBLISH command, as shown in the following steps.

7. Click the Publish Options button at the bottom left.

   The vast majority of the Publish Options dialog box is related to DWF output. There are features for Single or Multi-sheet DWF files and an option for naming a multiple-sheet DWF file.

   Also, there is a feature for assigning a password and associated prompt to a DWF file, providing a reasonable level of security for enabling the viewing of a DWF file. The last item at the bottom of the Publish Options dialog box is the option to enable Layering information to be stored in a DWF file made with the PUBLISH command.

8. At the top of the Publish Options dialog box, change the Default output directory to be Publish locally in the C:\IAC2005 directory you made earlier, as shown in Figure 20.12.

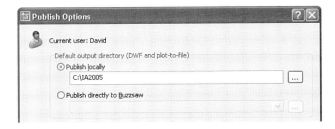

**Figure 20.12**    The Publish Options dialog provides a method to determine where to put your plot files.

This saves our plot files in the same location as the drawings, but that is not required; they can be saved to wherever they are needed.

When the directory has been edited to C:\IAC2005, press the OK button to close the dialog.

9. Click the Show Details button on the Publish dialog box. The dialog then expands downward to display information about the selected sheet, as shown in Figure 20.13. This can help identify problems that don't appear as a standard error. Click the Hide Details button to collapse it again.

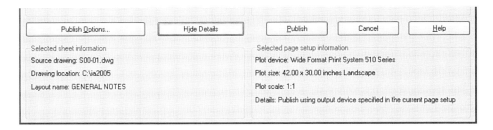

**Figure 20.13**    You can see basic information about a selected sheet in the Publish dialog box.

At this point, we are ready to publish. However, it is good practice to save your DSD file again. After clicking the Publish button, this list is erased. Typically, you will need it again.

10. Once again, click the Save Sheet List button and, in the Save List As dialog box, accept the default Bank Project.dsd entry. Click Save. Answer Yes at the prompt to replace the file.

Over at the right side of the Publish dialog box are two more options. One enables you to plot multiple times, and the other enables you to reverse the listed order of sheets. Both of these options only apply if you are not plotting to DWF files through the PUBLISH command.

**11.** Click the Publish button. The dialog dismisses, returning you to AutoCAD.

Plotting all those sheets was not that fast, really. What you are experiencing now is background plotting. The key to knowing this is the little plotter icon, as shown in Figure 20.14, over in the Communication Center of the AutoCAD application dialog box.

The icon in the Communication Center imitates a plotter while background plotting is occurring. If you try to plot or publish while it is still working, AutoCAD prompts you with a warning, as shown in Figure 20.15.

**Figure 20.14**
The Background Plotting activity icon shown in the AutoCAD Communication Center.

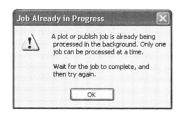

**Figure 20.15**   AutoCAD still takes time to plot your drawings. This is the alert displayed when you try to plot before it is ready.

The number of plots in this exercise is only 10, so unless your machine is very slow, the time to complete should be about 1 to 2 minutes. When AutoCAD finishes plotting, the Communication Center displays a notification balloon, as shown in Figure 20.16, informing you of that fact.

**Figure 20.16**   When AutoCAD finishes plotting, the Communication Center notifies you.

**I**NSIDER **NOTE**

It is possible to not display the balloon notifications. Just right-click over the tray icon and, using the shortcut menu, turn off the Enable Balloon Notification option. The feature can also be controlled by setting the system variable TRAYNOTIFY to 0 or 1.

12. After AutoCAD finishes plotting your sheets, you can use the balloon to view the plot details by clicking on the link provided. Click the detail link to display the Plot and Publish Details dialog box, as shown in Figure 20.17. If you had the balloon notification turned off or already closed it, you can also right-click over the tray icon and open the dialog from the shortcut menu.

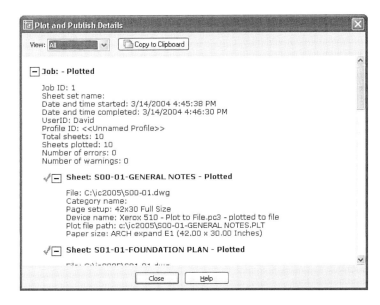

**Figure 20.17**    The Plot and Publish Details dialog enables you to see if your publish series was successful.

**I** NSIDER TIP

You can also use the VIEWPLOTDETAILS command to open the Plot and Publish Details dialog box.

Scroll through the information as desired. As you can tell, it is easy to find problems. If any exist, then go back and correct and rerun as needed.

You can close the dialog and AutoCAD if so desired.

The Publish command enables you to quickly edit an existing DSD file. You can modify plotting parameters to use for plotting each drawing in the list, and you can add drawings to or remove drawings from the list. You can modify the list of drawings to publish and the plotting parameters to use for each drawing.

## Plot Tracking

Depending on how long you have had AutoCAD 2005, you might be saving plot information and not even know it. If you go back to step 12 in the previous exercise, when you scrolled down, did you find entries for things plotted earlier in this AutoCAD session? The default AutoCAD setting for the tracking of plots is to have every plot tracked and to save this information in a single log file. Figure 20.18 shows this initial setting on the Plot and Publish tab on the Option dialog box.

**Figure 20.18**    The Options dialog has controls for background plotting and plot tracking.

As mentioned already, the log stores information for every plot or publish sequence within in a single AutoCAD session. However, you have the option to record only the most recent plot information. Either way, the log is refreshed the next time AutoCAD is opened.

As you begin to work with the AutoCAD 2005 PLOT and PUBLISH commands, you might find conditions where you want or don't want to store this information. If you don't need the logging at all, you can toggle the Automatically save plot and publish log option off. This halts repetitive tracking but does not stop the most immediate plot data from being viewable by using the Plot and Publishing Details feature.

## Background Plotting

When you plot in AutoCAD 2005, you can wait for the plot to finish as you normally would, or you can choose to enable to AutoCAD work tediously in the background. The previous exercises on the PUBLISH command showed that using background plotting can dramatically improve how fast you can get back to work.

AutoCAD 2005 empowers you with controlling the background plotting capability for both the PLOT and PUBLISH commands. Within the Options dialog box, as shown in Figure 20.18, in the Background processing options area is a toggle for both plotting and publishing. The background plotting setting is controllable at either command level.

# Summary

In this chapter, you learned about using AutoCAD's DWF plot feature to publish drawings on the Internet or in email. You also learned how to configure a DWF plot device and about creating a DWF plot file. Additionally, you experienced the PUBLISH command and learned how to create and edit DSD files. Finally, you learned about using DSD files to plot multiple drawings by picking a single button and how to review the Plot and Publish procedure. By using AutoCAD's DWF features and the AutoCAD PUBLISH command, you can enhance your ability to quickly create and share plots with colleagues and clients and ultimately increase your productivity.

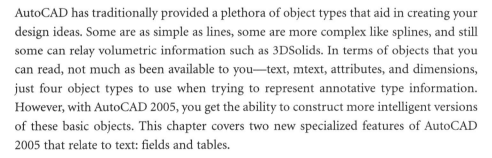

# Chapter 21

# Using Fields and Tables

AutoCAD has traditionally provided a plethora of object types that aid in creating your design ideas. Some are as simple as lines, some are more complex like splines, and still some can relay volumetric information such as 3DSolids. In terms of objects that you can read, not much as been available to you—text, mtext, attributes, and dimensions, just four object types to use when trying to represent annotative type information. However, with AutoCAD 2005, you get the ability to construct more intelligent versions of these basic objects. This chapter covers two new specialized features of AutoCAD 2005 that relate to text: fields and tables.

- Discovering fields
- Fields and text
- Fields and attributes
- Fields and tables
- Property-based fields
- Placeholder fields
- Tables and table styles
- Working with tables

These new features of AutoCAD 2005 revolutionize many areas of AutoCAD. In fact, you will probably be shocked at the many ways these two features can be used together.

# Understanding Fields

What is a *field*? That is tough to answer because fields can be described in many ways. A good description is what a field is not—it is not an object type. It is more like an internal AutoCAD call for data that is presented within a text-based object type. Many types of fields are available that can be applied in different formats for different needs. In fact, the Sheet Set Manager (discussed in Chapter 4, "Managing Your Drawing Projects") and the Table feature (discussed later in this chapter), both of which are new to AutoCAD 2005, would not be as nearly as valuable if not for the application of fields.

The term *field* may be very familiar to some because the concept is borrowed from Microsoft Word. AutoCAD fields are similar to the ones in Word because they provide a way to insert document or system information into a document (drawing) as text in AutoCAD. A field is made up of a field expression, which consists of escape characters, field codes, and format codes. This expression is not editable, but it can be created with normal text.

## Fields

Because no field object type exists, you don't really create a field so much as insert one within any text-based object. Text, mtext, dimension, and attribute values all can contain fields. We explore actually inserting fields in objects later in this chapter, but first, we need to look at the multitude of fields. As you can see in Figure 21.1, the Field dialog box is rather large but very basic in structure.

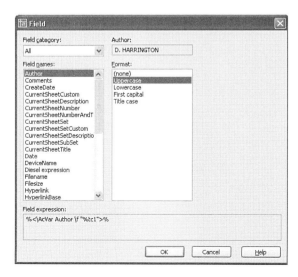

**Figure 21.1**    The Field dialog box is used when placing fields.

The basic premise of applying the desired field is to choose the proper Field category first. Then you choose the Field name needed. This is typically followed by the Format type, but sometimes you choose a Property and then a related Format. Tables 21.1 and 21.2 help explain the extensive list of fields available.

**Table 21.1   Field Categories and Names**

| Field Categories | Field Names |
| --- | --- |
| Date & Time | CreateDate, Date, PlotDate, SaveDate |
| Document | Author, Comments, Filename, Filesize, HyperlinkBase, Keywords, LastSavedBy, Subject, Title |
| Linked | Hyperlink |
| Objects | NamedObject, Object |
| Other | Diesel expression, SystemVariable |
| Plot | DeviceName, Login, PageSetupName, PaperSize, PlotDate, PlotOrientation, PlotScale, PlotStyleTable |
| SheetSet | CurrentSheetCustom, CurrentSheetDescription, CurrentSheetNumber, CurrentSheetNumberAndTitle, CurrentSheetSet, CurrentSheetSetCustom, CurrentSheetSetDescription, CurrentSheetSubSet, CurrentSheetTitle, SheetSet, SheetSetPlaceholder, SheetView |

**Table 21.2   Field Names and Formats**

| Field Names | Format or Type Example |
| --- | --- |
| *Date | M/d/yyyy or similar |
| Diesel expression | $(getvar, Dimscale), for example |
| NamedObject | Block, Dimstyle, Layer, Linetype, Tablestyle, Textstyle, View |
| Object | Any property value of any object you select |
| *Scale | (none), #:1, 1:#, #" = 1', #" = 1' - 0" |
| SystemVariable | All system variables (including Dimensioning) |
| Text (ex. Author) | No case, Uppercase, Lowercase, First capital, Title case |

*Indicates possible prefix such as Create or Plot.

Whereas some fields only permit the simplest of data types, others, such as a field displaying the properties of a dimension object, enable you to retrieve every possible value setting within a object. That is the beauty of this feature; nothing is left out because everything is available. If there is a property of your drawing that you can currently review or adjust, you can also "see" that data in the form of a field placed within a text-based object.

## Inserting Fields

As stated before, a field is not really an object type. The FIELD command, after you select a field from the dialog box, actually starts the MTEXT command with the field as the mtext content. In the following exercise, you experience firsthand the ease-of-use fields provide and discover the power they hold.

### Exercise 21.1   Using the *FIELD* Command

1. Open the 21EX01.dwg file from the accompanying CD. As shown in Figure 21.2, it contains a series of text organized as a small title block.

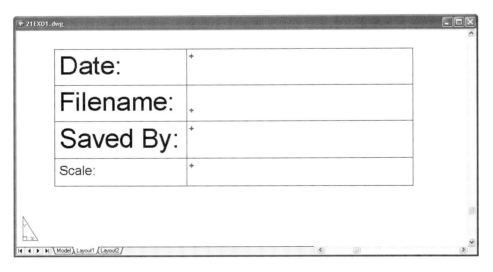

**Figure 21.2**   The exercise drawing used for implementing fields.

**I**NSIDER  **N**OTE

> You should set an active object snap mode for Node to help during this exercise.

2. Using the Insert pull-down menu, select Field, initiating the Field dialog box.

When you first open the Field dialog box, all the fields from all Categories are listed together. You can simply scroll through the Names list or change to a specific Category, thereby reducing the Names list to the only applicable items.

**3.** In the Field Names listing, select SaveDate. Then in the Examples list, choose MMMM d, YYYY. Click the OK button, closing the dialog.

You can create your own style using the Date format edit box.

**4.** The new field object is now attached to your cursor, awaiting placement. You might need to turn off Ortho mode to have unrestricted on-screen dragging of the mtext object. Using the Node osnap mode, place it on the point in the box adjacent to the Date: text.

You now have a field that always displays the date when the drawing is saved. This is the advantage of fields—the content can change as needed without user intervention.

The shaded background is on by default as a visual aid to show you where you have fields in an annotation type object. Without a background, fields are visually indistinguishable from plain text. You can turn this feature on and off by using the Display background of fields option found on the User Preferences tab of the Options dialog box. However, the field background does not plot, so leaving it on is usually good practice.

The system variable FIELDDISPLAY can also control the display of the shaded background.

**5.** Start the FIELD command again. This time, from the Field names list, pick Filename. Choose Uppercase in the Format list. This controls how your field text is capitalized.

6. On the right side of the Field dialog box, a few options became available for the Filename Field type. Select the Filename only option and make sure the Display file extension is active, as shown in Figure 21.3.

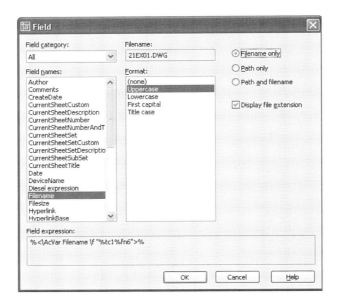

**Figure 21.3**   Controlling how the Filename field data is presented.

7. Click the OK button, closing the Field dialog. Notice that at the command prompt, AutoCAD provides prompts for what properties to use:

```
MTEXT Current text style:  "Arial"  Text height:  0.2500
Specify start point or [Height/Justify]:
```

It also prompts for a location but does enable changes for text height and justification. Type **J** and press Enter.

▌NSIDER TIP

You can use the right-click shortcut menu to answer option prompts for the FIELD command.

8. At the Enter justification [TL/TC/TR/ML/MC/MR/BL/BC/BR] <TL> prompt, choose **BL**. This sets the text justification to bottom left, which is better suited for the next point location. Again using a Node osnap mode, pick the point in the box adjacent to the Filename: text.

As shown in Figure 21.4, you now have text that displays the name of the file as opened from the CD-ROM.

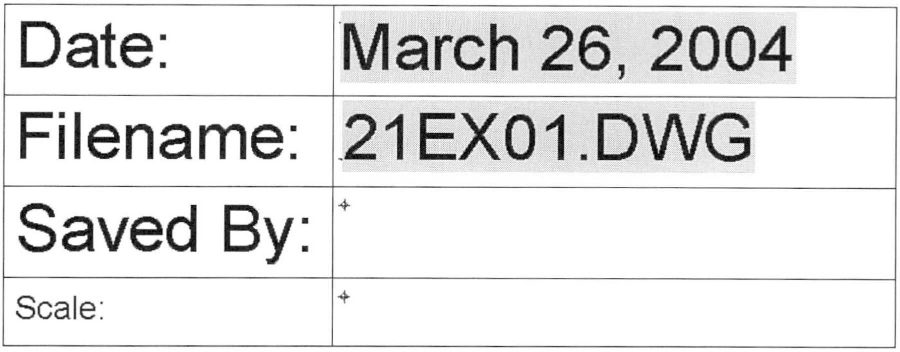

| Date: | March 26, 2004 |
|---|---|
| Filename: | 21EX01.DWG |
| Saved By: | ✦ |
| Scale: | ✦ |

**Figure 21.4** Displaying the current filename with a field.

9. Start the FIELD command again. Using the Field category drop-down list, choose the Document option. The Field names list then reduces to just those types.

10. Select from the Field names list the LastSavedBy option. In the Format list, choose the Title case format and click the OK button.

**INSIDER TIP**

Knowing what type of data you will be viewing ahead of time makes it easier to choose the proper case style. For example, names may be one or two words, so in order to have a name such as "Joe Cadman," you should choose the Title case format.

11. Again, use the Node osnap mode and pick the point to the right of the Saved By: text.

**INSIDER TIP**

The FIELD command always resets the default justification to top left. The previous Height value, however, is recalled.

12. Perform a ZOOM extents to see more of the exercise drawing. To the top of the block area is a typical viewport.

13. Restart the FIELD command once more. From the Category list, choose Objects and then pick Object in the Field name list.

14. Click the Select object button (next to the Object type edit box), which dismisses the Field dialog box, and pick the red viewport on the drawing. The Field dialog returns with many Property entries.

15. As shown in Figure 21.5, pick the Custom scale property type. In the additional Format box to the right, choose #" = 1'–0". Click the OK button.

**Figure 21.5**   Objects contain many properties that can be used with fields.

16. With the scale attached to the cursor, use the right-click shortcut menu and select the Height option. Change the height to 0.125 and press Enter.

17. Use the Node osnap mode and pick the point object in the box next to the Scale: text. You may need to ZOOM previous to clearly see it (see Figure 21.6).

    You now have some text that shows the scale of the viewport in this drawing, providing a great way to eliminate the coordination of detail scales in title lines/blocks and their corresponding viewports. You will see how powerful this is in a moment.

    Keep this drawing open for the following exercise.

| Date: | March 26, 2004 |
|---|---|
| Filename: | 21EX01.DWG |
| Saved By: | David |
| Scale: | 1' = 1'-0" |

**Figure 21.6**   All fields have now been placed.

With this single exercise, you should now have a good idea of the applications for creating dynamic text values within your drawings. As you have just witnessed, it is very easy to place fields into a drawing. The default object type of mtext allows for typical justification and sizing as needed. Fields are limited only by your imagination.

## Editing Fields

Inserting fields is easy, but how does the field redisplay changed data? There are several ways to update fields, and the majority of fields do so without your intervention. The following exercise explores the dynamic nature of fields.

### Exercise 21.2   Using Updateable Field Data

1. Continue from the previous exercise, or if needed, open 21EX02.dwg from the accompanying CD. It displays a title block with various mtext containing fields.

2. Zoom out a bit. Use the PROPERTIES command and select the viewport. Change the Standard scale property to 1/4"=1'-0". You can tell that the viewport updated because of the objects within it, but what about the field displaying the viewport's scale?

3. From the Tools pull-down menu, choose Update Fields and then select the 1' = 1'-0" text. Instantly, it is updated to read the new scale of the viewport, 1/4" = 1'-0", as shown in Figure 21.7.

**INSIDER TIP**

Executing a REGEN also suffices to update most fields.

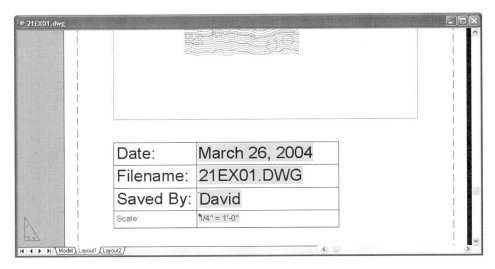

**Figure 21.7**    The new viewport scale is now reflected in the field embedded in the mtext object.

**INSIDER NOTE**

Unfortunately, fractional values in fields are not stackable.

4. Using the File pull-down menu, select Drawing Properties. Select the Statistics tab. Notice the Last saved by entry. Click OK to close the dialog. Save this to your local disk (anywhere will do) and name it **Fields.dwg**.

Immediately, your Filename field changes to match. Also, if you loaded 21EX02.dwg, the SaveDate field should change as well. The LastSavedBy field changes if you ran the DWGPROPS command at least once in the AutoCAD session (as we just did). Most fields update when certain events occur.

**Figure 21.8**   The Field Update Settings dialog box controls which events cause all fields to update their content.

The updating of fields is controlled through the Field Update Settings dialog box, as shown in Figure 21.8. The default setting has a number of instances that cause fields to update. Adjusting this will probably never be required, but if so, you can find this on the Options dialog under the User Preferences tab.

**I** NSIDER NOTE

Certain fields, such as Date, can only be updated through the UPDATEFIELD command.

Each field in this drawing is dynamic and connected to something else in the drawing. If the LastSavedBy field doesn't update to match your login name, it is because the command DWGPROPS wasn't used at least once during the AutoCAD session. The LastSavedBy field only displays the login name of the user. What if you want to support a full name instead? There is a field you can use.

5. Using the File pull-down menu, select Drawing Properties. In the Summary tab, as shown in Figure 21.9, fill in the Author edit box with **Joe  Cadman**. Click the OK button to close the DWGPROPS command dialog box.

6. Double-click the mtext that holds the LastSavedBy field. Because these objects are simple mtext, the Text Formatting dialog box appears.

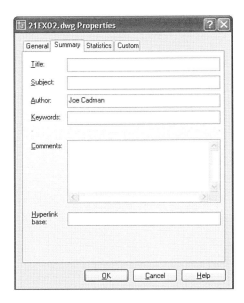

**Figure 21.9**    The Drawing Properties dialog box contains many user-modifiable values that can be used for fields.

7. Right-click on the field (see Figure 21.10) and select Edit Field. This opens the Field dialog box again, enabling you to adjust or replace the Field.

8. Select the Document Field Category, followed by Author. Notice in the Author box above the Format option that the current Drawing Property's Author value is displayed. Make sure that the Title case format is applied. Click OK to dismiss the Field dialog.

9. Instantly, the new field's data is reflected in Text Formatting dialog box. It now shows Joe Cadman because that is what was entered earlier. Click OK to dismiss the Text Formatting dialog.

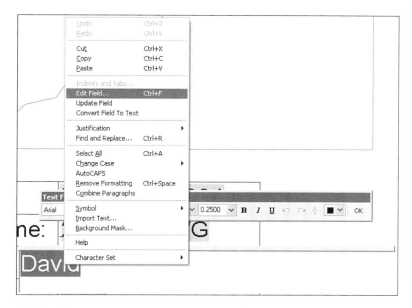

**Figure 21.10**   When you use the right-click shortcut menu on a field, the menu includes field-related options.

As shown in Figure 21.11, the drawing now contains correct field data. The Date should match your current date, the Filename should match the current drawing filename, the Saved By setting should be Joe Cadman as just entered, and Scale should match the viewport scale and display it in a style that is easily understood. You can close this drawing without saving.

| Date: | March 26, 2004 |
|---|---|
| Filename: | FIELD.DWG |
| Saved By: | Joe Cadman |
| Scale: | 1/4" = 1'-0" |

**Figure 21.11**   The completed title block with fields displaying current data.

There are many types of fields. Experimentation should be done to find values you find useful. As demonstrated in this exercise, when placed, they are easily updated and can be replaced if incorrect.

## Annotation Objects and Fields

This section examines the different text-based objects where fields can be applied. For most conditions, the default mtext object will do. But what if you need to meet other object type needs? Well, fields can be used in any text-based object except for tolerances.

### Exercise 21.3 Placing Field Code in Title Blocks

1. Open the 21EX03.dwg file from the accompanying CD. It contains a number of different objects to apply fields to.

   There is a title block, similar the one used in the previous exercise. We also have a POLYLINE rectangle with a couple of dimensions and a leader pointing to it. First, we need to utilize some attributes for our title block.

2. Open the Draw pull-down and select Block, Define Attributes. On the Attribute Definition dialog box, click the icon to the right of the Value edit box. This opens the Field dialog box.

3. Using the Field Category option, choose Document and then the Filename Field name. Make sure the format is Uppercase and the Filename only and Display file extension options are on. Click OK to close the dialog.

   Notice in the Value edit box the current filename is shown as well as a shaded background. This is your visual clue that this is a field.

4. Now use Figure 21.12 to fill in the rest of the Attribute Definition dialog options. Be sure to get the proper justification! When complete, press OK to close.

**Figure 21.12** Fill in the Attribute Definition dialog box to match.

5. AutoCAD places the attribute definition object on the cursor, enabling you to place it as needed. Use the Node osnap mode and pick the POINT object in the empty box.

The Attribute Definition for the Filename is there, but notice that it isn't shaded. That is because you are seeing not the field but rather the attribute tag. We need to build a block next.

6. Using the Draw pull-down menu, select Block, Make. This opens the Block Definition dialog box.

7. Type **TB** as the Name. For the Base point, click the button and the pick the center of the little circle at the upper-left corner.

8. Click the button to Select objects and then window-select all the objects for the title block content. Select all the boxes, text, and points (11 objects).

9. Make sure the Convert to block option is on and then press OK to close.

The Edit Attributes dialog box automatically appears, enabling you to adjust the content for the two attribute  definition objects contained in the TB block.

**I NSIDER NOTE**

You can learn about using blocks and attributes in Chapter 10, "Creating and Using Blocks."

Notice in Figure 21.13 how both content boxes are shaded—that is because now you are seeing the fields. Click OK to close the Edit Attributes dialog.

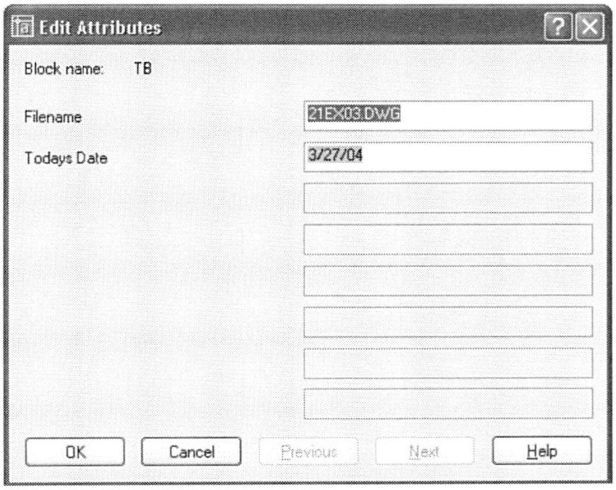

**Figure 21.13**   The shaded edit boxes indicate fields.

As shown in Figure 21.14, the block attributes display the fields, but it show the date when the Date field was originally applied.

**10.** Use the Tools pull-down menu and choose Update Fields. At the `Select objects` prompt, select the `TB` block and press Enter. Now the Date value should show today's date instead.

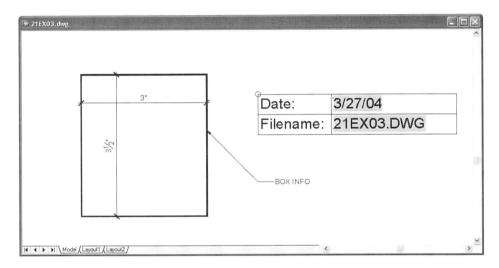

**Figure 21.14**    The drawing now has a block with attributes that contain fields.

---

**I**NSIDER **TIP**

You can overwrite or remove fields. Simply replace the shaded content with your own text. The field code is removed, leaving only your text. You can also convert the field to plain text using the right-click menu on the field.

---

Next, we work with some other forms of data and objects. We need the leader note to display dynamic information about the rectangle and dimensions.

**11.** Double-click on the `BOX INFO` mtext object. This opens the Text Formatting dialog box. Place the cursor after the word `INFO`, add a space, and then using the right-click shortcut menu, select Insert Field.

**12.** In the Field dialog box, choose the Objects Category. Select the Object Field, and then click the Select object button adjacent to the Object type display box. The Field dialog disappears for the moment.

**13.** Select the rectangle object. The Field dialog comes back. In the Property list, choose Area and then in the Format list, choose Decimal (as shown in Figure 21.15). Click OK to close the dialog.

**Figure 21.15** Specifying an object property field.

**14.** Type a space and **SQ.IN.** after the field. Then press Enter to start a new line.

**15.** In the Text Formatting dialog editor, use the right-click shortcut menu and choose Insert Field (or Ctrl+F). Click the Select object button and pick the 3" dimension object. As shown in Figure 21.16, scroll and select the Measurement property and the Decimal format. Press OK when ready.

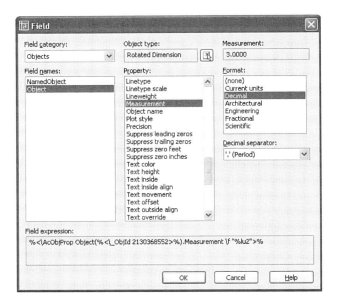

**Figure 21.16** Selecting the property Measurement from the dimension object.

As you can see, the mtext object now has a value representing the dimension calculated length. Even if you were to change the dimension text to something else, the field is reading the length of the dimension—not its text value. Click OK to close the Text Formatting dialog.

**INSIDER TIP**

You can also place fields in a dimension object, where they can reference other objects or properties in the drawing.

**INSIDER NOTE**

You cannot select property data from the current dimension object to which you are adding a field. A dimension's data cannot become circular in reference.

16. Use the Stretch command and stretch the left side of the rectangle 1.0 units to the left, changing the width to 4". Then perform a REGEN on the display.

As shown in Figure 21.17, the leader note now reflects that the rectangle area is equal to 14.0 square inches and that the width is 4.0 inches long.

You can close this drawing without saving.

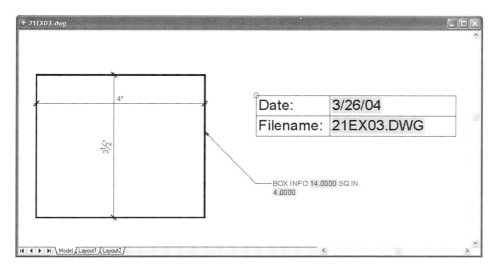

**Figure 21.17**   There are many possible uses for fields in just about every drawing.

Applications for fields are numerous. Odds are that your first uses will be to create your own Plot Stamp of sorts. Because they reside in the drawing and can be manipulated easily, drawing-based Plot Stamps are often preferred to the AutoCAD `Plot` command version.

**INSIDER NOTE**

> The last value displayed in a field is still displayed when the drawing is opened by earlier versions of AutoCAD. All field code is still attached after a round-trip through earlier releases.

It has not been covered yet, but you can also place fields in a simple text object. As you type in the content, just use the right-click shortcut menu to bring up the Field dialog box. From there, you can define a field as you normally would.

Additionally, if you need to remove a field but want the value to remain, use the right-click shortcut menu and select Convert Field To Text. The dynamic nature is removed, and it will read as last updated.

**INSIDER NOTE**

> Mtext objects can be exploded into separate text objects. Any fields within them are reduced to text. Other forms of annotated objects require the Convert Field To Text object to remove the field.

Fields have the potential to revolutionize how information is gathered in a drawing. Rather than having the user interpret information and type it as applicable, by using fields, the system can now do much of the work by itself. And because it reads information directly from other objects, it is 100% accurate and stays that way even as objects change. I encourage you to begin by placing fields into the title blocks of your sheets. Then, as you learn to appreciate that for its ease of use, try using them within the drawing area itself. The new Sheet Set Manager uses fields extensively, most of it automatically.

**I**NSIDER **N**OTE

> You can learn more about the new Sheet Set Manager feature in AutoCAD 2005 in Chapter 4, "Managing Your Drawing Projects."

# Understanding Tables

What is a *table*? It is a new AutoCAD entity type that is composed of lines and mtext objects arrayed in such a fashion as to resemble a schedule. This section discusses the methods used to develop how the table object should appear, how to place them into a drawing, and how to edit them afterwards.

Most industries and disciplines use some sort of tabular data. By using tables in AutoCAD 2005, you can bridge the gap between nice-looking schedules in Excel and the painful process normally used to get that same data into AutoCAD.

## Table Styles

As with other object types in AutoCAD, tables can be simple in appearance or highly intricate. By creating custom table styles, you can change the look that your table objects take when made. You can also apply a table style to an existing table just as you would with a text or dimension style.

Drafting standards are a necessary evil in most companies. Some argue that they curb creativity, but they also permit reliable results to be produced. Because schedules are typically graphically big and can contain hundreds of pieces of text, developing table styles that fit your needs is very important.

The following exercises walk you through the successful application of the new AutoCAD 2005 table objects.

### Exercise 21.4    Creating a Table Style

1. Open the 21EX04.dwg file from the accompanying CD. It has nothing but a few predefined text styles.

2. From the Format pull-down menu, choose Table Style. The Table Style dialog box appears, as shown in Figure 21.18.

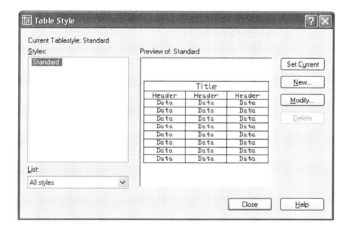

**Figure 21.18**    You utilize the Table Style dialog box to develop and modify your table styles.

3. Click the New button and then in the New Style Name edit box, type **Schedule-Small** (see Figure 21.19). Click Continue.

**Figure 21.19**    Create names for your styles that refer to how they will be applied.

In the New Table Style dialog box, you have a series of options and settings for each of three table structures: Data, Column Heads, and Title.

4. Using Figure 21.20, adjust the Text style to Arial, its Height to **0.10**, and its Text color to ByLayer. Also set the Alignment to be Middle Center. In the Border properties area, press the first button, All Borders, and then adjust the Grid Lineweight and Color to ByLayer as well. Lastly, change both Cell margin values to half the text height, **0.05**.

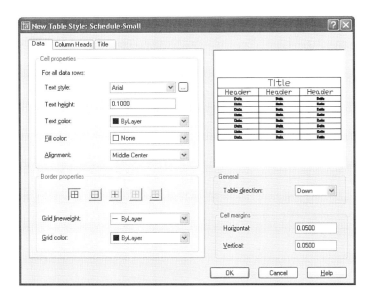

**Figure 21.20**   Adjusting the table style properties for the new Schedule-Small style.

5. Click the Column Heads tab. Select Arial-Bold for the Text style. For the Text height, type **3/16**. Notice as you click the Text color list that the height fraction is converted to 0.1875. Change the Text color to ByLayer. In the Border properties area, click the All Border button and then change the Lineweight and Color to ByLayer. Notice how the dialog assumes the text alignment and cell margins from the previous tab. Your dialog should match Figure 21.21.

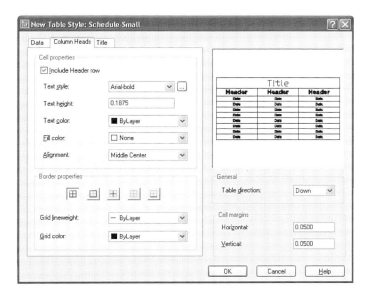

**Figure 21.21**   The Column Heads tab has similar settings to the Data tab.

6. Click the Title tab. On this final tab, change the Text style to Arial-Black. Leave the Height as 0.25 and change the Text color to ByLayer. Select the All Borders button followed by changing the Lineweight and Color to ByLayer. This tab should now look like Figure 21.22. Click OK when complete to dismiss.

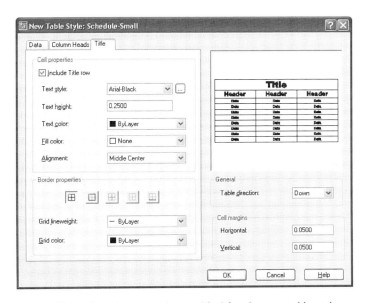

**Figure 21.22**   The Title tab is the last to be modified for the new table style.

7. Back in the Table Style dialog, the new Schedule-Small is listed but is not yet current. We don't need it to be current, so just click the Close button to dismiss it.

**INSIDER NOTE**

The best way to use this feature is to define your table styles in a template and then have them available in new drawings. If you do create one for use in the current drawing, be sure to make it current prior to leaving the Table Style dialog.

The new table style Schedule-Small is now defined within this drawing.

Leave this drawing open for the following exercise.

With that, you now have a table style that can be used in any other drawing. You can and should save your custom table styles in a single drawing as a template so they can be easily located and used.

## Creating a Table Object

After you have an acceptable table style you can use, you can begin to create the objects that use them. The following exercise goes through a typical use of this new object type.

### Exercise 21.5   Inserting a Table Object

1. Open 21EX05.dwg from the accompanying CD. It is a blank drawing with no user-defined styles at all. You also need to have open the previous exercise drawing. If needed, you can open 21EX04a.dwg from the CD, but make 21EX05 the active drawing.

2. Use the Tools pull-down menu and open DesignCenter. As shown in Figure 21.23, have the Open Drawings tab active so you can use DesignCenter to gain access to named objects (like table styles) stored in other drawings.

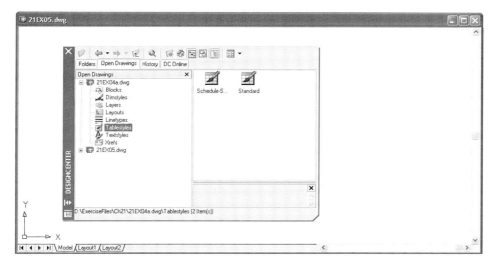

**Figure 21.23**   AutoCAD DesignCenter provides quick access to table styles.

3. While 21EX05 is the active drawing, double-click on the Schedule-Small table style stored in the other open drawing, 21EX04a, expanding the list by clicking the [(+)] button if need be. AutoCAD then loads the named object and provides the following report at the command line:

```
Table Style(s) added. Duplicate definitions will be ignored.
```

Somewhat generic, but it lets you know something was loaded. If you chose the correct style, everything is fine. You can close DesignCenter.

**INSIDER TIP**

When you loaded the Schedule-Small table style into the current drawing, AutoCAD also loaded the required text styles that are referenced in it. This is another great reason to use DesignCenter for loading table styles.

**INSIDER NOTE**

You can learn more about using AutoCAD DesignCenter in Chapter 12, "Applications for DesignCenter."

4. Using the Style toolbar, as shown in Figure 21.24, select the table style Schedule-Small, making it current.

5. Select the Draw pull-down menu and choose Table. The Insert Table dialog box then appears, as shown in Figure 21.25.

**Figure 21.24**
The Styles toolbar contains a drop-down list for activating a table style.

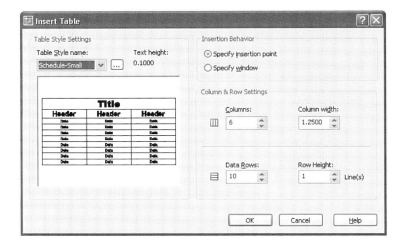

**Figure 21.25**    The Insert Table dialog box enables you to define the initial characteristics of the new table.

In the Insert Table dialog, you determine the basic structure of the new table object. In the left area, you assign the style to use. If needed, you can also click the [...] button and open the Table Style dialog box. This enables you to design a new style on-the-fly. In the right area of the dialog, you determine how to generate the table. If you choose Insertion point, AutoCAD uses the number of Columns and Column width to determine the overall width of the table. It also uses the number of rows multiplied by the text heights plus margins to determine the overall height of the table. If you choose the Window option, then all that applies is the column and row count; all cells are evenly divided up to create the various element dimensions. The Insertion point method is more accurate to use, as shown below.

6. Change the Column and Row values to 3 respectively. Change the Column width to 1.0. Leave the Row height at 1 line. Press the OK button to continue, closing the dialog.

7. The new table object then needs to be positioned on-screen; pick somewhere centered on your display. Immediately, the Text Formatting dialog box opens for the Title cell, as shown in Figure 21.26.

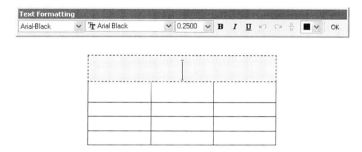

**Figure 21.26**   After the table object is placed, it uses the familiar Text Formatting dialog box to edit the various cell values.

8. For the Title, type in **Partition Types**.

When working with a table object, you can press the Tab key and move through all the cells one at a time, typing in the values as you go. Additionally, you can use the keyboard arrow keys to move about the table object, filling in as you go.

**I**NSIDER **TIP**

If you press Tab in the last cell of a table, a new row is started. You can then exit the editing mode, click in a cell on the new row, use the right-click shortcut menu, and select Delete rows.

**I**NSIDER **NOTE**

If you repeatedly press Enter, you move in a column direction, only editing the first column of cells, and eventually close the editing session after the bottom cell is reached.

**9.** Using Figure 21.27 as a reference, fill in all cell values using all the editing methods.

**I** NSIDER TIP

> If you accidentally exit the editing mode, just double-click within a cell to start editing that cell and then use the Tab or arrow keys as required.

You can close this drawing without saving.

| Partition Types | | |
|---|---|---|
| Mark | Width | Height |
| P-1 | 4" | 8'-0" |
| P-2 | 8" | 8'-0" |
| P-3 | 4" | 5'-0" |

**Figure 21.27** The new table object with all cells populated with information.

Inserting a new table object in AutoCAD 2005 is very simple, as you have just seen. After the individual styles have been designed, that effort pays dividends because the styles can be reused over and over. Cell content is primarily text, but you can also place fields if needed. As when working with normal mtext, use the right-click shortcut menu and choose Insert Field.

**I** NSIDER NOTE

> Remember that cell data is simply an mtext object placed into the cell box. All applicable mtext editing and style options apply and are available as needed.

You can insert a block or image into a cell as well. As shown in Figure 21.28, the Insert a Block in a Table Cell dialog box enables you to specify a block to place, how to align it, and if the block should be scaled to fit in the space. These blocks can be static and can have attribute values, and of course, the attributes can utilize fields. Your options and methods to apply are many indeed!

| Partition Types | | |
|:---:|:---:|:---:|
| **Mark** | **Width** | **Height** |
| P-1 | 4" | 8'-0" |
| P-2 | 8" | 8'-0" |
| P-3 | 4" | 5'-0" |

**Figure 21.28**    You can place blocks within table cells.

**INSIDER NOTE**

If you are comfortable with using Microsoft Excel, you can use it to fill in your cell data. Build a similar table structure in Excel, input all the data, and copy it to the clipboard. Then in AutoCAD, use the Edit pull-down menu and choose Paste Special. From there, select the AutoCAD entities format. AutoCAD recognizes this and creates a table object using the current table style, placing it on your cursor so it can be positioned properly.

## Modifying a Table

So far, you have learned how to create your own table styles and how to share a style with other drawings. You then experienced the ease with which a table can be populated. Lastly, you learned that additional data or object types can be placed within a cell itself.

Eventually, you also will need to adjust the structure of a table—not just change the content. AutoCAD 2005 has that covered as well. By using the right-click shortcut menu (see Figure 21.29) and choosing the appropriate action, you can adjust the table as required. The functions are similar to Microsoft Excel cell editing, so they are probably somewhat familiar.

You can also modify a table by using grips. Depending on the grip selected, you can adjust the structure of a table significantly. Use Figure 21.30 and Table 21.3 for descriptions.

**Figure 21.29**    The right-click shortcut menu contains various modes of cell editing.

**Figure 21.30**    Grip editing a table offers very flexible sizing controls.

**Table 21.3    Table Grip Editing**

| Grip Number | Editing Action |
| --- | --- |
| 1 | Table to be relocated |
| 2 | Resizing of adjacent column widths |
| 3 | Resizing of table width, columns equally spaced |
| 4 | Resizing of left column width |
| 5 | Resizing of right column width |
| 6 | Resizing of table height, row equally spaced |
| 7 | Resizing of width and height, equally spaced |

### Scaling a Table

If you remember, when you developed the table style, you assigned size properties for the text and cell sizes. This information is used when initially placing the table. But you do have the ability to scale a table object if needed. When you do, because this information is inherent in the style information, you can restore a given table to the original parameters by choosing the Remove All Property Overrides option (see Figure 21.31).

**Figure 21.31**  A few table commands are available on the right-click shortcut menu when the entire table is selected.

**I**NSIDER **N**OTE

The Remove All Property Overrides option does not restore specific font changes made in the Text Formatting dialog. Specifically, changes to Underlining, Bold, Italic, and Font File changes are not removed.

### Changing Table Styles

As expected, you can change the style used by an existing table object just by using the MATCHPROP command or the Properties palette dialog. By pasting one table style onto another, you can quickly change all your tables into a single uniform style.

### Exploding a Table

Although you lose all intelligence in the process, you can explode an object into its originating elements—mtext and lines. When in this format, you cannot return it to a table object.

## Exporting Table Content

You might have need on occasion to bring AutoCAD table data into another application such as Microsoft Excel. By selecting the entire table object and using the right-click shortcut menu, you gain access to the Export option.

The TABLEEXPORT command generates a comma-delimitated text file containing all text or field data from the table object. Of course, normal use of the Windows clipboard is always an option for direct information exchange from AutoCAD into Excel. Also on this shortcut menu is the added capability to adjust the rows and columns to be equally spaced.

# Summary

This chapter exposed you to two new major features of AutoCAD 2005. The ability to place fields into various objects is a very powerful tool. With it, you can do a better job of keeping up-to-date information in your drawings in a number of ways. The new table object in AutoCAD 2005 finally solves a big problem with AutoCAD—how to create tabular data that matches an AutoCAD graphics style. It also provides ease of use through standard mtext functionality as well as through tools for adjusting the cell structures as required. The combination of these two new features will surely impact your everyday AutoCAD use, raising your productivity to a higher level.

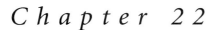

# Chapter 22

# Customizing Without Programming

One of AutoCAD's greatest assets is the level to which the program can be personalized. Users with little or no formal programming knowledge can learn to customize AutoCAD. Customizing to suit your needs is one of the best ways to increase your productivity. If you can make AutoCAD work in a manner that facilitates your needs, you will obviously be more productive. In fact, AutoCAD is so easy to customize that in a matter of hours, you can tailor this program to match your specific working process.

This chapter covers the following topics:

- Modifying an existing toolbar
- Creating your own toolbar
- Adding a customized tool to a toolbar
- Understanding the Tool Palettes interface
- Controlling and docking the Tool Palettes
- Hiding or making the Tool Palettes transparent
- Customizing the Tool Palettes

# Customizing AutoCAD Toolbars

Modifying AutoCAD's toolbars or creating a new toolbar of your own offers a way to increase your AutoCAD efficiency. Toolbars themselves can be great time-savers because they group a set of related tools into a single user interface that can be repositioned on-screen and even reshaped to fit a particular screen work area. Unlike pull-down menus, the individual icons on a toolbar are always visible (if the toolbar is on) and easy to select.

You can modify standard AutoCAD "factory" toolbars by rearranging the default tool layout, removing tools, or adding new tools. If you add new tools, they can either be from a library of standard AutoCAD tools and icons or "new" commands or macros that you have put together yourself. Figure 22.1 shows AutoCAD 2005 and the most-used command toolbars in their "out-of-the-box" default positions.

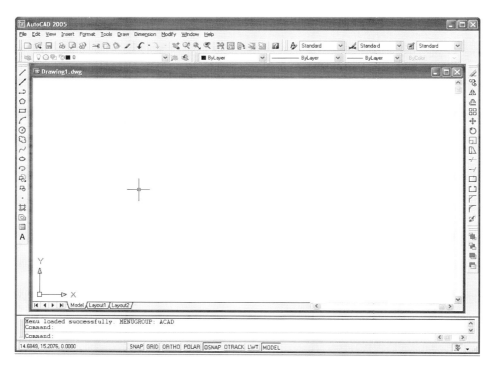

**Figure 22.1**    AutoCAD 2005's "out-of-the-box" toolbar arrangement.

# Modifying an Existing Toolbar

The capability to modify toolbars is one of AutoCAD's most powerful customization features. Adding a tool (icon) is easy to do. The following exercise demonstrates how to add a Donut tool and icon to the Draw toolbar.

**I**NSIDER **C**AUTION

> Modifying toolbars causes the modifications to be written to several AutoCAD menu files. It is advisable that you copy these files to a separate folder prior to modifying any toolbars, just in case. Assuming that your current menu is the ACAD menu, you need to copy the ACAD.MNU, ACAD.MNS, ACAD.MNC, and ACAD.MNR files found in the \Support folder. If you follow the steps in the next two exercises, the changes you make can be undone by replacing these files.

### Exercise 22.1    Adding an Icon to a Toolbar

1. In AutoCAD's default configuration, the Draw toolbar should be located on the left side of the screen (refer to Figure 22.1).

2. Right-click on any toolbar button to display the toolbar context menu (see Figure 22.2). The toolbar status menu displays all the available toolbars from the currently loaded menu and indicates their current On/Off status.

3. The toolbar Draw should be checked; if not, turn it on. Then select Customize at the bottom of the shortcut menu, displaying the Customize dialog box (see Figure 22.3).

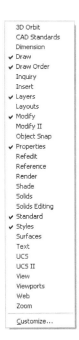

**Figure 22.2**
The right-click shortcut menu can display the toolbar status menu.

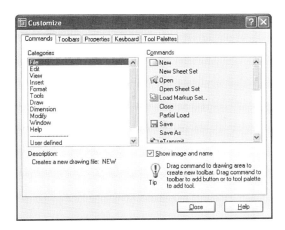

**Figure 22.3**   The Customize dialog box's Commands tab panel is displayed.

4. If not active already, click the Commands tab.

5. In the Categories section, select the Draw category in the list. The Draw command icons are then displayed, as shown in Figure 22.4.

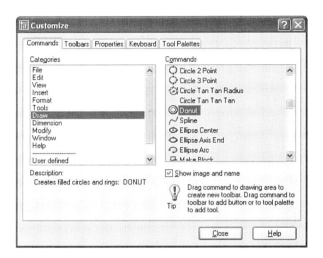

**Figure 22.4**    The Draw command icons available for placement on any toolbar.

6. Find and select the icon for Donut. A description for the tool appears in the Description area at the bottom of the dialog box (refer to Figure 22.4).

7. Drag the Donut icon onto the Draw toolbar under the Circle icon. This is where we want the button to appear. The new Donut button appears on the toolbar, as shown in Figure 22.5.

**Figure 22.5**
The modified Draw toolbar with the Donut tool added.

8. Click Close in the Customize dialog box. AutoCAD saves the new toolbar change to the MNS file and then recompiles the compressed MNC and MNR files.

Leave this drawing open for the following exercise.

**I**NSIDER **T**IP

To bypass the toolbar right-click shortcut menu and display the Customize dialog box focused on the Toolbar tab, using the View pull-down menu, select Customize, Toolbars.

You have just customized the standard Draw toolbar. On the assumption that you draw donuts frequently, this modification makes starting the command easier and quicker and therefore more time-efficient. The following exercise shows you how to remove icons from a toolbar.

**┃NSIDER NOTE**

> In some cases, it may not be a good idea to modify AutoCAD's standard toolbars, making them no longer "standard." Instead, consider making your own toolbar(s) with a collection of tools you find helpful for your work. Creating your own customized toolbars is covered later in this chapter.

### Exercise 22.2   Removing an Icon from a Toolbar

1. Using the View pull-down menu, select Customize, Toolbars, showing the Customize dialog box, as shown in Figure 22.6.

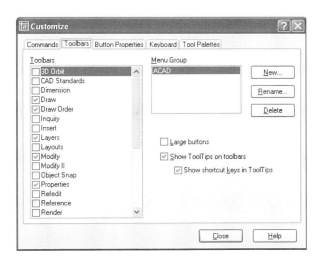

**Figure 22.6**   The Customize dialog box's Toolbars tab panel is displayed.

2. In the Customize dialog box, select the Commands tab to display the Categories and Commands listings, as shown previously in Figure 22.3.

**┃NSIDER TIP**

> It is not necessary to complete step 2 to remove an icon, but it's good practice to use because new icons come from this area.

3.  Click, hold, and drag the tool icon you want to remove from the appropriate toolbar (in this example, the Donut tool icon you added in the previous exercise) and release it on any portion of the drawing area. This removes the icon and its tool from the toolbar. At the confirmation prompt, click OK.

4.  Close the Customize dialog box. AutoCAD saves the new toolbar configuration to the MNS file and then recompiles the MNC and MNR files.

Leave this drawing open for the following exercise.

**I**NSIDER **T**IP

> Referring to the previous exercise, after you have activated the Customize dialog box (step 1), you can move or rearrange individual icons on any toolbar with a drag operation. Be careful not to drag (and release) an icon into the drawing area, or it will be deleted from the toolbar. After an icon is deleted, it must be added again manually; the UNDO command cannot restore your menu edits.

## Creating Your Own Toolbar

In AutoCAD, you not only can customize existing toolbars, but you also can create your own toolbars. You can place your new toolbars anywhere on the screen or even on other toolbars as a flyout. The following exercise demonstrates the steps used in the process of creating a customized toolbar.

**I**NSIDER **N**OTE

> With the introduction of AutoCAD 2005 comes a user-controlled menu named CUSTOM.MNU. By default, this menu is loaded and ready for use. It is intended to provide the user with a location to create and store pull-down menus and toolbars. The following exercises use the CUSTOM menu and not ACAD, although they are for the most part interchangeable.

### Exercise 22.3    Creating Customized Toolbars

1.  Verify that the CUSTOM menu is loaded and available. From the Tools pull-down, choose Customize, Menus. This opens the Menu Customization dialog box. Under the Menu Groups tab in the Menu Groups area should be listed both ACAD and CUSTOM. If so, click Close and skip to step 3.

2. If the menu is not loaded, type in the File Name edit box `CUSTOM.MNS` and then press Load.

   The CUSTOM menu loads, and AutoCAD creates related compiled menu files as needed. You can now close the Menu Customization dialog box.

3. Using the View pull-down menu, select Customize, Toolbars, showing the Customize dialog box. Be sure you are in the Toolbars tab panel.

4. Select the CUSTOM menu group and then click on the New button to display the New Toolbar dialog box (see Figure 22.7).

**Figure 22.7**   Naming the new toolbar for the CUSTOM menu group.

**I**NSIDER  NOTE

When you customize a menu, a warning dialog displays (see Figure 22.8), indicating that you are about to modify the ACAD menu file, even though it might not be the menu you are editing. Odds are this is something you want to do, regardless of the warning, but it is good to remember that your changes can make future migrations complicated. By all means, don't let future problems stop you—just be aware that they might happen.

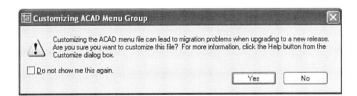

**Figure 22.8**   The warning dialog when you begin customizing ACAD menu toolbars. Make sure you understand this and then turn on the "Do not show me this again" option.

5. Type `Favorites` in the Toolbar Name field. This will be the name of your new toolbar.

**INSIDER NOTE**

When you right-click on a toolbar to open other toolbars, only toolbars that are in that menu are shown. For instance, if you right-click on the Favorites toolbar we just created, it's the only toolbar listed, and if you right-click on the Draw toolbar, Favorites is not listed. You can use the Toolbars tab in the Customize dialog box to find out which menu a toolbar is associated with.

6. Click OK to create the toolbar. A blank toolbar appears at the top of the screen, as shown in Figure 22.9.

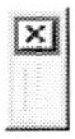

**Figure 22.9**
Relocate the blank new toolbar into the drawing area to make it easier to work with.

**INSIDER NOTE**

The new blank toolbar is small and appears somewhere on the AutoCAD screen. It is often difficult to see. To make working with the new toolbar easier, relocate it to the drawing area.

7. Select the Commands tab in the Customize dialog box.
8. Use the Categories list to select your specific categories and then find some commands that you would like to include in your new toolbar. Then you can drag the individual tools onto the new toolbar.

**INSIDER NOTE**

You can place icons from more than one category onto the new toolbar.

9. When you have placed all the tools that you want on the new toolbar, click Close in the Customize dialog box; this saves the new toolbar, and AutoCAD rewrites the appropriate menu files. When you return to the Customize dialog box, the new toolbar will appear as a choice on the Toolbars section. A possible configuration for the Favorites toolbar is shown in Figure 22.10.

**I**NSIDER **NOTE**

> Although many commands have associated icons, many don't. In those cases, when first placed, your icon will be blank. This can be remedied by using the Button Editor, enabling you to create or load a BMP from disk.

Leave AutoCAD open for the following exercise.

**Figure 22.10**
This is what my Favorites toolbar looked like after some quick customization.

**I**NSIDER **TIP**

> By carefully dragging an icon along the length of a new toolbar, you can cause a separator bar to be inserted next to the icon. A separator bar appears between the second and third tools in Figure 22.10.

The process of creating new toolbars is relatively easy and straightforward and requires no special knowledge of menu or AutoLISP programming techniques. By making one or more toolbars that contain the AutoCAD commands you use most often in your work, you can significantly increase your efficiency.

You can further customize your toolbar environment by creating flyout toolbars, such as the Zoom flyout toolbar found on the AutoCAD Standard Toolbar. You can also create tools and accompanying icons for commands or AutoLISP and DIESEL programming macros that you devise. See the online help documentation, "AutoCAD Customization Guide," for more detailed information about these more advanced customization topics.

# Creating Custom Tools

Creating new toolbars is an effective way to customize your AutoCAD interface and increase your efficiency. You might want to create a new toolbar that groups the tools you use most frequently. This not only saves time in selecting tools, but also saves space in the drawing area because you do not need to keep several toolbars open. After it is created, a new toolbar behaves as standard toolbars and can be hidden or displayed in either a docked or a floating position on the screen.

Toolbars that you create can have two general types of tools: existing icons, representing existing tools from other toolbars, and icons that you create, representing new macros that you define. Both types of tools can be placed on the same toolbar. In this respect, custom toolbars are similar to new or modified pull-down menus that you might add to AutoCAD's basic menu bar. Toolbars, however, have the added advantage of being able to be placed anywhere in the drawing area or even hidden from view.

**INSIDER NOTE**

You can also drag buttons from one toolbar to another while the Customize Toolbars dialog box is displayed. To copy buttons instead of moving them across toolbars, hold down Ctrl while you drag. However, always be cautious about which menu file you are editing.

## Adding a Customized Tool to a Toolbar

You can also add new tools composed of customized menu macros or AutoLISP routines to a new or existing toolbar. In the following exercise, you use a menu macro to create a new tool. You also design an associated icon and add the tool and the icon to the Favorites toolbar created in the previous exercise. Be sure the Favorites toolbar is displayed before beginning this exercise.

### Exercise 22.4   Adding a Customized Tool to a Toolbar

1. Using the View pull-down menu, select Customize, Toolbars, showing the Customize dialog box.

2. Click the Commands tab and then scroll down in the Categories list box. Select User Defined near the bottom of the list.

3. Referring to Figure 22.11, click and drag the User Defined button from the Commands area to the right end of the Favorites toolbar.

4. On the Favorites toolbar, right-click on the blank tool button to display the different button editing options and select Properties. This displays the Button Properties tab in the Customize dialog box, as shown in Figure 22.12.

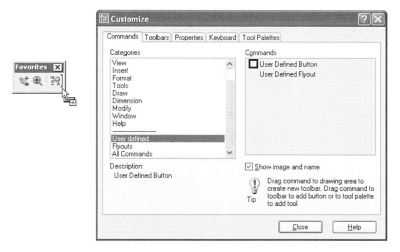

**Figure 22.11**   Adding a new blank tool button to a toolbar.

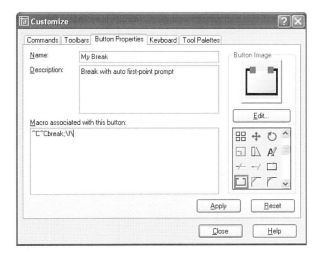

**Figure 22.12**   The Button Properties tab panel within the Customize dialog box with changes for the new button.

**I**NSIDER **N**OTE

> You must either right-click on a toolbar icon and select Properties or simply pick on that button to access its button properties. Only these processes will populate the Properties tab panel with controls.

5. In the Name input box of the Button Properties tab, type the name **My Break**, and in the Description input box, type **Break with auto first-point prompt**.

6. In the Macro input box of the Button Properties dialog box, type the following macro immediately following the ^C^C (refer to Figure 22.12):

   **break;\f\**

7. In the next steps, you define an icon for the My Break tool. In the Button Image area of the Button Properties tab, scroll down and select the icon for the BREAK command, as shown in Figure 22.12. It is typically found near the top third in the list, but it might not be in the exact location shown in the figure.

8. In the Button Image area of the Button Properties tab, choose Edit. AutoCAD displays the Button Editor dialog box with the BREAK command icon, as shown in Figure 22.13.

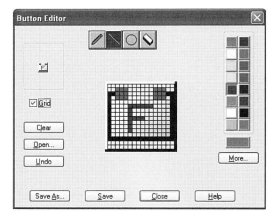

**Figure 22.13** The modified BREAK command icon.

9. In the Button Editor dialog box, choose Grid. AutoCAD displays a grid across the icon image.

**10.** Using the tools, palette, and preview window on the Button Editor dialog box and referring to Figure 22.13, draw a blue letter F in the icon editor.

**11.** When you are satisfied with your design, choose Save As in the Button Editor dialog box and save the icon to the name **MYBREAK-16.bmp** in your \Support directory. Note that the new icon design appears in the Button Icon area of the Button Properties dialog box. When ready, click Close to dismiss the Button Editor dialog.

**I**NSIDER  **N**OTE

> The MYBREAK-16.bmp file created in this exercise can be found on the accompanying CD.

**I**NSIDER  **T**IP

> Icons for use inside AutoCAD 2005 can be 16×16 pixels or 32×32 pixels in size. The default installation uses the 16×16 size, which enables more icons to be on-screen at once. It is good practice to create both sizes when customizing icons if you share your menus with others. A good way to keep track of both sizes is adding −16 or −32 to the end of your BMP filenames. That way, you can apply the proper icon when loading an image into the Button Editor dialog or when you do manual menu editing.

**12.** To save all of your changes in the Button Properties tab, choose Apply. Note that the new icon design appears in the My Break tool on the Favorites toolbar, as shown in Figure 22.14. Choose Close to dismiss the Customize dialog box.

You may now close AutoCAD if so desired.

**Figure 22.14**
The Favorites toolbar has a new addition.

**I**NSIDER  **T**IP

> If you use the Edit function of the Button Properties tab panel to design your own button icon and then use the Save button to assign a name to the icon's BMP file, AutoCAD assigns the resulting bitmap file a name and random number (for example, "RCDA2259.bmp") in the MNS file. You can replace the random bitmap filename with the name you saved by manually editing the icon's name in the toolbar definition of the MNS file. In the MNS file, search for the toolbar name and manually edit the BMP filename.

Of course, you can add other tools to your Favorites toolbar. Often, toolbars are more convenient to use than items placed on pull-down menus. In the next chapter, you create menu macros that you can duplicate onto new or existing toolbars. The menu macro code utilized in both menu pull-down items and individual tools on toolbars is exactly the same.

# Tool Palettes

Introduced originally in AutoCAD 2004, the on-screen Tool Palettes is an interesting user interface and customization alternative. The active display mechanism, after you get used to it, can be a great way to organize and retrieve tools. When you first installed and launched AutoCAD 2005, one of the things you probably did was turn off the on-screen dialogs that were "floating" above your drawing area. Learning to control these palettes enables you to take advantage of their usefulness.

## Controlling Palettes

The new Tool Palettes in AutoCAD 2005 is non-modal, which means it can appear outside of the AutoCAD application dialog. Unless you have a dual monitor station where you can put AutoCAD on one screen and the palettes on the other, generally this feature is of no use because you simply don't have the room to spare. But the various display controls offered can mitigate this problem.

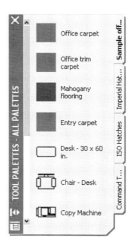

As shown in Figure 22.15, the default setting for the Tool Palettes is big—really big—and it eats up a lot of drawing area. The next sections cover some of the methods used to make palettes more display-friendly.

**Figure 22.15**
The Tool Palettes interface offer a very rich graphic-plus-named-icon user interface.

**I**NSIDER **T**IP

If the Tool Palettes interface is not active, you can turn it on (or off) with one of four methods. You can use the Tools pull-down menu, Tool Palettes Window option. You can also press the Ctrl button while pressing the number 3. There is also an icon on the Standard toolbar for Tool Palettes that, when clicked, turns it on or off. Lastly, you can type **TOOLPALETTES** at the command prompt. Generally, the Ctrl+3 option is the fastest.

## Docking Tool Palettes

When you locate the palette over to the edge of the screen, either right or left, the palette "stretches" to fill the vertical distance between the top and bottom of the AutoCAD window. The Tool Palettes interface loses its title bar and generally is able to show more of your palettes. As shown in Figure 22.16, the palette also pushes over any docked toolbars between it and the drawing area.

**Figure 22.16**   Docking the Tool Palettes moves it out of the way of the drawing area.

Now if you don't like losing two-plus inches of your screen, you can try resizing the palette to be thinner. In fact, the Tool Palettes interface can be resized to show only the icon; the icon names would not be visible at all. As you gain experience with your icons, where they are located and what they represent, this level of adjustment can help. Additionally, the icons have tool tips just like normal toolbar icons. As you hover above them, the name appears.

### Collapsing the Tool Palettes

It is possible to collapse the Tool Palettes down to just the vertical title bar. If you have found the palette helpful to your productivity but cumbersome because it can be so large, utilize the Auto-Hide option found on the right-click shortcut menu. When active, as you move away from the Tool Palettes, the content collapses away, leaving just the title bar. As shown in Figure 22.17, this dramatically reduces the screen area hidden by the palette.

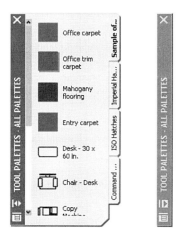

**Figure 22.17**   Auto-Hide makes the Tool Palettes interface much smaller when not in use. Note that when inactive, the title bar is lighter-toned.

**I**NSIDER **T**IP

> The non-docked Tool Palettes can be pinned to the edge of the display area outside of the toolbar icons. This positions it as close to the edge as possible without covering up the toolbars. This applies to the sides as well as top and bottom. Additionally, you can use the sides of the display area to flip the vertical title bar from side to side because in order to "stick" to a vertical edge, the vertical edge must be on the same side. You then can choose not to actually place it there and move it back into the drawing area.

## Making Tool Palettes Transparent

This naming convention is a bit inaccurate because "transparent" means "clear," which obviously would make the Tool Palettes interface very difficult to see. However, an option exists to control the *translucency* of the Tool palette. We know that the Tool Palette is big, and if you find the Auto-hide effect distracting, give the Transparency option a try. As shown in Figure 22.18, this "dims" the Tool Palettes components quite a bit, but they are still visible.

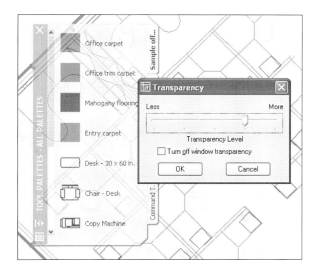

**Figure 22.18**    Adjusting the transparency of the Tool Palettes so that you can see through the dialog.

**I** NSIDER  TIP

> When this is applied, you can move objects, "rubber-band" selection windows, or drag new object profiles underneath this translucent palette, enabling you to still see where you are. You cannot, however, position your cursor under the palette. The assumption is that you always want the palette to be on top so that you can select something from it.

Now you should have a firm understanding of your display controls for Tool Palettes. Next up is to understand the various types of tool access and customization they provide.

## Customizing the Tool Palettes

The Tool Palettes interface gives you a location in which to contain your tools. It does not actually provide a way to create a tool on-the-fly—you must locate something and then drag it onto the Tool Palette. When it's there, though, you can organize the tools to better suit your needs.

The term "tool" might also be somewhat misleading because the "tools" that can be held on a palette can be any number of object types. On a given palette, you can place blocks, hatches, xrefs, images, gradients, menu macros, and toolbars. In the following section, you learn firsthand how to place tools, customize them as needed, and organize them for future access.

### Exercise 22.5    Tool Palettes and Blocks

1. If the Tool Palettes is not active, turn it on by clicking the Tool Palettes icon on the Standard toolbar.

2. Within an area of the palette with no content, use the right-click shortcut menu and select New Tool Palette (see Figure 22.19).

3. As shown in Figure 22.20, a small edit box appears in the palette area over the "New Tool Palette" you just created. In this edit box, type **Favorites**. If you happen to cancel or otherwise not provide a name, the tool palette will still exist, and it will be named New Tool Palette.

**Figure 22.19**
The Tool Palettes right-click shortcut menu contains various options for working with the Tool Palettes.

You now have a blank palette tab named Favorites. Time to add some tools! First, we'll implement block objects.

**Figure 22.20**
The rename window for editing the name of a tool palette.

4. Using the Standard toolbar (or Ctrl+2), open AutoCAD DesignCenter and browse to your AutoCAD installation directory. Double-click the \Sample directory and then double-click on the 8th Floor Furniture drawing.

5. Now select Blocks from the named objects within this drawing. The blocks contained in this drawing appear in the right preview area.

6. Click on and drag the Conference Seat from the DesignCenter window onto the Favorites tool palette. Your cursor will appear with a small + sign, indicating you are adding or copying that which you are dragging.

7. You now have a Tool Palettes-based tool to insert a chair block. Now use the right-click shortcut menu above the Conference Seat icon in the palette and choose Properties.

Using the Tool Properties dialog box, you can adjust various settings for blocks you place on a tool palette. Referring to Figure 22.21, you can preset the scale, rotation, and other values that a block uses when placed from a Tool palette into a drawing.

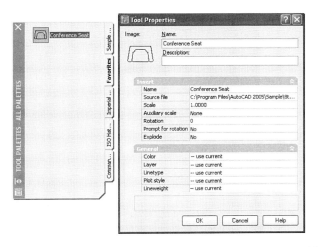

**Figure 22.21**   The Tool Properties dialog provides a means to control how blocks are implemented when dragged into the drawing.

**I**NSIDER  **N**OTE

> Notice in Figure 22.21 the Source file entry. The chair block does not actually exist in the current drawing, nor does it exist in some file controlled by AutoCAD such as a menu. The block still resides in the drawing it was *dragged* from. Using this approach greatly eases maintaining a library of symbols for your projects.

8. Press Close to dismiss the Tool Properties dialog box. Now that was easy to do, so let's add another tool.

9. Again, using AutoCAD DesignCenter, locate the Xref named object type from the 8th Floor Furniture drawing. Then in the preview area, click on and drag the xref drawing 8th floor plan onto the Favorites Tool palette.

**I**NSIDER  **N**OTE

> You can set an Auxiliary scale value for both blocks and xrefs, which provides a secondary scale factor matching either your current plot scale or your current DIM-SCALE setting. This is very handy for adjusting the scale of blocks to match a specific drawing scale, such as 3/4"=1'-0". A setting of 16.0 for the Auxiliary scale would bring in 1:1 blocks at the appropriate scale to be plotted.

Similarly to a block, you can adjust various settings for xrefs you place on a palette. Referring to Figure 22.22, you can even determine what attachment type an xref should use. Whereas a block tool is an object contained in another drawing, an xref tool is a direct link to another drawing.

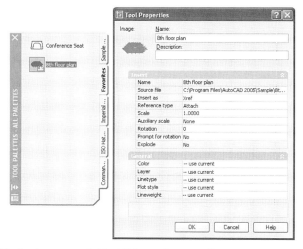

**Figure 22.22**    Xrefs placement via Tool Palettes is very efficient.

**10.** Close AutoCAD DesignCenter.

Leave this drawing open for the following exercise.

As you have seen in this exercise, the process of creating palettes is very simple, and adding content to a palette is typically just a process of dragging what you want onto the palette. We touched on placing blocks and xrefs, but there are a number of other object types to explore. The default palettes in AutoCAD 2005 contain examples of each type permitted except xref, so I would encourage you to test those as you build your palettes. Meanwhile, we continue to investigate some of the more interesting forms you can utilize.

### Exercise 22.6   Managing Your Tool Palettes

**1.** If the Tool Palettes interface is not active, turn it on by clicking the Tool Palettes icon on the Standard toolbar.

In the previous exercise, you created a new tool palette named Favorites. We continue to "play" with this palette in this exercise.

**2.** In an area of the palette with no content, use the right-click shortcut menu and select View Options. The View Options dialog appears, as shown in Figure 22.23.

As mentioned previously, palettes are big, but you can adjust the size of the icons and their names to gain more space. If your icons are very graphic by nature, you can choose to not display the titles, thus gaining dialog space.

**3.** Click the Icon Only toggle. We only want this change on this palette, so make sure the Apply to option is set to the Current Tool Palette. Then click OK.

**Figure 22.23**
You can control the size of tool icons as well the titles shown.

The icons then lose their titles, so you must rely instead on their visual appearance to determine what they are. Depending on your computer display resolution, you can also try increasing the image size on the View Options dialog if you have trouble recognizing your icons.

**4.** Click the Imperial Hatches tab on the Tool Palettes interface to display one of the default palettes in AutoCAD. Locate any hatch you prefer and then using the right-click shortcut menu, select Copy.

**5.** Click back onto the Favorites tab on the Tool Palettes. Right-click in a blank area and choose Paste. The hatch tool from the previous tab is copied to this palette.

6. Now right-click on the new Hatch tool and select Properties, displaying the Tool Properties dialog box, as shown in Figure 22.24.

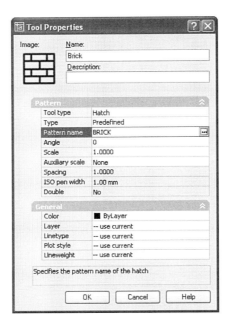

**Figure 22.24**    Hatch tools can have values preset, such as scale and angle, as well as what layer they should be created on.

A great feature of palette tools is their capability to contain layer information. If you utilize a standard layer-naming convention, embedding this information into your tools saves countless hours spent changing layers prior to placing objects or changing them after placement.

As you can see in Figure 22.24, you have the ability to change the hatch pattern after creating the tool. By using the [...] buttons found on the Type or Pattern name controls, you can choose different styles for different icons.

Refer to the Customize dialog box that was used earlier in this chapter for creating toolbars.

**7.** Select the Commands tab at the top and then from the Categories area select Draw. Then in the Commands area, click and drag the command Rectangle over onto the Favorites Tool palette.

You now have a tool for drawing rectangles. Not a big deal at first, but if you use the Properties option, you can preset what layer or other property should be applied when creating the rectangle. Let's add another!

**8.** Again, from the Customize dialog box and the Draw category, scroll down to Donut and drag it over to the Favorites tool palette. Just a silly icon for drawing donuts, right? Not if you make it a flyout.

**9.** Right-click on the donut icon and choose Properties. Then on the Tool Properties dialog, change the Use Flyout option to Yes. Now click the [...] button at the end of the Flyout Options control. As shown in Figure 22.25, a number of additional drawing objects can be accessed through a flyout on the one Donut tool.

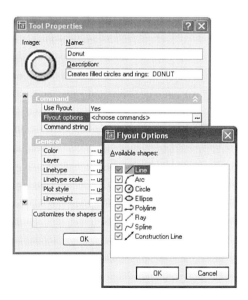

**Figure 22.25**   The flyout options for Draw commands provide basic object access.

**10.** Turn off the Ray and Construction Line icons and close the dialog. Then close the Tool Properties dialog followed by closing the Customize dialog.

**11.** Now if you click the Donut tool (do not use the flyout), the line command activates. Press Esc to cancel.

Probably not what you expected. You started with a Donut command, but when you turned on the flyout option, it was changed into a tool with limited draw functions, as shown in Figure 22.26.

You now have a Donut icon, but the commands available are controlled in the Flyout Options dialog box.

Leave AutoCAD open for the following exercise.

**Figure 22.26**
Various Draw tools available from a single icon flyout.

**INSIDER TIP**

If you change a command into a flyout, you would be wise to start with a similar command as the flyout commands. Having a donut icon start the Line command, for example, is obviously not good practice.

**INSIDER NOTE**

After quite a search of the available Tool palette flyouts, I located a flyout with the typical Draw objects such as Line, Arc, and Circle. I also found a flyout for basic dimension objects such as Linear and Aligned. In future versions of AutoCAD, there will probably be additional flyout collections or the capability to create your own. To find flyouts that you might find useful, you're invited to poke and prod around in the Customize dialog box.

As this exercise showed, you can add typical AutoCAD commands as icons to a tool palette. You can also leverage palette space by utilizing flyouts for Draw- or Dimension-related commands. There remain two more areas of special interest for this section. There is another icon type to expose as well as a method that can better organize your palettes.

### Exercise 22.7    Macro-Based Tools

I.  If the Tool Palettes interface is not active, turn it on by clicking the Tool Palettes icon on the Standard toolbar.

Previous exercises created a new palette named Favorites. This palette will continue to be enhanced in this exercise.

2. In an area of the palette with no content, use the right-click shortcut menu and select Customize. The Customize dialog appears, and if needed, select the Commands tab.

3. In the Categories area, choose Draw. Then, using the Commands area to the right, scroll down to Multiline Text. Click and drag it onto the Favorites Tool palette. You now have a tool to create mtext objects. Now for the controls! Go ahead and close the Customize dialog box.

4. Use the right-click shortcut menu on the Multiline Text tool and select Properties. The Tool Properties dialog box appears.

**I**NSIDER **NOTE**

It has been covered already, but utilizing the various settings for a given tool can greatly enhance your productivity. For example, you can predefine the layer and text style for the mtext object just by changing the value on the Tool Properties dialog.

If you examine the various settings for the mtext object, you will probably notice the absence of a size control. However, that is typically one of the most important values to change. It can still be accomplished though by using the Command string (menu macro).

5. Click in the Command string edit box and change it to

```
^C^Ctextsize;0.5;_mtext
```

6. Click OK to save changes and then click on the icon to execute the command. Pick a point on the screen and provide some basic text. Note the size of the text is 0.5. If you started these exercises with a new drawing, it normally would have been 0.2 in size.

That is a basic menu macro. This same code could also exist in an MNU/MNS file and accomplish the same thing. One major difference is the ease of editing that tool palettes provide. If this had been done in a true menu file, you would have been required to edit and save a separate file and then have AutoCAD recompile the various menu files, and if you had made a mistake, you would have had to repeat the whole process. However, tool palettes are very quick to create and fix.

But what if you need more size flexibility? Most users rely on a drawing scale to help determine what size text should be in a given drawing. In fact, this was recognized in the block and xref icon types by their Auxiliary scale value. This can done as well by using basic AutoLISP expressions.

7. Right-click on the mtext icon and select Properties, opening the Tool Properties dialog again.

8. In the Command string edit box, type the following:

```
^C^Ctextsize;(* (getvar "dimscale") 0.1);mtext
```

That little bit of stuff within the ( ) is AutoLISP. It gets the value of the DIMSCALE system variable , multiplies it by 0.1, and then uses that setting for the TEXTSIZE system variable. Then MTEXT executes and uses the current TEXTSIZE setting as its height.

You can put whole AutoLISP programs in the edit box, but for such programs, you are better off using separate LSP files and just putting their command names in the edit box.

Leave AutoCAD open for the following exercise.

**I**NSIDER NOTE

> Understanding AutoLISP and implementing it is a powerful skill to improve your AutoCAD productivity. However, it is outside the scope of this book to provide more than what was just discussed. Please refer to AutoCAD online documentation for more in-depth AutoLISP instruction.

As you develop your collection of tools, you might want to add a little more flair and structure to your customization efforts. If something is useful, you will probably want it to look nice and be well-organized. The last exercise deals with improving what you have already made so far.

### Exercise 22.8    Enhancing Your Tool Palettes

1. If the Tool Palettes interface is not active, turn it on by clicking the Tool Palettes icon on the Standard toolbar.

   Previous exercises created a new tool palette named Favorites. This palette will continue to be enhanced in this exercise.

2. On the "A" icon created in the previous exercise, use the right-click shortcut menu and select Properties. The Tool Properties dialog appears.

   The image used to represent this tool is very generic. Aside from the icon titles, which can aid in telling one from another, true speed is gained only by quick recognition, not by reading a title. Let's change the icon to improve this functionality!

3. Right-click on the actual "A" image; a link to Specify Image appears. Click the link to display the Select Image File dialog box.

4. Browse to the exercise files directory for this chapter on the accompanying CD and select the mtext-0.1.gif file. Then select the Open button to close the dialog.

   The image now appears in the Tool Properties dialog. It is a bit more specific to the functionality of the tool and much more intuitive, especially for a user who didn't create the original Tool palette.

5. Click the OK button to dismiss the Tool Properties dialog box.

   Notice the very clear and clean new icon for the 0.1-tall Mtext tool (see Figure 22.27). As you hover over the icon, it rises, indicating that tool will launch if you click it.

   **Figure 22.27**
   The before and after appearance of our Mtext 0.1" icon.

**I**NSIDER  **N**OTE

> This image was created 64×64 pixels as a GIF file where the background color (white) matched the transparency setting for the GIF file. Quality icons can be achieved with just a small amount of care, but you must use a third-party editor like Microsoft Paintbrush to create them.

After you create a number of tool palettes, accessing them will save you time and frustration. Because they can hold many tools, naming them appropriately is important. You then can gather related palettes into collections for even greater effectiveness.

6. In an area of the palette with no content, use the right-click shortcut menu and select Customize. The Customize dialog appears.

7. On the Tool Palettes tab, over in the Palette Groups area to the right side, right-click and choose New Group. In the edit box, type **My Favs**.

   This creates a group where you can organize your palettes.

8. Now over in the Tool Palettes area to the left, click and drag the Favorites Tool palette made earlier below the group My Favs.

9. Repeat this process for the Imperial Hatches Tool palette. Your new group now has two palettes.

10. Press the Close button to dismiss the Tool Properties dialog box.

    Now, you didn't see any change in the Tool palette. That is because you didn't make that group active.

11. Right-click over the vertical Tool palette title, and at the bottom will be listed your available groups. The last one, All Palettes, makes available every single palette, if so desired.

12. Choose the My Favs group. Now the Tool palette only contains the Favorites and Imperial Hatches palettes, as shown in Figure 22.28.

You may now close this drawing and AutoCAD.

**Figure 22.28**
The new My Favs tool palette group reduces the palettes that are available, streamlining access to the tools you need.

**INSIDER TIP**

Even though you can choose one of many types of image formats for your icons, AutoCAD converts them to a PNG format and stores these PNG files within the Palettes directory structure. That way, your original files can be stored wherever you like because they are not required for the display of the tool palette.

As you have just experienced, tool palettes are a great way to customize AutoCAD 2005. They are very intuitive and easy to create and modify. After you create some great palettes, you probably will want to share them, and this is easy to do as well. Using the Tool Palettes tab, right-click over the palette you want to share and choose Export. Using the Export Tool Palette dialog, browse to where you want to place the files and click Save.

Now, on the other user's station, right-click where you accessed Export and choose Import. Then locate the place you saved the tool palette. When located, choose Open on the Import Tool Palette dialog box.

**INSIDER CAUTION**

Custom icon images might not be saved when exported. When you export your tool palette to a specific location, review the files and directories made to verify that all the PNG files were copied as well. If any are missing, just copy them using Explorer from the Tool Palettes File Locations in your profile.

**I**NSIDER **NOTE**

You can store shared tool palettes on a server disk by changing the Tool Palettes File Locations search path within Options.

# Summary

There are many ways to customize AutoCAD. Creating toolbars and new Tool Palettes interface are the easiest and the most popular. Toolbars are a main user interface of AutoCAD with dozens of predefined icons and commands awaiting your implementation, and the tool palettes offers unparalleled functionality with its many tool structures and internal control options. With AutoCAD 2005, each user can create the optimal operating environment to increase his productivity. As this chapter demonstrated, these methods do not require any advanced knowledge of programming techniques and are easy to learn.

# Chapter 23
# Menu
# Customization

AutoCAD stands as the most popular CAD software in the world today, with millions of AutoCAD users in nearly all countries using it to generate high-quality engineering and architectural drawings. This extensive user base has made AutoCAD, and AutoCAD-based vertical products like Autodesk Architectural Desktop, the de facto leader in computer-generated drawings and models. One of the primary reasons is its so-called "open architecture," or its capability to be programmed and customized by its users. For example, users can easily change the appearance of the interface to suit their personal preferences. You can modify existing toolbars or add new ones. You can modify the way AutoCAD commands work and even develop an entire menu system to control specialized or sophisticated tasks.

As important as AutoCAD's open architecture is the ease with which most customization can be carried out. Even relatively inexperienced computer users can quickly learn to perform AutoCAD customization tasks that lead to significant increases in productivity.

This chapter includes the following topics:

- Creating command aliases
- Understanding AutoCAD menu file types
- Understanding and using AutoCAD menu file sections
- Understanding and creating menu macros
- Using AutoLISP expressions in menu macros

# Creating Command Aliases

The most rudimentary and historical method of AutoCAD customization involves creating command aliases, which provide a keyboard "shortcut" to access an AutoCAD command. Command aliases offer a powerful way to increase your productivity. Generally, when you work with AutoCAD, one hand is almost always on the mouse. Because the other hand is free for typing, command aliases offer a quick, alternate way to initiate commands.

There are over 200 command aliases predefined in an ACAD.PGP file located in your profile \Support folder. The PGP stands for ProGram Parameters, and this file is often referred to as the PGP file. The ACAD.PGP file is actually divided into two main sections: the Operating System Commands section and the Command Alias section. In a modern Windows OS environment, the Operating System Commands section is somewhat redundant, so this chapter only examines the Command Alias section. A sample section of the Command Alias section is shown here:

```
3A,        *3DARRAY
3DO,       *3DORBIT
3F,        *3DFACE
3P,        *3DPOLY
A,         *ARC
ADC,       *ADCENTER
AA,        *AREA
AL,        *ALIGN
AP,        *APPLOAD
AR,        *ARRAY
-AR,       *-ARRAY
ATT,       *ATTDEF
-ATT,      *-ATTDEF
ATE,       *ATTEDIT
-ATE,      *-ATTEDIT
ATTE,      *-ATTEDIT
B,         *BLOCK
-B,        *-BLOCK
BH,        *BHATCH
```

A short inspection of this excerpt shows the basic scheme of defining a command alias:

```
<Alias>,    *<Full command name>
```

<Alias> represents the one-, two-, or more letter keyboard combination that can be typed as a substitute for the official command name. A comma character must immediately follow the alias. Next, you enter the full name of the AutoCAD command for which the alias will stand. This name must be immediately preceded by an asterisk (*) character. There can be any convenient number of spaces between the comma and the asterisk. These spaces are inserted solely to visually separate the alias from its command so that the list is easier to read.

Although the number of predefined aliases is quite large, you might want to edit an alias to suit your own needs or add additional aliases for a command not included in the default list. In the following exercise, you create an alias for the QLEADER command.

> **I**NSIDER  **N**OTE
>
> The traditional method for modifying the PGP file is an ASCII text editor like Notepad, and it can certainly be used whenever needed. However, AutoCAD 2005 includes within the setup application the AutoCAD 2005 Express Tools Volumes 1-9. In this collection of tools is a program called ALIASEDIT, whose sole purpose is to provide a dialog-driven application for modifying a PGP file.

Because the possibility exists that you don't have the Express Tools loaded, the following exercise uses the tried-and-true method of using Notepad as the editor.

> **I**NSIDER  **N**OTE
>
> You should make a backup copy of your ACAD.PGP file before loading it into any editing application, just to be safe. Find out where your active file is located by typing **(findfile "ACAD.PGP")** at the command prompt.

### Exercise 23.1   Editing a Command Alias in the ACAD.PGP File

1. Open AutoCAD and, from the Tools pull-down menu, select Customize, Edit Custom Files, Program Parameters.

   AutoCAD then locates and opens your active ACAD.PGP file using your text editor.

> **I**NSIDER  **N**OTE
>
> Because AutoCAD 2005 is Windows XP-certified, it has user-specific profiles to contain user-customized files. One of these potential custom files is the ACAD.PGP file. Due to this, AutoCAD places original versions of standard support files in:
>
> C:\Program Files\AutoCAD 2005\UserDataCache\Support
>
> The first time you start AutoCAD under your login, AutoCAD copies folders and files located there to:
>
> C:\Documents and Settings\<LOGIN>\Application Data\Autodesk\AutoCAD 2005\R16.1\enu\Support
>
> This directory is where you will find your ACAD.PGP file, unless you are storing it elsewhere of course.

> **I**NSIDER **T**IP
>
> Another method for step 1 is to use an AutoLISP function to both find and open your file. At the command prompt, type:
>
> `(command "startapp" "notepad" (findfile "ACAD.PGP"))`
>
> This opens your active PGP file for editing.

2. Scroll down to find the Command Alias section and the list of command aliases. Find the line containing the definition of the alias for the REDRAW command.

3. Insert a new line immediately above it and type:

   `QL,          *QLEADER`

   This creates a shortcut for the AutoCAD QLEADER command. Save the file, overwriting the previous version.

4. Exit your text editor and return to AutoCAD.

> **I**NSIDER **N**OTE
>
> You can edit the ACAD.PGP file without AutoCAD running. In that case, you would not need to perform the following reinitializing step (step 5) because AutoCAD reads your changes the next time it is started. However, because the preceding steps were performed while AutoCAD was running, you need to make AutoCAD bring in the changes to the PGP file.

5. To load the modified PGP file, type **REINIT** and pressing Enter. AutoCAD displays the Re-initialization dialog box, as shown in Figure 23.1.

6. In the Re-initialization dialog box, select the PGP File option and then click OK. AutoCAD reads the edited PGP file and loads it into memory.

7. To test the new alias in AutoCAD, type **QL** and press Enter. Check that AutoCAD's QLEADER command starts. Then press Esc to cancel the command.

**Figure 23.1**
The Re-initialization dialog box of the REINIT command.

If the command doesn't start, you either edited the wrong PGP file, which does happen, or perhaps misspelled the alias QL. If you mistype the command name, AutoCAD reports back with "Unknown command (*what you typed*)," making this easy to determine.

If so desired, leave AutoCAD open for following exercises.

**I**NSIDER  **N**OTE

> Command aliases can only initiate commands; they cannot be used to specify command options. To automate both command initiation and subsequent options selection, you can create simple AutoLISP programs like:
>
> ```
> (defun c:ZP(/)(command "ZOOM" "PREVIOUS"))
> ```
>
> An ideal location to store this type of customization is in a file named ACADDOC.LSP that you would create and maintain. You would then store this in your profile support path. If you want to share it with others, you could place it on a network drive as well, as long as that network location is on AutoCAD's support path.

Editing your PGP file is a somewhat basic form of AutoCAD customization. Often, the hardest task is locating the file you are using and then loading it. But after you have added or changed the commands you use often, it is doubtful that editing it will be an ongoing effort.

# Understanding AutoCAD Menu File Types

Various menu files define the menus used by AutoCAD. The files that concern customization are in standard text-file format that you can easily modify. You can also define new menus. If you create or edit a menu, you assign items to the menu. You associate menu macros to these items that perform specific AutoCAD functions. A menu macro can be as simple as a sequence of standard AutoCAD commands or as complex as a combination of commands and AutoLISP or DIESEL code, or a combination of all three. Menu macros can be thought of as "command strings." If the user picks a menu item, the associated macro is executed. Later in this chapter, you learn how to construct menu macros. The menu files also describe the appearance and position of menu items in relation to the overall AutoCAD user interface.

There are several types of menu files, each distinguished by its file extension. These types include MNU, MNS, MNC, MNR, and MNL files. The base AutoCAD menu, for example, is called ACAD.MNU. For this base file, there is also an associated ACAD.MNS, ACAD.MNC, ACAD.MNR, and ACAD.MNL file. The function and format of the various menu file types are described in Table 23.1.

### Table 23.1    Menu File Types

| Menu Type | Description |
|-----------|-------------|
| .MNU | This is a template menu file in standard ASCII text format. |
| .MNS | This is a menu source file, in standard (ASCII) text format, which is generated by AutoCAD from the MNU file. |
| .MNC | This is a binary format file compiled from the MNS file. This file is the one actually loaded. |
| .MNR | This is a binary file containing the bitmaps used by the menu. |
| .MNL | This is a menu support file in standard ASCII text format containing the AutoLISP code to support the menu. |

**I**NSIDER **N**OTE

> AutoCAD uses one menu as its base menu, but other menus can be loaded at the same time as partial menus. The MENU command is only used to load the base menu. The MENULOAD command is used to load partial menus (when no base menu is loaded, this command can be used to load the base menu).

When you start AutoCAD, all the menus loaded in the last session are automatically loaded. The name of this menu is stored in the system registry. You can manually load a different base menu using AutoCAD's MENU command. Use the MENULOAD command to load partial menus in addition to the base menu. The CUSTOM menu is an example of a partially loaded menu. Whether the menu is loaded automatically or manually, AutoCAD finds and loads the specified menu using the following search sequence:

1. AutoCAD looks for an MNS source file of the specified name, following the AutoCAD library search path.

    - If an MNS file is found, AutoCAD looks for the compiled (MNC) version of the same file in the same directory. If AutoCAD finds an MNC file with the same or later date and time as the MNS file, it loads this MNC file. Otherwise, AutoCAD compiles the MNS file, generating a new MNC file, and then loads this file.

    - If an MNS file is not found, AutoCAD looks for a compiled (MNC) menu file of the specified name in the library search path. If AutoCAD finds this MNC file, it loads it.

    - If AutoCAD finds neither an MNS nor an MNC file, it searches the library search path for a menu template (MNU) file of the specified name. If found, the MNU file is used to generate an MNS source file. This MNS file then generates a compiled MNC file, and AutoCAD loads this MNC file.

- If AutoCAD finds no menu files of the specified name, it generates an error message prompting for another menu name.

2. After finding (or compiling) and loading the MNC file, AutoCAD searches the library search path for a menu LISP (MNL) file. If AutoCAD finds this file, it evaluates the LISP code and loads it into memory.

3. Any time AutoCAD compiles an MNC file, it also generates a new resource (MNR) file, containing the bitmap (toolbar icons) definitions used by the associated menu.

**I**NSIDER **N**OTE

> The library search path consists of the support files search path specified under Support File Search Path on the Files tab of the Options dialog box and the following locations: the current directory (typically, the "Start In" setting on your shortcut icon), the directory that contains the current drawing file, and the directory that contains the AutoCAD program files. Some of these search locations might overlap.

**I**NSIDER **T**IP

> You might assume from the preceding information that the menu files must reside somewhere on the support files search path. However, AutoCAD remembers the location of loaded menus, and it reloads the menu, even if it is not on the support files search path. If you must maintain both AutoCAD 2004/2005 and older versions of AutoCAD, place your menus in folders that are not on the support files search path. This avoids the issue of an incompatible version of the MNR file being created accidentally.

As you can see in Table 23.1 and in the menu-loading procedure, it is the compiled MNC version of any given menu that is loaded. Also, note that the MNC file is compiled from the MNS, not the MNU, file. In fact, the MNU template file is essentially useless in a Windows environment, and as you will see when we discuss custom toolbars later in this chapter, the MNU file itself can be dangerous. It is therefore recommended that you move the MNU file (for example, ACAD.MNU) out of the support files search path so that AutoCAD never reads it when menu files are loaded or reloaded. Perform all your menu customization using an MNS file.

**I**NSIDER **T**IP

There are several ways that you can keep an MNU file from interfering with the MNS and MNC files. You might leave the MNU file in its original location and rename it to <menuname>.ORIG-MNU, for example. Alternatively, you could create a new directory named \Backup and move the MNU file there. The second method has the advantage of providing a directory to store other AutoCAD files that you want to protect, such as the original ACAD.PGP or ACAD.LIN files. Never delete the original MNU file. In an emergency, it can be used to rebuild the MNS file, although you lose all your AutoCAD-generated menu customization.

# Understanding AutoCAD Menu File Sections

All AutoCAD menu files are made up of one or more major sections. Each section is associated with a specific area of the AutoCAD menu interface, such as the pull-down menus, the toolbars, and so on. Each menu section contains menu entries, providing instructions for the appearance and action associated with the menu entry. Each menu section is identified by a section label having the form ***section_name. The various section labels and their associated menu areas are listed in Table 23.2.

**Table 23.2   Menu Section Labels**

| Section Label | Menu Area |
|---|---|
| ***Menugroup | Menu group name |
| ***BUTTONS | Pointing-device button menu |
| ***AUX | System-pointing device menu |
| ***POP | Pull-down/shortcut menus |
| ***TOOLBARS | Toolbar definitions |
| ***IMAGE | Image tile menus |
| ***SCREEN | Screen menus |
| ***TABLET | Tablet menus |
| ***HELPSTRINGS | Text displayed in the status bar if a pull-down or shortcut menu item is highlighted or if the cursor is rested on a toolbar item |
| ***ACCELERATORS | Accelerator key definitions |

Within a given menu section, there can be one or more alias labels in the form ``**alias``. Note that section labels have the three-asterisk prefix, ``***``, whereas alias labels have a two-asterisk, ``**``, prefix. For the purposes of the customization done in this chapter, you can ignore the alias labels.

You can include comments within a menu file for documentation or notes by placing the comments on a line that begins with two slashes, ``//``. These lines are ignored by the AutoCAD menu interpreter. Such notes are often useful if viewing the file in a text editor. There are several useful and informative comment lines found in the ACAD.MNU file, for example.

**I**NSIDER **N**OTE

> Comments found in the MNU file are stripped from the MNS when the MNS file is created automatically. Comments added to an MNS file after it has been created remain there, as long as the MNU file is never reread automatically.

The various sections of an AutoCAD menu differ in their functionality and appearance. A description of the ``***BUTTONS``, ``***AUX``, and ``***POP`` sections appears later in this chapter. Several of the menu types are shown in Figure 23.2. We limit our menu file customization to the ``***POP`` section in this chapter and create macros for ``***POP`` sections later.

## Using the ***BUTTONS and ***AUX Sections

The ``***BUTTONS`` and ``***AUX`` sections appear near the top of the standard ACAD.MNU and ACAD.MNS files, and they are used to customize your system-pointing device. These two sections are functionally identical, and the section that your system uses depends on the type of pointing device you use. The standard Windows system mouse uses the ``***AUX`` section, and any other input device (a digitizer puck, for example) uses the ``***BUTTONS`` section. In this chapter, we confine our discussion to the ``***AUX`` (mouse) section.

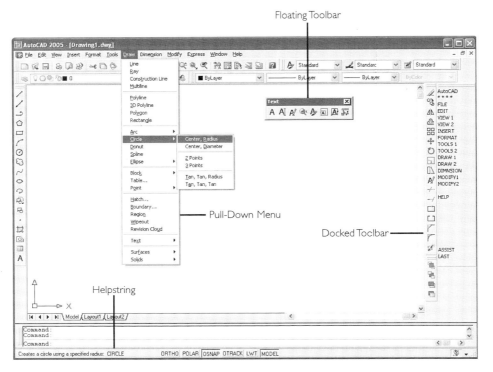

**Figure 23.2** The various AutoCAD menu components.

All input devices have a pick button, used to specify points and to select objects on the screen. On a normally configured, standard Windows mouse, this is the left button. On most digitizing pucks, this is normally labeled button 1. This pick button is not customizable, and no accommodation for its function is found in AutoCAD menus. The remaining button(s) can have commands, functions, or macros assigned to them.

The ***AUXn sections of the menu file define the actions (commands or macros) associated with the buttons on your mouse. Each line in any given section (***AUX1 or ***AUX2, for example) represents a mouse button. You can access each button menu with the key/button combination shown in Table 23.3.

**Table 23.3    Buttons and Associated Menu Sections**

| Key/Button Combination | Menu Section |
| --- | --- |
| Simple click | ***AUX1 and ***BUTTONS1 |
| Shift+click | ***AUX2 and ***BUTTONS2 |
| Ctrl+click | ***AUX3 and ***BUTTONS3 |
| Ctrl+Shift+click | ***AUX4 and ***BUTTONS4 |

**I**NSIDER **N**OTE

> The first line after the menu section label ***AUX1 or ***BUTTONS1 is used only if
> the SHORTCUTMENU system variable is set to 0. If SHORTCUTMENU is set to a value
> other than 0, the built-in menu is used. Similarly, the second line after the ***AUX1 or
> ***BUTTONS1 label is used only when the MBUTTONPAN system variable is set to 0.

Consider a typical ***AUX1 section. Refer to Table 23.4 for a listing of menu macrocodes:

```
***AUX1
$M=$(if,$(eq,$(substr,$(getvar,cmdnames),1,5),GRIP_),$P0=ACAD.GRIPS $P0=*);
$P0=SNAP $p0=*
^C^C
^B
^O
^G
^D
^E
^T
```

Remember that the pick button cannot be assigned and is therefore not included in the
menu. The first line after the ***AUX1 section label ends with (;) and therefore represents the next button after the pick button, usually button 2 or the right button. Thus,
on a two-button mouse, only the first line of this listing has any meaning. The third line
(^C^C) after the section label applies to button 4 on a four-button mouse, with the
remaining lines having no meaning. Later, you see that the semicolon (;) and the ^C^C
codes represent an Enter and a Cancel command, respectively.

Now consider a typical ***AUX2 section:

```
***AUX2
$P0=SNAP $p0=*
$P0=SNAP $p0=*
```

Referring to Table 23.3, the ***AUX2 section defines the actions taken when a combination of Shift and a button is pressed. In this AUX2 listing, there is a defined action for
Shift+button 2 and Shift+button 3. Again, with only a two-button mouse, the second
code line has no meaning. Each line in this example is the same, and the code causes the
POP0 cursor menu to be loaded and displayed using the following menu code format:

```
$Pn=name $Pn=*
```

In the previous code, $ is the special character code for loading a menu area, Pn specifies the
***POP menu section with n being the number of the section, and =* forces a display of the
specified section. You learn more about ***POP menu sections later in this chapter. This section and this code display the ***POP0 cursor menu if you Shift+right-click the mouse.

The ***AUX and ***BUTTONS sections of a menu provide several opportunities for the customization of the functions performed by your input device. If you use a 10- or 12-button digitizer puck, you can program up to 27 or 33 button functions, respectively. Moreover, even with the standard two-button mouse, the right button can be programmed to perform three different tasks.

**I**NSIDER **N**OTE

> The ***AUX and ***BUTTONS sections can be added to your CUSTOM.MNS file, which is discussed later in the chapter. However, only one ***AUX and ***BUTTONS section may be active at a time, no matter how many menus have those sections.

**I**NSIDER **T**IP

> Although you can add ***AUX and ***BUTTONS sections to any partial menu, by default only the primary menu's ***AUX and ***BUTTONS are used. This can be changed by using the menucmd AutoLISP function in your partial menu's MNL file:
>
> (menucmd "A1=CUSTOM.AUX1")
>
> In the previous code, A1= is used to replace the current ***AUX1 section, CUSTOM is the menu group name, and .AUX1 is the partial menu's section that you want to use for the substitution.
>
> Repeat that line and modify as needed for each section that you need to substitute.

## Using the ***POP Section

The ***POP menu section contains the definitions for the pull-down and shortcut menus. This section is perhaps the most frequently customized section. These menus are displayed in a "pull-down" or cascading fashion, as shown in Figures 23.3 and 23.4. Pull-downs have the advantage of being easy to read and use and do not permanently use up screen space.

Shortcut menus are usually displayed while commands are in progress, and they often duplicate the various command options that are available and displayed at the command line. Shortcut menus are displayed at or near the crosshairs or the cursor in the screen area. A typical shortcut menu (for the PEDIT command) is shown in Figure 23.4.

**Figure 23.3**
A typical pull-down menu.

Pull-down menus are defined in the ***POP1 through ***POP499 menu sections. Shortcut menus are defined in the ***POP0 and ***POP500 through ***POP999 sections. AutoCAD constructs the menu bar across the top of the screen from the ***POP1 through ***POP16 menu sections. If no ***POP1 through ***POP16 definitions are found, AutoCAD constructs a menu bar containing a default File, View, Window, and Help menu.

The following example shows a typical pull-down menu. The specific syntax and menu code for pull-down menus is discussed later in this chapter. However, generally there are three sections to each line in a menu item—the name tag, the label (text enclosed by square brackets), and the menu macro. The actual appearance of the menu is shown in Figure 23.4.

**Figure 23.4**
A typical command-related right-click shortcut menu.

```
***POP8
**DIMENSION
ID_MnDimensi [Dime&nsion]
ID_QDim      [&Quick Dimension]^C^C_qdim
             [--]
ID_Dimlinear [&Linear]^C^C_dimlinear
ID_Dimaligne [Ali&gned]^C^C_dimaligned
ID_Dimordina [&Ordinate]^C^C_dimordinate
             [--]
ID_Dimradius [&Radius]^C^C_dimradius
ID_Dimdiamet [&Diameter]^C^C_dimdiameter
ID_Dimangula [&Angular]^C^C_dimangular
             [--]
ID_Dimbaseli [&Baseline]^C^C_dimbaseline
ID_Dimcontin [&Continue]^C^C_dimcontinue
             [--]
ID_Leader    [L&eader]^C^C_qleader
ID_Tolerance [&Tolerance...]^C^C_tolerance
ID_Dimcenter [Center &Mark]^C^C_dimcenter
             [--]
ID_Dimedito  [Obli&que]^C^C_dimedit _o
ID_MnAlign   [->Align Te&xt]
ID_DimteditH   [&Home]^C^C_dimedit _h
ID_DimteditA   [&Angle]^C^C_dimtedit \_a
               [--]
ID_DimteditL   [&Left]^C^C_dimtedit \_l
ID_DimteditC   [&Center]^C^C_dimtedit \_c
ID_DimteditR   [<-&Right]^C^C_dimtedit \_r
             [--]
ID_Ddim      [&Style...]'_dimstyle
ID_Dimoverri [O&verride]^C^C_dimoverride
ID_DimstyleA [&Update]^C^C_-dimstyle _apply
ID_Dimreasso [Reassociate Dime&nsions]^C^C_dimreassociate
```

In this example, all lines contain simple menu labels. We discuss menu macros in the following section.

# Creating Menu Macros

Now that you have a basic understanding of the `***AUX`, `***BUTTONS`, and `***POP` sections of an AutoCAD menu, it is time to learn how to build new menu items and place them into a menu. To do this, you need to know the special codes used in menu macros. If you want to include command parameters in a menu item, you need to know the sequence in which the command expects its parameters. Every character in a menu macro is significant, even blank spaces. We devote our attention to the `***POP` menu section; however, with little or no revision, most menu macros work equally well in other menu sections.

**INSIDER NOTE**

If command input comes from a menu item, the settings of the PICKADD and PICK-AUTO system variables are assumed to be 1 and 0, respectively. This preserves compatibility with previous versions of AutoCAD and makes customization easier because you are not required to check the settings of these variables.

A menu macro is a kind of shorthand or coded method of representing the keystrokes that you would type at the command prompt. Often the macro merely contains what you would actually type. There is, however, a group of codes that is used to represent certain keyboard entries. These special characters are listed in Table 23.4.

## Table 23.4    Special Characters Used in Menu Macros

| Character | Description |
|---|---|
| ; | Issues ENTER. |
| ^M | Issues ENTER. |
| ^I | Issues TAB. |
| SPACEBAR | Enters a space; a blank space between command items in a menu entry is equivalent to pressing the spacebar. |
| \ | Pauses for user input. |
| . | A period can be used immediately before a native AutoCAD command to override any redefinition of that command that might be in effect. |
| _ | An underscore character; translates the AutoCAD commands and keywords that immediately follow. |
| + | Continues menu macro to the next line if it is the last character on a line. |
| =* | Displays the current top-level image, pull-down, or shortcut menu. |
| *^C^C | Prefix for a repeating item. |
| $ | Loads a menu section or introduces a conditional DIESEL macro expression ($M=). |

| Character | Description |
|-----------|-------------|
| ^B | Toggles Snap on or off (Ctrl+B). |
| ^C | Cancels command or prompt (Esc). |
| ^D | Toggles Coords on or off (Ctrl+D). |
| ^E | Sets the next isometric plane (Ctrl+E). |
| ^G | Toggles Grid on or off (Ctrl+G). |
| ^H | Issues backspace. |
| ^O | Toggles Ortho on or off (Ctrl+O). |
| ^P | Toggles MENUECHO on or off. |
| ^Q | Echoes all prompts, status listings, and input to the printer (Ctrl+Q). |
| ^T | Toggles Tablet on or off (Ctrl+T). |
| ^V | Changes current view port (Ctrl+V). |
| ^Z | Null character that suppresses the automatic addition of SPACEBAR at the end of a menu item. |

Several of the special characters in Table 23.4 are rarely used, but others are used frequently. You should refer to Table 23.4 until you become familiar with the more common codes.

The general form of functional menu entry items is consistent in most menu sections. The general format is as follows:

```
Name_tag        [label]menu_macro
```

The following line is an example taken from the Draw pull-down menu:

```
ID_Line         [&Line]^C^C_line
```

At least one space should separate the Name_tag element from the label element. There can be no space between the label and the menu_macro. The label must be enclosed within a set of square brackets. In the example, the first item, ID_Line, is the name tag for the entry. The label, [&Line], displays the word Line on the pull-down. The ampersand character, &, appears immediately before the alphanumeric character in the label that appears underscored on-screen, indicating that that character is the Alt+character hotkey for the entry. The menu macro in this example consists of the code ^C^C_line, which issues two cancels and is followed by the LINE command. If the Line item is selected from the standard Draw pull-down menu, this menu macro is executed.

**INSIDER NOTE**

> Name_tag elements are used as "aliases" or shorthand methods of referring to the associated menu macro from other portions of the menu, most notably from the Accelerator key definitions. You can see them in various chapter examples.

> **I**NSIDER **N**OTE
>
> On some systems, the access key does not appear underlined until you press the Alt key. This is because of a setting in your Windows operating system.

# Using the Custom Menu

For the most part, the kind of menu customization that most users do is creating new pull-downs and adjusting or creating new toolbars. Historically, at upgrade time, this entails quite a bit of work to extract the user customization and inject it into the new version menu file. However, AutoCAD 2005 has addressed this concern with an out-of-the-box menu just for the user.

> **I**NSIDER **C**AUTION
>
> Before performing modifications to any AutoCAD menu file, make a backup copy and place the copy in a separate folder. You might want to consider establishing a dedicated folder in which to store copies of all the AutoCAD support files that you use in customization.

There is a new partial menu named CUSTOM that is automatically loaded in AutoCAD 2005. This new menu is just for you, the user, and initially contains next to nothing in it. Here is what the CUSTOM.MNS file looks like originally:

```
***MENUGROUP=CUSTOM
***TOOLBARS
***ACCELERATORS
***HELPSTRINGS
```

As you can see, the primary purpose of this file is to be wide open for the user's own preferences. You should also notice that there is no section other than ***TOOLBARS, but the other sections are fully supported. Of the various elements in this custom menu, only the toolbars can be created from within AutoCAD itself. All the remaining menu components require editing in Notepad or another text-based editor.

> **I**NSIDER **N**OTE
>
> During a standard AutoCAD installation, Notepad is usually associated with MNS files. Double-clicking this file type in Windows Explorer causes it to be opened in Notepad or another file editor application that you might have designated during installation.

Although it is not the purpose of this chapter to explore AutoCAD's menu macro language extensively, by studying the ACAD.MNS file, you can start customizing your menu structure to increase your efficiency. See the online document "AutoCAD Customization Guide" for more detailed information about these more advanced menu customization topics.

## Building Menu Macros

In this section, you actually construct several menu macros and place them in a separate pull-down menu that you incorporate into your AutoCAD display interface. As you work with menu macros, you are modifying the base menu. It is important that you make a backup copy of this menu so that you can restore a known working menu if necessary.

We use the new AutoCAD 2005 CUSTOM partial menu for our editing. This provides a platform for toolbars and pull-down menus and keeps the average user away from the ACAD base menu.

### Exercise 23.2    Adding a New Pull-Down Menu

1.  Open AutoCAD and, at the command prompt, type **ai_editcustfile**. Then at the Custom File to edit prompt, type **custom.mns**.

**I**NSIDER **N**OTE

> The ai_editcustfile command is not an everyday user command. It is used by AutoCAD and the ACAD menu to enable the user to open files. In fact, on the Tools pull-down menu, Customize, Edit Custom Files, is an entry called Current Menu. Choosing this opens your ACAD.MNS file for editing (sadly, not your CUSTOM.MNS file).

2.  In the CUSTOM.MNS file, under the ***MENUGROUP=CUSTOM line, type the following:

```
***POP1
My_Favorites        [F&avorites]
My_Break_f          [&Break First]  ^C^C_.Break;\_f;
```

**I**NSIDER **N**OTE

> Notice the & in front of the a. This enables an Alt+a key combination to open this pull-down menu. Because the File pull-down menu uses Alt-F, we logically moved to the next available character.

3. Check your typing closely. The number of spaces between the name_tag and the label elements is not important. Format these elements so that they are easy to read.

4. Save the changes that you have made to the file and minimize Microsoft Notepad.

5. From AutoCAD's Tools pull-down menu, choose Customize, Menus to display the Menu Customization dialog box. Ensure that the Menu Groups tab is active, as shown in Figure 23.5.

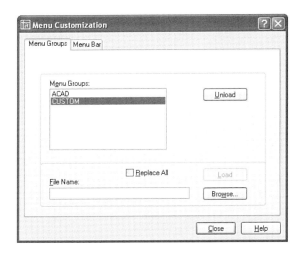

**Figure 23.5**    The Menu Customization dialog box.

6. If CUSTOM is listed in the Menu Groups list, select it and press the Unload button.

7. In the File Name edit box, type **CUSTOM.MNS**. Then press the Load button to make AutoCAD locate and load the modified menu.

8. Select the Menu Bar tab at the top of the dialog box.

9. Verify that CUSTOM is the selected Menu Group. Note the Favorites menu listed below. In the Menu Bar listing on the right side, click the Window item (see Figure 23.6) and then click the Insert >> button. The new Favorites menu item is positioned to the left of the Window pull-down.

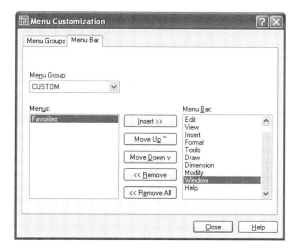

**Figure 23.6**    The Menu Customization dialog box enables you to organize
your pull-down menus however you want.

Even with this dialog open, you should now see Favorites
the left of the Window pull-down menu.

10. Select Close to dismiss the Menu Customization dialog
box. You can now click the Favorites pull-down menu, as
shown in Figure 23.7.

**Figure 23.7**
The new Favorites
pull-down menu.

Leave this drawing and AutoCAD open for the following exercise.

### Using the Break First Menu Macro

AutoCAD's native BREAK command has often been the subject of menu macro customization. In the BREAK command, if you select the object using your pointing device, AutoCAD both selects the object and treats the selection point as the first break point. At the next prompt, you can continue by specifying the second point, or you can override the first point by typing an **f**. In many cases, this default mechanism (having the object-pick-point become the first specified break point) is inconvenient. The following menu macro automatically enters the overriding **f**:

```
[&Break First]^C^C_.Break;\_f;
```

Refer to Table 23.4 and the following list for an explanation of this macro:

- **[&Break First].** This is the label for the macro as it appears on the menu. The
  &B signifies the character that appears underlined and is the Alt+Character
  shortcut for the macro.

- **^c^c.** The double ^C duplicates two cancel commands (Esc) to ensure that any ongoing commands are canceled.

- **_.Break;.** This supplies the BREAK command. The semicolon issues an Enter. The leading underscore character permits foreign language translation. The period makes sure to use the AutoCAD BREAK command. (The initial uppercase character is optional.)

- **\.** This pauses the macro to enable user input, that is, selecting the object to be broken.

- **_f;.** This supplies an f to skip the default Specify second break point prompt. The leading underscore character permits foreign language translation. The semicolon issues an Enter. AutoCAD then issues the Specify a first break point prompt.

**INSIDER TIP**

As noted in Table 23.4, a semicolon, ;, and a space both act as keyboard Enters in a macro. Using a semicolon is preferred because it is visually less ambiguous than a space. This is especially true when a space is used as the last element in a macro or when two spaces are used successively. If you use a semicolon, there is no question as to whether an Enter is intended.

This menu macro is given a tag name of My_Break_F to impart some sense of its function and to distinguish it from the standard BREAK command.

My_Break_F is a typical menu macro. It uses only standard AutoCAD command input and represents nothing more than a means to automatically supply the equivalent of conventional keyboard input. In constructing a menu macro such as My_Break_F, it is useful to run the command sequence "manually," noting the exact keyboard input you supply in response to each issued AutoCAD prompt. It is often helpful to write out the prompt and keyboard response sequence before attempting to duplicate the procedure in macrocode. It is easy to forget, for example, that in the place of every keyboard Enter, you must use either a semicolon or a space in the macro, or that the backslash character is used to represent either screen picks or user-typed responses to prompts.

**INSIDER TIP**

Reviewing the command and response sequence for macros that you want to construct is often easier if you carry out the procedure and then use AutoCAD's Text window to visually review the sequence as it took place at the command prompt. Remember that the F2 key displays or hides the text screen.

Like many menu macros, the My_Break_F macro is quite simple. It gains its effectiveness through the time and effort it saves. In the next section, you see how AutoLISP can be utilized in another simple but effective menu macro.

## Using AutoLISP Expressions in Menu Macros

You can use AutoLISP expressions and variables to create menu macros, ranging from the very simple to the extremely complex. One of the principle advantages of AutoLISP programming is the capability to "branch" into two or more programming directions depending on user input or the state of the drawing environment. This can lead to rather complex macros that possess "intelligence" and the capability to make "decisions." Shorter, less complex AutoLISP macros can also exhibit this decision-making capability as well. Often, these less complex macros utilize the state of AutoCAD's system variable settings to perform useful tasks that would be more cumbersome and time-consuming to perform from the keyboard or through a series of toolbar or menu picks.

For example, the system variable VISRETAIN controls if changes to xref layers in the current drawing are kept after the drawing is closed. When set to 0, all changes in the current editing session are discarded. When set to 1, these changes will still be in effect when the drawing is once again opened.

In the following menu macro, AutoLISP functions are used to manipulate the value of the VISRETAIN system variable. If the current value is 1, an AutoLISP function is used to set it to a value of 0. If it has a current value other than 0, it is set to 1. By utilizing this macro, it is easy to flip the value of the system variable back and forth. The macro is as follows:

```
^C^C(setvar "visretain" (abs (1- (getvar "VISRETAIN"))))
```

It is important to realize that this macro is a combination of menu macrocode (as outlined in Table 23.4) and AutoLISP code. The ^C^C is standard menu macrocode, although the remainder of the macro is expressed in AutoLISP code. The two are compatible and work together very effectively.

In the following exercise, you add the VISRETAIN menu macro to your Favorites pulldown menu.

### Exercise 23.3    Adding an AutoLISP-Based Menu Option

1. Return display focus to your text editor and the CUSTOM.MNS file.

2. Immediately below the `My_Break_F` macro, which you added previously, add the following all on one line:

```
My_Visretain    [&Visretain On/Off]^C^C(setvar "visretain"
(abs (1- (getvar "VISRETAIN"))))
```

3. Check your typing and then save the file.

---

**I**NSIDER **TIP**

> Because the menu we are working with is a partial menuload and not the primary or main menu AutoCAD is using, we must unload and then reload the menu for our changes to show. You could also just exit and reenter AutoCAD and achieve the same results.

---

4. Type **MENULOAD** at the command prompt. The Menu Customization dialog appears.

5. On the Menu Groups tab, select CUSTOM and click unload. The menu is removed.

6. In the File Name edit box, type **CUSTOM.MNS** and then click the Load button.

7. Click the Menu Bar tab on the Menu Customization dialog box. Then change the menu group if needed to CUSTOM.

8. In the Menu Bar listing on the right side, click the Window item (refer to Figure 23.6) and then click the Insert >> button. The Favorites menu item is now positioned to the left of the Window pull-down menu.

9. Select Close to dismiss the Menu Customization dialog box. You can now click the Favorites pull-down menu and see the new entry for Visretain On/Off.

    You can now close your text editor and AutoCAD if so desired.

Of course, other menu macros can be devised to perform tasks that require repetitive user input. The special menu macrocode `*^C^C` serves as a prefix for macros that repeat themselves until either canceled at the keyboard or canceled by choosing another menu item. The following macro is a typical example:

```
[&Repeat_Circ]*^C^CCircle;
```

In this example, the `CIRCLE` command is automatically repeated until canceled by the user.

Menu macros can become complex if they are designed to perform a series of AutoCAD commands and to require user input as well. For example, a user might find that he or she needs to perform the following series of operations frequently:

1. Draw a circle of fixed radius.

2. Pause for alphanumeric user input (text) centered within the circle.

3. Start a line from a user-specified point on the circumference of the circle.

4. End the line at a user-specified point.

5. Attach a solid donut (dot) of fixed size at the end of the line.

Performing this task manually takes as many as 32 separate input steps. The following macro accomplishes the tasks with as few as six input steps:

```
^C^C_.Circle;\1;_.Text;m;@;0.5;0;\_.Line;nea;\\;_.Donut;0;0.125;@;;
```

Although this "Bubble" macro is complicated, it is composed of a series of simpler steps utilizing basic AutoCAD commands translated into macrocode. Figure 23.8 diagrams the entire macro.

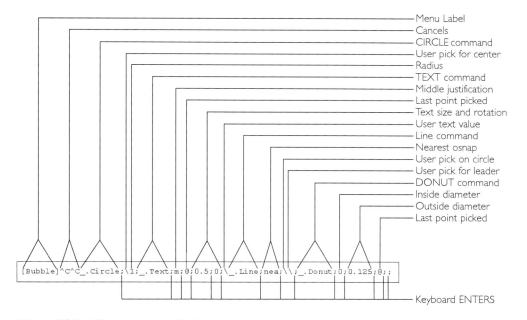

**Figure 23.8**   The diagrammed Bubble macro.

Menu macros are intended to save the user's time and effort. Frequently, the macros that increase efficiency the most are simple in concept and in the amount of macrocode required. As you have seen in the macro exercises, placing macros into a menu is a relatively simple process. The time and effort that you spend developing and implementing the macros that apply to your particular work requirements is quickly repaid, enabling you to work faster and smarter.

# Summary

AutoCAD offers a myriad of ways to customize both its commands and its command interface. Such customization offers the advantages of saving time and increasing your drawing efficiency. In this chapter, you have gained the basic understanding of AutoCAD menus and the special language used to build time-saving menu macros. Also, you were introduced to the new CUSTOM partial menu, which is provided to store a user's personal menu customizations. You now have the tools to build simple menu macros or to use in investigating menu customization further.

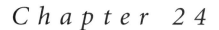

*Chapter 24*

# Implementing CAD Standards

Everyday, gigabytes of CAD data are created, and then much of it is used by others immediately or at some point in the near future. It is the policy of a standard that determines if this data created today will be usable tomorrow or years later. This chapter takes a look at tools that are included in AutoCAD 2005 known as CAD Standards. The following topics are discussed in this chapter to give you a understanding of these new features:

- Configuring CAD standards
- Checking standards
- Completing layer translations

All the various components that you create within AutoCAD can be customized to your specific needs. You can change layer colors, text styles, dimension appearances, and so on. It is the very ease of these changes that requires the development of some level of standard. Generally, these are defined by those responsible for the drawings—an architect or CAD manager. After your drawing *look* has been determined, which in itself can very difficult, you then can leverage the built-in mechanisms in AutoCAD to help you and your fellow coworkers follow them.

# Configuring Standards

To use any set of standards, you have to first define those standards. Creating an AutoCAD Drawing Standards file is simple: Open a drawing that conforms to your standards and then use the SAVEAS command to create a new file with the extension of DWS.

AutoCAD 2005 also comes with a toolbar for CAD Standards commands, and it provides a menu under the Tools pull-down menu named CAD Standards. Figure 24.1 shows where you can locate these tools.

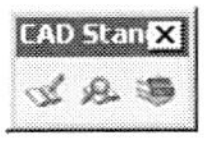

**Figure 24.1**
The CAD Standards commands can be accessed through the Tools pull-down menu or a toolbar button.

Any "standard" starts with documentation of the standard. Within AutoCAD, this is done by creating a drawing that emulates your desired standard. The following exercise covers the process of creating a Drawing Standard (DWS) file.

### Exercise 24.1    Developing a CAD Standard

1. Using Windows Explorer, create a directory on your C:\ drive and call it **IAC2005**. You will use this directory for files created during these exercises.

2. Open the 24EX01.dwg from the accompanying CD. This drawing has layer names and other user-defined items in it.

3. From the File pull-down menu, choose Save As. From the Files of type list, choose AutoCAD Drawing Standards (*.dws). Name the file **MASTER** and save it to your local hard disk in the IAC2005 directory, as shown in Figure 24.2.

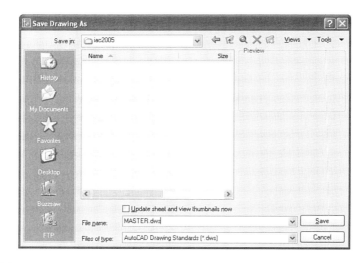

**Figure 24.2**    The Save Drawing As dialog enables you to create Drawing Standards files.

4. Open the Layer Properties Manager dialog by choosing the Layers button on the toolbar. These are the layer names and properties that you want other drawings to have (see Figure 24.3). Close the Layer Properties Manager dialog.

Other components you want others to follow are the text and dimension styles. They are also set properly in this drawing already.

Close this DWS file; you do not need it to be open for the following exercises.

As you have seen, the process of making a DWS file is simple. You might have noticed that the drawing you started with had no objects, but that is just how it was made. You could very well have standards files with all sorts of objects to help you define your named object properties. A named object is anything that the user can *name*. Examples of these are layers, blocks, text styles, and so on. In order to remove these named objects, you can use the PURGE command. PURGE is covered in Chapter 9, "Object Selection and Manipulation." Only named objects that are not being used in a drawing can be purged.

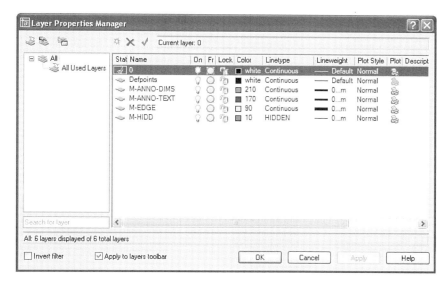

**Figure 24.3**    The Layer Properties Manager shows the layer names, colors, and linetypes of your "standard."

# Checking Standards

After you discover a standards problem (such as a misnamed layer or text with the wrong font style), you typically must fix it. However, the time needed to fix a drawing—or many—can be the difference between missing a deadline or getting that bonus. Having the best drawing does nothing if your client refuses it because it did not meet project standards.

In the previous exercise, you created a Drawing Standards file. This file now contains the all-important information that needs to be followed. After you have your standard files ready, you can link them to a drawing and take advantage of their internal information.

### Exercise 24.2   Applying a CAD Standard

1. Open the drawing 24EX02.dwg from the accompanying CD. This contains various objects that you will check against your Drawing Standards file.

2. From the Tools pull-down menu, choose CAD Standards, Configure. This starts the STANDARDS command and displays the Configure Standards dialog, as shown in Figure 24.4.

   Note that on the Standards tab panel, nothing is listed. We first need to associate a DWS with this drawing before it can be checked.

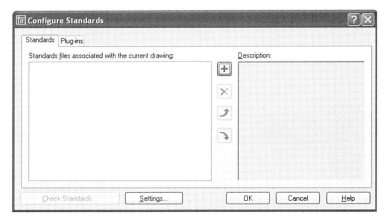

**Figure 24.4**   The Configure Standards dialog is the control center for standards application in AutoCAD 2005.

3. To associate a standards file, choose the plus (+) button near the middle of the dialog. This opens the Select Standards File dialog.

4. Using the Select Standards File dialog, browse to and select the \IAC2005\ MASTER.dws file you created in the previous exercise. You can also locate this file on the accompanying CD.

5. The standards file is read in, and some general DWS file information is listed in the Configure Standards dialog, as shown in Figure 24.5.

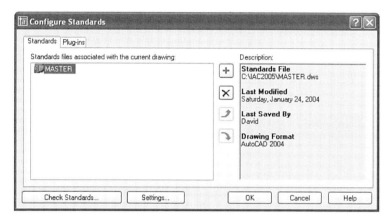

**Figure 24.5**   The Configure Standards dialog is used to attach DWS files to your current drawing.

**I**NSIDER **NOTE**

You can use both AutoCAD 2000 and 2004 drawing formats for standards files. The information they contain is fully compatible with all 200x versions of AutoCAD.

6. Select the Plug-ins tab. This panel shows you which plug-ins are loaded in the AutoCAD installation (see Figure 24.6). These are the areas that are evaluated when you check the drawing standards. Click the OK button to close the dialog.

**I**NSIDER **NOTE**

The installed plug-ins that come with AutoCAD 2005 are Dimension Styles, Layers, Linetypes, and Text Styles. Because this technology is extensible, the Communication Center can inform you of any new plug-ins that are released and even install them if so desired.

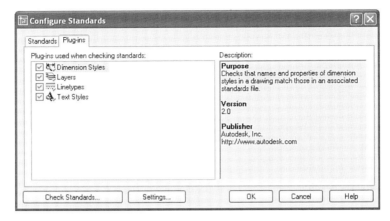

**Figure 24.6**   The Plug-ins panel in the Configure Standards dialog shows you what categories
will be checked for standards compliance.

**I**NSIDER **N**OTE

> Application of a standards file to a given drawing and the corresponding icon in the
> Communication Center are drawing-specific. As you change drawing files, you can
> quickly tell if you drawing has an associated standard by reviewing the
> Communication Center.

When you attach a standards file to the current drawing,
the Communication Center shows that fact with an icon
that resembles a book. Figure 24.7 shows the
Communication Center along with the Associated
Standards File(s) icon.

7. Next, execute a check of the current drawing against the
   DWS file you associated with it. Click the Associated
   Standards File(s) icon shown in Figure 24.7. The command name for this is CHECKSTANDARDS, in case you
   ever feel like typing it.

**Figure 24.7**
The Communication
Center contains an icon
to notify of an attached
standards file.

The Check Standards dialog has several areas for study (see Figure 24.8). At the
top is the Problem information box. This is where the program describes standards inconsistencies that exist in the current drawing.

**Figure 24.8**   The Check Standards dialog has several sections showing problems, solutions, and previews of proposed changes.

In the Replace with area, you get a suggestion of a fix for the current problem. When you select the item in question, in this case the correct Dimstyle to use, the Fix button near the bottom becomes available. This is your way to "make it so;" you click the button, and the proposed change happens immediately without leaving the dialog.

**INSIDER NOTE**

After you click the Fix button, the current problem is corrected immediately. Note that there is no Cancel button on the dialog, only a Close button. When you leave the dialog, the changes made already exist. You can, of course, UNDO all the changes if needed.

The Preview of changes area shows any collateral information. In this case, the text style also will be changed so that dimension style can be applied properly.

Also of note is the Settings button in the lower left. This displays the CAD
Standards Settings dialog box (see Figure 24.9). Here, you can choose to fix
problems automatically (used when the names of named objects match, such
as layers), turn off the display of ignored problems, and specify the default
standards file to use with the Replace With section in the dialog.

**Figure 24.9**   The CAD Standards Settings dialog has a number of options to speed up
making changes.

**I**NSIDER  **N**OTE

> You use the Notification Settings in the CAD Standards Settings dialog to control how
> "annoying" you would like the checking mechanism to be. The bottom option, Display
> standards status bar icon, is the most active. The top option removes all notifications.

8.  With that overview, select the M-DIM01 Dimstyle and then click the Fix button.
    This performs the change and then advances to the next problem.

9.  Now you see a problem with the layer Behind. Using the scroll bar, go down and
    select the M-HIDD layer. Looking in the Preview area, you can tell that the
    color, linetype, and lineweight are also wrong (Figure 24.10).

**Figure 24.10** The Check Standards dialog shows a typical layer problem that can easily be fixed with one found in the Standards File.

**10.** Click the Fix button to make this change and move to the next problem.

**11.** Another layer issue is the Edge Layer problem. Choose the M-EDGE layer and click the Fix button.

**12.** The next issue is with the Dimension Layer. In the Replace With list, choose M-ANNO-DIMS and click the Fix button.

**13.** For the Text layer problem, choose the M-ANNO-TEXT and click the Fix button.

**14.** The program then starts on any text style problems. It found that in the DWS, there was no text style named ROMANS. Because we have several text styles, you must select just one, similar to the way you work with layers (see Figure 24.11). Click the Arial text style and then the Fix button to proceed.

**Figure 24.11**    The Check Standards dialog with several Text Style options.

15. The program finishes. The Checking Complete dialog appears, showing the results (Figure 24.12).

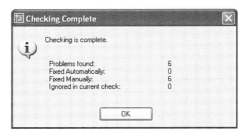

**Figure 24.12**    The results of the standards check and correction.

Now, even though the Check Standards dialog is not open, it is working for you at all times. As non-standard named items come into existence in your drawing, the Communication Center notifies you of them. For example, when you create a single layer not listed in your DWS file, the alert shown in Figure 24.13 appears.

**Figure 24.13**    The Communication Center provides notification of any standards violations that occur.

**16.** Click the Close button to end the command. All appropriate items from the attached DWS file have been incorporated into the current drawing.

You may close this drawing; there is no need to save.

You should have a fairly good understanding of the power of the CAD standards after that exercise. You learned that after you have defined a DWS file, you can easily modify a drawing to match that standards file. This technique can be used to update old drawings to new standards and to help new users learn your unique methods of organization. You can also open your DWS files later and correct them as needed.

Sometimes, you need the power of the CAD standards, but you have to develop DWS files to use them. So, what if your problems are solely layer-related? You could use a more streamlined feature for that. The following section covers this method.

# Layer Translation

Users of AutoCAD have been doing layer translations for years, usually by hand or through a custom script file. They would simply rename the layer to another name and then use the LAYER command to change any properties such as color and linetype. Obviously, for large drawings, this can be a time-consuming process.

AutoCAD 2005 has a feature called the Layer Translator (LAYTRANS). This program makes the process of changing layer names and properties nearly painless. The exercise that follows shows you how to use this new feature.

### Exercise 24.3    Using the Layer Translator

1. In AutoCAD, open the file 24EX03.dwg from the accompanying CD. This drawing contains objects on layers that need updating.

2. From the Tools pull-down menu, choose CAD Standards and then Layer Translator. The Layer Translator dialog opens (see Figure 24.14).

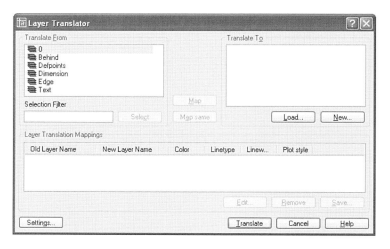

**Figure 24.14**    The Layer Translator dialog box shows all layers in the current drawing.

The Layer Translator dialog has three primary areas. The upper-left section lists all layers in the current drawing that could be translated. The upper-right section houses the layer names to which you can translate. The bottom section shows the series of translation mappings that will occur.

3. The first step is to get a list of layers to translate to. Click the Load button on the right. A Select Drawing File dialog appears; browse to the accompanying CD and load the 24EX01.dwg file. In the Translate To section, you can see a list of the layer names found in the 24EX01 drawing (see Figure 24.15).

**I**NSIDER **T**IP

You can load a layer translation set from a DWG, DWT, or DWS file. You can retrieve your prototype layer parameters regardless of how you store them.

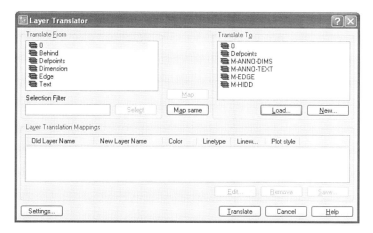

**Figure 24.15**    The Layer Translator dialog now shows layer names in the Translate To area.

4. Now you begin to match the layer names. Select the layer Behind in the Translate From area and then select the layer M-HIDD in the Translate To area. Click on the Map button, which was activated after both layers were selected. Follow this procedure for each of the items in the following list.

**INSIDER NOTE**

You can also double-click on the right layer list to map to the select layer in the Translate From list.

| Behind | = | M-HIDD |
| Dimension | = | M-ANNO-DIMS |
| Edge | = | M-EDGE |
| Text | = | M-ANNO-TEXT |

Did you notice that after each match, the layer on the left was removed from the list, but the layer on the right stayed? This enables you to see what has not been mapped but also enables you to combine two original layers onto one single layer.

On the right side is a New button. This button enables you to create a layer that does not exist in your prototype and match any layer to it.

5. You now should have two layers remaining, 0 and Defpoints. There is a quick way to clean them up. You can use the Map Same button to instantly match all layers that have matching names. This can be used for drawings in which you know the layer names are good, but the properties might be wrong. Click the Map Same button to match those leftover layers.

6. The Settings button at the lower left provides controls for forcing objects to take on the new properties. Click this button to open the Settings dialog (see Figure 24.16).

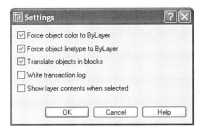

**Figure 24.16**    The Settings dialog provides controls for how to apply layer translations.

This dialog is helpful to clean up work where objects themselves have been given properties for color and the like. The default options make everything ByLayer.

7. The Settings dialog can be used to create a log and also to turn on all layers when finished, if desired. Turn off the Write Transaction Log option if it's checked and then click the OK.

If a layer to Translate To was not quite right, you can adjust it by selecting the layer in the Layer Translation Mappings area and then clicking on the Edit button. This opens the Edit Layer dialog and enables you to change a setting after you have mapped it (see Figure 24.17).

**Figure 24.17**    The Edit Layer dialog can be used to further adjust a layer translation.

Also after selecting a layer in the Layer Translation Mapping list, you can remove it from being processed. Doing so puts it back in the Translate From list. You then can translate it to another layer if needed.

8. Now that you have made all the mappings needed for your translation, you can take these layer changes and save them to a DWS file. Later on this file can be used for loading into the Layer Translator back in step 3, or you could use it for the Check Standards feature discussed earlier. Because you are done here, just press the Translate button. AutoCAD asks if you would like to save your mappings; after all that work you normally would, but reply No. The layer changes are made immediately, and the dialog closes.

9. To review what has changed, open the Layer Property Manager dialog and notice the new layer names and properties. Click Close when done.

You can now close this drawing; there is no need to save it.

Using the Layer Translator is only as difficult as knowing what your layer standard is supposed to be. As with any detail-oriented issue in AutoCAD, it is imperative that you document your layer names and their properties. If you do this, it is likely that you will never need to use this program unless wholesale changes are made to your standards. Alternatively, if you do get drawings from others and need to modify them for your use, using the Layer Translator dialog can reduce an hour-long process into minutes.

# Summary

In this chapter, you have been exposed to new features introduced for the purposes of CAD Standards. These new applications help you create Drawing Standards files and apply a DWS file to a drawing, thereby modifying its named object properties. You also learned about a quick tool for adjusting layer names and properties.

As time goes by, the level of collaborative work in your industry will undoubtedly increase. By mastering these features, you can take data from others and convert it quickly. Although the these tools in AutoCAD 2005 cannot solve all standard issues, they do solve basic layer, dimension, text style, and linetype problems that sometimes occur. By applying these features, you can handle the rogue drafter and still use what he or she produces.

# Part VI

# Three-Dimensional Techniques

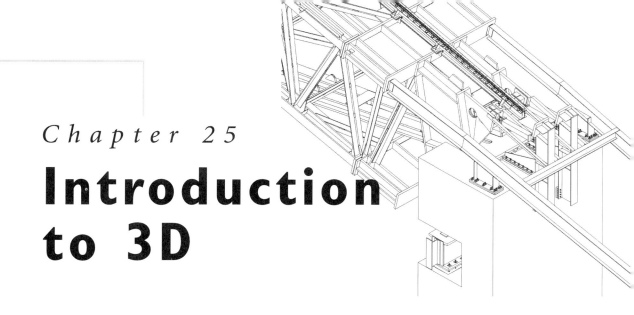

# Chapter 25
# Introduction to 3D

Up to this point, you have been learning about drawing 2D representations of real-world 3D objects. This method of designing and drafting is limited because a 2D drawing must be visualized as a 3D real-world object. Drawing 3D objects as 3D objects largely eliminates the need to mentally visualize the project because the 3D information is included in the design drawing. Drawing and designing in 3D offers other advantages as well. For example, the viewpoint can be changed to help define the form of the object. In addition, shaded and rendered presentations—and even animations—are possible (see Figure 25.1). Manufacturing and other information, such as Finite Element Analysis (FEA) data, can also be extracted.

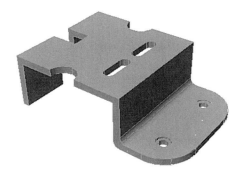

**Figure 25.1** A 3D solid model that has been shaded using AutoCAD's SHADE command.

The 3D capabilities of AutoCAD 2005 can be a valuable addition to your design skills. This chapter introduces you to the following topics:

- Understanding 3D coordinate systems
- Defining a User Coordinate System (UCS) in 3D space
- Using viewports
- Interactive viewing in 3D
- Shading a model

# Understanding 3D Coordinate Systems

Working in 3D is theoretically no more difficult than working in 2D. In practice, however, the presence of the third dimension greatly complicates your task. In 3D, you can work on an infinite number of drawing planes—not just the XY plane of 2D drawings.

Figure 25.2 shows the three axes that define AutoCAD's 3D world. These three axes can be aligned with any number of working planes conforming to the geometry of the 3D model.

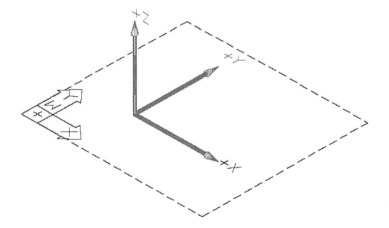

**Figure 25.2**   Working in 3D means working with an additional axis, the Z-axis.

Figure 25.3 shows a simple 3D model with five of the many possible coordinate systems that you might define for use while working on the model. Each coordinate system is called a *User Coordinate System,* or UCS. Of course, many other UCSs are possible with just this one model. It is the flexibility of the UCS that makes constructing and working with 3D models possible.

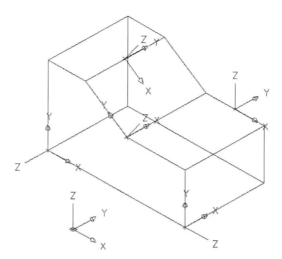

**Figure 25.3**    You can define an unlimited number of UCSs in a 3D drawing. This graphic shows possible locations; multiple UCSs cannot be active simultaneously in the same view.

Understanding how to position and manipulate 3D coordinate systems is the key to creating 3D models in AutoCAD, and the key to understanding 3D coordinates is an understanding of AutoCAD's User Coordinate System.

> **INSIDER NOTE**
>
> Within the UCSICON command is a Properties control that enables you to customize the look of the UCS icon. Refer to Chapter 7, "Using Coordinate Systems," for more information about this feature.

# Defining a User Coordinate System in 3D Space

The UCS command provides the means of changing the location of the 0,0,0 origin point of a coordinate system, as well as the orientation of the XY plane and Z-axis. Any plane or point in 3D space can be referenced, saved, and recalled, and you can define as many UCSs as you require. Coordinate input and display are relative to the current UCS. In AutoCAD 2005, if multiple viewports are active, you can assign a different UCS to each one.

Usually, it is easier to align the coordinate system with existing geometry than to determine the exact placement of a 3D point.

## Defining a New UCS

You can define a UCS in one of the following ways:

- Specify a new origin, new XY plane, or new Z-axis
- Align the new UCS with an existing object
- Align the new UCS with the current viewing direction
- Align the new UCS with the face of a solid object
- Rotate the current UCS around any of its axes
- Select a preset UCS provided by AutoCAD

**I**NSIDER **N**OTE

> The capability to align a UCS with the face of a solid is a powerful feature. Although you can align a UCS with a solid face using several other options of the UCS command, the "face" option is usually much faster.

In the following exercise, you use UCS command options that you might not be familiar with from work in 2D drawings to define UCSs on 3D objects.

**I**NSIDER **N**OTE

> Before exploring the methods of establishing 3D coordinate systems, you may want to review the basics of the World Coordinate System in Chapter 7.

### Exercise 25.1     Specifying a New UCS by Using the ZAxis, 3point, Object, View, Face, and Preset Options

1. Open the 25EX01.dwg drawing file on the accompanying CD-ROM. Your drawing should resemble Figure 25.4. Note the position of the World Coordinate System icon to the lower left of the model. Although it's not necessary, you may want to set a running endpoint osnap.

   In the following step, you use the ZAxis option to define a new UCS. The ZAxis option specifies a new UCS origin and a point that lies on the positive Z-axis.

2. Using the Tools pull-down menu, choose New UCS, followed by Z Axis Vector.

3. Specify the new origin point by snapping to the endpoint at ❶ in Figure 25.4. Specify a point on the positive portion of the new Z-axis by picking at ❷. The UCS should appear as it does in the upper-left viewport of Figure 25.5.

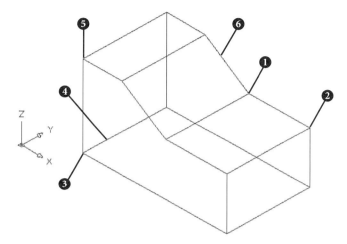

**Figure 25.4**    The 25EX01.DWG's 3D object with pick points for new UCSs.

In the following step, you establish a new UCS using the 3point option. The 3point option enables you to specify the new UCS origin and the direction of its positive X- and Y-axes.

4. Press Enter to restart the command-line version of the UCS command and type **New**.

5. Choose the **3point** option and specify the new origin by picking the endpoint at ❸ in Figure 25.4. Specify a point on the positive portion of the new X-axis by using a midpoint osnap and picking at ❹. Specify a point on the positive-Y portion of the XY plane by picking the endpoint at ❺. The new UCS should now be placed as shown in the upper-right viewport of Figure 25.5.

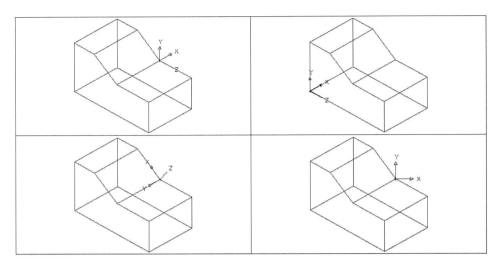

**Figure 25.5** Four possible UCSs for the 25EX01.dwg model.

**INSIDER TIP**

If you need to align a UCS with the end of an arc, a quick method exists using the 3point option. At the Specify new origin point prompt, pick the end of the arc to position the UCS icon. At the Specify point on positive portion of X-axis prompt, pick the center of the arc. At the Specify point on positive-Y portion of the UCS XY plane prompt, pick the other end of the arc (or somewhere on the arc). The icon should align with the arc; now just run UCS again and rotate the X-axis another 90 degrees. The UCS should now align perfectly tangent to the arc, ready for drawing!

In the next step, you use the Object option of the UCS command to establish a new UCS. The Object option defines the UCS with the same extrusion (positive-Z) direction as the selected object. The origin and orientation of the new XY plane depend upon the object chosen and are somewhat arbitrary.

6. Restart the UCS command and type **NEW**. Type **OB** and press Enter to select the Object option.

7. At the Select object to align UCS prompt, pick near ❻ in Figure 25.4. The new UCS should conform to that shown in the lower-left viewport of Figure 25.5.

   In the following step, you set a new UCS using the View option. The View option establishes a new UCS with the XY plane perpendicular to the viewing direction (parallel to the display screen). The origin stays unchanged.

8.  Start the UCS command and type **NEW**. Type the **V** option. The UCS aligns the XY plane with the display screen without changing the UCS origin, as shown in the lower-right viewport of Figure 25.5.

**I**NSIDER **TIP**

> The View UCS is useful when you want to add text to a non-orthographic view. The text is automatically placed parallel to the plane of the display screen.

In the next step, you establish a preset UCS using the Orthographic option of the UCS command. An orthographic preset UCS includes one of the six standard orthographic UCSs provided with AutoCAD.

9.  Start the UCS command and choose the Orthographic option by typing **G** and pressing Enter. Options for the six standard orthographic UCS orientations appear. Choose the Front option by typing **F** and pressing Enter. The UCS switches to the standard Front orientation, as shown in the upper-left viewport of Figure 25.6. Note that the Front UCS shares the World Coordinate System's origin.

    In the next step, you use the X,Y,Z rotation option to establish a new XY plane. The X,Y,Z option rotates the current UCS about a specified axis.

10. Start the UCS command, type **NEW**, and then type **Y** to indicate that you want to rotate the current UCS about the Y-axis. When you're prompted to specify the rotation about the Y-axis, press Enter to accept the default of 90. The new UCS retains the same origin, but the XY plane is rotated about the Y-axis 90 degrees, as shown in the upper-right viewport of Figure 25.6. (See the section titled "Right-Hand Rule" later in this chapter for rules governing rotations about a 3D-axis.)

**I**NSIDER **TIP**

> When establishing a new UCS by rotating the current UCS about the X-, Y-, or Z-axis, you can either specify a rotation angle or accept the default angle. This default angle can be changed using the UCSAXISANG system variable. Changing the angle to one you frequently use can save an input step when using the X-, Y-, or Z-axis rotation options of the UCS command.

The Face option can be used to quickly align a new UCS with the face of a 3D solid. This option is shown in the next step.

11. Start the UCS command, choose New, and then type **F**. At the Select face of solid object prompt, pick near ❶ in the lower-left viewport of Figure 25.6. Type **Y** and press Enter to flip the UCS 180 degrees about the Y-axis. Then type **X** and press Enter to flip the UCS 180 degrees about the X-axis. Then press Enter to accept the UCS, as shown in the lower-left viewport of Figure 25.6.

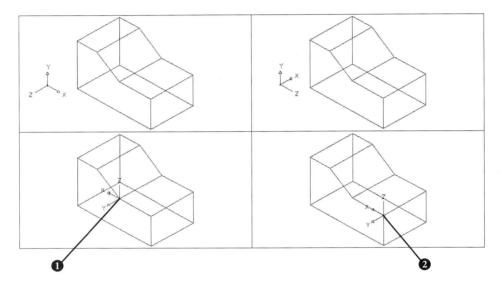

**Figure 25.6**   Moving the UCS around in a 3D model.

In the last step, you use the Move option of the UCS command. Just as the X,Y,Z option changes the XY plane without changing the origin, the Move option changes the origin without changing the XY plane orientation.

12. Start the UCS command and choose the Move option. When prompted for the new origin point, snap to the Endpoint at ❷ in the lower-right viewport of Figure 25.6. The XY plane orientation may differ from that shown in the lower-right image in Figure 25.6.

    Leave this drawing open if you plan to continue with the next exercise now; otherwise, close the drawing without saving changes.

**I** NSIDER **T**IP

> When using the UCS New option, you do not have to specify New if you don't want
> to. Instead, you can skip the New option and just indicate the New option you want
> such as **3** for 3point or **V** for view.

## Right-Hand Rule

In the previous exercise, you established a new UCS by rotating the current UCS about
one of its axes. The convention for defining the positive direction of rotation about an
axis is summed up in the so-called "Right-Hand Rule." To determine the positive rotation direction about an axis, point your right thumb in the positive direction of the axis
and then curl your fingers in a fist around the axis. The "curl" of your fingers indicates
the positive rotation direction of the axis. This sense of the direction of rotation about
an axis is used consistently throughout AutoCAD's 3D commands involving axes, such
as the REVSURF command in surface modeling and the REVOLVE command used with
solids. The positive rotation direction about the three axes is shown in Figure 25.7.

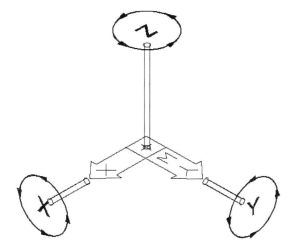

**Figure 25.7**   The direction of positive rotation about the X-, Y-, and Z-axes.

## Using the UCS Manager

Although the UCS command gives you maximum flexibility in setting, naming, restoring, and deleting a UCS, the UCSMAN (UCS Manager) command displays a multitabbed dialog box that presents a convenient, graphical method of restoring a saved UCS, establishing an orthographic UCS, and specifying UCS icon and UCS settings for viewports. In the following exercise, you use the Orthographic UCSs tab of the UCS dialog box to establish and position a preset orthographic UCS.

**Exercise 25.2    Specifying and Placing a Preset UCS with the UCS Manager**

1. Continue from the previous exercise or open 25EX02.dwg from the accompanying CD-ROM. If necessary, restore the WCS by using the World option of the UCS command. (Start the UCS command and press Enter.) Your drawing should resemble Figure 25.4 from the previous exercise.

2. From the Tools pull-down menu, choose Orthographic UCS, then Preset. AutoCAD displays the UCS dialog box with the Orthographic UCSs tab current (as shown in Figure 25.8).

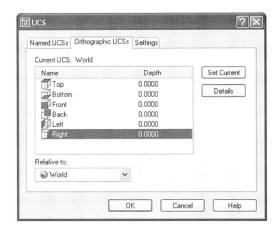

**Figure 25.8**    The UCS Manager's UCS dialog box with the Orthographic UCSs tab displayed.

3. Choose the Right option. Select the Set Current button and click OK. AutoCAD establishes a standard right orthographic UCS. Note that this UCS shares the 0,0,0 origin of the WCS.

    In the next step, you change the origin of the current UCS using the Depth feature of the UCS dialog box. This enables you to move the origin along the current Z-axis.

**4.** Press Enter to redisplay the UCS dialog box. With the Right orthographic UCS chosen, right-click and choose Depth to display the Orthographic UCS Depth dialog box, as shown in Figure 25.9.

**Figure 25.9**    The Orthographic UCS Depth dialog box of the UCS dialog box.

**5.** Click the button with the arrowhead (the Set Depth button) and, in the drawing, use an endpoint osnap to pick at ❶ in the upper-left viewport of Figure 25.10. In the Orthographic UCS Depth dialog box, click OK, then click OK in the UCS dialog box. AutoCAD moves the origin of the UCS along its Z-axis to equal the Z-axis value of the point at ❶.

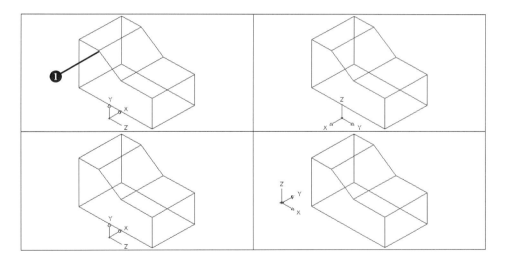

**Figure 25.10**    Moving the UCS around your model.

Now that you have established a new, non-preset UCS, you name and save it in the next step.

**6.** Type **UCS** and press Enter. Choose the Save option. When you're prompted for a name to save the current UCS to, type **MIDWAY** and press Enter. The UCS is saved with the name MIDWAY.

▌**NSIDER NOTE** _____

> You can restore named UCSs by using the Restore option of the UCS command or from the Named UCSs tab of the UCS dialog box. To access the UCS dialog box, open the Tools pull-down menu and choose Named UCS.

After you have named and saved a non-preset UCS as you did in steps 5 and 6, you can establish a new UCS relative to the named UCS, as shown in the next step.

7. From the Tools pull-down menu, choose Orthographic UCS, then Preset. On the UCS dialog box's Orthographic UCSs tab, choose the Back preset orthographic UCS. Under Relative To:, choose Midway from the drop-down list. Choose Set Current and click OK. The new UCS is changed to a "back" orientation relative to the previously named Midway UCS, as shown in the upper-right viewport of Figure 25.10.

▌**NSIDER NOTE** _____

> In the previous step, you also could have simultaneously changed the depth of the new UCS by using the Depth feature of the UCS dialog box, as you did previously in steps 4 and 5.

AutoCAD keeps track of the last 10 coordinate systems created in both model and paper space. Repeating the Previous option of the UCS command steps you back through the list. In the following step, you use the Previous option of the UCS command to return to the previous UCS.

8. Start the UCS command and select the Previous option. AutoCAD restores the most recent UCS (refer to the lower-left viewport in Figure 25.10).

In the last step of this exercise, you reestablish the World Coordinate System for the model.

9. Start the UCS command and accept the default World option by pressing Enter. AutoCAD restores the WCS, as shown in the lower-right viewport of Figure 25.10.

Close the drawing without saving.

**I**NSIDER **T**IP

> When you're working in the Orthographic UCSs tab of the UCS dialog box, be sure that the desired UCS is displayed in the Relative To: list before you change to any of the six preset UCSs. Orienting a new UCS relative to the World Coordinate System instead of to a UCS that you have named can produce very different results.

## UCSs and Viewports

The capability to have multiple viewports is helpful when you're working in 3D. Multiple viewports provide different views of your model and facilitate editing and visualizing your work. In addition to offering a different view, in AutoCAD 2005, each viewport can be assigned a different UCS. In addition, the UCS in one viewport can be transferred, or "copied," to any number of other viewports.

The UCS icon is normally visible in the lower-left corner of the viewport. It can, however, either be turned off or set to display at the origin of the current coordinate system on a per-viewport basis. You can also configure the UCS to automatically change to the associated UCS whenever an orthographic view is restored in a viewport. Lastly, you can set each viewport to generate a plan view whenever you change coordinate systems. Two of these viewport features are demonstrated in the following exercise.

### Exercise 25.3    Setting Different Coordinate Systems in Viewports

1. Open 25EX03.dwg from the accompanying CD-ROM. This drawing shows a solid model of a bracket. Your drawing should resemble Figure 25.11.

   The UCS applied in each viewport is controlled by the UCSVP system variable. When UCSVP is set to 1 in a viewport, the most recently used UCS in that viewport is saved and is restored when the viewport is once again made current. If UCSVP is set to 0 in a viewport, the UCS icon for that viewport always reflects the UCS in the current viewport model space.

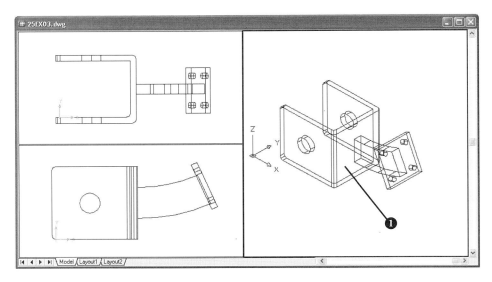

**Figure 25.11**  The multiview solid model drawing of the bracket.

The three viewports of this drawing show a top view, a front view, and an isometric view. The UCSVP system variable in all three viewports is set to 1, enabling each viewport to have a separate UCS active. In the next step, you set the UCSVP system variable for the right isometric viewport to 0.

2. Pick in the bottom-left viewport to make it current. Note that the UCSs in all three viewports remain unchanged. Now pick in the right isometric viewport to make it current. Type **UCSVP** and press Enter. When prompted, type in the value **0**.

3. Now pick the upper-left viewport to make it current. Note that the UCS icon in the isometric viewport changes to match the current viewport.

4. Pick the lower-left viewport and note that the UCS icon in the isometric viewport again changes to match the current viewport. Note that as you alternately pick the upper- and lower-left viewports, the UCS icon in the isometric viewport changes to reflect the UCS of the current viewport.

   In the next two steps, you establish a new UCS in the isometric view and then transfer the UCS to the top view's viewport.

5. Pick the isometric viewport to make it current. Start the UCS command and choose the New option. Select the Face option, and when you're prompted with Select face of solid object, pick on the face at ❶ in Figure 25.11 and press Enter. A new UCS is established on the side face of the bracket.

6. Start the **UCS** command again and choose **Apply**. When you're prompted with Pick viewport to apply current UCS…, pick the upper-left viewport and press Enter.

---

**I**NSIDER **N**OTE

If you are using the 2D UCSICON instead of the 3D version, the UCS icon turns into a broken pencil to show that the UCS plane is perpendicular to the display. Because it's a 2D type of symbol, it cannot be displayed—hence, the broken pencil icon.

---

7. With the top-left viewport still current, select the View pull-down menu, then 3D Views, Plan View, Current UCS. The upper-left viewport now shows a plan view of the new UCS.

8. Once again, alternately pick in the top-left and bottom-left viewports and note that the UCS icon in the isometric view changes to reflect the UCS in the current viewport. Your drawing should now resemble Figure 25.12.

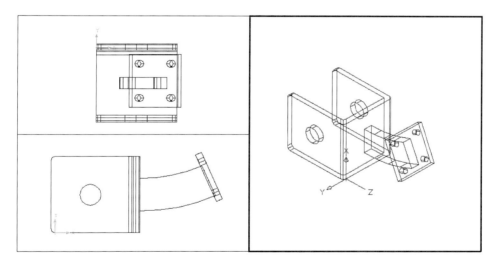

**Figure 25.12**    Transferring a UCS from one viewport to another.

> **INSIDER NOTE**
>
> Because you used the Face option of the UCS command, the orientation of the
> X- and Y-axes you obtained in step 5 may differ from that shown in Figure 25.12. As
> explained earlier in this chapter, using the Face and Object options of the UCS com-
> mand yields X- and Y-axis orientations that depend upon the geometry of the object
> or solid face. If axis orientation is important for your editing work, you can reorient
> the X- and Y-axes using the Next, Xflip, and Yflip options of the Face option or the
> Z-axis rotation option of the UCS command when the basic XY plane is established.

Being able to maintain separate UCSs on a per-viewport basis and being able to
transfer a UCS from one viewport to other viewports are effective tools to help
you quickly navigate to various planes and orientations in your model. In the
next step, you turn the UCS icon off in the active viewport.

9. Pick in the isometric viewport to make it active. From the View pull-down
   menu, choose Display and then UCS Icon. Select ON to remove the check mark.
   The UCS icon in the active viewport is now turned off.

   Close this drawing without saving.

## System Variables That Control the UCS

The ability to easily establish new coordinate systems and the ability to move, orient,
name, recall, and associate UCSs with individual views are among the most important
tools you have for working in 3D. The following list summarizes the many AutoCAD system variables that create or control User Coordinate Systems:

- **UCSAXISANG.** Stores the default angle when rotating the UCS around one of its
  axes using the X, Y, or Z option of the UCS command.

- **UCSBASE.** Stores the name of the UCS that defines the origin and orientation of
  orthographic UCS settings.

- **UCSFOLLOW.** Generates a plan view whenever you change from one UCS to
  another (also controlled from the UCS Manager dialog box).

- **UCSICON.** Displays the UCS icon for the current viewport (also controlled from
  the UCS Manager dialog box).

- **UCSNAME.** Stores the name of the current coordinate system for the current space.

- **UCSORG.** Stores the origin point of the current coordinate system for the current
  space.

- **UCSORTHO.** Determines whether the related orthographic UCS setting is automatically restored when an orthographic view is restored (also controlled from the View dialog box).

- **UCSVIEW.** Determines whether the current UCS is saved with a named view.

- **UCSVP.** Determines whether the UCS in active viewports remains fixed or changes to reflect the UCS of the currently active viewport (also controlled from the UCS Manager dialog box).

- **UCSXDIR.** Stores the X direction of the current UCS for the current space.

- **UCSYDIR.** Stores the Y direction of the current UCS for the current space.

# Using Viewports

Another important feature to help with your work in 3D is AutoCAD's ability to simultaneously display more than one model space viewport. In model space, AutoCAD usually displays a single viewport filling the entire drawing area. You can, however, divide the drawing area into several viewports. In model space, these viewports are "tiled" or fit together as adjacent rectangles much like tiles on a floor. Unlike the viewports of paper space discussed in Chapter 18, "Paper Space Layouts," model space viewports cover the entire screen and do not behave as editable boundary objects. Figure 25.13 shows a 3D drawing with three viewports defined.

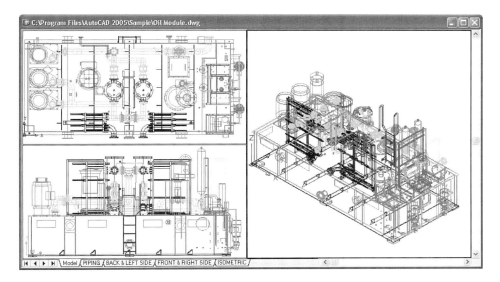

**Figure 25.13**  A 3D drawing displayed in three viewports.

Multiple viewports are especially useful when you're working in 3D because you can set up a top (or plan) view in one viewport, set up a front (or elevation) view in another viewport, and have yet a third viewport show an isometric view of your model. You can see the effects of changes in one view reflected in the other views, and as you learned in an earlier section of this chapter, you can also set the User Coordinate System (UCS) in one viewport so that it is always the same as the UCS in the active or current viewport. Each viewport is largely independent of other viewports, giving you a great amount of flexibility in viewing and editing your model. In each viewport, for example, you can independently:

- Pan and zoom
- Set grid and snap distances
- Control the visibility and placement of the UCS icon
- Set coordinate systems and restore named views

Most of the operations controlling tiled viewports can be carried out from the two tabs of the Viewports dialog box. To display this dialog box, shown in Figure 25.14, you can select the Display Viewports Dialog icon on the Viewports toolbar, or you can choose the View pull-down menu, then Viewports, followed by Named Viewports; you can also enter **VPORTS** at the command prompt.

The functionality of the New Viewports tab of the Viewports dialog box is summarized here:

- **New Name.** If you want to save the viewport configuration you are creating, enter a name here. A list of named viewport configurations is displayed on the Named Viewports tab.
- **Standard Viewports.** The standard viewport configurations are listed here by name.
- **Preview.** Displays a preview of the viewport configuration you select under Standard Viewports. The default views assigned to individual viewports in each configuration are displayed.
- **Apply To.** Enables you to assign the configuration to either the display or the current viewport. Assigning to the display assigns the configuration to the entire display area. Assigning to the current viewport applies the configuration to the current viewport only.

- **Setup.** You can choose either a 2D or 3D setup. When you select 2D, the new viewport configuration is initially created with the current view in all of the viewports. When you select 3D, a set of standard orthogonal views plus an isometric 3D view is applied to the viewports in the configuration.

- **Change View To.** Replaces the selected viewport configuration with the viewport configuration you select from the list. You can choose a named viewport configuration, or if you have selected 3D setup, you can select from the list of standard viewport configurations. Use the Preview area to view the viewport configuration choices.

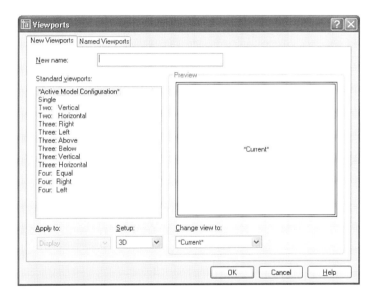

**Figure 25.14**   The Viewports dialog box controls most viewport operations.

In the following exercise, you learn about setting up multiple viewport configurations for work in 3D.

### Exercise 25.4   Configuring Viewports for Work in 3D

1. Open 25EX04.dwg from the accompanying CD. This drawing represents a model of a sliding glass door locking mechanism. Your drawing should resemble Figure 25.15.

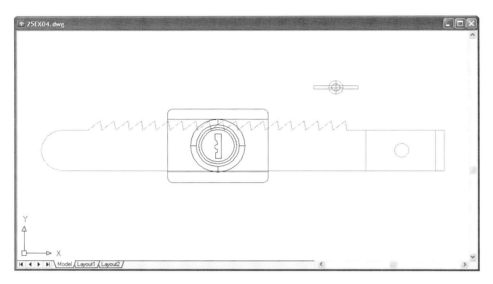

**Figure 25.15**    The initial single viewport view of 25EX04.dwg.

As mentioned earlier in this chapter, the UCSORTHO system variable determines whether the related orthographic UCS setting is restored automatically when a preset orthographic view is established in a viewport. In the next step, you ensure that this system variable is turned on.

2. Type **VIEW**, or from the View toolbar, choose the Named Views icon. In the View dialog box, choose the Orthographic & Isometric Views tab and, if necessary, select Restore Orthographic UCS with View option to place a mark in the check box. Click OK to close the dialog box.

**I**NSIDER **NOTE**

You can also display the View dialog box by opening the View pull-down menu and choosing Named Views. You can also set the UCSORTHO system variable by typing **UCSORTHO** at the command prompt.

In the next three steps, you establish and name a standard 3D three-viewport configuration.

3. From the Viewports toolbar, choose the Display Viewports icon. If necessary, select the New Viewports tab in the Viewports dialog box. In the New Name input box, type **INITIAL-3**.

4. In the Standard Viewports: selection box, select Three Right. Note that the Three Right viewport configuration is shown in the Preview window. The word *Current* indicates that the current screen view of your model will appear in each viewport.

5. To establish more meaningful views for 3D work in the three viewports, under Setup:, select 3D. Note that the viewports in the Preview window now have the standard Top, Front, and SE Isometric views assigned. Make sure Display is showing in the Apply To: selection box and click OK to exit the dialog box. Your drawing should now resemble Figure 25.16.

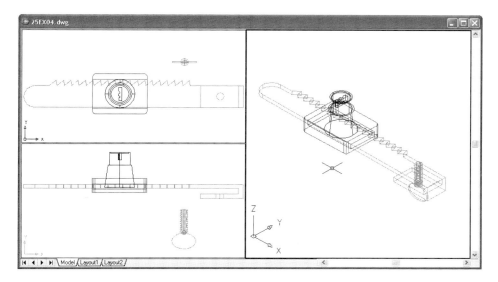

**Figure 25.16** You can easily establish standard Top, Front, and Isometric views.

In the next step, you establish a Right view in the lower-left viewport.

6. Press Enter to redisplay the Viewports dialog box. In the Preview window, pick in the lower-left viewport to make it current. Under Change View To:, scroll to find the Right view and select it. The viewport should display Right. Click OK to close the dialog box. Your display should have a right view in the lower-left viewport.

During the next step, note that the locking screw's position is dynamically updated in all three viewports as you drag it to a new position.

7. Set the upper-left viewport to current. Start the MOVE command, select the green locking screw, and press Enter. Drag the locking screw downward until it is approximately even with the screw hole at the right end of the main locking bar. Leave it in this new position.

8. To further divide a viewport, pick in the right isometric viewport to make it current. Redisplay the Viewports dialog box. In the Standard Viewports selection box, choose Two: Horizontal. Note the names of the proposed views in the Preview window. Select the top or upper viewport in the Preview window. Under Change View To:, select SW Isometric and note that the preview reflects the change. Under Apply To:, make sure Current Viewport is selected. Then close the dialog box. Your drawing should now resemble Figure 25.17.

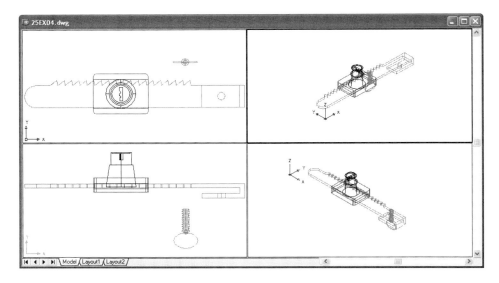

**Figure 25.17**   You can quickly restore a named viewport configuration.

In the next step, you name the current viewport configuration, then you return to a single viewport configuration. In the final step, you restore a named viewport configuration.

9. Redisplay the Viewports dialog box and type **4-SE-SW** in the New Name input box. Click OK to close the dialog box. Select the upper-left viewport to make it current. Then redisplay the Viewports dialog box. In the Standard viewports window, select Single. Be sure that Display is selected under Apply To: and close the dialog box. The previous "current" viewport is now a single viewport (refer to Figure 25.15).

10. Redisplay the Viewports dialog box and select the Named Viewports tab. Under Named Viewports:, select 4-SE-SW. The configuration is shown in the Preview window. Click OK to close the dialog box and restore the 4-SE-SW configuration (as shown in Figure 25.17).

Close this drawing without saving changes.

User-definable coordinate systems and the ability to quickly establish, name, and recall multiple viewport configurations represent two of the most useful tools in 3D modeling. Just as establishing a new UCS enables you to move the drawing's origin and XY plane to a position and orientation best suited for work on various parts or aspects of the model, multiple viewports enable you to see the model from the most advantageous viewpoint.

# Orbit Viewing in 3D

Whereas multiple viewports provide useful static views of a 3D model, the 3DORBIT command enables you to view 3D models interactively. When the 3DORBIT command is active, you manipulate the view with the screen pointing device (the mouse), and you can view the model from any point in 3D space.

The 3D orbit view overlays an "arcball" on the current view of the model. The arcball consists of a circle divided into four quadrants by smaller circles, as shown in Figure 25.18. The center of the arcball represents the target, which remains stationary. As you manipulate the view, the camera, or viewpoint, moves around the target depending upon where you place the pointing device. You click and drag the cursor to rotate the view.

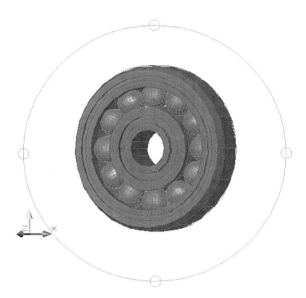

**Figure 25.18** The "arcball" symbol surrounds a 3D model.

Different cursor icon symbols appear depending upon the position of the cursor with respect to the arcball. Four basic movements are possible. The following list shows the cursor icons and their associated movements.

When the cursor is moved inside the arcball, a small sphere encircled by two arrowed lines appears. You can manipulate the view freely in all directions when this icon is active.

When the cursor is moved outside the arcball, a circular arrow surrounding a sphere is displayed. When this cursor is active, clicking and dragging in a vertical motion causes the view to move around an axis that extends through the center of the arcball and is perpendicular to the screen. If you move the cursor inside the arcball, it changes to the sphere encircled by two ellipses, and the view moves freely.

When you move the cursor over one of the small circles on either side of the arcball, a horizontal ellipse encircling a sphere appears. Clicking and dragging when this icon is active rotates the view around the vertical or Y-axis that extends through the center of the arcball. This axis is represented by the vertical line in the cursor icon.

When you move the cursor over one of the circles at the top or bottom of the arcball, a vertical ellipse encircling a sphere appears. Clicking and dragging when this icon is active rotates the view around the horizontal or X-axis that extends through the center of the arcball. This axis is represented by the horizontal line in the cursor icon.

With these four modes of movement, you can view the model from any position. Using any but the free movement mode that's available when the cursor is inside the arcball constrains motion to one axis. You practice manipulating 3D Orbit views in the following exercise.

### Exercise 25.5   Viewing a Model with 3D Orbit

1. Open 25EX05.dwg from the accompanying CD-ROM. This model shows a ball-bearing assembly from a side view (see Figure 25.19).

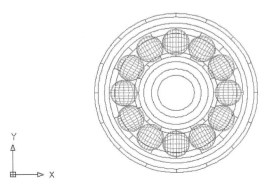

**Figure 25.19**   2D side view of a ball-bearing assembly.

In the following steps, note the shape and orientation of the 3D Orbit UCS icon as you manipulate the view of the model.

2. From the View pull-down menu, choose 3D Orbit to start the 3DORBIT command. Move the screen cursor to a position outside the large arcball circle and note the circular arrow icon. Remaining outside the arcball circle, click and drag the cursor in up and down motions. Observe that the model view rotates about an axis extending through the center of the arcball and perpendicular to the plane of the screen. Releasing the left mouse button "fixes" the view in a new orientation.

3. Right-click to display the 3DORBIT command shortcut menu. Select Reset View to restore the original view of the model.

4. Move the screen cursor over either of the small circles at the left or right edge of the arcball circle. Note the horizontal elliptical arrow icon. Click and drag the cursor in horizontal motions. Observe the view rotating about an axis extending vertically through the arcball. Note that dragging the cursor outside the arcball has no effect on the axis of rotation or the icon shape. Releasing the left mouse button "fixes" the view in a new orientation.

5. The current display is wireframe. Now we will change to another type. Right-click to display the 3D Orbit shortcut menu. Choose Shading Modes and select one of the five remaining shade modes.

6. Repeat the previous step four times, choosing one of the other remaining shade modes each time.

7. With the model in a shade mode other than wireframe, move the screen cursor over either of the small circles at the top or bottom edge of the arcball. Note the vertical elliptical arrow icon. Click and drag the cursor in a series of vertical up and down motions. Observe the view rotating about an axis extending horizontally through the center of the arcball. Note that the model remains shaded as the view changes. Releasing the left mouse button "fixes" the view in a new orientation.

8. Right-click to display the 3D Orbit shortcut menu. Select Reset View to restore the original view of the model. Now move the icon anywhere inside the arcball. Note the double elliptical icon with both a horizontal and vertical arrow. Click and drag the cursor in a series of horizontal, vertical, and diagonal motions. Observe the view rotating freely. Releasing the left mouse button "fixes" the view in a new orientation.

9. Right-click to display the 3D Orbit shortcut menu and choose Reset View. Close the drawing without saving changes.

## Model Interaction with 3D Orbit

The 3DORBIT command not only enables you to establish a shaded, static view of a model from virtually any vantage point, but also it enables you to view the model dynamically as you change the view. Shaded or hidden line removal modes persist even while the viewpoint is being dynamically and interactively modified. This capability enables you to gain new insights into the geometric relationships among the various aspects of even a simple model.

You should be aware of several features and limitations of the 3DORBIT command:

- Depending upon the complexity of the model and the efficiency of your particular CPU/graphics hardware, the components of the model may be reduced and displayed as simple 3D boxes during real-time manipulation of the view. These "bounding box" surrogates accurately represent the volumetric extents of the original elements. After dynamic motion input is stopped, the model reverts to its original geometric forms. Figure 25.20 shows this effect with 25EX05.dwg.

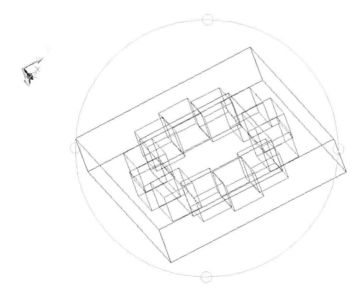

**Figure 25.20**    Bounding boxes may substitute for more complex shapes in slower systems.

- If you choose only individual elements of the model before entering the 3DORBIT command, only those selected elements will participate in the dynamic viewing and any subsequent presentations. Choosing only a few key elements may create a smoother, more accurate dynamic presentation.

- As described in the following section, placing your model in a perspective presentation is helpful for establishing spatial relationships.

- You cannot enter commands at the command line while 3D Orbit is active. However, commands such as ZOOM and PAN are available from the 3D Orbit right-click shortcut menu.

- Keep in mind that 3D Orbit alters only the view of the model; the model does not move during dynamic viewing.

- If the view of the model becomes ambiguous, the Reset View option available on the 3D Orbit right-click shortcut menu restores the view in effect when 3D Orbit was last entered.

When using the 3DORBIT command, you are in an inaccurate interface. However, AutoCAD has the capability to adjust the various viewing values using the Properties palette. If the Properties palette is active when you start the 3DORBIT command, you gain access to Camera, Clipping, Shading, and Visual Aids, all with the Properties palette. This can help in tweaking view properties not otherwise accessible. For more information about using the Properties palette dialog box, see Chapter 9, "Object Selection and Manipulation."

In addition to the modes of view manipulation and shading options demonstrated in the previous exercise, the right-click shortcut menu of the 3DORBIT command presents several other features and options. You can pan and zoom, turn two additional viewing aids on and off, establish standard preset views, adjust camera distance and swivel the camera, and set either a parallel or perspective view. A means of establishing clipping planes is also available. Several of these features are demonstrated in the following exercise. The clipping planes feature is demonstrated in a later exercise.

### Exercise 25.6    Additional 3D Orbit Viewing Options

1. Open 25EX06.dwg from this book's accompanying CD. This drawing represents a model of a battery canister. The initial view is shown in Figure 25.21.

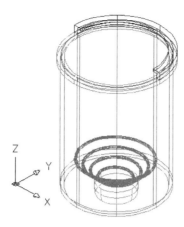

**Figure 25.21**   Isometric view of a battery canister.

2. From the View pull-down menu, choose 3D Orbit. The 3D Orbit arcball and UCS icon are displayed.

3. Right-click to display the 3D Orbit shortcut menu. Choose Visual Aids and select Grid. Note the 3D Orbit Grid display.

4. Repeat step 3 and select the Compass visual aid. While manipulating the view as you did in the preceding exercise, note the appearance of the grid and compass visual aids.

5. Use the right-click shortcut menu to turn off both the grid and compass visual aids.

6. Manipulate the view to resemble that shown in the right portion of Figure 25.22.

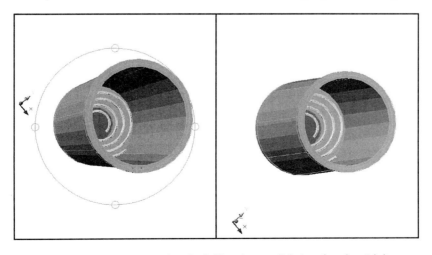

**Figure 25.22**   A perspective view (on the left) and a parallel view (on the right).

7. Right-click to display the 3D Orbit shortcut menu. Choose Projection and select Perspective. Your view should more closely resemble the model in the left portion of Figure 25.22.

8. From the 3D Orbit shortcut menu, choose Preset views and select Front.

   Leave this drawing open. You will continue from this view in the next exercise.

## Adjusting Clipping Planes in 3D Orbit View

You can establish clipping planes in 3D Orbit view. When you use clipping planes, objects or portions of objects that move beyond a clipping plane become invisible in the view. Adjustments to clipping planes are made interactively in the Adjust Clipping Planes window shown in Figure 25.23. To display this window, right-click to open the 3D Orbit shortcut menu, choose More, and then select Adjust Clipping Planes.

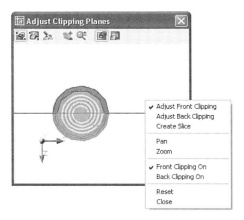

**Figure 25.23**   You adjust clipping planes in the Adjust Clipping Planes window.

The Adjust Clipping Planes window shows two clipping planes, front and back. These planes are represented by two horizontal lines, which initially may be superimposed upon each other. To choose the clipping plane you want to adjust and to turn clipping planes on and off, you use buttons on the toolbar in the Adjust Clipping Planes window or the options available from the right-click shortcut menu shown in Figure 25.23. The following options are available:

- **Front Clipping On.** Toggles the front clipping plane on and off. When the front clipping plane is on, the results of moving this plane are shown interactively in the main 3D Orbit display.

- **Back Clipping On.** Toggles the back clipping plane on and off. When the back clipping plane is on, the results of moving this plane are shown interactively in the main 3D Orbit display.

- **Adjust Front Clipping.** Adjusts the front clipping plane. The line nearest the bottom of the window shows the front plane. If Front Clipping On is active, you see the results of moving the plane up or down in the main 3D Orbit display.

- **Adjust Back Clipping.** Adjusts the back clipping plane. The line nearest the top of the window shows the back plane. If Back Clipping On is active, you see the results of moving the plane up or down in the main 3D Orbit display.

- **Create Slice.** When this feature is active, the front and back clipping planes move together at their current separation distance, creating a "slice" of the objects contained between the two planes. If both Front Clipping On and Back Clipping On are active, the slice is displayed in the main 3D Orbit display.

**I**NSIDER  **N**OTE

> Except when using the Create Slice option, you can adjust only one clipping plane at a time. If the Create Slice button is clicked, you adjust both planes simultaneously. On the toolbar, the button for the plane you are adjusting appears to be pressed.

**I**NSIDER  **T**IP

> Although you can establish clipping planes from any 3D Orbit view, standard orthogonal views such as front and side usually yield the most effective results.

The uses of front and back clipping planes and slices are demonstrated in the following exercise.

### Exercise 25.7    Establishing Clipping Planes

1. Continue from the previous exercise with a front view of the model in 25EX06.dwg. From the 3D Orbit shortcut menu, choose More and select Adjust Clipping Planes. Note that the view is rotated 90 degrees in the Adjust Clipping Planes window.

2. Right-click in the Adjust Clipping Planes window and make sure a check appears beside the Adjust Front Clipping and Front Clipping On options. Click in the Adjust Clipping Planes window to close the shortcut menu.

3.  In the Adjust Clipping Planes window, the bottom line represents the position of the front clipping plane, and the top line represents the position of the back clipping plane.

4.  Click and drag the special clipping plane icon upward and observe the view of the model in the main 3D Orbit display. As the clipping plane approaches the "middle" of the model, less of the model becomes visible because more of the model is "clipped." In this model, this effect is most evident in the spring element.

5.  With the front clipping plane line near the "front" of the model, select the Back Clipping On option from the right-click shortcut menu. You can also activate the Back Clipping On/Off button on the Adjust Clipping Planes window toolbar.

    The model is displayed as a slice, with only those portions falling between the current front and back clipping plane lines visible in the main display.

6.  Activate the Create Slice button or select Create Slice from the shortcut menu. Click and drag the icon to vary the position of the slice. Note that the front and back planes appear closer together when Create Slice is active. Figure 25.24 shows a typical front view slice of the model.

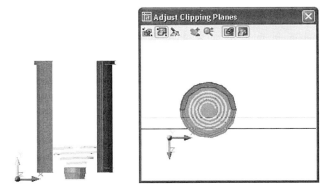

**Figure 25.24**   A slice view through the middle of the canister model.

7.  Close the Adjust Clipping Planes window by selecting Close from the shortcut menu. Manipulate the current view to observe the slice from different views. Restore the previous view by selecting Reset View from the shortcut menu.

8.  From the 3D Orbit shortcut menu, choose More and select Back Clipping On to turn the back plane off. Notice that the display now shows all portions of the model behind the front clipping plane.

    Leave this drawing open. You will continue from this view in the next exercise.

With clipping planes and the use of 3D Orbit's shading modes, you can establish new and informative views of your model. These clipped views remain when you exit 3D Orbit.

▌NSIDER  NOTE _____

> Clipped views are especially helpful when combined with shaded views in 3D Orbit. They may not be as effective, however, when you exit 3D Orbit and return to standard 3D and 2D views. The 3D Orbit shortcut menu offers you a quick way to disable the front and back clipping planes before you exit the 3DORBIT command.

## Using Continuous Orbit

While 3D Orbit is active, you can choose to establish a continuous motion of the view around your model. Such continuous motion studies can yield information about the structure and geometric relationships in the model that are less apparent in static views. Continuous orbit is demonstrated in the following exercise.

### Exercise 25.8    Establishing a Continuous Orbit

1. Continue from the previous exercise with a front shaded view of the model in 25EX06.dwg. From the 3DORBIT command right-click shortcut menu, choose Shading Modes and select Flat Shaded.

2. Again from the 3DORBIT shortcut menu, choose More and select Continuous Orbit. Note that the cursor changes to a small sphere orbited by two circles.

3. To start the continuous orbit motion, click and drag in the direction you want the continuous orbit to move and release the pick button. Observe that the model continues to move in the direction of the motion of the pointing device.

4. To change the direction of the continuous orbit motion, click and drag in a new direction and release the pick button.

5. To stop the motion at any point without leaving 3DORBIT, left-click while keeping the pointing device stationary.

6. To start a new continuous orbit motion, click, drag, and release again.

7. To change the projection type while in continuous orbit, right-click to display the shortcut menu and choose Projection. Then toggle the projection mode.

8. To stop the motion at any point and exit 3D Orbit, press the Esc key.

   You are finished with this model. Close the drawing without saving changes.

While continuous orbit is active, you can modify the model view by right-clicking to display the shortcut menu and choosing Projection, Shading Modes, Visual Aids, Reset View, or Preset Views. You can also turn the front and back clipping planes on and off. You cannot, however, adjust the clipping planes while continuous orbit is active. Choosing Pan, Zoom, Orbit, or Adjust Clipping Planes from the shortcut menu ends continuous orbit.

When using the 3DORBIT command, you can often flip the Z-axis upside-down accidentally. It can be very frustrating trying to get back a normal Z-axis—especially if you are in wireframe mode, because you can "see" through the object and can't tell if you are above or below it. A great feature is the Z-axis lock, and it is accessed by right-clicking the 3DORBIT shortcut menu. Under the More subject, select Orbit Maintains Z. This is a simple on/off toggle. When checked, the Z-axis cannot change as you rotate the model, helping you to keep things straight.

**I**NSIDER **N**OTE

> The speed with which you drag the pointing device to establish continuous orbit determines the speed of the orbit motion. If your model is very complex or your CPU/hardware is less efficient, you may want to make your orbit motions slower to yield smoother, less jerky results.

**I**NSIDER **T**IP

> Continuous orbits are frequently more realistic with the projection mode set to Perspective.

# Shading a Model

The SHADEMODE command provides you with the same hidden line removal and enhanced shading options that are available inside the 3DORBIT command. As with the 3D Orbit shade modes, the shading provided by SHADEMODE uses a fixed light source over your left shoulder. The various SHADEMODE command options are shown in Figure 25.25. Those options are described here:

- **2D wireframe.** Displays the model objects using lines and curves to represent boundaries. This is AutoCAD's default display mode for 2D and 3D objects.

- **3D wireframe.** Same as 2D wireframe, but also displays a shaded 3D User Coordinate System icon.

- **Hidden.** Same as 3D wireframe, but hides lines representing back faces. Similar to the results obtained with the `HIDE` command.

- **Flat.** Shades the objects between polygon faces. Objects appear flatter and less smooth than Gouraud shaded objects.

- **Gouraud.** Shades the objects and smoothes the edges between faces. Yields a smoother, more realistic appearance.

- **Flat+edges.** Combines the flat shaded and wireframe options. Objects appear flat shaded with wireframe showing.

- **Gouraud+edges.** Combines the Gouraud shaded and wireframe options. Objects appear Gouraud shaded with wireframe showing.

The options offered by the `SHADEMODE` command are also available from the View pull-down menu. Choose Shade and then select one of the six shading modes. You can also return your display to standard 2D Wireframe mode from this menu. `SHADEMODE` is also available from the command line.

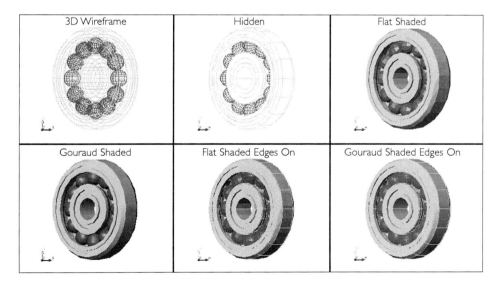

**Figure 25.25**   Shading and hidden line removal options available with `SHADEMODE`.

The behavior of shaded models in AutoCAD 2005 differs in important ways from that of releases prior to AutoCAD 2002. In general, it is now much easier to work with shaded models. The AutoCAD 2005 shaded model changes include the following:

- **3D Grid.** When any of the shade modes (including 3D Wireframe) are active, a distinctive "3D" grid is displayed if the grid feature is enabled. The grid features major (heavier) grid lines, with 10 horizontal and vertical lines drawn between the major lines. The number of major lines corresponds to the value set using the grid spacing option of the GRID command and stored in the GRIDUNIT system variable. The 3D grid is displayed coincidentally with the current X-Y plane and "tracks" UCS changes. The 3D grid is shown in Figure 25.26.

- **3D UCS Icon.** When any of the shade modes are active, a distinctive 3D UCS icon is displayed whenever the UCS icon is enabled, as shown in Figure 25.26. This icon is shaded and the X-, Y-, and Z-axes are labeled. The X-axis is red, the Y-axis is green, and the Z-axis is blue.

- **3D Compass.** When any of the shade modes are active, a Compass feature can be activated. This feature superimposes on the model a 3D sphere composed of three lines representing the X-, Y-, and Z-axes. The apparent center of the sphere coincides with the center of the viewport. The display of the 3D compass, shown in Figure 25.26, is controlled by the COMPASS system variable.

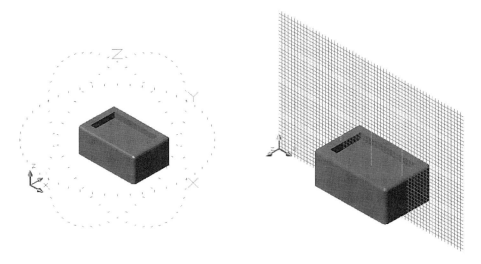

**Figure 25.26**   The 3D Icon, Compass, and Grid features are available in 3D shade modes.

- **Regeneration.** Regenerating the drawing does not affect shading.

- **Editing.** You can edit shaded models by selecting them in the normal manner. If a shaded object is selected, the wireframe and grips appear on top of the shading.

- **Saving.** You can save a drawing in which objects are shaded, and when you open it again, the objects are still shaded.

**I**NSIDER  **N**OTE

> If you exit 3DORBIT with a shade mode active, the only means of changing to a different shade mode or of returning to standard 2D wireframe mode is through the SHADEMODE command or the Shade options of the View pull-down menu.

# Summary

Understanding the orientation of AutoCAD's 3D axes is the first step toward working comfortably in 3D space. The UCS command sets the orientation of the UCS in three-dimensional space. Understanding and using multiple viewports enables you to easily orient yourself in 3D space, and it provides an easy means for switching views of your model. AutoCAD's 3DORBIT command lets you move around and view a shaded model in real-time. Together, these 3D tools make working in 3D space more efficient.

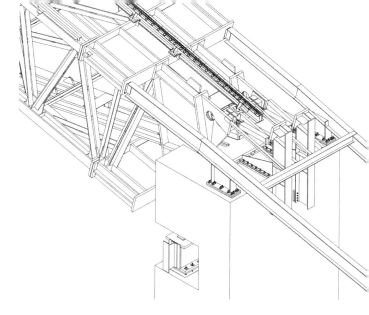

# Drawing in 3D

As you work with 3D models in AutoCAD, you will soon find that two skills enable you to quickly become as comfortable working in 3D as you are working in 2D. The first required skill is the capability to move around inside the 3D model, which you learned about in the previous chapter.

The second required skill is the ability to generate the geometry within 3D space that is used to build a 3D model. In this chapter you learn about using AutoCAD commands already familiar to you from your work with 2D drawings in a different way as you apply these commands to 3D work. Familiar commands, such as LINE and PLINE, can be used in 3D work as well—you just use them a little differently. Likewise, edit commands such as ROTATE, MIRROR, and ARRAY have 3D counterparts in 3DROTATE, MIRROR3D, and 3DAR-RAY. You also learn that tools such as point filters and object snaps are even more important and necessary as you work with 3D space.

Last, you learn how to create a special AutoCAD object called a *region*, which acts like a 2D object in some ways and like a 3D object in others.

The following topics are discussed and demonstrated in this chapter:

- Working with lines, polylines, and 3D polylines
- Using object snaps and point filters
- Using 3D editing commands
- Using EXTEND and TRIM in 3D
- Creating regions

# Working with Lines, Polylines, and 3D Polylines

A standard line in AutoCAD is usually drawn in two dimensions and exists in the World Coordinate System or the current UCS. Each endpoint of this line is defined by a set of coordinates: X, Y, and Z. If you have spent most of your time drawing in 2D, then you have probably always left the Z value set to 0. By adjusting the Z value of either endpoint of the line, it becomes a line using all three dimensions.

The fact that the line is now in three dimensions, however, becomes apparent only by observing it from a different viewpoint. For example, a line can appear to be two-dimensional when viewed from the top but three-dimensional when viewed from other angles (see Figure 26.1).

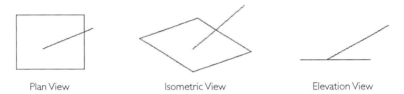

Plan View                    Isometric View                    Elevation View

**Figure 26.1**    Three views of the same line, showing the importance of correctly viewing a 3D model.

The following exercise shows you how to draw a wireframe version of a box in 3D by using the `LINE` command. In the last chapter, you created a similar object, but you changed the UCS frequently. In this exercise, you create the object without changing the UCS, which is significantly faster.

### Exercise 26.1    Using the *LINE* Command to Draw a Wireframe Box

1. Load AutoCAD if it is not already loaded and start a new drawing.

2. Select the `LINE` command from the Draw toolbar.

3. Type the following coordinates:

   `0,0`

   `5,0`

   `5,5`

   `0,5`

   Type **C** to close the line command.

4. From the View pull-down menu, choose 3D Views, SW Isometric to switch to an isometric view of the drawing.

5. Select the COPY command from the Modify toolbar. At the Select objects prompt, select the four lines and press Enter. Specify a displacement by typing **0,0,4** and press Enter twice. The four lines are copied "up" five units on the Z-axis. Perform a ZOOM Extents to view the entire drawing. Figure 26.2 shows the drawing at this point.

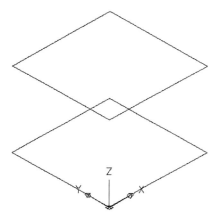

**Figure 26.2** The "top" and "bottom" of the 3D box from an SW Isometric view.

6. Start the LINE command again. Type the following coordinates:

   **0,0,0**

   **0,0,4**

   Press Enter to end the command.

7. Repeat step 6 three more times using these coordinate pairs for the From and To points:

   **5,0,0 & 5,0,4**

   **5,5,0 & 5,5,4**

   **0,5,0 & 0,5,4**

   Your drawing should now resemble Figure 26.3. You may now close this drawing without saving.

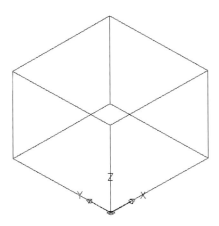

**Figure 26.3**    The completed wireframe box in an SW Isometric view.

**INSIDER NOTE**

> During Exercise 26.1, you created what is called a wireframe model of a box. A wireframe model does not have any 3D surfaces. It represents only the edges of the object you have drawn. These edges, however, can have surfaces applied between them later.
>
> You can also give a line or polyline a thickness (similar to an extrusion) by changing the properties of the line with the PROPERTIES or CHANGE command.

As you can see from the previous exercise, drawing a line in three dimensions with the LINE command is relatively easy; you just type in the coordinates. However, it is also very tedious and potentially inaccurate. As you see later in this chapter, the use of drawing aids can dramatically increase your 3D drafting speed and accuracy.

A standard polyline is not quite as flexible as a regular line in 3D work. When you create a standard polyline, the vertices must lie on the same two-dimensional plane. If you start a polyline at three units above the XY coordinate system, for example, all the vertices of the polyline would be at that height, regardless of where you select the points in the drawing. This makes polylines very useful for creating outlines or other planar construction elements that can later be surfaced with a variety of commands in AutoCAD.

**INSIDER NOTE**

> *Surfacing* is the process of creating continuous surfaces between boundary edges, such as lines. These surfaces can then be used to hide objects such as lines that exist behind them.

A new feature introduced in AutoCAD 2004 was Hidden Line Settings, the HLSET-TINGS command. It enables you to control the linetype and lineweight of edges that are hidden by other faceted geometry such as surfaces, 3D faces, regions, and solids. Learn more abut this feature in Chapter 28, "Solid Modeling in 3D."

Because of the planar limitation of a polyline, AutoCAD also includes a 3D polyline object. This polyline differs from a standard polyline because you can place each vertex of the polyline at a different point in 3D space. Several of the polyline editing commands, however, are not available with the 3D polyline. For example, although you can still use PEDIT to create a spline curve from a 3D polyline, you cannot create a fit curve by using PEDIT. Figure 26.4 shows a 3D polyline that has been changed into a spline curve by using PEDIT.

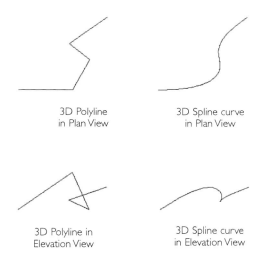

**Figure 26.4**   A 3D polyline changed into a splined curve. The curves are smoothly translated in both 2D and 3D space.

Now that you have an idea of how lines and polylines can be used to create three-dimensional drawings, it is time to look at how those lines and polylines can be created using snaps and point filters.

# Using Object Snaps and Point Filters

Drawing a line in three dimensions is relatively easy if you type in the coordinates for the endpoints of the line rather than pick those points with a mouse. However, typing in points is not overly intuitive and can become tedious very quickly. To get around this, you need to make use of AutoCAD's drawing aids—in particular, object snaps and point filters.

## Object Snaps

An object snap (OSNAP) is used to accurately input a point based on an existing piece of geometry. Using object snap modes make it easy to draw elements using the geometry of previously drawn items. When you consider this concept from a three-dimensional perspective, object snaps become critical to the drawing process.

**INSIDER TIP**

> AutoCAD 2005 introduced a new object snap that helps reduce excess construction lines. The Mid between 2 Points osnap enables you to pick two points, and AutoCAD returns a point exactly between them, even 3D point locations! You can find this new object snap mode on the right-click shortcut menu.

For example, if you draw a box in 3D by just entering the endpoints of the wireframe, you can draw only so much of the box in a 2D plan view. To create the rest of the box, you must switch to a three-dimensional view, such as an SW Isometric view, to see the model in its three-dimensional form. You must make this switch because any lines that extend along the Z-axis appear as dots in a plan view. Only from a 3D view, such as an Isometric view, are you able to truly see the model. Because this is an Isometric view, however, what you see in the view might not be apparent. Figures 26.5 and 26.6 illustrate this problem.

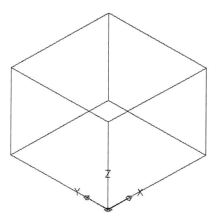

**Figure 26.5**   A drawing that looks like a 3D box when viewed from an SW Isometric view.

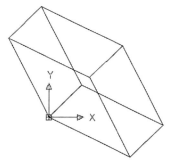

**Figure 26.6**   The same box view in Plan. Now you can see that this never was really drawn in three dimensions.

As you can see from Figures 26.5 and 26.6, it is very easy to draw lines that appear to be three-dimensional, but that really exist only in the flat plane of the current UCS (instead of in three-dimensional space). This is where object snaps come in handy. By snapping to geometry that exists in three-dimensional space, you ensure that you avoid this problem.

### Exercise 26.2   Using Object Snap Modes to Draw a 3D Box

1. Start AutoCAD if it is not running and begin a new drawing.

2. Select the LINE command from the Draw toolbar. Now create a line with the following coordinates:

```
0,0
5,0
5,5
0,5
```

Type **C** to close the LINE command.

3. Now from the View pull-down menu, select 3D Views, then select SW Isometric to switch to a 3D isometric view.

4. Start the COPY command and select the four lines. You will duplicate these "up" 3 units on the Z-axis. Specify a displacement of **0,0,3** and press Enter twice to complete the copy. Now perform a ZOOM Extents. Figure 26.7 shows the drawing at this point.

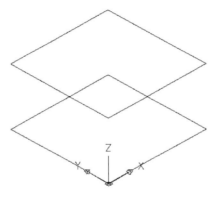

**Figure 26.7**    The box with completed "top" and "bottom."

Now that you have built the "bottom" and the "top" of the box, it is time to use object snap modes to create the lines in between.

5. Right-click over the OSNAP button found on the Status bar and select Settings. This displays the Drafting Settings dialog box and makes the Object Snap tab current, as shown in Figure 26.8.

**Figure 26.8**    The Object Snap tab of the Drafting Settings dialog box.

6. Click the Clear All button if necessary to remove any checks from snap modes, then place a check next to the endpoint osnap mode only. Click OK to exit the dialog box.

7. Select the LINE command from the Draw toolbar.

8. Draw a vertical line from the endpoint of each corner on the lower portion of the box to the corresponding upper portion, as shown in Figure 26.9. This creates your 3D wireframe model.

Close this drawing without saving.

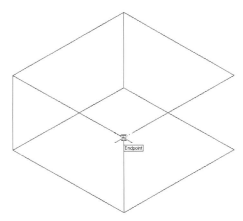

**Figure 26.9**    Constructing the vertical lines of the box using endpoint osnaps.

As you can see from this exercise, the use of object snap modes almost immediately gives you a performance gain. It becomes quite easy to "snap" to a point in 3D.

Even object snaps can be troublesome from certain 3D viewpoints, though. Consider the box example again. Depending on the dimensions of the sides of the box, when you view the box from an isometric view, you can have overlapping endpoints, as shown in Figure 26.10. To get around this problem, you can change the view of the 3D model so that the endpoints do not overlap visually.

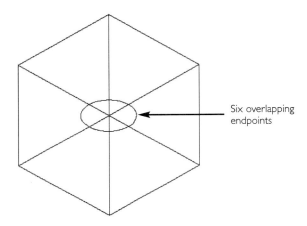

Six overlapping endpoints

**Figure 26.10**    A view of a wireframe box showing how endpoints can overlap in certain views.

**INSIDER TIP**

3D views of wireframe models are notoriously ambiguous. When working in three dimensions, it is always a good idea to check your model from different views to make sure you have drawn it correctly. What looks correct in one view actually might be incorrect, but the view hides the problem. Because of this, even experienced AutoCAD users occasionally unintentionally draw something incorrectly in three dimensions. Using the 3DORBIT command described in Chapter 25, "Introduction to 3D," can be very useful for correcting this problem.

## Point Filters

Point filters are a handy method of drawing three-dimensional lines without having to enter all three coordinates. A point filter, such as the .XY (pronounced "dot XY") point filter for example, is used to isolate one or more of the three coordinates of a point selected or *picked* with the mouse. For example, when you use the .XY filter, AutoCAD accepts only the X and Y coordinate values from the point you select. You then type (or pick) a .Z point filter to supply the Z coordinate. Because of the way they work, point filters—and especially the .XY filter—are extremely useful in 3D work.

Up to this stage, you have drawn lines in three dimensions by relying on existing geometry or by typing in all three coordinates. By using point filters, however, you can create 3D lines even more quickly and easily.

### Exercise 26.3  Constructing the Vertical Lines of a Box with a .XY Filter

1. Start a new drawing in AutoCAD.

2. From the Tools pull-down menu, choose Drafting Settings and on the Drafting Settings dialog box's Snap and Grid tab, turn on both your grid and snap, with both set to 1 unit. Then set an active endpoint osnap mode as you did in step 6 of the previous exercise.

3. From the View pull-down menu, choose 3D Views, SW Isometric.

4. Select the RECTANGLE command from the Draw toolbar and draw a rectangle by dragging the mouse. The size of the rectangle should resemble that shown in Figure 26.11.

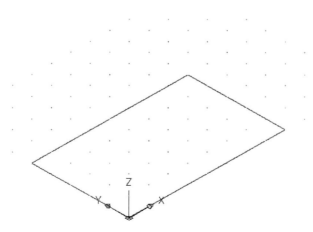

**Figure 26.11**  The "base" of the box prior to using point filters to construct the vertical elements.

5. Choose the LINE command.

6. Select a corner of the box to set the start point of the line.

7. At the To Point prompt, type **.XY** and press Enter. AutoCAD then prompts with OF, meaning .XY "of" what point.

8. At the OF prompt, select the same point that you picked in step 6. AutoCAD then prompts you for a Z value.

9. Type a value of **3** and press Enter to end the command. Figure 26.12 shows the box at this point.

10. Repeat steps 5 through 9 for the remaining three corners, or use the COPY command to copy the vertical line to each corner.

11. Use the LINE command with the endpoint osnap mode to complete the top of the box.

   Close this drawing without saving.

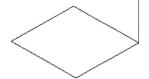

**Figure 26.12**
The box with one vertical line segment drawn using a .XY filter.

Point filters are always relative to the current UCS; therefore, make sure that you are aware of your current UCS orientation before using them, or you can get results you did not expect. Refer to Chapter 25, "Introduction to 3D," for a description of the UCS command.

Now that you have explored some of the basic commands used to draw lines and polylines in 3D, it is time to look at how AutoCAD handles editing in three dimensions.

# 3D AutoCAD Editing Commands

Like the line and polyline commands, most AutoCAD editing commands can also be utilized to work in three dimensions. In addition to the standard editing commands, AutoCAD also provides you with several 3D-specific editing commands. We first look at the basic 2D editing commands to see how they are utilized in three dimensions.

## Using *MOVE, COPY, SCALE,* and *ROTATE* in 3D

The basic 2D editing commands in AutoCAD include MOVE, COPY, SCALE, and ROTATE. Depending on your view of the 3D model, each command can be used easily in 3D as well. For example, consider the MOVE command. If you are working in an isometric view, you can use the MOVE command in combination with object snap modes to move and place objects in three-dimensional space. This works well when you have existing geometry to use—that is, when you have a point to move from and to.

Suppose, however, you have drawn the outline of a table top and want to move it into the correct position in three-dimensional space, but you have no existing geometry to work with. In this situation, you have two options. First, you can combine the MOVE command with a .XY point filter to correctly move the tabletop. A second method involves using a shortcut in the MOVE command. When you select the MOVE command in AutoCAD, you are first prompted to select the object(s) you want to move. Then AutoCAD prompts you for the base point from which the move occurs. Rather than a base point, you can specify a displacement. If, for example, you type in a displacement of 0,0,10 and press Enter twice, the selected objects move 0 units in the X and Y axes but 10 units along the Z-axis. The COPY command offers the same option at its Specify base point prompt. Rather than specifying a base point, you can enter a three-dimensional displacement vector and press Enter twice, and the copy appears at the displaced distance. In some instances, even when reference geometry is present in the model, it is more convenient to specify displacements when moving or copying objects.

In the following exercise, you use the displacement option of the COPY and MOVE commands with 3D objects.

### Exercise 26.4    Working with *MOVE* in 3D

1. Load the file 26EX04.dwg from the accompanying CD-ROM. The model consists of a box within a box, as shown in Figure 26.13.

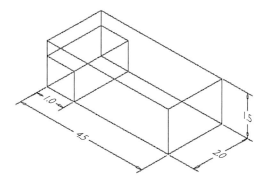

**Figure 26.13**    A 3D model showing a box within a box.

2. Choose Move from the Modify toolbar.

3. Select an edge of the smaller box in the corner and press Enter.

4. When prompted for the base point or displacement, type **0,0,1.5** and press Enter twice. The smaller box is displaced 1.5 units in the current Z direction, as shown in Figure 26.14.

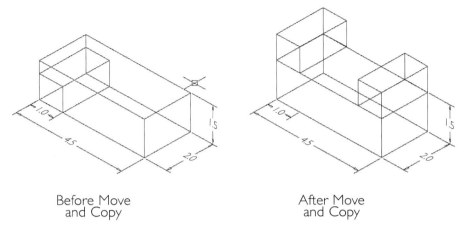

Before Move
and Copy

After Move
and Copy

**Figure 26.14**   The 3D model after a move and copy displacement.

In the next steps, you displace a copy of the box you just moved 3.5 units along the X-axis.

**5.** Choose Copy from the Modify toolbar.

**6.** When prompted to select objects, type **P** for previous and press Enter.

**7.** When prompted for the base point or displacement, type **3.5,0,0** and press Enter twice.

A copy of the box is placed at the specified displacement (refer to Figure 26.14).

Close this drawing without saving.

As you can see from this exercise, using the MOVE and COPY commands with the displacement option is a fast and easy way to specify displacements of objects in 3D space. There are situations in which the displacement method is not practical, and in these situations, using object snaps, perhaps with point filters, and existing geometry reference points is the most efficient method.

Both the SCALE and ROTATE commands can also be used in three dimensions and work essentially as they do in a "flat" 2D model. Keep in mind that, when editing 3D models, it is essential that you move away from plan views and utilize isometric views so that the 3D geometry can be fully seen.

In addition to the standard 2D editing commands, AutoCAD provides several editing commands specifically intended for use in 3D modeling. These include MIRROR3D, 3DRO-TATE, ALIGN, and 3DARRAY. We examine these specialized 3D editing commands in the following sections.

## The *MIRROR3D* Command

The MIRROR3D command is a modified version of the standard MIRROR command. In the standard 2D command, the mirror line always lies in the XY plane of the current UCS. In the 3D version, a provision is made to mirror about any plane in 3D space.

After selecting the objects you want to mirror, the following prompt appears:

```
Specify first point of mirror plane (3 points)
or[Object/Last/Zaxis/View/XY/YZ/ZX/3points] <3points>
```

There are several methods of specifying the 3D mirroring plane:

- **Object.** Use the plane of a current planar object as the mirroring plane. Qualifying objects include a circle, arc, or 2D polyline.
- **Last.** Use the most recently specified mirroring plane.
- **Zaxis.** Define the plane with a point on the plane and a point normal to the plane; i.e., perpendicular to the mirror axis.
- **View.** Use the current viewing plane as the mirroring plane,
- **XY/YZ/ZX.** Use one of the standard planes through a specified point.
- **3-Points.** Define the plane by specifying three points on the mirroring plane.

The 3-Points method is the default and can usually be used when sufficient geometry is available.

### Exercise 26.5   Working with the *MIRROR3D* Feature

1. Load the file 26EX05.dwg from the accompanying CD. This drawing is shown in Figure 26.15.

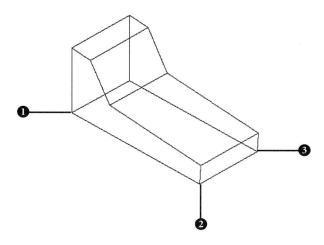

**Figure 26.15**   A 3D model for use with the MIRROR3D command.

2. From the Modify pull-down menu, choose 3D Operation, Mirror 3D.

3. Select anywhere on the model and press Enter. You are prompted with the Mirror 3D options.

4. Use the default 3-Points option to define the mirroring plane. Because 3-Points is the default method, you can immediately identify the first point.

5. Use an endpoint osnap to pick at ❶, ❷, and ❸ as shown in Figure 26.15.

6. When prompted to delete the old objects, press Enter to accept the default No. Figure 26.16 shows the mirrored result.

7. Use the right-click shortcut menu and choose Undo to undo the last command.

8. Next use the XY plane option to identify the mirroring plane.

9. Repeat steps 2 and 3 and specify the XY option.

10. When prompted for the point on the XY plane, use an endpoint osnap and pick at ❶ in Figure 26.15. Press Enter to accept the default No when asked if you want to delete source objects. Figure 26.16 again shows the same mirrored result.

    If you are not continuing with the next exercise, close this drawing without saving. Otherwise, leave it open to use in Exercise 26.6.

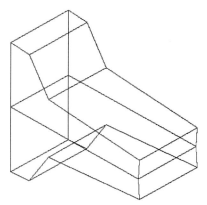

**Figure 26.16**   The model after using the MIRROR3D command.

As you can see from this exercise, the MIRROR3D command enables you to mirror one or more objects around any planar axis in 3D space, as long as you have three locations on that plane to select.

## The *ROTATE3D* Command

The ROTATE3D command is very much like the MIRROR3D command. It also differs from its 2D counterpart by enabling you to rotate an object around an axis, not just the current Z-axis.

After selecting the objects you want to rotate, the following prompt appears:

```
Specify first point on axis or define axis by
[Object/Last/View/Xaxis/Yaxis/Zaxis/2points]
```

**I**NSIDER **T**IP

> The right-click shortcut menu for the ROTATE3D command provides on-screen access to these options as well.

You have various methods of specifying the 3D axis of rotation:

- **Object.** Align the axis of rotation with an existing object. Qualifying objects include a line, circle, arc, or 2D polyline.
- **Last.** Use the most recently specified axis of rotation.
- **View.** Align the axis of rotation with the current viewing direction.

- **X/Y/Z axis.** Align the axis of rotation with one of the standard axes that passes through the selected point.
- **2-Points.** Define the axis of rotation by specifying two points.

The 3D rotation routine is accessed from the Modify pull-down menu by choosing 3D Operation, 3DRotate, or by typing in **ROTATE3D** at the command prompt. In the following exercise, you use the X/Y/Z axis method of specifying an axis of rotation for the ROTATE3D command.

### Exercise 26.6   Using the *ROTATE3D* Command

1. Continue from the last exercise or open the drawing 26EX06.dwg. This drawing (refer to Figure 26.16) is from the preceding exercise.
2. From the Modify pull-down menu, choose 3D Operation, 3D Rotate.
3. When prompted, select both halves of the mirrored model and press Enter.
4. From the command options, type **Y** and press Enter to select the Y-axis around which to perform the rotation.
5. When prompted for a point on the Y-axis, use an endpoint osnap to pick ❶ in Figure 26.15.
6. When prompted for the rotation angle, type **90** and press Enter. The model is rotated 90 degrees about an axis parallel with the current Y-axis and passing through the specified point, as shown in Figure 26.17.

   Close this drawing without saving.

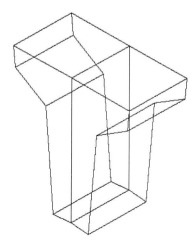

**Figure 26.17**   The model after using the ROTATE3D command.

In the previous exercise, you could have performed the same rotation of the model by first changing the UCS and then using the standard 2D ROTATE command. This would have involved changing the new UCS so that its Z-axis aligned with the desired axis. Although this would not have been a difficult UCS realignment, leaving the UCS intact and using an option of the ROTATE3D command is quicker and simpler. There are also circumstances when using the ROTATE3D command options provides the only convenient means of identifying the rotation axis.

## The *ALIGN* Command

The ALIGN command is used to cause one object to line up, or align, with another object based on the source and destination points specified on the two objects. The two objects need not necessarily line up exactly; the ALIGN command either makes the best alignment possible with the point you supply or scales the object being aligned to the object to which it is being aligned. The ALIGN command is a very powerful 3D tool and is probably underused. The command is accessed by choosing 3D Operation, Align from the Modify pull-down menu or by typing **ALIGN** at the command prompt. In the following exercise, you use the ALIGN command to align one 3D object with another 3D object.

### Exercise 26.7   Using the *ALIGN* Command

1. Open the file 26EX07.dwg from the accompanying CD. The model consists of a 3D wedge and box (see Figure 26.18).

   Because the ALIGN command is difficult, if not impossible, to use effectively without object snaps, you first need to set a running endpoint osnap.

2. Right-click over the OSNAP button on the status bar and choose Settings, which displays the Drafting Settings dialog box. On the Object Snap tab of the dialog box, ensure that a check appears beside Object Snap On and the endpoint mode. Click OK to close the dialog box.

3. From the Modify pull-down menu, choose 3D Operation, Align.

4. When prompted to select an object, select the box and press Enter.

5. You are then prompted for the first source point and first destination point. These points are shown in Figure 26.18.

6. Create the second source and destination points, as shown in Figure 26.19.

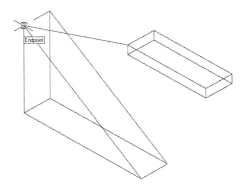

**Figure 26.18**    The first source and destination points.

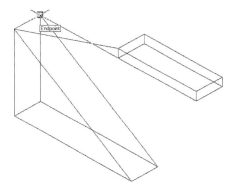

**Figure 26.19**    The second source and destination points.

7. Create the third source and destination points, as shown in Figure 26.20.

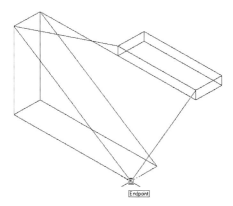

**Figure 26.20**    The third source and destination points.

After selecting the third destination point, the box is automatically aligned, as shown in Figure 26.21. You can close this drawing without saving changes.

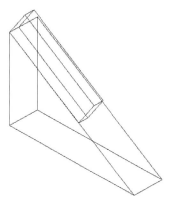

**Figure 26.21**   The newly aligned box.

The first destination point determines the final position of the first source point of the selected object. The other source-destination points determine the alignment. In the preceding exercise, for example, if you were to switch the first and third pair of points, the box would be positioned at the bottom of the wedge rather than at the top.

If you supply only two sets of points to the ALIGN command, you can cause the source object to be scaled to "fit" the destination object with the two sets of points acting as a "reference" for the scaling operation. This may not always lead to the alignment you want, but a subsequent ALIGN, MOVE, or 3DROTATE command can achieve the proper alignment.

## The *3DARRAY* Command

The last 3D editing command to discuss is the 3DARRAY command. Like the other 3D editing commands, this command is located on the Modify pull-down menu, or it can be typed at the command prompt as **3DARRAY**. This command is a modified version of the standard ARRAY command, but it can create objects quickly in the third dimension. This is accomplished in the rectangular array by adding levels to the rows and columns.

**INSIDER NOTE**

This command is called 3DARRAY, whereas the previous 3D commands where called ROTATE3D and MIRROR3D. This is not a typing mistake, just a poor command naming convention. If you find yourself typing it incorrectly, consider customizing your ACAD.PGP file to get the commands to be named similarly. Learn more about command customization in Chapter 23, "Menu Customization."

### Exercise 26.8    Using the *3DARRAY* Command

1. Load the file 26EX08.dwg from the accompanying CD-ROM. The file contains a three-element cell, as shown in Figure 26.22.

2. From the Modify pull-down menu, choose 3D Operation, 3DArray.

3. Select the three cylinders and press Enter.

4. Type **R** (for rectangular) as the type of array you want to create.

5. Set the number of rows, columns, and levels each to **4**.

6. Specify the distances between rows, levels, and columns each as **1**. When you complete this step, AutoCAD begins arraying the objects. Depending on the speed of your machine, this might take a second or two. You also may need to perform a ZOOM   Extents to view the entire array. Figure 26.22 shows the array after performing a HIDE command.

   You can close this drawing without saving changes.

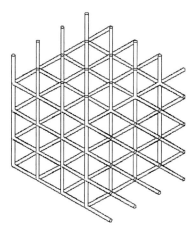

**Figure 26.22**   The completed 64-unit 3Darray.

The 3DARRAY command also supports a polar option. As with the other specialized 3D editing commands, the capability to specify an axis or plane in space provides the command's unique 3D functionality.

The special 3D editing commands, MIRROR3D, ROTATE3D, and 3DARRAY, combined with the ALIGN command enable you to easily edit objects in 3D space. Two other editing commands—TRIM and EXTEND—also have functionality that make them useful in 3D work.

# *EXTEND, TRIM,* and Other Editing Commands in 3D

AutoCAD's TRIM and EXTEND commands both have a Projection option that gives you some degree of flexibility when using these commands in 3D space. As shown in Figure 26.23, for example, the EXTEND command can extend a line lying on one 3D plane to another line lying on a different plane.

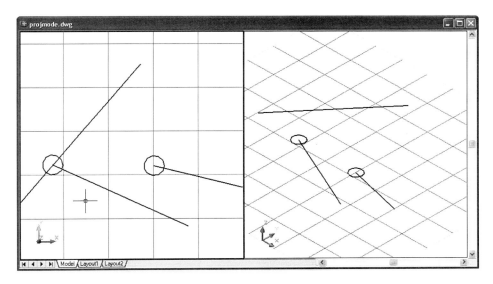

**Figure 26.23**   You can extend a line to another line on a different 3D plane.

In this case, the boundary line can be "projected" onto the plane of the line being extended. Alternately, you can cause the extension of one line to be taken to a plane perpendicular to the current viewing plane. Using the Project mode, you can cause TRIM and EXTEND to behave in the following ways:

- Using no projection causes `TRIM` and `EXTEND` to trim or extend to objects that actually intersect in 3D space.

- Using the UCS mode of Project causes objects to be projected onto the current XY plane.

- Using the View mode of Project causes the objects to be projected onto a plane perpendicular to the current viewing plane.

The following exercise demonstrates the UCS and View modes of the Project option of the `EXTEND` command.

### Exercise 26.9    Using the Project Mode of the *EXTEND* Command

1. Open the file 26EX09.dwg from the accompanying CD. The file contains three lines with a thickness applied. The longest line is drawn at a higher elevation, as shown in Figure 26.24.

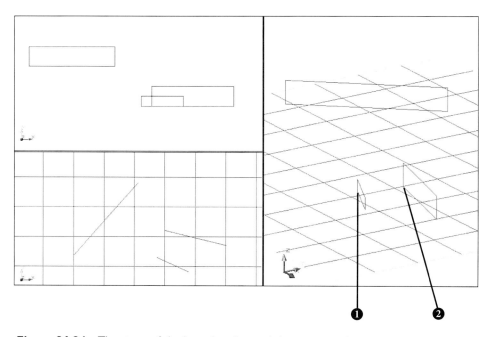

**Figure 26.24**   The views of the boundary line and the extension lines.

2. Click in the large right viewport, if necessary, to make it active.

3. From the Modify pull-down menu, choose Extend. Note that the current setting for the Projection mode is reported on the command line.

4. When prompted to select boundary edges, select the longest line near the top of the viewport and press Enter.

5. At the prompt to select objects to extend, type **P** and press Enter. At the next prompt, ensure that the Projection mode is set to UCS and press Enter.

6. When prompted again for objects to extend, select the shorter line at ❶ in Figure 26.25. Note that the line is extended to the USC projection of the boundary line down onto the current XY plane.

7. When prompted again for objects to extend, type **P** and change the Projection mode to View by typing **V** and pressing Enter.

8. When prompted for objects to extend, choose the now shorter line at ❷ and press Enter to end the command. Note that the line is projected to appear to end at the current view of the boundary line. Your drawing should resemble Figure 26.25.

Close the drawing without saving changes.

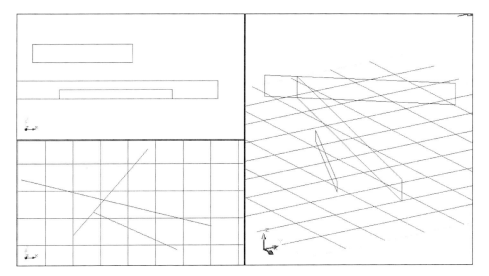

**Figure 26.25**   The views of the boundary line and the extension lines.

When working with the TRIM and EXTEND commands in 3D space, you may want to have the Project option of these commands set to UCS to ensure accuracy no matter what viewpoint you are using to view the 3D geometry.

Before looking at actual 3D objects constructed with surfaces and composed of solids in the following two chapters, we should examine a special 2D object that behaves like a 3D object.

# Working with Regions

*Regions* are special AutoCAD objects. In many ways, regions act like 2D planar objects; in other ways, regions exhibit many of the properties of 3D objects. Like 3D surfaces, for example, regions can hide objects "behind" them and can have materials applied to them for rendering purposes. Like 2D objects, regions have no third dimension or Z-axis information. In many ways, regions can be considered infinitely thin solids.

Technically, regions are enclosed 2D areas. The objects that compose a closed area can be closed themselves, such as circles, ellipses, 3D faces, solids (2D) or closed polylines, or they can form a closed area by sharing endpoints with other objects. Any combination of lines, open polylines, arcs, elliptical arc segments, or splines can form a closed area by sharing endpoints.

As you can see, a large number of AutoCAD objects can join together to form a closed curve from which a region can be created. The only restrictions are that the object must be *coplanar*, or exist on the same plane, and sequential elements must share endpoints. Assuming that the arcs and lines shown in Figure 26.26 are coplanar, the set of curves on the left could not be converted into a region, whereas the curves on the right could.

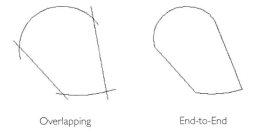

Overlapping                    End-to-End

**Figure 26.26**    Sets of overlapping and end-to-end curves. Only end-to-end curves can be used to create a region.

To convert a set of qualifying curves into a region, you use the REGION command. In the following exercise, you create a region from a set of straight polyline "curves" using the RECTANG command.

### Exercise 26.10    Creating Regions with the *REGION* Command

1. Open the file 26EX10.dwg from the accompanying CD. This drawing is composed of only a circle and a polyline drawn at an elevation of -1.0 units.

2. From the Draw pull-down menu, choose Rectangle. When prompted for the first corner of the rectangle, type **4,2**. At the Specify other corner prompt, type **@3.5,5.5**. Your drawing should now resemble Figure 26.27.

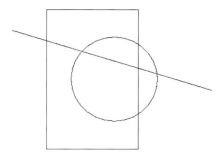

**Figure 26.27**   A closed polyline curve drawn over a circle and line.

3. From the Draw pull-down menu, choose Region. At the Select objects prompt, select the rectangle you just created and press Enter. AutoCAD reports 1 Region created at the command line. The polyline used to create the rectangle has now been converted to a region.

4. Type **HIDE** and press Enter to invoke the HIDE command. Note that the newly created region acts as a planar surface, hiding the circle and line objects behind it as shown in Figure 26.28.

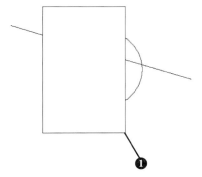

**Figure 26.28**   A region created with the REGION command. Regions hide objects behind them.

In the following step, you rotate the region in 3D space.

5. From the Modify pull-down menu, choose 3D Operation, Rotate 3D. When prompted to select objects, select the region and press Enter.

6. At the next prompt, type **Y** to indicate that you want to rotate the region about its Y-axis.

7. When prompted to specify a point on the Y-axis, use an endpoint osnap and pick at ❶ in Figure 26.29. To specify an angle of rotation, type **90** and press Enter.

8. From the View menu, choose 3D Views, SE Isometric. Your drawing should resemble Figure 26.29.

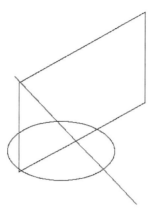

**Figure 26.29**    Regions can be moved and positioned in 3D space.

9. Again, type **HIDE** to invoke the HIDE command. Note that the region is rotated in 3D space and hides objects behind it as shown in Figure 26.30.

   You can close this drawing without saving changes.

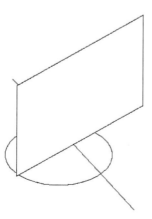

**Figure 26.30**    Regions behave like solids and hide objects behind them.

As you can see from the preceding exercise, regions have many of the properties of 3D surfaces—they hide objects behind them, and they can be easily moved in 3D space. One of the most interesting and useful properties of regions is their capability to undergo Boolean operations—a trait they share with AutoCAD solids. Boolean operations are discussed and demonstrated later in Chapter 28.

# Summary

In this chapter, you learned some of the basic principles of drawing in three dimensions. Starting with simple, basic lines and polylines, you learned the importance of using object snaps and point filters to ensure accuracy in 3D space. You learned that many of the editing operations you use in 2D, such as MOVE and ROTATE, have equivalent 3D commands. Finally, you learned about a special 2D/3D object called a region.

In the next chapter, you learn how to create 3D surfaces by using the AutoCAD surfacing commands.

*C h a p t e r   2 7*

# Surfacing in 3D

In the previous two chapters, you learned about creating simple 3D objects. By creating and manipulating these 3D primitives, you can create a wide variety of more complex objects such as chairs, tables, and so on. When you're modeling complex objects, however, you often may need more flexibility to create such things as irregularly curved surfaces.

Fortunately, AutoCAD provides a set of surfacing commands with which you can create the outlines of these types of objects in profile using lines or polylines and then create surfaces between these lines. This chapter takes a look at the various methods and techniques AutoCAD provides for creating both simple and complex 3D surfaces. This chapter covers the following topics:

- Basic surfacing techniques
- Working with advanced surfacing commands
- 3D meshes
- Editing mesh surfaces

# Basic Surfacing Techniques

In the previous chapter, the techniques used to create 3D lines and polylines were discussed. Objects modeled with such lines are called *wireframe* models. To create a true 3D object, however, surfaces must be applied across or around the edges of the wire frame. Such surfaces can then be used to hide lines and other surfaces that lie "behind" them in any particular view. Surfaces can also have hatch patterns and even materials applied to them to yield more realistic-looking objects.

In some cases, you need to create the wireframe "skeleton" of an object before you create the surfaces, using the wireframe as a starting point from which to apply the surfaces. This method employs two relatively simple 3D objects: 3D faces and polyfaces.

**I**NSIDER  **N**OTE

> All the surfacing commands discussed in this chapter are available from the pull-down menus. Most are also available on the Surfaces toolbar. When working with the exercises in this chapter, we usually refer to the menu commands. You can also use the corresponding tools from the Surface toolbar. The basic commands are also available by typing them at the command prompt.

## Using 3D Faces and Polyface Meshes

A 3D *face* is a surface defined by either three or four sides, forming either a rectangular or a triangular surface. In most instances, a triangular, three-sided face is preferable because a 3D face is a planar element. A rectangular 3D face can be either planar or nonplanar. Figure 27.1 shows a triangular and a rectangular 3D face with the upper-right corner of the rectangular face lying at a different elevation than the other three corners. Four-sided faces can be more difficult to visualize.

**Figure 27.1**    A three-sided (left) and a four-sided 3D face. Three-sided faces are planar, whereas four-sided faces can have vertices at different elevations.

You construct 3D faces with the 3DFACE command, accessed by selecting the Draw pull-down menu, Surfaces, 3D Face. Specifying the corner points creates the face. The 3DFACE command enables you to continue creating 3D faces by selecting more points.

3D faces can be difficult to visualize. To see if the 3D faces you created are correct, use the HIDE and SHADEMODE commands to check your drawing. Also check from different viewpoints to ensure that the faces are drawn correctly.

When creating your 3D face, always work your way around the perimeter of the face. This is especially important if you decide to create a four-sided face. If you select points in a crosswise fashion, a bow-tie effect occurs, as shown in Figure 27.2.

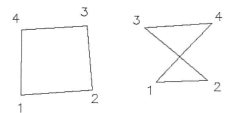

**Figure 27.2**    Always specify the corners of a 3D face in a clockwise or counterclockwise sequence.

Although you can construct a surfaced box with the AI_BOX command, sometimes you may need to place 3D faces on a wireframe, as shown in the following exercise.

### Exercise 27.1    Using the *3DFACE* Command to Surface a Box

1. Load the drawing file 27EX01.dwg from the accompanying CD-ROM. The file contains a wireframe box, as shown in Figure 27.3. This "box" consists of 12 individual polylines arranged in such a way as to represent a three-dimensional box.

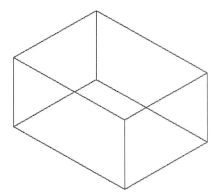

**Figure 27.3**    A wireframe "box" that you surface with the 3DFACE command.

2. At the command prompt, type **HIDE** and press Enter. Because there are no surfaces in this collection of polylines, the HIDE command has no visual effect.

3. From the Tools pull-down menu, select Drafting Settings and on the Drafting Settings dialog box Object Snap tab, ensure that the Object Snap On and Endpoint Object Snap options are checked. Click OK to close the dialog box.

4. From the Draw pull-down menu, choose Surfaces, 3D Face.

5. Select the seven corners of the box shown in ❶ through ❼ in Figure 27.4. Be sure to select the corners in proper numerical sequence.

6. When you have selected the corner at ❼, press Enter twice to end the 3DFACE command.

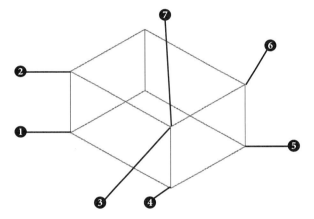

**Figure 27.4**    Choose the corners in sequence to apply 3D faces. Note the new diagonal line—the edge of a face object.

7. Type **HIDE** again and press Enter. Figure 27.5 shows the resulting box.

Leave this drawing open for use in the next exercise.

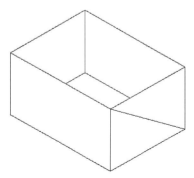

**Figure 27.5**    The box with faces applied to two sides.

In the previous exercise, you constructed only two of the six 3D faces required to completely cover the frame of the box. The other four sides could be applied in a similar manner. The second face actually consists of two three-sided faces with the diagonal line appearing between corners ❺ and ❼ representing the shared edge. Due to the manner in which the 3DFACE command works, four-sided faces are usually drawn this way because AutoCAD attempts to construct three-sided faces where possible.

AutoCAD provides two means to hide face edges. You can hide an edge during the construction of a face by typing an **I** just prior to specifying the first point that will create the edge. You can also make a 3D face edge invisible after it is formed by using the EDGE command. The following exercise shows how to use the EDGE command to hide a face edge after it has been drawn.

### Exercise 27.2    Using the *EDGE* Command

1. Continue in 27EX01.dwg from the preceding exercise.

2. From the Draw pull-down menu, select Surfaces, Edge.

3. When prompted, select the diagonal edge appearing between corners ❺ and ❼ in Figure 27.5. Notice that AutoCAD switches you to a midpoint object snap mode automatically.

4. Press Enter, and the edge is hidden.

   After an edge is hidden, you can no longer select it. To unhide an edge, you can use the Display option of the EDGE command.

5. Press Enter to restart the EDGE command.

6. Select an edge of the face containing the hidden edge. Select between ❹ and ❻, for example.

7. Type **D** (for display) and press Enter. You are then prompted with the Display options.

8. Type **A** (for all) and press Enter. All the edges of the face become visible and highlighted.

9. Select the edge you want to make visible and press Enter. The visibility of the edge is restored.

   Quit this drawing without saving changes.

---

**I**NSIDER **N**OTE

The AutoCAD system variable SPLFRAME can be used to control the display of the invisible edges of 3D faces. If you are having trouble using the EDGE command to change the visibility of an edge, change SPLFRAME to 1 to display all edges. Then you can more easily use the EDGE command to make edges visible or invisible.

---

3D faces are limited as surfacing tools, principally because they are limited to three or four sides and do not serve well for the creation of curved objects. Applying 3D faces to define a large surface would be tedious work and would likely yield less than satisfactory results. To get around this limitation, you can make use of the AutoCAD PFACE, or polyface, command. It enables you to create larger faces composed of many more individual faces by defining multiple faces that specify how the surface is created between points. Such a large non-planar surface is termed a polyface mesh. Again, to construct a large polyface mesh manually would be tremendously tedious and time-consuming. The PFACE command is therefore usually used by other applications. The application "communicates" with the PFACE command through an application programming interface, such as AutoLISP, to automatically construct the mesh.

# Working with Advanced Surfacing Commands

AutoCAD provides five true surfacing commands. These commands make use of existing geometry—usually polylines—to create surfaces. These surfacing tools include the following commands:

- EDGESURF
- RULESURF
- TABSURF
- REVSURF
- 3DMESH

## The *EDGESURF* Command

The EDGESURF command is used to create a 3D surface between four connected lines or polylines. Figure 27.6 shows an example of the result of using EDGESURF. The EDGESURF command can be accessed by choosing the Draw pull-down menu, Surfaces, Edge Surface or by typing **EDGESURF** at the command prompt.

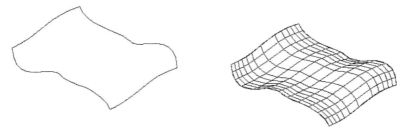

**Figure 27.6**   Four splined curves before (left) and after applying the EDGESURF command.

The resolution of the 3D surface generated by EDGESURF, as well as by the other surfacing commands, is controlled by two system variables: SURFTAB1 and SURFTAB2. These two variables represent the number of mesh faces in the M and N directions, respectively. The letters M and N are used to reduce the confusion with the standard X and Y axes. The M direction, however, is generally considered to coincide with the X-axis direction and the N direction with the Y-axis direction. The default value of both SURFTAB1 and SURFTAB2 is 6. By increasing these values, you get more accurate surfaces because more individual faces are generated between the bounding edges. Figure 27.7 shows the difference between a surface with both variables set to 6 and the same surface with both variables set to 24.

**INSIDER TIP**

> The SURFTAB variables do not always have to be set to the same values. For example, if you have a set of four lines that you want to surface, but in one direction the lines are more complex than in the other direction, you might want to increase the SURFTAB value in the more complex direction only. This results in a more accurate but not overly complex mesh.

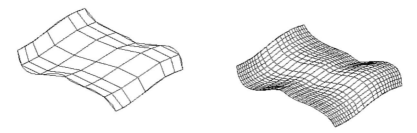

**Figure 27.7**   Two surfaces created with the EDGESURF command. The surface on the left was created with SURFTAB settings of 6; the surface on the right with SURFTAB values of 24.

The following exercise shows you how to use EDGESURF to create the canopy of an airplane.

### Exercise 27.3    Using *EDGESURF* to Create the Canopy

1. Load the file 27EX03.dwg from the accompanying CD-ROM. The file contains the outline of an airplane canopy, as shown in Figure 27.8.

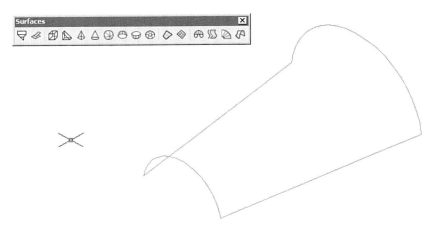

**Figure 27.8**    The outline drawing of an airplane canopy that is ready for the EDGESURF command.

2. At the command prompt, type **SURFTAB1**. Set the value to **24**.

3. Type **SURFTAB2** and set it to a value to **24**.

4. From the Draw pull-down menu, select Surfaces, Edge Surface.

5. Select the four lines in the drawing. The surface is then created, as shown in Figure 27.9. Because the SURFTAB variables are set to the same value, the order of selection is not important.

   Close this drawing without saving changes.

In this exercise, you set SURFTAB1 and SURFTAB2 to relatively high values. This resulted in a smoother surface at the expense of longer regeneration times and a larger drawing. If you change SURFTAB1 and SURFTAB2 to either higher or lower values, you must erase or undo the previous mesh and perform the surfacing operation again. Also note that the surface is generated on the current layer. As you work with EDGESURF, remember that the command neither removes your edges from the drawing nor attaches the mesh to them.

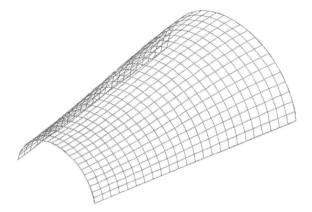

**Figure 27.9**   The canopy with the surface applied.

## The *RULESURF* Command

The RULESURF command creates a ruled surface. Unlike the EDGESURF command, RULESURF requires only two defining edges. Because RULESURF works only between two objects, it uses just the SURFTAB1 system variable to establish the mesh density. Figure 27.10 shows examples of typical surfaces created with RULESURF. The defining edges can be points, lines, splines, circles, arcs, or polylines. If one of the edge objects is closed—a circle, for example—then the other object must also be closed.

If you generate a surface between two open boundary edges, you must be careful about the points you use to select the boundaries. RULESURF starts generating the mesh at each boundary by dividing the boundary curve into a number of segments equal to the current setting of SURFTAB1, starting from the endpoint nearest the pick point. If you use pick points on opposite sides of the two boundary curves, the resulting curve is self-intersecting, as shown in Figure 27.11.

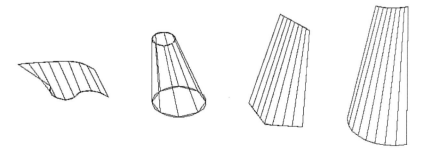

**Figure 27.10**   Typical surface meshes created with the RULESURF command.

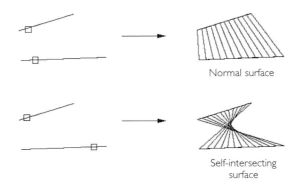

Normal surface

Self-intersecting surface

**Figure 27.11**    With open boundary edges, selecting objects at opposite ends creates a self-intersecting polygon mesh.

The following exercise shows how to use RULESURF to surface the contours of a site.

### Exercise 27.4    Using *RULESURF* in a Mapping Application

1. Load the file 27EX04.dwg from the accompanying CD-ROM. The file contains four contours, as shown in Figure 27.12.

2. From the Draw pull-down menu, select Surfaces, Ruled Surface.

3. Select the top two lines of Figure 27.12 in order: ❶ then ❷. The ruled surface is generated, as shown in Figure 27.13.

4. The smoothness of this curve is inadequate. Type **SURFTAB1** and set the value to 24.

5. Use the ERASE command to erase the surface. Repeat step 3 with the new SURFTAB1 setting. The surface should now resemble Figure 27.14.

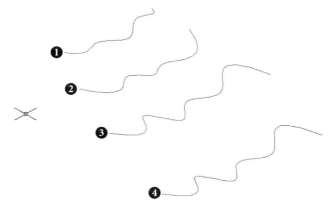

**Figure 27.12**    Four contour lines that you can surface with RULESURF.

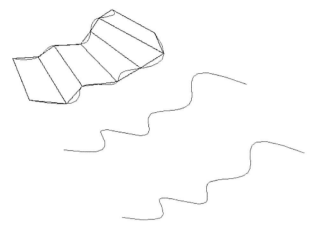

**Figure 27.13**   The first surface generated between the first two contour lines.

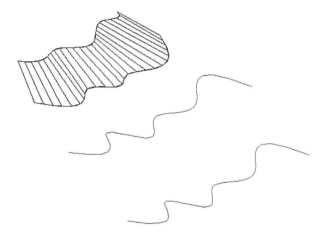

**Figure 27.14**   The first surface generated between the first two contour lines at higher density.

6. Select the new surface to grip it and change its layer from 0 to Surface. Note that the Surface layer is currently frozen. Click OK in the AutoCAD alert for frozen layer dialog box. The surface disappears when transferred to the frozen layer.

7. Repeat step 3, selecting at ❷ and ❸ of Figure 27.12. RULESURF generates a second surface.

8. Use the same procedure as in step 6 to transfer the second surface to the Surface layer.

9. Use RULESURF and the boundaries at ❸ and ❹ to generate the third surface.

10. Transfer the third surface to the Surface layer and thaw that layer. Your drawing should now resemble Figure 27.15.

    Close this drawing without saving changes.

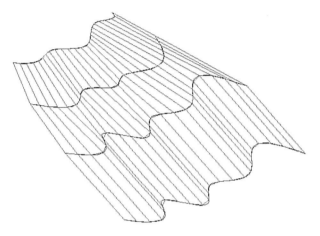

**Figure 27.15**   The completed contour surfaces.

This exercise demonstrates that the amount of detail necessary in a RULESURF mesh often depends on the boundary object(s). With curved boundaries, SURFTAB1 may need to be set to a higher value to cause the surface to follow the boundary edge more closely. With sequential boundaries such as in the preceding exercise, it is a good idea to create the surfaces on a separate layer and then transfer them to a frozen layer. This enables the boundary edges to be more readily selected.

## The *TABSURF* Command

The TABSURF command creates a tabulated surface, or a surface that is extruded along a linear path. TABSURF is accessed by choosing Draw pull-down menu, Surfaces, Tabulated Surface or by typing **TABSURF** at the command prompt.

To create a surface with TABSURF, you must have two elements: an outline or curve to be extruded and a direction vector indicating the direction and distance the curve is to be extended. Figure 27.16 shows several examples of tabulated surfaces.

The path curve can consist of a line, arc, circle, ellipse, or a 2D or 3D polyline. TABSURF draws the surface starting at the point on the path curve closest to the selection point.

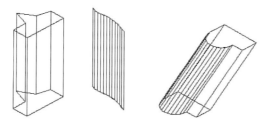

**Figure 27.16**    Typical surfaces constructed with TABSURF.

If the direction vector is a polyline, TABSURF considers only the first and last vertices of the line in determining the length and direction of the vector. In other words, TABSURF extrudes only a straight line. The end of the vector line chosen determines the direction of the extrusion. As with RULESURF, only SURFTAB1 affects TABSURF.

The following exercise shows you how to use the TABSURF command to create a stair railing.

### Exercise 27.5    Using *TABSURF* to Create a Stair Railing

  1. Load the file 27EX05.dwg from the accompanying CD. This drawing is shown in Figure 27.17.

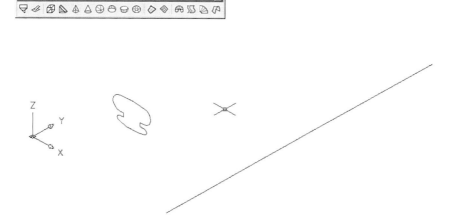

**Figure 27.17**    The path curve and direction vector for use in constructing a stair railing.

  2. From the Draw pull-down menu, select Surfaces, Tabulated Surface.
  3. Select the outline of the handrail.

4. Select the horizontal line. The profile is then extruded, as shown in Figure 27.18. Close this drawing without saving changes.

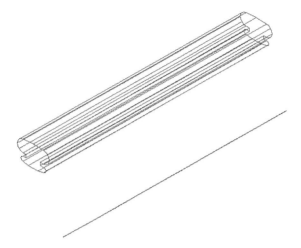

**Figure 27.18**   The completed railing.

---

**I** NSIDER **TIP**

The tessellation lines that are a part of curved solids are often problematic when viewing the model. However, the density can be controlled with the ISOLINES system variable. If you need even more clarity, try changing the DISPSILH system variable as well. Changing from a default of 0 to 1 suppresses the lines and dramatically improves the HIDE output quality.

---

## The *REVSURF* Command

REVSURF is perhaps the most useful of the 3D surfacing commands. REVSURF generates a 3D mesh object in the form of a surface of revolution by taking an outline—the path curve—and revolving it about an axis of revolution. As shown in Figure 27.19, the path curve is revolved around the axis of revolution to create the surface. The REVSURF command is accessed by selecting the Draw pull-down menu, Surfaces, Revolved Surface, or by typing **REVSURF** at the command prompt.

The *path curve* is the outline that will be revolved. It must be a single object: a line, arc, circle, ellipse, elliptical arc, polyline, polygon, spline, or donut.

The *axis of revolution* is the axis about which the path curve is revolved. The axis can be a line or an open 2D or 3D polyline. If a polyline is selected, the axis is assumed to be a line running through the first and last vertices.

REVSURF is made even more powerful by the fact that it can revolve the path curve through an included angle that can range from 0 to a full 360 degrees. The default angle is a full circle that results in the generation of a closed surface of revolution such as that shown in Figure 27.19. If you specify an angle less than 360 degrees, then the surface is generated in a counterclockwise direction. If you specify a negative angle less than 360 degrees, then the surface is generated in a clockwise direction.

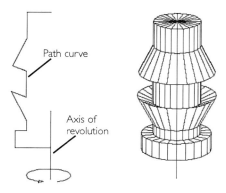

**Figure 27.19**   REVSURF revolves an outline around an axis.

You can also specify the start angle, which is the angular offset from the path curve at which the surface of revolution begins. The default value, 0, indicates that the surface of revolution will begin at the location of the path curve.

### Determining the Positive Direction of Rotation

To have a *start angle* other than 0 degrees or an included angle other than a full circle, you must be able to determine the positive direction of rotation. REVSURF follows these conventions: A negative value dictates an angular distance in the clockwise direction, and a positive value dictates an angular distance in a counterclockwise direction. You can determine the direction of rotation by applying the "right-hand rule."

According to the *right-hand rule*, if you point your right thumb in the positive direction of the axis about which you are rotating and wrap your fingers of your right hand around the axis, the curl of your fingers indicates the direction of positive rotation. But how do you determine the positive direction of the axis?

The positive direction along the axis of rotation runs from the endpoint of the object nearest the pick point used to select the object to the other endpoint. For example, in Figure 27.20, if you select the line at point ❶, then the positive direction of the axis runs from ❶ to ❷. If you select the line near ❷, then the positive direction of the axis runs from ❷ to ❶.

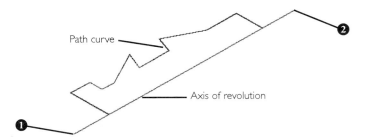

**Figure 27.20**    Where you select the axis of revolution determines the positive direction of revolution.

Unlike the surfaces created by TABSURF and RULESURF, but similar to the surfaces created by EDGESURF, REVSURF creates a two-dimensional mesh, and therefore both SURFTAB1 and SURFTAB2 influence the density of the resulting mesh. Keep both SURFTAB values as low as possible, but make sure the resulting mesh is still dense enough to meet your needs.

**INSIDER TIP**

> The original objects used to define the profile (path curve) and the axis are left untouched by REVSURF; they are not incorporated into the resulting mesh. They are often difficult to distinguish, however, because the mesh can obscure them. It is therefore a good habit to generate the surface mesh on a separate layer. This enables you to freeze or turn off the two layers and isolate the path curve and axis object, should you want to use them again. This tip applies equally to the TABSURF, EDGESURF, and RULESURF commands.

The following exercise shows how to use REVSURF to create a rivet.

### Exercise 27.6    Using *REVSURF* to Create a Rivet

1. Load the file 27EX06.dwg from the accompanying CD-ROM. The file contains an outline of a piston and its axis of rotation, as shown in Figure 27.21.

2. At the command prompt, type **SURFTAB1**. Set the value to 24. Type **SURFTAB2** and set its value to 24.

3. Change the current layer to Mesh.

4. From the Draw pull-down menu, select Surfaces, Revolved Surface.

5. When prompted for the object to revolve, pick the piston outline.

6. When prompted to select the object that defines the axis of revolution, pick the vertical line next to the outline.

7. Press Enter to accept the default start angle of 0 degrees.

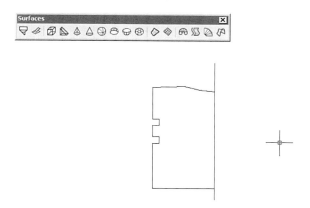

**Figure 27.21**   The outline of a piston and the axis of rotation line.

8. When prompted for the included angle, press Enter to accept the default of 360 degrees. REVSURF creates the revolved surface. Your drawing should now resemble Figure 27.22.

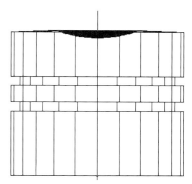

**Figure 27.22**   The revolved piston surface.

9. From the Modify pull-down menu, select 3D Operation, Rotate 3D.

10. Type **All** and then press Enter to select all objects for rotation. Press Enter again.

11. Type **X** and then press Enter to specify the X-axis as the axis of rotation.

12. When prompted for a point on the X-axis, use a midpoint osnap to pick the midpoint of the line representing the axis of rotation.

13. When prompted for the rotation angle, type **90**. The piston, its outline, and the axis line are rotated 90 degrees around the X-axis.

14. From the View pull-down menu, select 3D Views, SE Isometric. AutoCAD switches to an isometric view. Notice that the original piston outline and the axis line are visible.

15. From the View pull-down menu, select Shade, Flat Shaded. Your model should now resemble Figure 27.23.

    Close this drawing without saving changes.

**Figure 27.23**   The revolved piston surface in a shaded rendering.

REVSURF offers more options and parameters than the other commands presented in this chapter. Although it is a somewhat complicated surfacing command, it is one of the most flexible and useful 3D tools available.

## The *3DMESH* Command

Like the other 3D surfacing commands discussed in this chapter, the 3DMESH command creates a mesh of contiguous 3D faces. An M×N matrix, where M is generally associated with the X-axis and N with the Y-axis, defines the size of the mesh. To construct even a relatively simple mesh of this type requires a large amount of input and, if done manually, is quite tedious and error-prone. The 3DMESH command, therefore, is intended primarily as the avenue of input for external programs. In this respect, 3DMESH is similar to the PFACE command discussed earlier in this chapter. Programs written in programming languages such as AutoLISP are adept at supplying the vertex information required by the 3DMESH command.

## Editing Mesh Surfaces

After a surface has been created using one of the commands described in this chapter, there are two methods for editing that surface in addition to the standard editing commands such as MOVE, ROTATE, and SCALE. Those two methods are grip editing and the PEDIT command.

Grip editing works on a surface just as it does on any other AutoCAD object. The one difference is that surfaces generally have more grips that you can easily manipulate. However, all modes of grip editing, including Move, Scale, Rotate, Mirror, and Stretch, work with surfaces. Figure 27.24 shows the grip's density of a typical 3D surface.

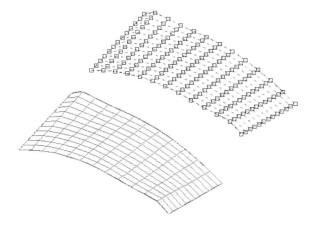

**Figure 27.24**   A typical 3D mesh surface with (right) and without grips displayed.

The PEDIT command provides the second method of editing any 3D mesh object. Just as you can edit a polyline with PEDIT, you can manipulate a mesh surface in certain ways. PEDIT can be used to perform the following functions on a 3D mesh surface:

- **Edit vertex.** This includes adding, moving, and deleting vertices from the mesh.

- **Smooth surface.** This is generally used with 3D meshes or other surfaces that are not already smoothed. This is very similar to the `PEDIT` spline command for polylines, but it works in three dimensions instead of two.

- **Desmooth.** This removes any smoothing from surfaces that have been smoothed with the `PEDIT` smooth command.

- `Mopen`, `Nopen`, `Mclose`, and `Nclose`. Basically, surfaces are created as polylines with 3D faces between them. These commands either open or close the polylines in the M or N directions. For example, if you create a surface that forms a dome, using `Mclose` and `Nclose` closes all the polylines in the M direction and forms a floor. An example of closing a 3D mesh in the M and N directions is shown in Figure 27.25.

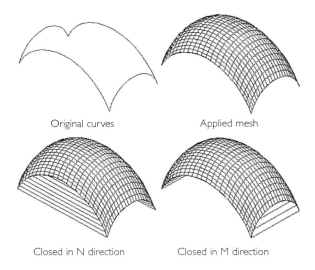

Original curves          Applied mesh

Closed in N direction          Closed in M direction

**Figure 27.25**   Closing a 3D mesh in the M and N directions with the `PEDIT` command.

Editing a 3D mesh surface is not easy. If you need to change a surface in AutoCAD, it is frequently more efficient to change the construction edges defining the surface instead of using grips or the `PEDIT` command to perform the editing.

# Summary

In this chapter, you learned how to create 3D surfaces based on existing geometry in your model by using a variety of 3D surfacing commands. Adjusting the SURFTAB1 and SURFTAB2 system variables controls the resolution of these surfaces. You also discovered how you can edit surfaces by using PEDIT. The 3DMESH and PFACE commands are used primarily by outside programs that provide the high amount of input that they require.

In the next chapter, you explore how to use AutoCAD's solid modeling commands to create many types of 3D solid objects that would be difficult, if not impossible, to create by using the surfacing commands covered in this chapter.

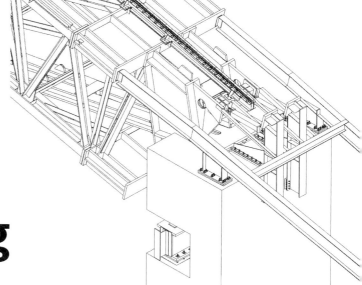

*Chapter 28*

# Solid Modeling in 3D

Solid modeling consists of creating fundamental three-dimensional elements (such as boxes, spheres, cylinders, pyramids, and so on), called primitives, and combining and manipulating those primitives into more complex objects. It is called solid modeling because your work has volume, and thus you can attach material information to the model so that you can find data such as an object's center of gravity, how much it weighs, and so on.

This chapter focuses on how the Autodesk Shape Manager in AutoCAD 2005 works as an integrated modeling tool. Specifically, this chapter explores the following concepts:

- The Autodesk Shape Manager
- Creating primitives
- Working with EXTRUDE and REVOLVE
- Working with 3D Boolean commands
- Using FILLET and CHAMFER
- Controlling surface resolution
- Advanced solid modeling commands
- Editing solids

# The Autodesk Shape Manager

The solid modeling system in AutoCAD 2005 is supplied by the Autodesk Shape Manager, the geometric engine that most Autodesk packages now use. The Autodesk Shape Manager uses an object-oriented approach for modeling, where the data is stored in a boundary representation. This modeler also takes advantage of the AutoCAD load-on-demand architecture, so the modeler program tools are loaded only when you access the commands.

The solid modeling commands are located on the Solids and Solids Editing toolbars, as shown in Figure 28.1. You can also access the solid modeling commands by selecting Solids from the Draw pull-down menu or by typing at the command prompt.

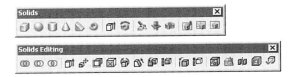

**Figure 28.1**    The Solids and Solids Editing toolbars.

# Creating Primitives

AutoCAD 2005 supports six different ACIS primitives:

- BOX
- SPHERE
- CYLINDER
- CONE
- WEDGE
- TORUS

These rather simple solid geometric forms are termed *primitives* because they are the most basic 3D objects that can be constructed. They then can be used in various combinations to produce hundreds of other, more complex solid geometric shapes. Primitives themselves are easy to construct.

Creating a solid box, for example, is as simple as selecting the BOX command from the Solids toolbar and specifying the two points that define the opposite corners of the box and the height. The resulting solid box appears similar to a 3D box created with surfaces.

The display of solid objects, however, is quite different in some cases. Consider, for example, a surface sphere and a solid sphere. The surface sphere looks quite different from the solid version, as shown in Figure 28.2.

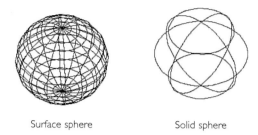

Surface sphere                    Solid sphere

**Figure 28.2**    A sphere made of surfaces compared with an ACIS solid sphere.

The displays differ because the solid modeler works with *boundaries*, whereas the surface modeler works with faces joined together to form surfaces. When you hide the solid sphere or render it, it is converted to a surface-like model for that purpose only. Figure 28.3 shows the spheres represented in Figure 28.2 after using the HIDE command.

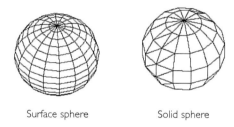

Surface sphere                 Solid sphere

**Figure 28.3**    A surface sphere and a solid sphere after using the HIDE command.

**I**NSIDER **N**OTE

> The lines used to visually display AutoCAD's solids are called *isolines*. The system variable ISOLINES controls the number of isolines used to show solids. Usually, four isolines per solid object adequately represent the shape and form of a solid; therefore, the default value is 4. For more complex solids, or in views containing a large number of solid objects, you may want to increase the number of isolines. If you alter the number of isolines, you must perform a regen to make the display change for solids already drawn.

> When viewing curved edges on solids, such as those on a cylinder, the lines displayed to show the curve are known as *tessellation* lines. You may find the displayed tessellation lines visibly bothersome. A trick some like to implement is to use a few system variables together to get better results. The system variable DISPSILH controls the silhouettes of curved objects; set it 1. This produces curved solid objects with fewer (if any) disturbing tessellation lines. Tessellation lines are discussed later in this chapter.

After you have two or more solid objects, you can use a number of Boolean commands to create complex shapes. The UNION command can be used to weld two or more objects into one. An interesting characteristic of this command is that these objects do not actually have to touch in order to be unioned; they simply become one object where formerly there were two. You can then use the SOLIDEDIT command, discussed later in this chapter, to separate them again.

The opposite of UNION is the SUBTRACT command. This command removes the volume of selected solids from a selection of other solids. For example, this command could be used to create a hole in a box—subtracting a cylinder from a box would do the trick.

Then there are two commands for building solids from the volume of shared 3D space. The INTERSECT command reduces any number of selected solids to only the shared volume. For example, executing this command on a sphere that is halfway into a solid box generates a hemisphere. The other command is INTERFERE, which is similar to INTERSECT but doesn't require removal of the original objects. The INTERFERE command is discussed later in this chapter.

As you may have guessed, modeling with primitives is not much different from modeling with surface primitives. As always, when working with 3D models, you need to change your view direction frequently in order to keep the spatial relationships of the model's components in view.

# Creating Solids with *EXTRUDE* and *REVOLVE*

As mentioned before, solid primitives, such as Box, Sphere, Cone, and so on, are frequently used in combinations to produce new solid shapes. In addition to primitives, AutoCAD provides two powerful commands that produce non-primitive, often complex, shapes from closed 2D curves: EXTRUDE and REVOLVE.

The EXTRUDE command is useful for objects that contain fillets, chamfers (discussed later in this chapter), and other details that might otherwise be difficult to reproduce except in a profile. The REVOLVE command creates a solid by revolving a two-dimensional object (profile) about an axis. 2D objects capable of being revolved include closed polylines, polygons, circles, ellipses, closed splines, donuts, and regions.

## Using the *EXTRUDE* Command

With the EXTRUDE command, you can extrude, or give thickness to, certain 2D objects. You can extrude along a path, or you can specify a height and taper angle. Objects must be "closed" to qualify for extrusion. Such objects can include planar 3D faces, closed polylines, polygons, circles, ellipses, closed splines, donuts, and regions. 2D objects such as these are termed *profiles*.

A common usage of the EXTRUDE command is the creation of 3D walls. The following exercise shows how to create a wall by using the EXTRUDE command.

### Exercise 28.1    Using the *EXTRUDE* Command to Create a Wall

   **1.** Load the file 28EX01.dwg from the accompanying CD. The file contains the outline of a wall, as shown in Figure 28.4. If the Solids toolbar is not active, turn it on.

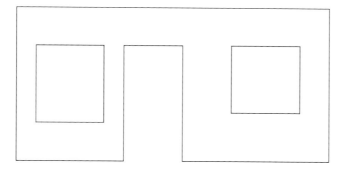

**Figure 28.4**   The outline of a wall with openings ready to be extruded.

   **2.** Choose Extrude from the Solids toolbar.

   **3.** Select the three polylines in the view (the wall and two window openings) and press Enter.

   **4.** When prompted for a height, type **0.5**.

5. Accept the default taper angle of 0 by pressing Enter. The objects are then extruded (although the display doesn't noticeably change).

6. From the View pull-down menu, choose 3D Views, SW Isometric.

7. From the View pull-down menu, choose Hide. The wall parts after the extrusion process are shown in Figure 28.5.

You may now close the drawing without saving.

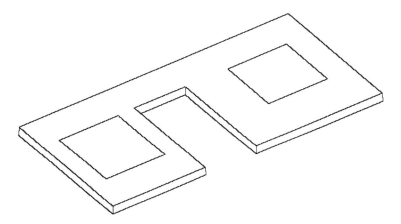

**Figure 28.5**    The hidden wall parts after extrusion. The windows are extruded as separate objects.

As you can see, using the EXTRUDE command to extrude a profile in the object's Z-axis is simple and straightforward. If you extrude a closed polyline that is itself enclosed within the boundary of another extruded closed polyline, as in the preceding exercise, you end up with multiple objects. This would be a common situation when extruding walls with window openings. The windows can be subtracted using the SUBTRACT command. You do this in an exercise in the later section, "Working with 3D Boolean Operations."

In addition to extruding straight up or down, with or without a taper, you can extrude a closed 2D object along a path. The following exercise shows you how to create a pipe by using the Path option. This exercise shows you some of the flexibility of the EXTRUDE command and how it can be useful for modeling many different objects.

### Exercise 28.2     Extruding Along a Path

1. Load the file 28EX02.dwg from the accompanying CD. The drawing contains a circle and polyline path, as shown in Figure 28.6.

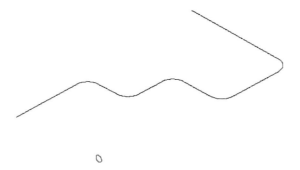

**Figure 28.6**   A circle and the polyline path along which it will be extruded.

2. From the Solids toolbar, choose Extrude.

3. Select the circle as the object to extrude. Press Enter to end the Select Objects prompt.

4. Type **P** for Path.

**INSIDER TIP**

> Many commands have a right-click menu that provides quick access to the command features. You can also start the Path option for the EXTRUDE command this way.

5. Select the adjacent polyline. The object is then extruded following that path. Note that the path is applied by AutoCAD to match the center of the shape.

6. From the View pull-down menu, choose Hide. Now shown is a hidden view of the extruded circle applied along the path, as shown in Figure 28.7.

   You can close this drawing without saving.

As you can see from this exercise, extruding along a path is relatively easy. Just make sure that the shape you want to extrude is truly perpendicular to the path, as it was in this exercise. If not, you might not be able to extrude the object, or you might get undesirable results.

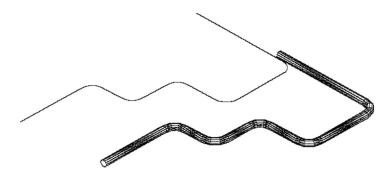

**Figure 28.7**    A new section of pipe after extruding a circle along a polyline object.

Extruding along a path works well with polylines and splines as long as they are not closed. When a closed polyline or spline is used as a path, the extrusion might not always work.

## Using the *REVOLVE* Command

The REVOLVE command produces solid objects from 2D profiles, much like the EXTRUDE command. With REVOLVE, however, an axis of revolution is specified. 3D objects produced with the REVOLVE command therefore have a radial axis of symmetry. You can revolve any number of degrees about the axis of revolution, although full 360-degree revolutions are most common. In the following exercise, you use two different amounts of rotation to produce two models of a piston.

### Exercise 28.3    Using *REVOLVE* to Produce a Piston

1. Load the file 28EX03.dwg from the accompanying CD. The drawing contains two identical profiles of a piston. The axis of revolution is indicated with both profiles, as shown in Figure 28.8. If the Solids toolbar is not active, turn it on.

2. Choose Revolve from the Solids toolbar.

3. Select the left piston outline and press Enter.

4. When prompted, type **0** for Object.

5. Select the vertical line associated with the profile. This line will serve as the axis of revolution.

**Figure 28.8**    Two profiles of pistons ready to revolve.

6. Press Enter to accept a full 360 degrees of revolution.

7. Restart the REVOLVE command by pressing Enter. Repeat steps 3-5 with the right piston profile.

8. When prompted to specify the angle of revolution for the right piston, enter **230**.

9. From the View pull-down menu, choose Named Views and click the Southwest Isometric view to make it current.

10. Again from the View pull-down menu, choose Hide. Figure 28.9 shows the resulting solid objects.

You may now close the drawing without saving.

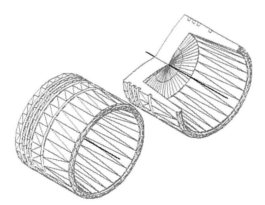

**Figure 28.9**    Piston profiles fully and partially revolved about an axis.

As you can see, the REVOLVE command can be a flexible 3D design tool. Similar to EXTRUDE, REVOLVE is useful for objects that contain fillets or other details that would otherwise be difficult to reproduce in a common profile.

**I**nsider Tip

> If you create a profile using lines or arcs that meet a polyline, use the PEDIT Join and Close option to convert them to a single closed polyline object before you use REVOLVE.

# Working with 3D Boolean Operations

Much of the power of solid modeling comes from the capability to use Boolean operations as modeling tools. 3D Boolean commands enable you to quickly and easily create complex objects from simple primitives.

There are three Boolean types that you can use: Union, Intersect, and Subtract. Figure 28.10 shows two primitives and the object that results when you apply each of the three Boolean operations to the primitives.

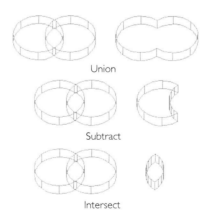

**Figure 28.10**   Examples of each of the three Boolean operations.

The following exercise shows how to use a Boolean Subtract operation to create holes in a wall that you built earlier in this chapter.

### Exercise 28.4    Using Subtract to Create Holes in a Wall

1. Load the file 28EX04.dwg from the accompanying CD. If the Solids Editing toolbar is not active, turn it on.

2. Choose Subtract from the Solids Editing toolbar.

3. Select the large wall object as the object to subtract from and press Enter. Then select the two boxes representing the windows as the objects to subtract and press Enter. Again, the display doesn't change appreciably, although significant changes to the model have been made.

4. To show the result of the subtraction, run the HIDE command from the View pull-down menu. The wall with window openings is shown in Figure 28.11.

   You may now close this drawing without saving.

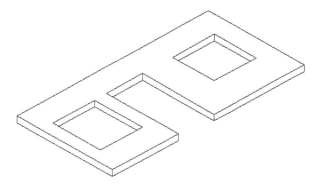

**Figure 28.11**   The wall after subtracting the window openings.

As you can see, Boolean operations are easy to carry out. In some instances, performing a Boolean intersect or subtract operation is virtually the only way to obtain the solid object you want. The following exercise shows a more complex example of another subtract operation.

### Exercise 28.5   Creating a Groove with Subtract

1. Load the file 28EX05.dwg from the accompanying CD-ROM. The file contains a box and a pipe, as shown in Figure 28.12.

2. Choose Subtract from the Solids Editing toolbar.

3. Select the box as the object to subtract from and press Enter.

4. Select the pipe as the object to subtract and press Enter. The subtraction is created.

5. Hide the drawing to achieve the result shown in Figure 28.13.

   You may now close the drawing without saving.

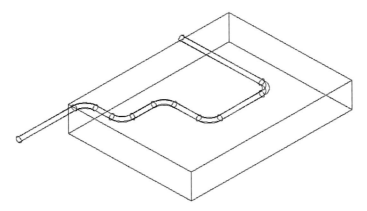

**Figure 28.12**    A solid box and the pipe that will form a groove when subtracted.

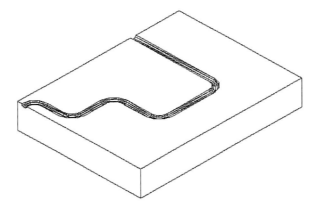

**Figure 28.13**    The box with the pipe subtracted to create a groove.

Imagine trying to create the 3D model in the last exercise without the Boolean subtract operation. This would be difficult if not impossible to do using simple surfaces.

# Enhanced Modeling with *FILLET* and *CHAMFER*

By their very nature, solids have edges in which two surfaces meet. However, there are many times when these edges will require further editing to represent a solid model properly. An example of this is a weld, where solder is laid into a corner. Now as a user, you could extrude a cove shape along this corner, creating a new solid, and then UNION it to the main object. A better technique would be to use the FILLET command with a radius. Both FILLET and CHAMFER can be used to "ease" an edge, both by adding material or removing material, depending on the model.

The following exercise shows how to use the FILLET and CHAMFER commands to edit the edges of a solid model of a phone handset.

### Exercise 28.6    Using the *FILLET* and *CHAMFER* Commands

1. Load the file 28EX06.dwg from the accompanying CD. The model consists of three unioned boxes, as shown in Figure 28.14.

   You first use the FILLET command to round the edges and refine the receiver end of the model.

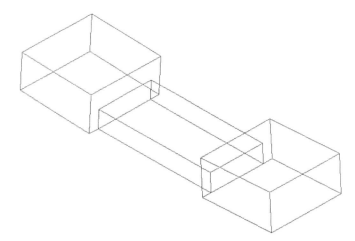

**Figure 28.14**    A set of three solid boxes representing a basic telephone handset design.

2. Choose Fillet from the Modify toolbar or simply type **FILLET** and press Enter.

3. At the prompt to select the first object, select the vertical edge of the receiver portion, as shown at ❶ in Figure 28.15.

4. Specify a fillet radius of **0.20** and press Enter.

5. At the Select an edge or [Chain/Radius] prompt, select the other three vertical edges shown at ❷ through ❹ of Figure 28.15, then press Enter. AutoCAD fillets the four edges as seen in Figure 28.16.

   In the following steps, you use the Chain option of the FILLET command.

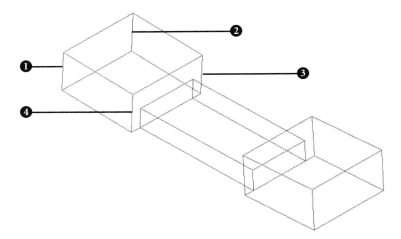

**Figure 28.15**    Preparing to fillet four vertical edges.

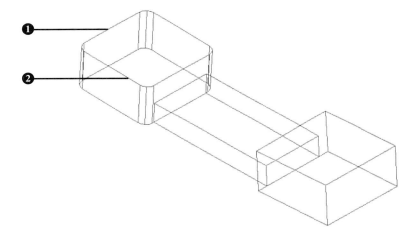

**Figure 28.16**    Preparing to fillet a chain of edges.

6. Repeat FILLET again by pressing either the spacebar or Enter.

7. Select the upper edge of the receiver portion, as shown at ❶ in Figure 28.16.

8. Accept the default radius of 0.2 by pressing Enter.

9. At the Select an edge or [Chain/Radius] prompt, type **C** for Chain and select any of the eight edges making up the top surface of the receiver, keeping in mind that the newly filleted corners now constitute edges. ❷ of Figure 28.16 is a valid choice. Note that selecting any edge selects all connected edges in the chain. Press Enter to complete the fillet operation. At this point, your model should resemble Figure 28.17.

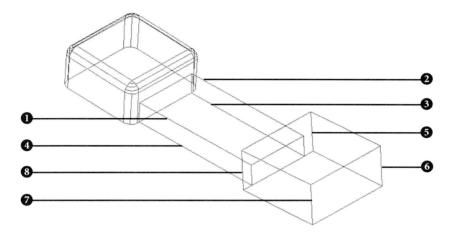

**Figure 28.17**   A total of eight edges is filleted at one time.

10. Repeat the FILLET command and pick the edge shown at ❶ in Figure 28.17 when prompted for the first object.

11. Enter a new radius of **0.15**.

12. Select the edges shown at ❷ through ❽ in Figure 28.17. Press Enter to carry out the fillet operation. Your model should now resemble Figure 28.18.

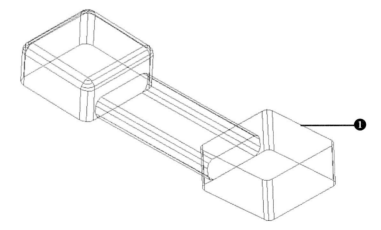

**Figure 28.18**   Preparing to chamfer the handle and transmitter portions.

In the following steps, you use the CHAMFER command to mold the top edges of the transmitter portion of the model.

13. From the Modify toolbar, choose Chamfer.

14. When prompted for the first line, pick ❶ in Figure 28.18. If necessary, type **N** and press Enter until the top surface of the transmitter portion is highlighted, then press Enter to OK the selection.

15. When prompted, specify a base surface distance of **0.10** and specify the other surface distance of **0.10**. At the next prompt, type **L** for the Loop option and pick ❶ shown in Figure 28.18 again to select an edge loop.

16. Press Enter to chamfer the top surface. Use the HIDE command to view your model now. A lot of tessellation lines display. Set the DISPSILH system variable to 1 and use Hide again. Your model should resemble Figure 28.19.

    You can now close this drawing without saving.

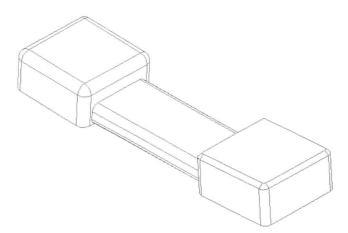

**Figure 28.19**    The finished model with filleted and chamfered edges and hidden lines removed.

As you can see from the exercise, adding a third dimension presents many more edges that can be filleted and chamfered. In this exercise you also took advantage of the Chain option of the FILLET command and the Loop option of the CHAMFER command. These options provide you with the ability to quickly fillet or chamfer any surface that has a continuous string of component edges that need to be chamfered or filleted.

# Controlling Solid Representations

As mentioned earlier, AutoCAD displays solid objects on-screen as boundary representations of the objects (see Figure 28.20). Solid objects are converted to surfaces only when you hide, shade, render, plot, or export the solid geometry.

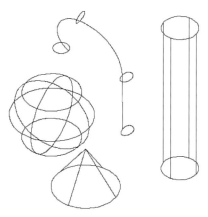

**Figure 28.20**    Solids are represented on-screen by lines and curves denoting boundaries.

The process of converting a boundary representation into a surface representation is called *tessellation*. Tessellation places a series of contiguous three- and four-sided tiles on the solid's boundaries, resulting in a surface mesh that can be shaded, rendered, and used in a hide operation. Figure 28.21 shows the same solids as in the previous figure with tessellated surfaces applied.

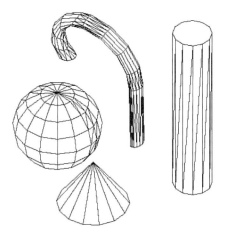

**Figure 28.21**    Low-resolution tessellation of solid objects.

The density of the surface mesh applied during tessellation is controlled by the system variable FACETRES (for facet resolution). The default value for FACETRES is 0.5, but can be set anywhere from 0.01 to 10. Higher values result in finer meshes generated from the solid objects, but higher resolution meshes also take much longer to hide, render, or export to other programs. Figure 28.21 has FACETRES set to a value of 0.5. Compare Figure 28.21 with Figure 28.22, in which FACETRES is set to a value of 2.0.

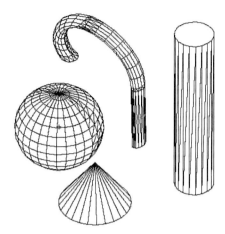

**Figure 28.22**    Increasing the value of FACETRES increases the resolution of the surface representation of solids.

## Hidden Line Conditions

Most traditional methods of representing solid models have lacked the completeness of showing *hidden* lines for items blocked by other objects (or themselves for that matter). So we would end up having to fill in these gaps with standard line work, being careful to match up to edges in the 3D model. However, AutoCAD 2004 introduced a new command called HLSETTINGS, which provides a good level of control over actually presenting these *hidden* lines as hidden lines instead of nothing. The Hidden Line Settings dialog is shown in Figure 28.23 and contains other controllers such as whether to hide text objects when you apply HIDE to your model.

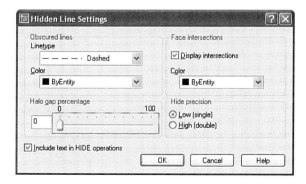

**Figure 28.23**    The Hidden Line Settings dialog provides easy access to adjust how your model appears when hidden or plotted.

The settings for the HLSETTINGS command that control hidden line appearance are stored in two system variables, OBSCUREDLTYPE and OBSCUREDCOLOR, and these variables are drawing-specific—they are stored in the drawing in which they are modified and do not apply to other drawing sessions. Figure 28.24 shows a simple solid model with example view conditions that are achievable.

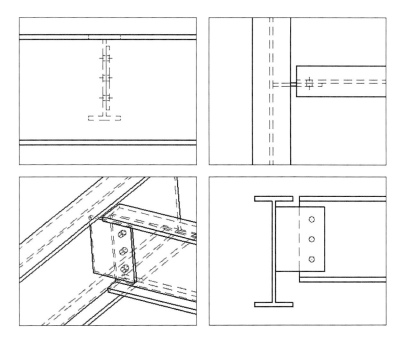

**Figure 28.24**    Various modes of viewing a single model with hidden viewports.

The last major component of the Hidden Line Settings dialog box is the Halo gap percentage. For some display needs, this can help the viewer visualize your model by creating gaps at the end of a line that ends at another physical object. Figure 28.25 shows an example of this effect; notice where the lines of the two objects cross.

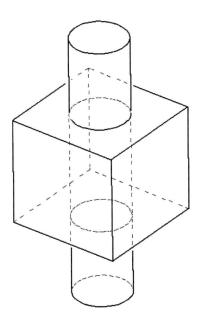

**Figure 28.25** A sample model implementing the Face Intersections and Halo gap features.

You can see the power of showing hidden lines—it greatly adds to the ability of the viewer to comprehend the model accurately. Although it can take some testing to get the right look, it can save you time in the long run and could be well worth it.

# Advanced Solid Modeling Commands

AutoCAD also provides three advanced solid modeling commands that can be useful:

- SLICE
- SECTION
- INTERFERE

The following sections define these advanced commands and take you through exercises designed to show how you can use each to help build your solid models.

# The *SLICE* Command

The SLICE command is used to divide solid objects on either side of a plane. If, for example, you create a complex model and want to cut it in half, the SLICE command will accomplish the task. There are five methods you can use to define the slicing, or cutting, plane:

- **3points.** Defines the slicing plane using three points. If the desired plane is not parallel with the current XY, YZ, or ZX plane, the 3points method is usually the best choice.

- **Object.** Aligns the cutting plane with a circle, ellipse, circular or elliptical arc, 2D spline, or 2D polyline. The object needs not be separated from the volume of the solid.

- **View.** Aligns the cutting plane with the current viewport's viewing plane. Specifying a point defines the location of the cutting plane along the Z-axis of the viewing plane.

- **Zaxis.** Defines the cutting plane by specifying a point on the plane and another point on the Z-axis (normal) of the plane.

- **XY, YZ, and ZX.** Aligns the cutting plane with the XY, YZ, or ZX plane of the current UCS. Specifying a point defines the location of the cutting plane.

Note that the 3points method defines the plane immediately; no further point is required. The other four methods first align the plane; you must supply an additional point to place the plane relative to the model.

After the slice has been carried out, AutoCAD prompts for a point on the desired side of the plane. You must specify a point to determine which side of the sliced solids your drawing retains. This point cannot lie on the cutting plane. You can also choose to keep both sides, which retains both sides of the sliced solids. Slicing a single solid into two pieces creates two solids from the pieces on either side of the plane.

Often, you can use more than one method to accomplish the same slice. The method you choose depends on the geometry available to you.

**I**NSIDER **T**IP

> The 3points method can be used even when a convenient third point is not available. Often, you can use a relative coordinate designation (such as @0,0,1) after specifying the second point to identify a point coplanar with the first two.

All you have to do to make SLICE work is create the solid model you want to slice and then determine a slicing plane. The following exercise illustrates this.

### Exercise 28.7    Using *SLICE* to Cut a Complex Model in Half

1. Load the file 28EX07.dwg. This is a model of a piston similar to the one you created earlier. Note that the line used to define the axis of revolution in forming the piston from its profile is also visible. The piston is sitting on a plane coincident with the XY plane (see Figure 28.26).

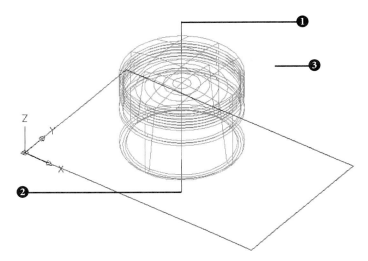

**Figure 28.26**    The 3D solid piston awaiting dissection.

2. Choose Slice from the Solids toolbar.

3. When prompted, select the piston and press Enter.

4. Type **ZX** and press Enter to indicate that you want to define the slicing plane parallel with the current ZX plane.

5. When prompted to specify a point on the ZX plane, snap to either endpoint of the line defining the axis of revolution (❶ or ❷ in Figure 28.26).

6. When prompted to specify a point on the desired side of the plane, pick a point near ❸. AutoCAD completes the slice.

7. Choose Hide from the View pull-down menu to see a result similar to the one shown in Figure 28.27.

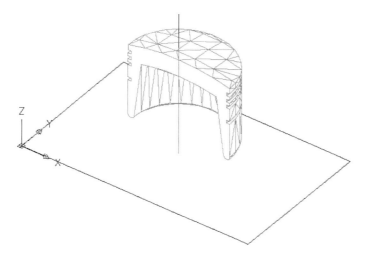

**Figure 28.27**   The hidden line display of the sliced piston.

**8.** Before closing this model, you might want to practice using other methods of specifying a slicing plane. Note that after a slice has been completed, you can use the Undo option of the SLICE command to restore the solid to its original state.

Close the drawing without saving.

**I**NSIDER **T**IP

> Keep in mind that when you are picking a side of the slicing plane to maintain, if you don't use an object snap, the point will automatically be picked in the XY plane, with Z set to the current elevation. When performing slices on complicated geometry, it's often easier to maintain both sides of the slice and then erase whichever side you want to delete.

**I**NSIDER **T**IP

> Often, the SLICE command can be used to build 2D line work that otherwise would require substantial geometry to create. For example, consider slicing a cone solid at an odd angle and then exploding it and erasing the sides and bottom. You are then left with a region object, which can be exploded down to an ellipse object, which you can then EXTRUDE along. It would take a long time to develop that ellipse size/location information without the SLICE command.

This exercise gave you practice in visualizing and specifying "invisible" slicing planes. With practice, you will be able to slice solids quickly and precisely.

## The *SECTION* Command

The SECTION command works almost exactly the same as the SLICE command, with only one major difference. Instead of slicing the object, the SECTION command generates a region that is representative of a cross-section of the selected ACIS solid object on the chosen plane. Suppose you model this great 3D part and want to draw a section of it for manufacturing purposes. The SECTION command can automatically generate most of the 2D drawing from your 3D model with very little effort.

The following exercise shows how to create a section of a solid object.

### Exercise 28.8   Creating a Section of a Solid Object

1. Load the file 28EX08.dwg. This is a completed telephone handset similar to the one you built earlier in this chapter. The model should resemble Figure 28.28.

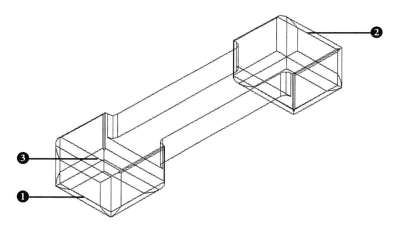

**Figure 28.28**   The three points of the section plane.

2. Select Section from the Solids toolbar.

3. Select the handset and press Enter. Press Enter again to define the section plane by three points.

4. When prompted for the first point, choose midpoint object snap and select the middle point of the end of the receiver at ❶ in Figure 28.28.

5. Select the next two points by using midpoint object snap, as shown at ❷ and ❸. AutoCAD then creates a region object that contains areas from the plane through the solid.

6. Now choose Move from the Modify toolbar.

**7.** When prompted to select objects, type **L** for last and press Enter.

**8.** Move the region object arbitrarily so it is outside of the solid. Figure 28.29 shows the solid object and resulting region.

You may now close this drawing without saving.

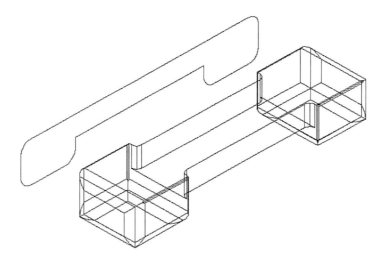

**Figure 28.29**   After creating a section of the model, use MOVE to relocate the newly created region.

As this exercise showed, the way the SLICE and SECTION commands are used is very similar. The difference between the two is revealed in their results. The SLICE command enables you to cut a model into pieces, whereas the SECTION command's result is a region. This region can be converted to a series of lines by exploding it if you need to further edit the section. You can also use it to develop new solids by extruding it. You could even hatch this region for further use.

## The *INTERFERE* Command

The last advanced command that is addressed here is the INTERFERE command, which is used to determine whether two solids overlap, or interfere, with each other. If they do, you can generate a new solid that is the volume of the area where the two solids interfere. This enables you to quickly calculate how much volume is interfering between the two solids. The INTERFERE command uses a Boolean intersect operation to generate any interference information.

# Editing Solids

Just as with all other AutoCAD objects, after you create solid objects, you might want to edit them. AutoCAD 2005 has a solid editing facility that enables you to easily edit or modify the size and geometry of AutoCAD solids. Through the SOLIDEDIT command, you can move, rotate, taper, resize, or even remove features of a solid. Blends created with the FILLET command, for example, can be removed.

Through SOLIDEDIT, you can also copy a face or edge of a solid as a body object or region object in the case of faces, or as a line, arc, circle, ellipse, or splice object in the case of edges (see Figure 28.30). You cannot, however, copy a feature, such as copying a hole in a solid to make a second hole. This is technically not a valid edit operation.

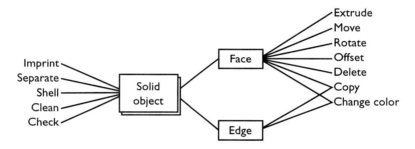

**Figure 28.30**    An overview of the SOLIDEDIT operations.

## *SOLIDEDIT* Operations

The following operations are performed by the SOLIDEDIT command. Two solid editing operations, Color and Copy, are common to both faces and edges. The Imprint, Shell, Separate, and Clean operations are performed on entire 3D solid bodies.

- **Extrude.** Extrudes selected planar faces of a 3D solid object to a specified height or along a path. You can select multiple faces at one time.

- **Move.** Moves selected faces on a 3D solid object to a specified height or distance. You can select multiple faces at one time.

- **Rotate.** Rotates one or more faces or a collection of features on a solid about a specified axis.

- **Offset.** Offsets faces equally by a specified distance or through a specified point. A positive value increases the size of the solid; a negative value decreases the size or volume of the solid.

- **Taper.** Tapers faces with an angle. The rotation of the taper angle is determined by the selection sequence of the base point and the second point along the selected vector.

- **Delete.** Deletes or removes faces, including fillets and chamfers.

- **Copy.** With faces: Copies faces as a region or a body. If you specify two points, AutoCAD uses the first point as a base point and places a single copy relative to the base point. If you specify a single point and then press Enter, AutoCAD uses the coordinate as the new location. With edges: Copies 3D edges. Every 3D solid edge is copied as a line, arc, ellipse, or spline.

- **Color.** With faces: Changes the color of faces. With edges: Changes the color of edges.

- **Imprint.** Imprints an object on the selected solid. The object to be imprinted must intersect one or more faces on the selected solid for imprinting to be successful. Imprinting is limited to the following objects: arcs, circles, lines, 2D and 3D polylines, ellipses, splines, regions, bodies, and 3D solids.

- **Separate.** Separates 3D solid objects with disjointed volumes into independent 3D solid objects.

- **Shell.** Creates a hollow, thin wall with a specified thickness. You can specify a constant wall thickness for all the faces. You can also exclude faces from the shell by selecting them. A 3D solid can have only one shell. AutoCAD creates new faces by offsetting existing ones outside their original positions. Specifying a positive value creates a shell from the outside of the perimeter; specifying a negative value creates a shell from the inside.

- **Clean.** Removes shared edges or vertices having the same surface or curve definition on either side of the edge or vertex. Removes all redundant edges and vertices, imprinted as well as unused geometry.

- **Check.** Validates the 3D solid object as a valid solid, independent of the SOLID-CHECK system variable setting.

### Picking Edges and Faces with SOLIDEDIT

SOLIDEDIT is the only AutoCAD command that requests that you select faces on 3D solid objects to perform some of its operations. Selecting individual faces while in the SOLIDEDIT command, however, can be tricky. If you pick an edge at a Select faces prompt, the two faces that share the picked edge are highlighted, and you must remove the unwanted face from the selection set.

To alleviate this inconvenience, an additional method of selecting, called boundary sets, is automatically available during SOLIDEDIT operations involving faces. With boundary set selection, you can pick on a face inside the edges that define the face. Whereas elsewhere in AutoCAD picking on "empty space" at best establishes one corner of a selection window (if the system variable PICKAUTO is set to its default value of 1), in editing operations involving 3D solid faces, you can successfully pick within the boundary of a face.

In the following exercises, the boundary set pick method is demonstrated as some of the options of the SOLIDEDIT command are examined.

**I**NSIDER  **N**OTE

> Even with the convenience of the boundary set selection method, if there is any ambiguity due to the view, picking on the two faces selects the "closest" one visually. Picking again selects the second, more "distant" face. You must then remove the "top" face from the boundary selection set.

In the following exercise, you explore some of the capabilities of the SOLIDEDIT command. This command enables you to perform common editing operations on AutoCAD solids that were not possible in previous releases of AutoCAD. You begin by moving the "front" face of a solid inward 20 units by performing a negative extrusion.

### Exercise 28.9   Using Boundary Selection to Edit 3D Faces

1. Open the drawing 28EX09.dwg. Your screen should resemble Figure 28.31.

2. From the Modify pull-down menu, choose Solids Editing and then Extrude Faces. When prompted to select faces, select the front face. Use a single pick boundary selection by picking at ❶ in Figure 28.31. Notice that using a boundary selection enables you to select the face by picking inside the face boundary.

3. Press Enter to close the selection set. At the prompt to specify the height of the extrusion, type **-20**. When prompted to specify the angle of the taper for extrusion, press Enter to accept the default value of 0. The front face is then extruded in a negative direction by 20 units with a zero taper angle. Press Enter twice to exit the SOLIDEDIT command.

   Next, you extrude the top of the block and all the countersink holes upward by 20 units. Because "auto-windowing" is disabled during solid face editing to allow boundary set selection, you must manually start a crossing window.

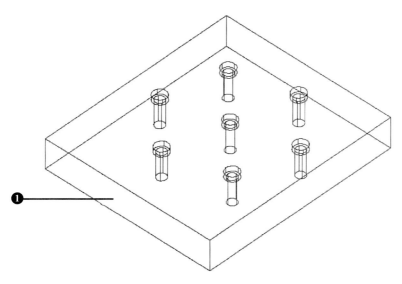

**Figure 28.31**   Using boundary sets to select faces.

4. From the Modify pull-down menu, choose Solids Editing, Extrude Faces. When prompted to select faces, start a crossing window by typing **C** and pressing Enter. Specify a crossing window that includes all faces and all countersink holes (see Figure 28.32).

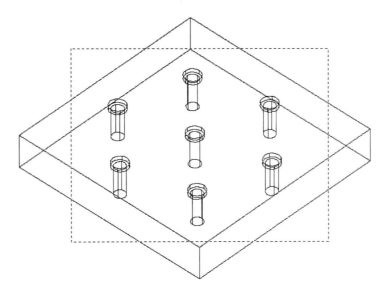

**Figure 28.32**   Choosing faces with a crossing window.

This step selects all 27 faces of the model. Because you want to extrude only the seven countersink holes and the top face, in the next step you remove the side and bottom faces.

5. While still being prompted to select faces, choose the Remove option by typing **R** and pressing Enter. When prompted to remove faces, pick the edges at ❶, ❷, ❸, and ❹ (see Figure 28.33). Press Enter to end face selection. Notice that the first edge that you select removes two faces: the side face and the bottom face.

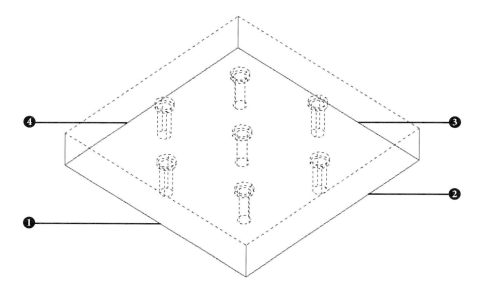

**Figure 28.33**   Removing faces by selecting common edges.

6. When prompted to specify the height of extrusion, type **20**, then press Enter to accept the default zero angle for the taper of extrusion. The top face and the seven countersink holes are extruded by 20 units. Press Enter twice to exit the SOLIDEDIT command.

   In the next steps, you rotate the array of countersink holes to align them better with the sides of the block.

7. Using the VIEW command, restore the view Rotate. From the Modify menu, choose Solids Editing, then Rotate Faces. When prompted to select faces, initiate a crossing window by typing **C** and pressing Enter. Specify a window enclosing all the countersink holes.

   In the next step, you take advantage of boundary set selection to remove faces from the current set.

8. While still being prompted to select faces, choose the Remove option. When prompted to remove faces, pick on the sides, top, and bottom faces by picking at ❶, ❷, ❸, ❹, ❺, and ❻ in Figure 28.34. Note that selecting at ❶ chooses the top face because it is "closest" in this view; picking at ❷ then removes the bottom face. Press Enter to end selection.

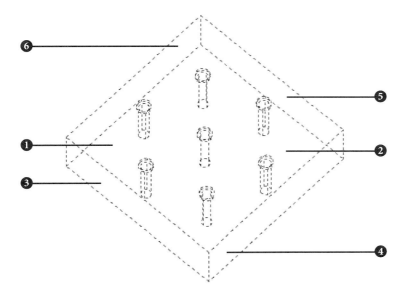

**Figure 28.34**   Using boundary set selection to remove faces.

In the next step, you specify the axis of rotation by picking the center of the array and then specifying a vector.

9. Respond to the prompt to specify an axis point by choosing a Center osnap and then picking at the bottom of the center of the central hole. Specify the second point on the rotation axis by typing the relative coordinate @0,0,1 and pressing Enter. Specify a rotation angle by typing -15 and pressing Enter. The array of holes rotates 15 degrees clockwise.

In the next steps, you use the Offset option of SOLIDEDIT to edit the diameter of the central countersink hole.

10. Choose Offset from the Face Edit choices by typing O. Select faces by typing C, pressing Enter, and then specifying a crossing window enclosing only the center countersink hole. Remove the top and bottom faces of the box as you did in step 8 and press Enter to end selection.

**11.** Specify the offset distance by typing **-1.5** and pressing Enter. Notice that supplying a negative offset distance decreases the volume of the solid by increasing the diameter of the countersink hole. End the command by pressing Enter twice. The model should now resemble Figure 28.35.

You may now close the drawing without saving.

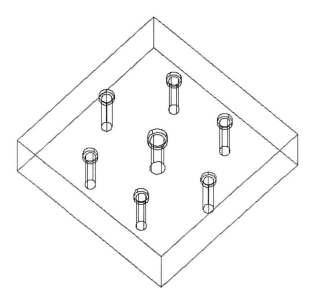

**Figure 28.35**    The completed model after editing.

### Distinguishing Between SOLIDEDIT *Extrude and Offset*

Although similar in their effects, the Offset and Extrude options of the SOLIDEDIT command can yield different results. In Figure 28.36, the faces highlighted on the center solid are extruded and offset by the same amount in the left and right solids. The solid on the left underwent an extrusion; the solid on the right was offset.

In the following exercise, you investigate the Move, Delete, and Taper options of the SOLIDEDIT command.

### Exercise 28.10    Using the Move, Delete, and Taper Options of *SOLIDEDIT*

**1.** Open 28EX10.dwg from the accompanying CD. The drawing should resemble Figure 28.37.

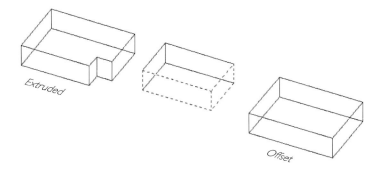

**Figure 28.36**   The Extruded and Offset options yield different results.

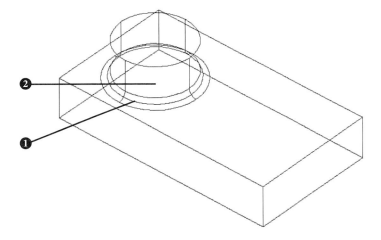

**Figure 28.37**   Using the Move and Delete options of SOLIDEDIT.

2. To move the filleted structure on top of the block, from the Modify menu, choose Solids Editing, Move Faces. Pick the filleted face at ❶ and the cylinder at ❷ in Figure 28.37. Press Enter to end selection. Specify a displacement by typing **25,10** and press Enter twice.

3. Specify the Delete option by typing **D**. Select the filleted face again and press Enter to end selection and remove the face.

4. To taper the cylinder, choose the Taper option. Pick the cylinder face using a boundary set selection method and press Enter.

5. Use a Center osnap and pick the lower or upper center of the cylinder. Specify another point along the axis of tapering by typing **@0,0,1**. When prompted for the taper angle, type **6**. Your drawing should now resemble Figure 28.38.

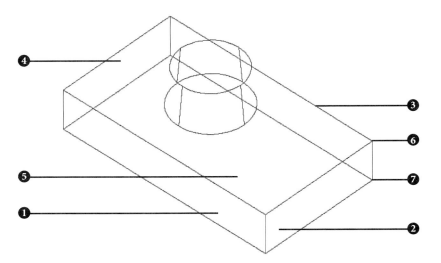

**Figure 28.38** Using the Taper option of SOLIDEDIT.

In the next steps, you taper the four side faces in the drawing.

6. Choose the Taper option again. Referring to Figure 28.38, pick the four side faces of the model by picking at ❶ and ❷ and at ❸ to select the top and back face; then pick at ❹. To remove the top and bottom faces, choose the Remove option and pick at ❺ twice. Press Enter to end face selection.

**INSIDER TIP**

You can also remove selected faces by pressing the Shift key and picking on the selected face or edge.

7. Specify the taper base point by using an endpoint osnap and picking at ❻. Specify another point along the taper axis by using an endpoint osnap and picking at ❼.

8. Specify the taper angle by typing **-12**. This completes your work on this layer. Your drawing should now resemble Figure 28.39.

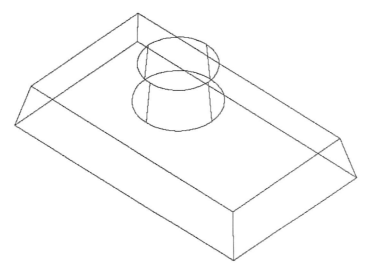

**Figure 28.39**    Finished model with faces moved, deleted, and tapered.

Note that the rotation of the taper angle is determined by the selection sequence of the base point and the second point along the taper axis. Tapering the selected face with a positive angle tapers the face in, and tapering the face with a negative angle tapers the face out. If the pick sequence of ❻ and ❼ in step 7 had been reversed, for example, the specified tapering angle of -12 degrees would have resulted in an "inward" taper.

You may now close this drawing without saving.


## Understanding the Imprint and Shell Options

The Imprint and Shell options of SOLIDEDIT provide ways to alter a solid object. You can, for example, create new faces or solids by imprinting arcs, lines, circles, and so on onto existing faces. After imprinting, you can use the imprinted face as the basis for extrusions. With the Shell option, you can "hollow out" a solid, forming a thin wall of a specified thickness.

In the following exercise, you use the Imprint and Shell options of the SOLIDEDIT command to further develop an object.

**Exercise 28.11    Using the Imprint and Shell Options of *SOLIDEDIT***

1. Open file 28EX11.dwg from the accompanying CD. Your drawing should resemble Figure 28.40.

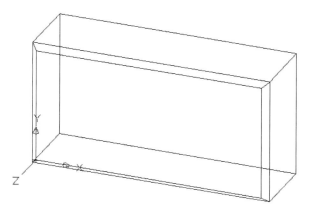

**Figure 28.40**    Preparing to add imprinted profiles.

Notice the UCS icon is turned on its side; this aids in creating an object on the box face. The creation of User Coordinate Systems (UCSs) is discussed in detail in Chapter 25, "Introduction to 3D."

In the next steps, you draw a rectangle on the face of the box.

2. Choose Rectang from the Draw pull-down menu. Type **F** to choose the Fillet option and specify a fillet radius of **5** units. When prompted for the first corner of the rectangle, type **8,40**. Enter a coordinate of **46,10** for the opposite corner.

3. To imprint the rectangle on the face, using the Modify pull-down menu, choose Solids Editing, Imprint. Pick anywhere on the solid. When prompted to select an object to imprint, select the rectangle. Then press Enter to retain the source object. Press Enter again to end the Select objects prompt. Your drawing should resemble Figure 28.41. You witnessed no difference when imprinting; however, it will soon be evident what you have done.

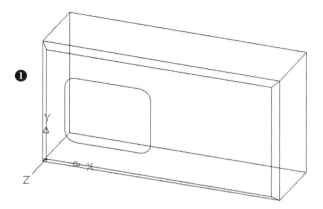

**Figure 28.41**   Imprinted figure on a solid face.

After objects are imprinted on a solid, they can form the basis for both positive and negative embossments.

4. Press Enter to display the parent SOLIDEDIT command-line prompts. Choose the Face option by typing **F**, then choose the Extrude option.

5. Select the rectangular imprint by picking at ❶ within the boundary of the rectangle and pressing Enter (refer to Figure 28.41). Press Enter again to end face selection. Specify a height of extrusion of **2.5** and press Enter to accept the default of 0 degree extrusion angle. Press Enter twice to end the SOLIDEDIT command. Your drawing should resemble Figure 28.42.

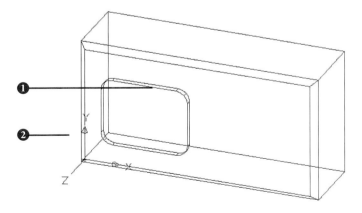

**Figure 28.42**   An embossed surface after extruding an imprint.

In the following steps, you use the Shell option to "hollow out" the solid.

6. From the Modify pull-down menu, choose Solids Editing, Shell. Because you do not want to remove any faces, pick anywhere on the solid and press Enter.

7. Enter a shell offset distance of **2** and then press Enter. Press Enter twice more to end the SOLIDEDIT command.

   In the next steps, you use the SLICE command to examine the effects of the previous shell operation.

8. Type **UCS** and press Enter twice to change the UCS to World. From the Solids toolbar, choose Slice, and then pick anywhere on the solid and press Enter.

9. Use the right-click shortcut menu, select YZ, and then use a midpoint object snap and pick on the imprint top edge at ❶ in Figure 28.42. When prompted to specify a point on the desired side of the slicing plane, pick near ❷.

10. Use the HIDE command to remove hidden lines from the view. Your drawing should now resemble Figure 28.43. Note that the original rectangle used to generate the imprint remains.

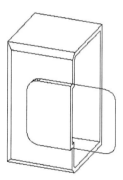

**Figure 28.43**    The result of using the Shell option and Hide.

You can now close this drawing without saving.

# Summary

Solid modeling is a powerful method of creating complex models by combining and editing solid primitives and extruded 2D shapes. To make these models, you can use the Boolean operation commands of UNION, SUBTRACT, INTERFERE, and INTERSECT as well as the EXTRUDE, SLICE, REVOLVE, and SECTION solids commands. The SOLIDEDIT command enables you to copy and modify solid edges and faces after they are created. You can also imprint shapes onto solid objects and create shells from parent solids. Chapter 29, "Rendering in 3D," takes 3D modeling a step further and adds rendering to the visual model "package."

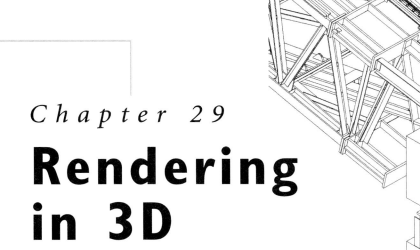

# Chapter 29
# Rendering in 3D

Up to this point, you have explored several different methods of modeling in three dimensions in AutoCAD. To produce a "picture" of the model, you will probably want to render it. *Rendering* is a process in which you attach materials to the surfaces of your 3D objects, create lights to illuminate the objects, establish a viewpoint from which to view the model, and then transform the scene into a realistic rendering, or picture.

The line of demarcation between shading and rendering is somewhat arbitrary. The shading modes available with the SHADEMODE command (discussed in Chapter 25, "Introduction to 3D") could be considered simple rendering because the surfaces of a model are depicted as they appear with a single light source. AutoCAD's RENDER command, however, takes up where simple shading leaves off, providing the capability to apply materials to surfaces, to supply various types of lighting, and to cast realistic shadows.

This process is generally straightforward, but it can require a bit of trial and error as well as an understanding of artistic and photographic principles to produce good results. This chapter focuses on the basics of rendering and the rendering tools, including how to set up and create simple renderings inside AutoCAD. In particular, this chapter addresses the following topics:

- Types of rendering supported by AutoCAD
- Creating a view
- Creating and assigning materials
- Creating lights
- Rendering the model
- Generating output

# Types of Rendering

AutoCAD 2005 incorporates a full-featured rendering engine that is capable of producing rendering ranging from simple shaded models to full photorealistic renderings. Generally, three types or levels of rendering are offered by the rendering facility inside AutoCAD:

- Render
- Photo Real
- Photo Raytrace

These three different types of rendering produce increasingly more realistic outputs, of which Photo Raytrace is the most realistic. You pay a price for realism, however: Increased realism requires increased rendering times.

The three levels of rendering offered with the RENDER command are summarized here:

- **Render.** Basic Render is the next logical step beyond the Gouraud shading mode offered by the SHADEMODE and 3DORBIT commands. Render mode has the added advantage of enabling you to assign materials to surfaces. You can assign materials such as brick, chrome, and wood to objects in the model on a per-layer, per-color, or per-object basis. In addition, you can add any of three types of light sources to the scene. In the basic Render mode, however, light sources are not capable of casting shadows. Other enhancements, such as backgrounds and plants, are also supported. Figure 29.1 shows a typical rendering using the Render mode.

**Figure 29.1**   Typical rendering using the Render mode of the RENDER command. Note the absence of shadows.

- **Photo Real.** The Photo Real mode shares all the features of Render mode, but it adds the capability to cast shadows and to use bitmaps for materials (see Figure 29.2).

- **Photo Raytrace.** Photo Raytrace provides the most realistic renderings. It adds the capability to generate reflections, refraction effects, and true detailed shadows. Figure 29.3 shows a rendering using the Photo Raytrace mode.

**Figure 29.2**  Typical rendering using the Photo Real mode of the RENDER command. Shadows and materials are present.

**Figure 29.3**  Typical rendering using the Photo Raytrace mode of the RENDER command. Note the presence of shadows and reflections.

# The Rendering Process

Rendering takes place after you have constructed a 3D model. The preceding chapters gave you the knowledge you need to build models you want to render. Now it is time to look at how to set up your scenes for rendering. In general, you can follow this simple process to render your scenes:

1. Create a view of the scene. Most of the views in AutoCAD are orthogonal, such as an SW isometric view. For true realism, you must create a perspective view by using DVIEW.

2. Create and assign the materials in the scene. A material is a set of surface attributes that describe how that surface looks at render time. You must define these attributes and assign them to the appropriate surfaces.

3. Create lights for the scene. Without lights, you do not have any illumination or shadows in the scene. Correct placement of lights adds to the realism.

4. Create test renderings of your scene. Here, you make sure the materials, lights, and geometry are correct. Most of the time, you will create your test renders with the Photo Real method. You might end up creating dozens of test renders before achieving the look you want.

5. Set up the final Photo Raytrace rendering and save the rendering to a bitmap file for printing or use outside of AutoCAD.

Now let's take a closer look at each step.

# Creating a View

Establishing a compelling view of the model is one of the most important steps toward creating an effective rendering. No matter how much effort and time you devote to selecting and applying materials and establishing realistic lighting, a rendering of the model from an uninteresting point of view will detract from your efforts. Put another way, an interesting or even dramatic view of the model can make the difference between an average-looking rendering and a memorable one.

During the construction of the model, you can effectively use the 3DORBIT command to view and study the various parts of the model. 3DORBIT's capability to dynamically change the viewpoint in real time is useful because it gives you a sense of the model's spatial relationships. For the final rendering, however, you generally will want more control of the viewpoint. Such flexibility and control are offered by the DVIEW command. Like

3DORBIT, DVIEW enables you to view the model from a perspective projection, which is almost always preferable because it is the way we view objects in the real world. In addition, DVIEW enables you to easily set and fine-tune such factors as the camera-to-subject distance and the field of view.

To use the DVIEW command to establish a perspective view of your model, you must know two things:

- **Camera point.** The location in the model from which you want to be looking.

- **Target point.** The location in the model that you want to look at.

As soon as you establish these points, you can adjust the perspective until you are happy with it. If you have any experience with 35mm photography, many of the concepts, such as focal length, that are used to adjust viewing angle of the camera will be familiar to you.

**I**NSIDER **N**OTE

> AutoCAD's CAMERA command prompts you for a camera point and a target point. These points only establish a vector along which the camera and target lie; you have little control over the exact placement of the actual camera position. You cannot adjust the focal length or the camera-to-target distance directly from within the CAMERA command. The DVIEW command gives you more control.

After you set up the view by using the DVIEW command, you use the VIEW command to save the view so that you do not have to re-create it later, as shown in the following exercise.

### Exercise 29.1    Setting Up a View with *DVIEW*

1. Load the file 29EX01.dwg from the accompanying CD. The file contains a model of a 12-story office building, as shown in Figure 29.4, with SHADEMODE on for Gouraud shading with edges. For reference, the floor is at elevation 0, and the roof of this building has an elevation of approximately 154 feet above ground. Turn off object snap modes if they are not off already.

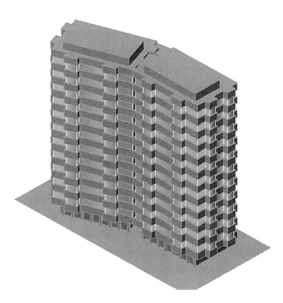

**Figure 29.4**    A model of a 12-story office building shown in an isometric, Gouraud + Edges shaded view.

2. From the View pull-down menu, select Shade, then 2D Wireframe. Select the View pull-down menu again and choose Named Views. In the View dialog box, right-click on view Top and choose Set Current from the shortcut menu. Click OK to exit the dialog box. The model should now resemble Figure 29.5.

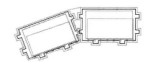

In the next three steps, you draw the "sight line," which establishes the viewpoint for the rendering. You place a line from the intended camera point to the target point. Zoom out a bit from the building to get some room, as shown in Figure 29.6.

**Figure 29.5**
A model of a 12-story office building shown in plan view.

3. From the Draw pull-down menu, choose Line. When you're prompted to specify the start point, type **.XY** and press Enter to indicate that you will specify the X and Y coordinates on-screen. Pick a point near ❶ in Figure 29.6. (This point should be near 163', –174'.)

4. When prompted for the Z value, type **8'5"**. This establishes the camera position for the view.

5. When prompted for the next point, again type **.XY** and pick a point near ❷. (This should be near 24', 33'.) When prompted for the Z value, type **83'**. Then press Enter to end the LINE command. The completed line-of-sight should

resemble that in Figure 29.6. This line starts 8'5" off the ground and aims at a point a little more than halfway up the building. Perform a ZOOM Extents to get all of it on-screen.

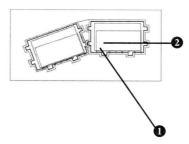

**Figure 29.6** The first step in establishing a view is drawing the line-of-sight from camera to target.

In the next steps, you use the Points options of the DVIEW command to establish a view along the line-of-sight.

6. To start the DVIEW command, at the command line, type **DVIEW** and press Enter. When you're prompted to select objects, pick only the line-of-sight line and press Enter. Note that all the model's objects except the line you drew in steps 3–5 temporarily disappear.

7. Type **PO** and press Enter to select the Points option of the DVIEW command.

8. When you're prompted for the target point, use an Endpoint osnap and pick at ❷ in Figure 29.6 to specify the target end of the line. When you're prompted for the camera point, again use an Endpoint osnap to pick at ❶. Although all the model's objects seem to have disappeared, DVIEW has established a view looking down the line of sight from camera to target point.

9. Type **D** and press Enter to choose the Distance option of the DVIEW command. Type **300'** to increase the default distance—the distance of the line-of-sight.

**10.** At the next prompt, type **Z** and press Enter to select the Zoom option. Specify a lens length of **33** mm and press Enter. Then press Enter again to end the DVIEW command. The resulting view of the model should resemble Figure 29.7.

**Figure 29.7**   The view resulting from looking "down" the line of sight.

**11.** To generate a nicer view of the building, open the View pull-down menu and choose Hide. Figure 29.8 shows a hidden line view.

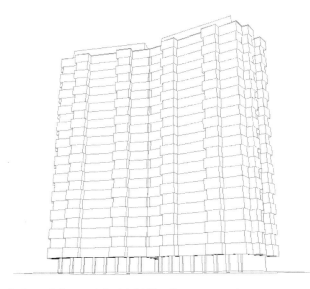

**Figure 29.8**   A view of the model with hidden lines removed.

**12.** Use the VIEW command to save this view under the name Camera1.

**13.** Save this drawing as 29EX02.dwg on your hard drive. You will use it in a later exercise.

The advantage to using the line-of-sight method with the DVIEW command is that you have complete control of the resulting viewpoint. Fine-tuning of distance, field of view, and target point and direction make establishing the exact view that you have in mind a straightforward matter of adjusting the line-of-sight line and then using the DVIEW command and the method in the preceding exercise to generate the view.

As discussed in Chapter 25, the 3DORBIT command can often be used to generate views of models. This is similar to the effect that can be created by DVIEW. However, DVIEW has a finer set of controls for determining your view and lens values.

**I**NSIDER  **C**AUTION

> If you're setting up a view using the line-of-sight method, be careful when adjusting the camera-target distance. If the objects represent a ground plane, increasing the distance using the Distance option of the DVIEW command may place the camera point below this plane. This will result in a rendering in which all the model's geometry is hidden.

# Creating and Assigning Materials

After you establish a view of the model, you can begin assigning materials to the model's surfaces. A *material* is a set of graphic attributes assigned to a surface. These attributes include such qualities as color, smoothness, reflectivity, texture, and transparency. When the model is rendered, the rendering engine takes into account those attributes accordingly.

Materials are handled through the Materials and Materials Library dialog boxes. The Materials dialog box is used to assign, create, or modify materials and their associated set of attributes. The Materials Library is used to store a group of predefined materials or materials you create.

You use the Materials Library to choose materials you want to import into your model for assignment to surfaces or for use as the basis for creating a modified or new material. You access the Materials Library by choosing Materials Library from the Render toolbar, or by selecting View, Render, Materials Library, or by typing MATLIB at the command prompt. Figure 29.9 shows the Materials Library dialog box.

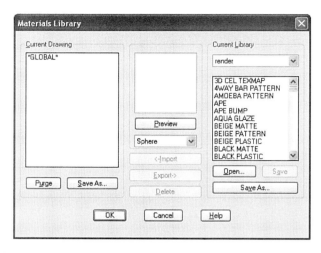

**Figure 29.9** The Materials Library dialog box.

The Materials Library dialog box is divided into three main sections:

- **Current Drawing.** This lists all the materials currently loaded for use or that are assigned in the current drawing.
  - **Purge.** Deletes all unassigned materials from the Current Drawing list.
  - **Save As.** Enables you to save the current drawing list to a material library (MLI) file.
- **Preview window.** This is a small window that gives you a preview of what a material would look like if you applied it to a sphere or cube object.
  - **<-Import.** Adds materials selected in the Current Library list to the Current Drawing list.
  - **Export->.** Adds materials selected in the Current Drawing list to the Current Library list.
  - **Delete.** Deletes materials selected in the Current Drawing list or the Current Library list.
- **Current Library.** A list of materials contained in the current library. All material libraries for AutoCAD have an MLI extension. By default, AutoCAD ships with one large library file—the RENDER.mli file. It also ships with one small one where you can place your favorites, MINI.mli.
  - **Open.** Displays a standard file selection dialog box listing MLI files.
  - **Save.** Saves the changes to the current MLI file in the current folder.

- **Save As.** Displays a standard file selection dialog box where you can specify the name of the materials library (MLI) file in which AutoCAD saves the Current Library list.

**INSIDER TIP**

The small preview window in the Materials Library is a 256-color display. This means the final rendering will invariably look better than this simple preview window. Keep this in mind when selecting materials. If you are not sure how a material will look, use the AutoCAD Multiple Drawing Environment to create a new drawing with a simple object in it. Use this second drawing to test how a material will appear in the larger model.

You use the Materials dialog box (shown in Figure 29.10) to manage the materials selected for use in your model. You access the Materials dialog box by choosing Materials from the Render toolbar, or by selecting View, Render, Materials, or by typing **RMAT** at the command prompt.

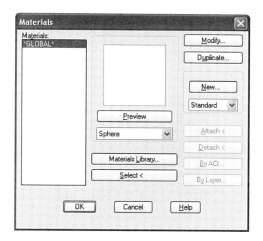

**Figure 29.10**   The Materials dialog box.

The Materials dialog box contains the following sections and buttons:

- **Materials.** Lists the available materials. The default for objects with no other material attached is GLOBAL.
- **Preview.** Displays a selected material on either a sphere or a cube.
- **Materials Library.** Displays the Materials Library dialog box, from which you can select a material.

- **Select <.** Closes the dialog box temporarily so you can select an object with the pointing device and display the attached material. After you select the object, the Materials dialog box is redisplayed with the method of attachment specified at the bottom of the dialog box.

- **Modify.** Displays one of four dialog boxes, depending on which material type is selected in the list under the New button: Standard, Marble, Granite, or Wood. Use the dialog box to edit an existing material.

- **Duplicate.** Duplicates a material and displays one of four dialog boxes, depending on which material type is selected in the list under the New button: Standard, Marble, Granite, or Wood. Use the dialog box to name the new material and define attributes.

- **New.** Displays one of four dialog boxes, depending on which material type is selected in the list under the New button.

- **Attach <.** Closes the dialog box temporarily so you can select an object and attach the current material to it.

- **Detach <.** Closes the dialog box temporarily so you can select an object and detach the material from it.

- **By ACI.** Displays the Attach by AutoCAD Color Index dialog box, from which you can select an ACI to attach a material to.

- **By Layer.** Displays the Attach by Layer dialog box, in which you can select a layer to attach a material to.

The following exercise shows you how to load a few materials from the Materials Library and assign them to objects in a scene.

### Exercise 29.2    Assigning Materials from the Materials Library to a Model

1. Load the file 29EX02.dwg, which you worked on in the last exercise. If you did not complete the last exercise, you can load the file from the accompanying CD.

2. Display the Render toolbar if needed and choose Materials. AutoCAD displays the Materials dialog box shown in Figure 29.10.

3. Click the Materials Library button to launch the Materials Library dialog box (refer to Figure 29.9).

4. If Render is not the active library, use the drop-list and choose it. Then select the material named Blue Glass.

5. Click the Import button. This places Blue Glass material on the list of materials available for use in the current drawing.

6. Repeat steps 4 and 5 for the Dark Brown Matte material.

7. Click OK. The materials you just imported now appear in the Materials list. The Materials dialog box should now look like Figure 29.11.

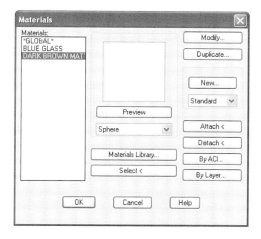

**Figure 29.11**   The Materials dialog box after you've selected materials for use in the model.

8. Select the Blue Glass material in the list.

9. Select By Layer and in the Attach by Layer dialog box, select the glass layer from the Select Layer list. Click Attach to attach Blue Glass material to objects on the glass layer.

10. Repeat steps 8 and 9 to attach Dark Brown Matte material to the concrete layer. The Attach by Layer dialog box should resemble Figure 29.12. Click OK to exit the Attach by Layer dialog box. Click OK again to exit the Materials dialog box.

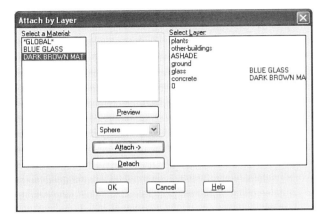

**Figure 29.12**    The Attach by Layer dialog box shows current layer/material attachments.

11. Choose Render from the Render toolbar to display the Render dialog box. Under Rendering Type, select Photo Raytrace. Under Rendering Options, make sure the Smooth Shade, Apply Materials, and Shadows options are all selected. The settings for this rendering are shown in Figure 29.13.

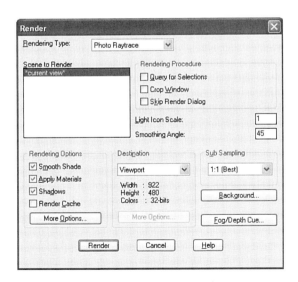

**Figure 29.13**    The Render dialog box settings.

12. Click Render, and the scene is rendered, as shown in Figure 29.14. Depending on your equipment, the rendering process may take a few seconds.

13. Save the file locally as 29EX03.dwg for use later.

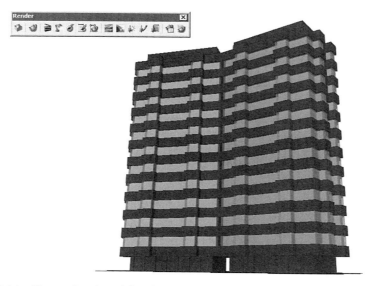

**Figure 29.14**   The rendered model with materials applied.

This exercise shows that even with simple "off-the-shelf" materials and no lighting effects, effective renderings are possible. The key to such renderings is the viewpoint. In this example, a perspective viewpoint from near the ground looking upward at the building yields a lifelike view—one you might see if you were standing in front of the building.

In this exercise, you assigned materials on a "by-layer" basis. You can also assign materials on a "by-color" or "by-object" basis. The advantage to assigning materials by-layer is a more orderly material assignment process. Just as using layers in 2D drafting helps you organize a drawing, placing objects in your model on layers that share a rendered material makes assigning materials much more orderly and easy. Because the "by-layer" method offers a distinct advantage, you should adopt a layer-conscious scheme as you construct a model.

## Basic Materials Versus Mapped Materials

Materials can be roughly divided into two categories: basic materials and mapped materials. Mapped materials make use of a bitmap, or image, to represent the color or some other attribute of a material. A brick material, for example, may have a bitmap of the brick pattern superimposed along with the other material attributes. Basic materials achieve their appearance without the use of bitmaps. Defining mapped materials can require more effort, but mapped materials can yield more realistic results with materials that exhibit prominent textures or patterns.

### *Basic Materials*

Generally, basic materials have no prominent surface textures or significant surface patterns. Examples of such materials include metals, paints, plastics, and glass.

Clicking the Modify button on the Materials dialog opens the Modify Standard Material dialog box shown in Figure 29.15. Here, you see the attributes you can modify. Each is briefly described in the following list:

- **Color/Pattern.** This is the general color of the material. It is defined in either the RGB (Red, Green, Blue) color system or the HLS (Hue, Lightness, Saturation) color system. The color can also be derived from the ACI Color value of the object to which it is assigned. The Value slider is used to control the overall intensity of the color.

- **Ambient.** This is the color of the material when it has a shadow cast onto it. Generally speaking, this is simply a darker version of the color/pattern color.

- **Reflection.** This attribute determines the amount of reflection the material has. The Value slider determines the strength of that reflection. In general, most reflections are subtle and have a value of .20 or less. The Lock check box can be used to lock all the colors together, and the Mirror check box can be used to turn the material into a mirror, based on the color. For example, a true mirror material would have Lock turned on, Mirror turned on, and a white Color/Pattern value.

- **Roughness.** This attribute adds roughness to the material. The adjustment you make here controls the value of the roughness. The higher the value, the rougher the material appears.

- **Transparency.** This attribute is used to determine the amount of light that passes through an object. For example, glass is highly transparent, whereas concrete is not. The amount of transparency is controlled with the Value slider.

- **Refraction.** Refraction is the bending of light as it passes through an object. You can set the Value slider to determine the amount of refraction.

- **Bump Map.** This is the only attribute that makes reference to a bitmap. A bump map is used to make the surface of the object appear to have more detail or texture, such as mortar joints, without having to model the joints themselves. This detail and appearance of texture comes from a bitmap such as one created from a photograph of a set of bricks.

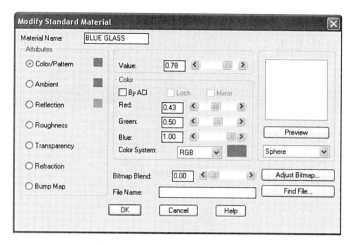

**Figure 29.15**   From the Modify Standard Material dialog box, you can assign attributes to a new material.

By setting one or more of these attributes, you can create just about any material you want. In the following exercise, you create a new glass material for use in the model from the preceding exercise. Because the new material is a modification of an existing material, most of the material attributes remain unchanged. Other attributes are changed slightly to yield a more appropriate material.

### Exercise 29.3    Creating a Simple Material

1. Open 29EX03.dwg from the preceding exercise if it is not already open or load the file from the accompanying CD. If necessary, display the Render toolbar. From the Render toolbar, choose Materials.

2. From the Materials list, select the Blue Glass material.

3. Select Duplicate. AutoCAD displays the New Standard Material dialog box.

4. In the Material Name input box, type **Dark Blue Glass**.

5. Make sure the Color/Pattern radio button is active. Verify that the By ACI check box is turned off. Then in the Color section of the dialog box, click on the color swatch to the right of the color system pull-down menu. This opens the Select Color dialog box shown in Figure 29.16.

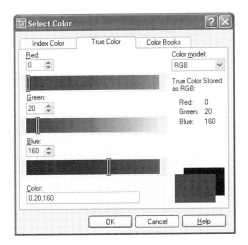

**Figure 29.16**    From the Select Color dialog box, you can choose from millions of colors and apply them to materials.

6. Make sure the True Color tab is active, change to the RGB Color Model if needed, and the set the Red, Green, and Blue values to 0, 20, and 160, respectively. This creates a dark blue color.

> **INSIDER NOTE**
>
> AutoCAD 2005 has not only the traditional 256 color palette that you use in the Index Color tab, but also selecting the Color Books tab enables you to apply vibrant colors from various print industry standards.

7. Click OK to return to the New Standard Material dialog box. With Color/Pattern still selected, set the Value slider to 0.15.

8. Click the Ambient radio button and select the Lock check box to place a check in it.

9. Click the Reflection radio button and set the Value slider to 0.10.

10. With the Reflection attribute still selected, select the color swatch in the Color section to display the Select Color dialog box (as you did in step 5). Set the Red, Green, and Blue values to 0, 7, and 77, respectively. Click OK to close the Color dialog box. The New Standard Material dialog box should now resemble Figure 29.17.

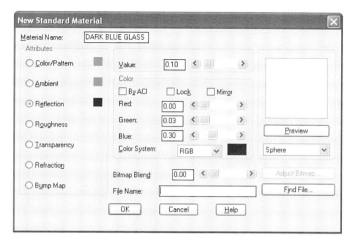

**Figure 29.17**   The New Standard Material dialog box after you define the new Dark Blue Glass material.

11. Click OK to return to the Materials dialog box. The DARK BLUE GLASS material now appears in the Material list.

**INSIDER NOTE**

Even though you may have typed your material name with lowercase letters, materials are only reported in uppercase and are saved that way as well.

12. With DARK BLUE GLASS selected in the Materials list, select the By Layer button.

13. From the Select Layer list, choose the glass layer, then select the Attach -> button to assign DARK BLUE GLASS to all objects on the glass layer.

14. Click OK to close the Attach by Layer dialog box, and click OK again to close the Materials dialog box.

15. From the Render toolbar, choose Render to display the Render dialog box. Verify that the settings duplicate those shown in Figure 29.13.

16. Click the Render button, and AutoCAD renders the model. The model should now resemble Figure 29.18.

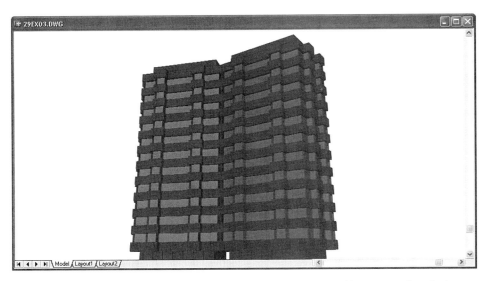

**Figure 29.18**   The office building model with the new Dark Blue Glass material applied to the glass layer.

>Save this drawing as 29EX04.dwg and leave this drawing open. You will use it in the next exercise.

As you can see from this exercise, creating a new basic material is not difficult. As in this exercise, you frequently can modify one or more attributes of a currently defined material to create the new material. The existing material serves as a template for the new material.

After you have created a new material, you may want to save it for use in other models. The following exercise demonstrates how to add a newly created material to the material library.

### Exercise 29.4   Saving a New Material

1. Continue from the previous exercise or open 29EX04.dwg from the accompanying CD. From the Render toolbar, choose Materials.

2. Click the Materials Library button.

3. In the Materials Library dialog box, select DARK BLUE GLASS in the Materials list.

4. Click the Export button to add the selected material to the Current Library.

5. In the Current Library list box, scroll down to find DARK BLUE GLASS added to the list.

6. Click OK. In the Library Notification dialog box, select Save Changes to save the modification. Then click OK to close the Materials dialog box.

You can close this drawing without saving.

## Mapped Materials

A mapped material varies from a basic material because one or more of the attributes is replaced with a bitmap image. For example, by replacing the color/pattern attribute with a photograph image of a wood pattern, you can make the surface of an object appear to have that wood pattern.

In AutoCAD, working with mapped materials is slightly more complicated because you also need to supply mapping coordinates. Mapping coordinates tell the rendering engine where and how to place the map on the surface of the object. Without correct mapping coordinates, the texture might not appear at the desired orientation or might not be on the same scale as the rest of the scene.

You can find the bitmap controls when you look at the lower right corner of the Modify Standard Material dialog box, shown in Figure 29.19. If you choose the Find File button, you can navigate to any directory on your system and select a bitmap file for use in the material. You can use any bitmap file format supported by AutoCAD. These include the BMP, JPG, PNG, TIF, TGA, PCX, and GIF formats.

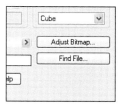

**Figure 29.19**   The Modify Standard Material dialog box bitmap controls appear near the bottom right.

**I**NSIDER  NOTE

To use a particular bitmap in your scene, that bitmap should reside in either the same directory as the drawing or one of the directories listed under Texture Maps Search Paths in the AutoCAD options. Otherwise, AutoCAD may not be able to find the file.

After you select the bitmap, you can click the Adjust Bitmap button to crop and trim the bitmap as needed. Figure 29.20 shows the dialog box that appears when you click this button.

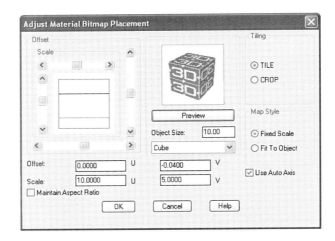

**Figure 29.20**    The Adjust Material Bitmap Placement dialog box.

Although in many instances you won't need to adjust the bitmap, in some circumstances, you will have to adjust the bitmap to obtain the effect you want. If, for example, you need to create a "decal" map—such as the label on a bottle of wine—you can set the tiling to CROP instead of TILE, and only one copy of the image will appear on the object. Figure 29.21 shows the difference between a tiled material and a cropped material. You learn more about mapping materials to objects later in this chapter.

**Figure 29.21**    A tiled material (left) and a cropped material (right).

The following exercise shows how to create a wood grain material with a bitmap.

**Exercise 29.5    Using a Bitmap to Create a Wood Grain**

1. Start a new drawing.

2. Open the Materials dialog box by choosing Materials from the Render toolbar.

3. Choose New to create a new material. Name the material by typing **Wood2** in the Material Name input box.

4. With the Color/Pattern radio button selected, choose Find File in the lower-right corner. AutoCAD displays the Bitmap File dialog box. Make sure that the Files of Type input box is set to *.* or *.tga in order to display targa files.

5. Navigate through the many textures available in your AutoCAD 2005 installation. Choose TEAK.tga and click Open to open the file. At this point, you are returned to the New Standard Material dialog box.

6. Set the Value slider to 1.00, select Cube shape from the drop-down list below the picture, and then choose Preview to view the teak bitmap. Figure 29.22 shows the dialog box at this point.

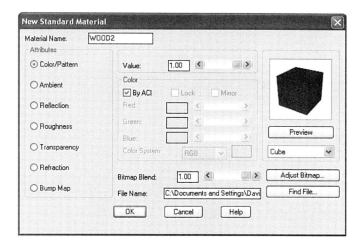

**Figure 29.22**    The New Standard Material dialog box displaying the new Wood2 material.

7. Click OK to accept the new material and return to the Materials dialog box. The new Wood2 material now appears in the Materials list.

8. To save the new material and add it to the materials library, first click the Materials Library button.

9. In the Materials Library dialog box, select Wood2 from the Current Drawing list. Then select the Export button to add the material to the current library. Save the changes to the library by clicking the Save button.

**10.** Click OK twice to close the Materials Library dialog box and the Materials dialog box. You can try this material out on a simple box, as shown in previous exercises. You can close the drawing without saving.

This exercise demonstrates that creating a mapped material is easy as long as you have the bitmap file and know its location. Several libraries of third-party bitmaps suitable for use in making new materials are available. You can also create bitmap files by scanning photographs of materials such as metals, woods, and construction materials, to mention just a few.

### *Applying Mapping Coordinates*

As mentioned earlier, when you use materials that are composed wholly or in part of bitmap images, you usually must apply mapping coordinates to the object. To do so, use the Mapping icon on the Render toolbar or type **SETUV** at the command prompt. You are then prompted to select the objects to which you want to apply the mapping coordinates. Select the appropriate objects, and the Mapping dialog box shown in Figure 29.23 appears.

**Figure 29.23**    In the Mapping dialog box, you select the type of mapping to apply to an object.

AutoCAD supports four types of mapping: planar, spherical, cylindrical, and solid (see Figure 29.24). The first three generally refer to how the bitmap is wrapped around the object to which the mapping is applied.

**Figure 29.24**   The four mapping types in AutoCAD: planar, cylindrical, spherical, and solid.

The last mapping type is called a solid mapping type and is intended for use with procedural materials such as wood, marble, and granite. These materials are generated based on mathematical formulas and do not make use of bitmaps. The solid mapping coordinates are used when you have a procedural material assigned to an object with highly varying geometry, such as a box with a sphere subtracted out of it. The curved inner portion of the subtracted area stretches the bitmap due to the mapping coordinates, but a solid procedural material always appears correct.

After you select the type of mapping you want to use, you can select the Adjust Coordinates button to fine-tune the mapping. Which specific dialog box appears depends upon whether you choose a planar, cylindrical, spherical, or solid mapped object. As an example of the scope of adjustments available for mapping and adjusting coordinates, Figure 29.25 shows the Adjust Planar Coordinates dialog box.

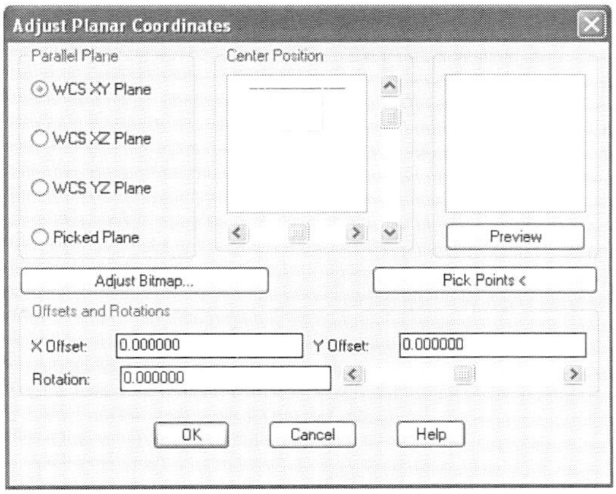

**Figure 29.25**   The Adjust Planar Coordinates dialog box for adjusting mapping settings on planar objects.

You can select the World Coordinate System plane along which the mapping coordinates are aligned. You can also pick your own 3D plane by picking three points on that plane, much as you can define your own UCS.

In the Center Position section of the dialog box, you actually see a wireframe representation of the selected object. A light blue outline, called the Mapping icon, appears around this box as well.

The blue outline represents the mapping coordinates and indicates the size of one copy of the bitmap on the surface of the object. By adjusting the slider to the right and bottom of the preview, you can control the position of the bitmap on the surface of the object. At the bottom of the dialog box, you can control the offset and rotation of the Mapping icon. If you want to control the scale of the bitmap, click the Adjust Bitmap button.

The combinations of geometric shapes and mapping planes make adjusting bitmapped materials a somewhat complex operation due principally to the number of choices available. The procedures are relatively straightforward, however, and by adjusting the offset, rotation, scale, and coordinates of bitmapped materials, you can exert a great deal of control over how materials based on bitmaps will appear in the rendered model.

# Working with Lights

After you select (and perhaps create) and then apply materials to the objects in your model, the next logical step is to add sources of light. Lighting is one of the most important aspects of creating an effective rendering. Without realistic lighting, the surfaces and materials of an otherwise realistic model look "flat." Lighting also provides the means for adding realistic shadows to your model.

You create lights by selecting the Lights button from the Render toolbar or by typing **LIGHT** at the command prompt. Either method displays the Lights dialog box, shown in Figure 29.26.

In the Lights dialog box, you see a list of all the current lights in the scene, as well as the Ambient Light controls, the Light Creation controls, and the North Location button.

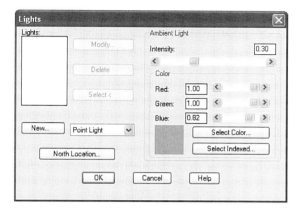

**Figure 29.26**   From the Lights dialog box, you can create, adjust, and manage all the lights in a model.

The ambient light is the overall brightness of the scene. By adjusting the ambient light, you can set the overall brightness of the scene. Higher ambient values are good for outside light, whereas lower values are good for interior or night scenes. Strive to avoid extreme settings of ambient light. Usually, values between 30 and 70 yield suitable amounts of ambient light. You can also adjust the ambient light color to provide basic color tinting to the scene. Keep ambient light color variations very subtle for the most realistic effects. Ambient light has no source and therefore is not capable of casting shadows.

The North Location button enables you to set the north direction in your models. By default, north coincides with the positive Y direction. You may want to alter the north direction in architectural models.

## Types of Lights
AutoCAD supports three types of lights:

- **Point.** This type of light is similar to a single light bulb. Light radiates from a single point in all directions. You can specify no attenuation or attenuation that is inverse linear or inverse square.

- **Spotlight.** This type of light is similar to the light emitted from a flashlight. The spotlight has a source and a target location. Light from a spotlight is cast in a cone fashion, and you can define the angle of the cone. You can specify no attenuation or attenuation that is inverse linear or inverse square.

- **Distant.** A distant light emits parallel light beams in one direction. Distant light sources cannot exhibit any attenuation; the light intensity remains constant regardless of its distance.

Typically, point lights are used for general illumination in the scene, spotlights are used to add special highlighting in a relatively small area, and distant lights are used to simulate sunlight.

## Creating a Light

As you can see in the Lights dialog box shown in Figure 29.26, you create a light simply by choosing the type of light from the drop-down list next to the New button and clicking the New button. Each of the three light types has its own dialog box for specifying the attributes of the light. The dialog box for a spotlight is shown in Figure 29.27.

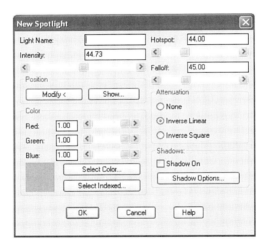

**Figure 29.27**   The New Spotlight dialog box, where you create and set the attributes of a spotlight.

Every light that you create in an AutoCAD model must have a name. You enter the name in the Light Name input box. Choose a name that is descriptive, such as Spot1 or Point-main.

With point lights and spotlights, you need to position the light in the model. Point lights require only the location of the light source. However, because spotlights are directional, you must specify the position of both the source and the target. You specify these locations by choosing the Modify button in the Position section of the dialog box. In the case of spotlights, you are then prompted to pick the target of the light, followed by the location of the light. AutoCAD temporarily hides the dialog box to enable you to pick these points in the model. Using point filters (as described in Chapter 26, "Drawing in 3D") makes specifying light locations easier. With distant lights, you need to specify the source direction as well as its height above the horizon.

After you position a light, you are returned to the New Light dialog box, where you set the remaining parameters associated with the light, which are explained here:

- **Intensity.** Sets the intensity or brightness of the light. Entering 0 turns off a light. The maximum point light intensity depends on the attenuation setting and the extents of the drawing. With no attenuation, maximum intensity is 1. If attenuation is inverse linear, maximum intensity is the value of twice the extents distance. If attenuation is inverse square, maximum intensity is twice the square of the extents distance.

- **Color.** You can assign a different color to each light in the scene. For example, fluorescent lighting often has a slight blue cast, while typical incandescent lighting tends to be slightly yellow. For special effects such as sunrise or sunset, you may want to give a distant light a slightly red color. Keep these color assignments minimal for the best results.

- **Attenuation.** In real life, light fades or grows weaker as the distance between source and objects increases. In AutoCAD, lights remain the same strength over a distance unless you specify an attenuation factor. There are two types of attenuation: inverse linear and inverse square. Inverse square drops off much faster than inverse linear does. For point lights and spotlights, inverse linear is the default attenuation factor and generally yields the most effective results. Direct lights exhibit no attenuation.

- **Shadows.** All lights in AutoCAD are capable of casting shadows. The type of shadow depends on the current render type (Photo Real or Photo Raytrace) and the settings in the Shadow Options dialog box. The shadow-casting capability of any light can be turned on or off with the Shadow On check box in the Shadows section of the new Lights dialog box.

In addition to these basic controls common to all light types, the New Spotlight dialog box enables you to adjust the angle of the cone and its falloff rate, and the New Distant Light dialog box provides settings for sun position.

The following exercise shows you how to create a spotlight for use in a model.

### Exercise 29.6   Creating a Spotlight

1. Load the file 29EX06.dwg from the accompanying CD. The drawing presents a model of a telephone handset unit, as shown in Figure 29.28.

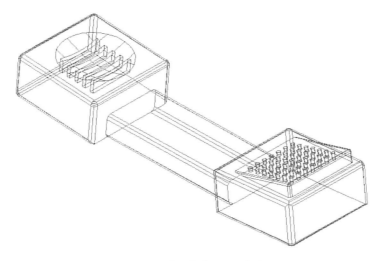

**Figure 29.28**   Model of a telephone handset before rendering.

2. From the View pull-down menu, choose 3D Views, Plan View, World UCS. This switches you to a plan view. From this view, you will add a spotlight.

3. Select Lights from the Render toolbar.

4. In the Lights dialog box, choose Spotlight from the drop-down list and click the New button.

5. In the New Spotlight dialog box, type the name **Spot1** in the Light Name input box.

6. In the Position section, click the Modify button. AutoCAD hides the dialog box and displays the drawing.

7. At the Enter light target prompt, type the coordinates **8.5,7.0**. At the Enter light location prompt, type **.xy** to indicate that next you will provide the X-Y location of the light location.

8. At the of prompt, type the coordinates **-2,14**. At the (need Z) prompt, type **25**. This places the light location 25 units above the model. AutoCAD returns to the New Spotlight dialog box.

**9.** Configure the remaining settings in the New Spotlight dialog box, as shown in Figure 29.29.

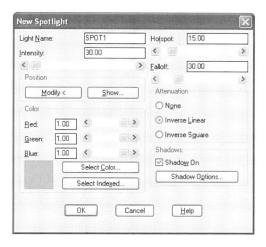

**Figure 29.29**   Settings of the New Spotlight dialog box for the model's new spotlight.

**10.** In the Shadows section of the New Spotlight dialog box, select Shadow Options, and in the Shadow Options dialog box, check the Shadow Volume/Ray Traced Shadows check box. Click OK to close the Shadow Options dialog box. Then click OK to close the New Spotlight dialog box.

**11.** In the Lights dialog box, set the Ambient Light Intensity to **0.5**. Click OK to accept the settings and close the dialog box.

**12.** From the View menu, choose Named Views. In the View dialog box, select View1 and then Set Current. Click OK to close the dialog box and restore the opening view.

**13.** From the Render toolbar, choose Render.

**14.** Configure the settings in the Render dialog box like those shown in Figure 29.30.

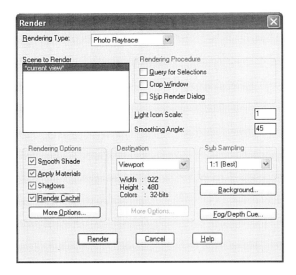

**Figure 29.30**    Settings of the Render dialog box prior to rendering the model.

**15.** In the Render dialog box, choose Render. After a few moments, the rendered model appears. The rendering should resemble Figure 29.31.

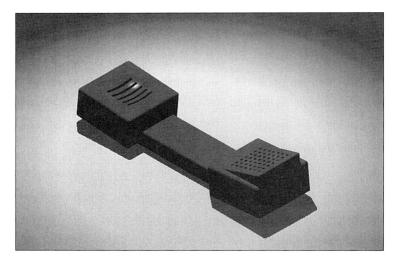

**Figure 29.31**    The rendered model is illuminated with the new spotlight.

**16.** You may want to render this model again after adjusting the Hotspot and Falloff angles as well as the intensities of the spotlight and ambient light.

You can then close this drawing without saving.

As you learned in this exercise, creating lights for a model is not difficult. Proper lighting of a model, however, is an art form in itself. Good results can be produced quickly, but great results take time and a lot of testing and adjusting of the lights in the scene.

When testing different light types, positions, and intensities, you can speed up your test renderings in several ways. First, you need not render the complete model or view. Often, rendering a smaller portion of the view gives you the information you need to decide if further adjustments are needed. In the Render dialog box shown in Figure 29.32, in the Rendering Procedure section, the Crop Window option enables you to window a portion of the model for rendering. In a similar way, the Query for Selections option enables you to select portions of the model for rendering on an object-by-object basis. Using one or both of these options can greatly speed the rendering of portions of the model as you make lighting adjustments.

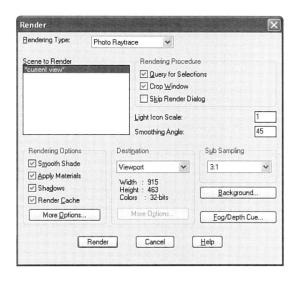

**Figure 29.32**   The Render dialog box offers methods for speeding up test renderings.

If you need to render the entire model view while making adjustments, you can make "coarse" renderings using the Sub Sampling options found in the Render dialog box. Sub-sampling reduces rendering time and image quality without losing lighting effects such as shadows by rendering a fraction of all of the pixels. A sub-sampling ratio of 1:1 renders all pixels and takes the most time. A sub-sampling of 3:1, however, renders only every third pixel, greatly reducing rendering times. Shadows also increase rendering times. Turning off the Shadow option in the Rendering Options section of the Render dialog box is yet another way to make successive test renderings easier.

# Creating Sunlight

Sunlight—in both exterior and interior views of your model—can be the most important light you use. You can manually set a distant light to simulate sunlight from any direction to yield any effect you want. You can also use AutoCAD's built-in Sun Angle Calculator to calculate the exact position of the sun for any point on Earth on any day of the year at any time of day. Being able to place the sun so precisely is often important in renderings of exterior architectural models where the exact position and extent of shadows cast by buildings or other structures may be important. In the following exercise, you learn how to create precise sun shadows using the Sun Angle Calculator.

### Exercise 29.7   Using the Sunlight System to Create a Distant Light

1. Load the file 29EX07.dwg from the accompanying CD. This drawing contains a model of an apartment building with an adjoining urban park.

2. Choose Lights from the Render toolbar. In the Light Type drop-down list, set the light type to Distant and click the New button.

3. In the New Distant Light dialog box, create a new distant light. Name this light **Sun**. Slide its intensity value to 1.00.

4. In the Shadows section, select Shadow On. Select Shadow Options and, in the Shadow Options dialog box, select the Shadow Volume/Ray Traced Shadows. Click OK to close the Shadow Options dialog box.

5. In the New Distant Light dialog box, select Sun Angle Calculator. AutoCAD displays the Sun Angle Calculator dialog box shown in Figure 29.33.

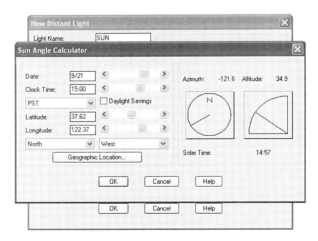

**Figure 29.33**   The Sun Angle Calculator dialog box, where you set the geographical location and date/time.

6. Select Geographic Location to display the Geographic Location dialog box. Select San Francisco from the City list box and click OK to close the dialog box.

7. In the Sun Angle Calculator dialog box, set the Date and Clock Time as shown in Figure 29.33, then click OK to return to the New Distant Light dialog box. Click OK to close this dialog box.

8. In the Lights dialog box, check that the Ambient Light intensity is set to 0.90. Click OK to close this dialog box.

9. Select Render from the Render toolbar.

10. In the Render dialog box, set the Rendering Type to Photo Raytrace. In the Rendering Options section, make sure the Shadows option is checked.

11. Click the Render button to begin rendering the model. After a few moments, your rendered model should resemble Figure 29.34.

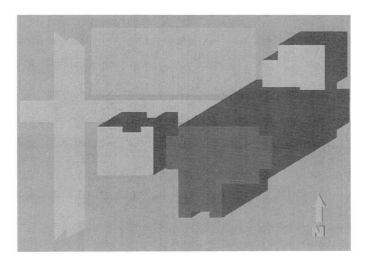

**Figure 29.34**    The rendered building model showing the cast shadows on a specific date and time.

You may now close this drawing without saving.

**INSIDER NOTE**

The Sun Angle Calculator takes its north as the current AutoCAD north direction. By default, this is the positive Y-axis direction of the current coordinate direction. You can change the north direction in the North Direction dialog box, which is accessible from the Lights dialog box.

This exercise demonstrates that the Sun Angle Calculator can be effectively used to place a distant light that's capable of producing accurate object shadows. Of course, a distant light can also be used more conventionally as a directional light source.

# Generating an Output

The Default Rendering method in AutoCAD renders the output to the current viewport. This is the method used in the exercises in this chapter. To print the image or use it in other programs, however, you must be able to save the rendered image to a file. You accomplish this by choosing File from the Destination drop-down list in the Render dialog box. After you select File, click the More Options button to define the file type.

AutoCAD enables you to render the image out to one of five different file types: BMP, PCX, Postscript, TGA, and TIF file formats. Below the File Type drop-down list, you can select the resolution to which you want to render. Higher resolutions, of course, take longer to render.

**I**NSIDER **T**IP

> You can also RENDER in a paper space viewport. Set the viewport Shade plot property to Rendered and then use the PLOT command to create rendered plot files.

**I**NSIDER **N**OTE

> There are other advanced features of the rendering system in AutoCAD to explore. These include fog, backgrounds, vegetation, and several others. This chapter gives you an introduction to the principles of rendering and the basic capabilities of the rendering feature in AutoCAD 2005. Rendering is as much an art as a science, and you can use this chapter's information to serve as a basis for individual exploration of rendering inside AutoCAD. You might considering utilizing either 3D Studio VIZ or 3D Studio MAX to take your imagery to a higher level.

# Summary

After you have constructed a 3D model using the principles discussed in the 3D chapters of this book, you can use AutoCAD to render the model. Rendering consists of applying materials to the objects in the model and setting lights to illuminate the model. One of the most important steps in carrying out an interesting and informative rendering is establishing an effective viewpoint. After you carry out these basic preparation steps, rendering is often a matter of trial and error and fine-tuning.

# *Index*

## Symbols

# M

# www.informit.com